Gilbert D. Nass
University of Connecticut

Marriage and the Family

ADDISON-WESLEY PUBLISHING COMPANY
Reading, Massachusetts • Menlo Park, California
London • Amsterdam • Don Mills, Ontario • Sydney

This book is in the Addison-Wesley Series in Sociology

Cover drawing, "Bond of Union" by M. C. Escher, Escher Foundation—Haags
Gemeentemuseum—The Hague

ISBN 0-201-02500-0
BCDEFGHIJKL-HA-798

Preface

If there is one thing almost everyone in the United States would agree on, it is that our society is constantly changing. Change occurs in superficial things like clothing fashions and favorite slang words, and in basic issues as well. The likelihood of being drafted is presently not a factor in the life choices of young people finishing high school, and this alone has made a tremendous difference in the way people are living their lives in the 1970s.

FOCUS OF THE TEXT

In this text, considerable emphasis is given to the notion of diversity and change in the United States, particularly as it affects marriage and family life. Our intention has been to prepare a functional text, one that can help students make effective choices in their own lives. In making such choices, people need to be aware of events and trends in American life which affect their personal lives. They also need to have a certain flexibility in behaviors and beliefs so as to adapt to changes around them. We hope this book will help students to achieve this flexibility.

A second major focus of the text is the acknowledgment of the hazards and difficulties of everyday interpersonal relationships. All of us are required to work toward interpersonal adjustment if we are to receive the rewards of intimacy and continuity in our relationships with other people. We also need to recognize that conflict is bound to arise in interpersonal relationships. It almost seems that the more intense the relationship, the more likely conflict is to occur. So we have tried to convey to students the realization that adjustment in interpersonal relationships is a continuing process, not a stable state to be achieved and held on to forever. It is our hope that students will thus be assisted in achieving maximum personal growth through their interactions with others. We think that the study of the sociology of marriage and the family provides a good start in this direction.

SCOPE OF THE TEXT

Our intention has been to provide a broad introduction to the study of marriage and the family, from which instructors can choose material best suited to the needs of their students. Individual instructors will, of course, vary the emphasis they give to different topics. Some may not wish to give class time to the chapter on alternatives to traditional marriage or the one on money management. Others may omit the materials on human sexuality, pregnancy, and family planning. Yet all chapters can be read by students on their own. In this way, the students can gain a basic knowledge of the subject even though a specific topic may not be regarded by every instructor as an essential part of the course.

CHARTS AND TABLES

Numerical data—both from government sources and from sociological research—have been used sparingly. In using the data we have tried to rouse the curiosity and interest of students. Much of this information is presented in the form of easy-to-read charts and tables which students will find helpful in understanding the text.

CASE STUDIES

Throughout the book, concepts are illustrated by short, everyday examples. In addition, ten brief case studies have been included in Part III, Relationships In and Out of Marriage. These are followed by suggested discussion questions to help students tie the abstractions of sociology to the realities of day-to-day marital relationships. We believe students will respond to these as an interesting feature of the book.

STUDY AIDS

To increase the effectiveness of the text as a learning resource, four study aids are included at the end of each chapter. The brief chapter summaries are presented in numbered paragraphs. Key concepts are listed to help students identify the most important ideas in the chapter. Review and discussion sections will help students become personally involved with the subject matter of the text. Annotated suggested readings are provided to aid students who want to pursue a particular topic beyond the limits of the text. Many of the readings are of general interest, and all are chosen for simplicity of language and presentation.

In addition, a substantial glossary is included at the end of the text to help students who have difficulty learning new terms. Each of these glossary terms is printed in boldface type when first introduced in the text. There is also an extensive bibliography listing all sources cited in the text.

SUPPLEMENTS

For students who want even more help in understanding the subject matter of the text, a *Student Workbook and Study Guide* is available. This separate booklet contains chapter objectives, topic outlines, review items, and self-tests. The study guide, keyed chapter by chapter to the text, has been prepared by Ronald Sabatelli of the University of Connecticut, as have the *Instructor's Manual* and the *Test Item Book,* to accompany the text. The *Instructor's Manual* gives particular emphasis to development of class discussion and enrichment of the course through references to additional source materials. The *Test Item Book* is available as an aid to professors in evaluating the work of their students.

ACKNOWLEDGMENTS

If ever a book could be said to be the result of a team effort, it is this one. Planning for the book was based on the results of a market research study to determine the needs and desires of people teaching courses in marriage and the family at a wide variety of colleges. We believe that, as a consequence, the content and organization of the book will find a warm response from people who are looking for a solid text with a contemporary point of view. In the development of the book, the assistance of my colleagues at the Department of Human Development and Family Relations of the University of Connecticut has been invaluable. I also want to thank Terry L. Swanlund and Rikke Wassenberg for many hours of research assistance, and Jeanette McIntosh for assistance on the human sexuality chapters. Writers Mary Pat Fisher and Gail H. Pool deserve much of the credit for the expression of some pretty complex sociological concepts in simple, direct prose, well suited to first-year and second-year college students for whom the book is mainly intended.

I also thank the reviewers who read the chapters carefully and made suggestions which improved the book immeasurably. Among these are Professors David Edens of Stephens College; Roger H. Rubin of the University of Maryland; Rita Sakitt of Suffolk County Community College; and Peter J. Stein of Lehman College, City University of New York. And finally, I want to acknowledge the contributions of a sizable group of able and cooperative editorial and production staff members at Addison-Wesley. In particular, I thank Elizabeth S. Mason, Project Editor for this book, who was a major driving force and provided splendid contributions for every aspect of the text. Without the assistance of all these people, the book could not have been done.

Storrs, Connecticut   G.D.N.
October 1977

Contents

Part III
The Physiology of Reproduction

Part III
Relationships In and Out of Marriage

Part IV
Will the Traditional Family Survive?

Marriage and the Family

Part I

The Family in Perspective

Family Group (1948–1949) by
the sculptor Henry Moore,
from the collection of the
Museum of Modern Art,
New York.

A family of Kung Bushmen in the Kala-hari Desert in Africa. Belonging to a hunting and gathering society, they move frequently in search of food, so the huts in the background are temporary homes. The man is playing the musical bow, an instrument which has a flutelike sound.

Variety and Change in Family Systems 1

CONCEPTUALIZING MARRIAGE AND THE FAMILY

The study of marriage and the family is about the problems of human existence: birth, survival, and death. Like all animals, we must reproduce if our species is to survive; and like certain other animals, our young are helpless at birth. But unlike any other animal, our young remain helpless for years, dependent upon adults for care and for instruction in the most basic elements of survival. It has been said that we are in a sense born too soon, before we are physically ready for life (Fox, 1967). If there had been no solution to this problem, we would also have died too soon. The human species might well be extinct. That we are not extinct we owe to the child-caring and child-rearing systems which have developed throughout the world—groups of varying size and form generally referred to as the family.

Social institution. A system of social relations organized to meet a basic societal need.

In view of the importance of the family's task of transforming the helpless infant into a mature human being, it is not surprising that the family is sometimes called the basic **social institution.** By social institution, we mean the set of customs and laws a **society** has established to ensure that some specific function is fulfilled. The term family, as a social institution, includes the customs of a society related to having and rearing children, for these are among the family's main tasks. It is the family that provides for the children's physical survival; it also provides for their emotional security. And it is through the family that children learn the values of their society—how they should think, feel, and act. By teaching children what society's demands upon them are, and what they will be as they grow up, the family provides the link between them and their society.

FUNCTIONS OF THE FAMILY

The benefits to a society which result from the way the family meets social needs are usually called the **functions** of the family, and these can be grouped in four categories.

Reproduction and Socialization. As a means of reproduction, the family ensures a society that its population will be maintained; a sufficient number of children will be born and properly cared for so that dying members will be replaced. Traditionally, the family has also been responsible for educating its children to become participating members of their society, though to a considerable extent this function is now shared with schools and churches. This transmittal of culture, a process called **socialization,** transforms the child from a biological organism into a social being.

Socialization. The process by which individuals learn a society's norms and values.

Economic Cooperation. Historically, the family has been central to the economic organization of most societies, both as a unit of production and as a unit of consumption. The cooperation between the sexes inherent in the marriage bond has been one means by which societies have provided for the efficient production and distribution of goods and services. Although today the home is less a producing unit and more a consuming unit for goods produced elsewhere, even in urbanized and industrialized nations family members still cooperate in meeting their economic needs.

Assignment of Social Roles.   In any social organization, the members must know what parts they are expected to play, what tasks they are expected to perform, and what they may expect others to do. It is through the family that children acquire a legal identity as members of the society; race, ethnic, and religious identification; and socioeconomic status. Even in contemporary American society, where status is more achieved than inherited, property, wealth, and power are often acquired through the family. Thus the family defines for people many of the major **roles** they will play in their lives.

Role. Expected behavior pattern associated with a particular position in a social system.

Personal Relationships.   A fourth major function of the family is to provide emotional security for its members. Through intimate and enduring relationships, anxieties about one's position in society and fears about one's purpose in life or one's death may be eased. The family is also the arena for our earliest practice in interpersonal relations.

In view of the fundamental needs met by the family, it is clear why people have wanted to marry and create families of their own. The marital relationship may provide not only a constant sex partner, but companionship and the moral support that accompanies the sense of being important to another person. The desire to have children is usually satisfied within the marriage partnership where a sharing of the work and responsibility of child rearing benefits both parents and children. To have taken on the rights and responsibilities of marriage signifies entry into the adult world.

WHAT IS A FAMILY?

So far we have been talking about the family as if everyone knows what it is—and, to some degree, everyone does. Most of us have grown up in families. We have observed families around us, and we have gathered a good amount of information on the subject. In fact, many people would say they not only know what a family is, they know what it should be, who is to be counted as family and who is not, and how these people should behave toward each other.

While most of this information is valid, it really concerns just our own family in our own society at the present time. This personally gained information provides only a small bit of insight into what the family is, for marriage and family systems vary greatly throughout the world. What one ought to do in one society may be strictly forbidden in another. As we examine the family patterns of different societies, we find that variation is a key word. Each variation might be viewed as a different solution to the same problem—human survival. While different customs in themselves are always interesting, they are also far more than that: they show us what is possible. Cross-cultural studies broaden our perspective and open our minds to the realization that different forms of the family serve best the needs of different societies. No one form is inherently superior to any other. Each must be studied in relation to the cultural and physical environment in which it is found. So, to be useful, the definition of the word family needs to be broad enough to fit the family systems of all different societies.

Family. A group of people related by blood, marriage, or adoption sharing a common residence and cooperating economically.

A Definition of the Family. As a sociological term, the word **family** refers to a social group sharing a common residence and cooperating economically. It is usually based on the marriage of one or more sexually cohabiting couples and usually there is the expectation of having children for whom the adults of the family accept responsibility.

Marriage. The set of laws and customs that specifies how family relationships should be established and carried out.

Marriage, also a social institution, is the set of laws and customs that specifies the ways in which the family relationship should be established, conducted, or terminated (Murdock, 1949). Broadly defined, it is the socially sanctioned union of sexually cohabiting adults such that children born to the wife are recognized as children of the husband. There is usually a public ceremony of some kind, and the relationship is characterized by economic cooperation and a degree of permanence.

We might distinguish between marriage and the family by saying that marriage is the institutionalized means of legitimizing offspring. It gives children a place in the society. The family is the institutionalized means of rearing them. It teaches children how to act out their roles in the society.

Of course, as our own observation tells us, there are times when the family circle is incomplete. A single parent and his or her children form a family unit and are counted as such by the Census Bureau, even though this grouping does not include a sexually cohabiting pair of adults. Other variations of the family often found in our society are the childless couple and the mature couple whose children are grown and living elsewhere, possibly with families of their own.

Difference Between a Family and a Household. A group of people is not considered a family simply because it is sharing a residence. To be a family, the people in the group must be related to each other by blood, marriage, or adoption. Thus the Census Bureau considers two sisters or a sister and brother living together a family. On the other hand, all those who occupy a housing unit are called a **household.** A household thus includes the related family members and all the unrelated persons, if any, such as lodgers, foster children, or employees living in the house. Two unrelated persons sharing a housing unit constitute a household but not a family. One person keeping house alone is also counted as a household.

Family of Orientation and Family of Procreation.   Most people participate in two families during their lifetime. The family into which one is born is called the **family of orientation.** Orientation, becoming acquainted with the existing situation or environment, is an aspect of the process of socialization previously discussed. The family established when one marries and produces offspring is called the **family of procreation.** The role change when one leaves the family of orientation and, through marriage, enters the family of procreation, is often dramatic. In addition, the formation of a new unit by two people reared in different families of orientation may require each to assume new role obligations based on the expectations of the other. The success of the new unit depends on the ability of the newly married couple to make these adjustments.

BIOLOGICAL BASIS OF THE FAMILY

No one really knows how the family originated. It does, however, seem to be a natural grouping because of the need for cooperation in mating and rearing offspring. Though the family has long been viewed as a particularly human institution, increased scientific knowledge of **subhuman** species has revealed that elements of family life exist throughout the animal world. So widespread are the examples of economic cooperation, enduring relationships, joint care of offspring, and socialization among lower forms of animal life that some researchers feel the differences between human and subhuman family life are only a matter of degree. Consequently, many think that the study of social behavior among subhuman species may eventually lead to a greater understanding of human social behavior, and even of the fundamental nature of human beings and the moral choices they make (Wilson, 1975).

Family Life Among Subhuman Species.   Various forms of economic cooperation are found among many subhuman species. When wolves are hunting a large animal such as a moose, ten or more individuals may band together for the chase and share in the spoils. Among the social insects, such as ants and bees, nestmates communicate to their fellows the discovery of food. Such communication is also found among chimpanzees, who will make an enormous racket upon discovering a fruit tree, drawing other groups to the place to share the food (Wilson).

A variety of family relationships are also found in the animal world. **Monogamy,** the permanent mating of one male and one female, occurs among many species and may derive from certain ecological conditions, as when the environment is so difficult that two adults are required to cope

Monogamy. The permanent mating of one male and one female.

with it if the young are to survive (Wilson). Crane "marriages" may last as long as 50 years, with the male and female sharing equally in care of the nest and eggs (Dossenbach, 1971). Among wild turkeys, brothers cooperate in finding a mate for the strongest male of the brood, and these bonds between brothers are maintained for life. Nor can we think of the role of mother as purely **instinctive**, even among subhuman species. Among certain **primates**, young female members of the group, referred to as "aunts" by some researchers, assist parents in the care of **offspring**, apparently learning a future role as mother by this process (Wilson).

Offspring. The young of an animal or plant; descendants; children.

There is other evidence that the process of socialization occurs among subhuman species. The term itself, first used by social scientists, is now being used by biologists. Among primates, both kin and nonkin relationships are established early and are differentiated from each other. Experiments such as the Harlows' famous studies with monkeys indicate early deprivation of these relationships blocks the animals' normal development. The play activities of the primate young, as of the human young, are an important part of socialization. This is especially true of tool-using animals such as the chimpanzee.

Differences Between Humans and Lower Animals. Although the differences between human and subhuman family life appear to be largely a matter of degree, still there are differences. To some extent, these may derive from differences in biological traits. The constant sex drive of humans and consequent desire for a constant sex partner, the relatively long period of human **gestation** (the period when the female is carrying unborn young), and the long dependency of human offspring make formal, legal family systems seem natural social developments.

Equally important, however, is the complexity of human culture compared to the lifestyles of other animals. To provide for the transmission of the cultural heritage of technical skills, tools, languages, and beliefs, complex and stable systems of social organization are required. Nor can biological factors account for the variation in form that human families take throughout the world. Whatever the **biological factors** in family life may be, they are always modified and influenced by **cultural factors**.

THE FAMILY AS A COOPERATIVE UNIT

The family as a social, rather than a biological, organization is basically a kinship system, an organization of people cooperating with each other to meet their common needs. The people in the system have certain duties they are expected to perform according to their position; and on the other hand, they have certain rights because of their position in the family structure. Thus a daughter may be expected to perform certain duties for her mother, but she also has the right to expect that her mother will perform certain duties for her.

Kinship system. The means of defining who one's relatives are and the mutual rights and obligations involved.

A modern extended family in Brazil. The man at the bottom center of the photo started out as a poor vegetable trader. Eventually he became a successful coffee merchant, sold his business for several million dollars, and bought a large cattle ranch on which his parents, sisters, brothers-in-law, parents-in-law, wife and daughters, grandchildren, cousins, nieces and nephews all live and work.

Of course, every individual occupies more than one position in a kinship system. For example, an individual is not only a son. He may also be a brother, a nephew, and a cousin. Moreover, he is a son to both his mother and his father. Each of these relationships has its own set of rights and obligations. What a son owes his mother may well differ from what he owes his father, and what he will expect from each of them may differ as well.

In the past, and especially in **primitive** societies, kinship units tended to control almost everything about a person's life. Who one's parents were determined a member's residence, social position, and occupation. The kinship system controlled **mate selection** for its members and also leadership, determining which people would succeed to specific ranks and offices. In exchange for the control an individual allowed the kinship group to have, certain benefits were received. The kinship group would provide automatic support in disputes; in health care, security, and sharing of resources; and in the determination of **social status.**

Social status. The individual's position in society in relation to the position of others.

As we examine different forms of the family later in this chapter, we will gain some idea of the variety of kinship systems that have developed throughout the world. Some are very complex. Compared with the kinship structures of many so-called primitive societies, our own family system appears to be quite simple.

Incest taboo. Prohibition of sexual relationships between certain closely related family members.

Restrictions on Sexuality. It is the very closeness of family contacts and the need for cooperation among kin that is thought by many social scientists to have brought about the regulation of sexual relationships called the **incest taboo.** Almost every society has rules prohibiting sexual contacts between certain closely related kin. Most commonly, these rules ban sexual intercourse and marriage between parent and child and between brothers and sisters. In some societies, marriage with a cousin on the mother's side of the family might be the preferred choice, while marriage with a cousin on the father's side of the family would be strictly forbidden. Some societies extend the restrictions to quite distant relatives and even to in-laws.

Ritual. A ceremonial act, especially a customarily repeated series of acts.

On the other hand, societies have been found where sexual intercourse between father and daughter is a **ritual** observed on special occasions. Researchers have also found evidence that in ancient Egypt and Old Iran, father-daughter and mother-son relationships were the preferred form of mating as well as instances of Egyptian kings marrying their sisters or half-sisters (Middleton, 1962; Slotkin, 1947).

Murdock, considering the wide variation in incest taboos found in different societies, expressed surprise that there has been found no society in which a married couple is forbidden to have sexual intercourse and each one required to find a sexual partner outside the marriage.

Reasons for the Incest Taboo. The reasons for incest taboos have been researched and debated for years. It has been suggested, for example, that humans have a natural aversion to incest, but in many societies the response to occurrences of incest, while not approving, is indifferent. It has also been proposed that because of the harmful effects of **inbreeding,** societies which practiced incest have died out. Another theory, also based on **natural selection,** has suggested that sexual relations within a family unit would result in extreme competition for sexual favors which would destroy the cooperation the family needs to survive—thus societies which did practice incest would be weakened by internal dissension and eventually die out (Fox). None of these **theories** or any others offered has provided a satisfactory explanation of the origin of the incest taboo or of its persistence. It may be that no **universal** answer will be found. Perhaps as the reaction to incest varies from one society to the next, so too did the motives for establishing a taboo.

Societies also vary widely in their rules about and reactions to **premarital** sex relations, premarital pregnancy, sexual activity among children, and **extramarital** sexual activity. What is considered highly desirable in one society may be merely tolerated in another and strictly prohibited in a third.

Rules of Endogamy and Exogamy. The incest taboo, where it exists, has usually applied to close blood relatives, and forbids both sexual intercourse

---

STRICT ENDOGAMY ENDANGERS THE KOTAS

The Kotas, a tribe of about 1200 people in the Nilgiri Hills in southern India, appear to be facing extinction because of their refusal to marry outside of their own community. Kota boys do not mix with outsiders and Kota girls are not permitted to go to school or leave their settlement after they grow up. Visitors to a Kota village may not enter the homes and are restricted to a special guest house.

A committee of Indian doctors investigated the tribe because of their high death rate—thirty per thousand, twice as high as that of the surrounding population—and estimated that inbreeding has been going on for nearly 1500 years.

The doctors noted that the common blood group "A" was missing from the community—a sign of prolonged inbreeding which eventually leads to extinction. Subsequently, the missing blood group was found in 23 Kotas from two families. However, a Kota leader opposes the idea of other Kotas marrying with the newly discovered "A" group tribesmen since they are probably linked to a woman who at some time had sexual relations outside the tribe. "The tribe's decline is the will of the gods and we can do little about it," this leader said.

The Kotas are bound by inflexible traditions. A 24-year-old Kota postal worker noted the advice of the doctors to marry outside the community, but said, "For the sake of a girl I will not forsake my parents and my tribe." A Kota chieftain told Samachar, India's national news agency, that he would rather see the tribe perish than have it grow by crossbreeding with other tribes.

Source: *Boston Evening Globe*, December, 1976.

---

and marriage. There are other, broader rules about who may marry whom, called rules of **endogamy** and **exogamy**, and these also vary from one society to another. Often they are based on membership in large social organizations called **clans, sibs,** or **moieties.** Rules of endogamy require that one choose a mate from a group of which one is also a member. In our society, this might be observed as the custom of marrying within one's own race, religion, or **ethnic group.** Rules of exogamy require that one's mate be chosen from outside one's own group. Rules of exogamy, by forcing an individual to find a mate outside the immediate circle of associates, ensure the formation of links between social units. And these links based on marital ties have helped to foster the cooperation necessary for the expansion of civilization.

VARIATIONS IN FAMILY ORGANIZATION

The model American family is a self-sufficient unit of mother, father, and children living in their own home sharing social events and family ceremonies with grandparents, aunts, uncles, and cousins but essentially an independent social group. This is called the **nuclear** or **conjugal family**. It is based on a strong husband-wife relationship, and ideally each adult mar-

Nuclear family. A close-knit unit of mother, father, and children living in their own home.

ries only one time, for life. Such a marriage—one man to one woman—is called monogamy. The family in the United States is usually a two-generation family. When the children grow up, they move away to establish their own nuclear families, and with the death of the parents, the original unit is dissolved.

This type of family is not the most common throughout the world, however. It has been stressed in this chapter that families vary widely in kinship structure, functions performed, rules of behavior, ways of selecting mates, and attitudes toward sexuality. They vary also in size. Nuclear units are combined in various ways to form larger familial groups, and these are called extended families. Sometimes the terms **compound** or **composite families** are also used to refer to these larger groupings.

Since family patterns are so variable, the research data about different societies do not always fit neatly into categories. Consequently, various researchers may have used the same term to refer to systems or social features that are really somewhat different. On the other hand, two different terms may exist which refer to the same concept and are used interchangeably. We are using the term **extended family** to refer to all family groupings more complex than the nuclear family.

Extended family. A large family structure combining a number of related nuclear families.

EXTENDED FAMILIES

Among extended families the ties between family members may be formed along marital lines—that is, based on **conjugal** relationships. Or they may be formed along blood lines, based on what are called **consanguineal** relationships.

Three or more generations of females may be living with all their husbands and children as an extended family. As the daughters marry, their husbands become new members of the household, and as the sons marry, they go off to become members of the households of their wives. The same structure may exist in reverse, with all males of the family remaining in the family home, bringing in their wives, and all females leaving the family of orientation upon marriage and moving to the new husband's home as their family of procreation.

The Joint Family. Another type of extended family formed along blood lines is the **joint family.** This family unit consists of a number of married couples, usually brothers and their respective wives and children, living in the same household. The family is joint in the sense that resources are pooled, rooms are shared, and mutual obligations exist between the different nuclear units of the family.

The Stem Family. The **stem family,** also formed along blood lines, is sometimes called the minimal form of the extended family. In this family system, only one child, usually the eldest son, inherits the family property. His sisters and brothers must find other homes and means of livelihood once they are adults.

The stem family ordinarily passes through several developmental stages over time. If the heir marries and has children before his parents' death, the household extends over three generations. While brothers and sisters are young and unmarried, they are living in the household. When the parents die, and as the **siblings** grow up and leave, the household diminishes in size so that it resembles the nuclear family of husband, wife, and their children. The process of expansion then begins again. Changes in the size and structure of the unit also occur in the joint family. Such a family may also pass through a nuclear phase if too great an increase in family size forces them to divide the family property and split up into separate groups.

Siblings. Brothers and sisters.

The Polygamous Family.   When extended families are formed on conjugal lines, it is through plural marriages. There are three possible types of plural marriage: (1) **polygyny,** in which a man has two or more wives; (2) **polyandry,** in which a woman has two or more husbands; and (3) **group marriage,** in which two or more men and two or more women are married in common to each other. While some societies, including our own, insist upon monogamy, most societies permit some form of polygamy. The most widespread form of plural marriage is polygyny; the family consists of several mothers and their children clustered around the male family head. Polyandry is rather uncommon, and there is debate as to whether genuine group marriages have ever really existed. Sharing of sexual partners does occur, especially among brothers, but there is uncertainty about whether this sharing constitutes group marriage.

RULES OF RESIDENCE

As we have seen, the wife may move to the home of her husband or the husband to the home of his wife. Sometimes they move periodically from one to the other, or, as in our society, they may set up an entirely new home. **Rules of residence** are those customs which determine where a newly married couple will live. These customs fall into three major patterns: (1) **matrilocal,** where the couple lives with or near the wife's family; (2) **patrilocal,** where the couple lives with or near the husband's family; and (3) **neolocal,** where the couple sets up a new household separate from that of either spouse's family.

Rules of residence. Customs, varying from one society to another, which determine where a newly married couple will live.

Rules of residence are important because they determine the alignment of kin and, often, the distribution of authority within the family. Whoever moves, whether husband or wife, is at a disadvantage because that person loses the support of relatives and moves to a family where he or she is an outsider to the relatives of the spouse. Thus rules of residence decide not only those with whom one will maintain social relations but what one's power within the family will be.

RULES OF DESCENT

Rules of descent. Customs of a society which define kinship in relation to the naming of children and the rules of inheritance.

Descent may be defined as **matrilineal,** through the mother only; **patrilineal,** through the father only; or **bilineal,** through both the male and female lines. Our society has a modified bilineal descent pattern in that children generally take the name of their father, but inherit through either male or female lines. They may take the religion of either the mother or the father, if there is a difference, and may consider relatives on each side equally close.

ARRANGED MARRIAGES

In our country it is generally believed that love should be the basis of the marital relationship if it is to endure and grow stronger over time. Although parents and grandparents may try to influence the choice of a marriage partner, and sometimes do exercise a good deal of control, the choice is generally left up to the individual. In other societies, and even in times past in the United States, marriages have been arranged by parents or family elders.

The difference between the two systems of mate selection relates to differences in family systems. In the nuclear family, the strength of the conjugal relationship is both necessary and desirable, because the married couple is the basis of the family. In extended family systems, however, what is important is the functioning of the entire family unit, of which the couple is only a part. If spouses in an extended family put each other's or their children's interests first, the larger family unit may suffer. Intense relationships between husband and wife therefore can pose a threat to the extended family. In the **arranged marriage,** the family will try to select a mate who is suitable not only for the spouse but for the whole family. By de-emphasizing marriage as a source of emotional gratification, and by denying the union a basis in personal preference or love, the custom of arranged marriages ensures that the marital union will be viewed as one union among many, a part of a system.

Arranged marriage. Selection of a mate according to economic and social criteria rather than through free choice of the persons being married.

Marriage as an Economic Alliance.   Often, marriage partners are also chosen as a means of creating alliances between kinship groups. The marital exchange forms the basis for other links—social, cultural, and economic—and establishes kinship ties between groups. It has been suggested that the exchange of **spouses** developed from the fact that in primitive societies there was little else to exchange, and friendly relations between neighboring groups were of critical importance (Fox).

In many societies, the marital exchange is accompanied by a payment of money, goods, or services on the part of either the bride's or the groom's family to the other family. If the woman brings goods, livestock, or money to her new home, this is called a **dowry**. It may be turned over to the husband's family, or it may be used by the young couple to help them get started in life. If the man or his family makes a gift to the woman's parents, this is called a **bride price**, or in cases where no goods are exchanged, the man may perform labor for his prospective father-in-law, and this is called **bride service.** The payment is made to the family who loses a valuable worker when a member marries and moves to another home. The payment also serves in some societies as a guarantee that the spouse will be well treated in the new home, for the payment may have to be returned if the marriage doesn't last.

With this listing of some of the variations in marriage and family patterns as background, we can now look in more detail at the way some of these variables have been combined in particular societies.

EXTENDED FAMILIES FORMED THROUGH PLURAL MARRIAGES

A polygynous society is one in which polygyny is not merely permitted but is the preferred form of marriage—that is, polygyny enjoy's higher prestige and there is some social pressure to marry more than one wife. Because of the natural **sex ratio,** a fairly equal number of men and women in a society, monogamous unions may outnumber polygynous unions even in societies where polygyny is preferred. Among Australian **aborigines,** a shortage of males due to their slaughter in warfare has been associated with polygyny (Berndt, 1965). Economic factors also force many men to remain monogamous. It is likely that a man will have to provide the families of each of his brides with a bride price, which usually represents a substantial quantity of goods, cattle, or money, and the provision for more than one bride price would be difficult for one man—virtually impossible for a poor man or for younger men who have not yet established themselves. The number of wives tends to be related to the man's social status. Among the Baganda in central Africa, for example, the king traditionally had hundreds of wives, chiefs had dozens, and commoners had two or three (Queen and Habenstein, 1974).

Sex ratio. The number of males in a society for every hundred females.

POLYGYNY
Characteristic of polygynous societies is a strong emphasis on a large number of children. Queen and Habenstein report that, among the Baganda, ten children for a wife was not considered abnormal, and a well-to-do man might have fifty children. The mother-child tie tends to be stronger than the father-child tie, and rivalry between children of different mothers may be intense. The husband tends to be more aloof and to exercise more au-

---

LARGE FAMILIES

In polygamous countries, the number of a person's descendants soon becomes incalculable. The last Sharifian Emperor of Morocco, Moulay Ismail (1672–1727), known as ''The Bloodthirsty,'' was reputed to have fathered a total of 548 sons and 340 daughters.

Capt. Wilson Kettle (born 1860) of Grand Bay, Port Aux Basques, Newfoundland, Canada, died on January 25, 1963, aged 102, leaving 11 children by two wives, 65 grandchildren, 201 great-grandchildren, and 305 great-great-grandchildren, a total of 582 living descendants. Mrs. Johanna Booyson . . . of Belfast, Transvaal, was estimated to have 600 living descendants in South Africa in January, 1968.

Source: *Guinness Book of World Records* ©️ 1976 by Sterling Publishing Co., Inc., New York.

Co-wives. One or more women who share the same husband.

thority in a polygynous union than in a monogamous one. But since more than one wife is the ideal, women may be highly valued, particularly in an agricultural society where women do most of the field work. This is true among the Baganda, where a wife is considered an economic investment.

Polygynous societies usually have a number of mechanisms for reducing interpersonal conflict. Since, in general, relationships among co-wives are more amicable where the wives are related, **sororal polygyny,** the marriage of a group of sisters to one man, is a widespread form of polygyny. Where co-wives are unrelated, they will probably have separate dwellings, another means of reducing tension. Sexual jealousy is frequently lessened if the husband is expected to cohabit with his wives in regular rotation. Whether or not he has sexual relations with each wife, none of them is humiliated by a public rejection. Another device to reduce conflict is to assign one wife, usually the one first married, a supervisory position in the management of tasks and the settlement of disputes.

It is difficult to see how a polygynous society could function harmoniously if it did not include mechanisms such as these, and it has been suggested that it was the lack of such measures that caused the failure of the nineteenth-century Mormon experiment with polygyny in the United States.

Polygyny as Practiced in the United States. In the Mormon church, established in 1830 by Joseph Smith, plural marriage was officially proclaimed in 1852 and may have been practiced as early as the 1830s. Some historians have suggested that the Mormons adopted the doctrine of polygyny for reasons of expedience. More women than men were attracted to the organization, and because they needed husbands for protection and assistance as the group moved west and the organization needed children in order to

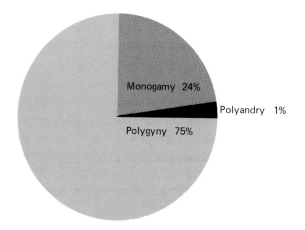

Fig. 1.1 Percentage of societies preferring plural marriage. Distribution of monogamous and polygamous marriage as the predominant form in Murdock's World ethnographic sample. (Source: George P. Murdock, World ethnographic sample, *American Anthropologist* 59:686.)

expand, polygyny was a highly functional family system for the group. The decision to enter a polygynous union was entirely voluntary on both sides and the practice was defended by both women and men (Kephart, 1972).

One of the major problems the Mormons faced, of course, was the difficulty of maintaining a polygynous system within a monogamous culture. Public opinion and the courts both exerted considerable pressure to end polygyny. But accounts written by Kimball Young, a grandson of the Mormon leader Brigham Young, suggest that the system was also weakened by internal troubles. Sexual jealousy, for example, was a problem. Not only did unrelated wives live together in one establishment, but their status was insecure. The newest wife was likely to be the favorite and the previous wives would be neglected. Moreover, whoever was the favorite wife of the moment might well exercise authority over her older co-wives because of her stronger influence with the husband (Murdock, 1949). Conflicts arose and the culture did not provide any standardized ways for handling them. In a society where polygyny is a long-established, integral part of the culture, such mechanisms have developed out of necessity.

It is important to remember that marriage and the family are social and economic, not merely sexual, institutions. The mutual protection and economic cooperation that characterized the large households formed through plural marriages have appeared to be less functional in industrial societies than in agricultural and hunting societies. But in rural areas where elimination of polygyny would seriously disrupt the established economy there has been resistance to abandoning this form of the family.

Mormons. Believers in the Book of Mormon; members of the Church of Jesus Christ of Latter Day Saints.

POLYANDRY

Although polyandry is practiced in some parts of the world, it is rarely the preferred form of marriage in any society. The World Ethnographic Sample, a comparison of 565 cultures from all over the world, lists only four poly-androus societies: the Nayar and the Toda of South India, the Marquesans of Polynesia, and the Tibetans of the Himalayas (Murdock, 1957). Other societies sometimes called polyandrous have been found upon examination to be somewhat different. Thus the Kota of South India, for example, have a sharing of wives, but not true polyandry; a man's brothers may have free sexual access to his wife, but they will not be considered the fathers of her children (Mandelbaum, 1938).

In **fraternal polyandry**, the husbands are brothers; in nonfraternal poly-andry, the husbands are unrelated. Some societies practice a custom related to fraternal polyandry called the **levirate**. This specifies that the preferred mate for a widow is her deceased husband's brother. This is not fraternal polyandry, since the woman is not married to the husband and his brother at the same time; but the levirate is a variant of the custom of fraternal polyandry in that all of the woman's offspring would be of the same male lineage.

Polyandry seems to occur in societies that are extremely poor. Where economic productivity is so low that a man is unable to support a wife and children by himself, the shared responsibility can assure the family's main-tenance. Polyandry is also related to other conditions in the society. It is advantageous, for example, where help in hunting is regularly required. It is compatible with a society in which the primary occupational category is military and the husband may be absent for long periods of time. This was the case among the Nayar, a warrior caste in India to be discussed later. It is also useful in places where there is a land shortage, since family property will be kept intact as it is passed along to the sons of the next gen-eration. One or more of these conditions have usually been associated with polyandrous societies.

Another characteristic of such a society must be an imbalance in the sex ratio. There must be more men than women. The surplus of men of marriageable age characteristic of polyandrous societies has been associ-ated with the practices of female **infanticide** and selling of women. But whether these practices cause polyandry to develop or are the mechanisms by which the number of women is kept low in order to maintain the marital system is uncertain.

The Toda Form of Polyandry.   Although there are certain functional ad-vantages associated with polyandry, as in any marriage system, there are certain disadvantages. Sexual jealousy or competition may be a problem and **paternity** cannot be accurately determined. The Toda, a tribe of India, developed an interesting set of mechanisms for dealing with these problems.

The Toda are a pastoral, hill-dwelling tribe whose main occupation is herding buffalo. They lived for centuries in some isolation, and their social

Infanticide. Socially ac-cepted killing of infants, usually by exposure or abandonment, often for economic reasons.

and cultural patterns, as well as their physical appearance, differ markedly from those of the people around them. Their traditional social organization was complex, as were their marriage customs. There were, in fact, three marriage institutions: fraternal polyandry, wife transfer, and the **consort-mistress union** (Queen and Habenstein).

When a Toda woman married a man, she became the wife of his brothers as well. The brothers would usually continue to share a household, and sexual privileges would rotate equitably among them. There was little jealousy and the determination of paternity was not viewed as a problem. For legal purposes, paternity was ceremonially established in the seventh month of a woman's pregnancy. In this ceremony, one brother, usually the oldest, would present the woman with a toy bow and arrow. He was thereby recognized as the legal or social father of the child and of all subsequent children who were born. After two or three births, another brother would present the bow and arrow and be father of all children born thereafter. The Toda were not upset that the legal father of the children was not necessarily the biological father; by means of this rite, paternity was established without hostility or conflict (Queen and Habenstein).

Giving the bow. A Toda ceremony for establishing who the legal father of a child will be.

In addition to fraternal polyandry, there were two other Toda customs which served to keep their marriage systems running smoothly. One was a form of wife transfer. There are always more widowers than widows in a polyandrous society. The Toda male who was seeking a wife was permitted to choose a mate from among those already married, and the husbands would be repaid with cattle for the loss of their wife. In this way, marriage partners were made available for nearly all members of the tribe at some time. This custom, together with the custom of consort-mistress union, which legalized certain prohibited marriages by means of a special ceremony, helped avoid the problem of a possible shortage of mates.

Many facets of the Toda system may strike Americans as highly unusual. But the system worked well for centuries. In recent years, Toda marriage customs have undergone many changes, but these have been caused largely by external conditions, not by problems within the marriage system itself.

GROUP MARRIAGE

There has been some debate among social scientists over whether or not true group marriage has ever existed. It has been reported to be a custom among the Kaingang of Brazil, the Dieri of Australia, and the Chuckchee of Siberia, though not the predominant marital form in any of these societies. Some anthropologists question the data; others question the interpretation of the data. Part of the problem arises from the difficulty of defining marriage. It is clear that to be called marriage, a relationship must involve more than the sexual privilege. But exactly what else must be involved? A shared residence? Shared economic responsibilities? In general, these characterize the marital union—but not in all societies.

The definition of marriage becomes extremely complicated when it involves a group. It may be clear that they share sexual privileges but difficult to assess their other responsibilities to each other. What has been called group marriage among the Marquesans, for example, has been described as involving a head couple and a number of men and women who live with them. While all share sexual rights, the ties binding the head couple seem to be stronger than those binding the other members of the group to each other or to the head couple (Kenkel, 1973). Do we say then that all are married, or that only the head couple have a full marital relationship?

Obviously, the problem of definition derives directly from the complexity and variety of the marriage and kinship systems found in various parts of the world and at different times in the history of human development. In the United States, our kinship system is so simple that we find it difficult to understand the complicated relationships of many primitive societies. We don't even have the vocabulary to describe these systems. Whether or not group marriage can be considered to exist depends finally upon how one defines marriage. However, as we will see in Chapter 16, some consider group marriage to be a viable alternative to traditional monogamous marriage in the United States at the present time.

Group marriage. Marriage of two or more people of each sex including sharing of sexual privileges and economic responsibilities.

EXTENDED FAMILIES FORMED BY DESCENT

Extended families formed by descent are those family groups that combine along a blood axis, as when several brothers and their wives, several sisters and their husbands, or several generations of the same blood line share a common household.

Extended families formed by descent share certain features with those formed by plural marriages. Both have the advantages of a large household which provides continuity over time and the economic, social, and political strength of numbers. And both have the disadvantages—the tensions of many people living close together, the need for strong authority, and the lack of personal freedom.

The particular form of the extended family that a society adopts is related to other aspects of its social system and also to its particular environmental circumstances. For example, because of its ability to transmit property intact over generations, the extended family based on blood ties tends to develop where immovable property constitutes the major form of wealth, as in economies based on landholding. Where a society's main form of wealth is immovable, and there is also such a shortage of this immovable property that there is really only enough for one heir, the stem family may develop. As we have mentioned, in this particular form of the extended family, only one child inherits the family property. This has been the case in Ireland where the average farm is too small to make subdivision of the land feasible.

THE STEM FAMILY IN IRELAND

The family and marriage patterns of the rural Irish represent an interesting version of the stem family system. One unusual feature is that there is no custom or law that specifies who shall be the heir. The father is free to choose which son will succeed him. This tends to keep the sons working on the father's farm well into their maturity, each hoping to inherit it. It also invests the father with strong authority, since he will leave the land to the son who pleases him most (Humphreys, 1965). His authority is further intensified in that it is he who determines when the transfer of property will take place.

In general, the father hands over the ownership and management of the farm to his heir at the time of the latter's marriage. The heir's marriage is the central event in the entire family cycle for several reasons. First, in Ireland, the dowry of the heir's bride belongs not to the couple but to the heir's father and is used to provide a dowry for the daughters of the family. Second, once the daughters' dowries are provided for and the management of the farm transferred, the parents generally retire. And third, at this point the other brothers usually leave the household to seek a living elsewhere.

Dowry. A payment of money or property from the family of the bride to the groom or his family.

The dispersal of the heir's brothers and sisters is inherent in the stem family system. In Ireland, both males and females used to find a vocation in the church. Nowadays, both tend to migrate to the city. Urban life in Ireland differs greatly from rural family life, and in Dublin, as in any industrial city, large impersonal organizations now perform the functions the rural family has traditionally fulfilled. Away from the structure of the family farm with its duties and responsibilities, the structure of the family has altered, and the conjugal family is replacing the stem family as the typical system (Humphreys).

THE JOINT FAMILY IN INDIA

Another variation of the extended family is the joint family. Historically, this system has been characteristic of rural areas and of the upper classes. It has traditionally been the ideal system among the Hindus in India.

The joint household in India consists of the father, if he is alive, his sons (a set of brothers), and their sons, their wives and unmarried daughters, and possibly other kinsmen. Legally, the property is jointly the possession of all males directly descended from the father. The joint household is generally a single producing unit and a single consuming unit as well. It is also the center of religious functions.

Bride price. A gift by a man or his family to the parents of the woman he is to marry.

Many features of the Hindu family are related to the pressure to keep the family unit and the family property intact. To reinforce the importance of the larger unit, marriages have traditionally been arranged by the elders of the group and the separateness of the conjugal pair has been strongly de-emphasized. Authority within the family is delegated strictly according to sex and age, and the position of the young girl entering her husband's home is subservient to all the older women of the household, especially her mother-in-law. This is counterbalanced only slightly by the bride price, which has served not only as a way of legalizing the marriage and the children and stabilizing the marriage, but also as a means of giving the bride some status in her new home.

In India, as elsewhere, family patterns are changing, and there is some debate concerning the direction of present trends. Some social scientists have linked the small size of modern Indian families to the decline of the joint family. The census of 1901, however, indicates that families then were equally small, averaging five members (Orenstein, 1961).

Cyclical. Characterized by a recurring succession of events which usually lead back to the starting point.

Statistics by themselves are often deceptive. The joint family, like the stem family, is **cyclical** in its structure. An increase in family size may lead to the division of the joint household into nuclear family units each of which in time develops into a new joint family. Thus at a given point in time, there may be a predominance of small units but this does not indicate that the joint family is declining. It is also important to note that the values of the joint family may exist although the joint household does not. By this we mean that the rights and obligations, sentiments and feelings that characterized relationships in the joint family may persist although the joint household has dissolved. As young Indians leave the family home for employment in the cities and for advanced education, the structure of the joint family is impaired. But there is some evidence that once young people get settled in new locations they tend to revert to the joint family structure (Khatri, 1975).

The joint family, like all of the forms of the extended family described, is a combination of overlapping units composed of father, mother, and children. These units are generally referred to as nuclear families and may be thought of as the building blocks of the various forms of the extended family.

IS THE NUCLEAR FAMILY UNIVERSAL?

Some social scientists have claimed that the nuclear family, the mother-father-child unit, performs tasks that are so essential to society that it is a universal structure. They say that the nuclear family, although it may be embedded in the larger kinship structure, is recognized as a separate and distinct unit by every society in the world (Murdock, 1949).

Others have questioned this. Not all societies have been fully investigated or adequately described. Moreover, before we can say whether or not a society recognizes the nuclear family as a unit, we have to know what properties characterize the family. For example, do the members of the nuclear unit have to live together to constitute a family? Do there have to be reciprocal economic obligations between husband and wife? We have already discussed the difficulties involved in finding definitions of marriage and family broad enough to include all variations of these patterns found throughout the world. Some **anthropologists** have suggested that whether or not the nuclear family is universal may depend upon how we define that institution (Stephens, 1963).

It is certainly possible to conceive ways of organizing society that would eliminate the need for the nuclear family. The tasks usually performed by the family could be performed by other institutions instead. There are two cultures that we know of where the nuclear family does not in fact perform the tasks usually associated with it. Among the Nayar of Southwest India and the kibbutzim of Israel, it is difficult to say whether the nuclear family is an important structural unit at all.

THE CASE OF THE NAYAR

The traditional marriage and family customs of the Nayar, practiced until the end of the nineteenth century, were very complex and highly unusual. Kinship in this warrior caste was traced through women; each person belonged for life to the mother's family group, called a **matrilineage.** All members of a matrilineage lived in one large house that was built upon a mound; both the mound and the kinship unit living there were known as the **taravad.** The taravad as a family group was headed by the oldest surviving male member of the matrilineage who was called the **karanavan** (Fox).

Both boys and girls, as they grew up, treated the taravad as their home and remained there after they had married. In other words, husbands did not live with their wives, but with the families of their mothers and sisters. They would visit their wives in the evening, but they had few obligations toward them or toward their children, who remained on the wife's taravad and came under the guardianship of the head of her household. Rather, a man had well-defined obligations toward the children of his sisters and female cousins in his own taravad (Gough, 1968).

Another aspect of the Nayar marital system that we must consider is that it was polyandrous. A girl was ritually married, before puberty, in a ceremony that lasted four days, at which point the union was terminated. After puberty, a woman was then free to take several husbands. The only requirement was that a husband be of a **caste** equal to or higher than her own. The question of paternity was of little significance among the Nayar, provided the woman could name a man of appropriate caste as the father, whether or not he was the biological father. If she could not name such a

Anthropologist. One who studies the science of human behavior in relation to physical character, environmental and social relations, and culture.

man, however, it was assumed she had mated with a man of lower caste and she was turned out of the family and disowned for having defiled the taravad.

It is clear, then, that the husband-wife relationship among the Nayar was a socially legitimate sexual union, but was it marriage as we usually define it? The couple did not share a residence, they had no reciprocal economic obligations, they did not share the responsibilities of parenthood (Stephens). A man had no rights concerning his children, nor obligations toward them. It would seem that among the Nayar the nuclear family did not function as a unit, nor was it recognized as such within the society.

THE CASE OF THE KIBBUTZ

The **kibbutz** of Israel provides another example of a society where the role of the nuclear family may lack significance. Many of the **kibbutzim** are agricultural collectives first established in the early part of the century, in which living, ownership of property, and the rearing of children are communal. Some follow the Marxist doctrine, "from each according to his ability, to each according to his needs," and discourage ownership of private property (Spiro, 1968).

Although marriage does exist in the kibbutz, there is usually no ceremony, and the couple, though they do share a room, continue to live communally. They do not function as an economic unit, for they are both part of the larger economic unit, the kibbutz; nor do they raise and educate their children, for this, too, is the task of the kibbutz which provides communal nurseries and dormitories for the children where all children are treated as equals (Spiro).

Kibbutzim. Agricultural communes in Israel which emphasize reclaiming the land or increasing productivity.

Children of an Israeli kibbutz located in a desert area. They are being raised in communal groups according to age level but visit with their biological parents daily.

Is the nuclear family a functional unit in this society? For the most part, the traditional roles played by the nuclear family are taken over by the kibbutz as a whole. Yet there is some indication that the family continues to play an emotional role in the people's lives. Children recognize their parents as their closest relations, and view their visits to their parents' room as an important part of the day. Thus the nuclear family in the kibbutz does seem to perform the important function of providing emotional security for children and strong emotional satisfactions for parents. Perhaps we might say that the nuclear family, though greatly reduced in importance, does continue to exist in this society.

WHY DO WE WANT TO KNOW? WHY DO WE CARE?

When we ask whether the nuclear family is universal, we are really asking whether a society can survive without it. This question is of particular significance in the United States at this time since the increasing instability of the family has caused some people to fear that it is a dying institution. As more and more of the family's traditional roles are assumed by large, impersonal organizations, such as day-care centers, schools, and hospitals, the family seems to be left with little real significance. Changing attitudes toward marriage are reflected in the high rate of divorce and the reluctance of many young people to marry. But can alternatives be found that will substitute for the family in meeting human needs? **Communes,** many of them similar in structure to the Israeli kibbutz, are providing an alternative to traditional monogamous marriage to thousands of people in the United States today, as are group marriages and extralegal **cohabitation.** Should we call these units families or not?

These questions, to which we will return in Chapters 16 and 17, cannot be answered with as much certainty as we would like. As we have seen, the nuclear family may not be universal. It is almost universal, though, which indicates just how effective it has been as a means of performing tasks necessary for societal and personal survival. Nevertheless, the great variation in family systems throughout the world is evidence that neither the family nor the functions it serves should be too narrowly defined. Family systems can be modified, changed, and even, as in the kibbutz, drastically reduced in importance, without necessarily impairing the functioning of the society as a whole.

Universal. Present or occurring everywhere.

THE IDEAL AND THE REAL

We have described the kibbutz in terms of the ideas on which these communities were founded: communal living, the equality of all individuals, and the minimization of family life have been their explicit goals. An investigation of daily life in the kibbutz, however, reveals some deviation

Values. Principles or qualities which are highly esteemed.

from these **values.** In fact, the kibbutz provides an interesting case of the divergence that exists in any society between the way people think life should be lived, the ideal, and the way it actually is lived, the real.

The kibbutz was originally founded on the basis of complete equality between men and women, and all jobs were rotated among all members on a regular schedule. Nowadays, however, the women are tending to do more of the domestic work than the men, and their job involvement seems to be weaker than their family involvement (Gerson, 1971).

Ideals. Standards of perfection; goals; the focus of endeavor.

We can only speculate about the causes of these deviations from kibbutz **ideals.** It may be that the task of caring for infants was most easily assigned to mothers and this led to the assignment of other domestic duties. It is also important to remember that the kibbutzim are small communities within the larger society of Israel, which has maintained the ideal of the nuclear family. Perhaps this has caused some conflict for the women of the kibbutz about what their role as mothers should be.

Whatever specific problems and tensions of life on the kibbutz have led to these particular deviations from the society's ideals, such deviations are to be expected. In any society, we are likely to find a difference between the way people think life should be lived and the way they actually live their lives.

IDEAL AND REAL IN JAMAICA

Norms. Principles of right action binding upon members of a group and serving to guide, control, or regulate behavior.

Although performance falls short of ideals, people do not necessarily relinquish those ideals. In this sense, ideals are normative: they represent values and standards of correctness (**norms**) toward which we strive. Insofar as our ideals are our goals, they have a strong influence on our lives (Goode, 1964). A study of family life in Jamaica vividly reveals the normative strength of the ideal.

Research conducted by Judith Blake (1961) indicated that among lower-class Jamaicans, a higher proportion of young men and women were living together unmarried than in legal wedlock. Yet the majority of those questioned felt that marriage was far more desirable than the **common-law** unions in which they were living. Moreover, among older couples, a majority had had a church wedding.

Exploring the question of why young Jamaicans did not marry although they said they thought marriage was best, Blake found that several economic and social factors were involved. For most Jamaicans, the cost of a wedding celebration and a gold ring is prohibitive, yet they feel that a marriage without these would be an admission of failure. Moreover, the cost of being married is very high, since Jamaicans feel that the couple should have a home of their own, that the husband should be able to provide support for the family, and that the married couple's standard of living should be higher than that of a couple living in a common-law union. Since poverty is the norm in Jamaica, these demands are difficult to meet, and most Jamaicans feel they would rather forego marriage if they cannot do it "in the right way" (Blake).

Social factors complicate the situation. Although it is believed that a woman should be a virgin when she marries, there are few social or family controls restricting premarital relations, and many women become pregnant while still in their teens. From then on, a woman's marital opportunities are limited, and from economic necessity she may consent to a common-law union. From the male point of view, this type of union may be all he is economically able to offer without opening himself up to the possibility of social ridicule.

Common-law marriage. A marriage based on the agreement of a cohabiting couple to present themselves as married.

Yet by the age of 65, 74.7 percent of the males and 66.7 percent of the females have had a church wedding and a reception afterwards. It seems that although socioeconomic factors may force Jamaicans to postpone marriage for many years, they do not lose sight of this ideal and eventually they do achieve it, with their children in attendance at the wedding (Blake).

In our own society, we can also find many ways in which our ideals are not matched by reality. Most Americans would say that monogamy is best; but with the high rate of divorce and remarriage, what we really have is **serial monogramy,** one spouse at a time. Although our ideal remains the conjugal family, we have, in fact, many single-parent families. And while the United States is a neolocal society and most people would say it is desirable for a newly married couple to have a home of their own, many young couples cannot afford it and stay on at least temporarily with one set of parents in an extended family situation.

CHANGE IN THE FAMILY

The separation between the ideal and the real should not be seen as entirely negative. It has been caused, in part, by changing social conditions which are in turn related to other changes in the society. What was ideal 50 years ago may no longer be economically realistic. As values change over time, what was once considered right may now seem undesirable. In this sense, reality may point the way to future ideals. Usually transitions are made slowly, but even when they are rapid, they need not be destructive. Social systems can often undergo major upheavals without being destroyed, as we shall see in a brief examination of China, which in recent decades has successfully endured extensive change.

THE ANCIENT CHINESE FAMILY

The ancient Chinese family, sometimes called the purest form of the extended family, served to meet all its members' societal and personal needs for survival. It was the basic economic unit in the society, both for production and for distribution. It was the basic political unit, directly responsible to the central government in all administrative matters. Socialization, education, and religious instruction all took place within the family. It was the family that conferred upon individuals their social position and, by defining all role expectations, their **identity.** It was by meeting family expectations that individuals could develop a sense of security, a feeling of worth in the group and in the society at large (Queen and Habenstein).

Identity. The sense of one's own uniqueness, consistency, and continuity over time.

Because of the importance of the entire family structure, the conjugal unit was de-emphasized. Marriage was regarded as a social arrangement not between two individuals but between two families. Marriages were arranged by heads of families and were concluded by contracts which required the signatures of the family elders, but not those of the couple. The purpose of the marital union was to provide male heirs who would carry on the male lineage and thus carry on the family.

The position of women in this society was very low. Of especially low status was the new wife, who was considered to be entering the service of her husband and his mother. Her position could improve slightly if she bore male children or if younger daughters-in-law entered the family. But it is important to note that her husband's position, though better than hers, was nonetheless subservient: he was considered to be in the service of his father, who was in turn in the service of the departed ancestors. In fact, the whole society was based on a hierarchy of domination and subservience (Sidel, 1973).

THE FAMILY IN MODERN CHINA

The Communist revolution of 1949 brought about major changes in the family system in China. Most of the functions formerly performed by the family have been transferred to the state. The family has diminished in importance and the government has assumed the authority the family once had. Families are no longer separate economic and political units, working to serve their own needs. Rather, people are supposed to be working to serve the good of the entire country.

Among the many significant effects of the changes in the family system has been the marked improvement in the status of women. Arranged marriages have been abolished, along with such practices as child marriages, and **concubinage.** The marital union is now considered a partnership between equals. Especially important for the status of women, the state provides child care to enable women to work, and they receive equal pay for equal work (Sidel).

Concubinage. A custom by which the head of a household takes an extra female sexual partner who then lives with the family.

One need only consider China's recent history to realize how radical the trend toward equalization of the sexes is, and how dramatic the changes undergone by the Chinese family system have been. Yet China has survived

A modern family in Hong Kong, China.

these rapid and overwhelming changes, and the society as a whole appears to be flourishing.

TREND TO THE CONJUGAL FAMILY

We have seen that family systems not only vary from one place to another, they also change over time. Natural disasters, political upheavals, economic conditions—all affect the social structure of which the family is a part. The changes may be temporary or they may be permanent. What is important for the society is that its institutions be sufficiently flexible to adapt to new conditions.

A trend of major significance observed throughout the world in recent years has been the increasing prevalence of the conjugal or nuclear family. Not only in Western countries, but in the developing nations of Africa and the Middle East as well, extended families are coming to play a less and less important role, and the conjugal family a more important one.

Conjugal family. A family which strongly emphasizes the bond of intimacy between husband and wife.

Many social scientists attribute this trend to the effects of industrialization and urbanization. An industrial economy by its very nature requires that individuals leave home and settle where jobs are available. This demand for physical mobility has weakened the extended family structure. And because the status individuals can achieve outweighs the status ascribed to them at birth, the family has less to offer. Equally important, commercial and civic organizations in urban society have now taken over many of the functions the family once performed, such as protection, education, or lending money, and the extended family is no longer such a necessary structure (Goode, 1963).

In the United States, the importance of the extended family has diminished but it has not altogether disappeared. Ties among kin are maintained through visits, letters, and gifts. Particularly in times of crisis, such as illness or unemployment, family members do provide services and even financial support for close kin who need it. These ties are generally considered to be voluntary, however, involving few rights and obligations. The element of control has been weakened, and the trend is toward more freedom.

Many people in other societies, as well as our own, view these changes in family patterns as signs of social disintegration. They say that if there wasn't freedom in the old system, at least there was order and security. But if we look closely at that order, we find that it was often geared to "keeping people in their place." One of the major changes associated with the trend to the conjugal family has been the improved status of women. It may be that what is disorder for some is a release for others from a rigid and repressive system. We might also ask to what degree a negative judgment of changing forms of marriage and the family is fruitful. Social organization must change as the total environment changes, or a society cannot survive.

REASONS FOR CROSS-CULTURAL STUDY OF THE FAMILY

Cross-cultural. Describing and comparing the customs and beliefs of two or more different cultures or cultural areas.

One reason for studying family systems in other societies is that it helps us to look objectively at problems of family life present in our own society and the possibilities for change. Marriage and the family is a subject with which most of us are intimately involved, and many people tend to get emotional about such issues as extralegal cohabitation, how to raise children, or terminating marriage through divorce. However, it is easier to be objective about the facts of a culture other than our own. What we might feel is improper for our own families or neighbors becomes interesting when it concerns people who are distant and personally unknown to us. And once we have learned how to look at the features of a society objectively, we have acquired a tool, a method of observation that can then be applied to our own society as well. In addition, the great variety of family patterns that exists makes it clear that no one system is the natural system for everyone. This realization opens up to us the possibility of alternatives for our own society (Queen and Habenstein).

Another advantage of cross-cultural studies is that they enable us to compare what is happening in our own society with what is happening in other societies. Such comparisons can sometimes provide insight into the broad patterns involved and help us to understand the directions in which our society is changing. The next chapter will describe some of the changes American family patterns have undergone in the past as they developed from colonial times to the present. And in Chapter 3, we will consider American family patterns in the seventies.

1. The main purposes of this chapter are to introduce and explain the concepts of marriage and the family; to examine various types of family organization found in other cultures; and to recognize that marriage and the family, like all social institutions, are affected by changes in other aspects of a society.

2. The family is a social group sharing a home and cooperating economically. It is commonly based on the marriage of one or more sexually cohabiting couples and usually involves the expectation of having children for whom the adults of the family accept responsibility. The family is sometimes called the basic social institution. As such it performs certain functions: reproduction and socialization; economic cooperation; assignment of social roles; and development of intimate personal relationships.

3. Marriage is a social institution consisting of laws and customs that specify the ways in which the family relationship should be established, conducted, or terminated.

4. The organization of the family varies from culture to culture. The most common form of family organization in the United States (but not throughout the world) is the nuclear or conjugal family. In other societies, the nuclear family can be combined in different ways into larger extended families, which can be based on conjugal (marital) or consanguineal (blood line) relationships. The joint family, the stem family, and the polygamous family are different forms of the extended family. In addition to establishing the basic organization of the family, societies have rules and customs governing mate selection and aspects of family life such as where the family lives (rules of residence) and how relationships are traced (rules of descent).

5. The nuclear family, whether as a single unit or as part of an extended family, may not be a basic unit in all societies, as witnessed by the Nayar and the Israeli kibbutzim. That it is almost universal indicates its effectiveness in performing functions for societal and personal survival.

6. Cross-cultural studies of family systems and their development in other societies help us to look objectively at the problems, possibilities, and alternatives of family life in our own society. The variations in family systems throughout the world and the changes in these systems over the years (such as those in the Chinese family) are evidence that neither the family nor its functions should be too narrowly defined.

Summary

Society	Marriage	Sex ratio
Institution	Monogamy	Norms
Cross-cultural	Polygamy	Values
Socialization	Nuclear family	Ideals
Roles	Extended family	
Family	Mate selection	
Household	Arranged marriage	
Kinship system	Incest taboo	

Key Concepts

Review and Discussion

1. Thinking of the four basic functions of the family, give specific examples of how your own family fulfilled each of these functions.

2. Describe some examples of how families in the United States are carrying on customs of other parts of the world brought here either by themselves or by previous generations.

3. Describe differences and similarities between the way each of your parents grew up in the homes of your grandparents (their families of orientation) and the way they have brought you up (their family of procreation).

4. Compare the Toda form of polyandry with that of the Nayar.

5. Would you enjoy living on an Israeli kibbutz? Why or why not?

Suggested Readings

FOX, R. (1967). *Kinship and Marriage.* Baltimore: Penguin.

This introduction to kinship systems in other cultures examines how kinship is determined, how marriage and inheritance are controlled, and social and economic conditions which have led to particular systems.

GOODE, W. J. (1964). *The Family.* Englewood Cliffs, N.J.: Prentice-Hall.

Covers the relationship between family systems and the larger social structure using a framework of sociological theory and data gathered from societies past and present.

HAMMOND, D., AND A. JABLOW (1976). *Women in Cultures of the World.* Menlo Park, Calif.: Cummings.

Studies women's roles in traditional societies using a cross-cultural approach. The book covers not only the institutional framework of women's roles but the quality of their lives as well.

STACK, C. B. ET AL. (1975). Review essay: anthropology. *Signs: Journal of Women in Culture and Society* 1: 147–159.

Eight women at the Department of Anthropology of the University of California (Berkeley) summarize contemporary anthropological analyses of the roles of women in various primitive societies.

QUEEN, S. A., AND R.H. HABENSTEIN (1974). *The Family in Various Cultures,* Fourth Edition. Philadelphia: Lippincott.

A study of the family systems of other cultures which combines the comparative and historical approaches. It covers the family life of Hopi Indians, Chinese, Ancient Hebrews, Black Americans, Canadians, Mexican-Americans, and many others.

Historical Antecedents of the American Family 2

The Love Scene is an illustration from a fourteenth-century German collection of lyrics sung by the troubadours in praise of love and chivalry.

Consider a common contemporary dilemma: a young mother is trying to decide whether to place her preschool children in a day-care center and go back to work. Even though her family needs the money, she is torn by conflicting feelings: that her children need her full-time attention while they are young; that woman's proper place is in the home; that women should have the same opportunities and responsibilities as men; that she is not really happy as a full-time housewife.

These contradictory notions concerning women's roles are part of the accumulation of ideas over many centuries about what family life should be. Some of our current ways of fulfilling social roles are novel solutions to contemporary problems, but many are not. When we behave in the same ways that our ancestors did, are we responding to basic realities of the human situation, or are we following traditions that no longer serve any social purpose? Or, we might ask, are some of our customs still valid, but for different reasons than in the past? Questions like these are basic to an understanding of contemporary marriage as well as to individual choices in interpersonal relationships.

Family customs have always had some link with the past. The early American colonists from Europe looked at courtship, marriage, childbearing, sexuality, and divorce from points of view shaped not only by the challenges of settling a new land but by their Old World traditions as well. How women and children are treated today in America is still influenced by **patriarchal** customs and values derived from early agricultural societies. The laws which are supposed to regulate our sexual behavior have developed from Greek, Roman, and Judeo-Christian traditions mingled with Puritan religious concepts and Victorian beliefs in self-restraint.

Despite its continuity with the past, the history of the American family has also been one of change in response to advances in scientific knowledge and new inventions. The course of change is not easy to trace, for evolution of the American family has not followed a straight path from ideas we now consider old-fashioned to notions we consider modern. Attitudes toward sexuality, for instance, have swung back and forth between repression and permissiveness. In order to trace the threads which have been woven into the complex fabric of today's family traditions, we must go back to the roots of our heritage in ancient cultures.

ROOTS OF THE FAMILY IN WESTERN CIVILIZATION

The story of the development of Western civilization to its present condition is divided into three major periods. **Prehistoric** times are so called because no written history remains of the preliterate peoples who lived then. The period is generally referred to as the Stone Age because of the

Patriarchal. Characterized by the supremacy of the father of the family and the legal dependency of wives and children.

Prehistoric. The period of human existence—prior to the invention of writing—for which no historical records exist.

primitive stone tools and weapons found at various sites where prehistoric peoples lived. Written history began about 5000 years ago. It is divided into B.C., meaning Before Christ, the 3000-year period before the birth of Jesus Christ, and A.D., the period of almost 2000 years since his birth. A.D stands for the Latin words *anno Domini,* which mean "in the year of the Lord." This division of time was adopted by the Christian church, as a part of other calendar reforms, about 500 years after the time of Christ (*Encyclopedia Britannica*).

A.D. **The period of time since the birth of Jesus Christ.**

B.C. **The period of time prior to the birth of Jesus Christ.**

We know almost nothing about the family in prehistoric times, though some things have been surmised from studies of primitive groups of people found living in isolated pockets around the world in more recent times. Even after the beginnings of recorded history, only a little is known about home life, since written documents are few. A fairly clear picture of family structure emerges among the ancient Greeks and Romans, beginning about 500 B.C. The importance of the family to the Hebrews is indicated by the numerous references to **betrothals** and marital relationships in the various books of the Bible and especially through the fact that two of the Ten Commandments relate to family obligations. One is the injunction to honor your father and mother; the other is the prohibition of adultery. In general, it is through the Bible that the Hebrew ideas about marriage and the family became so influential in Western civilization.

Jesus, the central figure of the Christian church, spoke Hebrew, the language of the Old Testament. Many books of the New Testament were originally written in Greek. This language had become important in the Mediterranean world through Greek conquest and colonization of the area (Rickard and Hyma, 1956). The language of the early Christian church, however, was Latin, the language of the Roman Empire. The cultural elements represented by these three major civilizations of ancient times, the Hebrew, Greek, and Roman, have blended into the customs, habits, and laws transmitted to America by way of Western Europe.

Following the decline of the Roman Empire in about the fourth century, European history became a series of barbaric struggles between warring Anglo-Saxon and Germanic tribes. Meanwhile, the Catholic church, centered in Rome, was gradually establishing its position of leadership and authority, and during the Middle Ages increased its influence over domestic life.

The intellectual darkness of the Middle Ages gradually gave way during the fifteenth and sixteenth centuries to urbanization, increasing trade and industry, and a renewal of interest in education and the arts. This cultural **Renaissance** was paralleled by changes in Christianity, as dissidents split from the established Roman Catholic church in the **Protestant Reformation.** Some of these Protestants called themselves **Puritans,** since they sought to purge their religion of clerical power and rituals and go back to the "pure" Biblical form of Christianity. Eventually outlawed in England, they began migrating to the New World in the seventeenth century in search of religious freedom, carrying with them ideas from the Old Testament about what the family should be—ideas which, in some ways, ran counter to English trends of the times. Other settlers, members of the established English Protestant Church, colonized the southern part of the new country, bringing with them a slightly different heritage. Spanish, Dutch, French, Germans, and representatives of many other nations eventually participated in the settlement of the American continent. It was against a historical background of reaction and continuity in Western civilization that today's American attitudes toward marriage evolved.

GENDER ROLES AND THE STATUS OF WOMEN

Gender roles. Behavior patterns expected of males and females on the basis of their sex.

In our society there is a growing trend toward more equal rights and responsibilities for women and men. Some people criticize this development, maintaining that a division of labor according to gender is biologically mandated because of women's childbearing function. Others support the trend toward equality, asserting that male dominance is a historical **artifact** which is no longer functional, and is in fact highly damaging to men as well as women.

The Role of the Patriarch.   The Hebrews, Greeks, and early Romans were strongly patriarchal. Everyone in the household—wife (or wives), **concubines,** servants, children—was bound in service to the patriarch, who exercised absolute control over them. In early Roman families, as in the ancient Chinese family described in Chapter 1, the power of the **pater familias,** the father of the family, extended down through all generations of his descendents. Even his grown and perhaps politically influential sons had no control over their property or income because the patriarch was the sole owner of all family wealth and lands (Bardis, 1964).

Patriarchs did not amass such total authority out of sheer love of tyranny. This authority had its burdens, too, and probably held some survival value for the family when community ties were weak and the difficulties of primitive life could best be dealt with through strength in organized numbers. The patriarch's responsibilities were those which held the family together and provided for its material support: he was the religious expert, manager of the herds or crops, family judge, camp chief, and general protector of group harmony (Kenkel, 1973).

The Status of Women in Early Patriarchies.   Despite the similarities of the strong male roles in Hebrew, Greek, and Roman patriarchies, the status of women was different in each culture. None, however, could escape their subservience to men, for in marriage authority over a woman was transferred from her father to her husband.

The subjugation of Greek wives was the most complete. They probably were as intellectually inferior to their husbands as men thought them, for they were not educated and their social lives were severely restricted. They were not allowed out of the house without the husband's permission; even with it, they could venture forth only veiled and chaperoned. At home, they had to stay in their own quarters most of the time, joining their husbands only at mealtimes, and then only when there were no guests. The repressed Greek wife's sole function was to provide her husband with offspring. For physical and emotional satisfaction, he turned to an elite group of concubines, the **hetaerae,** who were trained to provide the companionship and pleasure which men did not expect from their wives (Bardis).

Hetaerae. An elite group of mistresses or concubines in ancient Greece.

The Biblical Hebrews had developed a more idealized version of woman's role under a patriarch, one which is still held up to women as a rationale for keeping them at home. Marriage was viewed as a state which should bring a woman not only social respect but also emotional satisfaction, if she fulfilled her roles well. Bearing children was her major responsibility, one which she was supposed to regard as a sacred privilege rather than a hardship. She was also expected to care for her family willingly and capably in fulfilling her domestic role (Murstein, 1974).

In the early years, Roman women were respected as mistresses of their husband's households and treated as their social and intellectual companions. But while the men were off fighting long wars during the middle years of the Empire, Roman women began to have higher status in their own right. They were left to manage the family estates and often did so capably. Roman wives also became increasingly educated and politically active. Changes in the male-female balance of power made marriage less important to a woman's status, and many women began to shun marriage unless a prospective husband could offer both emotional satisfaction and economic gain (Bardis).

Paradoxical Status Under the Christians.   Although the early Christians traced many of their ideas to the Hebrews of the Old Testament, they were also influenced by Roman thought and by the ancient Persian belief that the mind, or spirit, and the body were separate and opposed to each other. They thus introduced some paradoxical changes into the relationship between the sexes. Jesus taught that all people were equal in the sight of God because all had divine souls. Women were at first eagerly welcomed into Christian congregations to swell their numbers, and were respected for their good works. Virgins were especially respected and given important charitable tasks as brides of Christ (Bardis).

Yet, even as women's status seemed to be improving, a countertrend was developing toward pronouncing them morally inferior. At least partly in reaction to the increasing worldliness and materialism of the late Roman Empire, Christian men began to fear women as temptresses who would

The Temptation of Eve
from *Paradise Lost* by
William Blake, 1808.
Courtesy Museum of
Fine Arts, Boston. Gift
by subscription, 1890.

lure them to the pleasures of the flesh, which they considered incompatible
with spirituality. Women came to represent original sin, since the Christian
leaders decided that Adam's fall from grace was Eve's fault. After all, according to the Bible, she gave him the apple. To keep females from tempting
men into the evils of sex, women were to "adorn themselves in modest
apparel, with shamefacedness and sobriety." Women could not teach the
Gospel, but they could perhaps learn about God's teachings from men if
they listened "in silence with all subjection" (1 Timothy 2:9–11).

The only ways in which the relative status of women could be said to
have improved under the influence of the early Christians were as a result
of the new restrictions placed on men. **Divorce,** formerly a male prerogative,
was forbidden, and men who engaged in extramarital affairs were for the
first time considered as sinful as women who did.

Position of Women in the Middle Ages.   Ambivalence toward women became even more confusing during the Middle Ages. In the period after the

fall of Rome, the Christian clergy became so negative toward women that in 585 the Council of Macon seriously debated whether women had souls as men did (Murstein). During the twelfth century the church fathers engaged in a hysterical campaign against women in their efforts to win the clergy over to **celibacy.** In their distrust of women, they linked them with sexual insatiability, irrationality, and temptation from the devil (Kaufman, 1973).

Celibacy. Abstention by vow from sexual intercourse and from marriage.

Meanwhile, the feudal aristocracy was developing an opposite but equally stereotyped view of women. The literature and ritual behaviors of **chivalry** and **courtly love** elevated women to a pedestal of spiritual sublimity and beauty which men could only worship with a hopeless love. But this inversion of the male-female balance of power occurred only in fantasy, not in fact. For all practical purposes, aristocratic women were still treated as mere property in the exclusively male power structure. Often, upper-class women were traded to husbands of somewhat lower class in marriages which enhanced the man's economic and social class, while denying women both romantic fulfillment and social advancement (Kaufman).

Chivalry. The customs of medieval knighthood, marked by courtesy and high-minded consideration, especially to women.

Most of what we know about life in the Middle Ages has come down to us through the courtly literature of adoration of aristocratic ladies on the one hand and the clerical literature of antifeminism on the other. Neither is likely to portray accurately the everyday reality of most women's lives in that period. Research into other documents of the times—legal proceedings, family letters, clerical records, and guild bylaws—shows that women of the lower classes worked alongside men as partners in the family's struggle for survival. In agrarian villages, where there was little division of labor, wives worked with their husbands in the fields. In towns, wives cooperated with their husbands in cottage industries such as weaving or held positions in their own right as merchants, teachers, doctors, tailors, barbers, and apothecaries.

Back to the Home in the Renaissance.   After a period of relative equality, women of the new middle class were once again relegated to a subservient position during the Renaissance. The shift from an agrarian society to an urbanized economy disrupted peasant farming patterns, forcing men to look for work in the cities. In the movement of work out of the home, women were squeezed out of the working world and told that their proper place was in the home as their husbands' subordinates, with child rearing and housekeeping their natural roles. The division of sex roles which both men and women were supposed to find most fulfilling—the husband as master, protector, and economic supporter of the family and the wife as childbearer and domestic servant—was emphasized in the late sixteenth century in a stream of books about how the ideal household should be set up (Kaufman). Although these are ideas that grew out of the social realities of ancient Hebrew times and the Renaissance, they are still with us in the twentieth century. Arguments that many women, and men, too, are unable to find fulfillment in this kind of sex-typing are just beginning to gain credibility.

MATE SELECTION AND MARRIAGE

Just as the position of women has risen and fallen repeatedly in the past, the value placed on marriage has seesawed with the times. For the early Hebrews, marriage was a responsibility, expected of everyone, which bound two families together and ensured the continuation of family lines through childbearing. It had little to do with love between the two principals. Their union was usually arranged by the parents. Although the young pair had to give their consent to the match, it is unlikely that many vetoed their parents' arrangements. The transfer of the woman from her father to her husband was a private ceremony between the families. Church and state did not assert control over marriage until the **Middle Ages** (Kephart, 1972).

Middle Ages. The period of European history from about 500 A.D. to about 1500.

Under the Romans, marriage could be an elaborate religious ceremony with priests and witnesses, a secular agreement between parents in which the bride was "sold" to her husband, or even, in the case of lower-class couples, the declaration that an unmarried couple who had lived together for at least a year were to be considered married from then on (Bardis). This legalization of long-term cohabitation was the ancestor of the common-law marriage still recognized today in parts of the United States. In the late days of the Roman Empire, marriage became more a matter of individual desire and less a matter of consent between two families. Since many chose not to marry at all, marriage rates fell and nonmarital sexual activity increased.

Christian Attitudes to Marriage. Viewing marriage as chiefly a sexual union and valuing the spiritual life more than the physical, the followers of Jesus felt that marriage really was not a very desirable state after all. Those who remained virgins were the most exalted; those who married but managed to stay celibate anyway were next in line; those who married and engaged in sexual intercourse were only one step higher than those who had sex outside of marriage. By the beginning of the fifth century, priests were forbidden to marry lest sexual activity should distract them from their spiritual duties (Bardis).

The Church fathers tried to deal with what they considered lustful relationships by asserting control over conjugal sexuality. In the second century, a church leader decreed that people could only have intercourse after supper; to do so during the day was sinful. Even today, many couples seem to be inhibited by this lingering taboo. In 398 A.D., the church fathers announced that out of respect for the sacred nature of the wedding benediction, newlyweds should not have intercourse on their wedding night, although if they paid a fee to the church, they would be excused from this prohibition (Murstein).

Increasing Church Control.   The early Christian church basically followed the Roman law regarding marriage. The essential thing was that the partners consented with affection. Gradually, through the time of Peter Abelard (1079–1142) to the Council of Trent in 1563, the Roman Catholic Church developed the notion that marriage was a **sacrament.** Thus marriage became a sacred union and its formation was claimed to be under the control of God's representatives (Brundage, 1975).

> **Sacrament.** A formal religious act symbolic of a spiritual reality, especially one begun or recognized by Jesus Christ.

Traditionally, marriage had been an agreement between two families, with the bride's father handing her over to her new husband. But from Roman times on into the Middle Ages, some unions had been formed through **"self-marriage"** by couples who recited their vows to each other, with the bride giving herself away. In some cases, they did so secretly, without any witnesses, forming alliances which were easily undone. As it came to look on marriage as a sacred union, the now-established Roman Catholic church began to insist that marital vows be exchanged at the church entrance with a priest in attendance. He would give the union his benediction and by his presence supposedly lend the occasion a sense of holiness and seriousness of purpose. By the thirteenth century, the ceremony had moved inside the church, with the clergy actually performing the rites and pronouncing the couple husband and wife. The father's traditional role in transferring authority over his daughter to the groom was cut back to a token appearance on the cue, "Who giveth this woman to be wedded?" By the sixteenth century, marriage was officially declared a sacrament, a divinely graced bond which could not be broken by divorce (Kephart).

> **Self-marriage.** A custom in the Middle Ages when some couples recited their marriage vows to each other and the bride gave herself away.

The Roman Catholic church also extended its influence over who could marry whom. Moses had commanded Hebrew men not to have sexual relations with close blood relatives or even in-laws such as their uncles' wives, for to do so was "unclean" and would cause "confusion" (Leviticus 20:12, 21). The Romans relaxed these incest taboos, allowing even first cousins to marry. Under the Roman Catholic church, the pendulum swung back to greater restrictiveness than ever before with the declaration, in 506 A.D., that no two people who were known to be at all related could marry. In-laws were as taboo as blood relatives; even unrelated people who agreed to act as godparents for a child's baptism were thought to be spiritually related and therefore forbidden to marry. Since this extreme prohibition could have made finding a marriage partner almost impossible in some small communities, half a century later a slightly less restrictive prohibition to the seventh degree was substituted; by this decree, those more closely

Banns. A public announcement, especially in church, of a proposed marriage.

related than third cousins could not marry (Murstein). To make sure that no one violated these restrictions, **banns** announcing a couple's intent to marry had to be posted in the church before the wedding so that anyone who thought they were too closely related could object to the marriage.

Growing church control over marriage was undermined to some extent by the Protestant Reformation. Martin Luther held that the patriarchal family was the center of world order. He and his followers helped set into motion changes which eventually resulted in establishment of civil control over the right to marry (Friedenthal, 1967).

DIVORCE

Today there is great concern about the high rate at which marriages break up and the effect that instability of the family has on children, the marriage partners, and society itself. It is often assumed that divorce is a relatively new phenomenon only recently invented by a decadent society. A look at history shows that this is not true.

Cultures of the past in which marriage was a highly esteemed state did not necessarily forbid termination of marriage through divorce. Hebrew men had the right to divorce their wives for any reason, though Hebrew women had no such recourse. Although incompatibility or adultery were considered plausible grounds for divorce, **barrenness,** which was presumed to be the woman's fault, was the reason most often given for breaking up a marriage. However, the Hebrew husband was subject to severe social disapproval if he left his wife for frivolous reasons (Bardis).

Barrenness. Failure to produce offspring; sterility.

Among the Greeks, if it was the husband who committed adultery, his wife could be granted a divorce only if she could prove that by doing so he had deprived his own family of adequate support. In the late days of the Roman Empire, married couples saw little reason to stay irrevocably together. Women as well as men could seek a divorce, and wives could even use as grounds the husband's departure for military service (Bardis).

The Christians' stand on divorce was not clear at first: Jesus seems to have rejected divorce when he stated that married people "are no more twain but one flesh. What therefore God hath joined together, let not man put asunder" (Matthew 19:6). However, by 140 A.D. divorce was accepted by leading Roman Christians. Conditions for divorce included adultery and worship of idols. But Christian policy regarding divorce involved continuing debate in the early centuries after Christ (Bardis).

In the fifth century, the Roman church officially proclaimed that marriages could not be dissolved, but it wavered in enforcement of this doctrine for 500 years, accommodating itself to the view of the Germanic tribes that divorce was a personal privilege and not subject to interference by the **clergy.** By the tenth century, however, the Catholic church was better established, and it insisted on judging all requests for marital dissolution. Bishops' courts were willing to grant approval only for **annulments** and **separations.** An annulment was a public statement that the marriage had been illegal in the first place, perhaps because the bride and groom were related closer than the seventh degree or because they had previously been involved in a secret self-marriage. Separation—the ending of cohabitation but without the privilege of remarriage—was allowed in cases of adultery, cruelty, or religious heresy. The regulations were, however, open to false claims by unhappy couples and ready granting of clerical dispensation to end the marriage if a substantial gift was made to the church (Leslie, 1973).

Annulment. A judicial pronouncement that a marriage is void and does not exist.

ATTITUDES TOWARD CHILDREN

One of the reasons society has been interested in preventing divorce has been to ensure provision of a stable home for the rearing of children. But despite this concern, children have not always been treated as human creatures with needs and rights of their own.

To the early Hebrews, large families were a blessing, a fulfillment of a divine commandment to increase and multiply, insurance that the family line would not die out, and extra hands for the herds, the fields, and the housework. Children were expected to be obedient, but since this was not considered to be their natural state, instilling respect for their parents was thought to be a matter of curbing willfulness through severe punishments. According to the command of Moses, any child who struck or cursed his parents should be killed (Exodus 21:15–17). Although this punishment was probably used rarely, if at all, beating apparently met with social approval: "He that spareth his rod hateth his son: but he that loveth him chasteneth him betimes" (Proverbs 13:24). Despite the absolute nature of parental authority, especially that of the father, the stories of the Old Testament give the impression that there was a large measure of love and devotion in the bonds between parents and children.

Under the Greek and Roman versions of patriarchy, treatment of children seems to have been severe. The patriarch not only could but apparently did sometimes sentence a disobedient child to death. He had the right to abandon them outdoors as infants, ensuring their death, and frequently did so if they were **illegitimate** or sickly. Female infants were exposed more often than males. Greek and Roman fathers could sell their offspring into slavery, and Roman fathers could have children married and divorced without their consent (Bardis).

Illegitimate. Born of parents not married to each other.

The early Christians strongly opposed these practices since they valued each human life. As the power of the patriarch declined, the status of children rose. **Abortion,** infanticide, child-selling, and sentencing children to death were all condemned. Nonetheless, Christians expected children to obey their parents and to care for the parents when they became old (Bardis).

Despite this trend toward more humane treatment of children among the early Christians, the status of children fell again during the Middle Ages. Fathers in Germanic and Anglo-Saxon tribes were permitted to kill or **expose** their infants if they did it before the infant had tasted food. Germanic fathers could sell both wives and children in the event of a famine. Anglo-Saxon fathers could sell their children into slavery, marry off their daughters without their consent, and commit sons and daughters to convents and monasteries (Leslie).

Even when children of the Middle Ages were not being sold or killed, they were subjected to child-rearing practices which seem unnecessarily cruel and restrictive by modern standards. According to **psychohistorian** Lloyd de Mause, for perhaps 2000 years infants in most cultures were customarily swaddled so tightly in long cloths that they could not move. **Swaddling** was supposed to keep babies from tearing themselves apart, but it was also a matter of adult convenience. Swaddled babies became passive and untroublesome, neat packages which could be hung on pegs or stuck in corners (de Mause, 1974). Severe beatings, by both parents and teachers, were apparently so common that most children of earlier times would probably qualify as "battered" by today's standards. The idea of the innate sinfulness of children was thought to require breaking their will. If children could be broken—directed how to behave with respect to little events— then they could be directed in the important events of getting an education, choosing a mate, and developing a career (Stone, 1975). Adults engaged in these nightmarish child-rearing practices, according to de Mause, not only because they did not understand child development, but also because they did not realize how intense children's terrors and frustrations can be. Shorter (1975) says that even in the eighteenth and nineteenth centuries, infants were left entirely alone for long stretches of time while their mothers worked in the fields, and parental indifference to infants was the custom among ordinary people. Enlightenment in child rearing has been slow to develop.

ATTITUDES TOWARD SEXUALITY

Even though Judeo-Christian influences are responsible for much of what is humane in American marriage, the sexual **double standard** inherited from the Hebrews and the restrictive attitude toward all sexuality introduced by the Christians have burdened sexual activities with negative meanings which many people now reject.

To the early Hebrews, sexuality was an accepted part of human nature. Relationships outside of marriage met with strong social disapproval, but within marriage, intercourse for its own sake as well as for **procreation** was

Expose. Deprive of shelter or protection; abandon, especially by leaving in the open.

Double standard. A code of morals which applies more restrictive standards of sexual behavior to women than to men.

considered divinely willed (Murstein). However, the early Hebrews held a double-standard of sexual conduct for men and women which is still with us. While brides found to be nonvirginal and wives found to have committed adultery could be stoned to death, men were allowed to have sexual relationships with as many wives and concubines as they could support. They were not supposed to have intercourse with another man's wife, not because of the effect on their own marital relationship, but because to do so would be a violation of the other man's property rights and a confusion of blood lines. An illegitimate child and that child's future offspring could not be part of the Lord's congregation "even to the tenth generation" (Deuteronomy 23:2) and could not honorably carry on the family name.

The double standard was even more exaggerated under the Greeks. They allowed men, married or not, to have sexual relations with female concubines, **prostitutes,** and **mistresses,** and also **homosexual** relationships with male lovers. For men, the social ideal seemed to be a full expression of sensuality with a minimum of restraints; for women, committing adultery was a criminal act, grounds for divorce and justification for being put to death (Reiss, 1960). The early Romans forbade polygyny and frowned on the taking of concubines, but later on adultery, concubinage, informal sexual **liaisons,** and homosexuality all thrived (Bardis).

Among the Christians, the double standard was replaced by sexual repression for everybody. Jesus and his followers urged rejection of the material aspects of life, popularizing an intellectual tradition which had its roots in the 2000-year-old Persian philosophy of **dualism,** the idea that the demands of the spirit and the flesh are in conflict with each other. Christians chose to reject the needs of the flesh in order to elevate the life of the spirit.

In this, as in other matters, Jesus was more tolerant of human weakness than his followers. Although he felt that earthly entanglements made it difficult to do God's work, he acknowledged that some were called to celibacy and some to marriage. But some of his followers preached a rejection of bodily needs which bordered on insanity. In order to prove that they were superior to the temptations of the flesh, some men married virgins and then tried to remain celibate, even when sharing the same bed with them. Some even shunned eating and washing as being too worldly. St. Jerome maintained that both food and baths were invitations to lust and recommended eating just enough to keep from starving but never enough to feel full. But the attempt to repress natural bodily urges led to constant thinking about them. Nuns complained that the devil had come to tempt them to indecent acts in their dreams, and for all his self-denying willpower, St. Jerome was plagued by visions of dancing girls and inflamed with **lust** as he fasted in the desert (Murstein). However, the extreme Christian attitude to sexuality may have strengthened marriage in the long run. Forced

Dualism. A view of humanity which holds that the demands of the spirit and of the flesh are in conflict with each other.

to accept the fact of marriage—except for the clergy—in order to keep the population from dying out, the Church fathers ended up increasing the incentive to marry and to keep the conjugal relationship strong among Christians by declaring marriage the only state in which sexual intercourse was not sinful.

LOVE AS A BASIS FOR MARRIAGE

Hedonism. The doctrine that pleasure or happiness is the chief good in life.

While current sexual mores are an intricate mixture of the Hebrew sexual double standard, Greek and Roman **hedonism,** and Christian guilt, the notion that mate selection and marriage should be based on love and mutual happiness is a modern addition to the concept of the family. Until relatively modern times, marriage was generally regarded as a serious institution which carried out social and economic functions and provided a vehicle for raising a family. Parental matchmaking disregarded romance; the object was to select a partner who would bring honor to the entire family and perhaps enhance its financial and social status as well.

Nevertheless, love was not unknown among the ancients. Many married couples apparently did grow fond of each other with time; others formed love relationships outside of marriage. The Greeks even had three words for three different kinds of love: **philos,** or profound and enduring friendship; **eros,** which meant sexual attraction; and **agape,** or altruistic, nondemanding, spiritual love. By now we have added a fourth—romantic love, or intense emotional responsiveness to an idealized loved one—and hope to find all four in our marriages.

THE COURTLY LOVE COMPLEX

Troubadours. Poet musicians of the 11th to 13th centuries in France and Italy whose major theme was courtly love.

Idealization of romantic love came to us from the courtly notions of the Middle Ages. During the twelfth and early thirteenth centuries, upper-class people in parts of France and Germany developed a literary tradition which did not correspond to reality, but which they began to believe and act out anyway. Spread by **troubadours,** the courtly love story usually had a handsome knight falling helplessly in love with a beautiful noblewoman. Because she was inevitably married, she could not return his affection physically but allowed him to wear ribbons and carry trinkets she had given him as he went off to do battle or engage in tournaments in her honor. He was supposedly inspired to greatness and heights of heroism by her beauty and noble character. Since their love was never **consummated,** it existed —supposedly forever—on a spiritual plane above sexual gratification and such everyday realities as child rearing, financial problems, and domestic chores. In keeping with their dreams of this sort of romantic destiny, men of the court began to act out a ritualized adoration of noblewomen. Almost

"The first knight among you to slay the horrible dragon will win the hand of my daughter, plus two thousand golden ducats. Void where prohibited by law."

playing the part of servants by opening doors for them, picking up things they had dropped, and performing other gracious services, they introduced a new pattern of behavior known as **courtoisie.**

It is easier to see why women would have enjoyed this reversal of traditional male-female roles than to imagine why men, too, would have embraced it. Kaufman speculates that the courtly love tradition acted as a socially acceptable substitute for adultery, a ritualized expression of extra-marital passion rather than a physical act of adultery. Other scholars have suggested that courtly love may have grown out of frustration with arranged marriages, boredom with castle life, or perhaps an urge to add nobility to human relationships in times of harshness and cruelty (Beigel, 1951).

Moller (1959) traced the reasons for the rise of the courtly love complex to the social and economic characteristics of the times. He believes that the French troubadours and German **minnesingers** who sang of idealized love drew on themes and traditions derived from eleventh-century Muslim Spain. There a male preoccupation with **eroticism** apparently had its roots in the chronic shortage of women. Because of female infanticide, monopolizing of available women by the polygynous wealthy, and constant immigration of Arab soldiers, there were never enough women to go around.

Minnesingers. The German equivalent of the troubadours in France and Italy.

Things were somewhat the same in the particular regions of France and Germany where the courtly love tradition flourished. The need for armed knights and administrators drew great numbers of unattached young men to the castles of these regions, creating an imbalanced sex ratio. It would help these men to realize their ambition of rising into the lower nobility if they could marry above themselves. Competition for upper-class women and the anxieties of social climbing created, according to Moller's theory, a sense of insecurity about being socially acceptable. Thus the approval and sponsorship of a well-born lady was highly prized as an assurance of worthiness and a symbol of admittance into courtly circles.

The pattern of sexual restraint, Moller says, was an attempt by upwardly mobile men to assume a nobility of manners to match their social aspirations. As the practical need to expand the nobility opened the class to the lower-born, good character came to be considered a substitute for inherited wealth and status and self-willed **chastity** was regarded as an ennobling virtue (Beigel).

Chastity. Abstention from all sexual intercourse.

Whatever its causes, romantic love always occurred outside of marriage. The nobility during the Middle Ages rejected the idea that bodily sexual fulfillment and "spiritual" romantic attraction could coexist in the same relationship, and the courtly tradition did little to bring love within the scope of marriage. But it did set the stage for this to happen. While courtly rites themselves degenerated into empty rituals in the twelfth century—once the historical reasons for the tradition had disappeared—chivalry had raised men's concept of female virtues. It made men willing to be voluntarily loyal, restrained, and gentle toward women, and suggested the possibility that intimate relationships between men and women could provide other benefits besides sexual satisfaction (Kephart).

ROMANTICISM

By the sixteenth and seventeenth centuries, a new business class had emerged, enriched by foreign trade and urban commerce. This new class, influenced by the ideas of romantic love which had filtered down to them from the nobility, developed the art of "courtship." Employing the vocabulary and behaviors of courtly love, middle-class men began to use them on the maidens to whom they had been betrothed through parental matchmaking. During the months between their betrothal and their marriage, young men "courted" their future brides with adoring talk, gifts, and romantic poety (Beigel).

Courtship. Participation in social activities leading to engagement and marriage.

Some apparently began to fall in love with each other, further calling into question the notion that love and marriage could not coexist. This gradually led to rebellion against parental mate choice, since young people discovered that it would be more emotionally gratifying to marry for love. Finally, they were successful, and by the end of the nineteenth century, people in parts of Europe and especially in America were choosing their own mates, with love the main basis for their choice. Today, people elsewhere in the world point to the high divorce rates in America as proof that love is a shaky foundation for a family. Romantic lovers were once considered slightly insane, and even now, people in cultures other than ours find it absurd that we use such a fragile emotion as the basis for choice of a lifelong mate (Reiss). On the other hand, people in a highly urbanized and industrialized society like ours seem to feel a great need for emotional satisfaction to counteract the tensions and impersonal nature of workaday life.

To see how old norms were replaced in America and marriages began to be based on more contemporary human needs, we will look briefly at social conditions at two points in American history: first, the time of the earliest settlement, and then the nineteenth century, when the shift was made from a primarily agricultural to a primarily industrial economy.

AMERICAN FAMILY LIFE IN COLONIAL TIMES

English colonists began settling the American continent at the beginning of the seventeenth century, with New England initially colonized by Puritans seeking religious freedom, and the South settled by people who had not broken with the Church of England but who hoped to increase their wealth in the New World. Social scientists are cautious in generalizing about what family life was like then. Variations existed between different areas of the country, the pace of change was rapid, and there is difficulty in weeding out long-lived but inaccurate myths passed down as facts by earlier generations of historians. Nevertheless, some conclusions can be drawn.

Puritans. Members of an early Protestant group opposing ceremonial worship and the ceremonial activities of the bishops of the Church of England.

COURTSHIP AND MARRIAGE
Social conditions in early America accelerated the trend begun in Europe toward individual, rather than parental, mate selection. Immigrants to America were generally young and physically removed from the patriarchal control of the families they left behind. On the continually expanding frontiers, people were separated even more from kin ties, and from land ties as well as they moved on. The movable household replaced the clan as the basic social unit.

In addition to the increased independence of the nuclear family, frontier American life also encouraged a spirit of individualism. Class structure was fluid, for immigrants from all social classes were equalized by the hardships of frontier life. Individuals advanced or failed according to their own capabilities and efforts rather than according to their family's social standing. Mates tended to be chosen on the basis of their personal qualities, although financial considerations were not entirely overlooked.

Under primitive early conditions, romance at first had little room to grow. Because population was sparse and transportation poor, people usually ended up marrying neighbors. Courtship was brief and could not even begin until the girl's parents had agreed to her betrothal. Despite their spiritual aspirations, the Puritans were shrewd about money, and betrothals often included detailed contracts laying out the financial and property rights of each party (Kephart).

Bourgeoisie. People of the middle class in Europe, often associated with commercial and industrial interests.

In keeping with the trend among the **bourgeoisie** during the sixteenth century in Europe, many Puritans seemed to think that ease and mutual comfort could be found in marriage (Schnucker, 1975). But while they felt that love should flower within a good marriage, given enough time, they did not see romantic love as a prerequisite for mate selection. As Puritanism declined, marriages were increasingly built on preexisting romantic attraction.

Romance was always more highly prized in the South. There the climate was more benign, the soils were richer, and the slave-owning plantation families lived like aristocrats. Courtship in the South was patterned after the rituals of courtly love, but potential suitors nonetheless pursued love with an eye toward increasing wealth through careful marriage arrangements (Kephart).

Bundling. A New England courting custom whereby an engaged couple would spend the evening in bed together but physically separated from each other.

Bundling. In spite of the strict Puritan disapproval of premarital sex, restrictions were relaxed for the betrothed, once the terms of the marriage contract had been spelled out, since they were considered nearly married. Many engaged in the extraordinary colonial practice of **bundling,** spending the evening or even the whole night lying together in bed, fully dressed.

Bundling began because warmth and fuel were at a premium. What the bundling couple were supposed to be doing in bed together was keeping warm while they talked. To make sure that nothing else happened, parents sometimes slept in the same room or separated the couple with a low bolster or board placed down the middle of the bed. Mothers occasionally even tied their daughters' ankles together before leaving them to their bundling (Kenkel).

Regulation of Marriage. Puritan couples were wed in **civil ceremonies.** In this, as in other matters, they had broken with the Church of England by declaring that marriage was not a sacrament and should not be performed by the church. Instead, civil authorities set forth rigid laws requiring the posting of banns, parental consent, and registration before marriage could take place. Since the Southern colonists had not broken with the Church of England, they were married by clergymen when this could be arranged. But ministers were few and population sparse between plantations and on the frontier. When there was no one available to marry them, some couples simply began to live together until a circuit-riding clergyman came by to formalize the relationship. By that time, some were so fully accepted as husband and wife that it seemed unnecessary to go through the motions of being officially married. Although some of the colonies tried to discourage these "common-law" marriages, most begrudgingly recognized them as valid. Once a common-law wife became pregnant, there seemed to be no advantage to declaring the couple legally unmarried (Leslie).

ATTITUDES TOWARD SEXUALITY

Although we now use the word puritanical to mean something like **antisexual,** Morgan, in his classic study "The Puritans and Sex," concluded that the Puritans had a more realistic view of sexuality than is commonly supposed. Like the Hebrews of the Old Testament, from whom many of their ideas were derived, they did not worship virginity and instead apparently saw sex as one of God's blessings. The Puritan minister John Cotton, for instance, wrote that "Women are Creatures without which there is no comfortable Living for man . . . . They are a sort of Blasphemers then who despise and decry them, and call them a necessary Evil, for they are a necessary Good" (Morgan, 1973). Sexual satisfaction was an acknowledged human need—but it was to be indulged only within marriage, and only when it did not interfere with glorifying God. Intercourse was to be shunned along with recreation on the Sabbath, which was to be spent in religious activities.

Intercourse outside of marriage was punishable by fines, whipping, and forced marriage between the guilty parties since they were considered unfit to marry anyone else. Even married people were punished for breaking sex codes. A sea captain, for instance, was bound in the **stocks** for two hours as punishment for having kissed his wife on the doorstep of their house on a Sunday—on returning from a three-year voyage (Kenkel). The strictest penalties were reserved for adultery. It was officially punishable by death, and this sentence appears to have been carried out at least a few times. The death penalty gradually gave way to whipping, imprisonment, banishment, or the forced wearing of scarlet *A*'s on the clothing or branding on the forehead with a hot *A*-shaped iron.

New England colonists apparently continued to break Puritan sex codes despite the shame and punishment they were likely to suffer if discovered. Many even confessed voluntarily in church to **fornication** and occasionally to **adultery,** for public admission would save their illegitimate offspring from being forever excluded from the church and therefore from society.

While the Puritans punished men as severely as women for sexual misdeeds, there were clear double standards in the South, perhaps because the landed aristocracy was at first short of women and later had access to large

Antisexual. Opposed for moral or religious reasons to the enjoyment of sexual activity.

Fornication. Sexual intercourse between unmarried persons.

numbers of black slaves. Men of the upper class were allowed great sexual freedom outside of marriage. They carefully guarded their own women against all nonmarital sexual involvement, pampering them with courtly attentions but at the same time spreading the **myth** that well-bred women had no sexual passions of their own and instead regarded lovemaking as a duty. Perhaps this long-lived fiction became a self-fulfilling prophecy, for men of the aristocracy frequently looked elsewhere for satisfaction of their own needs. Taking of mistresses was common, and wives actually met with social disapproval if they did not graciously accept this fact.

Miscegenation. Marriage or cohabitation between a white person and a member of another race.

Laws against **miscegenation,** or racial mixing, were ignored when white men sought out black women for sexual fulfillment. They usually did so at their own convenience, though there were some long-term liaisons in which both the black mistress and her illegitimate children were well provided for by the white father. But a strict black-white double standard was nonetheless operating, for if a black man showed any sexual interest in a white woman, he could be put to death.

GENDER ROLES AND THE STATUS OF WOMEN

Whereas in the South, upper-class women were elevated to a pedestal, freed by servants from menial work, and encouraged to develop social graces, New England women appeared to be more subjugated to men. Like the early Christians, the Puritans tended to suspect women of hidden evil. Women were far more likely to be accused of **witchcraft** than men, although the opposite is true in some cultures (Demos, 1974). Under the patriarchal rule of men, wives usually could not own property, except as widows, and even their clothing was considered to belong to their husbands. For their part, Puritan men were expected to support their wives and forbidden to beat them or even tongue-lash them. Both partners were allowed to take legal action against each other for undue "cruelty" (Leslie).

Although they sometimes helped the men with farm chores, Puritan women's place was in the home, busily turning raw goods into the things their families needed: spinning, weaving and sewing cloth, making candles, and preserving and cooking food. In the absence of doctors, they also had to act as medical experts, preparers of healing potions, and nurses for the sick.

While the lives of colonial women were narrowed by custom and by sheer lack of time, they were apparently not as restricted as we have long thought. It is true that most colonial women received less formal education than men; but men received relatively little of it themselves by modern standards. Higher education was designed principally for future clergymen. However, under frontier conditions, teaching went on everywhere, and girls as well as boys received much of their schooling informally from parents, ministers, shopkeepers, craftsmen, and other adults who had knowledge to share. Contrary to our stereotyped notions about which jobs are "women's work," colonial girls were granted apprenticeships just as boys were in such positions as barbers, carpenters, wheelmakers, and brewers. Some women were also the "masters" to apprentices (Long, 1975). While most colonial women stayed in the home, not all did. Thanks to the chronic labor shortage in newly settled areas, women could be found in all areas of economic life, working as everything from botanists and lawyers to managers of sawmills and taverns. They may even have held greater authority at home and enjoyed more emotional closeness and equality with their husbands than did their female Victorian descendants, but this speculation cannot be proved without further research (Somerville, 1974).

ATTITUDES TOWARD CHILDREN

Whatever their mothers' functions, colonial children were prized economic assets, for families needed all the help they could get in forcing the wilderness to support human habitation. Because colonial children's labor outweighed the cost of feeding and clothing them, large families were considered more desirable then than they are now. In 1790, the year of the first U.S. Census, the average household (all those living in a single dwelling unit, possibly including unrelated people) consisted of 6.6 people, about 2.7 of them white children and 0.8 of them slaves (an average boosted by Southern states like South Carolina, whose average household included 4.1 slaves). By 1970, the average white household in the U.S. had shrunk to 3.2 people, only 1.0 of whom was a child and none of whom were servants or slaves (Wells, 1974).

While some knowledge of do-it-yourself **contraception** and abortion was available to colonial women as a relief from the burden of continual childbearing, they were apparently unwilling to make use of it. Procreation might not have been the main reason for marriage, but it was nonetheless a serious responsibility. In addition to the economic advantages of having children, there was the Old Testament commandment to be fruitful and multiply and the Hebrew belief that children were a blessing from God. The larger the family, the more the parents had been blessed. Furthermore, the more Puritan children who were born, the greater the body of the elect and of the commonwealth. And as for themselves, Puritan women were willing to put up with pregnancy and the pain of childbearing because these burdens were seen as a means of salvation from Eve's original sin (Schnucker).

Though wanted, Puritan children were not indulged. They fell under the strict patriarchal control of their fathers, according to family patterns handed down from Old Testament times. Since children were thought to enter the world with inherently evil natures, raising them to be good adults was thought to be a matter of crushing their will, teaching them obedience, humility, and religious faith.

Contraception. Prevention of conception; voluntary and intentional prevention of pregnancy.

After they were about six to eight years old, colonial children began to wear small-sized adult clothes, serve as apprentices, and perhaps learn adult roles by working with their parents (Demos, 1973). Nevertheless, Beales (1975) comments that "The transition from the dependence of childhood to the self-sufficiency of adulthood was not made suddenly in early New England." Many Puritan churches expected youths to be age 14 and older before being examined about their religious understanding. Economic and political independence through apprenticeships and various laws were only gained after age 20. Beales pictures colonial New England youth as involved in a "chusing time," a time to set their sights for adult objectives, although in this process they did not have as many options separate from their parents as today's adolescents have.

DIVORCE

Despite the esteem with which the Puritans held marriage and the family, they made relatively liberal provisions for divorce. This seeming contradiction can be explained as part of their rebellion against the Church of England, which had only allowed separations. And even though the South had not broken with the church, it was unwilling to set up church courts in the New World. Since there was thus no institution to hear requests for separation, some Southern couples simply separated on their own.

Most Puritans, while entitled to divorce, did not take advantage of this provision. There were only 25 divorces in Massachusetts in the 53 years between 1639 and 1692, an average of one every two years, even though men were allowed to divorce their wives for adultery, desertion, or even cruelty. It was harder for women to win a divorce. As was true of the Greeks, a wife could not divorce her husband for adultery unless she could prove that he had endangered his family's security by deserting or failing to support them. Despite this double standard, more colonial women than men instigated divorce proceedings, perhaps because marriage was more central to their lives and a bad marriage was therefore more intolerable (Leslie).

NINETEENTH-CENTURY FAMILY LIFE IN AMERICA

Even when we get closer to our own times in the history of the family, it is hard to separate fact from fiction. Americans are fond of the nostalgic myth of the good life on grandma's—or great-grandma's—farm. As Goode (1963) describes the **stereotyped** picture of life several generations ago, the large family lived together happily in a big, old farmhouse. Most of what they ate they grew or raised themselves. Everyone worked hard but cheerfully. All the children married young; the girls were virginal as

Stereotype. A conception of a group or category of people that represents an oversimplified, rigid opinion or attitude.

brides and faithful as wives. Young couples lived with or near the husband's parents and eventually inherited the land. Marriages were harmonious; there were no divorces. It is important to recognize this picture as a myth, for it is one which each successive generation seems to hold of the "good old days."

In trying to see what family life was really like in the last century, when America was transformed from a rural, agricultural society to a predominately urban, industrial one, social historians generally accept the period from 1800–1850 as a time when the country was still largely agricultural, a baseline against which the later changes associated with industrialization can be measured. However, Furstenberg (1974) has pointed out that trends often associated with industrialization were already present in preindustrial America. The sources he analyzed were the observations of foreign travelers to this country from 1800 to 1850. Smith and Hindus (1975) have sifted through old records of births and marriages for statistical data on the incidence of premarital pregnancy as a clue to changing sexual **mores**. And Lantz, Keyes, and Schultz (1975) examined all the issues published between 1825 and 1950 of 47 different nationally read magazines for clues to the balance of power in husband-wife relationships, attitudes toward nonmarital sexual activity, and popular reasons for getting married. Efforts like these to go to original sources are helping to form more exact and detailed pictures of family life in America.

Mores. The fixed, morally binding ideas of a particular group in regard to correct and incorrect behavior.

Table 2.1. Premarital pregnancy in America, 1680–1910   Though collected from incomplete and widely scattered records of marriages and births, this data gives some indication of the extent of premarital pregnancy in the North American colonies and in the U.S. through the nineteenth century. Each time period represents a span of 40 years. Note that the peak period was 1761–1800, including the time of the American Revolution.

HISTORICAL PERIOD	TIME BETWEEN MARRIAGE AND BIRTH OF FIRST CHILD					
	UNDER 6 MONTHS		UNDER 8½ MONTHS		UNDER 9 MONTHS	
	%	N	%	N	%	N
−1680	3.3	511	6.8	511	8.1	663
1681–1720	6.7	445	14.1	518	12.1	1156
1721–1760	9.9	881	21.2	1146	22.5	1442
1761–1800	16.7	970	27.2	1266	33.0	1097
1801–1840	10.3	573	17.7	815	23.7	616
1841–1880	5.8	572	9.6	467	12.6	572
1881–1910	15.1	119	23.3	232	24.4	119

Source: Adapted from Smith and Hindus, 1975, p. 561. © *Journal of Interdisciplinary History.* Used by permission.

Morality. Conformity to ideals of right human conduct.

SEXUAL MORALITY

Smith and Hindus characterize the nineteenth century as a time of anti-sexual **morality.** According to their findings, premarital pregnancy reached a low of about 10 percent of first births in the Victorian mid-nineteenth century, matching that of the seventeeth-century Puritan period. Between these two lows, premarital pregnancy reached an all-time high in the second half of the eighteenth century: 30 percent of all first children were conceived outside of marriage. In contemporary America, the figure has risen again to 20–25 percent of first children.

In trying to find reasons for this up-and-down pattern, Smith and Hindus suggest that two different kinds of sexual controls were operating during the periods when illegitimacy was low, while the rate of premarital pregnancy rose in between because neither kind of control was operating fully in the interim. Puritan morality was enforced by external social controls—the high visibility of every member of the community to the others. Victorian morality was accomplished by religious socialization to internal controls, or self-repression. In the nineteenth century, increasingly independent unmarried people were bound to chastity by the Victorian belief in self-restraint which was more antisexual than Puritanism had ever been. The new sexual restrictiveness was based on Protestant, rather than Old Testament, teachings, and it extended to all aspects of sexuality, including an exaggerated horror of **masturbation** (Smith and Hindus).

THE MAN-WOMAN RELATIONSHIP

At the same time that Victorian women were absorbing the antisexual teachings of the churches and asserting their superiority to sexual temptation, they were also becoming more assertive and persuasive in their relationships with men. According to the magazine analyses of Lantz, Keyes, and Schultz, the patriarchal power structure was weakening even before industrialization took most men out of their homes into factories and stores and separated work life from family life. Before 1850, women were already exercising considerable authority in the family in the areas of morality and child rearing, controlling some domestic financial decisions, and manipulating the love relationship by being teasing and flirtatious. Popular magazines were advocating mutual, rather than patriarchal, decision making (Lantz et al.).

REASONS FOR MARRYING

Judging from the content of magazine articles and stories, the trend toward individual choice and romantic love in mate selection was continuing and even intensifying during the nineteenth century. Happiness was now by far the main reason for marrying. In 89 percent of fiction and nonfiction pieces

which touched on this issue, happiness was the prevailing concern, compared to only 8 percent mentioning financial gain and 3 percent advocating marrying to improve one's status. Pleasing parents was only occasionally mentioned as a motive for marriage (Lantz et al.).

TREATMENT OF CHILDREN

European travelers to preindustrial America frequently remarked on the loving attention that was lavished on American children. Some saw America's young as spoiled and undisciplined, as a result, and holding a degree of power over their parents considered shocking by European standards. To other observers, American parental **permissiveness** was producing delight-fully spontaneous and independent children; their rejection of parental authority was seen as a necessary preparation for being citizens of a democracy. If all this sounds familiar, it is because the controversy between restrictiveness and permissiveness in child rearing continues in twentieth-century America.

Most of the European criticism of American youth seems to have been aimed at young children; there was little written about **adolescents.** Fursten-berg speculates that a "youth culture" did not stand out in the nineteenth century because teenagers were quickly absorbed into the responsibilities of adulthood rather than being left, as happens today, in a suspended state between childhood and adulthood while they completed their education.

Permissiveness. Toler-ance; the giving of con-sent or approval by someone in authority.

FROM THE NINETEENTH CENTURY TO THE TWENTIETH

From this brief description, it can be seen that there are many differences between nineteenth- and twentieth-century American family life, but also many continuities. The influence of Victorian ideas about sex persisted strongly until the 1920s, when Freudian psychology became popular, and still lingers in many people's minds today. Clothes were different; modes of transportation were different; but the belief in romantic love as the proper basis for marriage was strong. Independence and self-reliance were highly valued. Rapid industrialization and the expanding frontier in the West offered opportunities for people who were dissatisfied at home to set out and make new lives for themselves, a choice not so readily available in the twentieth century. At each point in American history, family relationships can be seen as resulting from the interaction of preceding ideas and traditions with changing conditions of life.

In our own times, sociologists are divided in their opinions about what is happening to the family. Some theorists believed in the 1950s that the trend to the conjugal family of husband, wife, and children living in a separate household was worldwide. These conjugal families are seen to be cut off from the extended kinship groups and social ties which theoretically helped to hold families together under earlier living conditions. In the American past, boarders, servants, apprentices, and numerous children within the household all kept a watchful eye on family affairs. Work life

Fig. 2.1 Size of households in the United States: 1790–1970. The proportion of four-person households has varied by only three percentage points at these widely separated time periods in U.S. history. However, the proportion of one-person households has risen by over 13 percent while the proportion of households with seven or more members has declined by over 30 percent. (Source: U.S. Bureau of the Census, *Historical Statistics of the United States, Colonial Times to 1970,* Part I, Washington: 1975.)

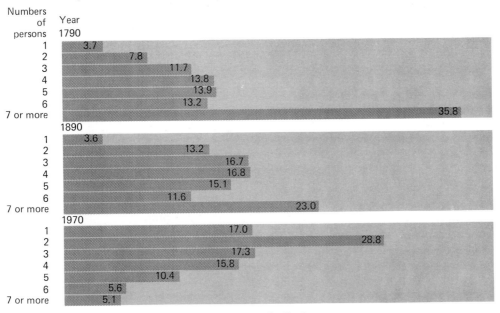

Numbers of persons	Year
	1790
1	3.7
2	7.8
3	11.7
4	13.8
5	13.9
6	13.2
7 or more	35.8
	1890
1	3.6
2	13.2
3	16.7
4	16.8
5	15.1
6	11.6
7 or more	23.0
	1970
1	17.0
2	28.8
3	17.3
4	15.8
5	10.4
6	5.6
7 or more	5.1

Percent distribution

and home life were intertwined in one location. By comparison, under urban and suburban living conditions today's average household has shrunk in size and withdrawn from public view. This privacy increases the potential for violation of cultural norms, such as the Puritan belief that home life should be peaceful and harmonious and that husbands and wives should not strike or verbally abuse each other (Laslett, 1973). There is also concern that in its isolation the nuclear family is now subject to impossible demands: complete responsibility for care and socialization of its children and total fulfillment of each other's emotional needs by husbands and wives who married for the sake of romantic love and expect the love relationship to be a permanent part of the marriage (Birdwhistell, 1974).

On the other hand, some sociologists maintain that nuclear families have never really cut themselves off from their extended kinship groups. Even though household size is smaller, exchanges of services and financial aid among relatives, advice, and visiting and/or living in the same neighborhood help to maintain extended family relationships. From this point of view, it is in spite of the **geographic mobility** which characterizes open-class, industrial societies that American families have managed to keep in touch with each other and to maintain at least some degree of mutual support (Sussman, 1974).

Debate will continue as to whether the trend to the isolated nuclear family is inevitable and worldwide, in response to continuing urbanization and industrialization, or whether traditional patterns of family life in different cultures will persist. But no one denies that the American family is changing in **structure** and function, that there is an increasing fragility in man-woman relationships and increasing freedom for either partner to terminate one marriage and enter another. What are the factors that are bringing about these changes? The next chapter looks more closely at contemporary family organization in the United States, beginning with a discussion of the laws which govern formation and dissolution of the family at the present time. Chapter 4 examines some of the theories social scientists have developed to explain variations in family form and the behavior of family members in relation to each other, and then examines the **sociocultural** environment surrounding the family in the United States. Through understanding the changes taking place in American society as a whole, a better understanding can be gained of changes now taking place in the institution of the family.

Summary

1. The purpose of this chapter is to give historical perspective to patterns of marriage and family in the United States at the present time. It traces the general historical background of marriage and family in Western civilization, grouping ideas under the topics of gender roles, sexuality, mate selection, di-

vorce, and attitudes toward children. The chapter also looks briefly at marriage and family in early colonial times in America and in the late nineteenth century, considering the same topics listed above.

2. Traditions and attitudes associated with marriage and family life in the United States today developed from cultural traditions of three ancient civilizations—the Hebrews, the Greeks, and the Romans. These traditions were brought to America by way of Western Europe, undergoing many changes along the way in response to religious, political, and economic currents. One example of this is the change from parental to individual mate selection and the increasing importance of love as a basis for marriage, a change which developed slowly over a long period of time out of the court customs of the Middle Ages.

3. Social scientists are cautious in generalizing about the development of family life in America because of the variations between different areas of the country, the rapid pace of change, and the difficulty of weeding out myths from facts. However, some notion of changes in American family life can be obtained by looking briefly at colonial times and then late nineteenth-century America.

4. Prior to the American revolution, social conditions of frontier life led to increased independence of the nuclear family and accelerated the Western European trend toward individual mate selection. Between the colonists in the North and those in the South, there were differences in attitudes reflecting differences in religious beliefs and the organization and orientation of the society.

5. In the nineteenth century, America made the change to a predominantly urban-industrial society, based on rigidly defined gender roles. There was a new sexual restrictiveness. Women began to exercise more power in domestic matters, and children, valued as economic assets but not indulged in colonial times, were treated more permissively.

6. Today, sociologists are divided in their opinions concerning the fate of the family in an increasingly urban-industrial society. All agree, however, that the American family is changing in structure and function in response to the changes in the sociocultural environment of the United States.

Key Concepts

Gender roles	Antisexual	Stereotype
Status	Celibacy	Mores
Patriarchal	Betrothal	Courtly love
Illegitimate	Sacrament	Courtship
Infanticide	Divorce	
Sexuality	Annulment	
Double standard	Separation	
Dualism	Myth	

1. Compare the attitudes toward children in one of the following societies with current attitudes in the United States.

   Hebrew   Greek   Middle Ages in Europe   Colonial America

2. Compare Hebrew and early Christian attitudes toward women.

3. Thinking of the early Puritans and the late-nineteenth-century Americans, discuss the differences in their attitudes toward sexuality.

4. What differences can you find between your attitudes toward marriage and family life and those of your parents? Your grandparents?

5. What problems and adjustments might you have to face if your mate was chosen for you by your parents for economic and social reasons rather than chosen by you on the basis of love? Would it be an easier or more difficult situation? Why?

ARIES, P. (1965). *Centuries of Childhood: A Social History of Family Life.* New York: Random House.

Examines the development of the modern conception of family life and the modern image of the nature of children. Deals primarily with the family, child, and school in pre-nineteenth-century France and England, using paintings, diaries, the history of games and skills, and the development of schools and their curricula.

DEMAUSE, L. (ed.) (1974). *The History of Childhood.* New York: The Psychohistory Press.

Ten psychohistorians discuss what childhood was like in various countries and time periods. They discuss how parents acted toward, cared for, and loved their children, and how the parent-child relationship has changed.

LASLETT, B. (1973). The family as a public and private institution. *Journal of Marriage and the Family* 35:3, 480–492.

Compares the twentieth-century American family and the American family of earlier times in terms of the amount of privacy family members have. Also, discusses the effects of this increased privacy on the patterns of family life in the twentieth century.

ROSENBERG, C. E. (ed.) (1975). *The Family in History.* Philadelphia: University of Pennsylvania Press.

A collection of essays on the influence of the family on society throughout history ranging from medieval China to the mid-twentieth-century United States. Examines various functions of the family and the environments which have shaped and influenced it in different cultures and time periods.

SHORTER, E. (1975). *The Making of the Modern Family.* New York: Basic Books.

A comprehensive history of the family in Western culture, including courtship and sexual practices, child care, and the division of labor. Covers the development of lower, middle, and upper-class families over the past 300 years.

Contemporary Family Organization in the United States | 3

The family is a set of intimate and personal relationships, but it is also a **legal entity.** Marriage, although it may be based on love, is nonetheless a legally binding contract that requires the state's permission to be dissolved. As a social institution, the family occupies a unique position in U.S. society, in between the public and the private domains.

We might ask what is the state's interest in marriage and the family? Aren't such matters as the selection of one's mate, the rearing of one's children, or the decision to end one's marriage strictly personal issues? In view of the important role the family has played in societal survival, the answer to this last question must be a qualified "no." These are personal issues, but not strictly so, for communities have developed sets of expectations regarding appropriate family relationships and sometimes have made these into laws. For example, communities have established laws directed at the prevention of child abuse or the random dissolution of families that might leave children uncared for. The **legitimization** of children, the protection of the spouse from **exploitation,** the protection of property rights, the restriction of sexual activity, and the prohibition of incest and **bigamy** are also social expectations that communities have defined legally (Katz, 1971). And in general, our legal system has developed a rather narrow, **sexist,** and rigid **concept** of the family (Weitzman, 1975).

LEGAL REQUIREMENTS FOR MARRIAGE

Ceremony. A formal act dictated by protocol or convention and following a prescribed ritual.

License. A permission granted by the proper authorities to engage in an activity that is otherwise unlawful.

In order to be legally married, a couple must obtain—for a fee—a marriage license in the **jurisdiction** where the marriage will take place. The state also requires that a **ceremony,** either civil or religious, be performed and that the person officiating at the ceremony sign the **license.** There is one exception to the rule that legal marriage requires a license: in some states, when a couple has lived together for a period of time, presenting themselves as husband and wife to neighbors and associates, they are viewed by the law as legally married. The legalization of such unions, called common-law marriages, grants legitimization to any offspring and ensures survivors, should one spouse die, the rights of inheritance.

Contrary to popular thought, there is no legal requirement that the married couple take the husband's name. The woman may retain her **maiden** name, the man may adopt her name, or the couple may create a hyphenated combination of their names. In fact, if they wish, they may choose an entirely new name. The couple also has the right to give a name other than the husband's to their offspring.

State laws restricting who may marry tend to maximize the freedom of all to marry when and whom they choose while at the same time providing some assurance that only responsible and well-matched individuals

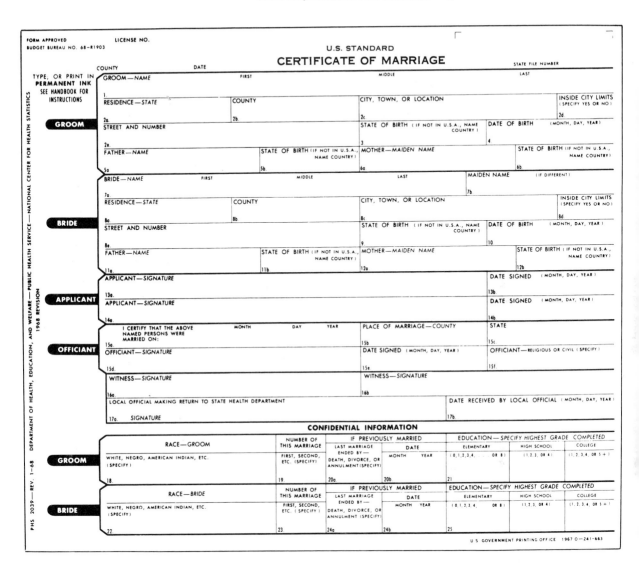

Fig. 3.1 Certificate of marriage.

will be joined in marriage (Drinan, 1969). An individual's marital status, age, health, and relationship to the prospective spouse are legal factors that influence his or her **eligibility** for marriage.

U.S. law requires that an individual, in order to marry, must be single at that time. If the person has been previously married, the former marriage bond must have been dissolved through annulment, divorce, or death before a new bond can be formed. Although this law has sometimes been challenged, notably by the Mormons in the last century, the standard of monogamy is strong in American culture and the law enforcing it shows no sign of weaking.

Although minimum-age requirements vary from state to state, all states have laws prohibiting individuals under a certain age from marrying. In some states, the individuals may marry at a younger age if they have parental consent. The specified age is often different for males and females, a highly questionable practice allowing for the greater **maturity** of young females and the necessity for the male to prepare for his career.

Maturity. The quality of being capable of making adult judgments, of being fully developed.

In addition to the almost-nationwide requirement of a premarital test for **venereal disease,** some states check on other health problems such as tuberculosis or **alcoholism.** Tests for **mental competence** also exist in some states; these are intended to ensure that only responsible individuals become parents. Because of the difficulty of proving or disproving mental competency, these tests point to a crucial problem with all restrictions in marriage law: to what degree do they interfere with the ideal freedom of all to marry and thus infringe upon the individual's basic civil rights? (Drinan).

Civil rights. Rights of personal liberty guaranteed to U.S. citizens by the Constitution.

This question of basic **civil rights** in free choice of marriage partners was raised in 1967 in the case of *Loving v. the State of Virginia* which challenged the long-standing law prohibiting **interracial** marriage. The United States Supreme Court's decision that such laws are **unconstitutional** reasserted the basic right of people to marry whom they want. The decision of the judges includes the statement that marriage is a basic civil right, fundamental to our very existence and survival. On the basis of the *Loving* decision, certain other marriage restrictions, if challenged, would probably be declared unconstitutional. Few question the laws forbidding marriage between close blood relatives because the incest taboo in our society is strong. But what about the restrictions on remarriage between **affinal relatives,** or in-laws? Presumably, these laws are based on a belief that family stability would be undermined if in-laws knew they could marry after the death or divorce of the related spouse. On the constitutional grounds established by the *Loving* decision, however, this restriction would seem indefensible. Similarly, it would be hard to justify the requirement of a waiting period before a person who has been divorced can remarry (Drinan).

Affinal relatives. People to whom one is related through marriage.

A new issue in marriage law has been raised in recent years: whether two people of the same sex have a right to be legally married in the same way that **heterosexual** couples are. And, conversely, whether a person whose spouse is a **transsexual,** operated on to accomplish a sex change, is thereby entitled to a divorce. So far, no state knowingly permits a marriage license to be issued to two persons of the same sex, and divorces have been granted to the spouses of transsexuals (Weitzman; Lentz, 1975).

Considering the important role marriage has played in our society, the legal restrictions imposed upon individuals are minimal. Moreover, those

MARRIAGE LAWS AS OF DECEMBER 31, 1975*

State or other jurisdiction	Age at which marriage can be contracted without parental consent		Age at which marriage can be contracted with parental consent		Blood tests and other medical requirements		Waiting period		Common law marriage	
					Max. period between examination & issuance of license (days)	Scope of medical inquiry	Before issuance of license	After issuance of license	May be contracted in State†	Recognized if valid at time and place where contracted
	Male	Female	Male	Female						
Alabama	18	18	17(a)	14(a)	30	(b)	....	....	Yes	Yes
Alaska	18	18	16(c)	16(c)	30	(b)	3 da.	....	1917	Yes
Arizona	18	18	16(c)	16(c)	30	(b)	(e)	....	......	Yes(f)
Arkansas	18	18	17(c)	16(c)	30	(b)	3 da.	....	......	Yes
California	18	18	18(a,c)	16(a,c)	30	(b,g,h,i)	....	....	1895	Yes
Colorado	18	18	16(c)	16(c)	..	(b,h,j)	....	....	(d)	(d)
Connecticut	18	18	16(c)	16(c)	35	(b)	4 da.	....	......	(d)
Delaware	18	18	18(c)	16(c)	30	(b)	....	(k)	......	Yes(f)
Florida	18	18	18(a,c)	16(a,c)	30	(b)	3 da.	....	1/1/68	(l)
Georgia	18	18	18(c)	16(c)	30	(b,g)	3 da.(m)	....	Yes	(l)
Hawaii	18	18	16	16	30	(b)	....	....	(n)	
Idaho	18	18	16(c)	16(c)	30	(b)	(o)	....	Yes	Yes
Illinois	18	18	16(c)	16(c)	15	(b,g,h)	....	....	......	(d)
Indiana	18	18	16(c)	16(c)	30	(b,g)	3 da.	....	1/1/58	(l)
Iowa	18	18	16	16	20	(b)	3 da.	....	Yes	Yes
Kansas	18	18	18(c)	18(c)	30	(b)	3 da.	....	Yes(p)	Yes
Kentucky	18	18	18(a,c)	16(a,c)	15	(b,g)	3 da.	....	(n)	Yes
Louisiana	18	18	18(c)	16(c)	10	(b)	....	72 hrs.	(n)	Yes(f)
Maine	18	18	16(c)	16(c)	60	(b)	5 da.	....	......	(l)
Maryland	18	18	16(c)	16(c)	..	...	48 hrs.	....	......	Yes
Massachusetts	18	18	18(c)	16(c)	30	(b)	3 da.	....	1/1/57	Yes(f)
Michigan	18	18	(q)	16(c)	30	(b)	3 da.	....	......	(l)
Minnesota	18	18	18(a)	16(r)	..	...	5 da.	....	4/26/41	(l)
Mississippi	21	21	17(c)	15(c)	30	(b)	3 da.	....	4/5/56	(l)
Missouri	18	18	15(c)	15(c)	15	(b)	3 da.	....	3/31/21	(d)
Montana	18	18	18(c)	18(c)	20	(b)	5 da.	3 da.	Yes	Yes
Nebraska	19	19	18	16	30	(b)	2 da.	....	1923	Yes
Nevada	18	18	16(a,c)	16(a,c)	..	...	....	....	3/29/43	Yes
New Hampshire	18	18	14(r)	13(r)	30	(b)	5 da.	....	......	Yes
New Jersey	18	18	18(c)	16(c)	30	(b)	72 hrs.	....	1/12/39	Yes
New Mexico	18	18	16(c)	16(c)	30	(b)	72 hrs.	....	......	Yes
New York	18	18	16	14(s)	30	(b,g)	....	24 hrs.(t)	4/29/33	Yes
North Carolina	18	18	16	16(c)	30	(b,u,v)	(w)	....	......	Yes
North Dakota	18	18	16	16	30	(b,x)	....	....	......	Yes(f)
Ohio	18	18	18(c)	16(c)	30	(b)	5 da.	....	Yes	Yes
Oklahoma	18	18	16(c)	16(c)	30	(b)	(y)	....	Yes	Yes
Oregon	18	18	17	17	30(z)	(b)	7 da.	....	......	Yes
Pennsylvania	18	18	16(c)	16(c)	30	(b,x)	3 da.	....	Yes	Yes
Rhode Island	18	18	18(c)	16(c)	40	(b,h,v)	....	(aa)	Yes	(l)
South Carolina	18	18	16(c)	14(c)	..	...	24 hrs.	....	Yes	Yes
South Dakota	18	18	16(c)	16(c)	20	(b)	....	....	7/1/59	(l)
Tennessee	18	18	16(c)	16(c)	30	(b)	(o)	....	......	Yes
Texas	18	18	14(c)	14(c)	21	(b)	....	....	Yes	Yes
Utah	18	18	16(a)	14(a)	30	(b)	....	....	......	Yes
Vermont	18	18	16(c)	16(c)	30	(b)	....	5 da.	......	(d)
Virginia	18	18	16(a,c)	16(a,c)	30	(b)	....	....	......	Yes
Washington	18	18	17(c)	17(c)	..	(b,v,x)	3 da.	....	......	Yes
West Virginia	18	18	(ab)	(ab)	30	(b)	3 da.	....	......	Yes
Wisconsin	18	18	16	16	20	(b)	5 da.	....	1913	(l)
Wyoming	19	19	17(c)	16(c)	30	(b)	....	....	......	Yes
Dist. of Columbia	21	18	18(a)	16(a)	30	(b)	3 da.	....	Yes	Yes
Puerto Rico	21	21	18(c)	16(c)	10(z)	(b,ac)	....	....	......	(d,f)

*Prepared by the Women's Bureau, U.S. Department of Labor.
†Common law marriages attempted after dates shown are not valid.
  (a)   Parental consent not required if minor was previously married.
  (b)   Venereal diseases.
  (c)   Procedure established whereby younger persons may obtain license.
  (d)   Legal status uncertain.
  (e)   Blood test must be on record for at least 48 hours before issuance of license
  (f)   If permanent residents of the State (domiciliaries) attempt to contract common law marriages in another State, such a marriage is not valid in State where domiciled.
  (g)   Sickle cell anemia.
  (h)   Rubella immunity.
  (i)   Tay-Sachs disease.
  (j)   Rh factor.
  (k)   Residents, 24 hours; nonresidents, 96 hours.
  (l)   Probably yes.
  (m)   Unless parties are 18 years of age or over, or female is pregnant, or applicants are the parents of a living child born out of wedlock.

  Recognized under some circumstances or for limited purposes, e.g., legitimacy of children.
  (o)   Three days if parties are under 18 years of age.
  (p)   However, a misdemeanor.
  (q)   No provision in the law for parental consent of males.
  (r)   Permission of judge also required.
  (s)   If under 16 years of age, consent of family court judge also required.
  (t)   However, marriage may not be solemnized within 3 days of date on which specimen for blood test was taken.
  (u)   Mental competence.
  (v)   Tuberculosis.
  (w)   Forty-eight hours if both are nonresidents of the State.
  (x)   Marriage prohibited in event of feeblemindedness, imbecility, insanity, or chronic alcoholism. In Washington State, an affidavit is required.
  (y)   Seventy-two hours if one or both parties are below the age for marriage without parental consent.
  (z)   Maximum period between examination and expiration of marriage license.
  (aa)   If female is nonresident, must complete and sign license 5 days prior to marriage.
  (ab)   No minimum age.
  (ac)   Insanity, epilepsy, idiocy (affidavit required).

Fig. 3.2 Variations in marriage laws for the fifty states, the District of Columbia, and Puerto Rico. (Source: *The Book of the States, 1976–77,* vol. XXI, The Council of State Governments, Lexington, Kentucky. Reprinted by permission of the publisher.)

which do exist can often be avoided. Since requirements vary from state to state, a couple may simply cross state lines to avoid some particular restriction. For most individuals, getting a marriage license is a simple matter, easier in many respects than getting a driver's license.

MARRIAGE AS CONTRACT

Contract. A binding agreement between two or more persons or parties.

The restraints involved in the **marriage contract** are primarily intended to protect women from sexual exploitation and children from abandonment. That the contract is **tripartite,** with the state as "third party," has added strength to the marriage bond; it has also meant that the state's permission is required for the bond to be dissolved. In most states, until recently, court permission to dissolve a marriage was difficult to obtain. One spouse had to provide evidence that the other had caused the marriage to fail in one of the ways designated by the state as legitimate grounds or reasons for divorce. Adultery, cruelty, and willful desertion were typical grounds for divorce in every state and, in some states, the only acceptable grounds. Thus divorce was an **adversary proceeding,** with one spouse filing suit against the other (Wheeler, 1975).

This system of divorce has been considered by many critics to be destructive and unsatisfactory. The emotional cost of the battle between spouses which the system not only encourages but requires is extreme. The cost of legal fees has been notoriously exorbitant. Since issues such as custody of the children, **alimony, child support**, and division of property have depended on proof of guilt, participants have gone to extreme lengths to win the suit, frequently resorting to **hypocrisy, perjury,** and even **blackmail.** Moreover, the very basis of the system has been questioned: to what degree is a failed marriage anyone's fault? If one spouse has committed adultery, has this caused the marriage to fail, or is it rather a symptom that the marriage has already failed? The erosion of a marriage is a gradual process and one cannot point to one particular act that destroyed it (Kargman, 1973).

No-fault. Pertaining to a system which settles legal claims without regard for the question of which party is to blame.

Widespread criticism of the very basis of the system as well as the practices it encourages has led to the adoption of a **no-fault** system of divorce. In California, for example, a dissolution of marriage is obtained on the basis of "irreconcilable differences which have caused the irremediable breakdown of the marriage." In a true no-fault system, the only grounds for divorce are irretrievable breakdown of the marriage; the only required proof of such breakdown is provided by either spouse saying that it has occurred. Many states have no-fault systems which fall short of this, for a judge may have the right to investigate a case and deny dissolution. In California, few judges have done so. It has generally been conceded that if a couple agrees to seek a divorce, the relationship has broken down beyond repair. If there is no disagreement between the spouses concerning custody of the children or division of property, divorce is granted almost on demand, with court appearance a mere formality (Wheeler; Robbins, 1973).

Opponents of no-fault divorce have claimed that ease in obtaining a divorce encourages marital breakdown. They cite statistics in California and other states which have adopted similar reforms where divorce rates have initially increased by as much as 46 percent. Closer examination of these **statistics,** however, leads to a different conclusion. Many couples who sought divorce under the new laws had already been living separately, some for as long as five years. It would seem that the new system simply permitted the legal termination of marriages long since dead (Wheeler). There is no evidence that the no-fault system of divorce encourages marital breakdown or that the traditional adversary system encourages healthy and stable marriages.

The personal and interpersonal aspects of divorce will be discussed in more detail in Chapter 14, Marital Problems and Marital Dissolution. Here we are looking at divorce from the point of view of the stake that society has in preserving stable marriages and how that interest has been **codified** into law. Changes in family law are indicative of changes in public attitudes, and in view of rapidly changing attitudes and experiences, further changes in divorce, alimony, and child custody laws can be anticipated.

> **Statistics.** A collection of data expressed in numerical terms and used for analysis and interpretation of actual events.

FUTURE OF MARRIAGE LAW

How big a role the law should play in marriage and the family is a difficult question to resolve. The issues involved are at once personal and of major societal concern; both individual civil liberties and public welfare are at stake. Some individuals concerned with these problems have advocated more control and others less. Reexamination of the minimum-age requirements for marriage has been urged. Some have suggested that the age be raised, others that the restriction be eliminated. The difference in the age requirements for males and females has also been questioned. If the later age for males has been to allow them time to prepare for a career, shouldn't females be given the same incentive for career planning? Since passage of the constitutional amendment guaranteeing the right to vote to citizens who are 18 years of age or older, most states have moved to set the same age for marriage of males and females without parental consent. The right to marry at age 18 may eventually become uniform in all states. Presently states vary in age requirements and in other requirements as well. In North Dakota, a couple may get the license immediately and go right out and get married. In Maine, there is a five-day waiting period before the license will be issued. Both of these states require a blood test, but South Carolina requires no physical examination at all (*Council of State Governments,* 1976).

A uniform marriage law for all 50 states has been proposed, and there have also been proposals for registration of all marriages with the federal government. Proponents of this law believe that **computerized** national records would be useful in eliminating illegal marriages, a sort of national "posting of the banns." People who have deserted their spouses and children would be prevented from entering a new marriage. So far, it does not appear that the states are willing to give up regulation of marriage and turn it over to the federal government.

People need to know more about the laws affecting their family experience. Yet Saunders reports that people in general have little knowledge about family law. There are two main reasons for this. First, the legal statutes pertaining to the family are spread around and are uncoordinated. Second, people in power and those making or changing the laws, such as state legislators, do little to publicize coherent sources of information that the public can clearly understand (Saunders, 1975).

The need for premarital education and marriage counseling has been widely recognized; but in what way is the law to fulfill this need? Is the law responsible for preventing marriages that will almost inevitably end in dissolution? On this premise, premarital counseling might be a **prerequisite** for obtaining a marriage license. If the state is considered responsible for maintaining a marriage as long as possible, marriage counseling might be a compulsory prerequisite for divorce. In a few states conciliation courts have been established to help families considering divorce. Court counselors help provide many families the chance to terminate marriage with dignity and minimal **trauma.** Additionally, in many cases, consultation with trained marriage counselors helps couples toward **reconciliation.** One measure of the success of such integration of the legal professionals with behavioral science professionals in the interest of assisting people can be illustrated in the report of the Conciliation Court of Los Angeles that about 40 percent of the families helped took no legal action to terminate the marriage (Elkin, 1973).

Marriage laws have not been sufficiently sensitive to the rights of children. If the state is responsible for the health and welfare of the child population, might it not require that a couple, in order to have children, first obtain a license, having proved themselves capable of handling parental responsibility? It has also been suggested that children should have more influence in deciding which parent they are to live with in cases of divorce. A more difficult question is whether children should have a say in their parent's **remarriage,** an event which will determine many aspects of their own lives. Stiffening the requirements for remarriage after divorce may provide protection for children, but it would restrict the freedom of people to marry whom they choose. Once again, the issue of public welfare versus civil liberties is raised.

It can be seen from this discussion that the legal requirements for marriage and divorce embody a set of ideals, some specifically related to the family, such as monogamy, and others related to broad beliefs, such as freedom of choice. As ideals change, the laws respond, evolving to meet new social needs. Laws generally change slowly, however. It is the tendency of the written law to lag behind the customs and behavior found in the society. Thus our study of the legal aspects of marriage and the family points us to the traditional set of ideals. Legal reforms which have occurred or are presently being advocated indicate areas of transition in our society and suggest perhaps where we are headed. The family in the United States today, in all its varied forms, is very different from the **legal construct** of the traditional U.S. family.

> **Legal construct.** A legal definition of the rights and obligations of persons toward each other in some specific context.

DIVERSITY IN U.S. FAMILY LIFE

The impression one often receives from the **media,** particularly television, is that the American family is white, Anglo-Saxon, and Protestant, consisting of one girl, one boy, one father, and one mother, with the father gainfully employed outside the house but coming home each night with a hug for his wife and children. In this model family, the husband's cheerful manner is shared by the wife who has serenely cooked, cleaned, and cared for her children all day. The children are progressing smoothly at school and in the community. However, the picture presented by this "typical" American family often corresponds so little to reality that major portions of the American public would not recognize themselves in it.

Correspondence between the myth and reality can be examined in your own family situation, which is of course dependent on age, income, race or ethnic identification, political orientation and education, and religious persuasion, to name just a few **social indicators.** There are a great many **variables** which describe the conduct of family life in America. The facts are that marital problems and divorce are common, that many families have only one parent, that many children live with stepparents, that some families have no children, and thousands upon thousands of women are combining jobs outside the home with their domestic duties. Families are often characterized by neglect, unhappiness, poverty, abuse, and stress as much as by firm, loving, tranquil support. Nevertheless, most people do marry, many of them more than once, and most couples do have children.

> **Variables.** Measurable elements or characteristics which influence and account for human behavior.

WHAT WE LEARN FROM STATISTICS ON THE U.S. FAMILY

The statistical picture of family living patterns in the United States reveals that there are many different variations of the family. **Demographic** statistics are hard to collect and often difficult to interpret. Nevertheless, trends are evident and offer some indications of what course future families will take.

Household. A group of persons occupying a housing unit, whether related to one another or not.

In collecting statistical data, as explained in Chapter 1, the U.S. Bureau of the Census distinguishes between households and families in the following way. All the persons occupying a housing unit are a household. A family is a more specialized designation and must include two or more persons residing together who are related by blood, marriage, or adoption. Everyone, then, who does not reside in an institution such as a hospital or prison lives in a household.

Households are divided by type. Of the 71.1 million U.S. households in 1975, 66 percent were husband-wife family households, 22 percent were households with unrelated members or just one occupant, and the remaining 12 percent were family households where no spouse of the head was present. This last category includes single-parent households, or sister-brother households, or any combination of related members that is not headed by a husband-wife team. The statistical relationship between families and households has undergone some changes in recent years. The total number of households has been increasing while the proportion of people living in families has decreased (U.S. Bureau of the Census, 1975, P-20: 282). In other words, more separate households are being established by people who would formerly have been included in a family living situation. This trend is explained by the growing number of young people who are leaving their families at a younger age and establishing homes with friends or by themselves. Also, older people whose families have dissolved are increasingly maintaining residences by themselves, away from relatives. There seems no doubt that the family has assumed less importance as a living unit.

Not only has the number of nonfamily households increased, but the average size of both families and households has decreased. In 1965, for example, the average number of people living together under one roof was 3.29. This had decreased by 1975 to 2.94 (U.S. Bureau of the Census, 1975, P-20: 282). Not only are people choosing to live away from their families, but they are increasingly choosing to live completely alone. This reflects a trend toward valuing individual freedom and personal space over family obligations and ties. Families have found their membership decreased for some of the same reasons that households have been declining in size. The falling **birth rate** has decreased family size so that even when the family circle includes all its primary members, there will be fewer children to be counted. In addition, the practice of neo-local residence, whereby a newly married couple will choose to establish its own home rather than live with one of the parents, is now firmly established. These young couples are being counted as separate families and are statistically decreasing family size.

Birth rate. The ratio of births to the size of the total population, usually expressed as the number of births per year per thousand people.

While the family forms the basis for the majority of households, the character of the family itself is changing. Of those households characterized by the Census Bureau as families, nearly 13 percent were headed by women without husbands as of March 1975. This is an increase from 11 percent in 1970. The number of white families headed by women has increased from 9 percent in 1970 to 11 percent in 1975, while the corresponding increase among black families has been from 28 percent in 1970 to 35 percent in 1975. Families headed by women represent a sizeable portion of the population and their number is growing.

Place of Residence. The American family is changing not only in regard to the composition of its members, but also in where it decides to live. The lifestyle of a family is dependent to a large extent on whether it lives in a city, suburb, or rural area. And this in turn is determined very largely by social-class factors such as income, education, and race or ethnic origin.

Lifestyle. An individual's typical way of life.

The largest proportion of Americans now live in suburban areas. The suburbs have experienced the largest population increase in the seventies, about 8.0 percent from 1970 to 1974. Rural areas increased their population by 5 percent between 1970 and 1974, and central cities lost 2 percent of their population during that same period. Fewer Americans live in cities than in suburbs or rural areas.

The well-known phenomenon of white flight to the suburbs is a reality, as can be seen from comparing the figures for city and suburbs. Blacks also are leaving cities and moving to suburban areas, however. About 20 percent of the blacks living in suburbs in 1974 had moved there since 1970. While some whites have been moving into cities, the trend away from cities remains pronounced. A distinctive difference in family structure between rural, urban, and suburban dwellers is the incidence of female-headed households. The proportion of female-headed households in cities is twice as high as in suburban areas. This difference in family composition is attributable in part to the differing racial composition of cities and suburbs. Income is also a factor. The proportion of female-headed families is about 19 percent in cities, as compared to 10 percent in rural and suburban areas (U.S. Bureau of the Census, 1975, P-23: 55).

Marriage and Divorce. In 1975, there were 69 divorced persons per 1000 people in intact marriages. This ratio includes only those divorced people who had not remarried at the time of the survey. The figure would be much larger, of course, if it included all people who have been divorced. The comparable rate in 1960 was 35 divorced people to 1000 people in intact marriages. Clearly, this is a significant climb in the rate of divorce. The proportion of divorced women is larger than that of divorced men, a reflection of the greater tendency of divorced men to remarry. The rate of divorce of nonwhites is nearly twice the rate for whites (U.S. Bureau of the Census,

1974, P-20:271). The increase in the divorce rate has occurred in all age groups but is more pronounced among those under 45 years old.

The rising divorce rate is usually considered to be related to two factors: changes in the attitude of Americans to divorce and changes in the status of women. Women are less likely now to stay in a marriage for reasons of financial security. The increased economic independence of women has made divorce a realistic alternative for an unhappy marriage, even one with children. And with the increase in the number of women holding jobs, a young couple can more easily afford the financial burden of a divorce. Americans also have begun to be less conservative on the question of divorce. Partly this is because more of their neighbors are doing it. Partly it is because religious groups have been treating the subject more tolerantly. Still another reason may be that a **humanist** element has crept into our expectations concerning marriage, and fewer people feel compelled to stay in an unsuccessful marriage because it is the "right" thing to do. Whatever the reason, the fact is that more Americans seem able to accept divorced teachers, doctors, and political figures than has been the case in the past.

Humanist. Centered on the human capacity for self-realization without dependence on supernatural forces.

Remarriage. Statistics show two common patterns of how divorced people live after dissolving their marriage. If they have no children, they usually live alone. If they have children, the woman is about four times more likely to have them living with her than is the man (U.S. Bureau of the Census, 1974, P-20: 271).

When and if a **divorcée** remarries, her children will join a fairly large number of children who are living with a stepparent. Only about 70 percent of the children under 18 years of age in 1970 were living with their two natural parents who had been married only once. Among black children the corresponding figure was 45 percent (Glick, 1976). Each year more than a million children are involved in divorce. The number of children whose parents were divorced was 562,000 in 1963 and 1,079,000 in 1973 (USDHEW, *Vital Statistics Report,* 76-1120, 24: 4). Family theories will have to be responsive to this as a reality of the socialization of young children. What will the consequences be when these children become adults? Will marriage have a stronger or a weaker value for them?

The rates of remarriage are an indication that while individuals may experience an unhappy marriage the first time, they are often willing to try again. Most second marriages occur between divorced rather than widowed people, and more men than women get married a second time. In 1973, there were 133 men who entered new marriages for every 1000 widowed or divorced men in the population, and 41 women who tried again for every 1000 widows or divorced women in the population (USDHEW, *Vital Statistics Report,* 76-1120, 24: 5).

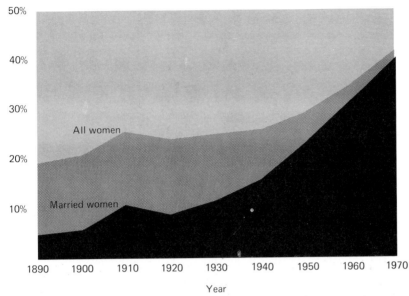

Fig. 3.3 Increased participation of females in the labor force. The chart shows the female labor force as a percent of the female population. (Source: U.S. Bureau of the Census, *Historical Statistics of the United States, Colonial Times to 1970*, Part I. Washington: 1975.)

Women in the Labor Force.   The number of married women in the labor force has more than doubled since 1950 and now accounts for almost three-fifths of all women workers. About one-half of all married women with husbands present work outside the home, and 59 percent of married women with husbands absent (separated, deserted, in the Armed Forces, etc.) are workers (*U.S. Bureau of Labor Statistics*, Bulletin 1880). Figure 3.3 shows how the percentage of women in the labor force has increased.

Women with preschool children are less likely to be workers than women with school-age children. Divorced or separated women, however, are somewhat more likely to find themselves working even with small children at home. In general, mothers have increasingly entered the labor force, with the sharpest rate of increase coming from mothers with preschoolers (*U.S. Bureau of Labor Statistics*, Bulletin 1880). The next few sections of this chapter discuss some of the consequences for family life of the participation of married women in the labor force, whether in **dual-career families** or as single parents.

Dual-career families. Families in which both husband and wife work at paid jobs.

DUAL-CAREER FAMILIES

Increased participation of women in the labor force is at variance with the traditional view of the American family. How are the women faring who have children and husbands and at the same time are pursuing careers? What are the stresses on the members of such two-career families? Rhona and Robert Rapoport attempted to answer these questions in their study of dual-career families. One of the first things they discovered is that there is a gap between the ideal and the reality in such marriages. Even where the husband-father is vocally supportive of his wife's career and expresses a desire for an **equalitarian** marriage, the wife-mother will retain the major responsibilities of home and children. Both husband and wife experience stress as a result of the additional energy required to maintain the home at a middle-class standard of cleanliness and order and the desire to be involved in the upbringing of the children. This is referred to by the Rapoports as **role overload,** as both husband and wife try to juggle their outside occupations with mothering, fathering, and domestic-maintenance roles. Most couples cannot afford domestic help so they cope by eliminating non-essential household tasks. Children in such families are frequently given increased responsibilities for domestic chores.

Problems of Childcare. Except in cases of economic necessity, U.S. mothers are still expected to stay home with their children, even if this leads to personal frustration and underutilization of the woman's talents and abilities. Women not staying home will often be made to feel guilty for neglecting their home duties and leaving their children in the hands of **surrogate** parents. Children tend to be highly valued in dual-career families, so this can be a major source of conflict and guilt. Unfortunately, there are nowhere near enough good, responsible, child-care facilities provided in this country to meet the demand. American society has, by and large, not yet adapted to the needs of working women with families.

Costs and Benefits. Dual-career families derive many benefits from their lifestyle, though they pay for it in stress. The Rapoports (1969) have come to the following conclusions. Role overloads result from taxing the energies of family members to an extent that would not be necessary if the wife did not work. Benefits derived, however, are the personal stimulation and development afforded the wife by working outside the home, the increased family income provided, and the closer relationship of the father and his children resulting from his greater participation in their upbringing. The costs for the working woman of diverging from the norms of society are psychic distress and the sacrifice of social relationships associated with the stay-at-home-mother role. The benefits she derives (and her husband benefits too) involve a sense of integrity in fulfilling her ideals and a sense that she has not wasted her capacities. This applies, of course, more to women in professional jobs than to those doing clerical or factory work.

The dual-career family gives up many contacts in the social network of kin and friends through lack of time. It may suffer from loss of contact with the outside world and from guilt at ignoring social obligations. A benefit derived is in priority-setting: by limiting the obligatory relation-

Role overload. Stress occurring when people are trying to fulfill more different roles than they have time or energy for.

Surrogate. Appointed to act in place of another, as a babysitter is a surrogate parent.

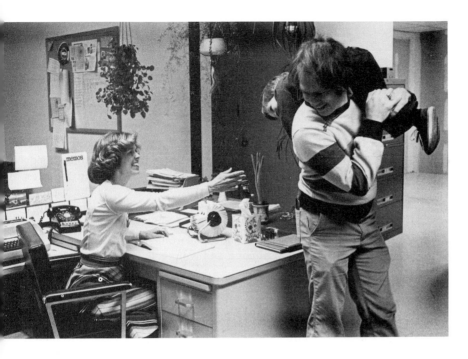

ships, the family pursues only those interests and relationships which are truly gratifying. Many a mother has used her outside job as the excuse for not participating in some community organization in which she has little genuine interest.

Limitations on the Woman's Career.   The more rigid the occupational demands are, the less likely it is that women will reach the top positions in their field. For example, a woman studying to be a doctor might put off having children until well past the median age of most childbearing. Or, having children, such a woman might not undertake to become a surgeon or other specialist requiring extra years and special effort. In demanding professions, women may be restricted from the top positions because, while they are able to put in 40–50 hours per week, they may be unable to put in the 70–80 hours per week necessary to climb to the top. Of course, married men would be unable to do this either without their wives and families' willingness to take a back seat.

Many dual-career families succeed despite the obstacles and stresses. Often, however, a dual-career family will end either by divorce or by the woman giving up her career. The problems of time, the difficulties of child care, and the guilt over not fulfilling normative role expectations all converge until the woman decides the career is not worth the effort. The third

Normative. Conforming to the society's norms.

mode of dual-career breakdown, that of the man giving up his career, is possible but a rare occurrence.

What societal forces contribute to the difficulty of maintaining a dual-career family? In Holmstrom's (1972) examination of academic families where both husband and wife were employed, she found that a sex bias exists in the problem solving of these families; dilemmas were most often resolved in favor of the men and needs of the women were treated as secondary. Women are further handicapped by sexist job discrimination, which makes a career more frustrating to pursue even for highly motivated women.

Hybrid model of equality. A more equalized definition of gender roles than the traditional assignment of tasks based on sex.

Holmstrom advocates changes in the family and changes in the occupational world. The so-called **hybrid model of equality** that she proposes involves changing the roles of both women and men in the home and at the job. There would be a hybrid or blended role, rather than separate male and female roles. The idea is not for women to join men in their struggle for success, but that both men and women learn to lead less status-dominated lives. Making work schedules flexible could free both men and women for the care of children. The roles of men and women would be more balanced and couples could more easily share domestic responsibilities. A basic requirement for this model of equality is an excellent child-care system, run by government, private companies, and organizations such as universities and hospitals. The hybrid model of equality presupposes that both men and women would benefit from an equalization of their statuses.

CHILDLESS MARRIAGES

Parenthood is a dominant cultural value in American society. There are many pressures upon married couples who have no children; often they are considered selfish or neurotic. Women who are childless by choice are accused of denying their so-called **maternal instinct.** Both men and women are cautioned that they are missing the greatest things in life, or that they will be sorry when they are elderly and have no children to look after them (Movius, 1976).

Child-free. Childless by choice; a rejection of parenthood.

To combat this cultural bias, NON, the National Organization For Non-Parents, was formed in 1971. Their purpose is to promote **child-free** marriages and make nonparenthood a viable option for individuals. The organization presents evidence gathered in various research studies that child-free couples have happier marriages and that many persons identify the periods before the birth of the first child and after the last child leaves home as the happiest times of their marriage. All in all, the major educational purpose of the organization is to reassure married couples that it is an acceptable alternative, and perhaps even beneficial, to remain child-free. The need to restrict population growth has given added credibility to non-parents.

A Census Bureau study in June 1974 revealed that 25 percent of childless wives aged 14–39 expect to remain childless. Most wives who have reached the age of 30 without having children expect to remain childless the rest of their lives (U.S. Bureau of the Census, 1975, P-20: 277). A separate analysis of 1970 census data reveals that the more education a woman has, the more likely she is to remain childless. Neither of these studies attempted to determine how many of these women were voluntarily deciding to remain childless and how many would be childless for various **physiological** reasons, but a sample study in Rhode Island in the late sixties, reported by Rao (1974), produced an estimate that 4 percent of married women living with their husbands are involuntarily childless. This study also investigated differences between Catholic and Protestant ever-married females and found that 13 percent of Catholics were childless compared to 21 percent of Protestants.

In a study in Canada, Veevers (1973) interviewed 52 voluntarily childless wives to see if regularities could be observed in the decision to remain childless. Volunteers for the study were solicited in newspaper advertisements and chosen on the basis of being voluntarily childless rather than sterile.

Deciding to Remain Childless.   Veevers found two routes to voluntary childlessness. Nearly a third of the women reported that they had decided before their marriage that they would remain childless and had consciously sought mates who would agree to this condition. A few reported that it was their husbands who had convinced them, before they were married, of the desirability of remaining childless. In contrast to the conscious decision of this group, more than two-thirds of the wives reported that their decision was the result of continuous postponement of childbearing; the childbearing of these couples was deferred to a future which never came.

All the wives reported that they felt pressure from others to have children, both by negative attitudes toward childless women and by explicit promotherhood comments. They further reported that after the first year of marriage, the pressure from friends and relatives increased, reached a peak in the third and fourth years of marriage, and leveled off after about the fifth or sixth years. Most of the wives said they had considered adopting a child. Veevers viewed this possibility as symbolically important rather than a serious alternative to childlessness. The women could use this theme of adoption to convince themselves and others that they were "normal" and liked children; further, it eased the anxiety of making an irreversible decision. The researchers also found that the decision to remain childless was a personal one. While some of the wives expressed interest in or support for **feminism,** or the **zero population growth** movement, none indicated that these movements in any way contributed to her decision.

There are already a significant number of childless marriages. It seems clear that the wider availability of abortion and improvements in **birth control** techniques will inevitably increase the ranks of the voluntarily

Physiological. Based on the function or malfunction of various systems of the body.

Feminism. Organized activity in behalf of women's rights and interests.

childless, just by virtue of the increased possibility of carrying out the decision once made. With the rise in feminism and the formation of groups like NON, the social climate is changing to accommodate increased variability in attitudes toward becoming parents.

SINGLE-PARENT FAMILIES

Society is organized in such a way that structural problems exist for families that do not fit the two-parent model. Yet, in March 1975, one out of seven children under age 18 were in families without fathers, up from one out of ten in March 1970 (McEaddy, 1976). The tasks that a family normally carries out on a daily basis—financial support, child care, and household maintenance—generally require the cooperation of two adults. Single parents must find a way to carry the double burden alone. If the single parent is male, he will generally continue to carry out his breadwinner tasks, leaving a gap in the traditionally female functions. If he is financially able, he may hire someone for housekeeping and childcare. If, as is more usual, the single parent is female, she may have to adopt the breadwinner role, and again a gap is left in the homemaking function of the family. Single parents may be able to shift some duties to the children, if they are old enough, but most tasks will need the attention of an adult. In any case, unless a family is quite well off financially, some tasks, especially those normally done by women, will be neglected.

Role models. Figures in the socialization process on which children can base their conceptions of how they should behave in given situations.

In a two-parent family, children generally have close daily contact with both sexes and learn how adults of both sexes act. They have both male and female **role models.** It is part of a child's socialization process to see how society is perceived by either parent and also how either parent is seen by society. Fathering and mothering typically denote different behaviors in our society. The children in a one-parent family may get a distorted view, seeing the world through the eyes of one sex only. The single parent may also be cut off from communication with the other sex. Many social occasions for adults are planned for couples. A single parent may be excluded or may choose to ignore such occasions, causing further blocks in communication with the surrounding society. Having two adults in a home means that more input is received; interests that are sometimes sex-limited, such as sports or shopping, are represented fully. The single-parent family may find itself out of touch with certain things just because it is operating on a single channel of communication.

The single-parent family is also understaffed in serving as a source of love and security for its members, and children cannot grow up in a healthy manner without these needs being met. The loss or absence of one member of the family can reduce the security of the others, and also put more strain on remaining members to keep negative feelings to themselves. Still, it is not the children who suffer as much from lack of emotional support as the remaining adult. A single parent can provide love and support for a child, but the parent may lack adult sources of love and companionship, and may suffer as well from a lack of sexual activity. Finally, the possibility exists that the child will come to identify one sex only as a source of love, making sexual and other adult adjustments more difficult.

Father-Only Families.   Aside from an occasional newspaper feature describing the plight of a father trying to raise children in a one-parent household, little is written about fathers operating without wives. Even less **sociological** research has been done. Estimates made by the Census Bureau put the number of father-only families at over 800,000, about one-third of which are headed by **widowers.**

Most fathers in this situation do not remain as single parents long. The majority of them remarry rather quickly. As single parents, men do suffer from economic difficulties, although seldom as much as women, and they find little community support for their one-parent situation. Both men and women suffer from the role conflicts of job responsibility, social life, and parental demands. Fathers in one-parent families, particularly if they are divorced, suffer from the same difficulties of loneliness, economic stress, and role overload as women in one-parent families. By remarrying, they resolve these conflicts by transferring duties and role demands to their new spouses. However, Krantzler, a **marriage counselor** discussing creative divorce, warns fathers that a hasty remarriage is a major impediment to sustained personal growth (Krantzler, 1974).

Mother-Only Families.   Whether a woman is a single parent through divorce, separation, desertion, death, or having never married, her life and that of her family will have features common to all woman-headed families. Poverty is a prevailing possibility. In families with a male head, 8 percent were below the **poverty level** in 1975, while in families with a female head, 35 percent (12.3 million people) were below the poverty level that year (U.S. Bureau of the Census, *Statistical Abstract of the U.S., 1976*). Even where the mother-only family is not in abject poverty, there is relatively little possibility that the members can achieve normal middle-class financial security. Dividing the father's income between two households after a divorce, when it previously provided for only one, almost always requires a major drop in the **standard of living** for both of them. For women with children living on **public assistance,** the financial situation is usually just short of hopeless, since only enough money is provided to keep from going hungry, but not enough to raise the family out of poverty. The single mother may not have anyone who can take over responsibility if she is sick. Because she is overloaded with the role of breadwinner and disciplinarian, she may not be able to satisfactorily carry out the activities of

Poverty level. The minimum income required for an individual or a family to provide an adequate diet and other necessities of life.

providing domestic comfort and love. The absence of another adult with whom to share decision making will be a strain. The role of the single parent puts heavy social, emotional, and economic demands on both women and men. A national organization has been formed called "Parents Without Partners" specifically to provide mutual assistance for these people.

Types of Mother-Only Families. Some features of mother-only families are closely related to the way in which the family came to lack a father:

1. The widowed mother has the distinct advantage of having the support and sympathy of the community behind her. On the other hand, she and her children have suffered a severe emotional blow in the loss of the husband-father that may be difficult to get over. She is likely to have about the same financial and role problems as other woman-headed families, but will probably receive more support from her kin and friendship network.

2. The unmarried mother will have all the problems of any single parent in addition to the outright disapproval of society. She is more likely than others to be receiving public welfare and she is more likely to belong to a **racial minority.** She thus suffers more from **racism** and poverty than other mothers. Her chances for a successful marriage are smaller than that of other single parents (LeMasters, 1974). She is least able of all these women to fit her family to the traditional norms of middle-class America. In 1975, there were 447,900 illegitimate births: 163,000 were white, 234,500 black, and 9,800 other races. Almost 11,000 of these were born to females under 15 years of age. Fourteen percent of all live births in 1975 were to unmarried females.

3. The **deserted** mother is likely to suffer the same financial problems as the never-married mother, since the father is unavailable for even minimal financial help. In addition, she is not legally free to remarry. Deserted mothers and their families may suffer more from emotional distress and feelings of rejection than the divorced woman and her family. In the case of the divorced woman, the marital dissolution was planned, expected, and probably a mutual decision. A deserted mother may find herself thrust into her new role with little warning.

4. The separated mother is in a position similar to that of the deserted mother. Her only real advantage is the fact that the man is still in the picture and may be able to provide some financial support. They can also get a divorce later on to clarify the family's legal status or to enable the partners to marry others.

5. The divorced mother is statistically the most numerous type of single parent. She has the advantage of a clear and legal split with her hus-

Desertion. The disappearance of a spouse; sometimes called the poor man's divorce.

band, with **custody** decided and financial obligations of the man spelled out by the court. One of her main problems, however, is that court orders to support often are not lived up to by former husbands. In a study in the late sixties, it was found that within one year of the divorce decree only 38 percent of former husbands were in full compliance with the court order to support their families, 42 percent contributed no support at all after one year, and 67 percent were contributing nothing within four years. Fully one-third of fathers are never ordered to pay anything at all to their families, a sharp contrast to the popular media view of husbands burdened by exhaustive alimony and child-support payments (Brandwein et al., 1974).

Custody. Immediate charge and control exercised by a person in authority.

Poverty in Woman-Headed Families.   As expected, the economic situation of the divorced woman and her family will be a crucial factor in predicting how successful or unsuccessful they will be. The poorer a couple is, the more likely it is that they will divorce. On the other hand, even if a family was not poor before divorce, the chances are good that it will be after. Kriesberg (cited in Brandwein et al.) found that poverty in woman-headed families is not as closely related to the socioeconomic status of the family before divorce as it is to current circumstances.

Women are expected to depend on men for their economic support, so they suffer economic discrimination along the lines of, "She's making a lot for a woman," or "Let's give that job to a man; he has a family to support." Stein reported in 1970 that only 9 percent of female-headed families have incomes over $10,000 while 55 percent of two-parent families are above this level (Brandwein et al.). Many divorced women depend on friends or relatives for financial assistance. Without adequate child care, the single mother's options are few. She has the choice of not working and thereby suffering the uncertainties of child support or public assistance. Or she can choose to go to work and leave her children with undesirable or unqualified caretakers. In the absence of relatives or friends, the single parent must seek out paid child care and this will, of course, further burden the family's strained income. It is not the lack of a husband that by itself causes financial difficulties: the economic hardship suffered by divorced families is the result of economic discrimination against women, combined with a reluctance of the fathers or public agencies to provide meaningful support.

The divorced woman and her family may be branded by the community. Her family is seen as "broken," deviant; there are expectations from schools, courts, and neighbors that her children will be undisciplined. The divorced woman herself is seen as a failure because she "couldn't keep her man." At the same time, she may be regarded as a predatory female out to get other women's husbands and may be left out of social activities as a result. The divorced woman is presumed to be less moral than her married sisters. There is no doubt that society is still uncomfortable with a divorced woman's situation and seeks to discourage the idea that such a family is a normal variant of the traditional American family.

As compared to a divorced man-father, the divorced woman-mother may suffer from a lack of authority in relation to banks, stores, schools, and courts. The reason for this is two-fold. First, the divorced woman will naturally suffer from the same discriminatory practices that lending institutions and businesses show to all women. Second, the mother is stepping into a role as authority figure in relation to courts and schools that is more usually held by the father. In contrast to her situation outside the home, however, the woman's authority within the family is greatly increased as a result of her divorce. Many women see the divorced state as an opportunity to come out from under the domination of men, perhaps for the first time in their lives. While divorced women are at a disadvantage when compared to men's freer exercise of authority, they generally have more opportunity to be independent than do married women.

It has been established that a woman-headed family has a hard time fulfilling the functions of the two-parent family, and father-absence does have significant negative effects on the family. On the other hand, mother-presence is an important force and woman-headed families do survive and function. It is the argument of Brandwein, Brown, and Fox that two parents are not necessarily better than one for the successful functioning of the family. They have examined the divorced woman and her family from this perspective and have concluded that the problems of woman-headed families are not in the absence of the father, but in society's relationship with the family.

MIXED MARRIAGES

It was common in the past, and still is common in some parts of the world, for extended families to play an important role in mate selection. Such extended families would choose marriage partners among other families who shared their social characteristics, and who would continue the cultural tradition of the family, whatever it was. While it is no longer usual for families to perform this function, **ethnocentric** preference and endogamy (marriage within one's social group) still characterize the mate-selection process. People tend to marry individuals much like themselves, but this is by no means an absolute rule. **Intermarriage** in many forms does occur.

Two social characteristics with strong influence on mate selection have been race and religion. Less than one percent of all marriages involve racial

Ethnocentric. Pertaining to the feeling that one's own culture is natural, right, and superior to all others.

intermarriage, although the rate is increasing. The exact rate of interfaith marriage is not known, since such statistics are not officially collected. However, research indicates that such marriages are increasing in frequency. Such a trend is important to the consideration of marriage and the family because exogamous marriages (marriages outside one's own cultural group) have traditionally been associated with a high divorce rate.

INTERFAITH MARRIAGES

Many religious groups discourage interfaith marriage, but recognizing that such marriages occur, offer guidance to couples of different faiths who are considering marriage. In a country such as the United States with so many diverse religious groups, intermarriage is almost inevitable. It is generally accepted that the smaller the religious group, the higher the rate of intermarriage. The obvious logic of this is that there would be a limited number of marriageable partners in a small population that practiced strict endogamy, so exogamy must be accepted. It has been found that in states where the proportion of Catholics is low, the rate of intermarriage is high. Where the proportion of Catholics is high, the rate of intermarriage is low (Nye and Berardo, 1973). Protestants, being the most numerous religious group in the country, have the lowest rate of intermarriage. Despite the fact that the Catholic church has actively opposed intermarriage, about one-quarter of marriages involving a Catholic are to someone outside the faith. While the causal relationship described may generally hold true, the premise must sometimes be modified in response to other variables. Among Jews, for example, the rate of intermarriage has traditionally been very small, despite the fact that they comprise only 3 percent of the population. There are strong cultural reasons why Jews would reject the idea of marriage with Christians. In spite of these reasons, however, the rate has been climbing in the last decade.

Intermarriage. Marriage between members of different racial or religious groups.

Religious groups oppose intermarriage because of fear that the member will be less active in following his or her religion than if married to a person of the same faith. They also fear that the children of the intermarried couple may not be brought up within that faith. Religious leaders and other critics of intermarriage point to the instability of such marriages as further proof of their inadvisability. If the religious identification of one partner in the marriage is high, this may in itself cause conflict unless the other partner is extremely tolerant. Perhaps even more important as a factor in divorce is the behavior in family-related areas that the religious organization expects. For example, Catholics are instructed by the church to treat the father as the head of the house, the mother as his helping hand, and to send the children to parochial schools, if possible. Birth control, except through unreliable "natural" methods, abortion, and divorce are prohibited. Lack of agreement between the partners on matters such as these can make family decision making a very thorny process.

INTERRACIAL MARRIAGES

Marriages between blacks and whites increased by 26 percent in the decade between 1960 and 1970, but still represent less than one percent of all marriages in the United States (Monahan, 1976). Analysis of data collected by the Census Bureau in 1970 has revealed a total of 64,789 such marriages in existence at that time. However, according to David Heer (1974), the increase in interracial marriages has been entirely in marriage between black men and white women. There has actually been an overall decline in the number of marriages between white men and black women.

A particularly interesting part of Heer's data is the decline in black-white marriages in the South from 1960 to 1970. Up to 1967, interracial marriages were legally prohibited in all Southern states. In that year, the Supreme Court declared these **statutes** invalid and an infringement of the civil right of persons to choose their own marriage partners. It is not known whether the 20,432 black-white couples reported in the Southern states in the 1960 census had been legally married in other states and moved to the South to live, or actually were in **consensual unions, not legal marriages**. All of the decline in marriages between white men and black women occurred in the South. Whether these unions were terminated, by divorce or by mutual consent, or whether a substantial number of such couples moved to other parts of the country is not known.

Obviously, partners in an interracial marriage sometimes encounter problems not common to marriages within the same race. The couple may be rejected by families and friends. Differences in cultural background may make adjustment of each to the lifestyle of the other difficult, since the family role behavior expected by each spouse may be different. Heer's data definitely indicates that interracial marriages are more hazardous than marriages between partners of the same race. Comparing census figures for 1960 and 1970, and including only couples who were in their first marriage, he found that after ten years 89.8 percent of the all-white marriages and 77.8 percent of the all-black marriages were intact, but only 63.4 percent of the marriages between white women and black men and 46.7 percent of the marriages between black women and white men had survived. There is evidence, however, that when an interracial marriage occurs between members of equal-status races (as in Hawaii between Oriental and Caucasian), the likelihood of the marriage failing is not greater than for other marriages (Nye and Berardo). It would seem that difference in status between races is more critical than specific cultural differences. However, in most marriages, the closer in cultural background the partners are, the more likely it is that they will stay married.

THE BLACK FAMILY IN THE UNITED STATES

In recent years, it has become common practice to present separate statistics for blacks and whites in reference to family-related issues. This is because black families and white families have some significantly different family-life patterns in this country. Blacks in the United States represent about 11 percent of the total population, an estimated 24 million people out of a total of 216 million in 1977. In general, black families differ more radically than white families from the idealized picture of the model American family.

The exact difference and its consequences is a matter of scholarly judgment. Heiss, using nationwide data, asserts that the dynamics of black family life are not identical to those of the white family, but there are many similarities (Heiss, 1975). Scanzoni studied 400 black households in the Indianapolis area, and concludes: "We have discovered fundamental similarities between black and white family patterns and we have found certain dissimilarities between these patterns. These differences, however, are not the result of culture, race, or of black ideology. They are, pure and simple, the consequence of white **discrimination**, especially against black males" (Scanzoni, 1971, p. 324). Our purpose here is to examine briefly some of these black family patterns.

Discrimination. Unfair or unequal treatment of individuals according to their placement in certain social categories.

Since many more black families than white are headed by women (35 percent compared to 11 percent), the proportion of black children living in homes with two parents is smaller than the proportion of white children living with two parents. In the period between 1970 and 1974, the proportion of black children living with two parents declined from 64 percent to 56 percent. The comparable statistic for white children is 88 percent living in homes with two parents in 1974, down from 91 percent in 1970 (U.S. Bureau of the Census, 1974, P-23: 54). Staples (1971) has suggested that the position of the black woman is affected by lower sex ratios in the black population than in the white. For whites aged 14–24, there are 102 males for every 100 females. For blacks, there are 96 males for every 100 females. The difference is even greater at ages 25–44: for whites, there are 98 males for every 100 females, and for blacks, only 84 males for every 100 females (U.S. Bureau of the Census, *Statistical Abstract of the U.S.*, 1976). These differences, when multiplied over the whole population, represent a substantial shortage of adult black males relative to the number of females. Dietrich (1975) notes that even though lower-class black males have problems in adequately performing the provider role, their bargaining power is increased by the low sex ratio.

For both black and white families, the likelihood of children living with both parents rises as family income rises. Family stability, if this is the meaning of two-parent presence in the family, appears to be a function of economic stability (Scanzoni, 1975). Black families are over-represented in the lower economic categories. But it is also true that black families need to have considerably more income than their white counterparts to equal the family stability of the white family as measured by the presence of two parents. In other words, black families with an income of $10,000–$15,000 have the approximate stability of white families with an income of $8,000–$10,000 (U.S. Bureau of the Census, 1974, P-23: 54).

Black women tend to have more children than white women. In 1973, the **total fertility rate** (defined as the lifetime bearing of children) was 2.44 children per black woman and 1.80 per white woman. However, the total fertility rate is declining for black women at about the same rate as it is declining for white women (U.S. Bureau of the Census, 1974, P-23: 54).

BASIS FOR DIFFERENCES BETWEEN BLACK AND WHITE FAMILIES
In the past, social scientists have frequently labeled black families as **deviant, pathological, and self-destructive** (Heiss). Lately there has been a growing realization among sociologists that these are value judgments. Such judgments have limited inquiry into the black family and encouraged misleading comparisons between the white middle-class "normal" family and the black "deviant" family. It has been proposed in this chapter that the "normal" middle-class white family, characterized by harmony and stability, is a cultural myth. The companion view of the black family as weak or sick is also a myth, or at least a distortion. Marie Peters, in an extensive review of sociological statements concerning the black family, argues that many myths are included in sociology texts about blacks. These presentations closely associate black people with poverty, illegitimacy, supersexuality, and female dominance (Peters, 1974). The fact remains that many black families do experience life differently from white families.

> **Total fertility rate. The number of children born to the average woman during her entire lifetime, computed only for those beyond childbearing age.**

Table 3.1.   Persons below the poverty level in the United States in 1975   The figures show that people of black and other races are far more likely to be living below the poverty level than are whites. They also show the greater likelihood that families with a female head will be living below the poverty level.

	NUMBER	PERCENT
All persons	25,900,000	12.3
White	17,800,000	9.7
Black and other races	8,100,000	29.3
In families with male head	13,600,000	7.8
In families with female head	12,300,000	34.6

Source: *Statistical Abstract of the United States,* 1976

Marital instability is a significant factor in black family life. Black wives tend to be less satisfied with their marriages than white wives (Staples). Both divorce and separation rates are higher among blacks than whites. Socioeconomic factors are an influence. As income, education, and job levels rise, the chances for a stable marriage improve. There are some who feel that the instability of lower-class black marriages is the result of the black wife sharing the provider role with her husband. According to this view, the man is thus made to feel unsure of his status and so withdraws from the family decisions and household functions (Staples). However, Dietrich provides considerable evidence that even in lower-class families husbands were perceived to be major participants in decision making and their influence was noted especially with respect to decisions about where to live. Actually, the predominant family power pattern reported by Dietrich's low-income black families was equalitarian, with husband and wife sharing in decision making.

Two Possible Explanations.   Most current research on the black family explains black-white differences in one of two ways: one **theory** presents the black lower-class family as part of an **autonomous subculture with folkways and values that are distinct from the larger society**. People who favor this theory assert that the black family became an unstable unit as a result of the black historical experience of slavery and economic deprivation. The unstable family lifestyle thus created is perpetuated by the usual channels of cultural transmission: role formation and socialization of the young. The other theory presents class as the most important variable in explaining the divergence of black families from white middle-class norms: the lower-class status of a large proportion of the black population is the reason for the high rate of divorce, desertion, and other family problems. By this view, black families do not differ significantly from white families in the lower classes, whose family life is also characterized by instability (Leacock, 1971).

Autonomous. Existing or capable of existing independently; having the right or power of self-government.

Frazier's Ideas.   An important influence upon the study of the black family was the work of E. Franklin Frazier, a black **sociologist.** The family patterns he identified as typical emphasized the destructive legacy of slavery, the absent husband, and the mother-oriented character of black family life (Furstenberg et al., 1975). According to Frazier, family instability was a heritage of slavery. The method of enslavement destroyed the African system of social organization. On the plantation, casual sex was the norm; and marriage, since slaves were property to be disposed of at the will of the owner, never acquired a strong institutional base. Even with the abolition of slavery, development of a stable family system was made difficult by problems of economic distress and racism. At the time of his research,

Sociologist. One who studies social organization and the behavior of humans in social settings.

Frazier believed that the problems of blacks would be solved when they entered the mainstream of U.S. life and succeeded in adopting white culture. Later, however, as the civil rights movement of the sixties was getting underway, Frazier modified his assimilationist views. Contemporary scholars such as Gutman (1976), Furstenberg, and others now assert that slavery did not create the tangle of pathology. Instead, they emphasize the impact of the harsh urban experience of black families—economic discrimination, poverty, disease, and high mortality rates.

Pathology. Deviation from the normal so as to constitute a diseased condition.

Moynihan's Ideas.   A restatement of Frazier's views of the black family was provided by Nathan Glazier and Daniel P. Moynihan in *Beyond the Melting Pot* (1964). These views later received a great deal of publicity when Moynihan was appointed to a policy-making role for the federal government. The major thesis for which Moynihan is known is his contention that American blacks are malfunctioning members of society because of their deviant family patterns, and he specifically identified **matriarchy** as the most destructive element in black family life (Furstenberg et al.). His thesis thus shifted blame away from the overall social structure in the United States and onto the black family. Using census statistics, he related the high incidence of mother-headed households (matriarchal in his terms) to juvenile delinquency, overlooking the fact that such families are among the poorest in our society and thereby ignoring the established relationship between poverty and crime. Moynihan's solutions to the problem of black and white inequality focused on strengthening the black family, rather than attacking the problems of unequal opportunity and discrimination in American institutions (Leacock).

Rainwater's Ideas.   In his 1966 study, Rainwater shares with Moynihan the belief that the black family structure perpetuates the low socioeconomic status of blacks. His analysis was limited to lower-class blacks, and he did not seek to generalize his findings to black society as a whole.

Rainwater looked for specific family patterns that perpetuate the victimization of blacks and started with sex. The high rate of illegitimate births in the ghetto, he said, is the consequence of a casual, uncaring acceptance of out-of-wedlock children. Staples, while agreeing that illegitimate children are more accepted in the black community than in the white, offers evidence that premarital pregnancies are viewed negatively both by the black mothers themselves and by their families. Rainwater reports that marriages in his research community most often broke up through failure of the husband to provide economic support. He further states that the black male role model presented to young boys discourages achievement and encourages exploitative, illegal means for achieving one's goals. Finally, Rainwater concludes that the main source of black children's low **self-esteem** is their

Self-esteem. One's sense of one's own worth or value.

unstable family background and the environment in which they are raised. Thus he blames the black family rather than prejudice and discrimination for this negative **self-image** (Staples).

ROLE RELATIONSHIPS IN BLACK FAMILIES

The alleged matriarchal character of the black family has been blamed for everything from **juvenile delinquency** to family instability to poor educational performance of children. The myth of the black matriarchy has gained currency for two reasons: first, the fact that more black than white families are headed by females; and second, the belief that black wives have a dominant role, even in the two-parent home. There is a great difference, however, between having a significant decision-making role in the family and being a matriarchal dictator.

The role of black women, to the extent that they are the center of the family, has evolved out of economic necessity. Joyce Ladner (1972) points out that because of the relative powerlessness of black men in the white culture, many of them have not had the opportunity to provide support for black women. Black women have often had to assume the role of breadwinner, both because men were absent and because black men have had a high rate of unemployment and underemployment. One of the results has been a high divorce rate, a feature that is becoming more typical of white middle-class life as the white woman finds more opportunity for employment outside the home.

For the black woman, the role of mother is an important one. Children, born in or out of **wedlock,** are highly valued, and having children is regarded as a sign of adulthood in the black community. There is some indication that black women value the role of mother more than the role of wife. The role of the black man has evolved through the same process of racism, lack of opportunity, and economic deprivation that has forged the woman's role. However, the black man has not focused his energies on family matters. Research indicates that for him, the role of father is intimately linked to the ability to earn a living (Staples). To the extent that he fails occupationally, the black man will be an unsuccessful parent.

Some writers discount the possibility that the cultural values of the black community have contributed to the role failure of black fathers. But cultural input is an important source of role behavior, and the male role models in parts of the black community tend to treat fatherhood lightly (Ladner). Even so, Aldous reports that lower-class four- and five-year-old black children without fathers in the home are still able to think of fathers as being wage earners, sources of affection, and competent parents (Aldous, 1972).

There is evidence that lower-class black children are expected to mature early and are typically freed from parental control at a young age. **Peer-**

group influence is important, especially in the formation of sexual attitudes and courtship patterns. In general, the peer group serves as an important vehicle of socialization along with the family. The influence of the peer group, particularly on adolescents, seems to be greater among blacks and lower-class whites than among middle-class whites (Staples).

Black children must learn two realities. In daily life, they must have the skills to interact with their environment. For many blacks the environment is the urban ghetto and the skills learned there are not consistent with white middle-class values. At the same time, black children are expected to acquire occupational skills and socially acceptable goals to make it in middle-class America.

Ladner has remarked with some bitterness that the dominant white culture has placed blacks in an isolated and subordinate position and then blamed them for living by a different set of cultural norms. A more objective view of the black family is needed. The unique features of black family life should be examined as adaptive variants in the American pattern—without which the black population might not have survived at all.

As can be judged from the foregoing discussion—which has introduced some facts and ideas about two-career families, childless marriages, single parents, interracial and interfaith marriages, and the black family in the United States—the contemporary American family is not one standard model of the family, but a very varied line, almost as varied as the multitude of car models the American public has to choose from. There are also many different options for modification, according to economic necessity or personal tastes, of whatever model of the family a couple chooses. The next chapter begins with a brief discussion of some major theories about family behavior in the United States and then goes on to place family life into the framework of an urbanized, industrialized society in the latter half of the twentieth century.

Ghetto. A section of a city in which members of a minority group live, especially because of social or economic pressure.

Summary

1. The purpose of this chapter is to give an overview of the public and private aspects of marriage and family organization in the United States today, taking into consideration laws governing the formation and dissolution of families, the diversity of U.S. families, and cultural differences between black and white families.

2. Certain legal requirements must be met before a marriage can take place. If these are met, the couple marries and enters into a tripartite marriage contract (with each other and the state) which can only be dissolved with the state's permission. Although the issues involved in marrying and raising a family are personal, the state has an interest in them because the family as a social institution is important to public welfare and the survival of the society. If the contract is broken, the marriage may be dissolved through divorce, usually a complicated and costly process. While many current marriage and divorce

laws are outmoded, some states are changing their laws to reflect changing public attitudes and experience.

3. Population statistics gathered by the U.S. Bureau of the Census provide valuable information about various characteristics of family life such as family size; place of residence; marriage, divorce, and remarriage rates; intermarriages; and family types (such as dual-career, childless, or single-parent families). From this statistical information, it is possible to see trends in family development which help us understand how families have responded to changes in their socio-cultural environment. This data can also help us see new problems and needs brought about by these changes.

4. Family life in single-parent, childless, and dual-career families differs significantly from the idealized version of U.S. family life, and many people are finding it difficult to adjust to new definitions of social roles in these variant forms of the family.

5. Black families and white families in the United States differ somewhat in their family life patterns. Research on the black family explains black and white differences in one of two ways: (a) The black lower-class family is part of an autonomous subculture with folkways and values that are distinct from the larger society. The black family became an unstable unit as a result of slavery and economic deprivation, and this instability continues because it is transmitted from generation to generation. (b) The lower-class status of a large portion of the black population (a result of discrimination) is the reason for the high rate of divorce, desertion, and other family problems that are divergent from white middle-class norms. According to this theory, black families are not significantly different from white lower-class families, whose family life is also characterized by instability.

Key Concepts

Statutes	Statistics	Intermarriage
Jurisdiction	Variables	Sexist
License	Birth rate	Racist
Ceremony	Standard of living	Matriarchy
Civil rights	Poverty level	
Alimony	Single-parent families	
Custody	Dual-career families	
Child support	Role overload	

Review and Discussion

1. What are the laws and requirements involved in marriage and divorce in your state? Do you think they should be updated or altered? If so, how and why?

2. What are some of the problems and benefits of a dual-career family? If your family is a dual-career family, what are some of the benefits and problems of your family experience?

3. Discuss the advantages and disadvantages of raising a family as a single parent. If your family is a single-parent family, what are the benefits and problems of your family experience?

4. In what ways have economic factors brought about differences between white and black families?

5. Compare your family experience with that of a close friend. How might your attitudes be different (religious and political views, attitudes to money, to education, to careers) if you had been raised in your friend's family?

Suggested
Readings

GUTMAN, H. G. (1976). *The Black Family in Slavery and Freedom, 1750–1925.* New York: Pantheon.

Presents evidence that disproves some common assumptions about the effects of slavery on black family life. Shows that enslavement and poverty did not shatter family ties and that most slaves did maintain familial and kin associations which sustained the developing Afro-American culture.

HILL, R. B. (1972). *The Strengths of Black Families.* New York: Emerson Hall.

Points out the weaknesses, misconceptions, and myths in many studies of the black family. Shows that black families have been able to adapt and survive in a hostile environment and provide a foundation for the positive aspects of the black experience.

HOLMSTROM, L. L. (1972). *The Two-Career Family.* Cambridge, Mass.: Schenkman.

Explores problems that arise when married couples attempt to balance pursuit of a professional career and maintenance of family relationships. How problems are handled and how social institutions and attitudes can change to help the two-career family become a workable reality are also discussed.

MINDEL, C. H., AND R. W. HABENSTEIN (eds.) (1976). *Ethnic Families in America.* New York: Elsevier.

Examines a variety of American ethnic groups and their historical reasons for coming to the United States. Discusses how the structure and function of family life has helped or failed to maintain ethnic identification and speculates on what lies in the future for various ethnic groups.

WILKES, PAUL (1975). *Trying Out the Dream: A Year in the Life of an American Family.* Philadelphia: Lippincott.

Wilkes studied an "average" American family (i.e., one that resembles the Census Bureau's statistical picture of the average family). He reports on their lives, their problems, successes, and disappointments and finds out how the ordinary family copes with life in America today.

Sociocultural Environment Surrounding the Family | 4

The discussion in Chapter 3 has shown that the family in the United States is taking many different forms. As we shall see in Chapter 16, many other alternatives to traditional family structures are being experimented with, such as heterosexual cohabitation without marriage, group marriage, and communal lifestyles. At the same time, the option of remaining single, or at least of postponing marriage or remarriage, is increasing in popularity. Social scientists try to understand the basis for all these changes, and one way they do it is by formulating theories of why family behavior takes the forms that it does and why it is subject to so much experimentation and change.

Some students may wonder why all this theorizing is necessary. The purpose of a sociological theory is to try to bring an orderly interpretation of events out of wide-ranging studies of human behavior. For sociologists, theory is important in helping to decide how to direct their research and what questions they want to try to answer. It also helps in formulating broad concepts from **empirical** data and discovering how these concepts are related to one another. Even for nonsociologists, an acquaintance with sociological theories is useful. To take the point of view of the **theorist,** to stand away from society and consider what is happening in an analytical way, provides a basis for understanding one's life circumstances and making personal life choices.

Empirical. Originating in or based on experience or observation.

Theorist. One who analyzes facts in their relation to one another in order to develop general statements or principles.

THEORETICAL APPROACHES TO THE STUDY OF THE FAMILY

So far several different **theoretical frameworks** have been proposed to describe and interpret the various forms the family has taken. Four of these will be briefly sketched: **structural-functional analysis, conflict theory,** the **symbolic-interaction approach,** and the **family-development approach.** These theoretical frameworks help to clarify our perception of the extraordinary multitude of customs, rules, and patterns of behavior associated with the family relationships of men, women, and children.

THE STRUCTURAL-FUNCTIONAL APPROACH

Structural-functional theorists frequently start their explanation of **social organization** by suggesting an analogy between society and the natural world. Society is a system similar to a tree or a plant, and this system, far from being haphazardly arranged, is composed of parts that stand in a particular relation to one another. The relationship of the various parts of the **organism** is called the structure of the system. Like the leaves of a tree, or the parts of any living organism, the constituent parts of the system may undergo change, but the structure itself remains fairly continuous and is recognizable over time (McIntyre, 1966). An organism maintains itself;

that is, survives, through its life-sustaining systems of digestion, respiration, and adaptation to its environment. Similarly, society has subsystems, of which the family is one, that are crucial for its survival.

This analogy cannot be carried too far, however, because social systems are not visible in the same way as a tree or a piece of machinery. The structure of a social institution such as an insurance company or a hospital or a family is basically a set of relationships between people performing certain functions within the organization. The structure can be described and theorized about, but it cannot always be seen. It is particularly important not to think of a social system as a living organism, in the same way that fish or cats or human beings are living organisms, because structural-functional theory does not presuppose a purposeful intelligence, such as the brain, to be ruling the system. It is more closely related to the old Darwinian idea of survival of the fittest. What works for the system—that is, what is functional—will survive; what doesn't work will drop out and disappear.

Three Categories of Functions. The main question asked by structural-functional theory is what function does a subsystem serve for the maintenance of the organism? What contribution does it make to the whole? For example, the respiratory system serves the function of providing an animal with oxygen. In reference to the family, what role does this subsystem play in the larger framework of society and how does this contribute to the maintenance of society?

It should be emphasized at this point that the parts which make up this organism, society, are themselves systems and the same question of function can be asked about each of these parts. In considering the family, McIntyre points out three main categories of function to be considered:

1. Functions of the family for society.
2. Functions of the family for the family itself as a subsystem.
3. Functions of the family for the individual family member.

In the first category, the family's most important tasks are providing new members of society and providing for their socialization into society. Whatever else a family may or may not do, it does serve as the vehicle of procreation and is also largely responsible for transmitting the cultural values of the society to young children. In Chapter 1, it was made clear that there is a very wide range of family behavior in different cultures, but these basic functions of the family are considered to be universal.

In the second category, the family itself is the system being maintained, and anything contributing to the survival of that system may be termed functional. For the family itself, the major stabilizing mechanism is con-

Structure. Arrangement or interrelationship of parts as dominated by the general character of the whole.

Function. The social purposes or uses of customs, beliefs, and objects.

Division of labor. The assignment of tasks according to the skills and abilities of the workers.

sidered to be the sex- and age-related **division of labor** (McIntyre). According to this view, for any small group to function effectively and survive, it is necessary that tasks be allocated and role-differentiation occur. It is a tendency of small groups, according to Talcott Parsons, Robert Bales, and others, to develop spontaneously a structure of interlocking roles—that is, for leaders and followers to emerge. In the family, this need has traditionally been met by the distribution of power along age and sex lines, with men as breadwinners and women as caretakers of children. These are the predominating **gender roles** in the world, and have been considered by some people to be functional necessities for the continuance of the family.

The third category, the functions of the family for the individual member, is perhaps the most obvious one. In the family of orientation, the individual receives protection, training for survival, a place in society. Personality and skills in social interaction are developed within the family as these needs are being met. In the family of procreation, both social and biological needs are also met.

The relation of structural-functional theory to the family may be summarized as follows:

1. Society has functional requirements that must be satisfied if it is to survive, and these are satisfied through subsystems called social institutions. The family is such a subsystem and serves in various ways the functional requirements of the larger society.
2. At the same time, the family is a system unto itself with its own functional requirements which are met by the family members.
3. Finally, the family is composed of individuals who are provided with functional necessities by the family system.

Objections to Structural-Functional Theory. One of the main criticisms of the structural-functional approach is that it is deceptively simple. It is not always possible to determine what is or is not a functional necessity for a social system. Unlike a biological organism, there are few readily agreed-upon vital functions. For instance, divorce has traditionally been viewed as **dysfunctional** for the society, the family, and the individual. But seen in another light divorce may also be considered functional because it provides for the orderly separation of the lives of family members from each other, and it permits people to escape from potentially destructive relationships.

Dysfunctional. Having undesirable effects for some individuals, groups, or the society as a whole.

Perhaps the most significant complaint against the theory has stemmed from the high value it seems to place on stability and equilibrium. If equilibrium is valued, then a bias develops toward conventional roles that do not rock the boat. These conventional roles are seen as functional; others are dysfunctional or disruptive of social harmony. The theory has been used at times to explain that social-class differences, poverty, even the illness of a child within the family maintain the social structure, undesirable though they may be from the individual's point of view (McIntyre).

There have also been objections to the strong emphasis structural-functional family scholars have placed upon defining men as **instrumental** and women as **expressive** (Broderick, 1971). The instrumental designation for men suggests that they are task oriented and concerned with providing for the survival of the family. The expressive designation for women suggests that they contribute primarily to the emotional content of family life. Such linking of gender with family-role activity overlooks a great many variations and options in family behavior.

CONFLICT THEORY

Conflict theory has a long history, going back even before Thomas Hobbes' seventeenth-century writings about human competition and struggle as the war of all against all (Martindale, 1960).

Concern with Social Problems. Conflict theorists tend to look at large social units, such as whole societies, and attempt to find conflicting forces which explain the behavior of individuals and families. In doing so, they are likely to use the materials of history, geography, and economics, along with the data of sociology. This tendency to focus on social forces in conflict leads to placing greater emphasis on the disruptive aspects of society and on social problems. The sense of estrangement or alienation in urban-industrial society is one such problem. Danger to the quality of life from misuse of the environment is another.

Urban environments provide excitement and diversity but also frustration. The anonymity of urban environments may seem an advantage to some and a source of isolation to others. Sociologists differ in their approaches to the study of social institutions but all agree that human behavior is modified by the total environment in which people live.

Conflict theory. A sociological theory which emphasizes the social consequences of conflict between individuals, groups, or societies.

A major difference between **functionalists** and conflict theorists lies in their attitude toward how sociologists should react to solve society's problems. Should they become involved and offer solutions, or should they remain apart as scientific observers and collectors of data? (Chambliss, 1973) Conflict theory invites students of society and the family to question existing norms and behaviors by asking whom the existing norms and behaviors benefit. The answer to such a question may suggest that we should not accept things as they are, but rather work to establish rules that assist people with different interests to cooperate in producing a more humane social world (Young, 1976).

Power Struggles that Lead to Change. Functional theorists believe that gender-role differences, the particular tasks assigned to men and to women in each society, stem from the functional requirements of the family as a unit and from the biological differences between males and females. Conflict theorists take an entirely different view. According to them, there is in all social systems a relationship between the powerful and the powerless, with the dynamics of the system flowing from the struggle by one party of the relationship to achieve and maintain dominance over the other (Chambliss). Karl Marx and Friedrich Engels, two nineteenth-century **socialists** who contributed to the development of conflict theory, thought that men and women had a basic conflict of interest that was integral to **capitalist** society; in fact, they viewed it as the first and most basic example of class antagonism. According to their view, women were dominated and exploited by men because of their economic dependence on men through the institution of monogamous marriage. Gender-role differentiation, according to conflict theory, far from being a stabilizing functional mechanism, is the result of outright exploitation and is itself a source of conflict that is bound to produce social change. While the disadvantaged position of women is functional for some elements of the economic system, it fails to utilize the full potential of women to contribute to the society.

Conflict within the Family. In the study of family relations, most previous scholarly work assumed that getting rid of conflict was a primary goal. Couples were told that fighting was bad, and often felt guilty if they did fight. Conflict theory, by contrast, assumes that the differing attitudes, preferences, and goals of various family members make the family inescapably a system in conflict (Sprey, 1969). Family members' life perspectives vary. A teenage daughter will not always want to do what her 40-year-old father expects, let alone care about the things that fascinate her 10-year-old brother. The conflict theorist does not ask, "How do we get rid of family conflict?" but rather changes the basic question to, "How do we manage the existing family differences?"

This focus leads to exploring how family members go about making rules of daily operation which allow them to cooperate even though they disagree. That includes considering the impact of even insignificant differences like how to squeeze the toothpaste tube. Without rules between couples, little issues can get blown up out of proportion and lead to marital breakup. The conflict theorist is also interested in studying the subtle tensions between one's need for privacy and the obligation to be involved intimately with loved ones. These "separate" versus "togetherness" issues are especially crucial in family relations (Sprey, 1971). It follows, then, that the conflict theorist also does not assume that the family is a haven from the pressures of mass society. Actually, there are many different places and ways we can find rewarding relationships with other people. Conflict theory suggests that the family need not and probably cannot bear the brunt of providing the primary emotional support for everyone (Sprey, 1969).

In summary, conflict theory suggests that we seriously negotiate differences and hostilities among family members in order to achieve the benefits of family cooperation. It suggests we realistically examine the full range of human behavior and not idealistically shut our eyes to the unpleasant family experiences.

SYMBOLIC-INTERACTION THEORY

Where the functionalist considers systems in society, arranged in an organized structure, and the conflict theorist considers people involved in confrontation, the interactionist focuses attention on individuals reacting and interacting with one another in a network of social roles. The interactionist approach arose out of the field of **social psychology,** and this determined the focus of interaction theory. Interactionists have found that the recurring contacts between individuals are the significant sources of information and understanding about social behavior. Interaction is defined as a complex process whereby the social behavior of one person is dependent on and modified by the other's actions. Interaction thus bears some similarity to a simple stimulus-response mechanism or a series of such mechanisms. However, the added element of **symbolic communication** through words, gestures, and facial expressions, and interpretation of these symbols by the people communicating makes the study of human behavior a very complicated procedure (Heiss, 1976).

To some extent, behavior is predetermined by the roles the individuals have in relation to each other. A social role is a pattern of behavior that is appropriate to a particular social setting and exists outside the personality of the role-player. For example, at a party, the role of host would exist even if no one assumed it. It is an element of the **social structure** of a party. The related concept of role-playing adds the element of group norms and expectations. In our party example, it would be usual for a person playing

Social psychology. An academic discipline which focuses especially on the study of behavior of individuals within groups.

the role of host to behave in certain expected ways consistent with the group's norms; there might also be individual variations in the way the role is played. **Role-playing** is the process of modifying and adapting one's role to the roles of other individuals. In any two-person conversation, it is possible to observe the interchangeable roles of listener and speaker. These roles are interdependent. One cannot exist without the other, and each of them involves different though corresponding behavior. Each person assumes many, many roles during the day, as a student, passenger, customer, employee, stranger, friend. What happens as a consequence of the interaction depends on the interpretation each party to the exchange gives to the words and gestures, in fact, the total behavior, of the other.

Attitudes. Learned mental positions toward objects, events, or issues.

Symbols. Acts, sounds, or objects having cultural significance and the capacity to excite a response.

Emphasis on Meanings of Words and Gestures.   Interactionists attempt to study both the observable behavior of the family and the **attitudes** and expectations family members have regarding each other. They concern themselves not only with the **symbols** used in interpersonal communication within the family, but with the meanings these symbols have for the different family members. Language and gestures are the tools people use in defining their family relationships and the rest of their world. This focus on activity within the family differs from that of the functionalists, who attribute family behavior to social realities outside the stage of the family.

The basic assumptions of the symbolic-interaction framework, according to Schvaneveldt (1966), are:

1. People act in response to both physical stimuli and symbolic meanings.
2. An individual deliberately uses symbols to evoke expected responses from others. Problems sometimes arise from lack of agreement on the meaning of the symbols, so the desired response may not be forthcoming.
3. A relationship is seen by interactionists as being more than the sum of its personalities. The interaction gives the relationship itself a different identity which, in turn, affects the participants. The whole process of a relationship is dynamic rather than static.

Relation to Family Therapy.   Symbolic-interaction theory has been one of the most widely used approaches for studying the family. Much of the work utilizing this approach has dealt with **marital adjustment, dating** and mate selection, and parent-child relationships—in general, with how families get along and why they do not (Schvaneveldt). Interactionists have had a significant influence on **clinical psychologists,** family counselors, and **social workers.** The concept of the family as a unity of interacting personalities has created an in-context basis for understanding the individual patient or client. The interactionists have shifted the focus of family theory from the broad institutional views of marriage and parenthood to the more practical illumination of families as groups of individuals.

THE DEVELOPMENTAL APPROACH

The developmental approach to the study of the family evolved primarily as a system to be used in the analysis of census data. It is a composite theory which has borrowed liberally from several schools of thought in sociology, psychology, and anthropology. From the structural-functionalists, developmentalists incorporated the idea that the family is a **social system** functioning by its internal laws, and yet subject to the demands of the large society of which it is a part. From the interactionists, they have incorporated the view that the family is a unity of interacting personalities, and have also recognized the significance of social roles in the conduct of family life (Hill, 1974). The developmentalists have added to these concepts a time dimension: the explanation for a family's behavior can be attributed to the **developmental stage** the family is in (Rowe, 1966).

The Life Cycle of the Family.   Developmentalists describe the family as being analogous to the human organism in its process of birth, maturation, and death, and focus on the fact that families have careers or histories (see Fig. 4.1). A distinction can be made between the **lifetime family** and the

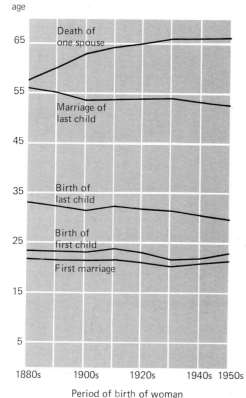

Fig. 4.1 Median age of mothers at the beginning of selected stages of the family life cycle.   The graph shows historical trends from 1880 to 1950 in the timing of five major events in the life cycle of a family. Indications are that the trends represented by these five lines have continued their downward or upward directions in the decades since 1950. (Source: Paul C. Glick, Updating the life cycle of the family, *Journal of Marriage and the Family* 39:1. Copyright 1977 by the National Council on Family Relations, reprinted by permission.)

Developmental tasks.
Steps to be accomplished
at various stages of the
life cycle in accord with
physical state, age, and
social expectations.

lineage family. The lifetime family history is concerned with people aging and their sequential filling of roles as they get older. The lineage family history refers to the continuities of successive generations (Feldman and Feldman, 1975). At each stage in a family's growth, a family has certain **developmental tasks.** These developmental tasks arise partly from human needs and partly from cultural norms (Rodgers, 1973). An example of a developmental task for the family would be the provision for economic support as a requirement for establishing a new family. Developmental tasks arise at particular points in the career of a family. A young couple in our culture may live with one of the sets of parents at the beginning of their marriage but would later, especially with the addition of children, consider it a necessity to establish a home of their own. This would be a developmental task. The family life career is the series of stages that a family will go through: before children arrive; as children are born, mature, and enter school; as they leave home; as the original couple adjusts to itself again; until both the partners die. The career is then completed (Rodgers).

Family study from a developmental perspective poses some interesting questions. For example, if you think of a family composed of four generations from an infant to great grandparents, each generation was probably born 20–25 years apart. Are differences between these family generations a result of the age differentiation only, or do they reflect the fact that each generation lived in a different historical-cultural environment? Undoubtedly both factors play a part, and developmentalists emphasize both the history of the family members and the current social situation. A given set of people, a **cohort,** born in 1940, will experience family careers differently from the cohort born in 1990. While effects of aging on these two cohorts may be similar, the effects caused by the time period are likely to be quite different. The time period in which we enter history can dramatically influence family careers (Elder, 1975).

Family Research Based on the Developmental Approach.   Like other theoretical frameworks, the developmental approach has been the basis for a substantial body of family research. Researchers have tended to study a particular segment of the family life cycle, attempting to base present behavior on past stages and predict future behavior. The early marriage period has received some attention, as has the transition from this early period to the birth of the first child. In studying the parent-child relationship, developmentalists have found that family crises often arise because parent and child are simultaneously trying to accomplish their respective developmental tasks. The husband-wife relationship has also been studied from the perspective of the time/stage cycle as the children are born, reared, and sent on their way. As in the interactional approach, the internal dynamics of the family are the main focus of study with the larger social system contributing the input of role expectations and norms.

A weakness of the developmental approach is that it has been worked out most thoroughly in reference to a contemporary suburban, middle-class American family. It remains to be seen how broadly this framework can be applied. Another difficulty is that having children is an implied value of the developmental approach. The stages of development have been established with the ages of the children in mind, and studies of childless couples have only entered the framework as examples of the early stages of family development or as control groups. Permanently childless couples are largely excluded from study, the implication being that such couples do not merit the term family. This position will become increasingly more difficult to defend as the incidence of childlessness increases in our culture. A modified theory of family development may be proposed with stages created to describe the changing husband-wife relationship as it progresses and matures through the years. The theory of marital development can be based on the premise that a marriage goes through stages as a result of the needs for companionship and security, as well as, for example, early romantic needs.

A final word should be added concerning the difficulty of testing the theories of the developmental framework. Several methods have been proposed, among which the soundest involves investigating a group of families throughout their life histories. This approach is, of course, costly and time-consuming. **Retrospective** family histories have been used (what people recall about earlier periods of their lives) as has **cross-sectional data** about families. But, in order to be complete, research findings of all segments of the family life cycle will have to be arranged in a consistent and coherent manner. This has yet to be done (Schaie and Gribbin, 1975).

Retrospective. Based on what individuals recall about earlier periods of their lives.

Cross-sectional. Based on responses of a representative sample of a social group or category at some point in time.

Sociological theories are abstractions formulated from observation and analysis of human behavior. Behavior in family situations is not abstract. It is real behavior in response to real situations. The behaviors and the changes in family forms described in Chapter 3 are responses to the total environment in which the family is embedded. To better understand how and why the family is changing, we need to look now at the total society and examine some of the characteristics of that society which affect people's attitudes and behavior, especially in relation to family life.

MAJOR FACTORS IN HOW PEOPLE LIVE

One of the most cherished myths of American life is expressed in the image of the United States as "the melting pot." Persistence of the myth is based on our strong desire to believe in one distinctive national culture, one true-blue American style of life. Cultural uniformity within a society eliminates one possible basis for conflict. At the same time, however, it sacrifices an important source of strength and creativity. Unity and diversity both have their advantages. And both concepts can be used to describe American life, for each one tells part of the story.

DIVERSITY IN U.S. SOCIETY

At most times in our history, diversity, or **cultural pluralism,** has probably been a stronger force than unity. The melting pot was successful only to a limited extent. Instead of blending together to form one dominant American type, many of the racial, religious, and national groups who immigrated to this country have maintained distinctive cultural traditions. It has not always been easy, though. Many groups have found that the preservation of their unique heritage requires a struggle.

One recent example is the Spanish-speaking Americans. Starting in the late 1960s, they began organizing to fight economic discrimination and to reestablish a sense of cultural identity. Native American Indians are also struggling for social recognition of their heritage. Some representatives of this cause have called for restoration of all ancestral lands and a return to their traditional culture.

The fact that cultural values can be difficult to maintain indicates a certain ambivalence toward pluralism. On one hand, there is a desire to respect and preserve differing traditions, while on the other, we tend to speak of "the average American family" or "an American way of life" as if there really were one basic style. But is there a typical American way of

Native American Indians are trying to maintain their ancient cultural traditions at the same time they adapt to the urban-industrial society in which they live. Some contrasts between the two cultures are illustrated in this family scene.

living? The answer is almost certainly, "No." The idea of a strictly uniform society conflicts with the American emphasis on individual rights (Berger, 1966).

Americans think highly of patriotism, yet resist a strong commitment to centralized national institutions. Although some ethnic groups stress family solidarity more than others, the idea that every individual should be free to pursue his or her own destiny is one of our deepest shared beliefs. Independence and initiative are reinforced virtually from the time of birth, and American children are trained to exercise personal freedom much more than children in other parts of the world (Slater, 1970). The result of this emphasis on **individualism** is clear. It leads to a very competitive society. Our training in individuality and independence makes it difficult for us to cooperate in meeting common goals in recognition of our interdependence, especially if it involves any personal sacrifice for the common good (Slater).

Individualism. A doctrine giving prime importance to individual rights and freedom to pursue personal goals.

We maintain a society characterized by **cultural diversity**, especially along racial, ethnic, and religious lines. In the next few pages, we will consider three other factors that have substantial impact on how different groups of people live in our **urban-industrial society:** (1) the kinds of jobs which are available, (2) the physical settings in which people live, and (3) the availability of public service (Warner, 1966).

Cultural diversity. Variability in customs, beliefs, and standards of behavior.

KINDS OF JOBS AVAILABLE

In looking for basic indicators which determine any family's social position, sociologists have turned to the area of jobs, or more specifically **occupational status** (Otto, 1975). Most people's economic resources are completely determined by their job, and the amount of money a person makes obviously has a strong impact on the lifestyle which that person can afford to maintain. In particular, occupational status has a strong influence on a family's area of residence. Economic factors are involved here since most housing in a given neighborhood is in the same general price or rent range. A great deal is known about a family's social status simply by knowing its address and the type of housing occupied.

Exploring the impact of work on family life further, we begin to find important differences between men and women. For American men, work tends to be seen as the primary area for developing a sense of self-worth. Males in our society are taught to perceive their jobs in this way to such an extent that job satisfaction and marital adjustment are usually closely related. For women, the situation is more complex. Many American women still tend to consider wife and mother to be the dominant roles in their lives, with work roles of secondary importance. Other women, however, regard their work as significant to their own development, and in these cases job satisfaction is linked to adjustment in marriage in much the same way as it is for men (Ridley, 1973).

Work and the Pathology of Modern Life.   For most men and some women, feelings about work play a powerful role in shaping an overall outlook toward life. To investigate this idea further, one sociologist has defined four levels of orientation to work (Fried, 1966). At the first level, work is seen as a job. The job brings certain restrictions in one's freedom, but also provides income with which to buy the necessities of life. At the next level of orientation, work is seen as a task. Here a worker begins to gain a sense of mastery, deriving pleasure from the exercise of task-related skills. At the next level, work as an occupation, work is seen in a broader context. Through work at this level, a person gains a feeling of social participation, a sense of contributing to society. Finally, work can be seen as a career. At this level of orientation, work becomes a major vehicle for gaining individual fulfillment.

Work-role orientation. Variable attitudes to work as a job, a task, an occupation, or a career.

It is not too surprising to find that these differences in **work-role orientation** are strongly related to social-class differences. Members of lower social classes tend to remain fixed at lower levels of work-role orientation and tend to find correspondingly less satisfaction in their work. **Job fragmentation,** or the division of a work process into minute parts, such as on an automobile assembly line, is a major feature of lower-level work roles and contributes to lack of interest in the job. At higher job levels, in professions such as law or engineering, there is high social status and greater opportunity for personal satisfaction. Nevertheless, job fragmentation is a factor which often detracts even from the rewards of high-status jobs.

Many researchers have looked at work orientation as an explanation for people's feelings of **alienation**—a sense of powerlessness, a feeling of inability to control one's own destiny. It may also lead to **self-estrangement,** or a discrepancy between an individual's ideal self and his or her actual situation (Otto and Featherman, 1975). While it was once believed that these feelings were related to low socioeconomic status, it is now recognized that even people of high social position suffer from a sense of alienation. Since high social status and high pay usually involve heavy responsibilities, it is possible that fear of failure lies behind the alienation in these cases.

The key to reducing feelings of alienation has two aspects. First, people must learn realistically what society expects. Second, they must learn to work toward goals which are actually attainable with the resources at hand. Otherwise, they will have difficulty in relating to people around them and fulfilling the social roles they are expected to play.

Effects of Occupational Mobility.   It is important to recognize that changes in a person's work-role orientation usually involve a whole set of adjustments to a new life situation. New work roles and higher occupational status tend to bring about fundamental shifts in relationships within the

Table 4.1. Feelings of individual control of life circumstances Nationwide surveys of people 18 years old and over by the Institute of Life Insurance indicate that people's feelings of control over key aspects of their lives have been declining. In only one area—family size—did the data for 1975 show an increase in feelings of control, doubtless the result of increasing acceptance of birth control. People with the lowest socioeconomic status—low family income, low education, nonwhite—felt the least individual control and had the greatest desire for government and industry to do more.

CONTROL OF LIFE CIRCUMSTANCE	VERY LITTLE %	SOME %	A GREAT DEAL %
Preventing inflation	72	19	8
Ending discrimination in employment	55	33	11
Improving availability and quality of medical care	59	28	13
Getting a better paying job	23	42	34
Improving neighborhood you live in	28	49	22
Accumulating funds for retirement	19	35	46
Number of children you have	7	21	71
Providing for children's college education	15	33	51
Obtaining good services and products at reasonable prices	46	36	17

Source: Adapted from Institute of Life Insurance, 1976

family and with friends. It can even mean a change of residence. For this reason, **occupational mobility,** a highly valued concept in American society, can be seen as creating a crisis of transition for the family (Fried).

In studying the occupational mobility of lower working classes, it has been found that the social network which surrounds a family can influence its ability to withstand a crisis of transition. Simply stated, the support which comes from a stable family and close friends helps a person's movement to higher levels of work-role orientation. On the other hand, many working-class families think more about maintaining their current position than improving it. There is in these cases a fear of **downward mobility** and a concern with "getting by" rather than "getting ahead" (Schnaiberg and Goldenberg, 1975).

Discrimination in Job Markets. Job discrimination, felt most strongly by members of minority groups, is a major barrier to occupational mobility. As we have seen in Chapter 3, discrimination can also be a significant factor

Occupational mobility. Movement to a different social class position based on changes in work status.

in limiting the income from jobs of women in dual-career or single-parent families.

Insofar as job discrimination results in either unemployment or under-employment, the problems which a worker experiences can become very serious. First, and most obvious, is the problem of low income. In some ways, however, the social and psychological problems produced by jobless-ness are even more serious. A strong work ethic exists in American society. Work is highly valued and productivity is generally considered to be a vir-tue. For this reason, an out-of-work person often feels out of touch with the values of society as a whole. The person may feel rejected or inferior, and the frustrations produced can have a dramatic effect on the quality of family life.

THE PHYSICAL SETTINGS IN WHICH PEOPLE LIVE

For most families, the home environment is a major factor, like work, which affects the quality of life. Friendship ties, sense of belonging, socialization of children—these and other functions are often based on a family's place of residence.

Surprisingly, the geographic mobility of Americans has served in some ways to strengthen the influence of the local community. Families do tend to move a great deal, much more than ever before, but they usually make an effort to be near others who share similar values and life-styles. As a result, age and social status often form the basis for patterns of residential **segregation.** This trend, sometimes called **residential differentiation,** is re-sponsible for living environments which are specially equipped to fit the needs of the particular type of individual or family they contain. As an individual grows older or as a family's social status improves, a move to a more appropriate residential setting may take place. One sociologist de-scribes this form of geographic mobility as a game of musical chairs (Po-penoe, 1973).

Residential differentia-tion. The tendency for people to select their housing on the basis of their age, income, ethnic identity, and stage in the family life cycle.

Factors Affecting Choice of a Place to Live.   Many factors are involved in the selection of a place to live, and middle-class families in particular are able to exercise a great deal of choice. Purchase price or rental fee, type of housing available, and nearness to work are major factors. For families with children, the quality of schools is important. Often the prestige associated with a neighborhood is an important consideration for middle- and upper-class families.

Lower-income families are much more restricted in their choice of a living area. The physical settings available will be those which other, more wealthy families have rejected. This narrow range of residential options is also experienced by members of some ethnic minorities. Some groups, such as blacks, have been forced into **ghetto** living situations. Other groups, however, live separately by their own choice in an effort to maintain a particular way of life against change from the outside world.

In addition to social status and ethnic ties, stage of life cycle has become a major factor in determining where people live. Young, single adults tend to cluster into the same areas. Families with children choose other neighborhoods. The **elderly** live off by themselves in entirely different living environments. Differentiation can even continue within these groups. That is, newer families with very young children and older families with teenagers, for instance, will often be found in distinct areas.

This pattern of segregation by stage of life cycle is a recent, predominantly American phenomenon. One problem it produces is a lack of variety in the environment. Neighborhood values, tastes, and styles tend to be very similar. Another problem is the sense of unreality about other stages of life. When young adults, middle-aged people, and the elderly live apart, each group tends to miss a subtle sense of life's wholeness. People lose part of their psychological bearings and forget that they are part of a universal process (Popenoe).

Pros and Cons of Urban Living. Can families establish a sense of community in the modern urban environment? Many urban sociologists would say no, for it is a widely held belief that urbanization and neighborhood solidarity are incompatible.

To explore this **hypothesis** further, a study was recently conducted in an inner-city neighborhood in Rochester, New York, which replicated a study of the same neighborhood done 25 years earlier. In 1952, Donald L. Foley published the original study, which included three **indexes** he developed for measuring the degree of neighborhood orientation. These indexes were labeled "Use of Local Facilities," "Informal Neighboring," and "Sense of Community." In 1975, Albert Hunter conducted an identical survey so that exact comparisons could be made of changes over the period of time.

Hypothesis. A tentative assumption that a researcher seeks to test through empirical research.

Index. A ratio or other number derived from a series of observations and used as a measure of a condition or characteristic.

The neighborhood under study was a middle-class, racially integrated section of the city adjacent to the University of Rochester. Urbanization had produced significant changes in the area, including an increase in multiple-family dwelling units, an increase in the black population, and a decrease in total population. Among the residents who were moving away or thinking about leaving, two basic reasons were cited—concern for safety and quality of schools.

Hunter's follow-up study focused on Foley's three indexes. First, Hunter discovered that the residents' use of facilities located close to home had declined. Grocery shopping, movies, and visits to the doctor took more people out of the neighborhood in the recent survey than in the original. With respect to informal neighboring, however, there was actually a slight increase over the 25-year period. Neighbors were visiting each other more often, exchanging things with a greater frequency, and spending more time together at picnics or parties. Moreover, the sense of community, or identification with the neighborhood, was quite a bit higher in the later study. Residents were aware of the boundaries of their community and referred to it by a special name. Within the neighborhood, there were many activities which took place solely for local residents. In short, while the community had changed in many ways, socially and culturally it was very much alive.

The strength of this urban community was represented by a neighborhood association, organized in the 1960s to protect the area. Through its formal activities, such as checking for zoning violations, and its social aspects, the association is a major force in preserving the local identity.

Trying to explain these changes, Hunter found three basic reasons behind the decision to move into the neighborhood, factors which seem to represent a trend which is opposed to dominant American values. First, many people were not interested in suburban living and simply preferred an urban setting. Some were motivated by a desire to live in a racially integrated area. And, finally, some were strongly attracted by the neighborhood spirit, its sense of community.

THE AVAILABILITY OF PUBLIC SERVICES

A third factor which affects American family life as strongly as work and residential setting is the availability of public services. Such services are provided in our society by a variety of agencies at the federal, state, and local levels. Some of them, such as transportation and education, have come to be taken for granted. Others, such as maintenance of recreational facilities, have only recently been seen as public responsibilities. These essential services vary widely in quantity and quality over different parts of the country. Protective services, such as police and fire departments, also vary widely in terms of the adequacy of service provided, even though these tasks are accepted as legitimate governmental functions. There is less **consensus** in other areas, such as health care, income maintenance, and provision of adequate housing. Debate is intense concerning where the responsibility for these should rest. Meanwhile, the quality of life in American homes ranges widely—from bare poverty to extreme luxury.

Consensus. Group solidarity in sentiment and belief.

Transportation.   Public services in the area of transportation include transit systems, such as commuter trains, subways, and buses, as well as development and maintenance of streets and roads. Public transportation is for many the primary means for reaching schools, shopping, and recreational facilities, and commuting to work. Unfortunately, expansion of public-transportation facilities has not kept pace with the increasing demand for service.

A 1974 government survey showed that public transportation is the basic neighborhood service most frequently found to be inadequate. Nationally, 41 percent of the households surveyed complained of insufficient mass-transit services. In contrast, only 14 percent reported inadequate shopping facilities at the neighborhood level, and only 5 percent mentioned inadequate schools. The survey also found that high-income households ($15,000 or more in yearly income) were more critical of public-transit services than were middle- ($5,000–$14,999) or low-income households (less than $5,000) (U.S. Bureau of the Census, 1976, CB 76-256).

With respect to public streets and traffic problems, however, the positions were reversed. Here, low-income households had the most complaints. Thirty-eight percent of the low-income group reported severe traffic congestion in their neighborhoods, a condition seen by one sociologist as a symptom of the failure of the city to perform its housekeeping function (Johnson, 1973).

Education.   In its broadest sense, the public commitment to education can be considered to include any activity which furthers social adjustment by aiding individual self-development. This commitment is very strong in our society and personal educational attainment is highly valued. Education provides access to jobs and the opportunity for **social mobility.** Personal resources for utilizing leisure time can also be developed through educational channels. For all their importance, though, educational opportunities vary widely within and among urban, suburban, and rural areas. Educational policies are implemented primarily at the state or local level, a factor which contributes to the lack of consistency.

Social mobility. Movement of an individual upwards or downwards in the social class structure.

Health Services and Income Maintenance.   Until very recently, it has been taken for granted in U.S. society that income maintenance and medical care are individual, not public responsibilities. While it seems as though a country as wealthy as the United States could provide adequate health and income-maintenance services to all of its citizens, thus far there has not been a strong national desire to do so.

The American system of private medical and psychiatric services, in spite of its sophistication and technical expertise, faces some serious problems. First, the geographic distribution of health personnel and facilities is uneven, with rural areas the least adequately served. Second, the cost of health services has grown to such an extent that their availability has become a function of income. Limited national programs do exist to help provide care for the elderly and the very poor, and higher-income families are able to make their own arrangements. In many cases, however, lower-middle-class families are ineligible for free care and often unable to pay for it on their own. The result is that many children suffer from a lack of needed medical and dental care. Furthermore, preventive services such as

Income maintenance. The provision of income by governments or private organizations to enable people to obtain the necessities of life.

prenatal examinations, well-child clinics, and dental check-ups are usually completely out of reach.

There are problems in our present system of **income maintenance** that are of the same magnitude as the problems in our health-care systems. Like severe illness, a prolonged period of insufficient income can have a devastating effect on all aspects of family life, psychological and material (Pumphrey, 1966). There are, of course, well-established programs intended to help individuals and families through times of unemployment or temporary financial need, but the eligibility rules are strict. Moreover, many forms of income maintenance are regarded as charity or as a handout, rather than a form of commitment to the welfare of the nation as a whole. Thus, the American ideal that rewards should be based on individual achievement is in conflict with the American dream of equality for all. At the same time, emphasis on self-reliance results in differences in family life that provide very unequal opportunities for personal growth and advancement of the members.

In many aspects of the sociocultural environment explored in this section, change has been an important theme. In the next section we consider another feature of the social environment which is also in transition—the new definitions of social roles which are bringing new patterns of interaction into marriage and family life.

RELATION OF GENDER ROLES TO HOW PEOPLE LIVE

Throughout much of American history, gender roles have been rather rigidly defined. Certain types of work and ways of behaving were supposed to be natural to each sex, and individuals were expected to perform accordingly. The traditional roles assigned to women have been those of housewife and mother. The major tasks associated with these roles have included taking care of the house and providing for the physical and emotional needs of the husband and children. These tasks represent forms of service, and thus they are consistent with behaviors that were assumed to be characteristic of the female sex, such as nurturance, passivity, and emotional sensitivity. The traditional roles assigned to men have been those of worker and head of household. The man's tasks have included providing economic support and social position for his family. The male has been characterized as creative, tough, and achievement-oriented, traits that are consistent with the tasks that society assigned to him.

CHANGING DEFINITIONS OF SOCIAL ROLES
There is in fact no evidence that the characteristics attributed by our society to males and females are in any way innate. There is no proof that girls are naturally more passive than boys or that boys are naturally more cre-

ative or productive than girls. But these beliefs supported the economic and social systems on which our society was based, and as long as those systems functioned efficiently few Americans questioned the underlying beliefs. The majority of Americans accepted the idea that certain behavior was truly feminine and other behavior truly masculine, and many Americans still believe this.

Gender Roles as Learned Behavior.   Until recently, most men and women in this country did behave according to the typical patterns assigned to them. But this was not because these patterns were inborn; rather they had been taught. Gender roles are among the earliest roles learned by children because of their close association with their mothers and fathers. Not only do children learn by observation what a man or a woman is supposed to do and not do, but imitation of the appropriate behavior is rewarded, while inappropriate behavior is punished or at least discouraged. Thus a girl who plays football with the boys might be criticized by her parents for being a tomboy. Similarly, a boy who wants to play with dolls may be called a sissy. The parents thus teach the child what behavior they consider appropriate to each sex.

The process of socialization is a subtle one. Parents may be tolerant of shyness in a little girl but embarrassed if their little boy is shy. Parents

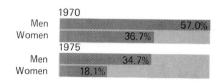

Fig. 4.2 Proportion of first-year college students who think married women should remain in the home. Though more men than women think married women should confine their activities to home and family, there has been a substantial decrease over a five-year period in the percentages of both men and women who agree with this statement. (Source: Beverly T. Watkins, This year's freshmen reflect new views of women's role, *The Chronicle of Higher Education*, January 12, 1976.)

may send a daughter as well as a son to college, but their attitudes and motives may differ. They may send the daughter to college because it is a good place to meet a husband, or it will add to her poise in social situations, while they send the son in order to prepare him for a career. They may ignore the girl's expression of career aspirations, encouraging her to concentrate on looking and being attractive to men, while they respond to the boy's aspirations with great seriousness. The typical patterns of behavior taught in the family are reinforced in other areas of society, such as schools and the media. Literature, movies, and television portray men and women behaving as they are supposed to behave in regard to their traditional roles.

Function of Gender Roles. For a long time, the traditional system of gender roles seemed highly functional for American society. The division of labor it established efficiently fulfilled society's basic needs. In the agricultural society that preceded industrialization, the family had served as an economic unit. But industrialization separated productive labor from family life functionally and sometimes geographically, with jobs taking the worker far away from home. The solution was to assign to men the fulfillment of the economic function and to women the fulfillment of the homemaking and child-rearing function (Palme, 1972).

During the twentieth century, the traditional system of gender roles has become increasingly less functional. As industrialization has made domestic life easier, the maintenance of the home has required less of the housewife. This has been particularly true as typical family size has decreased. More and more of the societal functions, such as education and care for the sick, take place outside the home. Not only do child rearing and household tasks absorb less of a woman's day; because of the longer life span, women may enjoy many productive years after their children have grown up and left home. Thus women's traditional role in our society has become increasingly less challenging and less fulfilling (Palme).

The traditional gender roles have become less functional during the twentieth century, not only in practical terms but in **ideological** terms as well. The emphasis on equality that developed during this century has led women to question the lower status assigned to their role. Why was child rearing viewed as inferior to factory work? What could be more important than raising children? Probing still further, modern thinkers challenged the ideal that the female was more suited to child rearing and domestic work than the male.

The Feminist Viewpoint. <u>The women's liberation movement organized</u> <u>these challenges into an **ideology.**</u> Women began to view themselves as a group who shared certain problems rather than simply as individuals, each dealing with her own unique situation. They began to challenge not only the domestic role assigned to them, but also their usual restriction to low-paying jobs, the lower pay they received for performing the same work men performed, and, perhaps most important, the **personality** traits expected of them.

Once women became aware of the inequality that existed between the sexes, they began to notice examples of it in all spheres of life—economic, political, and social. Women held few decision-making jobs in political life and few high-paying jobs in business, education, or the communications media. Not only were these fields almost exclusively limited to men, but masculine control led to presentation of an image of femininity that discouraged women from seeking power. The image of women depicted on television, both in the programs and in the commercials, is very limited.

Current medical textbooks omit recent research findings on feminine sexuality and present instead such myths as female passivity and lesser sexual desire and potential (Safilios-Rothschild, 1974).

Recognition of the widespread inequality between the sexes, whether subtle or open, has led some women to take a **radical** view of male-female relations. In an interesting article, Janis Kelly raises the question whether love between men and women can actually exist in our society. <u>Kelly defines love as the opening up of one person to another rather than the surrender of self.</u> The trust and mutual openness necessary for personal growth can only exist between equals. Given the imbalance of power between men and women in our society, Kelly concludes that "where women are concerned, the highest development of the ability to love can occur only in a homosexual context" (Kelly, 1972, p. 473).

Consequences for Family Life. <u>The **women's liberation movement** has had a profound effect on family life. By challenging her traditional role, the female has challenged the very basis on which the American family has been built.</u> If she does not stay home to care for the children, who will? If her main goal is to live her own life, what will happen to her husband, accustomed to her constant emotional support? Many men have reacted to the women's movement with a mixture of hostility and fear. This has been most evident in their use of ridicule against it. While their reaction is understandable given the extent of the threat, it is also futile. Women have not destroyed the family pattern by refusing to fulfill their roles; the pattern itself has ceased to be functional. Thus the women's movement might be viewed as an effort to create a new, more functional definition of gender roles. The success of the effort depends not only upon women's ability to

Ideology. The integrated beliefs, assertions, and aims that constitute a sociopolitical program.

Radical. Extreme; marked by a significant departure from the usual or the traditional.

free themselves from stereotypes but also on the ability of men to do so as well.

MEN'S LIBERATION

The liberation of men has not developed into a full-scale movement, in part because of the emphasis given to women's issues where the problems are seen to be more clear cut. Yet the gender role historically assigned to men is no less confining than that assigned to women; and if it is more powerful, it is nonetheless limited and limiting.

One of the major characteristics imposed upon the male in American society is repression of emotions. Taught from boyhood that showing their feelings is feminine and weak, males have no means to express negative or, to some degree, positive feelings. Striving toward the masculine ideal of independence and self-sufficiency, refusing to show any signs of weakness, men in our society are prone to disorders associated with tension, such as ulcers and heart attacks, and have, on the average, a shorter life span than women. Although it is generally thought that women in our society suffer more mental depression than men because more women seek psychiatric help, it may be that men, resisting the image of being weak, are less able to seek help (Goldberg, 1973).

The pressure on men to achieve, to be economically successful, leads to intense feelings of anxiety. Both the man's ego and his desirability as a mate depend upon his success. Herb Goldberg (1973), in "The Liberation of Men From Traditional Roles," remarks that as women are treated as **sex objects,** men also are treated as objects: "... the male is a status symbol whose attractiveness is measured by his earning capacity, the status of his profession or job, and the amount of his power." The man's fear of having

© Medical Economics Company.
Used by permission of Jerry Marcus.

"Don't ask me what happened. I started out helping with
the dishes, then scrubbing the floor for
her, then doing some ironing . . ."

his position taken over by younger men is equivalent to the woman's fear of losing her sexual desirability or attractiveness as she grows older.

Employment usually requires the husband to spend long hours away from home, and the more ambitious he is, the more time will be required. Many American fathers scarcely know their children. A standard complaint of adolescents in our society is that their fathers provide economic but not emotional support. Inept at expressing affection, tired and distracted after a long day of work, out of touch with the daily lives of his wife and children, the traditional father has often been a stranger in his own home, deprived of some of the most basic emotional rewards of human existence.

As the need to redefine the gender roles of both men and women in our society becomes more evident, changes are seen to be required in virtually every area of our society. Our processes of socialization and education—our culture itself—are altering the images of male and female roles presented, as girls get to play in the Little League and women become business executives and political leaders. Recent polls taken among first-year college students show increasing numbers of women now plan careers in business, engineering, law, and medicine; that fewer women—and men—think that married women should confine their activities to home and family; and that an almost equal number of men and women consider raising a family essential or very important (Watkins, 1976).

The trend toward equality between the sexes has been made possible to a large degree by our urban society which both values and permits individual freedom and personal growth. If the movement has produced some instability in our social system, it nevertheless seems to be a positive step toward a more satisfying and ultimately more stable system.

ATTITUDES TOWARD HOMOSEXUALITY

One effect of changing gender roles can already be seen in changing attitudes toward homosexuals. Homosexuality has long been viewed in America as an **abnormality.** Classified as sex offenders by the law and viewed by the majority of Americans as dangerous to society, homosexuals have been forced to live secret lives. This attitude toward homosexuality is by no means universal: in ancient Greece, for example, love between two men was considered to be the highest possible form of love. The American attitude toward homosexuality as deviance was founded in our Judeo-Christian tradition and reinforced by our Puritan heritage (Weinberg and Williams, 1974). These very strong religious and cultural influences condemned homosexuality because it emphasizes sexual pleasure for its own sake rather than sexual activity for reproduction only.

Abnormality. A state or quality deviating from the normal or average; a psychological or behavioral disorder.

In recent years, the definition of homosexuality as an illness has been challenged. The research of Kinsey and his associates in the forties and fifties revealed that homosexuality was far more prevalent than people had believed. Recent research using homosexual subjects indicates that homosexuality is a sexual pattern which is within the normal range psychologically (Weinberg and Williams). Homosexuals, like heterosexuals, vary in regard to personality traits and psychological problems, and these features are not necessarily related to their homosexuality either as a symptom or a cause.

Prejudice. An adverse opinion or leaning without just grounds or without sufficient knowledge.

During the last decade, homosexuals, both women and men, have challenged the public and legal **prejudice** against them. The **gay liberation movement** can be expected to influence both the **stereotype** society has of homosexuals and the homosexual's self-concept. Most homosexuals have productive jobs. Many live in stable, long-lasting relationships resembling marriage with other homosexuals and are no more or less emotionally unbalanced than heterosexuals.

Homosexuals, like blacks and women, have demanded the right to think of themselves as equal. Black women have two aspects of social discrimination to cope with, as do black homosexuals. The ideologies of each of these groups have been helpful to the others in their search for equality and personal freedom. Changes in one set of beliefs affect other beliefs in the culture. Thus, as homosexuality becomes more acceptable, people in our society will become less fearful of giving expression to all the varying aspects of their personalities. The changing sex roles of men and women will offer both sexes greater variety in how they carry out their other roles as workers, friends, and family members, redefining our concept of masculinity and femininity, and enabling all individuals to live fuller, less restricted lives.

THE INDIVIDUAL'S PERCEPTION OF SELF

The changes in gender roles are reflected both in the way we interact with others and in the way we think of ourselves. Thus they affect our responses to other pressures in the sociocultural environment. The constant bombardment of ideas, things, and people in **technologically** advanced societies puts great stress on the individual. The social and political environment easily produces feelings of loneliness, alienation, insecurity, and confusion. Some individuals feel helpless in the situation. They may view circumstances as arbitrary (it's all a matter of luck) or controlled by other people, but they see themselves as powerless. Others feel they have considerable control over their lives, that they can alter their own patterns of behavior, influence others, and act upon their environment in effective ways. What is it that differs for these two kinds of people? Are their situations, in fact, different —or only their perception of themselves?

Whether or not people have a sense of power and effectiveness depends upon how they think of themselves. Those who think highly of themselves, who have high self-esteem, are more likely to feel that they are in control of various aspects of their lives. But self-esteem is not based solely on performance, the actual organization of actions and behavior. It is based instead on the individual perception of self, the way a person sees the self. This image is referred to as the **self-concept** (McDavid and Harari, 1974).

How one sees himself.

HOW THE SELF-CONCEPT IS FORMED

The formation of the self-concept begins when, as an infant, one first differentiates one's own body from the surrounding world. Initially, the self is perceived as a physical identity. Even as the self-concept expands, the physical aspect of one's identity, referred to as the **body image,** continues to play a major role in determining one's opinion of oneself. Whether one has learned to view oneself as attractive or unattractive, ordinary or unusual looking, will affect one's self-esteem (McDavid and Harari).

The child's self-concept continues to develop through the acquisition of language. As babies learn their own names, other people's names, and the personal pronouns, they further distinguish between other individuals and themselves. The development of the self-concept is mainly a process of interpersonal communication. Parents and others involved in children's socialization teach them the values of their culture, rewarding certain behaviors and punishing others. The parents' evaluation of them forms their evaluation of themselves. Success or failure, their approval or disapproval, will tend to raise or lower the child's sense of worth. Thus the attitudes of others toward people shape their attitudes toward themselves.

The development of personality is strongly influenced by the type of family into which the child is born. The family initially locates the child in the social fabric of the community. It provides the definitions of what is important and what is appropriate behavior and thinking. It is the major factor in defining roles and shaping the self-concept. Had a person been born into another family, that person's self-concept would be different. This is especially true in societies such as ours where families vary greatly in socioeconomic status, cultural heritage, and type of community in which they live.

As the child's world enlarges, people other than the immediate family begin to become important and their evaluation of the child further influences the self-concept. Studies indicate that a child's definition of self tends to stabilize or become consistent mostly through interaction with other children. It has been suggested that peer groups play the largest role in determining an individual's standards for success or failure (McDavid and Harari).

Stability of the Self-Concept.   The stability of a person's self-concept is influenced by the stability of the person's relations with family members and others in the society. Often, having a consistent personality is simply the consequence of living in a stable system. However, the self-concept should not be seen as merely a sponge absorbing and taking its shape from the role-evaluations others provide. Actually, people are quite active in making or selecting the settings in which they participate in social interaction. As Secord and Backman (1974) note, there are a number of techniques we use, as unique individuals, to maintain a stable self-concept.

1. **Cognitive restructuring.** Suppose we do something we consider wrong, such as telling a lie, and create a situation which contradicts parts of our self-concept which say we are honest and straightforward. To deal with the conflict, we can restructure the event by telling ourselves that most everyone lies in that kind of situation, so it isn't so bad that we did. Or we did it to protect someone else. This is a frequent human means of adjusting behavior to agree with the self-concept.

2. **Selective evaluation.** Sometimes we change our assessment of ourselves and others to avoid an inconsistency in the self-image. Perhaps we have purposely hurt someone in the excitement of a game when usually we present ourselves as a good sport. To keep a consistent self-concept, we might tell ourself, "He had that coming. He's a dirty player."

3. **Selective interaction.** Using this strategy to maintain a consistent self-concept, we may choose to meet only with those people who will support our self-concept and allow us to behave in ways that are consistent with our notions of ourselves, avoiding those who put us down.

4. **Self-preservation.** Using this technique, we dress and stage ourselves selectively by doing things that will bring forth a certain desired response from family or friends. An example might be a child acting tearful and injured to get extra sympathy and attention from the mother—and support for the image of the self as someone who is always treated unfairly.

5. **Selective comparisons.** Finally, we often work for consistency in our self-image by using comparison processes favorable to ourselves. A man might avoid thinking that his brother has a better income than he does, and think instead that he is a better golfer than his brother or has more attractive children.

Modifying the Self-Concept Through New Experiences.   Although an individual's self-concept tends to be consistent, it is nevertheless subject to change. One's self-concept is revised in response to new expriences or new stages in one's life, such as adolescence, entering the work world, becoming a parent, retirement, and old age. **Consciousness raising,** such as the "Black is Beautiful" movement or the women's liberation movement, affects the self-concept. In an experiment performed during the 1940s, a majority of black children, when presented with two dolls, one black and one white, chose the white doll as the nicer of the two. In a repetition of this study in 1969, the majority of black children preferred the black doll. The improved image of blacks as a group has raised the self-esteem of individual members of the group (McDavid and Harari).

If an individual's self-concept is excessively rigid, there will be a tendency to resist change or fail to incorporate new experience into the view of self. One will thus have difficulty adjusting to new situations, a particular problem in the rapidly changing contemporary world. For instance, the husband whose self-concept depends on his ability to support his family may be unable to adjust to the fact that his wife's income is larger than his. Too flexible a self-concept, on the other hand, is also a problem. If people's feelings about themselves vary constantly with other people's approval or disapproval, they are likely to experience feelings of instability and have difficulty knowing what they want to do.

Setting Personal Goals.   Although people evaluate themselves in relation to other people's attitudes toward them, they generally differentiate between those people whose judgment matters to them and those whose opinion does not. George H. Mead, one of the pioneers in defining the self-concept, called these important people **significant others**. People also distinguish those areas in which they want to excel from those which they don't care about. Sometimes, however, the decision of where to place their major efforts is determined more by where they think they can succeed than by where they really want to succeed.

> **Significant others.** Those people whose judgment and opinion have the most influence in the formation of an individual's self-concept.

What matters most to the individual in regard to values, morals, personality traits, or social roles is largely determined by the particular cultural or socioeconomic environment. Different cultures and subcultures place different emphases on the various aspects of life, such as education or material wealth, which will influence the individual's personal goals. Cultural environments also vary in terms of the standards of behavior which determine for an individual what the ideal self should be. Thus the self-concept is related to the various social groups to which we belong. Some groups, like the family, we belong to automatically; others, we select. Which groups we seek to enter, what might be called our **level of aspiration**, is influenced by our self-concept. We go, generally speaking, where we feel we will be accepted.

> **Level of aspiration.** The highest position in the social structure at which we expect to be able to gain acceptance.

MAINTAINING THE SELF-IMAGE

Maintaining a favorable self-image in employment situations where one is just a small unit in a huge corporation, or in student situations where one is a series of punches on an IBM card, is extremely difficult. For parents, a child's failure in school, especially when the neighbors' children are doing well, is damaging to the self-concept. In urban-industrial society, where one interacts with dozens, even hundreds, of people a day, each encounter with a stranger is a potential threat to the self. It is in this environment that the need for intimate personal relationships between people who share the same values and goals becomes most intense. But the people who need these relationships most, due to problems of low self-esteem, are frequently those least able to maintain them.

One's attitude toward oneself influences the ability to relate to others. Low self-esteem encourages a sense of frustration and helplessness, and these negative feelings toward the self are often projected upon others. Thus the prejudice in our society against people who are low on the socio-economic scale—those on welfare, the unemployed, the undereducated—contributes to the hostility that is so prevalent in contemporary society. It should be emphasized that the problem of self-esteem is not only a personal problem. It is a social and political problem as well. The liberation movements of recent years have perceived the need to change societal conceptions associated with certain groups. In a sense, what these groups are striving to liberate is the self-concept: to free individuals from the limitations of a negative self-concept and, by raising their sense of self-worth, enable them to realize their life goals.

Self-concept. The mental image one has of one-self, including physical features, personality, and ability.

CHOICES AND PROBLEMS IN FAMILY LIVING

The scientific and technological developments of the last century have had both desirable and undesirable consequences. Medical discoveries have enabled people to live longer, yet overpopulation and the need to support large numbers of the aged are creating severe social problems. Machines have removed much of the drudgery from everyday life, yet the development of **mass production** and the assembly line have destroyed much of the pleasure in work, and **automation** has deprived many people of jobs.

The urban society created by the technological revolution is similarly two-sided in its effects. Urban life depersonalizes, but it also offers diversity and personal freedom. It provides many educational and recreational activities, but it is characterized by unequal distribution of resources. The social problems which have arisen in this setting are numerous and complex. The uses to which **technology** has been put have raised many moral issues. Should money be spent on exploration of space when people are starving on earth? To what degree have technological developments polluted the earth and come to control, and possibly destroy, humanity?

Changes in the nature of work, social customs, and values have presented a challenge to traditional goals and caused people to question their identity. Nowhere is this more apparent than in the institution of the family.

The isolated nuclear family is a comparatively recent phenomenon in American life. Characterized by freedom of roles, movement, and lifestyle, the nuclear family is also beset by loneliness, uprootedness, and a sense of instability. The main function of the family today is that of satisfying interpersonal needs. This puts a heavy burden on interpersonal relationships within marriage and the family. It would be unreasonable to suppose that the family would remain untouched while the sociocultural environment around it changed. New elements in the culture demand that new needs be met by its organizational structures and the family must adapt to serve these needs. The reverse is also true. Our societal structures must provide for the new needs of the family, such as child care outside the home and flexible employment schedules for parents.

Despite the many problems of the family and its apparent instability, a happy family life is still the goal of most Americans (Institute of Life Insurance, 1976). Since they do not inherit a clear definition of what a happy family is, they must work out many solutions to family problems for themselves. Individuals now have to think out what they want and expect in the way of marriage and family living—particularly whether sex and marriage can be viewed as two separate aspects of human life or whether they must necessarily be linked in the family as they have been in the past. Other basic issues, such as parenthood, are also being examined. No longer can it be assumed that because two individuals marry, children will eventually follow. The next three chapters on human sexuality, pregnancy, childbirth, and family planning provide some basic information on which to base one's personal life choices in an increasingly impersonal world.

Summary

1. The purposes of this chapter are, first, to look briefly at several different theoretical approaches to studying the family and, second, to outline the sociocultural environment in which American families develop and some of the influences and pressures that affect their development.

2. In order to understand why family behavior takes the forms it does and why it is subject to experimentation and change, social scientists formulate theories. Sociological theories are useful because they help us to stand away from society and look at what is happening in an analytical way. This objectivity provides us with a basis for understanding our life circumstances and helps us make personal choices.

3. Many theories have been proposed to describe and interpret the various forms the family has taken. Four of the major ones are (a) structural-functional theory, (b) conflict theory, (c) symbolic-interaction theory, and (d) developmental theory.

4. In discussing the cultural and social environment of American life, it is important to realize that we are an urban-industrial society characterized by ethnic, religious, and economic diversity. In addition to a family's cultural heritage, there are three other basic factors that influence how people live: (a) the kinds of jobs available to them, (b) the physical settings in which they live, and (c) the availability of public services, such as education, transportation, recreation, and health care.

5. Another factor bringing about change in family life is the changing definitions of gender roles, the cultural norms of appropriate male and female behavior. As these definitions have become less rigid, partly in response to the women's liberation movement, patterns of family life are changing too.

6. People's behavior is also influenced by how they see themselves. Whether or not they have a sense of power and effectiveness or feel helpless in the face of problems depends largely upon their self-concept, which begins to form in infancy and continues to develop throughout a lifetime. The self-concept is established through many interacting influences—communication with parents and others involved in socialization; the cultural, social, and economic environment; and unique personal experiences. Interpersonal relationships within the family are strongly affected by the self-concepts of the various family members and each person's self-concept is also affected by interaction with other members of the family.

7. The factors of the environment we have discussed are changing in American society. In response to altering pressures, family functions and responsibilities of the family to itself, its members, and society are also changing.

Key Concepts

Theory	Expressive
Hypothesis	Attitudes
Empirical data	Individualism
Cohort	Cultural diversity
Structural-functional analysis	Urban-industrial society
Conflict theory	Alienation
Symbolic interaction	Social mobility
Family development	Personality
Division of labor	Self-concept
Instrumental	Significant others

Review and Discussion

1. Think of the cultural, economic, and social environment in which your family has developed, including jobs available, physical setting, and use of public services. How has the environment affected your family life?

2. Do you feel you and your family would have been better off living in a different place or in a different time? Why?

3. Relate the idea of gender roles as learned behavior to your upbringing. Try to think of experiences where you were influenced to behave in an expected way rather than as you wanted to behave.

4. Do you agree with the current challenges made by women concerning traditional gender roles? Why or why not?

5. Describe some of the influences and experiences you feel were important to the development of your self-concept. Can you think of any ways in which your relationships to other people have been affected by those experiences?

FILENE, P. G. (1975).   *Him/Her/Self: Sex Roles in Modern America.* New York: Harcourt, Brace, Jovanovich.

Explores what it has meant to "be a woman" or to "be a man" today and throughout history. By analyzing the interactions of both sexes at once and using history, social psychology, and fiction, Filene examines the experience of middle-class Americans as they performed, defined, redefined, or defied their female or male roles between the Victorian era and the 1970s.

JAMES, M., AND D. JONGEWARD (1973).   *Born to Win: Transactional Analysis with Gestalt Experiments.* Reading, Mass.: Addison-Wesley.

Explains Transactional Analysis, the popular psychological method which promotes self-understanding in a way that helps individuals and groups increase their self-awareness and their ability to interact constructively with friends, family, and coworkers.

JONGEWARD, D., AND D. SCOTT (1976).   *Women as Winners.* Reading, Mass.: Addison-Wesley.

Transactional Analysis for women: contains information on games women play, women in history, women with fairy-tale lives. Readers can learn techniques for dealing with jealousy, improving relationships, becoming better parents, feeling good about themselves.

MCGRADY, M. (1975).   *The Kitchen Sink Papers: My Life as a Househusband.* Garden City, N.Y.: Doubleday.

A humorous account of what happened when one man switched roles with his wife—taking care of the house and children while she worked. A record of his experiences, discoveries, and observations and the effects on their children and their marriage.

RUBIN, L. B. (1976).   *Worlds of Pain: Life in the Working Class Family.* New York: Basic Books.

An account of the life of American white working-class families today. Considers their childhoods, marriages, work, and leisure, and examines the pressures and strains put on marriages and families by social, psychological, and economic realities.

Suggested Readings

The Physiology of Reproduction

Biological Aspects of Human Sexuality | 5

Is sex overrated? Is enthusiastic lovemaking life's greatest pleasure and the cornerstone of all strong marriages? The experts are divided in their opinions. Sociologist William M. Kephart, for instance, holds that not only sex but also love, marriage, and children are overrated. He claims that people expect far too much from them in the way of emotional rewards. Psychiatrist Natalie Shainess, on the other hand, feels that to view lovemaking as "the scratching of an itch," the mere satisfying of a physical need, is to vastly underrate "one of the potentially most rewarding of human experiences—the bliss of sexual activity related to warmth or love" (Kephart et al., 1974). Ideally, sex can be the ultimate in open and loving communication between two people who are deeply committed to each other. But in reality, the complexities of individual behavior and pair interaction permit this ideal to be reached only rarely in many relationships and never in some.

There is a clear relationship between pleasure in lovemaking and satisfaction with marriage, but which is the cause and which the result is hard to say. According to a 1973 survey by the Research Guild (commonly known as the *Playboy* survey), a large majority of the married men and women who described their marriages as being emotionally very close rated their sexual activity very pleasurable. Very few who called their marriages very close or even fairly close described sex as lacking in pleasure or unpleasant (Hunt, 1974, p. 230). In a 1975 survey of over 100,000 women, only 4 percent who found their sex life poor or very poor claimed to have good marriages (Levin, 1975a, p. 58).

The changing sexual standards which have made intercourse among single people so commonplace have also had a profound effect on marital lovemaking. Compared to the people interviewed by sex researchers Kinsey, Pomeroy, Martin and Gebhard back in the 1940s and 1950s, married Americans of both sexes now find the search for sensual pleasure in marriage far more acceptable. Couples are making love more often, making it last longer, and enjoying it more. Husbands are more considerate of their wives' special needs, women are now taking more responsibility for successful lovemaking and are having more orgasms, and both feel freer to experiment with new arousal and coital techniques. The focus seems to be shifting from an emphasis on **orgasm** to a richer enjoyment of all aspects of lovemaking (Hunt, 1974).

Physiology. The functioning of the life processes of an organism.

Although lovemaking is not a mechanical function, for the sake of clarity we will separate the physical aspects covered in this chapter—**physiology**, techniques, possible physical problems, and venereal disease—from the sociological and psychological aspects to be discussed in Chapter 11. Reproduction, which is part of **sexuality** too, is discussed in two short chapters. Chapter 6 covers **pregnancy** and **childbirth.** Chapter 7 concerns **family planning.**

THE PHYSIOLOGY OF SEX

Despite the obvious physical differences between men and women, their **genitalia** (sexual or reproductive organs) have interesting similarities. All human fetuses are structurally female until the fifth or sixth week after conception. If male hormones are then released, according to the genetic code, the primitive undifferentiated genital structures will begin to develop into the **penis** and **testicles** of a boy. If not, the same sexual structures will become the **clitoris** and **ovaries** of a girl. Despite their eventual differences in shape and size, these structures are both similar in function and similar in embryonic origin.

While the penis and clitoris are the most important of the erogenous zones (areas which cause sexual excitement when they are stimulated), other parts of the body may also contribute significantly to sexual arousal. Lovers may find each other exquisitely sensitive in places like the mouth and tongue, breasts (in both men and women), **anus, perineum** (the area between the anus and the genitals), ears, inner thighs, nape of the neck, hollow of the throat, and even the eyelids.

FEMALE SEXUAL ANATOMY

The external genitalia are smaller in a woman than in a man, but when stimulated they are no less capable of extreme erotic sensation. They are normally almost hidden by the hair on the **mons veneris,** or "mountain of Venus," the fat-covered area over the pubic bone. At the base of the mons is the tiny but intensely sensitive clitoris, whose sole function is to initiate or increase sexual tension. Although it has a shaft and a **glans,** or head, like the penis, the clitoris is less than an inch long and is partially covered by the **clitoral hood.** But the clitoris is rich in nerve endings, and when stimulated, its hollow areas of **erectile tissue** fill with blood, making it stiff just like an erect penis. This **engorgement** of erectile tissue is the primary bodily response to sexual stimuli; the secondary reactions are contractions of certain muscle groups. These responses can occur in a woman even if only her breasts or **vagina** are stimulated, but direct stimulation of the clitoris is the most effective way to female orgasm. This is the intense climax of sexual excitement, with involuntary rhythmic contractions in the vagina, anus, and **uterus,** followed by release of pressure in the erectile tissue.

The clitoris is shielded not only by the **pubic hair** but also by inner and outer "lips" **(labia minora** and **labia majora).** The outer lips are covered with hair like the mons; the inner lips contain erectile tissue and become engorged (filled with blood) during sexual arousal. As they do, they spread outward, clearing the way to the opening to the vagina which lies within the inner lips along with the urinary opening. The vagina is an

Genitalia. The organs of the reproductive system, especially the external genital organs.

Engorgement. In the genitals, filling of erectile tissue with blood as a result of sexual stimulation.

Fig. 5.1 External genitalia of the human female.

Fig. 5.2 Variations in shape of the hymen. The hymen, a membrane which partially covers the opening of the vagina in most females prior to first intercourse, varies widely in shape and thickness.

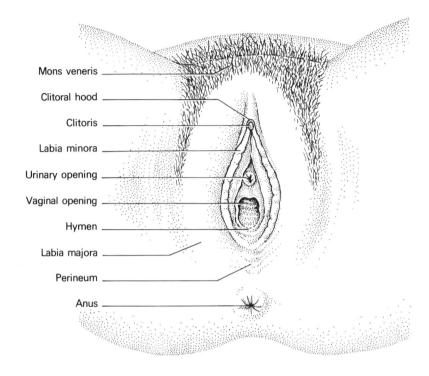

Mons veneris

Clitoral hood

Clitoris

Labia minora

Urinary opening

Vaginal opening

Hymen

Labia majora

Perineum

Anus

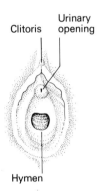

Clitoris

Urinary opening

Hymen

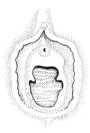

elastic tunnel normally about 3½ inches long which can stretch during sexual excitement to accommodate any size of penis. It is a potential, rather than full-time, cavity, for except during sexual arousal and during childbirth, its flexible walls fold and relax so that they are touching.

A small **membrane** which partially obstructs the vaginal opening, the **hymen** or maidenhead, seems to serve no physiological function, but it has traditionally been assigned great cultural significance. Since the hymen usually ruptures with the first intercourse, the slight bleeding that results has long been thought to be positive proof of virginity. But in some women the hymen is flexible enough to stretch during intercourse without breaking, or it may have been torn earlier during athletic activity or by manual stimulation of the vagina. In others, the tissue of the hymen is so strong that it cannot be broken by the insertion of the penis and a surgical incision must be made by a doctor.

Two small mucus-producing bodies, **Bartholin's glands,** lie at each side of the vaginal opening. Once thought to be the primary source of lubrication for intercourse, they have been found to contribute very little fluid and that only late in sexual arousal. Most of the fluid which makes it easier for the penis to enter the vagina apparently comes instead from water droplets squeezed through the vaginal walls from the engorged blood vessels which line them (Masters and Johnson, 1966).

The vagina leads to the uterus, a thick-walled organ the size and shape of an upside-down pear. It can expand considerably to accommodate the nine-months' growth of a human **fetus.** But like the vagina, the uterus is normally a potential, rather than actual, cavity with its sides touching each other. Its narrow neck, the **cervix,** protrudes downward into the upper end of the vagina. The opening between the two, the **os,** is normally no wider than a thin straw, but it is capable of stretching wide enough to allow a baby to pass through during childbirth.

Two **fallopian tubes** lead from the upper sides of the uterus to the ovaries, the almond-sized organs which store the eggs for reproduction and produce the female sex hormones, **estrogen** and **progesterone.** Rather than connecting directly to the ovaries, the fallopian tubes partially surround them with fingerlike projections. They create currents which draw the eggs into the tubes, where muscular currents propel them to the uterus.

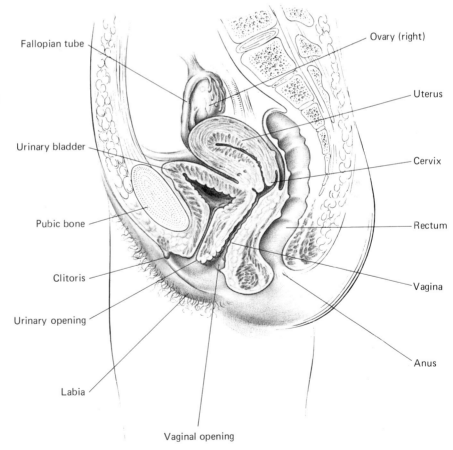

Fig. 5.3 Internal view of the female pelvis showing the reproductive system and other closeby organs. (Source: Eric T. Pengelley, *Sex and Human Life,* Reading, Mass.: Addison-Wesley, 1974.)

Fallopian tube

Ovary (right)

Uterus

Urinary bladder

Cervix

Pubic bone

Rectum

Clitoris

Vagina

Urinary opening

Anus

Labia

Vaginal opening

MALE SEXUAL ANATOMY

Men have no potential cavities equivalent to the vagina and uterus, but in other respects their sexual organs parallel those of women. Instead of ovaries, men have testicles, plum-shaped organs which produce both **sperm** cells for reproduction and the male hormone, **testosterone,** which influences sexual activity. Normally, the testicles move down from the body cavity into the **scrotum,** a sac-like structure below the penis, when the male fetus is seven or eight months old. If they did not drop—and this sometimes happens—body heat would prevent them from producing viable sperm cells. The insulating scrotum contracts in cold weather and relaxes in hot, to retain or dissipate heat so that the testicles are always about 2°F cooler than the interior of the body (Guttmacher, 1970).

An estimated 50,000 microscopic sperm cells are produced in the testicles of the average mature male every minute (Gordon, 1974). If one of them eventually collides with an egg cell in the fallopian tube of a woman

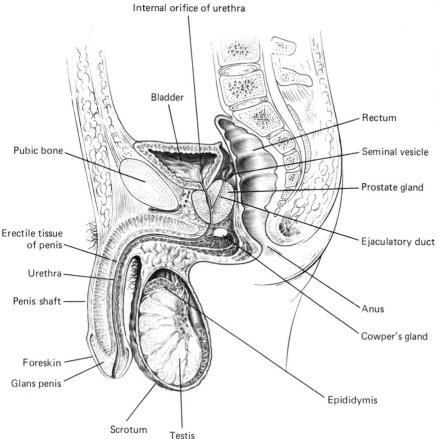

Internal orifice of urethra

Bladder

Pubic bone

Erectile tissue of penis

Urethra

Penis shaft

Foreskin

Glans penis

Scrotum

Testis

Rectum

Seminal vesicle

Prostate gland

Ejaculatory duct

Anus

Cowper's gland

Epididymis

Fig. 5.4 Internal view of the male pelvis showing the reproductive system and other closeby organs. (Source: Eric T. Pengelley, *Sex and Human Life,* Reading, Mass.: Addison-Wesley, 1974.)

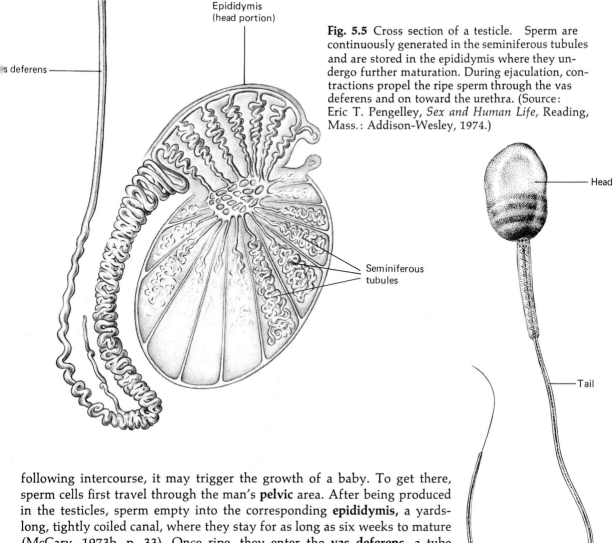

Epididymis
(head portion)

s deferens

Seminiferous
tubules

Fig. 5.5 Cross section of a testicle. Sperm are continuously generated in the seminiferous tubules and are stored in the epididymis where they undergo further maturation. During ejaculation, contractions propel the ripe sperm through the vas deferens and on toward the urethra. (Source: Eric T. Pengelley, *Sex and Human Life*, Reading, Mass.: Addison-Wesley, 1974.)

Head

Tail

Fig. 5.6 Greatly enlarged drawing of a human sperm cell. (Source: Eric T. Pengelley, *Sex and Human Life*, Reading, Mass.: Addison-Wesley, 1974.)

following intercourse, it may trigger the growth of a baby. To get there, sperm cells first travel through the man's **pelvic** area. After being produced in the testicles, sperm empty into the corresponding **epididymis,** a yards-long, tightly coiled canal, where they stay for as long as six weeks to mature (McCary, 1973b, p. 33). Once ripe, they enter the **vas deferens,** a tube which leads to a pouch called the **seminal vesicle.** Sufficient sexual arousal causes **ejaculation,** the forceful exit of the sperm from the body through the **urethra,** a canal running down the center of the penis. There are two epididymides, two vas deferens, and two seminal vesicles, in parallel systems, one attached to each testicle.

During ejaculation, a valve at the entrance to the **bladder** closes, preventing urine from leaving the bladder through the urethra as it normally does. Instead, the sperm cells mix with fluid from the seminal vesicles and the nearby **prostate gland,** forming the **semen,** or ejaculate. Milky and thick, the prostate fluid activates the sperm to help them swim through the vagina. It also provides an alkaline medium that helps to offset the vaginal

Fig. 5.7 Circumcision—
the surgical removal of
the foreskin covering
the glans penis.

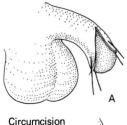

Circumcision

acidity which would otherwise kill the sperm. A few drops of alkaline fluid
to neutralize the acidity of the urethra itself are excreted into the urethra
by the **Cowper's glands** before ejaculation. The average ejaculation releases
only about a teaspoonful of semen; of this total volume, the sperm cells
take up no more space than the head of a pin (Guttmacher).

Externally, the penis is a long shaft with a cone-like glans at the end.
The glans, particularly the **corona** where it flares out before joining the
shaft, and the **frenum,** the thin ridge of tissue where it is joined to the shaft
on the underside, are extremely sensitive to sexual arousal because they are
laced with nerve endings. A cheesy secretion called **smegma** may accumulate under the foreskin, a loose fold of skin which covers the glans. Since
this causes a strong odor and sometimes irritation and infection, the foreskin is often removed. This operation—circumcision—is usually performed
shortly after birth in our society.

The penis, which contains most of the urethra, is otherwise composed
largely of spongy erectile tissue. The blood vessels react to sexual excitement by allowing more blood to flow into this erectile tissue than out of it.
This makes the penis enlarge and become stiff and erect so that it can
penetrate a vagina. After ejaculation, the dammed-up blood empties from
the erectile tissues, and the penis again becomes soft and limp.

Despite the fears of an estimated 15 percent of American men that their
penis is too small (Berscheid et al., 1973), there is little relationship between
the size of the limp penis and its size when erect. Small penises commonly
double in size with erection; larger penises expand less (Masters and Johnson, 1966). Penis size has nothing to do with **impotence** (inability to have
an **erection** stiff enough to allow intercourse) or **homosexuality.** And it has
little bearing on a man's ability to satisfy or be satisfied by a woman, for
vaginas are usually elastic enough to fit snugly around penises of any size.

LEVELS OF RESPONSE

In 1966, Dr. William H. Masters and Virginia E. Johnson published the
first clinical study of what happens during orgasm: *Human Sexual Response.* It was based on actual laboratory observation at their Reproductive
Biology Research Foundation in St. Louis of the physiological changes in
382 women and 312 men volunteers as they were being sexually aroused.
Despite the unromantic atmosphere of the clinical setting, the volunteers
were able to achieve orgasm through various kinds of stimulation: **intercourse** in several positions; masturbation; and for the women, breast stimulation alone (which worked for some), and simulated **coitus** (intercourse)
with an artificial penis of clear glass fitted with a special optical system
for observation and filming of internal changes.

Masters and Johnson found that no matter what the means of stimulation, sexual response always followed the same basic pattern, which was
similar for men and women. They found that this response cycle consisted

of four phases, which they called excitement, plateau, orgasm, and resolution. While this cycle can be triggered by a variety of physical and psychological **stimuli,** including sexual fantasy alone, it can be shortened, prolonged, or even turned off by adverse stimuli, distractions, or changes in the stimulation techniques being used. Failure to orgasm once some sexual excitement has been built up may result in restlessness and irritability from continued tension.

The Excitement Phase.   The beginning of sexual response for men is erection of the penis as it fills with blood, enlarging and lifting away from the body. This change from its limp state takes only a few seconds, whether it

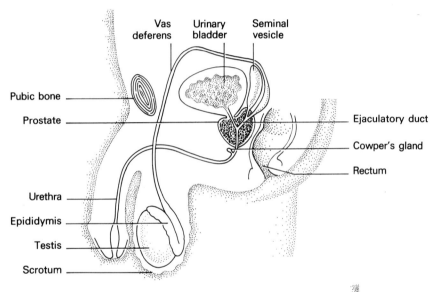

Fig. 5.8 Male pelvic organs during the unexcited or normal phase.

Fig. 5.9 Male pelvic organs during the orgasmic phase.   Note the rising of the testicles into the scrotum and the extension of the penis from its normal resting position.

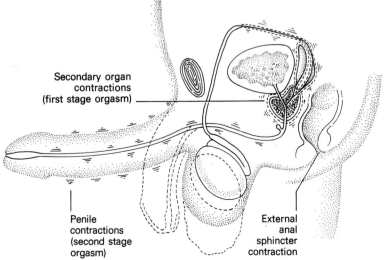

is stimulated by physical contact or by erotic thoughts. The skin of the scrotum grows tight and thick, and it pulls closer to the body.

In a woman, sexual stimulation causes engorgement of the vaginal area. The lips swell and open outwards, as if to make way for the penis. The vaginal walls sweat from engorgement, causing a **lubrication** response which can usually be detected ten to thirty seconds after stimulation begins. The fact that moisture has collected in the vagina does not, however, mean that a woman is fully prepared for intercourse, because this is only the beginning of her responses. If stimulation is continued after lubrication, the clitoris swells from engorgement. Direct contact with the clitoris may be unnecessary to this reaction and may even inhibit it if stimulation is too rough. The clitoris is so sensitive that indirect friction on the clitoral hood —either through penile thrusting or manual rubbing of the mons—is often sufficient for orgasm.

Inside, the uterus begins to expand to two or three times its normal size. It rises into the body cavity, pulling the cervix up and lifting the upper end of the vagina. This tenting effect causes the upper two-thirds of the vagina to balloon up and out to perhaps three times its usual diameter, adding about an inch to its length.

In both men and women, response during the excitement phase gradually involves the whole body. Muscles contract, the pulse accelerates, the blood pressure rises, and a rash called the sex flush often appears on the abdomen and breasts.

During the excitement phase, engorgement and muscle contraction in women's breasts cause the nipples to enlarge and erect; late in the excite-

Fig. 5.10 Female sexual organs in the normal position prior to sexual excitement.

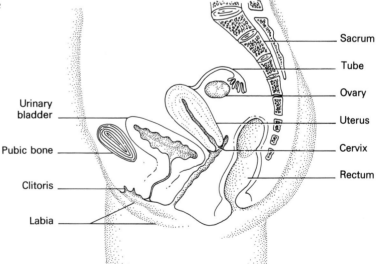

Sacrum

Tube

Ovary

Urinary bladder

Uterus

Pubic bone

Cervix

Rectum

Clitoris

Labia

ment phase, the whole breast swells. Masters and Johnson even noted some degree of nipple erection in three-fifths of the men they studied (Masters and Johnson, 1966).

The Plateau Phase.   There is no clear dividing line between the excitement phase and the plateau phase, but the plateau sensations are generally more intense.

In a man, the penis is already fully erected before the onset of the plateau phase, but the ridge of the corona now grows larger. The testicles swell and rise farther into the scrotum. A few drops of fluid may be secreted from the Cowper's glands, sometimes containing enough active sperm cells to cause pregnancy. The sex flush spreads and muscular tension throughout the body causes distorting contractions in the face and neck and strong grasping responses in the hands. The abdomen and buttocks tighten, increasing sexual tension, and thrusting pelvic movements which may have started voluntarily become almost involuntary, that is, beyond the man's control.

In women, the strained, grasping muscular responses of the plateau phase are linked with other changes. The vagina responds to continued sexual stimulation by forming what Masters and Johnson call the **orgasmic platform.** Engorgement so swells the lower third of the vagina that its diameter is decreased by up to 50 percent, providing pleasurable friction for both partners during intercourse. While the outer or lower third of the vagina closes in to grip the penis, the upper or inner two-thirds retains its ballooned-out shape. The clitoris temporarily disappears by withdrawing

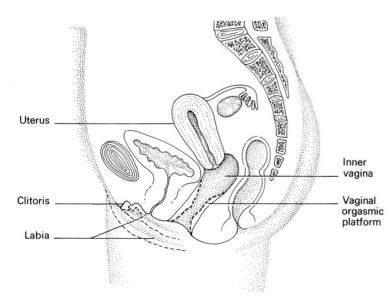

Uterus

Clitoris

Labia

Inner vagina

Vaginal orgasmic platform

Fig. 5.11 Female sexual organs showing changes during the orgasmic phase of sexual excitement.   The expansion and erection of the uterus causes a ballooning of the upper two-thirds of the vagina. The lower third of the vagina, swollen to possibly half of its normal diameter, forms the orgasmic platform.

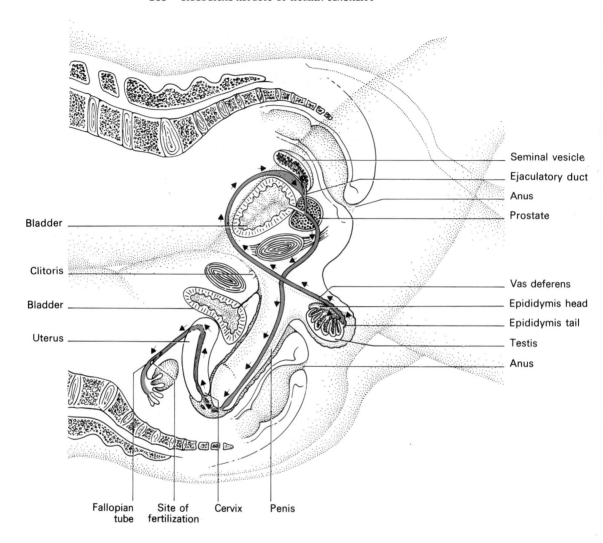

Seminal vesicle
Ejaculatory duct
Anus
Prostate

Bladder

Clitoris

Bladder

Uterus

Vas deferens
Epididymis head
Epididymis tail
Testis
Anus

Fallopian tube   Site of fertilization   Cervix   Penis

Fig. 5.12 Cross section of the male penis inserted in the female vagina, with related organs. Arrows indicate the route the sperm take to the site of conception.

under the clitoral hood. But it is still responsive to stimulation, either from direct rubbing on the mons veneris or from indirect traction on the clitoral hood caused by the penis as it rubs against the inner lips.

Late in the plateau phase, the heartbeat of both men and women may rise dramatically to 110 to 175 beats per minute. Their blood pressure rises, and they may begin to **hyperventilate,** breathing so fast or so deeply that they experience a slight loss of hearing, tingling feelings in the hands and feet, and even a partial loss of consciousness.

The Orgasmic Phase. When engorgement and muscular tension reach their peak, both men and women respond by explosive release of accumulated tensions through strong rhythmic contractions. In the woman, contractions in the vagina are joined by deep rhythmic contractions in the uterus. There may be as few as three contractions in a mild orgasm or as many as fifteen or more, gradually decreasing in intensity and occurring farther apart. Before the actual contractions begin, many women feel a momentary sensation of suspension at a point of extreme sensual awareness, and then a single explosive spasm of the orgasmic platform, followed by the rhythmic contractions. In both men and women, spastic contortions of the muscles in the neck, abdomen, buttocks, and even the hands and feet during the ecstasy of orgasm may be so extreme that they cause muscular aches the next day. During intense orgasms, normally placid people may so lose their self-awareness that they moan, scream, talk gibberish, cry, laugh uncontrollably, or thrash about wildly.

Orgasm. The peak release of sexual tensions, characterized by involuntary, rhythmic muscular contractions giving intense sensory pleasure.

The initial orgasmic contractions in a man occur at exactly the same rate as in a woman—eight-tenths of a second apart. Contractions of the urethra and muscles at the base of the penis cause ejaculation of the semen which collects in a bulb in the urethra at the base of the penis just prior to ejaculation. The contractions which have forced sperm cells from the seminal vesicles and prostatic fluid from the prostate gland down to the urethral bulb produce a first-stage sensation of orgasm before ejaculation actually occurs.

Although most men orgasm with almost every intercourse, the Research Guild found that 8 percent of married men over age 45 fail to orgasm occasionally to most of the time, 7 percent aged 25–44 fail to orgasm at least a quarter of the time, and 15 percent under age 25 fail to orgasm a quarter or more of the time. In older men, orgasmic failure is common because of the effects of aging; in younger men, erections are sometimes lost because of anxiety, awkwardness, distractions, or too-frequent attempts at coitus (Hunt, 1974).

Among women, many are unable to orgasm until they are at least 20 and have had several years of sexual experience (Toolan, 1975). Only 53 percent of the married women in the Research Guild survey orgasm with all or most lovemaking sessions; 15 percent never do (Hunt, 1973a). Data collected by Shere Hite suggests that the proportion of women who orgasm regularly from intercourse is only about 30 percent (Hite, 1976).

But 29 percent of the women in the *Redbook* survey who never experience orgasm nonetheless rated their satisfaction with marital sex as "good" or "very good" (Levin, 1975a). Many women find satisfaction in physical closeness during intercourse and the containment of the penis in the vagina, whether they orgasm or not. Some fake orgasm to please their partners, though this practice inhibits their chances of achieving full sexual satisfaction. A common problem for women is that if **erotic** stimulation has brought them to plateau levels of response, it may take hours for tensions which

Climax. Another term for orgasm, the high point of sensory pleasure in sexual intercourse.

are unrelieved by orgasm to ebb away (Masters and Johnson, 1966). However, many women who are unable to orgasm through intercourse alone can be brought to **climax** by specific oral or manual stimulation of the clitoris, techniques which are a legitimate and pleasurable part of sexual intercourse.

The Resolution Phase.   Soon after orgasm, muscular tension begins to subside. The sex flush disappears, and the woman's breasts, uterus, and vagina shrink to their usual size. Pulse rate, blood pressure, and breathing slow down. The penis returns to its normal size gradually after ejaculation; full loss of engorgement may take a few minutes or it may take longer, depending on how long the erection was held and whether sexual stimulation continues after orgasm (Masters and Johnson, 1966).

After orgasm, men enter a **refractory period** during which sexual stimulation cannot produce another erection; continued stimulation may even be irritating. In young men, this rest period may last only a few minutes; in older men it may last several days. Women have no refractory period, and most are capable of orgasm again and again under continued stimulation. Multiorgasmic women often report that the second or third climax is even more sensually satisfying than the first one. Even when men are capable of repeated orgasms, the first one is always the most satisfying, probably because of its greater release of accumulated semen (Masters and Johnson, 1966).

While some men are capable of holding an erection and thrusting long enough for their partners to have more than one orgasm, repeated orgasms for the women are often possible only through manual, oral, or mechanical stimulation. Masters and Johnson report that while most women are satisfied with three to five orgasms, women masturbating with mechanical **vibrators** may want and achieve twenty and even fifty orgasms in a single session (Brecher, 1966).

TECHNIQUES OF LOVEMAKING

While people can share a great deal of sexual pleasure without being experts, knowledge and use of a variety of techniques may increase both partners' enjoyment. Although sex seems to be a natural function, many forms of lovemaking are actually learned behaviors. Some of the how-to can be learned from books, but much of what is satisfying in lovemaking is what partners learn from each other.

Building a mutually satisfying sexual relationship takes time, practice, and openness about what feels good and what doesn't. Things that may have to be worked out include individual differences in timing, varying needs for stimulation, preferences for certain techniques, and differing levels of sex drive.

Foreplay. Enjoyable lovemaking depends heavily on developing both partners' responsiveness. Otherwise, nothing happens when they touch each other. If a woman is not turned on sexually, intercourse is mechanically possible but relatively unrewarding. If a man is unresponsive, his inability to develop the physical excitement necessary to an erection makes intercourse impossible.

Intentional development of sexual responsiveness is called **foreplay.** People kiss, caress, lick, and nibble each other's sensitive body areas for an average of 15 minutes before actual intercourse begins (Hunt, 1973c, p. 256), although foreplay sometimes lasts much longer. This alternate giving and receiving of sensual pleasure is satisfying in itself, but it also prepares both partners for intercourse. It takes an average of 11 minutes for women to become fully sexually aroused, including the vaginal lubrication and ballooning necessary for comfortable penile penetration, but one woman in seven needs more than 15 minutes of foreplay (Bell, 1974). Men's response—penile erection—is generally quicker and more automatic.

Foreplay. Development of sexual responsiveness in preparation for sexual intercourse through kissing and caressing of sensitive body areas.

Touching. Some adults in our society are still inhibited by childhood taboos against touching an unclothed body, their own or anyone else's. Others regard touching only as a mechanical means to bring on orgasm. But trying to handle the sensitive human instrument in this way, wrote French novelist Honoré de Balzac, is like giving a violin to a gorilla (Masters and Johnson, 1974).

To help couples experience the full potential of loving strokes, some **sex therapists** have them try what Masters and Johnson call **pleasuring.** Each gently explores the other's body with caresses, without aiming for orgasm. If the exercise works, the giving partner discovers that there is considerable pleasure in giving as well as in receiving, and that touching can communicate tenderness, understanding, and respect as well as desire. The receiving partner learns how to relax and experience sensual feelings without guilt or fear. Guiding the partner's hands, the receiver is to indicate what is pleasurable without worrying about the requests being selfish or disgusting.

Pleasuring. A technique used in sex therapy in which each sexual partner gently explores the other's body without aiming for orgasm.

Direct Genital Stimulation. When Kinsey gathered his data, American men with less than a college education generally regarded rapid erection, insertion, and ejaculation as a sign of masculinity. Foreplay was almost nonexistent among the less-educated, with body contact (other than a few kisses), kissing of the breasts, and **oral-genital contact** frequently avoided out of suspicion or disgust (Kinsey et al., 1948). The behavior of college-educated couples was only slightly more liberated.

With increasing cultural sexual openness, married men and women of all educational levels are now much more likely to use direct genital stimulation to prepare their partners for intercourse—and sometimes to trigger orgasm without coitus. According to the Research Guild survey, nine-tenths of American wives caress their husband's penis manually, and one-half to three-quarters of those with high school and college education, respectively, practice **fellatio,** arousing the male genitals with their mouth and tongue. Between 56 and 66 percent of husbands use **cunnilingus** (oral stimulation of the woman's genitals) to help their wives achieve orgasm (Hunt, 1974).

If they can shake off their inhibitions about such practices, lovers usually find direct genital stimulation a source of extreme sexual gratification. Contrary to common parental injunctions against handling the genitals because they are "dirty," the human mouth contains more bacteria than a washed penis or vagina (Fink, 1975).

INTERCOURSE

When both partners have had enough of the pleasures of foreplay, one of them guides the man's erect penis into the woman's moist vagina. Gradually, by rolling and thrusting hip movements and continued caressing, they build this joy of togetherness into the extreme muscular tension and then explosive release of orgasm.

Rarely do they reach this point simultaneously. The ecstasy of mutual orgasm is difficult to achieve because of differences in timing and seemingly incompatible needs for different kinds of movement as orgasm approaches. At the point of orgasm, men like to penetrate the vagina deeply and then hold this position except for perhaps a few more deliberate thrusts. Women, on the other hand, often prefer continued friction with an acceleration of thrusts and pressure on the **pubic area** (McCary, 1973).

Since women are capable of multiple orgasms with no rest period, couples often arrange their foreplay and intercourse patterns to allow the woman several climaxes before the man has his. For women who find it difficult to orgasm through intercourse, this may include use of manual or oral stroking, or positions which maximize clitoral stimulation while relieving muscular tension for the man, allowing him to delay ejaculation.

The duration of intercourse has changed dramatically in the past few decades. Kinsey estimated that about three-quarters of all men ejaculated within two minutes after insertion of the penis into the vagina. This speed was thought to be a sign of **virility,** despite its ill effects on wives who were unable to be orgasmic with so little stimulation (Kinsey et al.). But so many men have learned to control ejaculation that Research Guild figures indicate the median duration of marital coitus is now ten minutes for people of all educational levels. Rather than a sign of decreased virility, this is apparently a result of men's motivation to prolong their own enjoyment of coitus and to allow the women to catch up as well. Younger males, for whom ejaculatory urgency is strongest, now spend even longer in coitus than older men (Hunt, 1974).

Virility. Manly vigor and forcefulness.

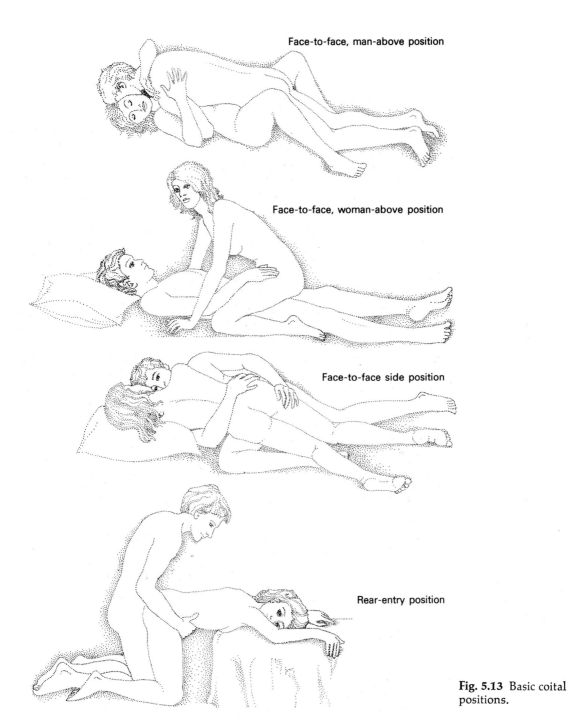

Face-to-face, man-above position

Face-to-face, woman-above position

Face-to-face side position

Rear-entry position

Fig. 5.13 Basic coital positions.

Positions.   There are hundreds of ways a man and a woman can intimately fit together, most of them variations on the four basic positions shown in Fig. 5.13.

The standard position for intercourse in our culture was labeled the "missionary position" by non-Western people. In this face-to-face, man-above position, the woman lies on her back, with her legs bent, straight, wrapped around her partner's body, pulled up to her shoulders, or propped against his. This position allows eye contact, embracing, and kissing. However, it affords relatively little clitoral stimulation unless the woman arches her back and the man presses down on the pubic area or takes one of her legs between his. If the man supports himself to keep from pinning his partner down and restricting her movements, he is unable to use his hands to caress her.

In the face-to-face, woman-above position, the woman sits, kneels, or lies on top of the man. She is free to move her hips to increase clitoral friction and to control the depth of penetration, but her partner is restricted in his movements and may find this position relatively unstimulating. It does, however, give him a chance to relax, prolong his erection, and fondle his partner's body.

The face-to-face, side position gives both partners freedom of movement as they lie side-by-side facing each other, with arms and legs variously entwined or free. Since neither supports the weight of the other, this is a relaxing posture well-suited to prolonged intercourse and mutual caressing. Since no weight rests on the woman's abdomen, it is often the preferred position during pregnancy.

In the rear-entry position, the woman can either lie or kneel with her back to the man, sit on his lap, or lie beside him, facing away from him. Clitoral stimulation is usually lacking, but the man or the woman herself may be able to provide this **manually,** and the position provides a sensation of pressure on the entrance to the vagina which many women enjoy.

Manually. By use of the hands.

Anal sex. The anus, because of its association with bowel movements, has long been regarded in our civilization as the most forbidden part of the body. But many Americans seem to be freeing themselves from this strong taboo, for in the Research Guild survey, only 27 percent of all men and women agreed with the statement, "Anal intercourse between a man and a woman is wrong." Over half of the couples under age 35 have used manual anal stimulation during foreplay, over a quarter have engaged in oral stimulation of the anus, and about a quarter have tried **anal intercourse** (Hunt, 1974).

Anal sex carries several dangers. There is normally no **fecal matter** in the end of the **rectum,** though this area should be washed as carefully as the genitals before lovemaking. But if the man puts his fingers or penis in his partner's vagina after they have been in her rectum, without washing in between, she may get a vaginal infection. And because the opening of the anus normally tightens when it is touched, anal intercourse can be painful for the woman.

Anal intercourse is not professionally regarded as "sick" behavior if both partners want to try it rather than one's being forced into the experience by the other. However, most heterosexual couples now using anal intercourse do so only rarely (Hunt, 1974). According to a 1975 survey, only 1 out of 100 women have anal intercourse often; women voted it the least-liked of all sexual activities (Levin, 1975a). Pregnancy, of course, could never result from anal intercourse.

AFTERGLOW

After intercourse, partners often find great joy in lying together in a state of warm mutual affection and appreciation. Men usually enter a refractory period which varies in length, during which they are unresponsive to further sexual stimulation. But women often continue to be capable of erotic arousal, and their sexual excitement ebbs away only gradually. Masters and Johnson (1974) have noticed that even if both partners fall asleep after lovemaking, the woman moves toward the man in her sleep, reaching out for him in what seems to be a subconscious attempt to remain in touch with him. Men, on the other hand, tend to stay put and show less need for continued body contact.

PHYSIOLOGICAL INFLUENCES ON SEXUAL ACTIVITY

What happens during lovemaking is not just a matter of who strokes whom where. As we will see in Chapter 11, people's responses are subject to social learning and psychological factors. And to some extent, they are also influenced by hormones, aging, drugs, and alcohol.

THE INFLUENCE OF THE BRAIN

Orgasm is a relatively uncomplicated physical response coordinated by the part of the spinal cord which lies in the pelvic area. But sexual response is also subject to a great degree of control by higher parts of the brain, which receive messages from the **sense receptors** and decide whether or not to interpret them as erotic. Since physical sensations are projected into the conscious part of the brain, the responses that normally follow can be consciously controlled to some extent. Men can, for instance, choose to delay ejaculation or even remain celibate for life.

Sense receptors. Bodily structures that receive stimuli from the external or internal environment and transmit the message to the brain.

Learned reactions, emotional states, and conscious thought can inhibit as well as trigger sexual response, regardless of sensory input. A man who is worried about his performance may find it impossible to achieve an erection, no matter how much physical stimulation he receives. And a woman's anxiety about sexual relations may actually cause her vagina to tighten in involuntary muscular spasms called **vaginismus,** effectively preventing intercourse.

On the other hand, sexual responses can be initiated by erotic suggestion to the brain alone without any tactile stimulation of the genitals. Despite the overriding importance of the sense of touch to human sexuality, people also respond through the brain to certain erotic cues they can see, taste, hear, or smell. American men are particularly excited by the sight of a woman's breasts (Stember, 1975). Hard-driving music has powerful effects on some people. There is some evidence that humans secrete and are subtly influenced by **pheromones,** genital odors which may excite or repel their partners (Kaplan, 1974a). And Kinsey found that young boys have erections as responses to everything from **pornographic** materials and athletic activities to receiving report cards and being chased by the police.

Inhibition. Restraint from free or spontaneous activity through social controls.

Inhibition of Female Sexual Awareness. Women may be just as responsive to psychic stimulation as men. But their arousal takes a less obvious form (subtly felt genital lubrication and swelling as opposed to penile erection) and their awareness of sensual desire has not been culturally encouraged as it has for men.

Using special devices to measure engorgement of the penis and vagina, researchers have discovered that while women can be "turned on" by sexual fantasies and scenes of sex acts just as men can (explicit sex without romance being the most effective turn-on for both sexes), many women are unable to recognize the signs of sexual arousal in themselves. Well over half of the women in one study said they felt neither vaginal swelling nor lubrication after listening to an erotic tape, although instruments showed that they had these responses (Heiman, 1975).

This lack of sexual awareness in women probably has something to do with the relative insensitivity of the vagina to anything but pressure, but it may also be caused by cultural repression of female sexuality. Pornography has traditionally been aimed primarily at men, for their arousal has long been socially approved. Erotic magazines for women have begun to appear, but it is not yet generally acceptable for women to read and derive the same enjoyment from them that men do. Only a few generations ago, it was not nice for women to enjoy sex. Sexual intercourse was a husband's right, but it was an experience to be accepted passively by the wife.

Lingering signs of this attitude were apparent in a recent survey comparing men's responses to *Playboy* to women's responses to *Playgirl.* Whereas all the males sampled had read *Playboy* before and almost two-thirds owned a copy of the magazine, only half of the females had read *Playgirl* before and little over a quarter owned a copy of it. When asked if they thought people would generally approve of their reading *Playboy*, 80 percent of the men answered "yes"; only 34 percent of the women thought their reading *Playgirl* would be culturally approved. While most men responded favorably to the sex-oriented parts of *Playboy*, a third of the women said that reading *Playgirl* made them feel "dirty," "cheap," "guilty," or "bad." Another third seemed to be ambivalent, listing both positive and negative responses to the pictures of male nudity. And while a third of the men said they liked to look at pictures of nude women because they were just normal, only 2 out of the 50 women surveyed considered it normal for them to enjoy looking at pictures of naked men. Since women are physically as capable of responding sexually to erotic materials as men, these significant differences in their reactions testify to the still-strong influence of traditional social pressures (Stauffer and Frost, 1976).

THE INFLUENCE OF HORMONES

The differences in male and female responsiveness may also have something to do with hormonal differences, though to what extent is unclear. The **hormone** most significantly related to sexuality is testosterone. It is produced in the testicles of males and also in the adrenal glands above the kidneys in both men and women. In boys, testosterone production begins at puberty, causing the development of male secondary sex characteristics such as deep voice, broad chest, and hair growth on the face and chest. High concentrations of testosterone also seem to cause typically masculine behavior patterns of aggressiveness and competitiveness. In girls, the effects of testosterone are neutralized to some extent by estrogen, the female hormone, usually rendering them less aggressive, more responsive to smells and touch, and more likely to be **nurturant** toward babies. But there may be great individual differences in the degree of masculinity and femininity (Kaplan, 1974a).

Hormones. Glandular products that circulate in body fluids and evoke responses in the body far from the glands where they originate.

In addition to influencing masculine development and behavior, testosterone is also essential to **libido** (sexual desire) and the ability to orgasm in both men and women. At times of erotic stimulation, it is testosterone which activates certain brain centers to cause sexual desire and effect sperm production, erection, and ejaculation in males and vaginal secretions in females. Men suffering from testosterone deprivation because of **castration** (removal of the testicles) gradually lose interest in sex and are usually unable to have erections. Women cut off from their testosterone supply may lose their sexual desire, stop having erotic fantasies, and usually can no longer be sexually aroused by stimuli which were once effective. If they are given supplemental testosterone, they become highly capable of sexual arousal. But they also become more masculine in behavior and appearance —becoming more aggressive and growing hair on their faces, for instance (Kaplan, 1974a).

THE EFFECTS OF AGING

Males and females also react differently to the effects of aging. While men usually reach the height of their sexual capacity between the ages of 17 and 21, many women do not become fully sexually responsive until they are in their late thirties and early forties. In young couples, it is often the husband who wishes that his wife were more responsive. But by the time women are between 35 and 39, according to one survey, one out of every three strongly religious wives and one out of every two nonreligious wives wish that their husbands would make love more often (Levin, 1975a). Although it is not clear whether their delayed responsiveness is a matter of biology or of slow unlearning of culturally induced inhibitions, once women have reached their peak, their sexual desire and capabilities do not begin to dwindle until they reach their sixties. Men's sexual performance declines slowly but steadily after its peak in early manhood.

Men respond to aging by taking longer to achieve erections and ejaculating with less force. Although sperm production ordinarily never ceases altogether, it decreases with aging. The testicles shrivel slightly and become softer, the prostate gland enlarges, and the ejaculate becomes thinner and decreases in volume. By the time they reach 70, perhaps two-thirds of the men in this country are impotent (Rubin, 1966). But Masters and Johnson (1966) have found that the sexual capability of a high percentage of men who have become impotent after the age of 50 (secondary impotence) can be restored through training. Psychological factors to be discussed in Chapter 11 may be more to blame than biological ones for their loss of sexual functioning.

Menopause. The time in a woman's life, usually around age 50, when menstruation ceases.

When women are about 50, their ovaries gradually cease to produce female hormones and release eggs. After this **menopause,** or "change of life," the vaginal walls become thin, the vagina narrows and shortens, the outer lips shrink, lubrication is less plentiful, and uterine contractions during orgasm become stronger. These changes, which result from estrogen deficiency, can make intercourse painful for women. They can be corrected by estrogen-replacement therapy, although there is currently some concern that estrogen supplements may increase the risk of uterine cancer. Despite their physical changes, many women experience a renewal of sexual interest after menopause because it frees them from the fear of pregnancy (Rubin, 1966).

According to Masters and Johnson (1966), there is no time limit drawn by the advancing years to female sexuality, and men have a capacity for sexual performance that frequently may extend to and beyond the 80-year age level. The notion that a man's body only produces a finite amount of semen which should be carefully rationed out so that some will be left for old age is only a myth. To the contrary, the more sexual activity a man engages in during his youth and middle age, the more likely he is to be able to continue to function sexually in his old age. And women over 60 who have had intercourse once or twice a week have longer orgasms and more vaginal lubrication than those whose sex lives have been less active. Kinsey found a 70-year-old man who was still averaging seven ejaculations per week and an 88-year-old man who was still enjoying intercourse with his 90-year-old wife (Brecher, 1966). According to Isadore Rubin, a specialist on the effects of aging, our society's assumption that sex, love, and marriage are the exclusive privileges of youth is denied by medical evidence to the contrary.

DRUGS AND SEX

Throughout history, people have tried to enliven sexual experiences or revive waning potency by subjecting themselves to a variety of foods and drugs. But many legendary **aphrodisiacs** (reputed sex stimulants) like raw bull's testicles and pulverized rhinoceros horn contain nothing which would affect sexual performance. The only lift that results from their use is probably psychological, due to the power of suggestion. Certain other substances do seem to affect sexuality, but not always in the way they were intended.

> **Aphrodisiac. A food or chemical which is thought to increase sexual desire and enjoyment of sexual activity.**

Although many people seem to think that alcohol improves their performance, alcohol is actually a depressant which slows physical reflexes and makes erection more difficult. In numbing the brain, however, alcohol removes mental inhibitions which block full sexual expression for many people. For them, the freedom they feel when influenced by alcohol more than offsets its effects as a depressant.

The same is true for marijuana, used in conjunction with sex by 30 percent of the women in one survey, including 63 percent of those under 20 (Levin, 1975a). A depressant, marijuana actually decreases sexual performance, but at the same time it loosens inhibitions and produces euphoria and a slowed sense of time which may make people interpret sex as being better. Some users claim that marijuana sharpens their awareness of muscular sensations, especially those associated with orgasm (Kaplan, 1974a). But according to recent studies, chronic heavy marijuana use may have a negative effect on sexual functioning, depressing both desire and the ability to orgasm (Ellinwood et al., 1975).

Amphetamines and cocaine do seem to stimulate sexual activity, but their long-term use may diminish this effect and actually decrease sexual interest and performance. Those who have sexual relationships while under the influence of LSD experience a warping of perceptions but not necessarily intense eroticism. Some feel detached from their own orgasms, while those on "bad trips" may lose all interest in sex (Kaplan, 1974a). L-dopa, a drug used chiefly in the treatment of Parkinson's disease, gained brief notoriety as an aphrodisiac because two percent of the male patients using it unexpectedly experienced hypersexuality as a side effect. But this effect cannot be consistently produced in clinical studies of L-dopa with humans or animals (McCary, 1971).

The legendary aphrodisiac "Spanish fly," an extract of crushed dried beetles, is actually a dangerously corrosive irritant which acts on the urinary tract, causing painful congestion. It may indeed produce an erection, but one which is anything but pleasant and usually devoid of any feelings of sexual desire. Use of Spanish fly may cause permanent damage to the kidneys and penis, and perhaps even death. Yohimbine, an extract from an African tree, seems to stimulate the pelvic area of the spinal cord which controls erection, but it also acts as a diuretic, stepping up the elimination of fluids from the body, and should only be used under a doctor's supervision (McCary, 1973a).

Dysfunctions. Abnormal or impaired functioning, such as inability to participate satisfactorily in sexual intercourse.

DYSFUNCTIONS AND THERAPY

For some couples, lovemaking is not the pleasure it could be. Masters and Johnson (1970) have estimated that up to 50 percent of all American marriages are marred by inadequate sexual responses in one or both partners. But most people apparently do not consider their own marriages sexually inadequate. Ninety-four percent of married men aged 45 and over find marital intercourse mostly pleasurable to very pleasurable, and the percentage is even higher in younger age groups, increasing to 99 percent among married men between 18 and 24. Among married women, satisfaction is highest between the ages of 35 and 44, a peak figure of 93 percent. It is lower for younger women, starting at 88 percent for those under 25. Ninety-one percent express satisfaction between the ages of 45 and 54, and the proportion is still 83 percent between the ages of 55 and 64 (Hunt, 1974).

No one is sure what a normal sexual relationship is. And it is difficult to tell which is the more reliable indicator of the health of sex in America— the clinical impressions of professionals who see mostly people with severe problems, or the self-evaluations of those who are comfortable enough with their sexuality to answer surveys.

Although we will return to psychosocial problems in a sexual relationship in Chapter 11, we will devote a section here to some physical manifestations of sexual difficulty: premature ejaculation, retarded ejaculation, impotence, female inability to orgasm, and intercourse which is painful for the woman. Until recently, people with these problems accepted them or didn't even recognize them as inadequacies. But there is enough said and written about sex today for them to know that their relationship could be improved.

Many are now seeking professional help in improving their sex lives at thousands of sex-therapy clinics across the country. The names of legitimate sex counselors can be obtained through physicians, city, county or state medical societies, or family service organizations. Most sex therapists regard sexual inadequacies as a problem for the couple rather than an individual one. They usually prefer to work with both partners rather than only the one who claims to be having trouble. However, some therapists work with individuals singly or in group-therapy settings (DeLora and Warren, 1977).

The kinds of treatment vary also. Some therapists deal only with the specific behavioral problem, prescribing exercises to help a couple overcome it. They feel that inadequate responses are learned and can therefore be unlearned. Other therapists link work on behavioral problems to analysis and treatment of the emotional conflicts and defenses thought to be blocking enjoyment of lovemaking (Masters and Johnson, 1970; Kaplan, 1974b).

PREMATURE EJACULATION

One of the **dysfunctions** that may require therapy is the inability of some men to control their ejaculatory reflexes. Once they begin to be sexually excited, they orgasm very fast, often ejaculating as soon as—or even before —they enter the vagina. They can tolerate very little foreplay before attempting intercourse. By contrast, an effective lover is able to continue foreplay for some time after he erects, withholding his own climax until his slower female partner is fully aroused.

Ejaculation. The forcible, rhythmic discharge of seminal fluid from the penis during the male orgasm.

Premature ejaculation occurs in many different kinds of men and often in otherwise sound marital relationships, so analysts are unable to provide a single explanation for what causes it. Some blame neurosis, some marital hostilities, some physical oversensitivity to stimulation, and some traumatic experiences during early attempts at intercourse. It has also been suggested that early experimentation in secret places conditions males to orgasm rapidly before being discovered, and that this pattern of rapid ejaculation is carried over into adult life (McCary, 1973b). These factors may cause premature ejaculation by blocking awareness of the sensations which precede orgasm. Just as children cannot learn to control urination until they learn what it feels like to have a full bladder, some men cannot consciously control ejaculation until they can identify what it feels like to be on the verge of orgasm. With therapy, though, most men can learn the control required (Kaplan, 1974a; Masters and Johnson, 1970).

RETARDED EJACULATION

While men who ejaculate prematurely cannot prevent orgasm, those who suffer from retarded ejaculation cannot achieve it. Although they are capable of erections, they get stuck at the plateau level and cannot find orgasmic release, much as they want it. Many men have mild forms of this problem and are only able to ejaculate after very lengthy stimulation or under the influence of fantasy. Some can only reach climax through masturbation or **oral** or manual stimulation by their partner.

Retarded ejaculation can usually be traced to psychological, rather than physical causes. A strict religious background, unresolved childhood sexual feelings toward one's parents, suppressed anger, conflicting feelings toward the spouse, fear of rejection, and specific traumatic sexual experiences are commonly found to inhibit the ejaculation reflex. But therapy can help to solve this problem by relieving ejaculation of damaging associations (Kaplan, 1974a).

IMPOTENCE

Impotence. Inability to have an erection of the penis as a means to copulation, due to either physical or psychological causes.

Nothing is more devastating to a sexually active man's sense of masculinity than to be unable to achieve or maintain an erection. No matter how much he might want to have intercourse, no matter how much stimulation he receives, his penis remains limp. At least half of the men in this country have had this experience (Kaplan, 1974b), and in some circumstances it can be humiliating. For most it is a temporary reaction to factors like fatigue or too much to drink. But if they allow themselves to worry that it may happen again, their anxieties may be self-fulfilling. If repeatedly unable to produce an erection, they may try to withdraw from sexual contacts out of the fear of failure. Sometimes the problem is a symptom of low hormone levels, fatigue, or other biological factors. But more often the cause is social in origin. The snowballing fear of failure, an overly demanding wife, depression, preoccupation with a career, or boredom with repetitive marital sex can make a formerly virile man impotent, as can overindulgence in food, drugs, or alcohol. Those who have never had an erection at any time may have been subjected to restrictive religious teachings or had a traumatic experience during the first attempt at intercourse. The chance of recovery from impotence now seems to be about 60–80 percent with therapy (Kaplan, 1974a; Masters and Johnson, 1970).

GENERAL FEMALE SEXUAL DYSFUNCTION

The sexual responses of women are usually less automatic than those of men, being more dependent on a reassuring emotional atmosphere. Whether for physical or cultural reasons, a woman's arousal seems to develop more slowly. Not recognizing these male-female differences, men have often begun intercourse long before their female partners were ready, and then labeled them frigid when they displayed little passionate involvement. In addition to insufficient stimulation, inability to experience sexual interest may have its roots in childhood learning, with cultural injunctions to female children to hide their erotic impulses under a good-girl front. Despite increasing sexual openness and the achievements of the women's liberation movement, traces of the double standard which represses female sexuality still remain, and some women themselves have not yet accepted their rights to equal sexual experience.

Women who have never experienced sexual arousal may view intercourse as a frightening or disgusting ordeal to be endured only for their husband's sake, or they may enjoy its closeness without really feeling anything. Some women labeled frigid were aroused by early lovemaking but lost their sensitivity when marital sex became solely a matter of mechanical copulation. Some nonresponsive women accept coitus neutrally; others feel used by their partners and may develop hostility toward them and dislike of sex in general. Men may accept female passivity as confirmation of what they assume to be the natural state of women; some even find their partner's submissiveness exciting. Others may feel personally rejected by a woman's lack of response, complicating the dynamics of their relationship.

Treatment for general female sexual dysfunction usually requires starting over carefully from the beginning. Therapists encourage partners to communicate openly and without guilt about what they feel and want. In the absence of deep mental disturbances or hostilities between the partners, most nonresponsive women who undergo treatment gradually find that sex is enjoyable; many are eventually orgasmic (Kaplan, 1974b).

Therapists. Persons trained in methods of treatment and rehabilitation other than the use of drugs or surgery.

FEMALE ORGASMIC DYSFUNCTION

Many women are capable of extreme erotic arousal but, like men suffering from retarded ejaculation, have problems in reaching orgasm. Some can do so only in masturbation when they are alone or with oral or manual manipulation by their partner, but not with coitus; some never experience orgasm under any circumstances.

Since women's inability to reach climax does not prevent intercourse, the female orgasm has not received much attention until recently. It was Masters and Johnson who successfully focused public attention on the fact that women have the potential for multiple orgasms and sexual capacity far greater than that of males. In the ensuing publicity, women who had previously accepted infrequent orgasm began to feel deprived.

While many women resent the current equation of orgasm with satisfaction in lovemaking, insisting that they are very contented with the closeness of intercourse and opportunity for giving pleasure to their husbands, others feel a real need for orgasmic release. As indicated earlier, 29 percent of women who never orgasm still rate their sex lives as being good to very good, but 40 percent who are inorgasmic rate the sexual aspect of their marriages as poor to very poor. By contrast, 81 percent of women who are orgasmic all or most of the time describe their satisfaction with marital sex as good to very good (Levin, 1975a).

Current explanations for the frequent failure of women to reach climax include fears of being hurt or hurting the man, cultural conditioning against having sexual feelings, inadequately reassuring emotional atmosphere during lovemaking, insufficient foreplay, and inadequate clitoral stimulation before and during intercourse. Men are frequently blamed for failing to accommodate their wives' slower responses by delaying their own and providing the kind of gentle, continuing stimulation their partners need.

Women can ask for this kind of stimulation, but some are too inhibited to find out what their own needs are. Even if they know, they cannot bring themselves to ask their partners to help satisfy them. Masturbation helps women to identify how they can best be stimulated to orgasm; sexual fantasies intensify their reactions. But these aids to sexuality have long been so taboo for women than many are embarrassed to use them. Some women inhibit their own orgasms by trying to rush them to keep from displeasing or asking too much of their husbands, but the female orgasm can be built up only slowly. Tensing of the wrong muscles at the wrong time out of anxiety or the wish to speed things along can prevent orgasm.

Taboo. Banned on grounds of morality or taste.

Many therapists feel that women who can orgasm only through non-coital means may be holding back out of unconscious fears of coitus; fear of body penetration and physical damage, fear of hurting the partner, hostility toward the mate, or negative feelings about the penis (Fisher, 1973). Fear of pregnancy is a powerful block to orgasm; some women only reach climax during intercourse after they have undergone sterilization operations or have passed menopause (Sorg, 1975). The sense of security has a great bearing on whether or not a woman can be orgasmic; a feeling of privacy and freedom from intrusion as well as a warm, trusting relationship with the partner head the list of factors listed by women as important conditions for sexual responsiveness (Fisher).

Except in cases of severe mental or physical illness or deep animosity toward the partner, all women are capable of sexual responsiveness, including orgasm. Rarely does treatment fail to help women who learn to relax and let themselves enjoy climax. But some may be unable to orgasm until after the birth of their first baby, since the physical changes of pregnancy and childbirth increase the blood supply to the pelvis (Masters and Johnson, 1974). Therapist Helen Kaplan suggests that women who are highly sexually responsive and free from psychological problems but who can orgasm only through manual or oral stimulation may simply have orgasmic thresholds which are too high to be reached during the less intense stimulation of coitus. They should not consider themselves sexually inadequate, because their pattern seems to fall within the range of normal female sexual functioning. Trying too hard for coital orgasm may make lovemaking a tense and anxious act rather than a loving form of communication (Kaplan, 1974a).

VAGINISMUS AND DYSPAREUNIA

A small number of women are unable to enjoy intercourse because they find it frightening or painful. In some, an involuntary spasm of the muscles in the outer third of the vagina, called vaginismus, constricts the opening so severely that penile penetration is impossible. In others, intercourse causes intense pain in the clitoris, vaginal barrel, or soft tissues of the pelvis, a condition called **dyspareunia.**

There are no known physical causes for vaginismus. It appears to be an entirely **psychosomatic** response to anticipated vaginal penetration. It may be linked to dysfunction of the male partner (out of anxiety or to avoid frustration), a restrictive background, specific traumatic experiences, or attempts at heterosexual intercourse by women who have previously been exclusively homosexual (Masters and Johnson, 1970).

Dyspareunia may stem from unconscious muscular tension associated with traumatic sexual experiences, conscious faking to avoid unwanted intercourse, or any number of true, unimagined physical causes for pain. They range from an unbroken hymen and insufficient vaginal lubrication to heavy-handed manipulation of the clitoris and vaginal infections (Masters and Johnson, 1970). A woman suffering from dyspareunia should be checked by a doctor. If he finds no indications of physical problems, her condition may respond to behavioral therapy and progressive psychological relaxation.

Masters and Johnson report 100 percent success in curing vaginismus. Whether the problem stems from restrictive upbringing, sexual dysfunction of the partner, rape, or a history of homosexual relationships, it can be cleared up through reeducation as to the facts and acceptability of human sexuality.

Psychosomatic. Controlled by the influence of the mind or emotions upon the functioning of the body.

VENEREAL DISEASE

Although therapists are counseling people to relax and enjoy sex, one aspect of lovemaking may be cause for legitimate anxiety: venereal disease. **Syphilis,** almost eradicated in 1956, has climbed back up to an incidence of 11.7 cases per 100,000 population (Fleming, 1975); **gonorrhea** has reached epidemic proportions, affecting an estimated 2-1/2 million new people in 1972 and still growing (Sgroi, 1974); and genital **herpes** virus, almost unknown ten years ago, infected an estimated 250,000 to 1 million people in 1975 (Subak-Sharpe, 1975). Two-thirds of the reported cases of VD occur in people under 25, and males are more likely to contract VD since they tend to be more active sexually than females (Sgroi). These virulent infections attack the genital areas and may cause serious complications elsewhere in the body. They are referred to as venereal diseases (from the Latin word *venus,* which means love or sexual desire) because they are spread by sexual contact. The bacteria can be found in the mouth, throat, vagina, cervix, urethra, and anal canal (DeLora and Warren). The more sexual partners a person has, the greater the chances for contracting—and then spreading—some form of VD.

Aside from limiting sexual contacts, the only ways to eradication of venereal diseases are rapid reporting to doctors or VD clinics by those who think they may have contracted one of the diseases, prompt treatment of

Venereal diseases. Dangerous infections spread mainly by sexual contact.

them and all their sexual contacts, and use of hygienic measures during intercourse with possible carriers. For men, this means using **condoms** and washing the genitals immediately after intercourse; for women, antiseptic **douching** and thorough soap-and-water genital cleaning are said to be fairly effective preventive techniques.

GONORRHEA

Men should suspect gonorrhea, sometimes called **clap,** if there is a thin discharge from the penis which becomes thick and greenish-yellow. Urination may be compelling but painful. If untreated, the infection can spread, swelling the testicles until they are very sore and the size of oranges.

Sterility. Inability to produce offspring. Further complications may lead to **sterility** and death if antibiotics are not used.

In women, early symptoms of gonorrhea include discharge from the vagina, inflamed genitals, and the need to urinate frequently, but painfully. These signs appear two to seven days after contact with an infected person. Because the symptoms are similar to those in common nonvenereal vaginal infections, four out of five women who have gonorrhea are unaware of it until more serious complications set in (Sgroi). If the infection spreads, it may cause permanent sterility or require surgical removal of the pelvic organs.

Gonorrhea can usually be diagnosed through laboratory examination of vaginal or penile discharge samples. One or two injections of **penicillin** or **tetracycline** usually clears up the symptoms if no complications have set in, but there are reports of new strains of **gonoccocus** which are resistant to antibiotics (McCary, 1973a).

SYPHILIS

The symptoms of syphilis are so subtle at first that the United States Public Health Service estimates that there are at least half a million Americans who have syphilis and don't know it (Sgroi). The disease develops in four stages. The primary stage, which appears 10–40 days after contact with an infected person, is characterized by a **chancre** or sore in the anal-genital or mouth region, with a nonpainful swelling in the nearest **lymph gland.** If the infection is untreated, the chancre goes away in 4–10 weeks, but the syphilis itself has merely gone underground temporarily. It surfaces again in the secondary stage as a slight non–itchy rash on the body, sometimes accompanied by swollen glands, sore throat, headache, and low fever. Sometimes people's eyelashes, eyebrows, and hair start to fall out. At this stage, syphilis can be transferred by kissing as well as by coitus.

The secondary stage gradually disappears spontaneously, resulting in a **latent** or third stage of untreated syphilis which may last for years. During that time there are no symptoms and the disease cannot be spread to sexual partners. But if still untreated, it eventually erupts—as much as 30 years later—as crippling, disfiguring **lesions** in the skin, central nervous system, cardiovascular system, bones, joints, eyes, and other organs.

Untreated mothers may pass on syphilis to their unborn children, sometimes causing mental defects or syphilitic symptoms which appear years later. During the first three stages of syphilis, one or two injections of antibiotics are usually all that is needed to prevent this chain of events; even in the fourth stage, treatment can stop its progressive destructiveness, although damage already done to the body cannot be repaired (Boston Women's Health Book Collective, 1976).

HERPES

Herpes is a serious modern venereal disease for which there is no known cure. It is caused by a virus known as Herpes Simplex, type 2, which is closely related to Herpes Simplex, type 1, the cause of cold sores or fever blisters. Symptoms show up two to six days after contact with an infected person. The most common symptom—in both sexes—is the outbreak of one or more very painful sores on the genitalia, similar to fever blisters or cold sores on the lips. There may be other generalized symptoms as well at the time of the first attack, such as tiredness, leg swelling, watery eyes, and difficulty in urinating. Herpes infection triples the chance of **miscarriage** in women, may cause death or incurable brain damage to babies carried to full-term, and may even cause cancer of the cervix. Outbreaks may come and go in an infected person for months and even years (Subak-Sharpe).

Miscarriage. Expulsion of the human fetus before it is able to live independently.

It would be misleading to conclude this chapter on biological aspects of human sexuality by emphasizing dysfunctions and diseases, serious though they are. The physical enjoyment of sexual activity is far more significant in the lives of most people. Nor is it desirable to stress the biological fact of sexual intercourse without considering the social meanings associated with it. Although we have focused on the biological components of sexuality in this chapter, this is only part of the picture. Human sexual behavior is not truly natural in the sense of being a strictly biological function. Unlike hiccuping or reflex knee-jerking, lovemaking does not have any instinctive predetermined pattern. Like most human behaviors, it is culturally learned and prescribed, and therefore unnatural. As we will see in Chapter 11, human sexuality is a complex condition that involves ability to think, to act, and to remember, and the human need to be with other humans (Gagnon and Simon, 1974). In the meantime, we will continue our discussion of the physiology of reproduction with pregnancy and childbirth, the subjects of Chapter 6.

Summary

1. The purpose of this chapter is to describe and discuss the biological aspects of human sexuality: sexual anatomy and physiology; techniques of lovemaking; possible problems in sexual activity; and venereal diseases.

2. Knowledge of male and female sexual behavior has been expanded by recent research conducted by Masters and Johnson on the levels of responses that occur during sexual intercourse and the physiological changes that accompany them. Masters and Johnson distinguish four phases of sexual response: excitement, plateau, orgasm, and resolution.

3. Knowledge of male and female sexual responses and use of a variety of techniques during intercourse can increase both partners' sexual pleasure. Some techniques are employed before intercourse to stimulate sexual response (foreplay), and others, such as different positions, are used during intercourse. The development of a mutually satisfying sexual relationship requires the cooperation of both partners and takes practice, time, and openness about what feels good and what doesn't.

4. Sexual responses can be either inhibited or intensified by a variety of factors: activity of the brain, hormones, effects of aging, and use of alcohol or drugs.

5. Some sexual relationships are marred by physical difficulties or dysfunctions, such as premature ejaculation, impotence, female orgasmic dysfunction, and dyspareunia. These problems can often be treated successfully by sex counselors and therapists. Their approaches vary from dealing only with specific behavioral problems to combining treatment of behavioral problems with analysis and treatment of psychological conflicts and defenses.

6. Venereal diseases—gonorrhea, syphilis, and herpes—present a severe national health problem in the United States. These infections are spread by sexual contact and attack the genital areas. Later they may cause serious complications elsewhere in the body, such as sterility, crippling, and eventually death. Gonorrhea and syphilis are curable if diagnosed and treated early enough, but herpes virus has no known cure. Aside from limiting sexual contacts, the only ways to stop the spread of VD are: (1) rapid reporting to doctors or VD clinics by those who think they may have contracted one of the diseases; (2) prompt treatment of them and all their sexual contacts; and (3) use of hygienic measures at the time of intercourse.

Key Concepts

Sexuality
Physiology
Erogenous zones
Sexual intercourse
Coitus
Engorgement
Erectile tissue
Orgasm
Ejaculation
Hormones

Glands
Masturbation
Foreplay
Inhibitions
Libido
Castration
Aphrodisiac
Sexual dysfunction
Sex therapists
Venereal disease

1. List the basic components of the male and female reproductive systems and their functions.

2. At what age do you think children should be taught about human sexuality? Who should do this teaching?

3. How does our social and cultural environment reflect our society's attitudes toward sexuality and sexual relations? Discuss behavior you observe around you as well as clothing styles, advertising, films, books, and TV programs.

4. Compare current attitudes toward female sexuality with attitudes toward women in late-nineteenth-century America described in Chapter 2. Taking into account the woman's place in society, and her view of herself, what changes good or bad do you think have occurred?

5. What steps should be taken to reduce the incidence of venereal disease? Whose responsibility is it to control this serious health problem?

Review and Discussion

BOSTON WOMEN'S HEALTH BOOK COLLECTIVE (1976). *Our Bodies, Ourselves: A Book By and For Women.* New York: Simon and Schuster.

Covers various aspects of a woman's experience in the United States today, and gives basic and helpful information on many topics such as anatomy and physiology of sexuality and reproduction; sexual relationships; lesbianism; health care; birth control; childbearing; menopause; and self-defense.

HITE, S. (1976). *The Hite Report: A Nationwide Study of Female Sexuality.* New York: Dell.

Presents the results of questionnaire studies that asked women how they feel, what they like, and what they think of sex. The first part of the book discusses orgasm; the second part is a new cultural interpretation of female sexuality.

HUNT, M. (1974). *Sexual Behavior in the 1970s.* New York: Dell.

Reports recent changes in sexual behavior and attitudes in the United States. The information, on a variety of subjects, was gathered from questionnaires and in-depth interviews.

MASTERS, W. H., AND V. E. JOHNSON (1966). *Human Sexual Response.* Boston: Little, Brown.

Provides scientific data on the physical reactions of men and women to sexual stimulation which disproves many myths and misconceptions about human sexuality. Was the first in the field of the anatomy and physiology of human sexual response and it established a basis for current sex therapy and treatment.

MASTERS, W. H., AND V. E. JOHNSON in association with R. J. LEVIN (1974). *The Pleasure Bond, A New Look at Sexuality and Commitment.* Boston: Little, Brown.

Discusses ways in which couples can strengthen and intensify their sexual relationship over a period of time. Includes group discussions held by Masters and Johnson with men and women of varied backgrounds about how they seek sexual satisfaction and how they approach marital problems.

Suggested Readings

Pregnancy and Childbirth

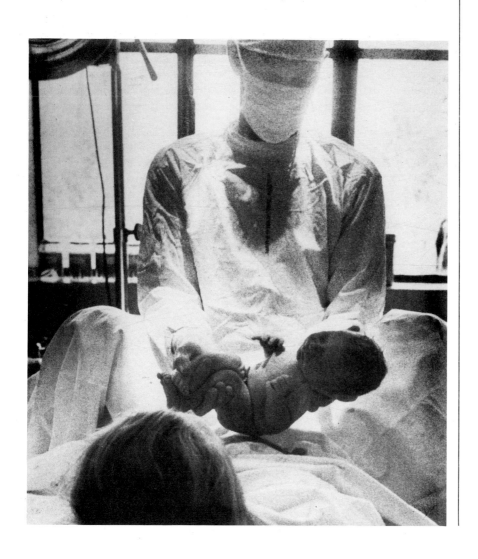

Fig. 6.1 Conception is the fertilization, development, and implantation of an ovum. Once during each menstrual cycle, a ripe ovum is released from one of the ovaries and drawn into the fallopian tube. Fertilization takes place in the fallopian tube if a sperm arrives and penetrates the egg. As a result of repeated cellular divisions, a hollow ball of cells, the blastocyst, is formed and imbeds itself in the thickened wall of the uterus approximately one week after fertilization.

While sexual intercourse is a means of expressing deep affection and of gratifying physical needs, it also serves a basic biological function: providing new members of the human race. If no **contraceptives** are used, and if the timing is right—or wrong, depending on your point of view—intercourse frequently triggers a series of events which results in the birth of a baby nine months later. This creation of new human life is an extraordinary responsibility but it can also be a deeply rewarding experience which adds a new dimension to love.

CONCEPTION

Human babies are the product of the union of an egg cell from a woman and a sperm cell from a man. These cells are so small that a shoebox could hold all the eggs which produced the earth's current population and a thimble all the sperm. But when united, they "know" how to develop into trillions of cells differentiated into the complex systems of the human body

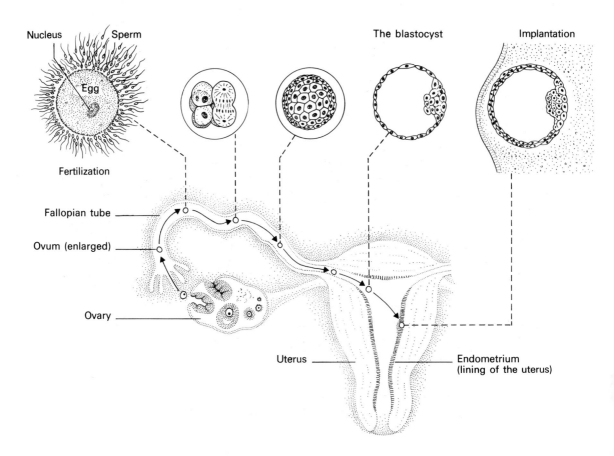

(Rugh and Shettles, 1971). The point at which the egg is fertilized by the sperm and they begin this incredible process is called **conception.**

THE FEMALE MENSTRUAL CYCLE

Every month a woman's body prepares itself for the possibility of conception. One-celled eggs surrounded by nurse cells have waited in an undeveloped form in her ovaries since before she was born. Of an initial supply of perhaps 400,000 potential eggs at birth, only about 400 will eventually mature (Rugh and Shettles). They are doled out one at a time once a young woman reaches **puberty.** Every 28 days, on the average, though the length of the cycle may vary from 24–35 days, one of her two ovaries is stimulated by hormonal cues to release an egg cell. As the egg is released, it is drawn into the nearer of the two fallopian tubes by the waving, hairlike projections which surround the opening of the tube. For several hours it waits at the top of the tube where **fertilization** might take place, then begins its travels down the tube toward the uterus. There hormonal secretions of estrogen and then progesterone have stimulated the uterine lining to

Fig. 6.2 Regular changes occur in the lining of the uterus during the menstrual cycle. The ripening egg follicle in the ovary produces a rising level of estrogen which causes the uterine lining to become thicker and more richly supplied with blood. Once the ripe egg has been released, the secretion of a hormone, progesterone, continues to prepare the uterus for pregnancy and prevents the development of a new follicle. Should fertilization not occur, production of progesterone declines, the uterine lining breaks down, and the menstrual flow begins. A new egg follicle begins development and the cycle starts again.

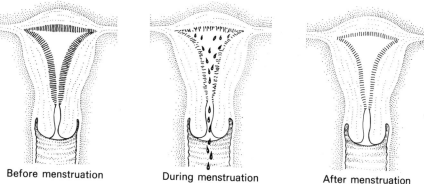

| Before menstruation | During menstruation | After menstruation |

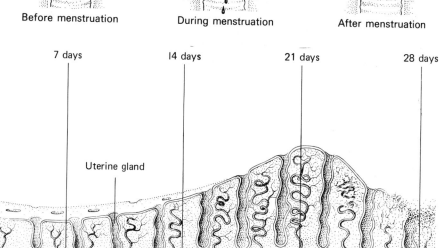

7 days   14 days   21 days   28 days

Uterine gland

Fig. 6.3 Diagram of a cross section of the uterine lining showing variations in thickness during the menstrual cycle. (Source: Eric T. Pengelley, *Sex and Human Life,* Reading, Mass.: Addison-Wesley, 1974.)

thicken, increase its blood supply, and secrete nourishing substances to aid the development of a fertilized egg. But if no sperm has fertilized the egg within 18–24 hours, it quickly degenerates, the bloody lining is shed in the process called menstruation, and the cycle begins again.

The onset of **menstruation** is regarded as the beginning of the menstrual cycle. **Ovulation,** the release of another egg from one of the ovaries, occurs 10–18 days after the beginning of the cycle. Some women feel a slight pain when they ovulate, and some report increased sexual desire at this time. But due to the subtlety of such clues and the great individual differences in body timing, most women are unaware of when they are ovulating and thus of when they are most likely to become pregnant.

SPERM PRODUCTION IN MALES
Although testicles in males develop before birth from the same primitive reproductive organs as ovaries in females, they operate under a different set of hormonal cues. Girls are born with all the eggs they will ever have. These eggs mature, on a monthly schedule, in the process called ovulation from puberty at the age of 10–14 until menopause at about age 50. At that time, hormonal cues result in a decline of ovarian function and the woman is no longer capable of conception. But in boys, sperm production does not begin until the average age of 13 or 14, when the changes of puberty include hormonal instructions from the pituitary gland to the testicles to begin forming sperm cells. Unlike the cyclical instructions sent to the ovaries from control centers in the woman's brain, hormonal cues sent to the testicles tell them to produce sperm constantly from puberty until death. They do so at the astounding average rate of 300 million sperm cells per day (Rugh and Shettles).

FERTILIZATION
When a man has an orgasm during vaginal sexual intercourse, hundreds of millions of his sperm cells are forcefully ejaculated through his urethra and into the upper part of the woman's vagina. Since there are many casualties along the way, few sperm ever reach the point where an egg might be waiting. As the whip-tailed cells swim about in every direction, some die as a result of the acidity of the vagina, some become tangled in the **mucus** of the cervix, some do not survive the long swim through the uterus, and some head down the wrong fallopian tube. Those which do enter the tube that contains that month's egg must swim against the currents which propel the egg toward the uterus. Many of the remaining sperm cells become trapped in crevices in the body tissue where they are destroyed as alien matter by the woman's **white blood cells.**

Nevertheless, sperm cells can live for two to three days in the upper fallopian tubes. Fertilization may take place up to two or even three days after intercourse if an egg arrives in time. If a live sperm cell manages to

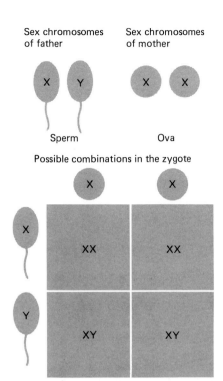

Fig. 6.4 Determination of gender. The sex chromosome of the ova or egg is always X, while that of the sperm may be X or Y. If the sperm carries an X sex chromosome, the child will be female; if the sperm carries a Y sex chromosome, the child will be male. Thus it is the father's sperm which determines the sex of the child.

Sex chromosomes of father

Sex chromosomes of mother

Sperm

Ova

Possible combinations in the zygote

collide with a viable egg during the period of 12–24 hours during which a woman is fertile in each cycle, it makes its way through the outer layers of the egg, which then seals itself off to penetration by any other sperm. But the collective effect of enormous numbers of sperm cells in the vicinity of the egg is apparently necessary to its penetration by a single cell. They seem to secrete an **enzyme** which dissolves the covering of the egg (Tortora and Anagnostakos, 1975).

The genetic material from the male, carried as 23 **chromosomes** in the nucleus of the sperm, joins the 23 maternal chromosomes of the egg. The 30,000 **genes** carried on the 23 pairs of chromosomes of the fertilized egg serve as a blueprint for the development of a new and unique human being. These chromosomal instructions will become part of every body cell in the baby. They will determine a broad range of traits from the color of its eyes to some of its personality characteristics.

One chromosome from each parent is a sex chromosome which tells the fetus whether to develop male or female characteristics. Those contributed by the woman are always X chromosomes, while those from the man may either be X, which means that the baby will be a girl (XX), or Y, in which case the baby will be a boy (XY).

FROM ZYGOTE TO EMBRYO
Once fertilization has occurred, the egg—now called a **zygote**—begins to produce more cells through a complex series of divisions. As it does, it is

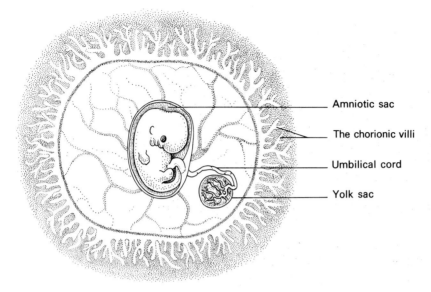

Amniotic sac

The chorionic villi

Umbilical cord

Yolk sac

Fig. 6.5 The developing embryo at about three weeks. The chorionic villi invade the uterine lining and together with the attached lining form the placenta.

moving down the fallopian tube to the uterus, a journey of about four inches. Approximately seven days after conception, it implants itself in the uterine wall, drawing nourishment from it until an external fetal organ called the **placenta,** can be formed. The placenta acts as an intermediary between the mother and the fetus, allowing the fetus to draw nutrients and oxygen from the mother's bloodstream and excrete wastes into it. The mother's blood never mixes with that of the fetus, for the exchanges take place by **diffusion** across membranes. So efficient is the transfer that nourishment just digested by the mother can reach the fetus within an hour (Rugh and Shettles).

One month after it is conceived, the **embryo** which began life as a one-celled pin point, has already developed a head, a curved trunk, and something which looks like a tail (the end of a developing spinal column which has temporarily outgrown the rest of the body). Though only a quarter of an inch long, the month-old human embryo has a primitive digestive system in the form of a food tube, a tiny heart that really pumps, 40 pairs of miniature muscle blocks, a primitive brain, a kidney similar to that of a frog which helps with excretion but will later be replaced, and gill slits —structures suggesting that humans share some common ancestry with the fish.

The development of the embryo is so complicated that an estimated 30–50 percent of all fertilized eggs die from imperfections or failures to implant. Many of these deaths occur during the first two weeks after conception before the mother has even missed a menstrual period or knows that she has conceived (Guttmacher, 1973). She cannot feel the embryo at first and is unaware of its fragile hold on life.

PREGNANCY

The symptoms of pregnancy may be deceptive. By the time that the embryo is a month old, the mother's menstrual period may be two weeks overdue, although some women have a light spotting of blood even when they are pregnant and a missed period is not always an indication of pregnancy. Emotional upheavals, sickness, the fear of getting pregnant, and other factors can inhibit the menstrual flow in nonpregnant women. Increased tenderness and enlargement of the breasts, darkening of the area around the nipples, nausea or morning sickness, sleepiness, fatigue, and the need to urinate frequently may all be signs of pregnancy—or they may not. Occasional women have all these symptoms, even a gradual swelling of the belly and, eventually, labor which "delivers" only air and fluids, without ever being pregnant. Such false pregnancies may last a full nine months— a psychosomatic phenomena which may stem from either the great urge to have a child or the great urge not to (McCary, 1973).

TESTS FOR PREGNANCY

Suspicion of pregnancy can and should be medically confirmed, for a woman unaware of her pregnancy might take drugs which could be dangerous to the embryo in its critical early development.

Gynecologists (doctors who specialize in female disorders and pregnancy) and **obstetricians** (who specialize in pregnancy and childbirth) can make out the shape of the fetus by vaginal examination after the twentieth week of pregnancy. Between the twelfth and twentieth weeks, they can detect the fetal heartbeat, find its skeleton by X-ray, and perhaps even map its shape with **ultrasonic** equipment. But most women prefer earlier proof of their pregnancy. Most doctors and clinics therefore diagnose early pregnancies by means of urine sample tests for the presence of a hormone called **chorionic gonadotropin.** Used for women whose periods are at least two weeks overdue, they are about 97-percent accurate in determining pregnancy (McCary, 1971).

There is another kind of test in which a progesterone injection is used to stimulate an overdue menstrual period. If no bleeding occurs, there is a 95 percent chance that the woman is pregnant (Guttmacher). But recent reports indicate that the progesterone test may cause birth defects and may complicate the hormonal problems of a woman whose period is merely late (Montreal Health Press, 1974).

If pregnancy is confirmed, the expected date of the baby's birth can be calculated by adding 280 days to the date when the last menstrual period began. This is an average figure—vigorous athletes may give birth 20 days earlier than women who get little exercise, girls are often born several days earlier than boys, and 3 percent of all pregnancies last 300 days or more (McCary, 1973).

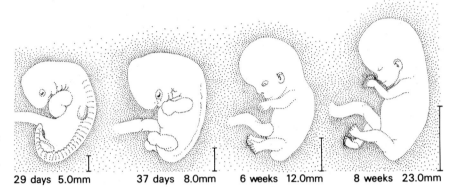

Fig. 6.6 The size and development of the embryo during the first eight weeks, greatly enlarged to show details.

29 days 5.0mm   37 days 8.0mm   6 weeks 12.0mm   8 weeks 23.0mm

FETAL DEVELOPMENT

While the woman is discovering that she is pregnant, the small being she has conceived is undergoing dramatic transformations daily. The term embryo is generally used in referring to the developing human organism in its first eight weeks of existence. Its arms appear as buds, which develop hand plates and then definite finger ridges by the time it is six weeks old. The gill slits turn into **Eustachian tubes** for ears. At seven weeks, its primitive reproductive organs have differentiated into either ovaries or testicles. By the time two months have passed, the embryo, about an inch long, has developed distinctly human features, and from this time until birth is called a fetus. The bumps which will become the penis or clitoris appear in the third month (Rugh and Shettles).

By the end of the third month after conception, the fetal nervous and muscular systems are sophisticated enough to coordinate movement in response to stimuli. If we could touch its lips, the fetus would try to suck as though it were nursing. It can now turn its head, curl its toes, make a fist, and kick its feet, although at 3-1/2 inches it is still so tiny that the woman is usually unable to feel these movements. The fetus is free to move about and grow because it is suspended in the **amniotic fluid** or **"bag of waters"** which fills the uterine cavity during pregnancy.

Studies of infants born **prematurely** at seven months show that reflexes which may be of survival value to them are already well-developed. If held erect, they will try to walk. They know how to search for food by turning toward a touch on the cheek and sucking when their lips are stroked. Some fetuses are so skillful in this respect that they suck their thumbs within the womb. Infants have even been born with callused thumbs (Rugh and Shettles). If startled, seven-month-old "preemies" will throw their arms and legs out and cry as though trying to find something to cling to. Their

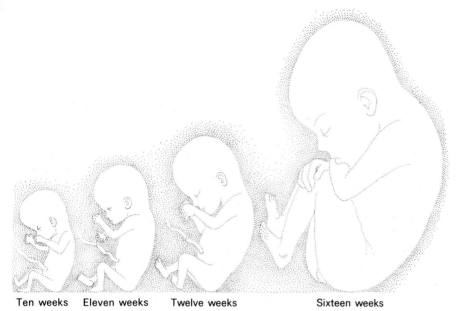

| Ten weeks | Eleven weeks | Twelve weeks | Sixteen weeks |

Fig. 6.7 The development of the fetus from ten to sixteen weeks, shown actual size. After 16 weeks' growth, the fetus is still little more than three inches long in its curled position.

fingers and toes curl around any object placed across them, another apparent adaptation to clinging which probably served our hairier ancestors well. So powerful is the grip of the premature infant that it can hang by its hands and toes from a clothesline (Eibl-Eibesfeldt, 1970).

Despite the sophistication of their motor reflexes, seven-month-old fetuses have only a 10 percent chance of survival if they are born prematurely. They weigh only two or three pounds and, due to the immaturity of their central nervous systems, they are unable to regulate their own body temperature. Both their breathing and their temperature maintenance must be aided by an **incubator** if they are born at this point. By eight months the chance of survival increases to 70 percent, although breathing and temperature control are still a problem.

By the time the fetus reaches full term, it weighs six to eight pounds. It so fills the grossly enlarged uterus that there is very little room for its movement. Although it may be comfortable enough during the day, rocked to sleep by the motion of the woman's body as she goes about her daily activities, it may wake up with a start when the woman lies down to try to get some sleep herself. Forced against her hard backbone, the fetus wriggles vigorously in search of a more comfortable position (Liley, 1969). But despite the crowded conditions within the womb, the fetus somehow manages to turn itself upside down to assume a headfirst position in preparation for its birth.

THE PREGNANT WOMAN

Meanwhile, the woman is hardly aware of the complexity of the changes taking place within her. But from the fifth month on, she can feel the fetus kicking, perhaps to her delight that it is alive, or perhaps to her despair of ever being able to get to sleep or to sit comfortably for any length of time.

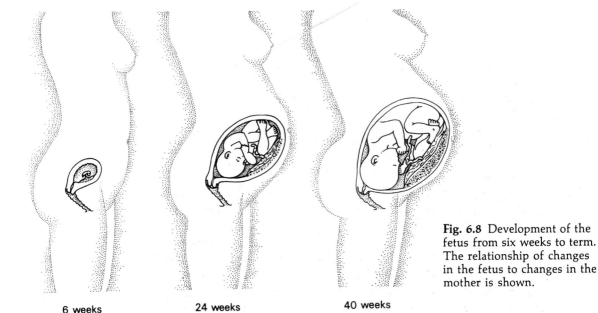

6 weeks   **24 weeks**   **40 weeks**

Fig. 6.8 Development of the fetus from six weeks to term. The relationship of changes in the fetus to changes in the mother is shown.

Aside from the fetal movements, the woman experiences pregnancy as a gradual swelling of her abdomen, often coupled with changes in the way she feels and acts which may be perplexing to both herself and her husband. She feels a need to urinate frequently because of the extra wastes she has to excrete for the fetus and because of its pressure on her bladder. The increased weight and crowding on her internal organs may also cause constipation, numbness in her legs from pinched nerves, and spasms in her abdominal **ligaments.** Since the demands of nourishing and carrying waste products for a fetus step up the volume of blood circulated through her body by about a third, her blood vessels may protrude visibly beneath her skin. She tires easily and should get more sleep than usual (Bradley, 1965).

The high levels of hormonal output during pregnancy may make a woman excitable and jumpy or unexplainably depressed. Pregnant women often find themselves crying for no particular reason. They may feel puffy all over as their increased circulation combines with water retention, which in turn results from salt retention. Increased food demands by the fetus may make the pregnant woman feel dizzy and nauseous, especially during the first three months. Frequent light meals help. A high-protein snack before bed and crackers to nibble on help to ward off morning sickness the next day.

Problems experienced during pregnancy can often be traced to biological factors but a woman's feelings about her pregnancy are just as important to her sense of well-being. Many psychologists claim that unconscious rejection of pregnancy and motherhood may underlie physical symptoms such as nausea, swelling, and constipation (Zemlick and Watson, 1953). Ignorance of what is going on during pregnancy and childbirth may make a woman tense and fearful for herself and the developing fetus. If a child is unwanted, its vigorous movements and the discomforts it causes may make the pregnant woman feel angry and put-upon. Some women worry that pregnancy makes them ugly and lessens their sexual appeal. On the other hand, some women feel—and look—unusually voluptuous during their pregnancies. To some it is a joyful, expectant time; to others, it is frightening or depressing.

In some cases, feelings of depression and anxiety may not disappear after the baby is born, and may even get worse. Fatigue from the extreme efforts of childbirth, rapid hormonal changes, and the sudden responsibilities of parenthood frequently cause a condition known as **postpartum depression.** The fluctuations of mood, feelings of inadequacy or resentment as a new parent, fears about the baby's helplessness, and inability to sleep are severe enough to cause hospitalization in one out of every thousand women who give birth in this country (Boston Women's Health Book Collective, 1976). It is a time when a mother needs all the support she can get from relatives, close friends, and a sympathetic husband. But relatives may be geographically scattered and the father lacking in understanding, jealous of his wife's attentions to their new child, and perhaps overwhelmed himself by his new responsibilities. A ten-year study headed by psychoanalyst Grete Bibring indicates that childbearing may constitute a maturational crisis for the mother similar to puberty and menopause. The physical and psychological imbalances of the postpartum period can lead to emotional growth in the mother if they are eventually resolved, but this may not happen until some time after the baby is born (Bibring, 1961).

Some men undergo the same emotional and even physical upheavals as their wives during pregnancy. A decrease in sexual intercourse during pregnancy may aggravate tensions within a marriage, unless it mirrors decreased sexual desires on the part of both partners. Until recently, doctors routinely forbade intercourse for six weeks before and six weeks after the baby was born. They were worried that either orgasm in the mother or thrusts of the penis might induce labor prematurely—which they sometimes do, but usually when the baby is almost ready to be born anyway—or rupture the membranes of the **amniotic sac,** causing infection. Despite continuing medical disagreement about the safety of intercourse late in pregnancy, many doctors now feel that gentle intercourse throughout pregnancy in positions which do not put the man on top is usually harmless. But they caution that intercourse and genital stimulation of the pregnant woman to orgasm should be avoided if she has abdominal pain, uterine bleeding, expectation of miscarriage, or if the amniotic sac has ruptured prematurely.

Intercourse may usually be safely resumed three or four weeks after childbirth, if the postpartum vaginal bleeding has stopped. But vaginal soreness, low estrogen levels, fear of another pregnancy, depression, and fatigue may often make a woman reluctant to resume sexual relations. If she can help her husband to achieve orgasmic relief from his sexual tentions by means other than intercourse, he may find it easier to accept her reluctance.

DAMAGING INFLUENCES

Old wives' tales to the contrary, most women are not in a delicate condition when they are pregnant. Frequent mild exercise is healthful, good for their sense of well-being, and helpful in preventing backache and building muscle tone for labor. Since the fetus is well cushioned by the amniotic fluid, it will rarely be harmed by jarring even if the expectant mother falls. An extreme example of how well this shelter works is the Welsh woman who delivered a normal baby six months after she was struck by lightning (Tanner and Taylor, 1968).

Despite its cushioning and insulating properties, the uterus cannot shield the fetus from all dangerous outside influences. Many chemicals pass from the pregnant woman's bloodstream through the placenta to the fetus. While her thoughts cannot directly affect the fetus (for instance, her sighting a rabbit will not cause it to be born with a cleft lip, or harelip), her emotions may have some effect. Reactions associated with exhaustion or emotional stress in the woman may make the fetus overactive; although they will not mark the baby with **birthmarks** or predestine it to an unhappy life, they do not provide an optimal environment for the intricacies of human development.

One out of every sixteen babies born in the United States has some kind of birth defect (Kogan, 1973). Almost 1500 different abnormalities present at birth have been identified. They range from deformities such as birthmarks and clubfoot to mental retardation and fatal diseases. Twenty percent of these defects are **hereditary,** or passed on as some kind of genetic weakness from one generation to the next. The rest are **congenital,** caused by something wrong in the fetal environment and not transferable to the next generation. Most congenital defects could have been prevented if the parents had been more cautious.

If the pregnant woman is exposed to certain drugs, diseases, or **radiation,** their destructive effects may reach the fetus and interfere with its normal development. The woman's age may also be linked to fetal abnormalities. The optimal age for childbearing is the period between 20 and 30; babies born to older or younger women are more prone to birth defects. **Mongolism,** for instance, a set of symptoms which includes mental retardation, is found in 1 out of every 50 babies whose mothers are over age 45. Only 1 in 2000 babies born to 25-year-old mothers are mongoloid (Rugh and Shettles).

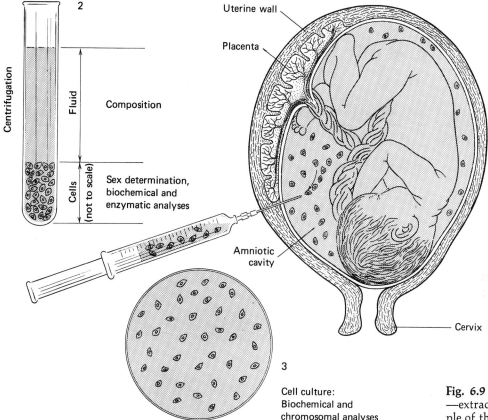

2

Centrifugation

Fluid

Composition

Cells (not to scale)

Sex determination, biochemical and enzymatic analyses

Uterine wall

Placenta

Amniotic cavity

Cervix

3

Cell culture: Biochemical and chromosomal analyses

Fig. 6.9 Amniocentesis —extraction of a sample of the amniotic fluid during pregnancy. This is a new technique for detecting severe hereditary defects in a fetus about midway through the pregnancy. If defects are indicated, the parents can then determine whether or not to have an abortion. The sex of the fetus can also be determined by this method. (Source: Eric T. Pengelley, *Sex and Human Life,* Reading, Mass.: Addison-Wesley, 1974.)

Certain diseases carried by agents small enough to slip through the placenta may infect the fetus during crucial periods in its development. German measles in the expectant mother may cause problems in the fetus ranging from dwarfed brain size and deafness to death. Chicken pox, pneumonia, scarlet fever, and syphilis may so damage the fetus that it is miscarried or else born dead at full term. If fetuses do not die from untreated syphilis in the expectant mother, they may be born with misshaped and shortened limbs, distortions in the face and teeth, severe brain damage, or blindness. Unlike syphilis, gonorrhea cannot cross the placenta to harm the fetus. Instead, it reaches the fetus as it is born, causing eye infections which may lead to blindness. Gonorrhea is so widespread that every state in this country requires that the eyes of all newborns be treated with medication immediately after birth (Grover, 1971).

So many drugs can have adverse effects on the fetus that women of childbearing age—even those who do not know that they are pregnant—are cautioned against taking any medication without the advice of a doctor.

The severe deformities caused by the tranquilizer Thalidomide provide a notorious example of what drugs can do. But it is not yet widely known that even aspirin may cause fetal heart abnormalities. Antihistamines may cause miscarriages or deformities, tranquilizers and antidepressants may have effects similar to Thalidomide, and diuretics may cause fetal kidney problems. Those who take LSD may have deformed babies with chromosomal abnormalities. Use of heroin may cause **convulsions** and sometimes death of the fetus, and morphine addicts may give birth to addicted babies with respiratory problems.

Materials in cigarette smoke can pass through the placenta, impairing the circulation of blood in the fetus and lowering its oxygen content. Women who smoke two packs of cigarettes a day may stunt the growth of the fetus by ten percent, endangering its survival. Smokers are more prone to having miscarriages, premature births, and babies with convulsions than women who do not smoke (Rugh and Shettles).

Modern life exposes pregnant women to many other unnatural influences which may inhibit the normal development of the fetus. Radioactive materials and X-rays may cause chromosomal abnormalities, leukemia, or brain damage. Anesthesia, insecticides, insect repellents, herbicides, defoliants, and food additives are all suspect.

It is extremely important that the pregnant woman eat enough of the right foods to build fetal health. In one study, 94 percent of the expectant mothers whose diets were excellent had perfect babies; 92 percent of those whose diets were deficient in even one food element had babies found to be defective (Hazell, 1969). Although until recently doctors insisted that pregnant women hold their weight gain down by rigid dieting, the Committee on Maternal Nutrition of the National Academy of Sciences and the National Research Council now urge that pregnant women be allowed to make the normal weight gain of about 25 pounds. Most of this will be lost when the baby is born or soon after; the rest will be quickly used up in milk production if the mother chooses to nurse her baby. Many studies have shown that if the pregnant woman is allowed to gain weight normally, labor, delivery, and nursing are likely to be easy for her. Her 7-1/2-to-8-1/2-pound baby is likely to be healthier, smarter, and easier to take care of than the smaller babies born to women who gained less than 20 pounds with their pregnancies (Davis, 1972). The pregnant woman's diet should be high in protein, vitamin- and mineral-rich vegetables, fruits, and whole grains. Protein deficiency in the expectant mother has been linked to low IQ in the child. Other nutritional inadequacies may be responsible for low birth weight, prematurity, infection, and brain damage in the infant and anemia and complications in the woman (Boston Women's Health Book Collective).

CHILDBIRTH

Despite the possibilities that something might go wrong, most fetuses carried full term in this country are born alive. As they leave the protection of their mothers' bodies, most successfully take over their own life-support

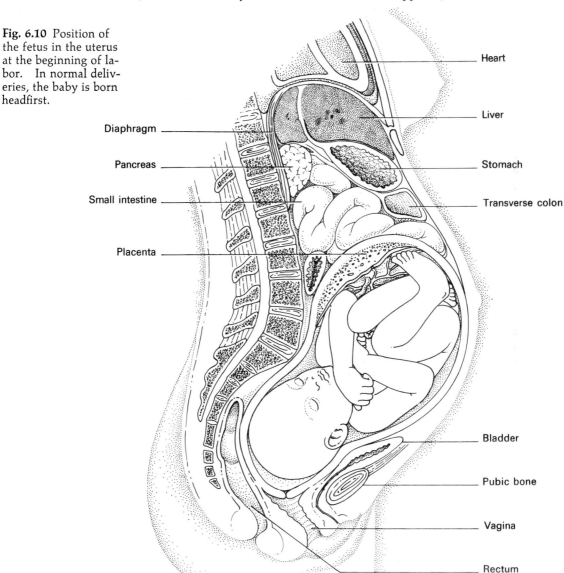

Fig. 6.10 Position of the fetus in the uterus at the beginning of labor. In normal deliveries, the baby is born headfirst.

Heart

Liver

Diaphragm

Pancreas

Stomach

Small intestine

Transverse colon

Placenta

Bladder

Pubic bone

Vagina

Rectum

functions. How the woman views her pregnancy, her physical and emotional readiness for the strain of childbirth, support or lack of it from the expectant father, hospital or home delivery arrangements, and physical factors in the course of the expulsion of the baby will make a difference in whether the birth of her child is a joyous occasion or a time of anxiety and unhappiness.

LABOR AND DELIVERY

The mother's body must work hard to expel a six-to-nine-pound fetus through the narrow **birth canal,** five inches of cervix and vagina hemmed in by the bony pelvis. The birth process, shown in Fig. 6.11 begins without any conscious effort on her part. Triggered by cues which may come from the "ripe" fetus, the uterine muscles begin a series of rhythmic **contractions** which reach a force of about 25-to-30 pounds during the first stage of labor. Pushing the head of the fetus against the cervix for an average of 10½ hours for first-time pregnancy and 6½ hours for women who have given birth before, these contractions normally succeed in stretching the neck of the cervix to a diameter of four inches so that the fetus can pass through. Once it does, the second stage of labor begins.

Usually lasting only 45 minutes to an hour and a half, the second stage is characterized by involuntary pushing efforts by the woman. Without being told to, she automatically holds her breath and bears down with her abdominal muscles as though trying to have a bowel movement, exerting a pressure of perhaps 60 pounds on the fetus (Guttmacher). As the head begins to appear in the vaginal opening, the attending doctor may make a slight incision called an **episiotomy** to allow the vaginal tissues to stretch without tearing. Alternatively, a midwife may have applied hot compresses and massaged the area with oil throughout labor to make it more elastic. As the fetus emerges fully, the doctor usually holds it upside-down by the feet and sucks mucus from its mouth and nose with a **syringe.** If all is well, the baby will gasp or cry as its lungs suddenly fill with air and it begins to breathe for the first time on its own.

The placenta follows the fetus out of the birth canal in what is called the third stage of labor. As it stops its nine-month work of supporting the fetus, the placenta is clamped off and cut where the **umbilical cord** connects to the baby at its navel. After being checked for heart rate, respiratory and muscle tone, crying (considered healthy), and color, and having its eyes treated for possible gonorrheal infection, the baby is wrapped in a blanket and either handed to its mother for her inspection or bustled off to the hospital nursery.

Birth does not always follow this normal pattern. If the pressure on the head of the fetus becomes too great or its oxygen supply drops too low during labor, its heart rate may slow dangerously and its intestines may

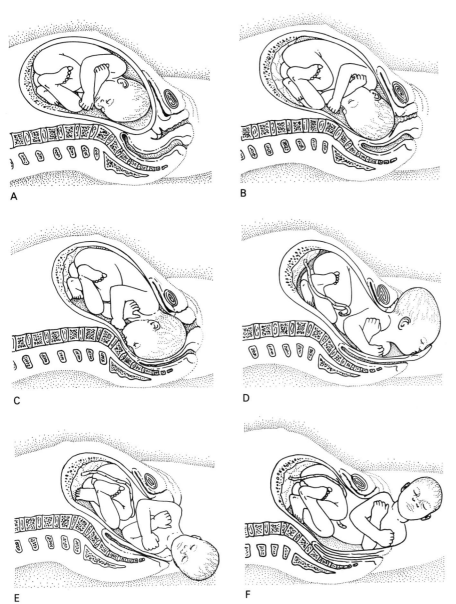

A

B

C

D

Fig. 6.11 The process of birth.   (A) The baby floats in the amniotic fluid before labor begins. (B) Rhythmic contractions force the baby's head against the cervix. (C) Descent through the birth canal begins, with the head gradually rotating and extending. (D) The head crowns and the baby begins to emerge from the birth canal. (E) and (F) Again the baby rotates as first one shoulder and then the other is delivered.

E

F

empty into the amniotic fluid. In such cases, many doctors feel it is wise to speed up the birth process in order to save the fetus by gently pulling it out with a **forceps,** a tong-like tool with two large curved blades. In 3½–4 percent of births, the fetus presents itself buttocks-first. Such **breech births** pose no added dangers to the woman, although they do lengthen labor somewhat, but they are slightly more dangerous to the fetus than birth

Caesarean. Pertaining to birth through an incision in the mother's abdomen, the way in which Julius Caesar was born.

from the better-fitting head-down position. Inadequate pelvic openings, breech presentations, and other conditions which might complicate vaginal delivery are now handled surgically in 6–7 percent of all births in the United States. Removed through an incision in the anesthetized woman's abdomen, babies thus born by **Caesarean section** are as likely to survive as infants delivered without complications through the vagina (Guttmacher).

RELIEVING PAIN

Labor contractions are painful to the pregnant woman. For those who find them unbearable, a variety of drugs may be used to ease the childbearing process. **Analgesics** decrease the sensation of pain; **amnesics** erase the memory of pain; and **anesthetics** block all sensation, either by producing unconsciousness or by cutting off the transmission of pain sensations to the brain. Anesthetics may be general, rendering the mother unconscious, or local, in which case they are injected at the base of the spine to numb sensation in the lower body.

Despite their benefits, so far as the woman's comfort is concerned, drugs can prolong labor by weakening the uterine contractions. They can also cross the placenta and endanger the fetus. Administered in dosages considered safe for the woman's body weight, but not for that of the fetus, analgesics and anesthetics may act as depressants on the fetus's respiratory system. This makes it difficult for newborn babies to begin breathing as they should after birth and may cause mild brain damage from a critical loss of oxygen at the moment of birth. Artificial respiration must often be used to get the baby's breathing started.

There is increasing evidence that the depressant effect of pain-relieving drugs given to the woman persists in the baby long after birth. The development of such behaviors as smiling, cuddliness, motor maturity, self-defensive movements, and habituation to neutral stimuli like the sound of a bell may be significantly interfered with for varying periods of up to one month after birth and perhaps much longer. Behavior patterns such as trembling and fearfulness seem to be linked to the long-term effects of certain tranquilizers (Aleksandrowicz and Aleksandrowicz, 1974).

Even before this evidence began to accumulate, some women questioned the need to be drugged for a natural process and to be asleep during the excitement of delivering their babies. Aided by the pioneering efforts of Dr. Grantly Dick Read and Dr. Fernand Lamaze, many women have learned to cope with the pain of childbearing without resorting to heavy medication. On the premise that pain is a result of muscular tension, which in turn comes from fear of the unknown, they, and their husbands, if they wish, attend special **natural-childbirth** classes which teach them what to expect during labor. The women are taught how to relax with each contraction, often through special breathing exercises, rather than tensing against it, and to take an active part in bearing down during the second

Natural childbirth. Birth without use of pain relievers and with the mother taking an active part in the delivery.

stage of labor. Awake in the delivery room, they may watch the birth of their babies in a slanted mirror. They may hold and even nurse their infants immediately. For many women who thus give birth naturally, with little or no medication to cloud their consciousness or sensations, giving birth is a supremely rewarding emotional experience.

FAMILY-CENTERED CHILDBIRTH

Hospital arrangements for labor, delivery, and the postpartum housing of mother and child are no longer as barren and impersonal as they used to be. The current trend is to approximate the natural family setting we once had in this country when most babies were born at home, without sacrificing the safety of the mother and baby. Recent research has confirmed what mothers have long suspected—that something is wrong with the hospital tradition of separating anxious fathers and stranded mothers during labor and delivery and isolating their babies afterwards in sterile rows in the hospital. Under these circumstances, the woman's labor is prolonged by fear and stress in unfamiliar surroundings, and the forming of crucial ties between mother, father, and baby is delayed until the mother's release from the hopsital, four or more days after she gives birth. Breast-feeding and leisurely body contact, special forms of early closeness between mother and child, are inhibited by such routines, causing physical discomfort and possible emotional damage to both.

There is evidence that the hours—perhaps the first day—after birth constitute a critical bonding period for mother and child. If the mother does not have ample opportunity to fondle and get to know her newborn at this time, she may not develop normal maternal caretaking responses. Maximum early contact with the baby is especially important in stimulating maternal feelings in women who have not been well mothered themselves, who are young or unmarried, do not want their babies, or do not have a good family situation to take them home to. It seems that the more contact the mother has with the baby after birth, the faster she recovers physically and emotionally from the stress of childbearing (McCleary, 1974).

Many hospitals now allow the father to be with the mother in the labor and sometimes even the delivery room. His presence can prevent her from feeling lonely, bored, and scared and often draws them closer together, strengthening bonds which must withstand the responsibilities of parenthood. Some men even act as coaches for their wives, helping them to breathe through the labor pains according to their training in natural-childbirth classes. Some hospitals also allow the father to handle the baby when he visits. If so, he is far more likely to become attached to his child than if he is only allowed to view it through the windows of a nursery.

"Rooming-in" arrangements are now offered as an additional option by some hospitals. Instead of the traditional separation of mother and baby in the maternity wing, broken only by brief periods during which the

Rooming-in. Placement of newborns in the hospital room with their mothers rather than in a communal nursery.

baby is brought to the mother for attempts at breast- or bottle-feeding (in which case she has been given pills to dry up the milk in her breasts), rooming-in allows the baby to stay with the mother in a bassinet next to her bed for most of the day. She can examine and cuddle it all she wants, feed it whenever it is hungry, and receive instructions in its care from nurses.

According to a study comparing 50 mothers rooming-in with their first-borns to 50 first-time mothers who did not have rooming-in, those with rooming-in felt more competent and confident in themselves as mothers when they left the hospital. They felt that they could understand what was wrong when their babies were crying and did not anticipate needing as much help when they got home as mothers who had less experience with their babies. Rooming-in mothers were also quicker to develop a strong maternal attachment to their babies. (Greenberg et al., 1973).

While rooming-in undeniably provides a baby with more loving attention than a nursery does, a new crusader is calling for more sympathetic treatment of the baby as a feeling person from the moment of birth. In his book *Birth Without Violence*, French obstetrician Frederick Leboyer argues that emergence from the hours of compression in the birth canal into a brightly-lit, noisy room is a terrible shock to the newborn. When Leboyer delivers babies, he dims the lights, asks for silence, and refuses to jar the baby into breathing by holding it upside-down and spanking it. Instead, he lays the infant on its mother's belly and allows it to begin breathing gradually before cutting off its life-support by severing the umbilical cord. To further ease the transition, he then immerses the newborn in a bath warmed to body temperature. According to his account, in this approximation of its former weightlessness, the infant relaxes, opens its eyes, looks about in awe and curiosity, moves its limbs tentatively at first and then almost playfully, and sometimes even breaks into a blissful smile. Such behaviors are in striking contrast to the terrified cries and grimaces of conventionally handled newborns. Leboyer's methods are attracting considerable attention in this country, but many doctors worry that babies handled so gently will not begin breathing properly.

HOME BIRTH

Hospitals in the United States have done a good job of protecting the mother from the physical dangers of childbirth. According to Rugh and Shettles, our maternal death rate of less than 3 per 10,000 live births may be the lowest in the world. However, many women are not satisfied with hospital provisions for meeting psychological needs of new parents and their babies. These women have the option of giving birth not in hospitals, but at home, as most women in this country did prior to the 1930s.

Giving birth in a familiar setting, attended by the father and sometimes by a physician or nurse-midwife, may be an intensely personal achievement which strengthens love bonds and the recognition of parenthood. The mother recovers faster at home, the father is given an important role rather than being excluded, and the baby is quickly integrated into the family.

On the other hand, home birth may be a nightmare if complications arise and no emergency care is available. Because of the dangers to both mother and baby, doctors urge that home birth be considered in only a narrow range of low-risk cases. The mother should not be younger than 20 or older than 30, she should have at least a high-school education, a fairly sound income, good nutrition, at least one but not more than three previous full-term births without any complications, and no potentially dangerous medical problems. Women who experience medical problems, vaginal bleeding after the first month of pregnancy, or progressively larger babies with each pregnancy should give birth only in hospitals under medical supervision (Ferguson, 1971; Edwards, 1973). This need not be a bad thing, for the new trend toward family-centered care in hospitals now makes it possible for people to experience the birth of their children as a personally meaningful introduction to parenthood.

Summary

1. The purpose of this chapter is to describe the processes of conception, pregnancy, and childbirth in humans.

2. A human baby is the product of the union of an egg cell from a woman, released once a month from her ovaries, and a sperm cell from a man, produced in the testicles constantly from puberty to death. The point at which the egg is fertilized by the sperm is called conception.

3. Once it is fertilized, the egg (now called a zygote) begins to divide into more and more cells. This cell mass implants itself into the uterine lining where it draws nutrients and oxygen from the mother's bloodstream through the placenta, and excretes body wastes in exchange.

4. The cell mass, known as an embryo until the eighth week and a fetus thereafter, in a normal pregnancy develops over nine months' time into a human organism with the potential to survive in the outside world.

5. During pregnancy, the mother must be careful to avoid exposing herself and the fetus to damaging influences such as diseases, drugs, radiation, or inadequate nutrition, since these may affect the fetus, through the mother, and interfere with its normal development. While the fetus is developing and changing, the pregnant woman also experiences physical and emotional changes due to hormonal changes, increased body demands, and her personal feelings about her pregnancy.

6. When the fetus is ready to be delivered, the mother goes into the first stage of labor—a series of rhythmic contractions of the uterine muscles which

forces the fetus out of the uterus through the cervix and into the birth canal. These contractions are painful and a variety of drugs may be used to ease the process, although "natural childbirth" is increasingly popular. In the second stage of labor, the woman involuntarily pushes down with her abdominal muscles and the fetus is pushed out of the birth canal and into the world. The placenta follows the fetus out of the birth canal in the third stage of labor, and the umbilical cord is cut.

7. In recent years, hospitals have tried to approximate the natural family setting. Fathers are allowed to be present during the delivery and mother and baby often stay in the same hospital room. These arrangements have beneficial psychological consequences for mother, father, and baby.

Key Concepts

Pregnancy	Amniotic fluid
Ovulation	Umbilical cord
Menstruation	Stages of delivery
Puberty	Postpartum depression
Fertilization	Hereditary
Conception	Congenital
Zygote	Caesarean birth
Embryo	Natural childbirth
Fetus	Rooming-in
Placenta	Home birth

Review and Discussion

1. Can you recall any myths you heard about where babies come from, or misconceptions you had relating to conception, pregnancy, or birth?

2. Give the essentials of sperm and egg development and fertilization.

3. How were you and your brothers and sisters born? In a hospital? At home? With or without anesthetic? How does this compare with the way your parents came into the world?

4. Is it necessary to have a medical doctor present for the successful delivery of a baby?

5. As a future mother or father, what circumstances for delivery do you think you would prefer? Why?

Suggested Readings

BEAN, L. A. (1972). *Methods of Childbirth: A Complete Guide to Childbirth Classes and Maternity Care.* Garden City, N.Y.: Doubleday.

Discusses methods of childbirth from Lamaze (natural) to totally anesthetized birth. Explains what occurs to mother and fetus during the process of birth and describes methods of preparation for childbirth (breathing exercises, physical exercises). Also covers how husbands can help, history of childbirth practices, and other birth-related topics.

FLANAGAN, G. L. (1962). *Nine Months of Life.* New York: Simon and Schuster.

This brief book on human development before birth is thorough and easy to read and understand. Liberally illustrated with black-and-white photographs of fetuses at various stages of development.

LEBOYER, F. (1975). *Birth Without Violence.* New York: Alfred A. Knopf.

Leboyer's method of childbirth is described in a lyrical, poetic manner. Illustrated throughout with black-and-white photographs of a delivery.

RUGH, R., AND L. B. SHETTLES (1971). *From Conception to Birth.* New York: Harper & Row.

Verbally and visually describes the growth and development of the human fetus. Illustrated with drawings and color photographs taken at different stages. Also covers the basics of genetics and heredity, reproductive anatomy, prenatal care, and family planning.

TANZER, DEBORAH, WITH J. L. BLOCK (1972). *Why Natural Childbirth?* Garden City, N.Y.: Doubleday.

Using tests and interviews with expectant couples, Dr. Tanzer studies the psychological impact of childbirth in two groups, one using the natural method, the other using anesthesia. Outlines the benefits of natural childbirth method to father, mother, and family unit as a whole.

Family Planning:
Contraception, Abortion, Increasing Fertility
7

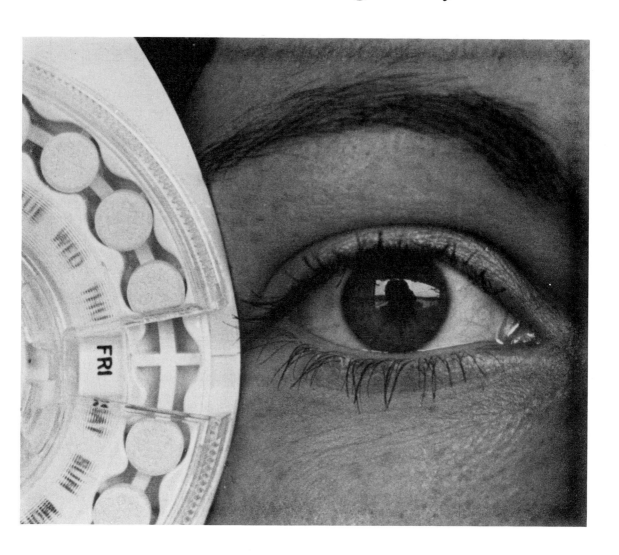

If the average woman began having intercourse at the age of 17 and never made any attempt to prevent pregnancy, she would eventually give birth to 13 children (Guttmacher, 1973). Before the industrial revolution, the large families thus produced were an asset. Children were useful as free labor for jobs ranging from churning the butter to working in the fields. Large families were a symbol of a man's virility, a secure identity for a woman, and a fulfillment of what was seen as a duty to God to increase and multiply.

But times have changed, and with them, attitudes about unrestrained human reproduction. In an urban, industrial society, children are an economic burden. Each new baby stretches the family's available money thinner in its needs for food, clothing, housing, health care, and schooling. On a global scale, more babies are straining already limited resources. Food production is particularly critical. At its present rate of growth, the earth's population could double within 33 years; the supply of land available for farming cannot (Meadows et al., 1972).

**Zero population growth.
A condition in which
the number of births
equals the number of
deaths, thus creating a
stable population size.**

To ward off famine as well as the environmental problems of overcrowding, advocates of zero population growth now urge that couples voluntarily limit their families to two children. ZPG pleas have coincided with a growing awareness on the part of women that they may find fulfillment outside the home as something other than baby-making machines.

EFFECTS OF FAMILY PLANNING

The result has been a dramatic reduction in the U.S. birth rate. Between the **baby boom** high reached in 1957 and the year 1973, there was a 44 percent drop in the general **fertility rate**—down to 69.3 births per 1,000 women aged 15 to 44 from the 1957 high of 122.9. Wives in the United States now expect to have an average of 2.5 babies. Young wives (aged 18–24) expect an average of only 2.2 births, many of them stating that they prefer to remain childless or to have only one child (*Family Planning Perspectives*, January/February 1975). As the Census Bureau optimistically predicted in its fertility expectations report for 1973, "It appears that the two-child family will be the wave of the future." But even if today's couples only replace themselves by limiting their families to two children, it will still take many years for our population to stop growing. This is because the number of couples having babies is now being swollen by the young adults born during the baby boom of the fifties.

FEWER UNWANTED CHILDREN
This rapid decline in fertility reflects a sharp reduction in unplanned births, an advantage for society as well as for unwilling parents. A study was made recently of 212 nine-year-old children who were known to have been unwanted since they were born to mothers who had been denied abortions.

Compared to other children their age, the unwanted children "suffered significantly more illness, were less socially acceptable to their peers and teachers, and seemed less able to live up to their inherent intellectual capacities" (Dytrych et al., 1975, p. 165).

From the parents' point of view, a survey of 2,164 adults has revealed that while Americans seem to be far happier married than single, couples rate their general life satisfaction highest in the period before they have children, and next highest when their children are over age 17. For the majority of adults, the stresses of parenthood—little time to be alone together, being tied down, harassment by noise and squabbling, economic burdens—seem to offset the emotional rewards. Americans continue to have babies (84 percent of all married couples have at least one child), in order to keep the family line going, to enjoy caring for them and watching them grow up, to satisfy grandparents, and often by accident—but children are not as popular as they used to be (Campbell, 1975).

BENEFITS FOR CHILDREN

Methods of birth control now available make it possible for couples not only to limit the size of their families, but also to space their children as they like. Even though it is biologically possible to have a baby each year, a planned interval of two or three years between pregnancies is best for the health of both the mother and her children. Statistics show that a gap of two years between the time one pregnancy ends and another begins yields the lowest rates of newborn deaths and prematurity. An interval of three years or more is linked with the highest chances of surviving childhood (Day, 1967).

In Holland, careful study of 386,114 people has indicated that those who come from small families are brighter than those from large ones. When separated into families of white-collar, blue-collar, and farm workers, these results still hold up (Zajonc, 1975). And contrary to the popular notion that children from large families are more well adjusted, a survey of 256 rural Midwestern fifth-graders showed that those from smaller families had better relationships with their parents and siblings and were somewhat less likely to be socially maladjusted. (Hawkes et al., 1958). According to Ivan Nye (1952), when small-family children reach adolescence, they will be far more likely to have good relations with their parents than those from larger families.

Putting all these things together, it seems that today's optimal family would consist of two children born about three years apart while the mother is between 20 and 30 years old (when there is the least possibility of birth defects). Such children would stand the greatest chance of being smart and healthy, and they would be most likely to get along well with each other and their parents.

Birth control. Limiting the number of children born by use of various procedures for preventing conception or terminating unwanted pregnancies.

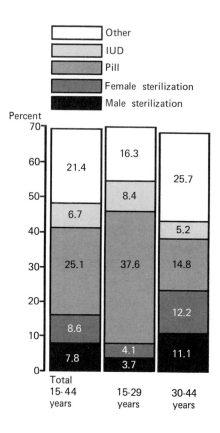

Fig. 7.1 Methods of contraception in use by currently married women, United States, 1973. An estimated 18.5 million, or 69.6 percent, of all married couples in the United States were using contraceptive methods to plan their families in 1973, representing a continuing increase in the proportion of married couples using contraception which has been observed through the sixties. The two columns at the right show differences in method used between couples aged 15–29 and those 30–44. (Source: USDHEW, 1976, Monthly Vital Statistics Report 25:7 Supplement.)

CONTRACEPTIVES

Whatever their intentions, couples cannot limit their family size unless they have access to an effective means of birth control. The only alternative is total **abstinence** from sexual intercourse, for there is a 2–4 percent chance of pregnancy with each unprotected intercourse at any time in the menstrual cycle (Lippes et al., 1975). Avoidance of intercourse has been the socially prescribed way for unmarried couples to avoid pregnancy. However, many people are unwilling to forego the pleasure and intimacy of sexual intercourse just because they are not prepared to undertake the responsibilities of parenthood at that particular time.

ANCIENT MEANS OF BIRTH CONTROL
People have tried to prevent conception of unwanted children throughout recorded history. If their primitive methods were unsuccessful—as many were—they often resorted to infanticide. Females were especially likely to be killed because they would not be hunters but they would still have to be fed. Even as late as 1932, there were only 48 females under age 18 for

every 100 young males among the Netsilik Eskimos, who practiced selective infanticide (Guttmacher).

Women of other times and other cultures have been instructed to prevent pregnancy by wearing magic charms, jumping up and down or sneezing after intercourse, and nursing their children for years in the hope of preventing ovulation. They have coated or plugged their vaginas with a variety of substances, including animal ear wax, elephant or crocodile dung, whitewash, grass, feathers, rags, pepper, and balls of lint soaked with acid liquids. They have stoically drunk concoctions like infusion of gunpowder, froth from a camel's mouth, honey laced with dead bees, and water left from the washing of dead bodies. There have always been attempts at home-made abortion, often with disastrous results. Occasionally, it was the man who was given the responsibility for preventing conception, by methods such as rubbing his penis with onion juice, tar, or rock salt (Havemann, 1967; Rugh and Shettles, 1971).

Contraception—the prevention of pregnancy—is now much less rigorous and far more effective than these ancient methods, thanks to our understanding of the biological processes involved. "The Pill" offers almost 100-percent effectiveness if used properly; other measures are nearly as successful.

OPPOSITION TO CONTRACEPTION

Despite the fact that contraceptives now available are not only effective but also relatively safe, cheap, convenient, and free from interference with intercourse, a 1971 survey of sexually experienced women between the ages of 15 and 19 showed that 80 percent of them had engaged in intercourse without taking any contraceptive measures. As a result, 3 out of 10 of them became pregnant. Most had their babies; most were illegitimate. Why? Seven out of 10 of these young women said they did not think they could become pregnant either because of the time of month, the infrequency of their sexual encounters, or their youth. Three out of 10 had no contraceptives either because they did not know where to get them, thought they were probably too expensive, were unaware that they could prevent pregnancy, or simply did not have them available when they needed them. Almost a fourth said that using contraceptives would have been inconvenient, would have made intercourse less spontaneous or less pleasurable. Nearly one-sixth (17 out of 100) stated that they were either trying to become pregnant or did not care if they did (many in this category had marriage plans). Only about one-eighth (about 12 out of 100) claimed to have moral or medical objections to contraception (Shah et al., 1975). Most of these arguments against birth control hold little weight, and even those with serious religious objections usually have available a limited choice of contraceptive measures.

While the Protestant and Jewish faiths now uphold the right to family planning with unlimited personal choice of contraceptives, Pope Paul reaffirmed in 1968 the traditional doctrine for Catholic couples: procreation is the most important reason for marriage and for the sex act, with companionship of only secondary importance. Only abstinence or the rhythm method of temporary monthly abstinence can be used to interfere with this goal by preventing pregnancy. On the other hand, Catholic theologians at all levels have indicated that they feel that the number and spacing of children and the means of birth control should be personal decisions. According to the liberal Catholic view, conjugal love is of equal importance in marriage to having and rearing children, and the use of chemical or mechanical contraception in responsible family planning is not morally wrong. Birth control is desirable, in this view, in the face of legitimate concerns about world population pressure, the difficulties of providing the necessities of life and loving personal attention for too many children at once, and the need to preserve the love bond between parents which holds the family together (Guttmacher et al., 1969).

Even when there are no religious objections, The Group for the Advancement of Psychiatry points out, there may be unconscious psychological factors which keep people from using contraceptives, even when they do not really want children. They may subconsciously want to test their fertility or perpetuate the excitement of taking a chance. Women may have subtle resentments about pills or foreign objects inside their bodies. In one experiment, 70 percent of the women who had been given sugar pills which they were told were oral contraceptives developed side effects. Pregnancy may be subconsciously sought by women who are uncomfortable about intercourse and would like an excuse to abstain from it. Some feel guilty about sidestepping motherhood or denying their husband's virility by preventing pregnancy. Others may feel most fulfilled as women when they are carrying life within them or caring for a young child. Social pressures to have at least two children, especially by would-be grandparents, may intensify such feelings. As a result of these various social and psychological factors, an estimated 30 percent of the children born in 1970 were unwanted by at least one parent (Group for the Advancement of Psychiatry, 1973).

VARIETY OF METHODS AVAILABLE

Failure rate. The likelihood of pregnancy occurring during one year in 100 sexually active women using a particular method of contraception.

To complicate matters further, the science and politics of birth control are in a state of flux. Research into the effectiveness and safety of newer methods turns up new considerations—and new possibilities—so rapidly that information on this subject is soon out of date. The carefulness with which contraceptives are used makes a big difference in their effectiveness, so different surveys have turned up different **failure rates** for the methods currently in use. Effectiveness also seems to vary with the age of the woman, with younger women incurring more unwanted pregnancies than older but still fertile women using the same contraceptive method. There is at least general agreement on the order of effectiveness, with the Pill always rated first, usually followed by the IUD, condom, diaphragm, foam, withdrawal, rhythm, spermicides other than foam, and the douche.

Other methods being investigated include plastic devices impregnated with a pregnancy-preventing hormone which can be either inserted into the uterus or the vagina or implanted in a muscle; reversible surgical placement of plastic bags over each ovary to trap eggs as they are released; vaccines which make a woman immune to sperm; and pills to inhibit sperm production or transportation in men without altering their sexual responsiveness. Much current research centers around **prostaglandins,** hormone-like substances found in both men and women which, among many other functions, seem to affect muscle activity. Since prostaglandins can produce contractions of the uterus, they may be used to induce labor, bring on delayed menstruation to terminate possible early unwanted pregnancies, and stimulate abortions.

Birth control advice is available from doctors and from Planned Parenthood—World Population (PPWP) chapters in 190 United States cities. PPWP offers not only contraceptives but also counseling and services in relation to sterilization, abortion, sex education, infertility, and **genetic defects.** The aim of PPWP is, "each child wanted joyfully by responsible parents." To further this aim it feels that no one who seeks contraceptive advice should be denied it, regardless of age or marital status (Guttmacher).

METHODS IN CURRENT USE

Though contraceptives are widely used, there is still resistance to artificial means of preventing pregnancy. It sometimes seems that the more effective a method of contraception is, the more controversy there is about its use. In the following discussion of commonly used methods, we begin with the least controversial.

The Rhythm Method. **Rhythm,** the only method of birth control officially sanctioned at this time by the Roman Catholic Church, is based on avoidance of intercourse during the woman's fertile period. The problem is to figure out just when that is. Ovulation usually occurs in the middle of the menstrual cycle, about 12–16 days before menstruation begins. As a Planned Parenthood manual points out, knowing when that will be is like saying to a passenger on a bus who asks for directions, "Watch me and get off one stop before I do" (Planned Parenthood of New York City, 1973).

The time of ovulation can be guessed by keeping track of the dates when menstruation starts and stops over many months. If menstrual peri-

Rhythm. A method of birth control based on exact timing of the phases of the menstrual cycle.

Method	Failure Rate: pregnancies per 100 women per year	How It Works	Possible Side Effects	Drawbacks	Physician Involvement
Sterilization	Tubal ligation: 0.04 Vasectomy: 0.15	Female (tubal ligation): Fallopian tubes are cut, tied, blocked or removed to prevent eggs from reaching the uterus. Male (vasectomy): Small piece of vas deferens is removed to prevent sperm from getting from testes to prostate.	None known.	Intended to be permanent rather than reversible.	Operations must be performed by a physician.
Oral Contraceptives ("The Pill")	4	The pill, taken daily, contains a synthetic progesterone and estrogen, which prevent ovulation from occurring. Should it occur, the progestin and estrogen make enough changes in the uterine environment to make it hostile to implantation.	*Bad:* Possible thromboembolism (blockage of major blood vessel by blood clot) may increase risk of gallstones; raise blood pressure. *Good:* Lessens risk of benign breast tumors, ovarian cysts; menstrual cycles more regular; lessens premenstrual tension and depression; may help control acne.	Must remember to take the pill every day; not safe for all women to take (esp. after 40); may have nuisance effects, e.g. color changes in skin; fluid retention; increased appetite and weight gain. May cause delays of up to a year in regular ovulation after discontinuing its use.	Doctor's prescription required. Periodic check advised.
Intrauterine Device (IUD)	5	Small plastic device inserted into uterus by doctor; precise reason it works is not known — thought to prevent pregnancy by disturbing uterine environment.	Can cause bleeding or cramps.	May be expelled by uterus without wearer knowing; some IUDs can't be used by women who haven't had previous pregnancy.	Doctor required for insertion of IUD into uterus. Periodic check advised.
Condom (prophylactic)	10	Sheath of rubber, latex, or animal membrane is placed over the erect penis before ejaculation; semen is caught in sheath and doesn't reach vagina unless some is spilled as man withdraws or condom ruptures.	None.	Foreplay must be interrupted to apply; some men claim it dulls sensation; must be careful when withdrawing from vagina.	None.
Diaphragm and Cervical Cap	17	A domed rubber cap, fitted to the vagina, forms a physical barrier that covers the cervix and prevents sperm penetration; spermicidal cream or jelly must be used with it; can be inserted up to 2 hours prior to intercourse and must be left in at least 6 hours after.	Spermicidal cream or jelly may cause vaginal irritation.	Diaphragm must be put in and taken out with each copulation; may become dislodged if coital position with woman on top is used; may slip due to widening of vaginal barrel if woman has an orgasm.	Doctor required for fitting diaphragm to the individual.

Method		How Used			
Chemical Contraceptives	22 for foam; up to 50 or more for others.	Spermicidal creams, jellies, foams, or suppositories that immobilize and kill sperm; must be inserted into vagina 5–15 minutes before ejaculation so they can disperse throughout the vagina.	Chemicals in the contraceptive may irritate vagina.	May be messy and leak out after intercourse; interferes with process of intercourse.	None.
Withdrawal (coitus interruptus)	20–25	Male withdraws from vagina before ejaculation; interferes with process of intercourse.	None.	Depends entirely on the man's self-control; can cause anxiety for both partners; drops of semen which leak from erect penis before ejaculation may contain enough sperm to cause pegnancy.	None.
Rhythm	21	Planned abstinence from intercourse during the female's fertile period after ovulation; to determine fertile period, she must keep track of her temperature daily and the length of her menstrual cycles to determine when ovulation may take place.	None.	Unpredictable irregular menstrual cycles make calculations inaccurate; planned abstinence is contrary to normal sexual urges.	Supervision by a doctor advised.
Douching	40	Female must flush all semen out of vagina *immediately* after intercourse with a syringe full of water and/or other spermicidal liquid.	None.	Has the worst record of any contraceptive method. Since sperm can swim into cervical canal as soon as 90 seconds after ejaculation, woman must rush to bathroom to douche.	None.
Morning After Treatment (diethylstilbestrol)	Undetermined	High dosage of estrogen taken within 72 hours of intercourse will prevent pregnancy; usually administered only in emergency cases, such as rape or incest.	Nausea, vomiting, bleeding, thromboembolism; if a woman is pregnant by previous intercourse and takes the morning after pill, the diethylstilbestrol may cause cervical or vaginal cancer in female offspring.	Severe side effects possible.	Must be prescribed by a physician.

Fig. 7.2 A comparison of various methods of contraception.

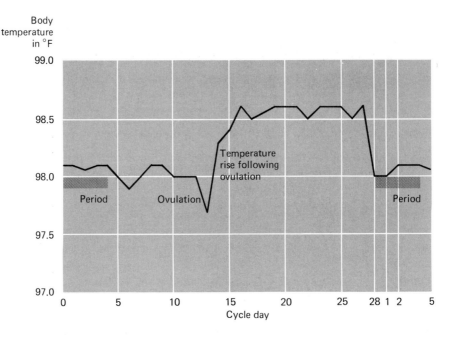

Body
temperature
in °F

Fig 7.3 A sample chart of changes in body temperature during a woman's menstrual cycle. There is an obvious drop at the time of ovulation and a sharp rise after ovulation.

ods are always about 28 days apart, the time of ovulation may be fairly predictable. Temperature-taking with a special thermometer may also help to establish the time of ovulation, since it is characterized by a slight drop and then a rise to about half a degree above normal. But if there is a variation of ten days or more over the course of one year in the intervals between periods, the rhythm method cannot be relied upon for birth control. (Rugh and Shettles).

To be at all successful, rhythm must be supervised by a doctor, records must be painstakingly kept, temperature must be taken every morning before even getting out of bed, and intercourse must be strictly avoided during the unsafe period. Because sperm can remain viable for up to 72 hours in the fallopian tubes, and the egg may be receptive to fertilization for 24 hours after it leaves the ovary, intercourse is unsafe not only during the five days when ovulation might take place, but also for an additional three to four days before this possible ovulation period and at least one day after it.

A new method for determining when the fertile period occurs is the Billings method—named after the Australian researchers John and Evelyn Billings who developed it. Instead of body temperature, it uses litmus paper to test secretions from the uterus as they flow down into the vagina, with colors telling whether intercourse could result in pregnancy. This procedure is said to be more reliable than the temperature method, but it requires abstention from intercourse for about half of each menstrual cycle (Askins, 1976).

Planned abstinence is contrary to normal sexual urges—which for the woman may be at their height during her unsafe fertile period—and may build tension within a marriage unless both partners are committed to the use of the method. Because of mistakes in calculation, unpredictable irregularities in the menstrual cycle, and failures of willpower, an estimated 21 out of 100 women using the rhythm method for a year will still become pregnant (Ryder, 1973).

Withdrawal.   In one of the oldest known methods of preventing pregnancy, the man withdraws from the vagina before he ejaculates. Although **withdrawal** (*coitus interruptus,* "being careful," or "pulling out") is medically safe for both partners and requires no equipment, it is entirely dependent on the man's self-control. If any of his semen touches even the lips of the vagina, the sperm may be capable of making their way up the fallopian tubes. And the drops of fluid which leak from the erect penis before ejaculation may contain enough sperm to cause pregnancy. The effectiveness of this method varies widely depending on the motivation of the couple (McCary, 1973).

Some couples are able to maintain a healthy, well-adjusted sex life using withdrawal. For others, it creates anxiety, with both partners worrying that the man may not make it out in time and the woman sometimes left unsatisfied by the interruption of intercourse. Despite its popularity elsewhere in the world, withdrawal is used exclusively by fewer than 5 percent of American couples; perhaps 18 percent use the method occasionally, particularly as an emergency measure when nothing else is available (Havemann).

Douching.   If withdrawal is disruptive to normal enjoyment of intercourse, **douching** may be even more so. This method requires that the woman rush to the bathroom immediately after the man ejaculates to try to flush all of his semen out of her vagina with water from a syringe or douche bag. Lemon juice, vingear, alum, or mild soap are sometimes added to the water as **spermicides;** other products may irritate the vagina if used frequently (Guttmacher; Pengelley, 1974).

Spermicides. Chemical substances, used as contraceptives, which immobilize or destroy sperm.

Since sperm can swim into the cervical canal as soon as 90 seconds after ejaculation (Pengelley), it is surprising that douching ever works at all. It has the worst rating of any contraceptive: 40 pregnancies per 100 woman-years. In other words, of 100 women using douching as their only method of contraception for a year, 40 will become pregnant during the year (Ryder). The best that can be said for douching is that it is better than nothing.

Condom.   The condom, sometimes called a rubber, safe, **prophylactic,** or skin, is a relatively effective method of contraception if used properly. It is cheap, medically safe, easy to use, and available without prescription from drugstores and family-planning associations. It consists simply of a 7-1/2-

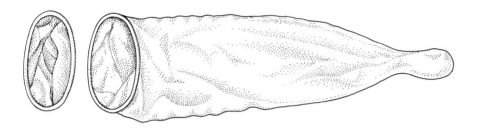

Fig. 7.4 Condom. This is a relatively safe and inexpensive contraceptive device. Worn over the penis during intercourse, it also provides some protection against spread of venereal diseases.

inch disposable sheath of rubber, latex, or animal membrane which is placed on the erect penis before ejaculation (see Fig. 7.4). Semen is caught and held within the sheath and thus prevented from reaching the vagina unless some is spilled as the man withdraws or the condom ruptures. Careful use, including grasping the ring at the base of the condom during withdrawal, will prevent the first risk, and the estimated 750 million condoms manufactured each year in this country (McCary, 1975) are carefully checked for flaws before being put on the market. Condoms fail to prevent pregnancy in 10 cases per 100 woman-years (Ryder).

The fact that foreplay must be interrupted for the application of the condom is considered a drawback by some couples. To others, it enhances excitement, especially if the woman helps to put the condom on. Some men claim that condoms dull their sensations, but those in current use are only 0.0025-inch thick (Montreal Health Press, 1974).

Diaphragm. Many women prefer that they themselves wear a mechanical barrier to sperm penetration of the cervix. The idea of covering the cervix to prevent conception is not new. Women once stuffed their vaginas with gums, leaves, seed pods, and wool; Casanova had his female partners place a squeezed lemon over the cervix to keep his sexual exploits from bearing fruit (Guttmacher).

The **diaphragm,** a removable domed rubber cap for the cervix, appeared in 1882 and is still widely used today. Used along with a spermicidal cream or jelly, it is harmless and prevents pregnancy in all but 17 cases per 100 woman-years (Ryder). It may be inserted up to two hours before coitus and must be left in place for at least six hours afterwards. It should be properly fitted by a doctor and carefully inserted so that it forms a sperm-proof dam across the cervix (see Fig. 7.5). Since the diaphragm rests at the upper end of the vagina, it does not interfere with intercourse and should not diminish the sexual pleasure of either partner or cause the woman any discomfort. It may, though rarely, slip out of place if the woman has an orgasm, due to the widening of the vaginal barrel. Coital positions in which the woman is on top may also dislodge the device (Montreal Health Press). Since diaphragms must be put in and taken out with each **copulation,** their effectiveness depends on the woman's motivation to prevent pregnancy.

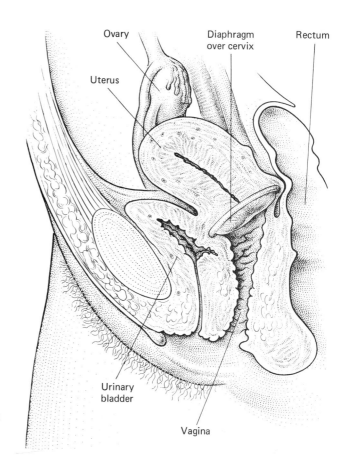

Ovary

Uterus

Diaphragm
over cervix

Rectum

Urinary
bladder

Vagina

Fig. 7.5 Cross section of the female pelvis showing diaphragm in position. Generally used in conjunction with a jelly or cream, the diaphragm blocks sperm from entry into the uterus and thus prevents conception. (Source: Eric T. Pengelley, *Sex and Human Life*, Reading, Mass.: Addison-Wesley, 1974.)

The **cervical cap,** far more popular in Europe than in the United States, helps to overcome the failures inherent in coitus-related devices like the diaphragm or the condom which may go unused if sexual excitement has progressed too far. It, too, fits over the cervix, but is smaller and deeper than the diaphragm and may be left in the vagina from one menstrual period to the next. The problem is that it is harder to position properly than the diaphragm; some women find its insertion impossible (Havemann). Used with a spermicide, the cap and the diaphragm are equally effective (Guttmacher).

Chemical Contraceptives. Creams, jellies, foams, **suppositories,** and tablets of spermicidal substances which immobilize and kill sperm may be inserted into the vagina before intercourse. The best of these are *aerosol foams* which easily spread throughout the vagina and have the additional advantage of acting as a physical barrier over the cervix. Foam carries a failure rating of 22 pregnancies per 100 woman-years (Ryder); creams and

jellies are considerably less effective and should only be used along with a diaphragm. All should be given 5–15 minutes to disperse themselves across the cervix before the man ejaculates. Suppositories and tablets must melt in the vagina before they can be effective, so must be inserted at least 15 minutes before ejaculation.

IUDs. A major problem with many of the contraceptives listed so far is that action must be taken shortly before intercourse occurs. This may call for extreme self-control at a time when sexual drives are strongly aroused. Only very strong motivation to avoid pregnancy ensures that **coitus-related** methods will be used with each intercourse.

The **intrauterine device** (IUD), one of the most effective contraceptives now used, has the advantage of being coitus-unrelated. A small plastic shape inserted into the uterus by a doctor, the IUD prevents pregnancy for several years with no action on the part of either partner, aside from occasional checks to make sure that it is still in place. Intercourse with an IUD as the contraceptive can be completely spontaneous and largely free from fear of pregnancy, for the best of the devices have a failure rate of only 5 pregnancies per 100 woman-years (Ryder).

Like the pebbles inserted into the uteri of female camels to keep them from getting pregnant during long desert treks, the intrauterine device prevents pregnancy by somehow disturbing the uterine environment. Although no one is sure just how IUDs work, the constantly irritating presence of a foreign body seems to cause an accumulation of scavenger white-blood cells in the uterus which destroy sperm cells. It also seems to inflame the lining of the uterus so that it becomes unreceptive to the **implantation** of a fertilized egg (Mishell, 1975).

IUDs come in a variety of designs. All-plastic models, like the double-S-shaped **Lippes loop** and the ram's-horn **Saf-t-coil**, have been used safely for many years. The smaller crab-shaped plastic **Dalkon Shield** gained popularity as a device which could be used by women who had never been pregnant, but it has been withdrawn from the market because of hazards connected with its use of a braided thread. The **Copper 7,** a plastic device in the shape of a 7 wrapped with thin copper wire, is small enough to be easily inserted in never-pregnant women. The copper seems to increase the concentration of sperm-destroying white-blood cells in the uterus (Guttmacher). A T-shaped IUD which continually releases tiny dosages of the hormone progesterone, making the uterus even more hostile to implantation, may soon be approved for general use. But the **Progesterone T** is not

Fig. 7.6 IUDs. Various forms of intrauterine devices inserted by a doctor into the female's uterus and worn continuously to prevent conception.

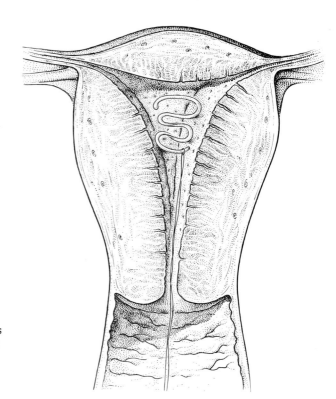

Fig. 7.7 Lippes loop in position in the uterus. The thread projecting from the cervix enables the woman to check at intervals to ensure that the IUD has not been ejected from the uterus. (Source: Eric T. Pengelley, *Sex and Human Life*, Reading, Mass.: Addison-Wesley, 1974.)

expected to significantly lower the risk of pregnancy, and it must be re-placed each year.

There are safety problems associated with IUDs. They sometimes cause excessive bleeding and cramps and, in about 10 percent of women, the uterus itself manages to expel the IUD within a year of its insertion (Guttmacher). Since this may happen without the user's knowing it, IUDs are provided with a nylon thread "tail" which is left protruding from the cervix (see Fig. 7.7). The woman should occasionally feel it to make sure that her IUD is still in place.

Despite drawbacks, IUDs are worn comfortably and safely by between 3 and 4 million United States women. Compared with the risk of death from pregnancy itself as well as from method-related causes, the IUD is the safest of all modern contraceptives. Among 100,000 women with IUDs engaging in intercourse for a period of a year, the death rate is only 0.74. This rate is lower than that of the Pill, 3 deaths per 100,000, all related to Pill use; and far lower than that of women who have used no contracep-tive at all and die from the dangers of pregnancy itself, 12 deaths per 100,000.

The Pill. Oral contraceptives, collectively known as "the Pill," are 96-percent effective in preventing pregnancy (Ryder) and allow complete spontaneity of intercourse, without specific precoital preparation as with the diaphragm or the condom. They are not safe for all women, however.

Most oral contraceptives contain **synthetic** progesterone (progestin) and estrogen which trick the ovaries into not ovulating, just as high levels of real estrogen and progesterone do during a true pregnancy, to prevent overlapping pregnancies. These synthetic hormones also cause changes in the uterus which make pregnancy impossible even if ovulation does occur.

Since estrogen causes most of the complications experienced by pill-users, attempts have been made to decrease the estrogen content to the lowest possible level which will still prevent pregnancy. The new, low-dose pills contain less than 0.05 milligrams of estrogen. A progestin-only mini-pill was developed to sidestep the problems associated with estrogen use, but it is less effective than those with estrogen and more likely to cause irregular or heavy bleeding. And if the mini-pill is not taken at exactly the same time every day, it will not prevent pregnancy. If one of the daily estrogen-progesterone, or combination, pills is forgotten, the chances of pregnancy are still very slim. However, if two combination pills are missed, it becomes necessary to use some other contraceptive for the rest of the cycle (Connell, 1975).

Use of the Pill may cause side-effects. The major complication doctors watch for is **thromboembolism,** the potentially fatal blockage of a major blood vessel by a blood clot. Although thromboembolism is uncommon among healthy younger women, the U.S. Food and Drug Administration now recommends that the Pill should not be prescribed for women over 40 (UPI, October 21, 1975).

Pill use is also linked to a number of nuisance side effects: color changes in the skin of the forehead and cheeks, swelling and tenderness of the breasts, enlarging of **varicose veins,** fluid retention, increased appetite and weight gain, and possible reduction of sexual desires. However, many of these problems disappear with a change in Pill brands (Connell, Montreal Health Press).

Anemia. Shortage of blood, or of red blood cells and/or hemoglobin, which results in a lack of vitality.

On the positive side, use of the Pill makes menstrual cycles more regular and reduces blood loss, thus helping to prevent **anemia;** it cuts down on **premenstrual tension,** the irritability and depression which often precede menstrual periods; and it even helps to cure acne (Connell). Physicians are warned against prescribing oral contraceptives for certain high-risk patients, such as those with a history of thromboembolism. But for the majority of the 10-million Pill-users in the United States, oral contraceptives, like IUDs, pose less danger than pregnancy itself.

Morning-After Contraception. People who get themselves involved in intercourse without any attempt at birth control often regret it the next day. It is now widely known that high doses of estrogen administered within 72 hours of unprotected intercourse will prevent pregnancy, probably by making implantation impossible. Patients are usually given ten 25-milligram tablets of DES (**diethylstilbestrol,** a different kind of synthetic estrogen than what is used in oral contraceptives) to take over a five-day period. Given within three days after unprotected intercourse, this dosage is almost sure to prevent pregnancy, but it is not considered safe enough to be used routinely.

The 250 milligrams of DES are equal to the estrogen content of an entire ten-month supply of some currently used birth-control pills. Since this raises the risk of estrogen-related side-effects, morning-after estrogen treatment is recommended only for emergency use, as in cases of rape or incest (*Family Planning Perspectives,* March/April 1975; Connell).

STERILIZATION

In 1973, of the married women under age 45 in this country who already had all the children they wanted, 29 percent were no longer at risk of becoming pregnant. Either they or their husbands had been surgically sterilized. An additional 14 percent of the presently married women in the United States indicated that they intended to seek contraceptive **sterilization** as a final solution to birth control (*Family Planning Perspectives,* May/June 1975).

TUBAL LIGATION

Present methods of permanently preventing pregnancy in women involve cutting, tying, blocking, or removing a portion of the fallopian tubes so

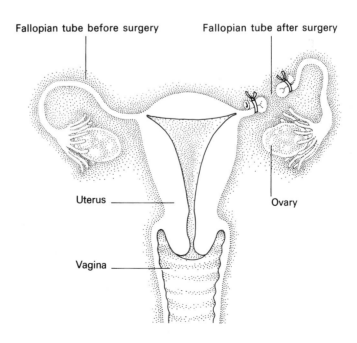

Fig. 7.8 A diagram of a tubal ligation. This is a relatively safe surgical procedure which is generally irreversible. In sterilization, the procedure is performed on both tubes.

Fallopian tube before surgery

Fallopian tube after surgery

Uterus

Ovary

Vagina

Sterilization. Altering or removing some part of the reproductive organs in either males or females so as to make conception impossible.

that eggs never make it from the ovaries into the uterus. **Tubal ligation** is easily performed through a small abdominal incision within 48 hours after a baby is delivered, when the tubes are most accessible.

The presently preferred method of sterilization outside of childbirth is **laparoscopy**, "band-aid" surgery which can be performed on an outpatient basis with only a few hours of hospitalization. The patient is anesthetized, her abdomen is inflated with carbon dioxide, and a slender instrument called a laparoscope is inserted through a small abdominal incision to allow the surgeon to see the tubes. They are then electrically seared or clipped and separated with special forceps inserted through another small incision. After being observed for a few hours while the anesthetic wears off, the woman is usually allowed to leave the hospital.

HYSTERECTOMY

Hysterectomy, major surgery in which the entire uterus and sometimes the ovaries are removed, is of course effective in preventing pregnancy, but it is subject to a 22-percent chance of complications. Deaths from the operation range as high as 300–500 per 100,000 hysterectomies. It is thus best reserved for medical problems rather than permanent contraception. With tubal ligation or laparoscopy, the chance of complications is only 1 or 2 percent, and normal menstrual and sexual functioning is undisturbed (Porter and Hulka, 1974).

VASECTOMY

More than a million men are now being voluntarily sterilized each year in the United States under a procedure which is simpler and even less subject to complications than laparoscopy for women. This minor operation, **vasectomy**, can be performed in a doctor's office under a local anesthetic. The doctor makes a small incision in each side of the scrotum to reveal the two vas deferens, which lie near the surface and are responsible for carrying sperm from the testicles to the prostate glands. He cuts out a small piece of each tube, ties the ends, sews up the incision with a few stitches, and applies a dressing. The whole thing only takes about 15 minutes, and the man can immediately resume all his normal activities except for heavy lifting. But until he has had 20 ejaculations and his semen can be tested to make sure all sperm cells have left the genital tract, some other method of birth control must be used.

Vasectomy will not affect a man's sexual functioning. His testicles will continue to produce sex hormones, and the blockading of sperm only reduces the volume of the semen by about 10 percent (Montreal Health Press). The great majority of both vasectomized men and sterilized women actually report an increase in their enjoyment of sexual relations after their operations, largely because of the new freedom from contraceptive hassles and fear of pregnancy (Thompson and Baird, 1972).

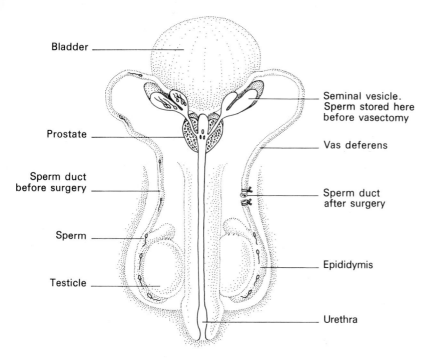

Bladder

Prostate

Sperm duct before surgery

Sperm

Testicle

Seminal vesicle. Sperm stored here before vasectomy

Vas deferens

Sperm duct after surgery

Epididymis

Urethra

Fig. 7.9 A diagram of a vasectomy.   This is a relatively simple operation which can be performed in a doctor's office under a local anesthetic, and it has no effect on sexual performance. However, attempts to reverse the procedure are generally not effective.

Fig. 7.10 Vasectomy. These drawings show the incision in the testicles and the removal of a small portion of the vas deferens on each side.

Vasectomy

Neither vasectomy nor tubal sterilizations in women are designed to be reversible. They should only be used by people who are certain that they do not want any more children. The chance of undoing sterilization in both men and women is now only about 25 percent (Davis, 1972; Porter and Hulka). If simple ways can be developed to open and close the tubes at will, temporary contraceptive sterilization may become a very popular form of birth control. In the meantime, men seeking vasectomy can take out fertility insurance by freezing a quantity of their semen prior to the operation. Kept in frozen **sperm banks,** human semen will probably retain its fertility potential for at least ten years and perhaps longer. If the couple change their minds and want a child after all, the wife can be artificially inseminated with her husband's defrosted sperm. Hundreds of children have already been born under these circumstances (Davis; Freund, 1972).

ABORTION

Despite advances in birth control, there are still many accidental pregnancies, many of them outside of marriage. If single women carry the fetus to term and then put the baby up for adoption, they are often unable to put the child out of their minds. Nonetheless, fewer and fewer choose to marry in order to keep their children, since the forced arrangement may not be a happy environment for parent or child. Those who keep their babies, though unmarried, face some degree of social disapproval and the burdens of the single parent described in Chapter 3. The only other choice is abortion, an option which is now legal, but which is rarely chosen without some degree of anxiety and ambivalence. Planned Parenthood of New York City says in its book on abortion (1973) that there is almost no such thing as a totally unwanted pregnancy.

Despite the emotional conflict involved, married as well as single women sometimes seek abortion. Unwanted or poorly timed pregnancy may force them to drop out of school or abandon career plans; or it may seem an unbearable burden on top of health problems, impending divorce, or difficulties in supporting and caring for the children they already have.

Abortion. Termination of a pregnancy by separating an embryo or fetus from a woman before it is capable of existing on its own.

THE LEGALIZATION OF ABORTION

Until recently, abortion was legal in this country only when the mother's life was threatened by her pregnancy. Desperate women nonetheless tried to end their pregnancies through dangerous illegal abortions or home-made remedies such as inserting crochet hooks and **caustic** douches, often causing their own deaths from acute infections in the process. But in January 1973, the United States Supreme Court overturned all restrictive state statutes on abortion. According to the Court, control of her own body is a woman's constitutional right. As Chief Justice Burger put it, "Elaborate argument is hardly necessary to demonstrate that childbirth may deprive a woman of her preferred lifestyle and force upon her a radically different and undesired future" (Wecht, 1975). The Court therefore legalized abortion on request by the mother during the first three months of pregnancy (called the first **trimester),** permitted second-trimester abortions subject to state regulations to safeguard maternal health, and allowed states to restrict abortion after six months (the 24th week) to cases in which pregnancy endangers the mother's life and health. After this decision, it is estimated that at least 745,400 legal abortions were performed in 1973, at a rate of 239 abortions for every 1000 live births, while deaths from abortion dropped by over 40 percent. In 1974, almost 900,000 legal abortions were performed (Weinstock et al., 1975; *Family Planning Perspectives*, March/April 1975).

ABORTION TECHNIQUES

Legal abortion is now a relatively simple and safe procedure, though never as safe or, to some people, as morally acceptable as contraception. Pregnancy can now be terminated, within two weeks of a missed period, by a technique known as **menstrual induction** (or menstrual regulation, menstrual extraction, or endometrial aspiration). The doctor simply inserts a slender tube through the cervix and sucks out the monthly menstrual lining, which may or may not include a fertilized egg. The procedure takes only two minutes, can be conducted on an outpatient basis, and can be done even before pregnancy can be confirmed, making it less traumatic than recognized abortions for some women. But because of the expense (about $80) and pain, many doctors and clinics advise their patients to wait until tests can accurately determine whether they are pregnant before going ahead with the extraction (Goldsmith, 1974).

Most abortions are now done by **vacuum curettage,** a method which does not require overnight hospitalization and can be used up to the twelfth week of pregnancy. Vacuum curettage takes only five to ten minutes and is generally preferred to the older method of **dilation and curettage** (D&C), in which the uterine contents are removed by scraping. Both the vacuum method and the D&C have a low mortality rate of 1.6 deaths per 100,000 (*Family Planning Perspectives*, March/April 1975).

After 12 weeks, the fetus is too large to be removed by these methods but too small to be aborted by other techniques. Once 16 weeks have passed, a saline (salt) solution may be injected through the wall of the woman's abdomen into the amniotic fluid. The fetus cannot live in the salt solution and the uterus begins to contract to expel the lifeless fetus through the vagina within 6 to 48 hours (Montreal Health Press). Another method is to inject prostaglandins **intravenously** or directly into the uterus, where they stimulate strong contractions so that the fetus is expelled within 5 to 72 hours (Kagan, 1975). If either of these methods fails, a **hysterotomy** (removal of the fetus through an incision) may be attempted. Mortality statistics are not yet available for the probably safer prostaglandin approach, but deaths from saline abortions average 15 per 100,000 patients and deaths from hysterotomies average 61 per 100,000 patients (*Family Planning Perspectives*, March/April 1975).

LEGAL COMPLICATIONS

Use of prostaglandins and hysterotomies have raised new legal and moral problems about abortion, for these procedures may in rare cases result in the delivery of live—though unwanted and almost hopelessly premature—babies. One issue is whether attempts must be made to save the life of aborted fetuses which are viable, or capable of survival, or even those which show some signs of life, no matter what their chances are. The Supreme Court has set the limit of viability at roughly 24–28 weeks and has permitted most abortions up to that point. But some experts say that viability is possible—though rare—as early as 20 weeks after conception. As modern care of the premature infant improves, the age of viability may be pushed back farther, although those artificially kept alive may never develop normally.

Curettage. A surgical scraping or cleaning by means of a scoop or, more recently, by use of a vacuum pump.

INFERTILITY

Those experiencing unwanted fertility during their reproductive years may find it hard to comprehend the anguish suffered by those who for physical reasons are unable to have children of their own. An estimated 15–20 percent of the couples in this country are either **infertile** or **subfertile.** Involuntary childlessness often creates tension, frustration, and resentment between marriage partners as well as grief. But infertility counseling and therapy can very often help a previously barren couple to have children.

Infertility may sometimes be the result of emotional barriers to relaxed sexual union. For instance, anxiety over intercourse may make it impossible for a man to achieve an erection, or it may cause muscular spasms which obstruct the fallopian tubes in the woman (Guttmacher et al., 1969).

Even if the sexual relationship is excellent, there may be physiological barriers to the union of sperm and egg, implantation, or the normal development of the embryo. In the man, infertility may be caused by an insufficient production of normal sperm. If there are fewer than 20 million sperm cells in his ejaculate, the chances of conception are slim (Rugh and Shettles). There must also be sufficient semen of the correct chemical composition, clear passageways from the testicles to the end of the penis, and the ability to have an erection and ejaculate inside the vagina. The woman must have at least one working ovary, a properly functioning uterus and cervix, appropriate chemical and hormonal factors to permit passage of sperm and implantation of the fertilized egg, and an open genital tract from the vagina to the ovaries (Guttmacher et al.). The absence of any one of these requirements has nothing to do with masculinity or femininity, but failure to conceive often leads to self-doubts in this regard.

After thorough testing to find the weak link which is preventing pregnancy, doctors may recommend hormonal, chemical, nutritional, or surgical therapy. Today these procedures have become sophisticated enough to enable almost 50 percent of involuntarily childless couples to have a baby (Kaufman, 1970).

Couples still unable to bear children may consider adopting a child, but the popularity of birth control and the legalization of abortion have made it more difficult now to find the right child for the right parents. In some cases there is another alternative: an estimated 100,000 Americans (Guttmacher et al.) have been conceived by **artificial insemination,** in which sperm obtained by masturbation are introduced into the woman's vagina with a syringe. For couples for whom intercouse is physically impossible, the husband's sperm is used. But if the husband's sperm production is inadequate or subject to possible genetic defects, the sperm may come from an anonymous donor. In **AID**—artificial insemination with donor sperm— the donor is chosen for his health, intelligence, and physical resemblance to the husband.

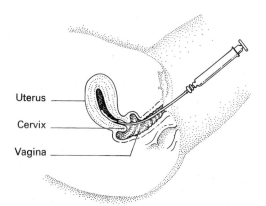

Fig. 7.11 AID. Artificial insemination of the female with donor sperm is sometimes used as a medical procedure in cases where a husband is unable to bring about a pregnancy in his wife.

Uterus

Cervix

Vagina

AID should seemingly be preferable to adoption of a child, since it allows the mother at least to contribute to the genetic pattern of the child. But the procedure may create subtle psychological problems within a marriage because it hints of adultery, reminds the husband of his biological inadequacy, and makes the child seem to be more hers than his. To ensure that the child will not be resented by the father, both parents should give their enthusiastic permission before AID is attempted. To avoid possible legal complications, several states have recently passed laws giving the children of AID full legitimacy and equal status to normally conceived children (Seligman, 1975).

Even though medical advances such as artificial insemination with donor sperm, outpatient sterilization, and menstrual induction are raising controversial moral issues, they are at the same time providing more and more couples with the chance to create what they consider an optimal family, into which all children born are warmly welcomed.

Summary

1. The purpose of this chapter is to discuss various aspects of family planning: its effects on population growth and family life; methods of contraception and abortion; and infertility.

2. Planning when and when not to have children is more common today than in the past due to economic and environmental concerns, and, to some extent, to women's increased awareness of the possibility of fulfillment outside the home.

3. In America, increased planning has resulted in a dramatically altered birth rate, and two-child families seem to be the wave of the future. As a result, there are fewer unwanted children, and those children born to smaller, planned families tend to be healthier and smarter than children in larger families.

4. Many contraceptive methods are available to prevent pregnancy. These methods vary in effectiveness, safety, and cost, and couples should consider all aspects of a method when deciding which to use. One method of contraception, usually permanent, is surgical sterilization—tubal ligation or hysterectomy in women, vasectomy in men.

5. Despite birth control advances, unwanted pregnancies still occur, many of them outside marriage. If the woman does not want to carry the fetus to term and keep the baby or put it up for adoption, the only other choice is induced abortion—termination of the pregnancy by artificial means. Abortion is legal on request by the mother during the first three months of the pregnancy, is permitted in the fourth to sixth month subject to state regulations to safeguard maternal health, and is restricted in the seventh to ninth months to cases where pregnancy endangers the mother's life or health.

6. Abortion is now a relatively simple and safe procedure, though never as safe or, to some people, as morally acceptable as contraception. There are both surgical and chemical ways to terminate pregnancy.

7. For many people, the problem is not unwanted pregnancy but infertility. This may result from physiological barriers to the union of sperm and egg or normal development of the embryo or there may be inadequate sperm in the male. After testing both partners to find out what prevents pregnancy, doctors may recommend hormonal, chemical, nutritional, or surgical therapy. If these methods are not successful, artificial insemination may be a solution to the problem.

Key Concepts

Family planning	Coitus-unrelated	Hysterectomy
Birth control	Rhythm method	Morning-after
Zero population growth	Oral contraceptives	contraception
Birth rate	Spermicide	Abortion
Fertility rate	Sterilization	Infertility
Contraception	Vasectomy	Artificial insemination
Coitus-related	Tubal ligation	Sperm banks

Review and Discussion

1. Compare your family experience with that of someone you know whose family is either larger or smaller than yours. What benefits and disadvantages do you see in a large family? A small family?

2. At what point in their relationship should a couple begin to discuss whether or not they want children or how many they would like to have?

3. Some countries, notably India, have considered passing laws to require sterilization after a couple have had a certain number of children. Do you think the problem of overpopulation justifies such a law in any country? Or do people have a right to have as many children as they want?

4. Pregnancies in unmarried teenagers are at an all-time high. What reasons can you give why these young people do not use contraceptives?

5. What are the regulations concerning abortion in your state? Is the general attitude toward abortion liberal or conservative?

FURSTENBERG, F. F., JR. (1976).   *Unplanned Parenthood: The Social Consequences of Adolescent Childbirth.* Riverside, N.J.: The Free Press.

Covers the effects of teenage pregnancy on education, finances, and career goals. Also discusses how children of teenage mothers compare with other children in terms of adjustment and the pros and cons of social agency programs for adolescent mothers.

GUTTMACHER, A. F., W. BEST, AND F. S. JAFFE (1969).   *Birth Control and Love, 2nd Ed.* New York: Macmillan.

A comprehensive book on conception and contraception which provides information about various methods of birth control. Includes sections on sterilization, abortion, infertility problems, and religious views on contraception.

PLANNED PARENTHOOD OF NEW YORK CITY, INC. (1973).   *Abortion: A Woman's Guide.* New York: Abelard-Schuman Ltd.

Gives the details of pregnancy termination from the diagnosis of pregnancy through the abortion. Gives details on various methods of abortion so women can know the advantages and risks and will be aware of what to expect. Contraceptive information is also given.

ZAJONC, R. B. (1975).   Birth order and intelligence: dumber by the dozen. *Psychology Today 8:8, 37–43.*

Describes and discusses research studies and theories on why intelligence may be related to a child's birth position in the family structure and the number of brothers and sisters a child has.

ZELNICK, M., AND J. F. KANTNER (1977).   Sexual and contraceptive experience of young unmarried women in the United States, 1976 and 1971. *Family Planning Perspectives 9:2, 55–71.*

Compares the results of two studies conducted to find out the sexual knowledge and experience and contraceptive practices of unmarried teenage women. Indicates a 30 percent increase in sexual activity of this group from 1971 to 1976.

Relationships In and Out of Marriage

Social Relationships
in Dating and Courtship 8

The search for intimacy is a major concern in U.S. society. To it we dedicate popular songs, films and books, TV commercials, and much of life's activity. The need for intimate involvement with other people seems to be present at birth and continues for a lifetime. Although some people learn to live without the warmth and emotional support of relatives, special friends, lovers, or spouses, those lacking intimate relationships are generally regarded as sad and lonely people.

Marriage is still viewed by many as the ultimate in the achievement of an intimate relationship, a peak reached through progressive involvement in dating and courtship from adolescence on. Recent social changes, however, especially changes in sex roles, have increased the incidence of other patterns of intimate involvement such as cohabitation and multi-partnered singlehood.

DEVELOPING HETEROSEXUAL INTIMACY

Intimacy. Close association or familiarity as in a relationship of a very personal or private nature.

The word **intimacy** refers to a close relationship with another person. Intimacy is the opposite of isolation and alienation. It involves closeness and sharing instead of distance. It is not simply physical nearness, though —for people can feel alone in a crowded elevator. Compared to more routine, everyday human contacts, intimacy triggers feelings of excitement, intensity, and association instead of neutrality and separateness. Although no relationship can produce such feelings all the time, even a few fleeting moments of intimacy can make life seem satisfying rather than random and meaningless (Mitchell, 1976).

The "best friends" relationship of childhood can be an important supplement to intimacy with family members. When children approach adolescence, they usually begin more actively to seek intimate relationships outside the family. As the emotional tides of adolescence in our culture begin to toss them from anguish to euphoria, they feel that they can barely live from day to day without someone in whom to confide their joys and problems. These early attempts to recognize and express their feelings are a step toward heterosexual intimacy.

In time, the urge to confide in a same-sex friend usually gives way to wanting to share emotional experiences with an intimate partner of the opposite sex. But adolescents have a hard time establishing intimate heterosexual relationships. Intimacy requires honesty and openness, and adolescents are often afraid to be open for fear of being rejected. Instead of revealing themselves, they wait behind a mask of reserve or affectation. Many are confused about who they are and, therefore, are unable to communicate honestly on an intimate level. However, the longing for intimacy will be at least partially expressed and satisfied by physical contact— touching and being touched, embracing and being embraced.

Adolescent couples may experience considerable physical passion and a degree of emotional sharing. Nevertheless, their romances are often short-lived, which is why they are often referred to as "crushes" or "puppy love." Full intimacy does not usually spring from insecurity. It requires, instead, openness between relatively mature people who know pretty well who they are and are not afraid of losing their own identities through joining with a partner (Mitchell).

KINDS OF INTIMACY

Even in mature relationships, intimacy may take many forms. One way of increasing our understanding of intimate relationships is to classify them in terms of breadth, openness, and depth. If two people have a relationship with great breadth, they spend a lot of time in each other's company doing a wide range of things, from studying or working, to dancing, to attending weddings and funerals together. By contrast, in a narrow relationship people share only a limited portion of each other's lives, such as attending classes together or only getting together for sex.

Openness is the degree of mutual disclosure in a relationship. It might include revealing one's goals and fears, being willing to take risks in expressing anger, and honestly attempting to deal with conflicts. Depth is the extent to which partners go beyond themselves to merge with each other. Examples of depth in a relationship might be relaxation and contentment when they are together, concern for the other as much as for oneself, and freely given commitments to each other without any guarantee of being loved in return.

These three dimensions are related to each other, for growing intimacy in breadth, openness, or depth of the relationship usually leads to greater intimacy in the other dimensions. They are also related to a different set of dimensions: intellectual, physical, and emotional expressions of intimacy. Kieffer has suggested that breadth in a relationship has intellectual, physical, and emotional components, and the same is true of openness and depth. A relationship with intellectual breadth might include activities ranging from discussions of what happened during the day and analyses of movies and books to joint attendance at political rallies. One characterized by physical openness might include nudity, free exploration of each other's bodies, and bathing, grooming, and eliminating body wastes in each other's presence. Couples expressing depth in emotional aspects of an intimate relationship might provide nonjealous support toward other intimate relationships each partner may have. Such an analysis helps us to understand the complexity of intimate relationships (Kieffer, 1977).

PATCHWORK INTIMACY

Patchwork. Something composed of miscellaneous or incongruous parts.

Psychologists say that we are happiest when our needs for intellectual, physical, and emotional breadth, openness, and depth in close human contact are regularly met. For some people, a patchwork of relationships of varying intensity and dimensions with a number of different people may fulfill these needs more adequately than any one relationship could, no matter how intense (Kieffer).

For example, a single woman might include among her intimates an older woman with whom she enjoys concerts and political discussions, a young boy with whom she enjoys outdoor activities and crafts, and a man whose sensuality answers her needs not only for sexual satisfaction but also for celebration of her femininity. A husband may find in his wife an affectionate partner with whom to make love, to share household and child-rearing responsibilities, and to enjoy certain leisure activities; but he may look to male and female companions at work for intimates who understand the intricacies of job-oriented problems.

Although marriage may provide a unique sense of security and daily fulfillment of most intimacy needs, it rarely fills all of them. Even in very happy marriages, there are times when one partner is preoccupied or needs to be alone but the other wants intimate contact. In addition, their personalities and interests may mesh at many, but not all points, so not all intimacy needs are met. Although monogamous marriage is traditionally expected to be an exclusive arrangement, in practice many married people move within a larger network of intimate relationships which may or may not include sexual intimacy.

Those who isolate themselves within marriage, trying to make it serve all their needs, may experience frustration when it doesn't. They might enjoy married life more if they expected less of it and shifted some of their needs to a patchwork of intimate contacts (Kieffer). But doing so without exciting jealousy may be tricky if what is lacking in the marriage itself is emotional depth. Unless partners feel secure in their commitment to each other, outside relationships may be seen as a threat to their marriage.

THE PURSUIT OF INTIMACY

People in the United States have a romantic preference for spontaneity rather than straightforward planning in their search for intimacy. In our stereotyped love stories, lovers meet by chance rather than by design, and commitment and contraception never enter the picture. The woman in these stories is especially likely to receive passively intimacies which happen to come her way, instead of actively seeking them.

According to Kieffer, it is unfortunate that so many Americans have accepted this stereotype as a guide for their own lives. In her view, full and rewarding intimate contacts are too important to our sense of well-being to be left to chance. Instead, we should try to exercise conscious control in this area. This means not only choosing intimates carefully from the variety of people we meet, but also actively seeking interaction with people who attract us. For women still bound by the traditional notion that they should play a passive role or by fear that men don't like aggressive women, this may be harder than it is for men. But people of both sexes stand to gain from rational efforts to tap the richness of intimate relations with others (Kieffer).

Assertiveness alone is not enough, however, for rewarding intimacy is not easily achieved. Building a relationship of any depth usually takes time. It also takes genuine respect for the other person, a mature sense of personal identity, a good meshing of personalities, favorable circumstances, and unselfish giving as well as receiving (Mitchell).

ADJUSTMENTS IN DATING

Being able to form intimate heterosexual relationships is a learned skill, and in U.S. society, much of the learning occurs through the dating process. Although dating, especially in the early years, may be more for recreation than for courtship, and although dating sometimes takes place in an artificial, games-playing atmosphere, it offers people the chance to experience intimacy in interpersonal relationships.

Spontaneity. Action arising from natural feeling or momentary impulse.

Dating. Taking part in social engagements—usually with people of the opposite sex—for recreational purposes.

LEARNING THE DATING CODE

Learning how to act on a date is an important part of adolescent socialization. Whether people get together in a movie theater, a pizza parlor, or a car on a back road, they find out which behaviors are appealing to those of the opposite sex and which are not. Since differences of opinion are bound to show up as a relationship continues, they may also begin to learn how to cope with interpersonal conflicts (Collins et al., 1976).

Studies of high school and college students reveal that many feel inadequate, ill at ease, and self-conscious when they go on dates, and nervous about taking the initiative in asking people out. Many report that they don't really understand people of the opposite sex and have problems establishing relationships with them. These concerns suggest that many young people have not made an adequate adjustment to dating (Herold, 1973). An alternate interpretation might be that the dating system itself is to blame—that its competitiveness and superficiality make formation of satisfying heterosexual relationships more, rather than less, difficult (Libby, 1977).

It seems, however, that experience with dating makes people more comfortable with its demands. A survey of 430 midwestern college students revealed that those who showed the greatest adjustment to dating—who were confident about their dating abilities, had no trouble getting dates, and were satisfied with their experiences—were those who had pushed ahead by being active. For both males and females, there was a strong correlation between high dating adjustment and four factors in the dating experience: (1) early age at their first date, (2) frequent high school dating, (3) frequent college dating, and (4) amount of emotional involvement with a dating partner. The last two factors, frequent dating in college and emotional involvement, seemed to be more important than an early start and high school experience (Herold).

EXPECTATIONS OF SEXUAL INTIMACY

A common problem in dating is disagreement between partners on how much sexual intimacy is acceptable. Adolescent boys have a greater tendency to seek physical satisfaction, whereas girls are more likely to look for affection. A recent study has shown that both males and females expect physical intimacy to grow as the level of affection progresses: first date, dating regularly, going steady, and considering marriage. But among 17–19-year-olds, males expect more sexual intimacy on a date than females. Expectations are more equal in older age groups, with 20–30-year-old males and females in near agreement on whether they expect kissing, necking, light petting, heavy petting, petting to orgasm, or intercourse at the different levels of affectionate involvement.

This smoothing out of differences in expectations occurs largely because of changed attitudes on the part of the female, not the male. With dating experience, women seem to become more liberal with less affectionate involvement in response to the man's less inhibited behavior. Males are less likely to respond to the female's need for greater emotional involvement before increasing sexual intimacy (Collins et al.).

The higher levels of sexual intimacy can be traced not only to changes in female expectations, but also to imperfect communication. According to various studies, college students tend to mislead each other as to how much permissiveness they expect. Men may assume an aggressive "line," regarding it as a bit of friendly deception advanced in hopes of making the woman become a little more permissive. Not catching on to the limited expectations that lie behind the performance, women tend to parry the line by pretending to be more permissive than they really feel in hopes of continuing the social contact. Then, in turn, men misread this pretense of permissiveness as a demand for increased sexual aggressiveness on their part. Sexual intimacy thus intensifies during the dating game on the basis of misperceptions and poor communication (Balswick and Anderson, 1969).

LEARNING TO COMMUNICATE

True intimacy cannot be built on such garbled communications. As dating progresses from casual get-togethers to serious relationships and perhaps commitment to marriage, couples seem to learn how to talk about difficult personal topics in ways that do not damage their relationship.

In one study, university couples ranging in commitment from second date to soon-to-be-married were asked to discuss several topics chosen for their personal content, such as what they would do if the woman found out she was pregnant. Videotapes of their conversations showed that conflicts were apparent between all couples. But those who were most advanced in their emotional involvement managed the conflicts in ways that did not disrupt their relationship, and sometimes even strengthened it. Evidence suggests that the involved couples had learned the communication skills necessary to sustain a romantic relationship through interaction with each other, rather than by being born with them or acquiring them as part of growing up (Krain, 1975). Thus the pairing off of couples in dating can be seen as beneficial to the establishment of intimate heterosexual relationships in later life. But what is it that draws people together in dating situations?

FACTORS IN HETEROSEXUAL ATTRACTION

Attraction. Pulling of others to or toward oneself through appealing to their desires and tastes.

Why are we strongly drawn toward some people but feel neutral toward others? Is it body chemistry, predestination, magic? Sociologists have examined the factors that make up heterosexual attraction for decades and have come up with two variables that seem to be more significant than any others—physical attractiveness and attitude similarity.

PHYSICAL ATTRACTIVENESS
Contrary to our democratic notion that everyone should have an equal chance to secure what life has to offer, it appears that in dating, those who are considered physically attractive will have a better chance than those who are less attractive. It should be kept in mind that there are no absolute criteria for physical beauty for men or women; there are only culturally accepted standards of what we mean, here in the United States, when we speak of a person as attractive or unattractive. Nevertheless, studies show that beautiful men and women are more sought-after as dates than less attractive people, no matter what other personality characteristics they may have.

The Matching Hypothesis. According to a sociological theory advanced in the fifties, people choose dates and mates who are like themselves in terms of social desirability. Total social value was presumed to be a combination of social skills, intelligence, wealth, prestige, physical attractiveness, and appealing personality traits. A number of experiments have been run to test this theory. They indicate that an overwhelming preference for physically attractive people throws the matching principle out of kilter, but that people's realistic assessment of their chances for success in dating tends to restore it to some extent (Berscheid and Walster, 1974).

In one test of the **matching hypothesis,** a computer dance was set up for first-year college students. Each subject was evaluated by the researchers on four points: personality, intelligence, social skills, and physical attractiveness. Pairs were assigned at random, except that as a concession to social custom, women were always paired with men taller than themselves. At intermission, subjects were asked to fill out a questionnaire indicating how well they liked their dates and whether they wanted to date that person again. The results: the more physically attractive the date, the better he or she was liked. No other variables seemed to make any difference. Those who were highly intelligent, socially skillful, or very personable were no more popular than those who were not, except on the basis of their physical attractiveness.

It seems likely that in computer dances people are not as afraid of rejection as they are in normal dating situations so their dating choices might be different from those in ordinary dating situations. Therefore, another experiment was set up to determine whether people would prefer dates more like themselves in terms of looks if actively required to choose a partner. They found that although highly attractive men and women were still strongly preferred, less attractive people did tend to choose less attractive dates than those chosen by highly attractive people.

The modifying influence of one's perception of one's own looks has been demonstrated in a number of other experiments. According to one study, men who consider themselves attractive rate more highly their chances of being accepted by attractive women than men who label themselves unattractive do. According to another study, men and women who think they are unattractive are more likely to consider going out with unattractive dates and less likely to try for dates with attractive people. Finally, observations of actual dating partners show that most are highly similar in physical attractiveness (Berscheid and Walster).

Attractiveness of Women.   Maybe it's not fair, but good looks seem to be more important to a woman's popularity than a man's. Compared to women, men are more likely to choose dates on the basis of physical attractiveness. Women who are popular and date frequently are statistically more likely to be attractive than popular men (Berscheid and Walster).

Although good looks earn a woman more dates, they also bring her greater sexual pressures. According to a study of Colorado University students, women who are highly attractive are less likely to be virgins than are less attractive ones. Although their attitudes toward sex are no more liberal and their backgrounds no more permissive than those of less attrac-

Matching hypothesis. Tentative belief that people choose dates and marriage partners who are like themselves in terms of social desirability.

Computer dance. Social event for which dates are paired off by a computer.

tive women, pretty women are likely to have more male friends, think that their friends have had intercourse, date more often, fall in love more often, and have more petting experience. This combination of popularity, frequency in dating, and petting experience greatly increases the opportunities for and pressures toward sexual intercourse (Kaats and Davis, 1970).

Why Is Attractiveness Valued?   Most of us take it for granted that attractive people will be more popular, but why should this be so? Sociologists suggest three reasons: (1) our cultural norms, (2) the prestige of a good-looking partner, and (3) the stereotyped notion that beauty is linked with other desirable traits.

Prestige. High standing in the eyes of other people.

We are drawn toward physically attractive people partly because of social learning. Advertisements, movies, and novels teach us that only highly attractive people are appropriate romantic partners. If a homely character in a book falls in love with someone beautiful, the homely one's feelings are rarely returned. If they are, it is made clear that the relationship is unusual. The cultural message transmitted is that we are supposed to respond with sexual desire and romantic love only to people who are good-looking.

Back in the thirties, the sociologist Willard Waller developed a theory that people also seek attractive dates for their prestige value. This was one element in what Waller called the rating and dating complex. Although generations of students have claimed that this is untrue, an experiment by Sigall and Landy (cited by Berscheid and Walster) has shown that we really are influenced by the appearance of a person's date in drawing an impression of that person. In the experimental situation, a man was seen with a woman made up to appear either very attractive or very unattractive. She was represented to some subjects in the experiment as his date, to others as a person who had no connection with him. Subjects who thought that she was the man's date were very much influenced by her looks in forming their overall impression of him. Those who saw him when she looked attractive had a far more favorable opinion of him than those who saw him when she did not. But those subjects who thought the woman had no connection with the man were not influenced by how she looked when they rated him. The experimenters concluded that, despite our high-minded ideals, it is better for a man in this culture to be associated with an attractive woman than not, and an unattractive date usually detracts from the impression a man makes.

Even though we are fond of the saying, "you can't judge a book by its cover," we seem to think maybe we can. Several studies have shown that we expect good-looking people to be personable and successful as well. When shown pictures of men and women varying in attractiveness, experimental subjects see the attractive individuals as more sexually responsive, sensitive, kind, interesting, strong, poised, modest, sociable, and outgoing than the less attractive ones. This assumption that beauty equals goodness and social competence even influences our predictions about people's futures. Those who are attractive are somehow expected to have better jobs, be more successful husbands and wives, and make happier marriages than the less attractive. The only area in which the beautiful people are not expected to excel is parenting. Subjects seem to think that they will make poorer parents than less attractive mothers and fathers (Berscheid and Walster).

Attractiveness and Marrying Well. Mate selection is thought by many sociologists to operate somewhat like the economic marketplace—people exchange their own desirable characteristics for those they desire in a mate. In one formulation of this **exchange theory,** the woman's market value is based on her attractiveness, the man's on his ability to raise her status by his job, wealth, and family background. On a simple level, this would mean that the most attractive females would marry the most prestigious males. Research has shown that the exchange is not this simple.

The attractiveness of women is only slightly related to their husbands' occupational prestige. Good looks are most important to a woman as a resource in the marriage market if she comes from a low-status background. Education is more important to the market value of high-status women than it is to those of lower social position. In addition, people are limited in their choice of mates to those who are available on the marriage market at a particular time. Some high-prestige men and highly attractive women who might marry if they met each other when both were single just never do. A final reason why female attractiveness and male prestige are not more closely linked may be that the match is usually made before the husband's eventual status is known. Although the prettiest girl in the class may marry the most popular boy from high school or the son of the best family in town, the boy may grow into a man who is downwardly mobile. And even if female attractiveness has been exchanged in the past for male prestige, current trends toward equality between the sexes may lead to a more equal exchange. Both looks and job status may eventually determine the market value of both sexes (Taylor and Glenn, 1976).

Although empirical research has demonstrated that a modified attractiveness-prestige exchange is often a factor in mate selection, no theory accounts for all the variables that may be operating. To some people, traits like warmth, sexual responsiveness, a sense of humor, supportiveness, intelligence, or peacefulness are more important in a mate than physical attractiveness or wealth. Unique needs and preferences probably affect a person's choice as much as the attractiveness-prestige scale (Taylor and Glenn).

Exchange theory. Formal expression of the idea that social interaction involves a give and take similar to the economic marketplace.

ATTITUDE SIMILARITY

A second major factor long thought to be important in heterosexual attraction is similarity of attitudes. We've all had the experience of being pleasantly drawn toward people who, we discover, share our opinions on things like music, clothes, literature, politics, or other people.

According to some sociologists, attitude similarity may be as important as physical attractiveness and perhaps even more so. They see attitude similarity as part of a process in which we are drawn toward those who meet our needs. One of these is a need for self-esteem—the need to feel valuable, capable, and socially acceptable. Finding that someone shares our views helps to make us feel this way, for their agreement "proves" that our feelings are appropriate and our opinions are sound.

Other sociologists play down the importance of attitude similarity. They hold that although it may be part of our initial attraction to certain people, its effect seems to diminish as relationships grow. For instance, a study of university couples by sociologist Richard Centers produced data indicating that the more intensely people are involved with each other, the less their attitudes are likely to agree. While couples who were at the most-preferred-date stage had similar opinions, those at progressively higher levels of intimacy (going steady, engaged, living together, married) were much less likely to agree.

Faced with this refutation of the attitude-similarity theory, Centers has proposed a different theory. Attitude similarity, he suggests, may be an important part of first impressions, but in intimate relationships, the need for self-esteem is less important than other needs. He therefore places the need for self-esteem in fifth position behind four other needs which he believes have greater influence in development of pair relationships:

1. Gratification of the sexual drive
2. Affectionate intimacy
3. Maintenance and enhancement of sexual identity
4. Interpersonal security
5. Self-esteem

Although attitude similarity as a factor in developing intimacy is chiefly associated with the fifth-place need for self-esteem, Centers believes it might also enter this list indirectly at other points. For instance, partners would have to agree to some extent on their attitudes toward sexual behavior before sexual gratification could be achieved. Nevertheless, he rejects the idea that attitude similarity is a crucial factor in the process of pairing off (Centers, 1975).

PROBLEMS IN PAIR RELATIONSHIPS

Although interpersonal intimacy is widely sought, the pathway to love is strewn with relationships that didn't work. Some have broken up because of troublesome differences in the attitudes of men and women in general, others because of unrealistic expectations regarding the relationship and subsequent disillusionment. Still others have ended because one or both partners have outgrown the relationship and the time has come to move on to a new experience or simply because of the availability of other partners.

BREAKING UP

A longitudinal study of 231 dating couples attending college in Boston revealed that almost half had broken up by the end of the two-year study period. Some relationships had lasted only a month, some had lasted as long as five years, with a median duration of 16 months before breakup. Dating is often a purely social activity, unrelated to eventual plans for marriage and family. Even couples who have been going together a long time don't necessarily expect the relationship to last forever. However, this weeding out of unworkable relationships is an important part of the mate-selection process. Even though withdrawing from a relationship in which a lot of time and emotion have been invested may be painful, couples who do so before marriage at least are spared the psychic and legal costs of divorce (Hill et al., 1976).

Longitudinal. Dealing with the growth and change of an individual or group over a period of years.

When they tried to find some basis for predicting which couples will stay together and which ones won't, Hill, Rubin, and Peplau found that sexual intimacy and living together are not related to the permanence of the relationship. Couples may become closer through sexual intercourse or cohabitation, but this positive effect may at times be offset by an increase in interpersonal conflict as the relationship becomes more intense. A factor which did emerge as significant, however, was matching. According to the Boston study, couples who are similar in age, education, intelligence, and physical attractiveness are less likely to break up than couples who are mismatched in these areas.

Very few break-ups are truly mutual. The results of the Boston study indicate that women are somewhat more likely to initiate the break-up than men, possibly because they are more sensitive than men to problems in the relationship. Even when the woman is the more emotionally involved partner, she may initiate a break-up because she recognizes that her commitment is not returned. Women are also more likely than men to consider alternatives to the relationship. Perhaps they are forced to be more selective because they can't afford to waste their best years with the wrong man. In our society, a woman's most marriageable period tends to be shorter than a

CASE STUDY—KATHY AND JOE

Kathy and Joe had been going together during the school year when she was a sophomore and he was a junior. Both of them agree that Kathy was the one who wanted to break up. She felt they were too tied down to one another, that Joe was too dependent and demanded her exclusive attention—even in groups of friends he would draw her aside. As early as the spring Joe came to feel that Kathy was no longer as much in love as he but it took him a long time to reconcile himself to the notion that things were ending. They gradually saw each other less and less over the summer months, until finally she began to date someone else. The first time that the two were together after the start of the next school year Kathy was in a bad mood, but wouldn't talk to Joe about it. The following morning Joe told Kathy, "I guess things are over with." Later when they were able to talk further, he found out that she was already dating someone else. Kathy's reaction to the breakup was mainly a feeling of release—both from Joe and from the guilt she felt when she was secretly dating someone else. But Joe had deep regrets about the relationship. For at least some months afterward he regretted that they didn't give the relationship one more chance—he thought they might have been able to make it work. He said that he learned something from the relationship, but hoped he hadn't become jaded by it. "If I fall in love again," he said, "it might be with the reservation that I'm going to keep awake this time. I don't know if you can keep an innocent attitude toward relationships and keep watch at the same time, but I hope so." Meanwhile, however, he had not begun to make any new social contacts, and instead seemed focused on working through the old relationship, and, since Kathy and he sometimes see each other at school, in learning to be comfortable in her presence.

Source: Charles T. Hill, Zick Rubin, and Letetia A. Peplau, "Breakups Before Marriage: The End of 103 Affairs," *Journal of Social Issues* 32:1.

For class discussion: (1) Do you think there might have been a different ending to this story if Kathy had expressed to Joe much earlier her concern that he was being too possessive? (2) Should Joe have been the one to bring conflicts out into the open when he realized in the spring that Kathy was not so much in love as he?

man's, for unlike her, he has the culturally accepted option of choosing a younger partner.

Outside circumstances may affect the timing of the break-up of a relationship which is already faltering. Among the Boston students, the academic calendar often seemed to have had this effect. In the 400 reported cases of previously broken-off relationships, the highest incidence of breakups occurred during September, December-January, and June. Changes in schedules and living arrangements, such as those that the beginning or end of a semester brings, may cause people to examine their relationship more closely to see what's in it for them. And changing circumstances may provide a handy excuse for ending a relationship that no longer seems viable (Hill et al.).

SEX DIFFERENCES IN INTIMACY GOALS

Some relationships apparently break up because of differences in the early socialization of men and women. Research shows that men and women tend to use significantly different slang terms for males and females and for sexual intercourse, that touching means different things to them, and that their motives for establishing intimacy are different. Another factor is that while the women's liberation movement seeks to equalize power between women and men, it may be causing new strains between them, for women's attitudes about sexual equality may be changing faster than men's. To the extent that these gender differences are merely leftovers from traditional gender-role socialization, they may become less important in the future.

Language Differences. Social scientists feel that the kinds of words people use are important clues to their state of mind, values, and ideas about other people. Language analysis has revealed important differences between the thinking of men and women, differences which may have been learned as part of their gender-role training. Male teachers, for instance, use words and language patterns which suggest active manipulation of objects (in line with their stereotyped roles as aggressors), while female teachers are more likely to use words that express concern with inner psychological conditions. A more obvious language difference has long been that women are less likely to use swear words than men, although this taboo is fading.

Analysis of the slang terms students use for members of the opposite sex and for sexual conduct shows clear differences by gender and an overall "sexploitation" of females. The expressions males use for "woman" often depict her as a sex object; it is uncommon for females or males to refer to a man as a sex object. Men are likely to use slang terms for intercourse which suggest male dominance of the female; women refer to intercourse euphemistically as "making love," "going to bed," "sleeping together," or "having relations." Such differences in the language with which females and males assign meaning to their behavior increases the possibility of misunderstanding in the relationship (Kutner and Brogan, 1974).

Sex objects. People viewed solely in terms of their usefulness in gratifying sexual desire.

Interpretation of Touching. Another place where understanding between the sexes may break down is in how they interpret physical contacts. For example, a man might mean to convey love when he squeezes his partner's arm, but she might interpret his touch as roughness instead.

To test whether men and women feel the same way about various forms of physical contact, Nguyen, Heslin, and Nguyen asked unmarried student subjects to indicate how they would interpret a pat, squeeze, brush, or stroke from an intimate of the opposite sex on each of eleven parts of the body (head, arms, thighs, genital areas, etc.). The five interpretations they could choose from were "playfulness," "warmth/love," "friendship/fellowship," "sexual desire," and "pleasantness."

The answers reveal some basic sex differences. Where she is touched is more significant to a woman; a man responds more to how he is touched, and can interpret a stroke almost anywhere on his body as an indication of sexual desire. Their interpretations also seem to form clusters which are different for each sex. For a man, the same touch can convey pleasantness, sexual desire, warmth/love, but not friendship. For a woman, the more a man's touch seems to convey sexual desire, the less she equates it with playfulness, warmth/love, friendship, and pleasantness.

If men link sexual desire with pleasantness and love, while women consider it the opposite of playfulness, friendliness, pleasantness, and love, the potential for interpersonal conflict is obvious. To feminists, female unwillingness to be an object for satisfying male sexual needs represents a refusal to submit to male domination. However, this interpretation of sexual approaches as unfriendly may be seen in another light. It may be a result of the double standard women have been socialized to accept: sex is okay for unmarried men but not for unmarried women. This interpretation is backed up by a study of married women which showed that dislike of sexual touching while unmarried gives way after marriage to strong positive responses to it (Nguyen et al.).

Differences in Motivation.   People date for many reasons: recreation (enjoyable social activity), socialization (establishing one's gender role and getting to know how to interact with the opposite sex), acquiring prestige (by going out with someone other people consider highly desirable), and courtship (in which dating is a prelude to mate selection and perhaps marriage). Problems in establishing intimacy may arise when the motivations of a dating couple don't match.

A study of student nurses by Skipper and Nass illustrates this point. The primary motivation of these young women for dating was found to be courtship—they wanted to get married and enter the wife-homemaker-mother role. But the men they had the opportunity to date—college and medical students—were primarily interested in recreation rather than courtship. To the men dating was an end in itself; to the women it was a possible means to a larger goal.

Both groups of males expected the student nurses to be sexually permissive—the college men because they held a stereotyped view of nurses as "knowing" and "easy," the medical students because they wanted release from work pressures without any emotional involvement. In either case, the women felt that in order to keep dating, they had to be more permissive than they wanted to be. This compromise distressed them, as did the fact that their dates usually did not share their interest in building

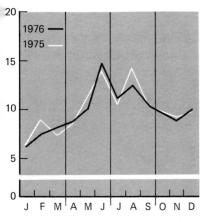

Fig. 8.1 Marriage rate per thousand of the population. The two lines compare month-by-month fluctuations in the marriage rate for 1975 and 1976. The lines show that the marriage rate is lowest in the first quarter of the year, then peaks in June, the traditional month for weddings, and again in August. When the marriage rate is calculated for the entire year, it averages 9.9 marriages per thousand of the population for both 1975 and 1976. (Source: USDHEW, 1977, Monthly Vital Statistics Report (HRA) 77–1120 26:1.)

a deeper emotional attachment which might lead to marriage. This difference in motivations was not always apparent to the women, however, for some of their dates considered it part of the dating game to pretend emotional involvement they did not feel in order to exploit the relationship. The males controlled these relationships since they were less in a position to be hurt and were often—especially in the case of interns—older and had more prestige than the student nurses (Skipper and Nass, 1966).

In this situation, it seemed to be the women rather than the men who experienced stress as a result of the different motivations each brought to the dating relationship. In other situations, differences in motivation might result in greater stress for the male.

Responses to Gender-Role Changes.   A marked shift toward feminist attitudes on the part of women has increased the likelihood of another source of conflict in male-female relationships. Undergraduate students at a women's college in New Jersey were surveyed by Parelius in 1969 and again in 1973. Their answers revealed that the women were attaching increased importance to sexual equality and self-fulfillment for women through careers, and were not accepting the traditional idea that a woman's main purpose is to marry, have children, and spend most of her time at home caring for them. But the woman's adoption of a less subservient role brings new strains to heterosexual relationships, if the man's attitudes have not shifted as well.

As far as the women students could judge, men's gender-role attitudes have remained basically traditional. Males were seen as willing to go along with females' shouldering part of the financial burden, but not as likely to accept other beliefs of feminism: the idea that a wife's career is as important as her husband's, the possibility that a wife might work outside the home all of her adult life, and the expectation that men take on some household responsibilities themselves. Men were seen as especially un-willing to accept feminism when it meant that a wife might put her occu-pation above her commitment to home and family in decision making.

The female students themselves were far more likely to support fem-inist goals. By 1973, a majority felt that their careers would be equally as important to decision making and family financing as their husbands'. They expected that they would work all their adult lives and that their husbands would help by doing up to half of the household chores. Al-though few thought they would entirely give up marriage or motherhood for career success, a majority said they would not consider the wife-mother role the most important part of their lives.

Even though these nontraditional college women thought that most men would not accept their feminist views in a wife, they seemed unwilling to compromise their own ideals. It may be that some will change their minds when faced with actual decisions. Another way out of this dilemma would be for men to change their minds. Research indicates that husbands and sons of working wives are already more inclined to believe in sexual equality than husbands and sons of nonworking women. As more and more women enter the work force, many men's attitudes will change in the direction of equality. As women see it, this is already happening, but at a slower pace than women's attitudes change (Parelius, 1975).

IDEALIZATION IN INTIMATE RELATIONSHIPS

Idealization. Giving an ideal form or value to a person, place, or thing in contrast to taking a realistic view.

Although clear conflicts of opinion pose one kind of problem in hetero-sexual relationships, couples who seem blissfully happy together and never disagree may face trouble, too. Social scientists have long worried that our culture's emphasis on romantic love may be partly responsible for our high divorce rates. They warn that engaged couples may idealize their partners, ignoring problem areas in the relationship and projecting their fantasies onto each other, only to break up after marriage when they see each other more realistically.

A recent study by Schulman of couples who were engaged or thinking seriously about marriage shows that many do seem to be in danger of falling into this pattern. Half the men and 68 percent of the women were found to be exaggerating the amount of agreement in values and attitudes between themselves and their prospective marriage partners. Subjects were asked to indicate their opinions on questions ranging from religion to rela-tives. They were also asked to predict what their partner's opinions would be, and to say what they thought the partner's prediction about their opinions would be. In line with Centers' data on attitudinal differences in involved relationships, all couples showed disagreements in their opinions. But they varied in the accuracy of their predictions. "Pessimistic" couples, a rather small group, predicted more conflict than there actually was, and "realistic" couples were fairly accurate in their predictions about each other's responses. A third group, the "idealistic" couples, did not seem to recognize their conflict areas, predicting much less disagreement in their answers than there actually was.

Although they claim to be very happy—as do the pessimists and realists—idealistic couples seem to block communication in situations where their ideals are threatened and thus are unaware of potential conflicts in their relationship. Their unresolved differences may surface only after marriage. When intimate daily contact with each other brings these problems into the open, they may be unable to cope with them. For such couples, premarital counseling may help to uncover problem areas where communication has been blocked. Once the conflicts are explored with the aid of a counselor, they can perhaps be resolved or new depths found in the relationship through negotiation of differences (Schulman, 1974).

HOW CAN WE TELL IF IT'S LOVE?

Although Americans stress the importance of love in intimate relationships, the word love means different things to different people. How can we tell whether or not someone loves us or, for that matter, whether the feelings we have for another person should be called love? The traditional signs of loving behavior are intense interest in and concern for another person, a desire for physical and emotional intimacy, and generosity toward the loved person. But these behaviors are not always reliable clues, for what appears to be loving behavior may not be. Opportunists may say "I love you" without meaning it; gift-givers may be motivated by habit or social expectations, rather than unselfish affection.

Opportunists. People who take advantage of opportunities or circumstances with little regard for moral principles.

In analyzing this problem, Judith Katz has suggested that people tend to use three criteria for determining whether an individual's behavior is an indication of love. First, the behavior being judged must be the other person's idea. If one had to ask, it's not love; the act must be voluntary. If one partner buys a gift the other one has asked for, that partner is obliging, but not necessarily loving. If one has to ask if one is loved, an affirmative answer probably won't be convincing.

Second, the unasked-for sign of affection must be appropriate and timely. It may not be love to give a box of candy to someone who is trying to diet. But perhaps it is love when one partner senses that the other is depressed and suggests going out to dinner. To meet this test, one must be observant as well as sensitive to the other's tastes, habits, and feelings.

Third, one must be willing to sacrifice one's own interests to give priority to those of the loved person. The chances that one partner in a pair relationship will suggest activities that the other considers appropriate and timely are pretty good; they may have the same tastes in clothes, restaurants, sports, movies, and music. But in order to meet this last test, there must be some differences in their interests, for one must be willing to participate in something he or she really doesn't enjoy for the sake of the happiness of the other. An example might be attendance at a sporting event when one would rather be at a concert, or vice versa. The sacrifice might also be financial in nature, such as spending money on a new car for one partner instead of on a trip the other wants to take.

Even if all three of the above criteria are met, the behavior still may not be perceived as a sign of love unless the recipient of the generosity is somehow aware of the possibility that love is the motivation for the behavior or perhaps is looking in that direction for love.

Once we have been convinced that people love us, we usually don't demand that they prove it in everything they do. Nor do we expect to submerge all of our own interests in those of the people we love. What we call love over a long time span is usually a series of ambiguous behaviors punctuated by a few instances that meet all of the above requirements and are regarded as "proof." How many are enough varies. For one person, a postcard might be proof that an out-of-town intimate still cares; others might be reassured only if they receive a phone call every night (Katz, 1976).

While some relationships progress smoothly through stages of increasing intimacy from first date to most-preferred date to going steady and then possibly to cohabitation and/or engagement and marriage, many others are terminated, for either serious or frivolous reasons. The most widely accepted reason for ending an intimate relationship in our society is likely to be, "we don't love each other," or perhaps, "we don't love each other any more."

COHABITATION

Increasing numbers of couples are now living with each other outside of marriage. According to the Census Bureau, the number of people sharing

Fig. 8.2 Median age at first marriage, by sex, for the United States. Between 1890 and 1960, the median age at first marriage declined for both males and females. For males the median age at marriage declined from 26.1 to 22.8, or 3.3 years. For females, the decline was almost two years, from 22.0 to 20.3. However, there has been a slight but steady upswing in the median age at first marriage since 1960. In 1976, it was 23.8 for males and 21.3 for females. (Source: U.S. Bureau of the Census, 1977, P–20:306.)

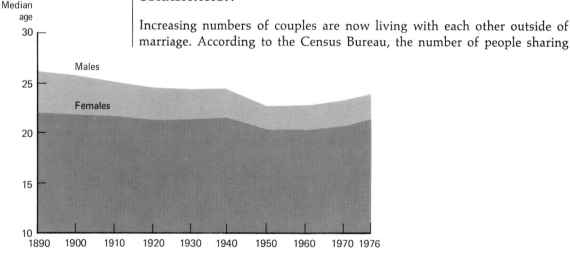

living quarters with someone of the opposite sex to whom they are not related almost doubled between 1970 and 1976, to an estimated 1.3 million people. Almost half had never been married (U.S. Department of Commerce, CB77-24). Although there is great variation in unmarried people's joint living arrangements, Cole's concise definition seems to cover most of the bases: cohabitation is "a more or less permanent relationship in which two unmarried persons of the opposite sex share a living facility without legal contract" (Cole, 1977, p. 67). The practice is now quite common in student populations, where the freedom of off-campus housing, coed dorms, and liberal student attitudes provides a supportive environment for cohabitation. A random sampling of Penn State undergraduates, for instance, showed that about 33 percent either were living with someone of the opposite sex or had done so at some time (Peterman et al., 1974).

COHABITATION AS A STAGE OF DATING

According to interviews with cohabiting students on several campuses, living together is for them neither trial marriage nor an alternative to marriage. Rather, it is considered a stage of dating, usually an extension of strong, affectionate involvement. At Penn State, 83 percent of the cohabiting men and 86 percent of the cohabiting women surveyed considered theirs an intimate or love relationship, rather than something less intimate, such as friendship.

Despite their often exclusive sexual involvement with each other, cohabiting students are unlikely to consider their relationship permanent. For a large majority, cohabiting lasts less than six months; half have cohabited with someone else before. Very few (6 percent) are committed to marrying their partner or even to working to build up a lasting relationship (7 percent). Instead, most are committed only to staying together as long as the relationship is mutually satisfying and personally enjoyable. Many keep their old dorm rooms in case living together doesn't work, or to provide an escape from too much togetherness.

This lack of commitment is especially noticeable among males and younger students. Cohabiting relationships of the later undergraduate years seem to be more durable and perhaps more like trial marriages (Peterman et al.).

EFFECTS OF COHABITATION

Surveys indicate that those who cohabit are very much like those who don't. Cohabitants are not significantly more likely than noncohabitants to have divorced parents or poor grades. There is no significant difference in their families' level of education, occupational status, or religion. Cohabitants are, however, more likely to hold liberal sexual views (Macklin, 1974; Peterman et al.).

Cohabitants. People sharing a household while unmarried.

Many cohabiting students don't tell their parents about their joint living arrangements, apparently for fear of upsetting them, and guilt over this dishonesty is one of the few negative results of the experience. According to various tests, cohabitants are actually better adjusted on the average than noncohabitants, and their heterosexual relationships are of higher quality. Even when couples have broken up, they usually feel that they have gained in self-understanding, personal growth, and understanding of the opposite sex as a result of cohabiting. There are probably some couples, however, who are not ready for living together, and for them, it may be a negative experience. The desire for intimacy is not enough. Living together also requires skill in communication, decision making, and conflict management, and these skills in turn require healthy, positive self-concepts (Cole; Peterman et al.).

Although student cohabitation is not usually regarded as trial marriage, it may nonetheless serve as a screening device which tends to prevent mismatched pairs from eventually marrying. Couples who live together have the chance to discover interpersonal conflicts and work them out in a marriage-like setting, with the option of breaking up without too much trauma if the costs of adjustment seem to outweigh the rewards of the relationship (Cole).

Trauma. An injury or wound, or a disordered behavioral state resulting from mental or emotional stress.

Despite increasing cohabitation, interest in eventual marriage is still strong. When a sample of undergraduates—including both cohabitants and noncohabitants—was asked what living arrangement they would prefer after they finished college, marriage was the most popular option. Cohabitation took second place, followed by living with someone of the same sex, living alone, and shifting arrangements; group marriage and other communal lifestyles were least desirable. However, when the responses of cohabitants were tabulated separately from noncohabitants, it was found that males who had experienced cohabitation thought they would prefer it to marriage, while females who had cohabited ranked cohabitation after college almost as high as marriage (Peterman, et al.).

The subject of cohabitation is discussed further in Chapter 16, along with other alternatives to traditional marriage such as communal lifestyles, group marriages, and remaining single.

THE DECISION TO MARRY

As cohabitation, voluntary childlessness, careers for women, and the goal of self-actualization increasingly challenge the value once placed on marriage and parenthood, couples in love find it difficult to decide whether or not to take the plunge—to commit themselves to each other in a legally binding compact. There are actually two aspects of such a decision. One is the question of whether or not to marry at all. The other is the question of whether to marry a particular individual or to seek someone else as a partner.

SINGLEHOOD: A GROWING CHOICE

The Census of 1930 revealed that well over a third of the American men and a quarter of the women over age 18 had never been married. That was the time of the Great Depression, and many people postponed marriage and parenthood because they simply couldn't afford it. After the 1930 high point, singlehood gradually dropped, reaching an all-time low in 1965, but the rate has been rising again in the last decade. By 1975, 20.8 percent of the men and 14.6 percent of the women in the United States were in the "never-married" category (*Statistical Abstract of the U.S.*, 1976). Even more have been married at some point but are now single again; those who remarry are waiting longer to do so than divorced people of ten years ago did (Stein, 1975).

The single people represented in these statistics vary widely in social characteristics. Some prefer to seek intimacy through a patchwork of varied and changing relationships rather than in monogamous marriage. This is now called "creative singlehood." Others have not rejected marriage, but are postponing it for various reasons or simply haven't yet found someone with whom they are willing to make the commitment to marriage. Still others were formerly married, have returned to the single state through divorce or death, and intend to remain single.

Creative singlehood, according to the definition of Roger Libby, is a state of availability to a variety of partners for companionship and sexual relationships. It is not cohabitation, which is usually monogamous as long as it lasts, and it is not singlehood because of lack of opportunity. Participation in this alternative lifestyle seems to be growing, particularly in cities where there are large singles populations.

Creative singlehood. The condition of being single by choice and exercising the options a single person enjoys.

Emerging Norms. According to Libby, creative singlehood is based on some emerging ideas which contradict traditional sexual norms. One is the recognition that regardless of marital status or affectionate involvement, people will be emotionally and erotically attracted toward others outside of these relationships. Another is the notion that human sexuality need not be tied to marriage and reproduction, so it is possible for individuals to be autonomous in determining their sexual conduct. A third idea gaining acceptance is that monogamous marriage is not the only way to legitimize sex—a wide range of sexual lifestyles are seen as workable and acceptable. A fourth is the recognition that if people are reasonably discreet, they can live their lives as they please without meeting social disapproval. A fifth is the feeling that changes in certain aspects of sexuality

—such as increasing social tolerance of premarital sex and co-marital sex in open marriages—should logically lead to greater tolerance of sexual expression among people who do not intend to marry.

Pushes and Pulls Toward Singlehood.   In the past, singlehood has generally been regarded as a negative status, resulting from an inability to participate in the good life. In Manfred Kuhn's analysis of the never-married in the 1950s, for example, it was suggested that they were likely to have personal and social problems. Some of the reasons proposed for why they had not married were: hostility toward marriage or people of the opposite sex, homosexuality, unnatural attachment to a parent, ill health or other physical problems, physical unattractiveness, refusal to accept responsibility, being too hard to please, ineptness in the dating-mating process, inability to finance a marriage, and extreme geographical or occupational isolation from potential mates (Stein, 1975). But in the view of many contemporary sociologists, people who remain single now often do so by choice.

Negative. Marked by prohibition, denial, or refusal.

Peter Stein, for example, interviewed 20 single men and women aged 22–45, all middle-class urban professionals, to explore their reasons for remaining single. He found little evidence of the negative motivations suggested in the 1950s study. None were unattractive, homosexual, overly romantic, or isolated from the dating market. None were inept at the dating-mating game, although some had rejected it as too old-fashioned, competitive, and exploitative.

What Stein found was an entirely different list of motivations for singlehood. Some he calls "pushes" away from unsatisfactory experiences with marriage or exclusive cohabitation; some he calls "pulls" toward the good features perceived in being single. The strongest of the pushes was the feeling that marriage or exclusive attachment to one partner restricted personal growth. The second major push was a sense of isolation and loneliness in monogamous relationships, a feeling of being cut off from other people and unable to share all one's feelings with one's mate. And a third push was the feeling that marriage would restrict friendships to people who were acceptable to one's mate as well as oneself. The majority of the single people interviewed felt that marriage represented restraint and compromise, limiting opportunities for variety of experience, independence, and learning.

The pulls toward singlehood included the desire for freedom, opportunity to develop multiple friendships, financial independence, sexual availability, and personal growth. Men were especially attracted by the possibility of trying out a variety of roles, instead of being restricted to those of breadwinner, husband, and father. In general, those interviewed felt that in singlehood they could find fulfillment and personal development, and that marriage was no longer the only avenue to emotional support, sexual satisfaction, and social activity (Stein).

Table 8.1   Choosing marriage or singlehood   The table may be read either vertically or horizontally. The pushes in the left-hand column represent felt needs not being met in one's present condition. That is, pushes toward marriage might be thought of as deficits felt by single people, while pushes toward singlehood might be thought of as deficits felt by married people. Pulls, in the right-hand column, represent positive values associated with the state of being married or the state of being single. Reading across the top two boxes, one becomes aware of the combination of pushes and pulls experienced by single people in U.S. society which may eventually result in marriage if a suitable partner can be found. Reading across the bottom two boxes provides a feeling for the combined pushes and pulls toward becoming or remaining single. The lists include a variety of social and personal factors in the decision to marry or to be single, and not every item will be relevant to the decision of every individual.

PUSHES TOWARD MARRIAGE	PULLS TOWARD MARRIAGE
Economic security	Influence of parents
Influence from mass media	Desire for family
Pressure from parents	Example of peers
Need to leave home	Romanticization of marriage

Interpersonal and personal reasons
  Fear of independence
  Loneliness
  Alternatives did not seem feasible
	Love
	  Physical attraction
	  Emotional attachment

Cultural expectations, Socialization	Security, Social Status, Prestige
Regular sex	
Guilt over singlehood	

PUSHES TOWARD SINGLEHOOD	PULLS TOWARD SINGLEHOOD

Restrictions
  Suffocating one-to-one relationships, feeling trapped
  Obstacles to self-development
  Boredom and unhappiness and anger
  Role playing and conformity to expectations
	Career opportunities
	Variety of experiences
	Self-sufficiency
	Sexual availability
	Exciting lifestyle

Poor communication with mate	Freedom to change and experiment
Sexual frustration	Mobility
Lack of friends, isolation, loneliness	Sustaining friendships

Limitations on mobility and available experience	Supportive groups
	  Men's and women's groups
	  Group living arrangements

Influence of and participation in women's movement	Specialized groups

Institution. A system of social relations organized to meet a basic societal need.

The Persistence of Marriage and Family Goals.   Despite the current trend toward singlehood, marriage and family life are still the chosen lifestyles of a majority of Americans. In 1975, 72.8 percent of the men and 66.7 percent of the women over age 18 in the United States were married (*Statistical Abstract of the U.S.,* 1976). And according to a representative sample of 2289 14–25-year-olds from across the country, marriage is still a desirable institution. Over three-quarters of those questioned felt either that "marriage is a great thing" or that "although many marriages are less than perfect . . . most people should get married." Only 18 percent felt that "most marriages are unhappy, and people should seriously consider remaining unmarried." The statement "Marriage is an outmoded institution and should be abolished," drew the support of only 4 percent of these young people.

When asked what lifestyle they aspired to, 52 percent of the males chose one which included marriage—either "successful executive or professional, living with wife and children in good neighborhood" or "average family man with routine job and time for family and own interests." An even greater number—69 percent—thought that despite the appeal of the unstructured single life, they are likely to be living in one of these conventional married lifestyles within 15 years. Among the females, 59 percent preferred marriage, either as a successful married professional or an average housewife with children and time to pursue their own interests; 78 percent expect to be living this way in 15 years (American Council of Life Insurance, 1976).

FINDING THE RIGHT PARTNER

Why is it that any two people choose to marry each other out of all the people they have previously known and many that they have perhaps dated? Curiosity about this question, and concern over the importance to later marital success of choosing well in the first place, have stimulated a great deal of sociological research. One of the problems in analyzing mate selection is that decisions are heavily influenced by personal quirks and chance factors. Pressures to marry at a certain point in time, a move to take a new job, a parent's death, or an identity crisis may propel a dating couple into a marriage they had not intended. Some relevant variables—such as values, social class background, psychological needs, and external pressures—are thought to influence mate selection. But no large-scale theory has yet been found which explains this complex process.

Robert Lewis has put together ideas from a number of previous theories in trying to develop a description of premarital dyadic formation which would fit the experiences of many different people. According to Lewis, middle-class American couples typically go through six developmental processes as they progress from dating to courtship.

1. Perceiving similarities in each other's backgrounds, values, and interests. This is a joint process, achieved through mutual exploration.

2. Achieving pair **rapport**: being able to talk easily, reacting positively to each other, finding the relationship satisfying, and feeling validated by each other's approval.

Rapport. A relationship marked by harmony, conformity, and shared interests.

3. Achieving openness in the relationship: mutual self-disclosure through open communication, revealing intimate thoughts and feelings to each other.

4. Achieving role-taking accuracy: judging correctly the roles that each expects the other to play and acting out roles in accord with those expectations. This is an essential preliminary to the next step of achieving interpersonal role-fit.

5. Achieving interpersonal role-fit: relating to each other in ways based on observed similarities of personality and discovery that each can meet the other's needs.

6. Achieving dyadic crystallization: experiencing deepening involvement, committing themselves to each other, and considering themselves a couple.

Dyadic crystallization. Becoming known as a couple and accepting this couple status.

Lewis found support for this theoretical framework in a longitudinal study of 91 dating couples. He also found that achievement of each level tended to require successful achievement of the one below. Most of us would agree with this on the basis of our own experience. For instance, we find it easier to talk and feel close to people (step 2) if we first perceive that they are similar to us (step 1). And we hesitate to disclose ourselves to someone else (step 3) unless we have already established some kind of rapport with that person (step 2). According to Lewis's findings, breakdown of the relationship can occur at any step if the requirements of that step toward progressive involvement in premarital dyadic formation are not achieved (Lewis, 1973a).

THE INFLUENCE OF FAMILY AND FRIENDS

One of the factors determining whether a pair on its way to dyadic crystallization will stay together and perhaps eventually marry is the influence of family and friends. Parents are usually eager to help their children select mates with whom they have a chance of building happy marriages. However, they are often torn between wanting the best for their children and cultural taboos against meddling in their adult offspring's private lives. Although parents in other societies may play an important role in the social placement of their children through marriage, parents in the United States are now expected to remain in the background.

Marriageable. Unmarried but of a suitable age and state of mind for marriage.

Mothers and Daughters.   One of the parent-child relationships in mate selection which has been studied in some detail is that of mothers and their marriageable daughters. Whether or not the mother works or expects her daughter to work seems to be an important variable. One researcher has found that mothers who work are less likely than mothers who don't to try to assist their daughters' courtship by encouraging potential suitors. The difference is not a matter of lack of time, for mothers who work part-time are no more likely to encourage courtship than mothers who hold full-time paid jobs.

It seems more likely that working and nonworking mothers view the social placement of their daughters differently. Working mothers are more likely to expect their daughters to work. The daughter's future thus will not be solely dependent on the efforts and status of the husband she chooses. Her participation in the rewards of society will be determined partly by her own career. Mothers who don't expect their daughters to have careers may try harder to help them marry well because marriage will be the sole basis of their status in adult society (Bruce, 1974).

Social Reactions.   Encouragement of possible marriage partners is not the only way outsiders influence mate selection. The general reaction of families and, to a lesser extent, of friends seems to help shape a couple's opinion of their own developing relationship.

According to a study of student couples, those who feel the most positive social reactions to their relationship are the most likely to continue it. When family and friends invite the two to social functions as a couple, comment on how nice a pair they make, and include the partner in family activities, this social approval reinforces the couple's feelings that they are a well-matched pair. Compared to those who meet with negative social reactions, they are more likely to commit themselves to their relationship, stop "playing the field," think of themselves as a couple, and act as a unit. But if family and friends reject the partner or avoid treating the two as an exclusive couple, they may internalize this implied judgment that their relationship is unworkable or undesirable and come to question it themselves (Lewis 1973b).

SOME GUIDELINES FOR MAKING THE RIGHT CHOICE

Family counselor David Olson traces much marital unhappiness to the fact that dating relationships are often superficial and the decision to marry is taken lightly. He also feels that the decision to marry may be due to pressures in the sociocultural environment rather than to a readiness to work at making the marriage a success. To improve the chances that careful mate selection will help to create marriages that will be vital and rewarding, he offers the following recommendations:

1. Not everyone should be encouraged to marry and no one should be pushed into marrying.
2. People should be encouraged to try out different lifestyles before deciding which one is best for them.
3. Couples should be encouraged to relate to each other openly and honestly, instead of using the traditional strategies of the dating-mating game.
4. People should not be encouraged to marry young. Instead, they should wait until they are emotionally mature and established in a profession.
5. Couples should not marry until they have built a meaningful relationship and resolved their biggest problems, for marriage will accentuate rather than erase them.

The title of this section, "The Decision to Marry," implies this should be a rational decision based on analysis of one's own needs and desires as well as the needs and desires of the other person. However, work to improve the chances of marital success does not end with careful mate selection. Chapters 9 through 15 provide information about some of the adjustments and problems which arise in marriage itself, requiring continuing efforts by both partners. Once the vows have been said, the task becomes one of adjustment to each other's needs and desires as these change over the years. And between deciding to marry and being married, there is a critical transition period in the couple relationship which requires a change from individual thinking to mutuality.

BONDING

The transition period between the decision to marry and the perception of the self as a married person includes the engagement period, the wedding, the honeymoon, and the first few months of the new marriage. Many people find it a period of great tension as well as a time of great happiness. The female especially may find herself the center of more attention and excitement than at any previous time in her life.

Bonding. Joining together in a state of mutual recognition of shared privileges and obligations.

ROLE TRANSITIONS OF THE ENGAGEMENT PERIOD

Marrying suddenly, without this period of preparation is likely to make the early months of marriage more difficult. Not infrequently, the couple discovers amid the anxieties and urgent preparations of the engagement period that they are not ready for marriage—at least not to each other—and the engagement is broken off. Rhona Rapoport has defined three important developmental tasks individuals should work on during the engagement period to prepare themselves for their new roles.

1. Getting ready to be a husband or wife—to live in intimate daily contact with another person, to carry on a joint economic life, and to cope with possible conflicts in the roles of worker and homemaker.
2. Disengaging oneself from other relationships that might compete with commitment to the marriage.
3. Preparing to give up the pleasures of single life or accommodating them to the different realities and rewards of married life.

In addition to these tasks that each partner must tackle as an individual, the couple as a unit faces other tasks during the engagement period. They must build a sense of identity as a couple, plan for the wedding, honeymoon, and early marriage periods, and work out mutually satisfactory patterns for financial support, family planning, communication, decision making, being with relatives, seeing friends, and fulfillment of obligations to employers.

PREMARRIAGE CONTRACTS

Some couples go even farther in their planning for marriage: they try to spell out the terms of their unique agreement in a personal premarriage contract. Exercising an option which was rarely considered by their parents' generation, these contemporary couples are negotiating beforehand on such matters as who will make the money and who will decide how it will be spent, who will do the housework, whose work will dictate where they will live, whether extramarital affairs will be allowed and under what conditions, whether there will be children, and who will get what in the case of divorce.

ENGAGEMENT AND WEDDING RINGS

About 75 percent of American women who become engaged wear a ring to prove it. The ring thing is thought to have begun with cavemen who tied up their women with braided grass to prevent escape. These bonds were eventually replaced with grass knotted around a finger. Rings were later made of leather, carved stone, and crude metals.

Among the ancient Romans, a signet ring was used at marriage to indicate that the husband was endowing the wife with his worldly goods and she had the right to seal all such goods. Among the Jewish people, wedding rings were first introduced in the eighth century, and Christians first used wedding rings when Nicholas was Pope, around 858 A.D.

Mary of Burgundy received the first diamond engagement ring in 1477 as a token from Maximilian of Austria. Today, two-thirds of engaged couples shop together for wedding and engagement rings.

Sources: *Seventeen*, February 1975, and *Boston Evening Globe*, April 28, 1976.

Although the idea of drawing up their own contract is highly appealing to some, the practice has its risks. For one thing, even though the document is written and signed by both parties, its legal validity is questionable, especially if it violates any existing state laws such as those providing for child support in case of a divorce. On the other hand, if such contracts are upheld by the courts as legally binding, they may tie couples into agreements they will later regret. The actual areas of conflict in a relationship usually cannot be anticipated ahead of time. It is difficult for unmarried people to predict what their married life will really be like, what unexpected crises will arise, or how they will react to them (Wells, 1976).

In addition to problems of doubtful legality and inability to see into the future, premarriage contracts may inhibit change, in the individuals and in the relationship itself. Studies of successful marriages show that both partners are continually changing. If their personal development—and corresponding growth in their marriage—were blocked by some clause in a contract, the document could become a source of conflict. A related problem is the contract's lack of flexibility, for successfully adjusted partners tend to continually renegotiate the terms of their relationship to meet changing personal and situational realities. And finally, by its assumption that two rational and caring people cannot continue their negotiations on such matters for the life of the relationship, but must instead fence off their rights and responsibilities ahead of time, the premarriage contract may set a pessimistic tone for the marriage.

Renegotiate. To confer again with another so as to bring about a readjustment of some matter.

However, the working out of a premarriage contract also has beneficial aspects, if a committed couple makes the effort to discuss together candidly and openly the problems they anticipate. This straightforward approach is an antidote to idealization and later disillusionment. Putting down agreements in black and white may prevent later misunderstandings. And the negotiating process itself can help to open lines of communication and clarify each partner's point of view.

The best use of the contract idea may be a flexible agreement which is open to continuous renegotiation. Instead of committing themselves to a rigid set of pre-established rules, the couple would be committing themselves to keep working together on matters that affect their family life. As children joined the family, they, too, could be included in the negotiating process, enhancing family communication and satisfaction (Wells).

RITUALS AND TRADITIONS

Marriage represents a critical transition from one social status to another in the life cycle of the individual. The variety of rituals associated with it is an indicator of the risks involved and of the importance placed on the formation of new families (Rapoport).

Traditions. Inherited patterns of thought or action.

Rite of passage. A ritual associated with a crisis or a change of status for an individual.

The wedding itself is a major rite of passage. Like birthdays, graduations, and death, it is usually marked by a public ceremony and embellished with special clothes, symbols, pageantry, and gifts which set the event apart from everyday life and emphasize its significance. Although some modern weddings are unique and sometimes bizarre personal statements—such as scuba divers' getting married underwater, and hikers' getting married on mountaintops in blue jeans—most still follow our society's traditional patterns. Among couples marrying for the first time in 1971, seven out of eight did so in a church or synagogue, seven out of eight brides received an engagement ring, and 85 percent of the brides wore formal wedding gowns (Seligson, 1973). Among the upper class, virtually all weddings are still held in churches (Blumberg and Paul, 1975). Although some couples are now writing their own vows and quoting Gibran's *The Prophet* instead of the Bible, they still express their commitment in spoken vows of some sort.

The money spent to support these traditions amounts to 7 billion dollars a year, over half a million dollars of which is spent on honeymoon travel and 2 billion on arrangements for wedding receptions (Seligson). Why do brides and wedding guests continue the old traditions—from the white wedding gown to throwing rice—whether the bride is a virgin and is wished fertility or not? Perhaps in the repetition of such traditional rituals, participants find a sense of stability and continuity with the past. In the face of soaring divorce rates and rapid social change, each new wedding seems to reaffirm the hope that marriage and family life have continuing validity. The realization of this hope is likely to depend upon whether couples about to be married understand themselves and what their own needs are and are successful in communicating their ideas and feelings to each other. Interpersonal communication is the subject of the next chapter.

Summary

1. The purpose of this chapter is to discuss the various stages and factors involved in the development of intimate, heterosexual relationships in dating and courtship.

2. Intimacy is usually learned first in the family, later with same-sex friends, and then friends of the opposite sex. There are different dimensions to intimate relationships in terms of their intellectual, physical, and emotional breadth, openness, and depth. Rather than expecting one person to fulfill all these needs, some people develop a patchwork of relationships.

3. The dating experience involves learning the codes of behavior, adjusting to different expectations of sexual intimacy, and learning to communicate with one's partner. Two important variables that influence the selection of dating partners are physical attractiveness and attitude similarity. Relationships are not always permanent and can break up for a variety of reasons, such as differences in male and female attitudes, different goals in the relationship, and idealization of the partner and subsequent disillusionment.

4. People tend to use three criteria for determining whether a partner's behavior is an indication of love: (a) the behavior must be the other person's idea, (b) the unasked-for signs of affection must be appropriate and timely, and (c) there must be willingness to sacrifice one's own interests to give priority to those of another person.

5. As a relationship develops, the couple may choose to live with each other outside of marriage (cohabitation) as a stage of dating and an extension of strong involvement. The number of people cohabiting almost doubled between 1970 and 1976.

6. A couple may eventually reach a point in their relationship where they are faced with deciding whether to commit themselves to each other in a legally binding compact. There are two questions involved: (a) whether or not to marry at all, and (b) whether to marry a particular person. Remaining single —remaining permanently available in the dating market—is a choice many people are making. The decision not to marry may be a result of either "pushes" away from unsatisfactory experiences with marriage or cohabitation or "pulls" toward the freedom and independence of being single.

7. When a person decides to marry, many factors influence selection of a mate: personal quirks, chance factors, values, social background, psychological needs, and pressures from family and friends. Careful and thoughtful mate selection can create vital and rewarding marriages, and there are guidelines that can help people make the right choice.

8. The period of transition—from the decision to marry through the first months of marriage—involves preparation for new roles, development of an identity as a couple and, finally, the perception of oneself as a married person. Some couples draw up premarriage contracts to outline their roles and responsibilities as a part of this bonding process.

9. Marriage represents a critical transition from one social status to another. The wedding is usually a major rite of passage. Rituals of the engagement and wedding may give participants a sense of stability and continuity with the past as they undertake establishment of a new family.

Key Concepts

Dating	Rating-and-dating	Cohabitation
Courtship	complex	Creative singlehood
Intimacy	Exchange theory	Lifestyle
Adolescence	Attitude similarity	Pair rapport
Patchwork intimacy	Feminism	Bonding
Matching hypothesis	Idealization	Premarriage contract
Longitudinal study	Love	Ritual

Review and Discussion

1. How is the idea of physical attractiveness as a basis for selecting a dating partner encouraged by our society and culture?

2. Does our popular culture (popular songs, books, movies, TV) present a realistic idea of love and marriage? Give some examples.

3. Do you think most people give careful consideration and planning to their choice of a marriage partner? Why or why not?

4. Do you think premarriage contracts are helpful to couples during the bonding period?

5. If you have been to any weddings, list or describe some of the traditions and rituals they involved or lacked. Be sure to include any ethnic traditions.

Suggested Readings

BERSCHEID, E., AND E. H. WALSTER (1978). *Interpersonal Attraction, 2nd Ed.* Reading, Mass.: Addison-Wesley.

Centers on interpersonal attraction—from attraction-rejection in a group to attraction-rejection in romantic love. Considers the problem of evaluating others and variables that affect attraction such as similarity and reward provided by the other person.

FROMM, E. (1956).   *The Art of Loving: An Inquiry into the Nature of Love.* New York: Harper.

Discusses the many aspects of love and presents love as an art which requires knowledge and effort, not as something one "falls into." Makes observations about the barriers that modern society puts between its members and the achievement of love.

KATZ, J. M. (1976).   How do you love me? Let me count the ways. (The phenomenology of being loved.) *Sociological Inquiry* 46:1:17–22.

How people in the United States determine whether or not someone loves them. The criteria are presented, explained and illustrated with sample situations and dialogue.

LASSWELL, M. E. (1974).   Is there a best age to marry? An interpretation. *The Family Coordinator* 23:3:237–242.

Interprets research on marriage age in the United States—the average ages of men and women; the relation to the success of the marriage; the best age to have children.

SELIGSON, M. (1973).   *The Eternal Bliss Machine: America's Way of Wedding.* New York: William Morrow.

The author reports and describes modern American marriage preparations and ceremonies, including discussions of ethnic traditions and honeymoons. Written in a lively, humorous style and peppered with sometimes unbelievable descriptions of marriage ceremonies the author attended.

Successful Interpersonal 9
Communication

Imagine two versions of a scene in a suburban kitchen at about 8 P.M.:

I.

Wife   (facing husband, hands on hips, as he enters the doorway) It's about time you came home. I've been waiting for you for hours and dinner's gotten ruined again. Why didn't you call me?

Husband I worked late. I don't want to eat now anyway.

Wife   After I went to all this trouble? I've been keeping this food warm so long it's all drying up. What's bothering you anyway?

Husband Nothing. (Turning away): Leave me alone.

II.

Wife   (putting her arms around husband as he walks in) I'm so glad to see you. I was worried about you.

Husband Sorry I'm late—we had to finish a rush order.

Wife   I wish you'd phoned. Next time you're going to be late try to call and let me know. Then I won't worry.

Husband O.K. I'll try.

Wife   There's a big pot of chili on the stove. Shall I warm it up for you?

Husband It smells good, but I'm not hungry right now. I'm still pretty tensed up. How about sharing a cup of coffee with me first? (As they settle on the sofa) So how were things with you today?

In both versions, the husband and wife are talking to each other about the same situation—his arriving home late from work. But it is easy to see that the second couple is communicating far more effectively in this situation than the first, turning a potential conflict into an opportunity for learning, understanding, and mutual support. Communication is more than shooting out bits of information: "You are late." Supper is ready." It is a complex process by which people exchange both feelings and facts as they try to understand each other and to express themselves.

FORMS OF COMMUNICATION

Words are not the only vehicles in interpersonal exchanges. Our **nonverbal behaviors**—such as gestures, postures, facial expressions, tone of voice, touching, listening, and physical distance between the speaker and the listener—all communicate messages about our feelings about ourselves, our subject, and our listener (Bienvenu, 1975; Chaikin and Derlega, 1974).

In the contrasting scenes, for instance, the wife who opens her arms to her husband as he comes in and then sits next to him on the sofa is communicating acceptance, affection, and interest in their relationship. The wife who greets her partner with an angry face and hands on hips communicates annoyance and accusation with her body as well as her words.

VERBAL AND NONVERBAL MESSAGES

Most human communication consists of both verbal and nonverbal signals, and the two forms of exchange may provide different kinds of information. (1) While language is usually better for discussing factual aspects of people, things, and events, nonverbal signals may be better for communicating emotions and feelings about the other person or the relationship. (2) Language tends to be more consciously controlled, whereas nonverbal behaviors are more spontaneous. This is so because language is a product of specialized higher areas of the central nervous system while nonverbal behavior often comes from lower, almost **involuntary** levels of the nervous system. (3) **language** is the assignment of meaning to arbitrary symbols. Nonverbal signals are uncoded. The meaning is directly indicated in the emotion (such as anger) or the act (such as kissing) (Argyle, 1969).

Language. A system for communicating ideas or feelings by the use of conventionalized sounds, gestures, or marks having agreed-upon meanings.

COMMUNICATION AND INTERACTION

Communication is not chance noise linked with random gestures. It is the purposeful—though not always successful—product of interaction between people. It is used to modify behavior ("Watch out, there's a car coming."), to give information ("The train to San Francisco will be ten minutes late."), to test reality ("I have the feeling that you are ashamed of me when we are with your friends—is that true?"), and to satisfy needs for self-expression ("I feel so happy.").

Any two or more people who are near each other are bound to be communicating. People cannot *not* communicate—there is always a message. Speech and activity are not the only ways messages are carried; silence and inactivity are also communications. Looking away from strangers in a supermarket or holding up a newspaper in front of your face at the breakfast table, for instance, may mean "Don't talk to me." The husband who tries to cut off his wife's, "What's bothering you?" by turning away nonetheless communicates something to her. She may interpret his refusal to answer as rejection of her, anger, deep hurt covered by defenses, or preoccupation with business problems. It may be that none of these is the message he wants to send, but how she responds next, or at least his **perception** of her response, will then influence his subsequent behavior, both **verbal** and nonverbal. Each of the participants is contributing to the behavior of the other, and the interaction between them is the product of

Perception. The process of becoming aware of the external environment or internal states by way of the sense organs.

their joint influence on each other. The fact that the message sent is often different from the message received makes this process all the more complicated.

Even when communication carries no spoken reference to the relationship, there is always a message about it in addition to the content of the message. "I can reheat your supper if you like," and "I worked all afternoon to cook this but now that you're so late it's probably dried up and no good," convey the same content: "Your supper is cold." But they say very different things about the nature of the relationship. While the first message makes a simple, affectionate statement which does not make reheating the supper a test of either partner's love, the second is self-pitying and sarcastic and invites a reply which can be interpreted as either support or rejection of the wife, her cooking, and the relationship itself. Unhealthy relationships, according to the research of Watzlavick, Beavin, and Jackson, are characterized by communications in which the struggle to shape the relationship tends to outweigh the content aspect of communication. Healthy **dyads**, they have found, are less likely to drag the nature of their relationship into every exchange of information (Watzlavick et al., 1967; Bolte, 1970).

Dyad. Two people interacting with each other.

IDENTITY AND COMMUNICATION

Communication, as explained in the section in Chapter 4 on the development of the self-concept, is the means by which we discover who we are, what our **identity** is. It is also the means by which we modify or reaffirm our identity as we carry out our various roles. We could not think about ourselves were it not for language. Words make it possible for us to define ourselves in our thoughts and plan our future behavior—"I am good at math, but I'd better study some more for that test anyway." However, these bits of information about what kind of object we are and how we will act are not altogether our own creations. They are largely the result of social interaction.

HOW IDENTITIES DEVELOP

As children gradually learn from the speech of others what symbols their culture uses for objects they see—"chair," "dog," "flower"—they also pick up the word-symbols for attributes and roles which they hear applied to themselves—"clumsy," "fat," "sweet," "artistic," "all boy." The self-image is developed in these terms—"I am a sweet little girl and I can draw pretty pictures."

The Expectations of Others.   Social interaction molds the identity in another way as well. In addition to seeing ourselves as others see us, we also come to measure our behaviors and looks in terms of what we think other people expect of us. The Sunday-school teacher thinks that he should be neat and proper; the judge that she should be sober; and the football coach that he should be tough and demanding.

Although our notions of how we should fulfill various roles are given some individual twists by our own perceptions and personality, they are still based heavily on conventional standards, social expectations that would apply to anyone in that role. For most of us, the responses of others keep our personal versions of our role-concepts from getting out of hand. If a man's performance in asking women to dance with him is so bizarre that he is continually turned down, he is bound to recognize that he will have to make some changes in it.

Demands of Different Roles.   At the same time that we are learning the duties and behaviors of our own roles, we are also learning to anticipate and **reciprocate** other people's role behavior. Even those of us who think we always act naturally have learned to behave differently toward people whose relationships to us are different.

Reciprocate. Return, usually in kind or degree.

Alterations in our behavior to fit with other's roles need not be false fronts. Instead, these changes in how and what we communicate reflect the important social ability of being able to see the other person's point of view. We learn it the same way we learn our own identities—by communication with others. Their role recipes and ours serve as the common vocabulary between us, a vocabulary which may be different when we interact with different others.

If we each had only one role for a lifetime, perhaps we could eventually get to be very good at it after years of dry runs and flawed performances. But each of us has many roles, confusing our communications with others because of our sometimes overlapping relationships to them. Each of us has certain roles within the family context (the same person could be father, husband, son-in-law, brother, uncle, and grandson), others within a community context (club treasurer, political activist, scout leader), others within a professional context (department head, typist, social worker) and so on. Each role has different requirements, but they are joined into the totality of thoughts and behaviors that is that person's identity.

What happens, though, when our role relationships with other people overlap and conflict? How do you act, for instance, if your employer is also your brother-in-law? Do you joke with him freely and give him advice, or do you maintain an employee's distance? Or if you are both mother and wife, do you react as the proud mother or as the jealous wife when your husband is being especially complimentary and affectionate to your teen-age daughter? In such cases, whichever role is more important or **salient** to our identity at that time governs our behavior. Our various roles seem to exist in a sort of **hierarchy,** some being generally more important to us than others, and the social situation brings out one role more clearly than the others in any particular interaction (Stryker, 1968).

Hierarchy. A graded or ranked series.

Functions of Role-Identities. Just as it is impossible to not communicate, it is impossible to have no identity. Even if we don't project one, other people will force one on us since they need to know how to interact with us. As McCall and Simmons (1966, p. 72) have written, "Our bodies get in the way of other people, and they have to identify us before they can know what to do to get past us." And the identity forced upon us may be less advantageous than one we could present for ourselves.

For most people, the identity, as a composite of all one's roles, is constantly undergoing change, because the roles themselves are subject to change. Moreover, each role is modified according to what McCall and Simmons refer to as a person's **role-identity.** By this they mean the combination of the role as society expects it to be played and one's own personal conception of how one should play that role. Often people rehearse their roles and fantasize how they will act them out. At other times the role performance is so stable and so ingrained that the person needs no rehearsal.

Whether rehearsed or not, role-identities serve three important functions. First, they get us ready for actual performances. In keeping with our concept of how we should play our part, we will smile, look stern, or shrug nonchalantly. If we have imagined another person's reactions to our performance beforehand, we may have already eliminated behaviors we think that person would find inappropriate, molding our communication skills to those best suited to the specific listener. It is highly desirable to obtain the support of others in the role we are playing. Acting like a glamourous dinner partner is much easier if the other person is responding to you as a glamourous individual. However, one's own feeling of being comfortable and skillful in the role is equally important to a successful performance. So knowing in advance how one is supposed to act on a glamourous evening out, possessing that role-identity, makes it much easier to plan one's behavior, including verbal and nonverbal communications.

In addition, role-identities serve a second function: they give us standards for evaluating our performances in our own terms. Our performances are designed as communications to another person, but they are supposed to satisfy us as well as others. The identity we want to project serves as a built-in censor, rejecting behaviors we consider personally embarrassing or inappropriate. A man who wants a date may reject the idea of begging a busy and very popular woman to go out with him because he wants to be a dominant rather than a dependent person.

Role-identities have a third function as well: they give meaning to our everyday lives. By serving as plans of action and standards for judging how we act and how other people react to us, they enable us to connect random events and interactions. We might say to ourselves, "They stared at me when I said that, and others have done the same thing. I'd better not say it again if I don't want to be considered childish." It is through our role-identities that we organize our responses to the various situations, events, and people we encounter in day-to-day living. However, fitting our role-identities to those of the others with whom we interact often requires a process called **identity bargaining.**

IDENTITY BARGAINING WITH OTHERS

In routine social interactions, people's reciprocal roles may fit together nicely so that they have no trouble accommodating them in the encounter. The customer is a person who has some money to spend and needs meat, the butcher is a person who has meat and needs money, so their transaction can take place fairly smoothly. But in many situations, the fit between people's roles is not nearly so neat; communication is likely to be unsuccessful unless they somehow agree on who can play what role in the encounter so that both can achieve their purposes.

All of us bring to social encounters an idea of who we are, what we want to achieve, and what part we want the other person to play. A man may approach a woman with the idea that he would like to take her to his apartment and make love to her, and that this is what she wants too. She on the other hand, may bring to their encounter the idea that she is his friend, that she would like to go out to dinner with him, and that his role

Identity bargaining. Negotiation for acceptance of one's identity through acceptance of the identity another person is projecting.

is that of friend, without any sexual ties. Since their self-perceptions, perceptions of each other, and purposes are not the same, the only way they can accommodate each other is through negotiation or "identity bargaining" (Blumstein, 1975; McCall and Simmons).

The Presentation of Self.   The first step in identity bargaining is establishing one's perception of oneself in the role one is playing in a particular interaction. The person seeking a writing job must have the characteristics of a capable writer. By carefully controlling what one says and the way one acts, an applicant may successfully convey the desired image. If the performance is a true reflection of what one is like, or if it is not but is, nevertheless, a skillful performance with no slip-ups, the publisher theoretically has little choice but to acknowledge the applicant as a skillful writer. This process of **self-presentation** is often exploited by those who are skillful at presenting themselves to be what they are not. People who have been fooled before are skeptical and have developed subtle ways of testing for deception. An ordinary job interview may therefore become a contest in which the employer tries to determine the accuracy of the image the applicant presents.

Casting Others into Roles.   The second aspect of identity bargaining is assigning a role to the other person. Like a director casting parts in a play, we place the person with whom we are interacting in a role that complements our purposes and our self-image. We then behave as though this person really fulfills the role we have assigned. In other words, the writer acts as though the publisher accepts the writer image; the would-be lover treats the woman as though she too thinks of herself as his lover. If the other person resists being cast in the role we have assigned, we may still persist anyway. If the woman wards off her "lover's" advances and suggests that they go to a restaurant instead of to his apartment, he may think she is just playing hard to get. If he persists in treating her as a lover, she may eventually decide to accept the role.

The Bargaining Process.   Often, however, neither the way we present ourselves nor the way we try to cast others makes them see us and themselves in the roles we have intended. Sometimes a negotiated settlement can be worked out. In such cases, indicating what our role is and what role we would like the other person to play succeeds in showing how we would like the person to act. The other responds by indicating how we should redefine our role. The result is usually a working agreement in which each person grants the other some of the identities claimed and cast but perhaps not all of them. The woman who feels that she does not want to become sexually involved with her would-be lover may manage to convince him

Presentation of the self.
Dressing and staging
oneself so as to facilitate
achieving one's goals in
social interaction.

that they can have a "very dear friends" relationship. And the publisher might conclude the interview with the writer by saying, "I'm not so enthusiastic about hiring you as you seem to think I should be (refusing to be the awed employer), but I do need another writer (accepting the part of an employer in need of an employee), and I'm willing to give you a chance to prove what you can do by having you try your hand at this short chapter here" (provisionally granting the would-be writer's claim to that role).

In this process, each person must strike two bargains—one with the self and one with the other. The publisher must determine how important a job can be entrusted to someone whose ability has not been proven and convince the applicant that it is worthwhile to take the job. The applicant, having convinced the publisher that a person with talent is available, must decide whether to give up the "great writer" role for the sake of a minor job which at least provides the opportunity to play the role of "paid writer." Identity bargaining thus has its costs as well as its rewards.

CHANGING SETS OF IDENTITIES

As we go through life, we continually acquire new identities. The first ones we take on are conferred by our social position—the sex, race, socioeconomic class, and religion we are born into. Others are placed on us by our parents' hopes ("This is my son, the future doctor"), others by our peers' judgments ("brain," "class leader"), and others by changes in our social position. When we marry, for instance, we drop the single status and take on new statuses with a whole new set of required behaviors.

New influences may introduce us to new roles or change our views of old ones. Teachers and peers may at some point become more important to children's definitions of themselves than their families. And movements like women's liberation may affect how we see ourselves—women may feel that they don't want to be referred to as girls anymore, or that the old role of housewife has somehow been devalued.

Performance in one role acquaints us with related or supplemental roles, as when a father becomes his son's scout leader. The new supplemental role may even at times conflict with the one it sprang from. The father, for instance, must communicate with his son as a member of the scout troop rather than as a family member, not showing favoritism to him at meetings because of their preexisting relationship.

As new statuses are acquired, old ones may be discarded. A woman who was a track star in college may stop competing after she graduates because she is so busy with her work as a medical student. The identities of the early years of life are especially likely to be outgrown with life cycle and physical changes.

Some identities are held onto even when they are no longer legitimate. The high school prom queen may still think of herself as a beauty at 59;

"Daddy's little girl" may still act childish with him when she is 20. Even when they should have been outgrown, the old roles may still affect the way a person relates to others—the faded beauty queen may still expect men she meets to be "slavish admirers." The old roles are clung to since they once brought pleasure, but they must eventually be recognized for what they are—former roles. They can still be savored, however. The 48-year-old ex-athlete can still think of himself as a former football star. As McCall and Simmons have written, "These formerly legitimate identities have a somewhat hollow ring about them, but they are nonetheless important as a source of comfort to the aging person and as a means of relating to the people who 'knew him when.'"

Whether people cling to an old identity or drop it largely depends on how important it is to their self-concept and whether other people still support them in that role. So long as a son acts the part of dependent child to support his mother's anxious parent role, she may refuse to let go of it, even when he is fully grown and living independently. Otherwise, their relationship may be progressively renegotiated, gradually phasing her out of the parental role over the years (McCall and Simmons).

In either case, the style and content of the communication between them will be determined by their joint agreement or disagreement on their reciprocal roles. Each will attempt to behave in congruence with a particular role-identity and to get acceptance of that role-identity from the other person. To the extent that the identity bargaining has been unsuccessful, the relationship will be unsatisfactory and communication will be ineffectual.

INTIMACY AND COMMUNICATION

A common complaint in dyadic relationships is "He (or sometimes she) never tells me anything." This does not mean that couples do not talk to each other. But two people may live together for years, eating together, making love, raising children, talking about repairs to the house, overdue bills, and in-laws without ever communicating on an intimate level about their feelings, fears, dreams for the future, and past experiences. Except for casual exchanges of information, they are still strangers to each other. What is missing in their relationship is **self-disclosure,** the process by which people reveal themselves to one another.

Self-disclosure. The process of revealing information about oneself to others.

Decisions about self-disclosure underlie much of our communication. Should I reveal my feelings and experiences to this person? How intimate can I allow this conversation to become? Is this the right time for this revelation? Such decisions will have a great bearing on our formation of friendships, ability to build an intimate relationship, personal growth, and mental health. In general, greater openness has a positive effect on these aspects of our lives. But in some cases too much self-disclosure may be as bad as too little (Chaikin and Derlega; Cozby, 1973).

VARIATIONS IN SELF-DISCLOSURE

People's ways of talking about themselves, of letting themselves be known by their listeners, may be very different. Self-disclosure can vary in at least three ways: the breadth, or sheer amount of information disclosed; the depth, or intimacy of the disclosures; and the time spent on each piece of information.

Who Discloses Most? In general, females seem to be higher disclosers than males. Although some studies reveal no sex differences in disclosure, many of them do, and it may depend on what is being measured. For instance, although it has been found that women don't use any more words to describe themselves than men do (their duration of disclosure is the same), they talk about themselves in more intimate terms than males (women have greater depth of disclosure). Another qualitative sex difference which has been found is that women tend to disclose themselves to someone they like, while men will only disclose themselves to someone they trust. Men in our society generally seem to feel they have to be very cautious about expressing feelings of weakness or tenderness.

Social class also seems to be a factor in self-disclosure. For instance, one study shows that middle-class women disclose more about their marriage problems than do working-class women. Another study indicates that middle-class mothers tend to speak and respond verbally to their children more than lower-class mothers, suggesting that the class variations in self-disclosure noticed in adulthood may be a result of patterns established in childhood (Cozby; Gilbert, 1976).

Disclosure in Marriage.   How much do marital partners disclose to each other? How much do they know about each other's inner lives? Shapiro and Swenson (1969), administered to 30 young married couples a test which measured self-disclosure and knowledge of the other in six dimensions: attitudes and opinions, tastes and interests, work or studies, money and possessions, personality characteristics, and body and sex.

These researchers found that both husbands and wives tended to overestimate how much information they had disclosed to each other. But despite the discrepancy between what one thought was told the other and what the other actually knew, partners did seem to have a fairly accurate picture of each other's personalities. This finding suggests that what these couples knew about each other's personalities came more from observation than from deliberate disclosures. Such observations probably included interpretations of clues from each other's nonverbal behavior, as well as inferences drawn indirectly from things the partner said. A woman might, for instance, know that her husband disliked dogs and would not want to own a dog more from observation of his response to other people's pets than from anything he had said.

THE COSTS OF NONDISCLOSURE

According to psychologists, failure to reveal ourselves to at least one other human is likely to block personal growth. When we hide ourselves from others, we cut ourselves off from the **feedback** and insight they could give us about ourselves. No one will know us well enough to tell us when we have behaved inappropriately. Without this feedback, we may keep on irritating people and making errors in relationships. Disclosers, on the other hand, learn important things about how they are perceived. They do not necessarily have to change their behavior, but at least they are given the information they need if they want to alter their interpersonal relationships.

By not disclosing ourselves to our friends, we also make it unlikely that the friends will disclose themselves in return. Our understanding is thus limited to our own insights and never enriched by theirs. And finally, we may be ignorant of our own needs and feelings, for verbalizing them helps bring them to conscious awareness. If we are unaware of ourselves, cut off from other people's understanding of us, and ignorant of their inter-

Feedback. Evaluative or corrective information about one's behavior supplied by persons with whom one interacts.

pretations of their own feelings and experiences, our chances of fully actualizing our unique potential are stunted.

In addition to its negative effect on personal growth, nondisclosure may have its psychic costs as well. The nondiscloser may be a lonely person, isolated from warm and open human contact. If we make conscious decisions not to reveal our true feelings, we commit ourselves to maintaining a false public image. Sustaining this fake image takes some effort and psychic energy. The more this false public self differs from what we are really like, the more being with other people causes stress in social contacts (Chaikin and Derlega).

THE LIMITS TO SELF-DISCLOSURE

Although open and honest communication about the self is considered valuable to personal growth, some observers feel that too much self-disclosure may hurt a person's relationships with other people. Intimate disclosures often occur within marriage. Many theorists have felt that this is as it should be, that frequent and totally open communication between partners will lead to the deepest intimacy and happiness in the marital relationship. But some studies have indicated that greater disclosure produces greater marital satisfaction only up to a certain point. After that, further increases in self-disclosure may actually decrease satisfaction.

The studies suggesting the negative effects of too much disclosure have made several points. One is that people tend to become less polite and restrained with each other after they marry, but open expression of hostilities and criticism at a very intense level may become intolerable. Cozby found that liking for people may decrease if they disclose too much about their intimate feelings and self-doubts. People are sometimes made anxious and uneasy, Cozby thinks, by overly intimate disclosures from another person, and may want to retreat from such a relationship. Several studies have shown that if husband and wife share their feelings about how each has failed to live up to the other's expectations, their marital adjustment may suffer rather than improve (Gilbert). Certain kinds of communication can be especially damaging. The results of a marital communication **inventory** developed by Bienvenu reveal that the item most likely to discriminate between happily and unhappily married couples was: "Does your spouse have a tendency to say things which would be better left unsaid?" Unhappily married persons were far more likely to answer yes to this question than those who were happily married.

Handling Criticism.   What, then, can be done with negative opinions in a close relationship? Sutton has suggested a compromise between brutal honesty and nondisclosure. She thinks that if a person expresses acceptance of the other before criticizing him, the disclosure will not be so likely to

Inventory. A list of preferences and attitudes used to evaluate personal characteristics or skills.

damage their relationship (Gilbert). In the examples at the beginning of this chapter, the second wife hugged her husband and said she was glad to see him before making a carefully worded complaint, softening its possible negative impact. The first wife, on the other hand, lashed out at her husband for being late without any attempt to reaffirm their bond to each other first. He reacted by becoming sullen and defensive instead of accepting her criticism, so complaining got her nowhere and soured their relationship as well.

Satir (1972) takes a different position. Partners in a truly trusting and nurturing relationship, she feels, are as straightforward about expressing criticism as they are about expressing their good feelings for each other. But she, too, places some qualifications on open criticism. People should be careful, she cautions, to express criticisms in descriptive rather than judgmental terms. Instead of "You look terrible in those pants," one might say, "Those pants are getting worn out." The success of this approach depends on whether the criticism has hit a sensitive spot. If a man is already self-conscious about being overweight, his wife's saying, "That overcoat is too tight," won't make him feel any better than if she says, "You're too fat for that overcoat now."

Ability to accept criticism—from a friend, a parent, a spouse—seems to be related to how we feel about ourselves. If our self-image is generally good, criticism will not be particularly threatening. But for a person whose self-esteem is low, critical disclosures, and the people who make them, may have to be avoided at all costs. Building and maintaining self-esteem for both partners, Satir believes, is the most important factor in any relationship.

The Quality of Self-Disclosure.   Self-disclosure may thus lead to greater intimacy—to a deepening exchange between partners within an atmosphere of trust and commitment to the relationship—or it may not. While self-disclosure does seem vital to an intimate relationship, unhappy relationships may be high in disclosure, too. The difference lies in the quality of disclosure. To study disclosure qualitatively, it is useful to consider three factors: (1) the subject matter of each person's disclosure, (2) whether what is said is favorable or unfavorable to the other person, and (3) the existing intimacy of the relationship in which disclosures are made.

Unhappy marriages tend to be high in negative disclosures: threats to alter the relationship, disappointments in each other, or conflicting opinions. But partners may also find there the greatest chance for intimacy. Handling such risky disclosures requires sensitivity to the other person's point of view and a commitment to preserving the other's self-esteem. A couple whose commitment to each other is very strong—and perhaps also long-lasting—may be able to discuss openly the feelings of jealousy aroused by the sexual relationship of one of the partners with someone outside the

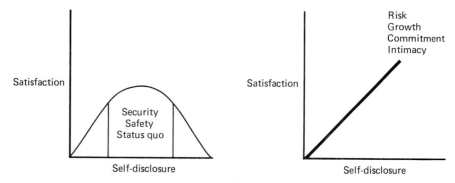

Fig. 9.1 Two interpretations of the relationship between self-disclosure and satisfaction.   The diagram on the left shows the curvilinear relationship Cozby believes to exist between increasing amounts of self-disclosure and satisfaction in a relationship. Gilbert suggests that maximum security and stability develops in relation to some specific quantity of self-disclosure, but further research will be needed to determine how much or what kind of self-disclosure produces such a relationship. Gilbert further suggests that optimal husband-wife relationships may be based not on safety but on willingness to take risks to achieve greater intimacy. The diagram on the right suggests a straight line rather than a curved line in the relationship of increased self-disclosure to satisfaction—provided a couple is willing to take risks to achieve growth and commitment. (Source: Shirley J. Gilbert, Self-disclosure, intimacy and communication in families, *The Family Coordinator* 25:3. Copyright 1976 by the National Council on Family Relations. Reprinted by permission.)

marriage. If both of them carefully and thoughtfully describe how they feel about the situation, they may be able to work through the dangerous disclosure, with the result that their relationship itself becomes more intimate than it ever was before. But many relationships are already too weak to tolerate mutual exploration of such high-risk topics (Gilbert).

CULTURAL BARRIERS TO SELF-DISCLOSURE
A couple's inability to share intimate thoughts with each other may be caused not only by the basic insecurity of their relationship but also by culturally acquired barriers to interpersonal communication.

Stereotyped Male and Female Roles.   During boyhood, males may actually be trained to be incapable of sharing their feelings. Although they are allowed to show anger and pride, boys are often socialized to believe that expressing certain other emotions is only for girls. Boys who cry or show tenderness, for instance, may be labeled "sissies," so they learn to conceal feelings of pain or affection. Their emotions may not be named, discussed, or explained except when they are being criticized. Girls, on the other hand, are often encouraged to talk about their feelings and are not laughed at when they cry over sad books, express feelings of loss when friends move away, or reveal that they have been hurt.

By the time a boy reaches manhood, socialization to a rigid notion of masculinity may have made him not only reluctant to reveal his unacceptable feelings but perhaps even unable to have them. Especially when their education is limited, men may be unwilling or unable to identify, interpret, or disclose their feelings. Taught that a strong man should bear his troubles silently, they consider talking about problems at work and admitting to being hurt signs of weakness. Men Komarovsky interviewed for her book *Blue-Collar Marriage* (1964) said things like: "After a man gets on his feet, he shouldn't be hurt deeply about anything," and "You ought to outgrow it." More men than women claimed, "Nothing can hurt me anymore." Komarovsky has labeled this rigid role behavior the trained incapacity to share.

In interviews with working-class wives, Komarovsky found that many complained of their husbands' reserve. Whereas the women believed in talking about their hurts and worries, their husbands refused to do so even under their wives' coaxing. According to one wife,

I think the good thing is to talk it (what's bothering you) out and get it out of your system. But I have to leave him alone because if I try to get him to talk he'll get really sore, or he'll go off the deep end and walk out of here. Or maybe he'd tell me something else, lying like, just so I wouldn't get at the thing that makes him sore. He is strictly hands-off if something hurts him. (Komarovsky, p. 157)

Class Differences in Communication.   The communication gap between husbands and wives is especially noticeable in lower-class marriages. Compared to the middle classes, working-class parents are more likely to bring up their children according to traditional notions of what behaviors are suitable for each sex. The childhood distinction between gender roles carries over into adulthood in marriages in which partners share few common interests and areas of knowledge. The impoverishment of their lives through limited education and little money for recreation gives them less to talk about anyway.

Comparing husbands who had graduated from high school, husbands with less education, high-school-graduate wives, and less-educated wives showed that the less-educated men were the most withdrawn, Komarovsky says. They disclosed themselves least to their spouses, were least likely to express emotions openly (other than anger), were most likely to respond to marriage conflicts by withdrawing from them, and were more likely to seek relief from their problems in physical activity rather than talk.

An important factor contributing to the gap between lower-class husbands and wives is the exclusion of the wives from occupational interests.

Blue-collar. Relating to factory workers or other laborers who often wear blue shirts to work.

The men in Komarovsky's study gave a number of reasons for their marked reticence in this area. Either they found their jobs too boring to talk about, felt that their jobs were too technical for their wives to understand, or felt that talk about their job would sound like complaining, which they considered unmasculine.

The exclusion of working-class wives from participation in their husbands' jobs contrasts sharply with the often noticed intimate involvement of **corporate wives** with their husbands' work. At the white-collar level, the wife may have a detailed knowledge of office politics and try to promote her husband's upward mobility by careful entertaining of his work associates and superiors. Whether this kind of involvement is good or bad for marriages is hard to say, but at least it does give these couples subjects of mutual interests to discuss (Komarovsky).

For couples who share the middle-class goal of companionship in marriage, but whose lives do not stimulate conversation, the lack of it may be distressing. Feeling that they should talk to each other, they may try, but find that they have nothing to say. According to one husband, "I wish we had more things to talk about, but when I try to think of something I don't know anything to talk to her about." Another man remarked wistfully, "If my wife and I had a little more education maybe we'd have what you call it—more interests? Maybe we could come together better, maybe life would be more interesting for us" (Komarovsky, pp. 155–156).

Inexpressive Males: The Cowboy and the Playboy.   Difficulty of communication between men and women has been increased by the development of a special breed: the inexpressive male. The inexpressiveness so often found in American men is not a natural male trait but rather one that is culturally induced. As indicated before, American boys learn to value expressions of what is thought to be masculinity—toughness, competitiveness, and courage—and to devalue traits considered feminine—gentleness, responsiveness, and expressiveness. This socialization to a rigid idea of masculinity may produce two basic kinds of inexpressive adult males: cowboys and playboys (Balswick and Peek, 1971).

The cowboy is epitomized by John Wayne's standard movie role—the strong, silent he-man. Even though this type may like women, he shows no tenderness or affection toward them since to do so would be unmanly. Instead, he is likely to treat a female with an uneasy reserve, placing her on a pedestal and being awkwardly courteous to her, or else he acts rough with her as though she were "one of the boys."

The newer playboy type, on the other hand, seeks to manipulate women as sexual objects. The playboy, as exemplified by James Bond, feels little affection for the women with whom he has affairs. His relationships are characterized by emotional detachment, as are the cowboy's. But the source of his behavior is different. While the cowboy may have warm feelings

White-collar. Relating to office workers and sales personnel who often wear white shirts to work.

Inexpressive. Lacking expression, especially expression of inner feelings.

toward women but be unwilling or unable to express them, the playboy feels nothing.

If such men marry, both forms of inexpressiveness are at odds with the contemporary American goal of affectionate companionship in marriage. For such a relationship to develop, both partners must contribute expressive characteristics to it. As Balswick and Peek point out, our society imposes conflicting demands on men: it teaches them to be inexpressive, but then it expects them to be expressive with their wives.

There are some indications that the inexpressive male stereotype may be on the way out, however. Distinctions between the sexes in dress and behavior are breaking down, and many critics are denouncing male inexpressiveness as a neurotic hang-up which blocks openness in interpersonal communication. According to Balswick and Peek, if personal-growth groups, psychiatrists, and marriage counselors have their way, the strong, silent male may soon be seen as a pathetic figure rather than the model of American masculinity.

IMPROVING COMMUNICATION

In a study of 172 married couples, Bienvenu found that couples who communicated well with each other could be distinguished from those who didn't by the way they expressed anger and handled their differences, the tone of voice they used, the extent of their understanding of each other, how well they listened, and the extent of their self-disclosure. Nagging, rudeness, and tight-lipped reserve were common patterns in poor communication. These patterns are unnecessary. Although destructive ways of relating are sometimes culturally induced, better modes of communication can be consciously learned and their use by couples seeking to improve their relationship is growing.

TECHNIQUES OF INTERPERSONAL COMMUNICATION
Miller, Corrales, and Wackman (1975) have grouped the requirements for good communication into five major categories: awareness, rules, disclosure and receptivity, skills, and esteem-building. For those who feel good-will toward each other, improvement in communication techniques in these five areas can ease handling of conflicts and enrich the relationship as well.

Awareness.   If people are to communicate effectively, they must know what is happening in the interaction. They must be conscious of their own feelings, sensitive to what their partner feels, knowledgeable about the subject, and aware of the dynamics of the relationship. Awareness, then, has four components: topic, self, partner, and relationship. It is impossible to

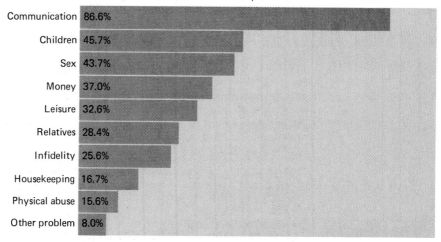

Percentage of all cases with a marital problem

Communication	86.6%
Children	45.7%
Sex	43.7%
Money	37.0%
Leisure	32.6%
Relatives	28.4%
Infidelity	25.6%
Housekeeping	16.7%
Physical abuse	15.6%
Other problem	8.0%

Fig. 9.2 Poor communication a major problem.   Analysis of the case loads of 266 U.S. family counseling agencies revealed that almost nine out of every ten couples with marital problems were faced with difficulties in communication. Clients would say, "We can't talk to each other"; "I can't reach him"; "She doesn't understand me"; or "Every time we talk to each other, it ends in an argument." Yet, Beck and Jones ask, without communication how can one know what the problems are, much less resolve them? (Source: Dorothy F. Beck and Mary Ann Jones, *Progress on Family Problems.* Copyright 1973 by Family Service Association of America, New York. Reprinted by permission.)

think about all four factors at once; we usually have to focus on one and then another at different times.

Topical awareness is required in specific references to people, places, events, ideas, and objects. Self-awareness requires recognition of our own sensory, mental, and emotional processes and how they are related to our behaviors. Awareness between partners requires perception of each others feelings, something akin to mind-reading. Sensitivity to both verbal and nonverbal cues, and a general willingness to understand other people's points of view can help us grasp what their feelings are.

To be aware of what is going on in the relationship itself, we have to focus on patterns of interaction rather than on indivdual behavior. Interaction is the product of the contributions and reactions of both partners. If the man, for instance, chooses to reveal his feelings in a certain situation, the effect on the relationship will be a combination of what he expresses and how the other reacts—whether she ignores him, responds empathetically, or reveals something about herself in return. Her disinterest or encouragement helps to set up a pattern of relating to each other that may become habitual.

CASE STUDY—SUE AND NED

Sue and Ned had been married about four years when Sue decided, on her way home from work one April evening, that they should try to cut down on their food bills by growing their own vegetables. Their little house had an equally little yard, but there was plenty of sun. When she told Ned of her plans, immediately upon his return from work, he was skeptical of how much money it could save and whether the return for their labor would be worth the effort. However, he went out into the yard with Sue to measure off the plot and agreed to dig it up for her.

As the garden progressed, it became obvious that Sue was putting in twice as much time on it as Ned was, and this became a source of some bickering between them. By June the weeding had become a demanding chore, and Sue decided on Friday evening that they should both spend all day Saturday working on the garden plot. Ned came home full of plans for an all-day trip to the beach with two other couples with whom they were friendly. The husbands had worked out plans for this together on their lunch hour.

A full-scale quarrel erupted between Sue and Ned, with many angry accusations. By the time dinner was over, both were miserable, but neither was showing any signs of going along with the other's plans. Ned was saying he had opposed the garden from the beginning and they should just forget it. Sue said she had developed the plan to save money and a lot had already been spent for tools, seeds, and fertilizer. To abandon the garden now would mean money wasted instead of money saved.

For class discussion: (1) What hints do you find in this case study that Sue and Ned are not doing a very good job of communicating with each other? (2) Do you think it would be a satisfactory solution to this problem for Sue to stay home and work in the garden while Ned goes alone to the beach with their friends?

Trying to discern these patterns may be very difficult for the actual participants, especially when they are caught up in interpersonal conflicts. An outside observer may spot them more readily. But couples can sometimes analyze their relationship on their own. They may, for instance, observe that the women tends to bustle around talking to the man in snatches as she does housework, and that he tends to respond by withdrawing into his shell, unwilling to follow her about in order to talk to her or beg her to sit down and talk with him. If brought to conscious awareness, such communication patterns can sometimes be altered, to the benefit of the relationship.

Rules. Awareness alone is not enough. It is one thing to recognize feelings and patterns of communication and another to do something about them. How a couple handles their awareness depends to some extent on the limits they have set on expression of certain kinds of information and behaviors.

For instance, some couples confront threatening topics directly and try to work them out; others try to avoid them. It has been suggested that people have little training for rule-setting in communication. Family counselors now feel that couples should bring the matter of rules out into the open and reach an agreement on how, when, where, and what they can talk about. They might decide, for instance, that they don't want to talk about touchy issues within an hour of their return from work, or in front of their children, and that they work things out best when they are talking in bed on a Sunday morning.

Disclosure and Receptivity.   In addition to settling with the partner what can be talked about and how, each person is faced regularly with the need to decide whether, to whom, and when one should disclose particular feelings and information. Some heavy topics—such as fears about pregnancy, or concern over a relative's drinking problem—might be postponed to a more appropriate time when the partner is more receptive. Some things—an observation that the partner is gaining weight, or feelings of jealousy without any real cause—might be kept to oneself. Candid self-disclosure by one can prompt the other to respond by listening carefully or by making disclosures in return, increasing intimacy in the relationship. But as we have seen before, some intimate disclosures may turn the other person off. It may be as important to know when to be silent in some situations as it is to reveal your feelings in others.

Skills.   If communication were successful only when people have accurate insights into their situations ("I think I resist talking about money problems in front of the children because my parents never did"), then it wouldn't be successful very often. But in recent years, observers have come up with ways that communication can be improved (Bockus, 1975; Miller et al., 1975). Some of these suggested conversation "skills" include:

- speaking for yourself and identifying your opinions as just that (Instead of saying, "You're really stingy," you might say, "It seems to me that you are more reluctant to spend money than I am.");
- using specific, descriptive examples to back up interpretations ("We don't seem to go out very often any more. We haven't been to a movie in over a year, and it's been at least five months since we've been to a restaurant.");
- making feeling statements, expressing how you feel at the moment ("I feel warm and secure with you next to me." "Perhaps it's irrational, but I feel annoyed that you are late.")

Certain listening skills have been suggested in addition to the speaking skills:

Empathy. The capacity for sharing another's feelings or ideas.

- using empathy to understand the other person's point of view;
- accepting the other's messages in a spirit of genuine respect, even if you don't agree with the opinions expressed;
- using feedback techniques of rephrasing what the other has said to check whether you have accurately received and understood the message (If one says, "Sometimes when I come home from work I'm still so busy thinking about what's gone on there that I don't pay much attention to what you're saying," the other might respond, "You don't really hear what I say when you're like that, do you?");
- questioning what the message means or how it should be interpreted ("I think I understand how you feel, but what do you want me to do about it?").

These and similar techniques make it possible to describe and interpret factors of awareness that would otherwise lie beneath the surface, clouding issues and provoking defensive reactions when the goal is open and responsive discussion. As we will see in the next section, specific skills of this sort can be practiced in experimental settings and then applied to everyday interactions.

Esteem building. Mutual efforts of partners in developing each other's self-esteem through emphasis on favorable aspects of personality and behavior.

Esteem Building Even though there are communication skills that can be learned, the most important factor in whether communication is successful is the spirit behind the messages—people's desire to uphold and improve their relationship and their own and their partner's self-esteem, or to destroy them. If people are basically fond of each other, even though they may make mistakes in what they say and when, their underlying affection and commitment to the relationship will still show through. In the examples used at the beginning of the chapter, it was obvious that the second wife was more committed to maintaining a good relationship with her husband than the first. The first made a point of belittling her husband; the second tried to get across the call-if-you'll-be-late message without putting down her spouse as a person.

In a healthy relationship, the partners take responsibility for what they say and when and how they say it, trying to make good choices in these matters. They also try to exercise some control over their responses to the other person's messages. If the husband of the complaining wife really cared about building and maintaining their marriage, he might have tried to understand her feelings—loneliness and boredom as a housewife, discouragement over cooking for someone who shows no appreciation, and fears about what his being late might mean. He might then respond to her in a spirit of concern for her and their relationship rather than one of defensive withdrawal. The second wife made it easier for her husband to react this way—praising her cooking, reassuring her about their relationship, agreeing to accommodate her needs, and expressing concern for her state of mind. By their responsible choice of disclosures and responses, the second couple added to the esteem-building aspect of their partnership. By their irresponsible choices, the first couple diminished esteem in their relationship.

THE NEED FOR BALANCE

For a relationship to be vital and growing, both partners must contribute. If one is noticeably lacking in disclosure, respect, and understanding, the relationship cannot develop, no matter how much the other person contributes. Either partner, then, can block the growth of the relationship.

This theory is supported by the results of several studies. One showed that there is greater satisfaction in marriages in which both partners display high disclosure levels than in those in which only one partner is likely to make intimate disclosures. Another study showed higher satisfaction in marriages in which each partner had a highly accurate understanding of the other's viewpoints on many issues than in marriages in which at least one partner was low on accuracy. Good communication is a shared responsibility. Neither partner can achieve it alone (Miller et al., 1975).

A PROGRAM FOR INVOLVED COUPLES

Many couples are capable of devising their own means of communicating well with each other. Evolving better ways of talking to each other may be a challenging and rewarding aspect of their relationship. But this takes internal resources which some people simply don't have. These people may need and appreciate some outside help in shaping their communication patterns. Building good communications also takes time—perhaps years of gradual opening up and learning how to speak to each other on ever more intimate levels without disrupting the relationship. But for some, the need to understand each other and to deal with conflicts is too urgent to wait for this gradual development.

Communication training which applies the principles discussed in this chapter is now widely offered. One interesting program is the Minnesota Couple Communication Program (Miller et al., 1976). Begun as a pilot project in 1968, it has now served over 1500 couples. It initially served small experimental groups of "engaging" couples—those seeking to communicate better while they were still in the process of forming an intimate relationship, whether they planned to marry or not. But the program has

since been found beneficial to committed couples at any stage—living together, planning marriage, married, or anticipating remarriage. The Minnesota program was not intended to help couples who were already in trouble
cope with their specific conflicts. Instead it sought participants who were
looking for an educational rather than a therapeutic experience.

THE GROUP CONTEXT

In the Minnesota program, volunteers were placed in groups of five to seven
couples. The group context was chosen over individual work with counselors for a number of reasons. (1) The group could serve as a safe environment for exploration and experimentation. Within an atmosphere of trust
and encouragement, couples could discover the possibilities of their relationship and personally guide its direction instead of obeying some authority's specific directions on how they should talk to each other. (2) Feedback
was maximized. Each couple's interaction was viewed by many observers
with many different points of view. (3) Couples served each other as models
of communication styles to copy or to avoid. Seeing that there are many
different ways of interacting on a personal level helps stimulate participants
to consider alternative modes for their own relationship. (4) Engaging couples are especially likely to lack support and advice at this time when they
most need it. Friends may be at different stages of falling in love, and fami-

lies may adopt a position of noninterference, cutting them off from feedback that could be valuable to them during this critical role-changing stage.

THE PROGRAM AND ITS GOALS

Two goals were set for the Minnesota program: to heighten couples' awareness—of self, partner, how each contributes to their interaction, their patterns of maintaining esteem, and their rules for handling conflicts—and to improve their ability to discuss their relationship clearly and openly. Groups got together once a week for four weeks for three-hour sessions. At these group meetings, one or two instructors directed exercises, discussions, and simulated situations, with focus on a different topic each week. Participants were also asked to read a book on improving communication, written by the organizers of the project, and to experiment at home with what they had learned within the group.

The first session concentrated on self-awareness—what it is and skills for developing and expressing it. The second focused on how to exchange information accurately. The third identified four different styles of communication—their intentions, behaviors, and impact—to stimulate consideration of alternative ways of relating. The final session focused on heightening awareness of the esteem-building or esteem-diminishing aspect of communication patterns, especially when critical issues are under discussion.

Self-awareness. Recognition of on's own sensory, mental, and emotional processes and how they are affecting one's behavior.

RESULTS OF THE PROGRAM

The success of the original program was evaluated by comparing 17 volunteer couples who went through the program with a control group of 15 couples who had not yet done so. All were at the "engaging" stage; all took pretests before training began and posttests after the sessions had ended. Substantial improvements in communication skills were found in the experimental group, who had the training, but not in the control group, who had none.

Specifically, couples were given two tests. One measured how well they recalled how they had interacted when asked to spend five minutes planning something they could do together. To fill out a 12-item question sheet, participants had to remember to what extent each had displayed behaviors such as agreeing, yielding, putting oneself down, putting the other down, expressing feelings, and making suggestions. The other test measured the couple's ability to sustain open communication about their relationship. They were asked to spend five minutes discussing things that each did that irritated the other. Their taped conversations were scored according to how many seconds of "hard-working" statements about their relationship they made.

In the first test, the experimental group's recall accuracy rose significantly with training, indicating substantial improvement in awareness. The control group's scores were the same in the pretest and the posttest. In the second test, the control group was actually higher to begin with but dropped by the posttest; the experimental group's scores rose significantly after training, indicating substantial improvement in disclosure and receptivity.

The experimenters concluded that successful interpersonal communication can be learned: through training (or perhaps even by giving conscious thought to these matters), people can become more aware of themselves and how they contribute to the interaction in a relationship, become more skillful in expressing their awareness, and recognize that they need not be stuck in the same old destructive patterns of interaction forever. Change is possible, and it is within people's power to make their ways of relating to each other mutually rewarding.

Summary

1. The main purpose of this chapter is to describe the nature of interpersonal communication: its forms, factors that affect its quantity and quality, and techniques to improve communication.

2. Communication is used to modify behavior, give information, test reality, and satisfy needs for self-expression. Communication may be verbal (through language) or nonverbal (through gestures, facial expressions, and tone of voice). Verbal communication tends to be consciously controlled, while nonverbal is more spontaneous and often on an almost involuntary level.

3. The relationship of communication and identity is complex. Through communication we discover, modify, and reaffirm our identity, which is a composite of all our roles and continually changes as our roles change. In turn, we communicate with others in terms of our particular identity, our concept of how a person with that identity should behave.

4. The combination of society's expectations and our own conception of how we should play our roles, called our role-identity, helps us prepare for actual performances, gives us a standard for evaluating our performance, and gives meaning to our lives. Establishing a role-identity often involves a process called identity bargaining through which people negotiate to resolve differences in their self-perceptions and their perceptions of each other and of the purposes of the social encounter.

5. Self-disclosure, the process by which people reveal themselves to each other, varies in breadth (amount), in depth (intimacy), and in the time spent on the information revealed. Quality of disclosure, as well as quantity, is important. Factors to consider in choosing whether to disclose information are: the subject of the disclosure, whether it is favorable to the other person, and the existing intimacy of the relationship.

6. While too little self-disclosure can have adverse effects on our personal growth and our relationships, there are limits as well—too much self-disclosure of a negative type may harm a relationship. When making criticisms, it is important to express acceptance before criticizing and to describe rather than judge when criticizing.

7. Our culture frequently puts barriers to intimate communication between people through stereotyped male and female roles.

8. Five major requirements for good communication are awareness, rules, disclosure and receptivity, skills, and esteem building. Communication skills can be learned, and there are communication-training programs that educate couples in these skills.

Communication	Dyad	Inexpressive male	**Key Concepts**
Verbal	Identity	Awareness	
Nonverbal	Reciprocal roles	Rules	
Symbol	Role-identity	Esteem building	
Involuntary	Identity bargaining	Receptivity	
Interaction	Presentation of the self	Empathy	
Perception	Self-disclosure		

Review and Discussion

1. Look around a place such as a post office or a cafeteria, where you cannot hear the verbal communications, and list or describe some of the attitudes and emotions being conveyed by nonverbal means.

2. Keeping in mind all your various activities, list all of the roles you played today and the reciprocal roles played by others in your interaction with them.

3. Try to recall a particular event in your life when you were involved in identity bargaining—perhaps with an employer, a teacher, or a new friend. Were you satisfied with the outcome?

4. Why do you think men tend to be lower in self-disclosure than women? How is the inexpressive male trait induced?

5. How can nondisclosure hurt a relationship? How can too much disclosure hurt a relationship? Give some examples.

Suggested Readings

FARRELL, W. (1974). *The Liberated Man—Beyond Masculinity: Freeing Men and Their Relationships with Women.* New York: Random House.
Discusses aspects of man's liberation such as limitations of masculinity, its values, and how they operate. The author also suggests ways in which men can benefit from women's liberation and how changes can take place through consciousness raising.

SATIR, V. (1972).   *Peoplemaking.* Palo Alto, Calif.: Science and Behavior Books.

The author covers aspects of family life and relationships which shape us into the people we are (self-worth, communications, and rules), and shows ways to find how these operate in a family and how to change them to increase the joy of family life.

SCORESBY, A. L. (1977).   *The Marriage Dialogue.* Reading, Mass.: Addison-Wesley.

Describes marital communication skills which can be learned and applied to improve dialogue between marriage partners. Covers the role of communication in marriage, interpreting marital messages, decision making, and other topics.

STEWART, J. (1977).   *Bridges Not Walls, 2nd Edition.* Reading, Mass.: Addison-Wesley.

A collection of articles about aspects of interpersonal communication, including verbal and nonverbal codes, self-perception, and self-disclosure. Concepts are presented in a clear and understandable style.

WILMOT, W. W. (1975).   *Dyadic Communications: A Transactional Perspective.* Reading, Mass.: Addison-Wesley.

Examines the nature of dyadic relationships and focuses on the complex processes that shape communication in social settings. The author uses knowledge from communication theory, family communication, psychiatry, sociology, and humanistic psychology to explore dyadic relationships, the effects on partners, and methods of improving communications.

Interpersonal Adjustments in Marriage | *10*

Interpersonal communication, as explained in Chapter 9, is the process by which people gain their identities as human beings. Without communication, socialization could never occur. It is also the tool by which people mold each other in the process called identity bargaining (described in Chapter 9) whereby people gain credibility in performance of whatever roles are relevant to a particular social encounter. At the same time, communication is the means by which people cooperate with each other in carrying out joint activities, whether they are for work, as in obtaining food, or for pleasure, as in playing tennis. Assignment of roles in any cooperative task is achieved through gestures, verbal exchanges, facial expressions, all kinds of visual and auditory signals.

Adjustment. Modification of a person's needs relative to those of another so as to achieve a mental and behavioral balance.

Even in very temporary encounters, as between a ticket seller and a purchaser, communication is the basis on which participants adjust their behavior each to the other, so that the purchaser ends up with a ticket and the seller gets the money. In long-term relationships, as between two sisters or between husband and wife, the process of adjustment is continuous and is achieved by the same means—effective interpersonal communication.

THE CONCEPT OF ADJUSTMENT

A couple may be described as very happy together, or perhaps as not getting along too well. But neither one of the conditions is likely to be a permanent state. Two people who are happily married will still be in conflict with each other at times over particular decisions or everyday events. Even people who are not getting along too well have their happy moments together when each one is well satisfied with the behavior of the other.

Process. A series of actions marked by gradual changes that lead toward a particular result.

In or out of marriage, dyadic adjustment—the adjustment of two people to each other—is a continuing process. Situations change. One partner gets a new job, with longer hours, or loses one; the couple moves; a widowed mother-in-law joins the household; they have a baby. With each change, new adjustments are required. Movement is not always in one direction, toward better adjustment or worse adjustment, but back and forth. We can think of this as movement along a continuous line, with extremely poor adjustment at one end and extremely good adjustment at the other. In some ways we might even think of this line as a tightrope, with partners balancing their way along the rope, sometimes helping each other, sometimes hindering.

Poor   ⟵————————————⟶   Good
Adjustment   Adjustment

A couple moves first in one direction, then the other, with perhaps an overall movement over a period of time, toward one end of the line or the other.

The total adjustment between the two members of the dyad at any particular time is a composite, or a balance, of a number of different elements. Social researchers have long been concerned with how to identify these elements so as to determine what makes happy marriages and what makes other marriages fail. Spanier (1976) has recently devised a Dyadic Adjustment Scale that measures factors found to be significant indicators of interpersonal adjustment. His questionnaire, which yields a total adjustment score, includes self-ratings on 32 items which fall into four general categories:

1. *dyadic satisfaction*—the extent to which the couple are satisfied with their relationship (measured by questions such as, How often do you and your partner quarrel? Do you confide in your mate? Do you ever regret that you married? Describe the degree of general happiness in your relationship.);
2. *dyadic cohesion*—the couple's feelings of togetherness (How often do you have a stimulating exchange of ideas, calmly discuss something, or work together on a project?),
3. *dyadic consensus*—the extent of agreement between partners (How often do you agree on handling family finances, household tasks, leisure activities, or ways of dealing with parents or in-laws?);
4. *affectional expression*—the degree of disclosure of feelings of love, affection, and concern (What is the extent of your agreement on sex relations? Has not showing love been a problem?).

In devising his **scale,** Spanier expected to include measures of two other kinds of variables—troublesome dyadic differences, and interpersonal tensions and personal anxiety—as part of his total adjustment score. But so far these negative elements have been less successful in measuring total dyadic adjustment than the four kinds of variables specified: satisfaction, cohesion, consensus, and affection. This should not be interpreted to mean that troublesome differences, tensions, and anxiety do not exist in well-adjusted relationships. Dyadic harmony can be achieved despite interpersonal conflict, depending on how people deal with their differences.

> **Scale.** A graduated series or scheme for ranking statistical data obtained in sociological research.

THE TENSION BETWEEN IDENTITY AND STABILITY

One ever-present problem in achieving a satisfying relationship in marriage is the tension most people feel between the need for intimate relationships and the need for personal privacy. Intimate relationships exercise restraints on the people involved in them, and these restraints are experienced as threats to the maintenance of one's identity as a separate individual. At the same time, needs for privacy and independence are a threat to the stability of the intimate relationship.

IDENTITY BUILDING

From the day of our birth onward, we gradually find out who we are by interacting with other people. We learn from social interaction that we are male or female, bright or dull, leader or follower, and what behaviors are appropriate to these roles. Constructing an identity, which may be thought of as the totality of all our different roles, depends upon our social relationships. To our intimates, friends, and relatives we reveal the complexities of our inner selves, seeking interpretation and encouragement.

While building and affirming our identity thus requires intimacy, it also requires periods of privacy. We need privacy from intimate interaction to reflect on what we have learned from it. Especially when the interaction with an intimate has been disturbing, we need to withdraw to figure out what it means—should we alter our future behavior or straighten out conflicts in our thinking, or does the problem lie more in our partner's inability to be realistic? It is only through such coming together to interact, withdrawing to reflect and perhaps change, and then interacting again that we develop our individuality. The process is a mutual one, for it influences our partner's personal growth in the same way.

According to Askham (1976), at least seven conditions are therefore required for maintaining a sense of personal identity:

1. An individual needs an intimate relationship in which both partners can talk about aspects of themselves that they usually keep hidden from others.
2. Within such a relationship, both people need an equal chance to develop their identity. Neither should impose an identity on the other or attempt to restrict the other's growth.
3. Both partners also need times of privacy to reflect on their interaction with each other and to distance themselves from the relationship in order to view it more objectively.
4. Because people's identities grow and change with experience, their relationship should be a developing one which is flexible enough to accommodate their individual changes.
5. Public perception of this relationship should not be allowed to freeze the partners into rigid roles. If it is a marriage, the man should not feel confined in the stereotyped role of husband nor the woman in the role of wife to the extent that it restricts their identity building.
6. The relationship should not restrict the partners from having new experiences. They grow by talking about their new perceptions. If they cease to have any, the exchange between them will wither away.
7. For fuller growth and a clearer view of the relationship, each of the partners should have the chance to discuss the relationship with at least one other person.

THE NEED FOR STABILITY

A second basic need that people seek to fulfill, also discussed by Askham, is a desire for stability. In a marital relationship, stability means security and a predictable way of life in which familiar situations require no new decisions. This base of predictable routines, habits, and events makes life easier and frees our energies for coping with new situations. If we seek the feeling of "home" or stability in our intimate partner, we want that person to be an accepting and permanent fixture in our life. If the partner changes, the change should be gradual without disrupting the tie to us. Neither partner should be absent for long periods of time. In general, anything that might damage the stability of this bond should be avoided.

Stability in an intimate relationship, according to Askham, therefore requires that:

1. Intimate conversations must avoid topics that threaten the relationship or reveal wide differences of opinion.
2. Actions which might make the other feel that the relationship is insecure must be avoided.
3. Behavior, such as sharing, which cements the relationship and makes it more legitimate in the eyes of others should be encouraged.
4. Third parties who might interfere with the stability of the relationship should not be allowed to form an intimate relationship with either partner.
5. Individual changes should not be encouraged, for there is no way of knowing what effect they might have on the stability of the relationship.
6. Partners may have to restrict each other's privacy and independence, since they might lead to redefinitions of reality which lessen one's commitment to the other.

RECONCILING CONFLICTING NEEDS

It is obvious that the sets of requirements for identity building and stability are at odds with each other. Yet, in marriage, people often hope to satisfy both needs in one relationship. The result may be a constant push and pull between the two desires. Identity building demands free and far-ranging conversation, some privacy or independence, the chance for each partner to have new experiences and to grow, trying out new roles, and the opportunity for involvement with third parties. Stability, on the other hand, appears to require that all these factors be inhibited in the relationship.

So how do couples meet the conflicting needs for both stability and identity? Askham found that people manage this problem in different ways. One method was to compromise both needs. Instead of fully realizing either goal, some couples settled for a limited amount of each. In one young

CASE STUDY—BARBARA AND TED

Barbara and Ted, both in their early forties, have been married for nearly 20 years. Their marriage has never been consummated through sexual intercourse.

Ted makes a good living, providing Barbara with financial necessities and some luxuries. She is a good cook and enjoys keeping house. Friends consider them happily married. In the beginning, questions were sometimes asked about why they did not have children, but now friends assume that they were simply unable to.

At times, Barbara is very depressed by her marriage to a man with whom she has little in common and longs for a more intimate relationship. However, she is reconciled to the situation because she feels she and her husband are sharing an exchange which is beneficial for both. She gets support; he gets a housekeeper. She has never found it possible to discuss with Ted how he feels about their arrangement. As far as she knows, he, too, is reconciled to a marriage in name only.

For class discussion: (1) What kind of a woman might be willing to settle for a marriage lacking both companionship and sexual intimacy? What kind of a man? (2) Do you see any advantages to this marriage compared with one in which there is a lot of emotional involvement but also a lot of conflict?

marriage, the husband continued to go drinking with his friends several nights a week; the wife's response was to spend a lot of time at her mother's or with women friends, so she was not always home when her husband returned. Finding this arrangement mutually unsatisfactory, since it threatened both partners' sense of security in the relationship, they agreed on a compromise: one night out a week with friends for each of them.

Another way of managing the conflict was to stress first one need and then the other. Askham found that for some, marriage begins with a strong need for building a sense of security—making certain that the relationship is really strong, not threatened by third parties, outside interests, or divergent opinions. This initial stress on stability begins even during the engagement period. After the wedding, the emphasis on setting up housekeeping reflects the need to provide a secure home base. Once this background of stability has been established, the couple may feel safer in allowing their relationship to change and grow by exploring formerly taboo areas of conversation together and by tolerating greater degrees of independent activity. It is also possible that they may shift to stressing identity and personal freedom, not out of a positive feeling of security, but out of frustration with the restrictions of the secure, stable relationship.

A third strategy Askham found couples using was to stress one need and sacrifice the other. Some people consider their independence and personal identity so important that they are willing to do without stability. Couples who share this feeling might live together for years without marrying, in order to grant each other freedom and keep their own options open. On the other hand, some people find stability so gratifying that they really don't regret their lack of independence. One married man Askham talked to, for instance, sprinkled his interview with remarks like "I'm quite content to stay at home" and "When I go out I'd rather go out with the wife."

A fourth means of dealing with the identity-stability conflict is to meet one need in one relationship and the other need in a different relationship. This is often the case in extramarital affairs, in which the married partner provides stability and the lover provides an opportunity for self-expression and personality expansion. This pattern is possible without extramarital sexual involvement. For instance, a woman might have a shallow but stable and happy relationship with her husband, coupled with an intimate relationship with a friend to whom she expresses her deeper thoughts. Askham speculates that continued contact with parents after marriage may be another way to give stability to a relationship within which the major stress is on identity building.

Whichever of the four strategies is used in a particular situation, some compromise between needs for identity and stability is likely to be involved.

Compromise. Settlement of differences through agreement to mutual concessions.

SOME MAJOR AREAS OF MARITAL ADJUSTMENT

The continuing push-pull in intimate pair relationships is a factor likely to affect all interactions between the partners. The decision whether or not the wife should have a paid job outside the home is especially likely to be affected by the separate needs of husband and wife for identity and stability. Relations with in-laws, sex-role adjustments, decisions about vacations and use of leisure time—some of the relationships to be discussed—are all made more complex by conflicting needs of family members for individual identity within a stable relationship with another individual.

ADJUSTING TO IN-LAWS

One of the first developmental tasks of marriage is the necessity that the pair come to identify with each other in their new roles of husband and wife rather than with the families they came from. Although their parents and other relatives have helped to shape their identities and may continue to be frequent visitors, the new couple must put the development of a good working relationship with each other before their loyalties to their families of orientation. Unless the bond between them is stronger than the bonds linking them to the families in which they grew up, the new family may be in trouble. And anything that a member of either of the original families does that hampers the cohesiveness of the new dyad can be looked upon as a potentially divisive in-law problem (Duvall, 1965).

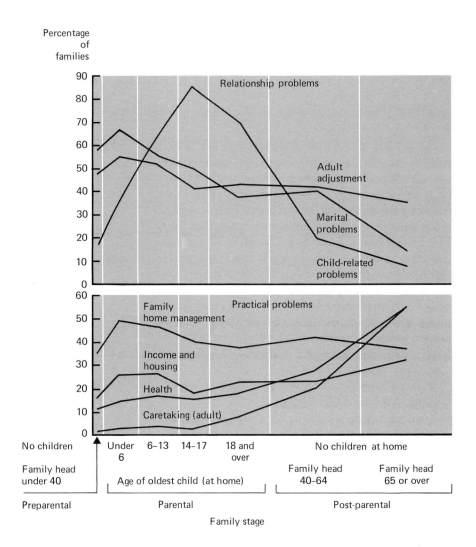

Percentage
of
families

Relationship problems

Adult
adjustment

Marital
problems

Child-related
problems

Practical problems

Family
home management

Income and
housing

Health

Caretaking (adult)

No children

Family head
under 40

Under 6-13 14-17 18 and
6 over

Age of oldest child (at home)

No children at home

Family head
40-64

Family head
65 or over

Preparental

Parental

Post-parental

Family stage

Fig. 10.1 Importance of common family problems at different stages of the family life cycle.   The types of problems for which families seek help from family counseling agencies differ markedly by the position of the family in the family life cycle. Relationship problems tend to decrease as couples move into the postparental stage, but practical problems tend to become more severe, especially for couples in which the family head is 65 or older. (Source: Dorothy F. Beck and Mary Ann Jones, *Progress on Family Problems.* Copyright 1973 by Family Service Association of America, New York. Reprinted by permission.)

Not much has been written by sociologists recently about in-law problems. Perhaps in-laws are no longer perceived as such a threat to marriages as they once were, perhaps because they are now less inclined to interfere or because new nuclear families find it easier to move away from them. Most of what we know about how in-laws affect adjustment problems in marriage comes from classic sources, such as Komarovsky's *Blue-Collar Marriage* (1964).

Patterns of In-law Conflict.   According to most studies, in-law problems are more likely to involve women than men. The mother-in-law is more often a problem than the father-in-law; daughters-in-law are more likely to have clashes with their in-laws than are sons-in-law (Kirkpatrick, 1963). But Komarovsky has found that for working-class men, in-law problems are as common as they are for women in general: one-third of each group have strained relationships with their in-laws.

Just as wives may be sensitive to controversies over housekeeping, child rearing, or the role of wife that seem to challenge their sense of adequacy, husbands' problems with in-laws seem to surface when their self-respect is threatened. For example, Komarovsky found that men who marry wives better educated than themselves are likely to experience in-law conflicts. Sometimes the wife's parents are clearly disappointed that she married "beneath her"; sometimes the educational imbalance in the marriage itself puts the husband on the defensive and makes him more sensitive to real or imagined criticism. Of course, less education does not necessarily mean less intelligence or less skillfulness in all areas, so educationally imbalanced marriages do not always lead to in-law conflict.

While in one pattern, a married person sides with the parent in cutting down the mate's self-respect, the triangle in other families may be weighted quite differently: sometimes the married couple side with each other against certain relatives, so that what hurts one affects them both. A taxi-driver Komarovsky interviewed, for instance, tried to be a barrier between his wife and her parents. As he put it, "I try to keep her away from her family as much as I can on account of they do hurt her a lot." In such cases, in-law problems, while certainly not desirable, may actually be a healthy sign of the couple's identification with each other.

Some partners may have been overly dependent on parents and they may continue to look to parents for advice on problems that should instead involve decision making within the nuclear family unit. They may also look to them for emotional support, stimulating competition between the spouse and the parents for affection and attention. A woman who visits her mother too frequently, or a man who will not make any decisions without consulting his father, is likely to have a spouse who has become jealous of the influence of in-laws.

In-law problems may be increased if the younger couple depend on their parents for economic support or share their home. Decisions that would otherwise involve only the husband and wife become everybody's business. There is also less chance that uncongenial persons can get away from each other. On the other hand, such interdependence may make it essential that they try to get along with each other, either for the sake of

In-laws. Persons to whom one is related by marriage.

everyday peace or out of financial necessity. One man Komarovsky interviewed tried to keep his wife from getting too angry with her mother, saying "We have to keep in good with her. We might need her real bad."

The Potential for Congenial Relations. Despite the opportunities for conflict, in-law relationships are not always or perhaps even usually a major problem. In Komarovsky's sample, for instance, the majority of men reported either a good relationship with the mother-in-law, characterized by affection, positive satisfaction, and only minor conflicts, or at least an average one—some favorable comments coupled with minor complaints.

The chances of running into in-law trouble are lessened if people choose wisely in the first place. In-law conflict is often minimized if the two families of orientation get along well together and if they come from similar cultures (Kirkpatrick). If a person comes from a background that fits well with that of his or her in-laws, they are likely to agree on the right way of doing things, to enjoy the same activities, to understand each other's jokes and concerns, and to grant each other the privacy that comes from trust and approval.

ADJUSTMENTS IN YOUTHFUL MARRIAGES

According to most studies, teenage marriages are subject to the same adjustment problems as later marriages, only more so. Marital satisfaction is usually found to be lower, the risk of disillusionment and failure is higher, and economic, social, and personal problems are greater. In order to assess this high potential for conflict, Vladimir DeLissovoy (1973) studied 48 rural or small-town Pennsylvania couples who married while they were in high school. Each couple was interviewed five times, starting within three months of their marriage, and ending with a visit about three years after the wedding.

DeLissovoy points out that these couples were not the sort whose weddings were celebrated in the society pages of their local newspapers. The average age of the girls at marriage was 16; for the young husbands, it was 17. Forty-one of the wives and 35 of the husbands dropped out of high school before they graduated; 46 of the 48 wives were pregnant before they married. Asked to rate their adjustment difficulties, they revealed that after only three months of marriage, they were experiencing a variety of problems and little of the bliss expected by newlyweds.

Money. The first of the problem areas these young couples were asked to evaluate was the degree to which they agreed on how to spend what money they had. On a scale in which 1 represented many quarrels about it, or mostly disagreement, and 5 represented complete agreement, the young wives gave money matters an average score of 2.12; the husbands rated it 2.52.

According to DeLissovoy, the central problem was not so much how to spend money as the fact that there wasn't much of it. Some of the couples received public assistance; most received surplus food from the government. After three months of marriage, one-third had already made credit purchases requiring regular payments, and more than half had borrowed from finance companies at high interest rates. Counteracting this bleak picture was the help that almost all the couples received from their parents in goods, money, services, and shelter.

Even at the three-year point, parents were still providing some form of financial assistance. But ratings of their adjustment in financial matters had worsened for both the wives and the husbands. The fact that money problems were continuing with no apparent end in sight seemed to be a major source of tension in these young marriages. DeLissovoy suggests that disagreements and worries in this area may have carried over into other areas as well.

Social Activities.   Although the teenage husbands and wives were in agreement that money was a serious problem, they had opposing views concerning their social lives. For the husbands, questions about their social activities and ability to keep up with friends drew an average score of 4.10, but for the wives, the average score was only 2.32, on the low end of the 1-to-5 scale. Apparently, marriage had changed the husbands' social lives very little. They continued to go out with their old friends, play basketball after school, and socialize in their part-time jobs. The wives, on the other hand, were more likely to be isolated from their schoolgirl friends by the differences of their housekeeping and childbearing roles and to feel left out even when their husbands' buddies came to visit. The wives' resentment against their husbands for not "settling down" was obvious in their conversation. And although most wives wanted to do things with other young couples, this had happened in only 7 of the 48 marriages.

Three years later, the social pattern was very much the same. Husbands still saw their old friends and wives generally didn't, but now the wives' attitude was more likely to be one of resignation rather than irritation. Busy with child care, they said they had little time for social activities anyway.

In-law Relationships.   Despite their isolation from peers, the young wives —and their husbands—had frequent contact with relatives. Although their parents (farmers, manual laborers, and housewives) had generally been shocked to learn that their children would be marrying so young, their initial disapproval gave way to resignation and then active support in most cases. Most, for instance, helped their children to arrange home or church weddings. As for the young couples, both husbands and wives gave their in-law relationships a slightly better than average rating, even those who were forced by economic circumstances to live in their in-laws' home.

By the three years' interview, DeLissovoy found that the husbands' satisfaction with their in-laws had increased slightly, while the wives' rating had dropped a bit. There were indications that the husbands were grateful for their in-laws' help and that they had begun to feel particularly close to their fathers-in-law, often calling them by their first names and enjoying mutual activities. But for the wives, the birth of the first child often brought resentment of the mother-in-laws' well-meaning interference in child-rearing matters. Nonetheless, 44 of the couples reported closer relationships with their parents once their first child was born.

Child Rearing.   These young couples, who became parents so early, seemed to know little about how a normal child develops and what child rearing involves. Before they had children, the couples gave themselves very high ratings on agreement on child training, an apparent reflection of their idealized, little-thought-out notion of parenthood. For those few who already had children at the time of the initial interview, self-ratings of agreement on child rearing were much lower. Asked at what age they thought a child would master specific developmental tasks, the sample as a whole revealed unrealistically early expectations. They thought, for instance, that a baby should smile at three weeks, achieve bladder and bowel training at about six months, and speak the first word at six to eight months.

By the time their first children were two years old (and some had more than one by this time), the mothers scored on the low end of a scale designed to test how well they accepted the child. DeLissovoy expresses concern that with few exceptions, they appeared to be impatient and intolerant with their children.

Sex.   Asked how much they enjoyed sexual relations with their partner and whether they were satisfied with the frequency of lovemaking, the young husbands rated their general satisfaction slightly below average and their satisfaction with frequency even lower. The wives, on the other hand, expressed higher than average satisfaction with their sexual activities, reporting that the amount of lovemaking, considered inadequate by their husbands, was plenty or even a bit too much for them. At the three years' interview, this pattern was even more pronounced. The husbands, apparently still dissatisfied with the frequency of lovemaking, gave their sexual relations a mean rating of only 2.10. But for the wives, too much sex rather than too little still seemed to be the main problem.

Religious Activities.   Even though the young wives in this study seemed generally isolated from their friends, irritated by their children, resentful of their husbands' outside activities, displeased about being asked to make love more often than they wanted to, and sometimes annoyed at in-law interference, they all reported one source of strength: their church. DeLissovoy reports that for 39 of the 48 couples, the decision to marry had been strongly influenced by their minister. And especially for the wives, church activities provided social as well as spiritual support, as a way to get out and see people. On a scale in which 1 represented no church attendance and the unimportance of religion in one's life, and 5 represented regular attendance and active participation in a religion considered to be an important part of one's life, the wives gave their religious activities an average rating of 4.27, close to the maximum possible rating. Their husbands also reported positive church involvement, with a mean rating of 4.01. But by the three-year point, the husbands' involvement had dropped and some had begun to stay home with the children while their wives went to church.

Conclusions. Many studies have confirmed the hazards of early marriage, especially when complicated by premarital pregnancy and economic hardships. DeLissovoy's findings suggest that in their immaturity and lack of experience, young people tend to romanticize marriage and child rearing. They quickly find themselves disappointed and discouraged, reaching a point of marital dissatisfaction at 30 months which for people who are older at the time of marriage usually does not occur until the middle years of a marriage.

But despite their apparent problems and signs of growing dissatisfaction with their marriages, perhaps the most remarkable thing about the teenage marriages in DeLissovoy's small, rural sample is that most of them had endured. By the time of the three-year follow-up, only 2 of the 48 couples had been divorced; 9 others could not be contacted, but parents reported that they were still married. The marriage DeLissovoy considered most likely to fail—one between a 14-year-old orphaned boy and a girl a year older—turned out to be a very happy one, three years and two babies later, despite their continuing financial hardships.

Generally, the chances for success in marriage between partners who are so young, so inexperienced, so financially pressed, so limited in education, and so poorly motivated (with existing pregnancy for the reason for most of the marriages) are low. For the young couples DeLissovoy studied, these negative factors were perhaps offset by some strong points in their favor. One was the kinship support which an unexpected pregnancy and the decision to marry evoked in their working-class rural families. Whether middle-class or urban teenage couples in the same situation—immaturity, premarital pregnancy, and dropping out of school—would receive as much support from their relatives is questionable. In addition to kinship aid, the young couples were sustained by their church ties. Religious activities may have helped to lessen guilt feelings and to provide a sense of security in a stable community institution at a time of personal crisis.

WORK-ROLE ADJUSTMENTS

The widespread movement of women into the labor force is having a substantial impact on couples' adjustment. In this section, we will consider the findings of some research on how some work-related variables seem to influence marital adjustment and the effect of the wife's working on husband-wife relationships.

Job Involvement and Job Satisfaction. It is sometimes thought that people who are highly involved in their work have little time for enjoying home life and that their marriages suffer as a result. On the other hand, it seems reasonable to suppose that people who are bored or dissatisfied with their jobs might be more likely to seek pleasure and satisfaction in their marriages. According to a study by Carl Ridley (1973) of dual-career families in which the wives are teachers, there is a relationship between involvement and satisfaction in work and happiness in marriage, but it is somewhat different than might be expected.

In testing his subjects for the three variables—marital adjustment, job satisfaction, and job involvement—Ridley defined job involvement as the amount of time devoted to thinking, reading, writing, and talking about the job beyond the normal workday. He felt that this kind of extended involvement was most likely to interfere with people's marital roles. He chose female teachers—and their husbands—as his subjects on the assumption that professional jobs are most likely to demand high involvement.

Ridley found that for men, the first two variables, job satisfaction and marital adjustment, were positively related. Satisfaction at work meant satisfaction in marriage; dissatisfaction at work was likely to mean dissatisfaction in marriage, contrary to expectations. Ridley suggests that because men in our culture are socialized to regard work success as the most important indicator of self-worth, happiness with themselves stemming from work satisfaction probably carries over into happiness with their marriages. For women, the work-marriage relationship depends on another variable; how important they consider their job. If women see their work role as only secondary in their lives, satisfaction from their job has no effect on their marital interaction. But for women who consider their work important, job satisfaction is significantly related to marital adjustment, just as it is for men.

In general, the couples Ridley interviewed had been more than moderately successful at keeping the third variable, job involvement, from interfering with their marriage. But their marital-adjustment scores were highest when both husband and wife scored low in job involvement. If either one was highly involved in his job, marital adjustment suffered.

Differences in Adjustment When the Wife Works. Other researchers have examined specific effects of the wife's working, compared with nonworking

Job involvement. The amount of time devoted to thinking, reading, writing, and talking about the job beyond the normal work day.

Job satisfaction. Positive attitudes toward one's work situation in terms of interest, feeling of accomplishment, adjustment to co-workers, and economic rewards.

wives. Although a lot is known about the stresses added to married life when the wife works, most of them involving a lack of time and various role dilemmas, the effects are not altogether negative.

Ronald Burke and Tamara Weir (1976) administered lengthy questionnaires to 189 Canadian couples. All the men in the study were professionally employed; 28 percent of the wives were working outside the home. The researchers found that the working wives were generally happier and more satisfied with their marriages than were the housewives, but their husbands were less satisfied than the husbands of nonworking wives.

On questions measuring marital adjustment, the working wives reported greater happiness in marriage, high agreement with their husbands on eight topics from sex to in-laws, and a greater likelihood of resolving disagreements by mutual give-and-take than by one person's habitually giving in.

The picture painted by the husbands of these working wives was not so rosy, however. Those with wives who worked reported themselves more worried about housing problems, the feeling of being in a rut, money troubles, and difficulties in communicating with and showing affection to their wives. Husbands of housewives, on the other hand, were more worried about general world problems and whether their children would live up to their expectations. Although those with working wives communicated more with their spouses, they were less happy with their marriages, lower in physical and mental health, and more likely to be generally depressed than were husbands of housewives.

In trying to figure out why the wife's working would have a beneficial effect on her marital adjustment but a damaging effect on her husband's, Burke and Weir suggest that when a wife takes on the responsibilities and time-demands of an outside job, the husband loses some of her emotional and physical support. In addition to missing the comforts of having her

DOONESBURY   **by Garry Trudeau**

serving and waiting upon him, he may have to help fill domestic roles, such as taking care of the children, cooking, and cleaning the house, to help compensate for the new demands on his wife's time. While his wife may gain in self-respect and status from a job that increases her feelings of accomplishment and competence, his position is altered to include support for her in her professional role. Despite the pleasure he may take in being closer to his children, seeing his wife grow as a person, and gaining competence in domestic matters, these factors are not as highly valued in our society as success in work roles. Although he may accept the shift in work roles out of a willingness to be fair and to see his wife happy, he may still

---

CASE STUDY—DAVID AND ELLEN

Ellen, at the age of 25, has a long history of mental instability, beginning about the time of her graduation from high school. She lives away from home and is somewhat estranged from her parents. Part of her emotional difficulties seems to be a need to come between her parents, to own them both for herself, instead of seeing the respect and loyalty of the parents for each other as a source of stability in the midst of her problems. The parents contribute to Ellen's support but refuse to allow her to return home, even for visits. Ellen has been hospitalized twice for treatment of her emotional problems, but always claims that she was just overtired and did not really need hospital treatment.

During the second hospitalization, Ellen became friendly with two black students from Africa who were attending college in the United States and working at the hospital. Upon leaving the hospital, she moved to the community where they were living instead of returning to the apartment she had occupied at the time of entering the hospital. She worked at a variety of jobs, though still receiving support from her parents.

After a few months, Ellen, who is white, moved in with David, one of the black students, much to the dismay of her parents. They refused to meet David or acknowledge her relationship in any way. Finally, a year after Ellen left the hospital, she and David were married. Both are working; both are continuing college studies. They have friends in the community and attend services together at a local Protestant church. David's parents have written from Africa that they welcome Ellen to their tribe and look forward to the time when she will come to Africa with David to live among them. Ellen's parents did not attend the wedding and refuse to meet their new son-in-law.

For class discussion: (1) Considering the difference in cultural background between an African black man and a white, upper-middle-class American woman, what do you think are the chances for success of the marriage? What strengths do you see in the relationship? (2) Ellen and David expect to have children, and Ellen has expressed to her parents, over the telephone and in letters, the belief that they will accept David as a part of their family once a grandchild is born. Do you think this is likely to happen?

feel himself devalued. His feeling of being somehow downgraded by his wife's activities may be especially troublesome if he has been accustomed to think in terms of traditional gender roles.

Burke and Weir conclude that the problems men experience in deviating from traditional gender roles should be given more attention. We can no longer maintain the myth that men are stronger, more independent, and more competent than women and, therefore, need less support. Their needs should be recognized in dual-career marriages as much as those of their wives and some kind of support provided for both. As Burke and Weir put it, "One individual in the marital pair should not have to suffer so that the other can grow."

GENDER-ROLE ADJUSTMENTS

Some problems in adjusting to work-role shifts stem from attitudes in general toward gender roles. The women's liberation movement and social change have altered some people's thinking about gender roles, but other people have held on to more traditional role conceptions. If one partner is becoming more modern in gender-role attitudes while the other maintains traditional views, the potential for conflict is increased.

The modern view of gender roles was once thought to involve only equality between the sexes, in contrast to the traditional view that women should accept a subservient position to men, waiting on them and letting them make all important decisions. But Marie Osmond and Patricia Martin (1975), along with other researchers, suggest that modern people of both sexes no longer regard gender as a relevant qualification for any social position or role. According to this view, equality for females is only part of a general opening up of all roles to both males and females. Some men who hold this attitude are now serving as nurses and telephone operators, traditionally women's jobs, while women are becoming carpenters and participating in government at high levels. Erasing of traditional gender stereotypes may be an essential part of equality for women, for as women's roles shift, men's roles must shift with them. As we have noted, when the wife takes a job, the husband must adjust his expectations of service from her and may have to assume more home and child-care duties. These jobs may have to be seen as "our" work rather than only "hers."

Whether people can and should be socialized to this position remains to be seen. The problem now is that some people have accepted the changes and some have not. The tendency is for men to be more traditional than women. Osmond and Martin confirmed this when they administered their 32-item Sex-Role Attitude Scale to 225 male and 255 female university students in Florida. The results parallel those of a nationwide survey of 22,000 college seniors by Bayer (1975).

The Osmond-Martin scale was broken down into four categories, listed here with some of the opinions on which students were asked to rate their agreement or disagreement:

1. *Familial roles*
   - Women with preschool children should not work, if at all possible.
   - It is possible for women to satisfy their needs for achievement through their husbands.
   - A man's self-esteem is severely injured if his wife makes more money than he does.
   - Men should take the same amount of responsibility as women in caring for home and children.

2. *Extrafamilial roles*
   - I would feel uncomfortable if my immediate supervisor at work was a woman.
   - Women are less capable of making important decisions than men are.
   - Females should be encouraged to plan for a career, not just a job.
   - Men are more capable of assuming leadership than women are.

3. *Stereotypes of male/female nature and behaviors*
   - Women really like being dependent on men.
   - Women are as capable as men of enjoying a full sex life.
   - Since men have a natural urge to dominate and lead, women who challenge this actually threaten the welfare of society.

4. *Social change as related to sex roles*
   - There should be low-cost, high-quality child-care centers for working women.
   - Women should have equal job opportunities with men.
   - Women should get equal pay with men for doing the same jobs.

Osmond and Martin found that even in their supposedly enlightened student sample, men were more likely than women to give traditional responses to these statements. There was only one item on which the men were much more modern than the women: the statement that a man's self-esteem will drop if his wife earns more money than he does. Women's general agreement with this statement (scored as the traditional response) may have reflected a lack of perception on their part. Or the modern opinion on the part of men may have been an unrealistic response about what was for most of them only a future possibility at the time.

This photograph of Rep. Max Baucus (D-Mont.) feeding his infant son, Zeno Ben, while listening to speeches in Congress brought sharp criticism from some of his constituents and praise from others. Many commented that a congressman makes a high-priced babysitter. The mother, Ann Geracimos Baucus, was not present on this occasion. The couple at the left are Rep. Andrew Jacobs (D-Ind.) and Rep. Martha Keys (D-Kan.) who are husband and wife.

Difference of opinion concerning appropriate roles for men and women can lead to conflict in marriage, and the potential for conflict is increased in situations where the wife is moving to the modern view while the husband is maintaining the traditional view. Osmond and Martin caution particularly that "females may well encounter strong resistance to sex-role changes which involve the assumption of supervisory, decision-making, and leadership roles outside the family" (p. 756). Bringing these conflicts out into the open may put stress on the marital relationship, but not to do so restricts the individuality of the partners and their opportunities for personal growth.

CROSS-SEX FRIENDSHIPS

Another potential for conflict lies in each partner's friendships with people of the opposite sex. While such friendships may enrich a marriage by bringing new ideas into it, they may still be perceived as a threat to the marriage, even when there is no sexual relationship involved.

Before marriage, close associations between males and females often involve courtship and sometimes sex. After marriage, it is hard for partners to see each other's cross-sex friendships as something different from this pattern, so such friendships may arouse feelings of jealousy. There may be a feeling of competition for the partner's affection, a reaction left over from courtship days, and there may be concern as well that the partner's interaction with a friend will limit interaction with the spouse (Booth and Hess, 1974).

A Study of Older Adults. In studying extramarital friendships in which there is no overt sexual expression, Booth and Hess defined friendship as a relationship that includes (1) a tendency to engage in a variety of activities with each other, and (2) favorable feelings toward each other, including mutual expressions of concern and the freedom to make demands on each other. They decided to sample adults over 45 years old in the hope that their cross-sex friendship patterns would have become stable, rather than temporary, phenomena for study. But because of this age restriction and the limited geographical scope of their data (from subjects in two Nebraska cities), their findings may not be applicable to younger dyads in other parts of the country and may reflect more traditional attitudes than might be found elsewhere.

The data that emerged from Booth and Hess's study showed that men were more likely than women to have cross-sex friendships, but that neither had very many. Married men had an average of 4.77 close friends, of whom only .71 were women. Married women had an average of 3.80 close friends, of whom only .53 were men. But for working women, the mean number of cross-sex friendships was the same as for men. Work alone is not the only important factor, however, for Booth and Hess speculate that true friendships are most likely to be formed when people are of equal status. Female secretaries, for instance, are unlikely to become close friends with their male bosses, although they may have some other kind of relationship. But in certain professions, such as teaching, women are likely to be on an equal footing with men and are thus more likely to form meaningful friendships with them.

Not only do the married people over age 45 in this study have fewer cross-sex than same-sex friendships, they also interact and confide within these relationships less than within their same-sex friendships. Even among those who do have cross-sex friends—for many in the sample did not—

Friend. One attached to another by common interests, affection, and esteem.

men interact an average of 123 times a year with one close male friend, but only 96 times with a female friend. For women, the difference is even greater: 113 interactions with a same-sex friend, but only 77 with a male friend. Confiding behavior was likewise less within cross-sex friendships. These limitations suggest that some constraints may have been imposed on these friendships because spouses view them as threats.

Friendships as a Potential Source of Strength.   Contrary to the traditional assumption that outside involvements threaten the marriage bond, sociologist Jetse Sprey (1971) argues that it is possible that they may actually strengthen it. He writes that the marriage relationship is special. But what makes it special is the fact that other options—the possibilities and sometimes realities of intimate involvement with other people—do exist. Continuing the central dyadic relationship in the face of these outside attractions requires partners to affirm the strength of what they feel for each other. This reaffirmation of the conjugal bond makes it seem more valuable and at the same time more vulnerable. Since outside friendships test their bond, partners must engage in a process of continuous mutual rediscovery which prevents them from taking each other for granted and keeps their marriage vibrant. According to Sprey, if you view the human capacity to love as limitless, as he does, then expressions of friendship outside the marriage do not subtract from the quantity of love which can be expressed within it.

Empirical evidence is lacking on how many marriages can survive the kind of continual testing Sprey talks about. Certainly the process could only work when both partners feel the same way about outside friendships. If one partner feels that they do not undermine their mutual love, but the other perceives them as threatening, there may be trouble.

LEISURE ACTIVITIES AND THE FAMILY

Dyads or families that take pleasure in mutual activities such as making music, going camping, taking walks, or traveling together enjoy an extra dimension in their relationship not experienced by those who habitually drift apart to follow their own interests in the free time left over from work and household demands. But periods of togetherness may present opportunities for interpersonal conflicts, as well as feelings of closeness, to show up.

Recreation has become more important to Americans than mere diversion. It is now regarded as an important arena for expression of people's respect, affection, interdependence, and awareness of each other. And the importance of recreation to the family has been heightened by three trends: (1) the family is based more on companionship now than in the past, with other functions having become less important; (2) the amount of free time available has increased as working hours have been cut and timesaving de-

Recreation. Refreshment of strength and spirits after work.

vices have become available; and (3) values have shifted from the work ethic toward acceptance of leisure as a life goal (Orthner, 1975).

It is generally assumed that joint recreational activities are good for a marriage. According to the National Recreational Association's slogan, "The family that plays together, stays together." But much more is known about precisely how and at what expense Americans spend their leisure time than about its actual effects on their marriages. Is skiing together at a crowded resort, for instance, more or less conducive to marital harmony than playing cards at home?

In an effort to pin down some of the variables in the leisure-marriage relationship, Orthner separated leisure activities into three different types:

1. *Individual activities*, such as reading or gardening, are those that require no interaction with others and may actually discourage it.
2. *Joint activities*, such as playing games, making love, and camping, are those that require a high degree of interaction and encourage communication.
3. *Parallel activities*, such as watching TV, listening to records, or visiting museums, may be little more than individual activities carried out in a group setting. They allow a minimum of interaction.

Orthner speculates that it is when they are engaging in joint activities that partners have the greatest chance of improving their relationships. Leisure activities have the potential to reduce people's anxieties, freeing them to see things in a different light and acting as shock absorbers and stabilizers in times of change. Joint leisure activities between partners encourage open communication and role interchange, increasing the possibility of understanding each other and of altering behaviors which may be causing problems.

When he surveyed 442 married upper-middle-class people in urban areas of the Southeast, Orthner found that the communication-increasing potential of joint activities was especially important at two points in the family life cycle. The first is the early years of marriage, when patterns of husband-wife interaction are being established. A high level of individual activities at this time cuts down on the amount of time left for joint activities and is associated with a low level of marital satisfaction. Conversely, a high level of joint leisure activities during the first five years of marriage is significantly related to positive marital satisfaction for both partners.

Joint leisure activities become significantly related to marital satisfaction again in mid-life when grown children are leaving the nest and parents again have the opportunity to be alone together. If they find joint activities which they both enjoy, their marital satisfaction is high. But if they are more likely to engage in individual leisure activities, marital satisfaction

Leisure. Time free from work or other duties.

will be low. Parallel activities can also contribute to marital satisfaction in the middle years, although they apparently did not in the early years. It may be that when people have known each other intimately for so long, they are communicating on a nonverbal level even if they are only reading books in the same room.

Between these two periods—during the years of child rearing and career building—patterns of leisure activity are only slightly related to marital satisfaction. Orthner suggests that the marital relationship may be placed on a back burner during these years, with couples defining their satisfaction more in terms of parental and career goals. While there is not the great need for joint activities at this time that we noted in the two periods of relational change, a preponderance of individual activities during these years may still make the wife feel deserted or rejected. It may not bother the husband, however, and he may be unaware of his wife's need for greater interaction.

ADJUSTMENT TO THE FAMILY HOME

Another area in which adjustment and decision making frequently produce stress is the couple's need either to accommodate themselves to where they live, change the structure to fit their needs, or move to a different place. According to Earl Morris and Mary Winter (1975), this process continues throughout marriage, with families constantly reevaluating their housing to see if it fits their current needs and expectations.

The American Ideal.   Morris and Winter state that Americans' ideas about optimal housing are very specific, widely agreed-upon, and supported by sanctions such as withdrawal of respect from those who do not measure up. People will thus go to great expense to try to meet the cultural housing norms, even though these norms have nothing to do with minimal shelter and safety requirements.

Sanctions. Punishments or rewards used as mechanisms for enforcing a society's standards.

In terms of space, Americans think they need rooms for cooking, eating, recreation, and entertaining, plus enough bedrooms to fit the family size. Whether some bedrooms will be shared depends on the number, age, sex, and family status of members of the household. The favorite housing unit is the single-family home, preferably owned rather than rented. Its quality depends on the family's income. According to the norms, the neighborhood should be mostly residential, with good schools, safe streets, and a population whose social class, racial, and perhaps ethnic makeup is similar to that of the family (Morris and Winter). These overall cultural norms are modified somewhat within particular families to conform to family tastes and values, but for the great majority of families, the broad cultural and family housing norms are identical (Morris, Crull, and Winter, 1976).

As a reflection of these norms, there are over 36 million owner-occupied single-family homes in the country. Almost a third are worth $35,000 or more; of these, almost nine out of ten have three or more bedrooms, and almost none lack inside plumbing (U.S. Dept. of Commerce, CB76-119).

Family Response to a Housing Deficit.   If, in its everyday judging of whether its housing fits cultural and family norms, a family feels that its home is **substandard,** it has three alternatives: adapt the residence, adapt the family, or move. Which option it chooses is determined by (1) family strengths and weaknesses in reaching joint decisions, (2) social factors such as housing discrimination, (3) economic considerations, and (4) ties that hold family members to their current home.

Families who for some reason do not move from a home they see as substandard may try to change it to fit their needs by building additions, remodeling, or changing the function of rooms. This residential-adaptation option is especially attractive when people like the community or house they live in but simply need more or different kinds of room.

Another alternative to moving is family adaptation—staying in the same structure and leaving it as it is, but trying to mold the family to fit into it better. If the house is small, couples may delay childbearing since it would cause overcrowding. Families with older children may encourage some of them to leave—to join the Army, or to take an apartment of their own, for instance—to ease the crowding. Conversely, if the family is "too small" for their house, the extra bedrooms may encourage childbearing or the taking in of foster children, lodgers, or relatives. Morris and Winter point out that while these efforts at adapting the family to fit the housing are usually not perceived as such, the principle may be operating all the same. Family adaptations may also take a more passive form—resignation to the existing housing deficit, with either a lowering of standards or just learning to live with a chronic low level of satisfaction.

The final option—moving—is acceptable to so many families that about 20 percent of them move each year. In a four-and-a-half year period between 1970 and 1974, almost half of all households in the country moved to a new dwelling (U.S. Dept. of Commerce, CB76-119). Some moved because of job changes and a quarter of the total were establishing new households, but for many of the rest the move probably reflected an attempt to increase housing satisfaction.

Several variables have been found to influence the propensity to move. People who rent are four times as likely to move as home owners. Renters may be less satisfied with their housing in the first place, unwilling or unable to make costly alterations in a building that does not belong to them, and freer to leave than a home owner who must first find someone to buy the house. But those of low income may be unable to move and may have to make do with the house or apartment they are living in, without any

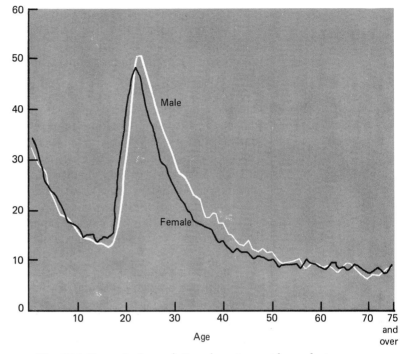

Percent
changing
residence

Fig. 10.2 Percent of population changing residence during a one-year period, by age and sex: average for 1966–1971. There is little overall difference in the mobility rates of men and women during their lifetimes. Differences which do exist probably reflect the movement of married couples wherein the wife is typically a few years younger than the husband. (Source: U.S. Bureau of the Census, 1976, P–23:58. Data include movers from abroad.)

resources to fix it up. People who move have a higher average income than nonmovers. And those who have recently moved are less likely to do so again soon, perhaps because they have temporarily solved their perceived housing deficit (Morris, Crull, and Winter; U.S. Dept. of Commerce, CB 76-210).

Moving as a Family Crisis. Moving to a new community, even if it brings greater satisfaction with housing, can still be a time of crisis for the family. It is becoming a common experience for Americans. In a study by Stella Jones (1973) of 256 couples of above-average income and education, the families had moved an average of five or six times, with 15 percent reporting eleven or more moves. Many of these moves were related to the husband's employment.

Wives are most likely to adjust well when the decision to move and planning for it have involved both husband and wife. Exploratory trips to the new community and gathering information about the schools and the cost of living there were regarded as helpful. So was previous moving experience. The wives Jones questioned indicated that the best training for the mechanical problems of moving—packing, selling the house, purchasing a new one, making arrangements with utility companies at both ends—is having done it before. Previous moving experience facilitates psychological adjustment as well, for Jones' subjects reported that it had helped them to cope with moving stress, to be more adaptable, to develop broader interests, to make friends more easily, and to understand and accept people of different backgrounds. Even though the experience of moving may be a trying one, it also provides the opportunity for personal growth and strengthening of the family through joint participation in working toward family goals.

THE PROCESS OF DECISION MAKING

Given the great potential for conflict within a dyadic relationship, it is surprising not that so many marriages break up but that so many endure. The question may be, not why so many couples split up, or, in the case of married couples, get divorced, but why so many couples stay together, why some marriages last a lifetime. In marriages that last, what have people done about their inevitable differences of opinion?

CONFLICT MANAGEMENT VS. CONFLICT RESOLUTION
It is more accurate to regard marital harmony as an achieved rather than a natural state of affairs. And as indicated earlier in the chapter, the achievement of harmony is only a temporary condition in a continual process of adjustment to meet new situations. Husband and wife, being two different personalities experiencing two different lives, are almost certain to change over the course of the marriage. And this change is likely to occur in ways which open up new areas of conflict that did not exist or were hidden at the beginning of their life together. Although partners may strive toward harmony, they are likely at any given time to have some sharply conflicting interests, so the process of negotiation over matters that involve them both continues for the life of the relationship.

> **Conflict management.** Control of conflict in a relationship through bargaining, compromise, and accommodation.

The way they make decisions has often been looked at in terms of power—one partner overpowers the other, either by making decisions unilaterally or by forcing the other to give up personal wants and needs. According to this view, if the husband wants to buy a house in a particular suburb, the wife will have to accept his choice if he has more power in the relationship. It may be a matter of living with him there or nowhere. One person wins, the other loses, and thus the conflict is resolved. Many think that resolution of the conflict is necessary to maintain the stability and

harmony of the relationship. But winning and losing are rarely so clear-cut in decision making. In this example, the wife may perceive some benefits in moving—such as a higher quality of life and interesting new experiences —and some losses in refusing to move—such as poor train service to the city or lack of adequate play space for the children in the present location. So her agreement to the move does not involve total sacrifice of her needs. The overall conflict between her interests and his is never finally resolved, but it may be managed through ongoing mutual give-and-take. Some sociologists therefore consider dyadic adjustment to be a process of **conflict management** rather than one of **conflict resolution** (Sprey, 1969; Sprey, 1971).

Conflict resolution. Final settlement of disputes, sometimes in ways not fully satisfactory to the parties concerned.

Powering in Conflict Management.   The theory that conflicts are managed rather than resolved in relationships that endure does not preclude the possibility that power may be used to influence some decisions. Both partners have power over each other because of the bond between them. Either partner can threaten to break the bond if the other refuses to give in or to change in some way. For instance, one might threaten to leave the other if extramarital involvement or excessive drinking doesn't stop. But threats of divorce or separation—or even lesser ones of walking out of the house or refusing sexual relations until the conflict is settled—must be used carefully, for they endanger the partner making the threat as well as the one being threatened. If both value the relationship, both would lose if the threat of separation were carried out. When such a threat is made, the person making it is actually at the mercy of the other, for the other has been given the power to sever the relationship. The one threatened may have more control of the situation than the person who makes the threat, since the threatened one has the choice of whether or not to conform to the wishes of the person making the threat.

If the choice is not to accede to the demand, the threatener then has to decide whether to carry out the threat or to back down. If a threat is made but not carried out—if, for instance, the alcoholic husband promises to stop drinking and doesn't, but his wife still doesn't leave him as she had threatened to—the wife's **credibility** will be undermined. Threatening thus tests the power of both parties to an argument. Such behavior should be undertaken cautiously and only when the threatener is really prepared to carry out the threat (Sprey, 1972).

Cooperation. A dynamic social process involving common effort such that mutual benefits outweigh the disadvantages.

Cooperation in Spite of Differences.   The objective in the negotiation is not to destroy the opposition or the relationship. According to Sprey (1972), decision making is a joint, reciprocal activity which can better be seen in terms of cooperation than of power. What is needed, Sprey writes, is not arrival at consensus, but ways of settling problems which allow people to maintain their differences but arrive at negotiated solutions they can both live with. This is where the communication skills described in the preceding chapter can be helpful.

Cooperation requires not agreement on values but agreement on a set of rules that can be used for decision making. Whether couples are able to manage their differences depends on their strength in using such negotiating tools as bargaining, compromise, **accommodation,** and even **mediation.** Separation is sometimes used to settle conflicts when all else fails, but this step represents conflict resolution, not conflict management. Conflict-management techniques are, in fact, used in an effort to avoid this final solution (Sprey, 1969).

BONDING—THE MOTIVATION FOR CONFLICT MANAGEMENT
Why do people engage in negotiating behavior to avoid separating over their differences? According to Sprey, the incentive lies in the bond between them. Once people have formed an intimate pair relationship, they are tied to each other not only by their mutual needs but also by the way the bond has changed them. They become to themselves and others different people, incomplete without each other. Thus linked to each other, they have a mutual need to maintain their bond, even though there will always be some tension about doing so.

According to Sprey's theory, the strength and workability of a dyadic relationship, therefore, cannot be judged so much by the degree of consensus (one component of Spanier's Dyadic Adjustment Scale) as by two other variables: the ability to negotiate differences in a spirit of cooperation rather than aggression, and the motivation to continue the relationship. If the bond does not mean much, if it is no more special than attractions to others outside the bond, then little effort will be made to manage differences in ways that will satisfy both parties and thus prevent breakdown of the relationship (Sprey, 1971).

Summary

1. The purpose of this chapter is to make students aware of some of the situations encountered in marriage that require interpersonal adjustment and help them understand the nature of the adjustment process. Conflict management is established as an important goal in interpersonal relationships.

2. Dyadic adjustment is a continuous process, changing as situations in a couples' lives change. The total adjustment between the two members of the dyad at any given time—whether they are happy with each other or not—is measured by the degree of satisfaction expressed, sense of togetherness, agreement between partners, and expression of affection within the dyad.

3. The tension between the need for stability and togetherness in intimate relationships on the one hand and the need for personal privacy and an individual identity on the other is a problem people continually encounter in dyadic relationships. Each need has its own requirements and they often conflict with each other. Couples may handle these conflicts by compromising both needs, by stressing first one need and then the other, by stressing one need and sacrificing the other, or by meeting one need in one relationship and the other in a different relationship.

4. Some major areas of marital adjustment are: (a) Relations with in-laws: couples must identify with each other and put the development of a good working relationship with each other before their loyalties to their families of orientation. (b) Work-role adjustment: the situation of the working wife adds the variables of job involvement and satisfaction in work to marital adjustment and happiness. (c) Gender-role adjustments: if one partner is becoming more modern in gender-role attitude while the other remains traditional, the potential for conflict increases. (d) Cross-sex friendships: these may enrich a marriage but are also potential threats to it. (e) Leisure activities and vacations: recreation is an outlet for expression of people's respect, affection, interdependence, and awareness of each other, but may also be a source of tension. (f) Adjustment to the family home: families accommodate themselves to where they live, change the structure to fit their needs, or move to a different place.

5. In teenage marriages adjustment is usually more difficult and economic, social, and personal problems tend to be greater. Early marriage, especially in

cases of premarital pregnancy, often limits educational opportunities and thus limits employment opportunities also.

6. The way to handle conflicts in decision making or adjustment in dyadic relationships is through conflict management, acceptance of differences, rather than through conflict resolution which may involve total sacrifice of the needs of one or both partners. The aim of conflict management is to avoid destruction of the relationship or the opponent through aggressive behavior. Couples can maintain their differences but still negotiate solutions with which both can live. The motivation for working out these differences lies in the bond between the couple which not only has tied them to each other by mutual needs but has changed them so they are incomplete without each other.

Key Concepts

Adjustment	Stability
Process	Developmental tasks
Dyadic Adjustment Scale	In-laws
Satisfaction	Job involvement
Cohesion	Cross-sex friendships
Consensus	Recreation
Conflict	Leisure time
Compromise	Decision making
Tension	Conflct management
Privacy	Conflict resolution

Review and Discussion

1. What kind of marital adjustment do you think could be worked out between two people who are both dedicated to maintaining a strong individual identity? If one partner is completely submissive to the other, would this necessarily lead to a happy marriage?

2. Why is in-law adjustment a problem for married couples? Given what you know about family structure and ideas in colonial and nineteenth-century America, do you think American couples always have had this problem?

3. Why do you think men tend to have more traditional attitudes concerning gender roles than women do? How much should a dating couple disclose about their gender-role attitudes?

4. The husband likes to play bridge, the wife likes to bowl. They feel they must do everything together and yet they argue every time one wants to bowl or the other wants to play bridge. When one partner gives in to the other's wish, there is a feeling of resentment and anger. Is it necessary for this conflict to occur? Why or why not? How might they manage this conflict?

5. Does your family engage in leisure activities together? Name some. How do these activities (or the lack of them) affect your family relationship?

LEDERER, W. J., AND D. D. JACKSON (1968).   *Mirages of Marriage.* New York: Norton.

Discusses many myths associated with marriage (e.g., "most married people love each other") and aspects of married life such as communication, sex, and destructive elements. Also includes section on how to make a marriage work, and uses examples (dialogues, scenes) to illustrate points.

DUVALL, E. M. (1964).   *In-Laws: Pro and Con.* New York: Association Press.

Presents valuable insights and information on in-laws in an interesting way. Discusses various problems of the mother-in-law relationship (including mother-in-law jokes), and also covers sisters-, brothers-, and fathers-in-law. Has sections on becoming a better in-law and on the meaning of in-law problems (where they come from, what to do about them).

CUBER, J. F., AND P. HARROFF (1965).   *The Significant Americans: A Study of Sexual Behavior Among the Affluent.* New York: Appleton-Century.

Explores sexual and emotional relations between men and women of the upper-middle class and their behavior in their marriages. In addition to statistics, the authors use long quotes to give an idea of how people feel about their marriages and relationships.

VISCOTT, D. (1974).   *How to Live with Another Person.* New York: Arbor House.

How to establish, nurture, and save a relationship with a loved one, spouse, or friend. The author feels that commitment must be renewed as growth continues, and includes bills of rights for couples, parents, and children. Written in a simple, personal style.

SUID, R., B. BRADLEY, M. SUID, AND J. EASTMAN (1976).   *Married, Etc.: A Sourcebook for Couples.* Reading, Mass.: Addison-Wesley.

An imaginative view of marriage and other couple relationships which encourages readers to question and share their experiences. Uses varied approaches (folk wisdom, cartoons, poetry, statistics, activities) to help readers look at their relationships and the issues and problems in them.

Suggested Readings

Human Sexuality: Implications for Marriage

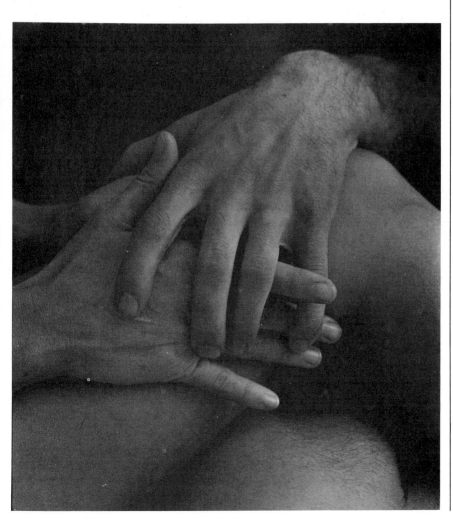

Sexual activity is becoming increasingly open in the United States. Some signs:

- Alex Comfort's *The Joy of Sex,* a collection of gourmet recipes for advanced loveplay techniques, sold over 3 million copies. It was then joined on its lengthy run on the best-seller lists by a sequel, *More Joy.*
- No longer restricted by curfews, college regulations, or community disapproval, an estimated 10 to 33 percent of single American male and female students are openly living together (Macklin, 1974).
- Sex research is such a respectable science that even doctoral candidates and government-funded projects are engaged in it.
- Scenes of intercourse, oral-genital contact, masturbation, and rape are now shown in legitimate movies, and male as well as female nudity now appears in mass-circulation magazines.
- An estimated 3500 to 5000 sex-therapy clinics have sprung up throughout the country (Masters, 1974). They offer to try to cure couples of problems preventing marital sexual satisfaction for fees ranging from $2500 to $4000. Even at these prices, their services are apparently in great demand (Holden, 1974).

THE DEVELOPMENT OF SEXUAL BEHAVIORS

Despite these increasingly liberal attitudes toward sex, social scientists consider the United States a relatively restrictive society, one which tries to keep its children from finding out about sexual matters and to block sexual responses in children. Permissive cultures, by contrast, allow children considerable freedom to handle their own genitals and those of others and may even instruct them in the techniques of lovemaking. On the Polynesian island of Mangaia, for instance, when boys are circumcised at the age of 13 or 14, they are taught how to orally stimulate the female genitals, hold back ejaculation until the female has had several climaxes, and time simultaneous mutual orgasms. They then spend some time with an experienced woman, practicing what they have been taught. Girls receive expert advice on such matters from an elderly woman. The young then begin such an active sex life that almost all have had substantial sexual experience with a number of partners before marriage. Eighteen-year-old boys are said to average three orgasms per night, seven nights a week, in encounters which may take place in the girl's home in the same room where the rest of the family is sleeping. If the parents wake up, Donald Marshall reports, "they anxiously listen for laughter and signs of enjoyment—indications that the girl will be happy with the man if the couple chooses to make the arrangement permanent" (Marshall and Suggs, 1971, pp. 107–131).

The contrasts between this encouragement of sexuality and attitudes in our country are obvious. But there are indications that we are becoming less restrictive, not so much through a more liberal explicit code for sexual behavior as by lack of enforcement of existing prohibitions. This looking the other way by adults may be partly out of sympathy with the long period of adolescence that exists in industrial societies like ours. Puberty comes early, perhaps because of good nutrition, and marriage may be delayed until career preparation is completed, ten or more years later. Between these milestones there is an uncharted region of contradictions between biological readiness for sex and social reluctance to allow its expression (Weiss, 1974).

Cultural standards of right and wrong in matters of sex are less clearly defined now, and parents—and their young—are trying to make their own decisions about how free sexual expression should be. For example, there is no current agreement on how masturbation should be treated. According to a recent national opinion study, 43 percent of adults think a boy or girl 12 or 13 years of age should be not discouraged from masturbating, while 40 percent would discourage masturbation, including 5 percent who think this behavior should not only be discouraged but punished (Cody W. Wilson, 1975) When their offspring reach a certain age, some parents turn them loose with cars and then co-ed dorms or apartments to devise in some way their own code of what is permissible and leads to happiness and what does not.

STANDARDS OF NORMALITY

The trend toward looking the other way instead of actively discouraging or encouraging sexuality among the unmarried is reflected in our laws governing sexual behavior. A few states, following the model penal code adopted by the American Law Institute in 1962, have dropped many or all private sexual acts between consenting adults from the list of crimes. In other states, the old laws against **sodomy** (which includes heterosexual and homosexual anal and oral intercourse as well as copulation with animals), cohabitation and sexual intercourse among the unmarried, and extramarital intercourse still stand but are rarely enforced unless these acts occur in public (Hunt, 1974).

In the face of growing permissiveness, there is now considerable confusion as to what is normal in sexual expression and what is not. Even the concept of normality is elusive. It may mean a sort of statistical **median** (i.e., if over half of the population masturbates, then it's normal). Or it may mean the liberal attitude currently popular among professionals: if a sexual activity is practiced by consenting adults who take responsibility for its consequences, doesn't hurt anyone, and is carried on out of the sight of people who don't care to watch, then it's acceptable.

Sexuality. Sexual activity, especially the expression of sexual receptivity or interest.

By this definition, masturbation, intercourse between unmarried people, homosexuality, and oral-genital contact may be acceptable; child-molesting and **rape** clearly are not. Only about one-fifth of all men and women in one survey agreed with the statement, "Masturbation is wrong." Three-fourths of the men and four-fifths of the women refused to label cunnilingus wrong; even more men and almost as many women considered fellatio permissible. And a Gallup poll taken in 1973 showed that only 48 percent of the population felt that premarital sex was wrong (Hunt, 1974).

EARLY EROTIC PLAY

Erotic. Related to sexual arousal; tending to arouse sexual love or desire.

The current professional opinion that sexuality is a natural human trait extends to childhood. As Freud pointed out, sexuality appears long before adolescence. Children's early discoveries of bodily pleasure are generally considered a normal part of their development. Many parents, however, still follow the traditional repressive script, so early sex play continues to be a more or less secret activity.

Kinsey found that 57 percent of the males and 48 percent of the females he interviewed remembered engaging in some form of sex play before they reached puberty, despite their parents' disapproval. Exploration and exhibition of their own and friends' sex organs is often embedded in social games, such as "playing doctor" and "playing house." Such activities peak at age 9 for girls, when 7 percent are involved in heterosexual play and 9 percent in homosexual play, and at age 12 for boys, when 23 percent are engaging in heterosexual and 30 percent in homosexual contacts, often in groups (Kinsey et al., 1953).

Self-stimulation is common among children. Some children discover on their own the possibilities of rubbing against furniture and toys or of contracting the buttocks, but boys are likely to learn effective self-stimulation techniques from others. Before they reach sexual maturity at puberty, boys are incapable of ejaculation, but they can orgasm. In fact, orgasm has been reported as early as five months in an infant boy and four months in a baby girl. Prepubescent boys are especially excitable, for they are able to erect faster and to have more orgasms in a row than either adolescent or adult males (Katchadourian and Lunde, 1972).

SEX EDUCATION

Since sexual activities before puberty in the United States generally occur in secret places, they add little to children's store of real information about sex. Less than 4 percent of the males and 3 percent of the females in the Research Guild sample reported that experience was the chief source of what they learned about sex as they were growing up. The major source of sexual information, or misinformation, continues to be the speculations and firsthand accounts passed down from slightly older friends, according to 59 percent of males and 46 percent of females. These accounts tend to be accepted as true, whether they are or not, by preadolescents who have no way of checking them against reality (Gagnon and Simon, 1974). Hearsay is followed by reading (20 percent of males and 22 percent of females). Information from parents takes third place. Attempts by today's parents to relieve their children of the guilt and ignorance that surrounded their own early sexual discoveries are apparently not yet very effective except in some mother-daughter relationships. Sixteen percent of the Research Guild's females but only 3 percent of the males named their mothers as their chief source of sexual information; 6 percent of the boys and only 1 percent of the girls learned about sex from their fathers. Sex-education programs in the schools are even less helpful. Only 3 percent of the boys and 5 percent of the girls said they learned anything useful from them (Hunt, 1974).

Part of the problem is a cultural uneasiness about what children should be taught. Even when growing adult permissiveness in the 1960s created a demand for sex education in the schools, adult reluctance to do anything that might encourage youthful sexuality gave a negative tone to this instruction. Stress was placed on the risks of sexual activity, perhaps in the hope that such instruction would lower the rates of illegitimacy and venereal disease. It didn't, and today there is professional demand for honest courses that explore the interpersonal aspects as well as the biological facts of lovemaking (Gagnon and Simon).

MASTURBATION

No matter how handicapped by misinformation, the American boy is likely to experience his first ejaculation between the ages of 11 and 15 with the changes of puberty. For some, ejaculation occurs as a spontaneous nocturnal emission or wet dream because of the pressure of unemptied seminal vesicles; but according to Kinsey's data, two out of three first ejaculations occur as a result of masturbation, or erotic self-stimulation (Katchadourian and Lunde). Gender has a substantial effect on the practice of masturbation. In one national sample, 66 percent of the males but only 17 percent of the females had masturbated by the time they were 17 (Cody W. Wilson, 1975).

Masturbation. The practice of sexual arousal by manual or other bodily contact exclusive of sexual intercourse.

While differences between males and females in incidence of masturbation may have some basis in biological differences, they are also the result of differences in socialization of each sex to masculine or feminine identity. Adolescent male peer groups experiment with masturbation and learn to associate sex with drive and achievement. Girls are encouraged to view sexual activity as service—something done for the sake of children, family, and love. Their initial responses may be not to their own desires but to the demands of males. For many females, interest in sexuality for its own sake may not develop until they are in their twenties or even later (Gagnon and Simon).

Masturbation is a form of early sexual behavior which is frequently carried over into adult life, especially for use as a sexual outlet when no partners are available. In the Research Guild survey, 94 percent of the adult males and 63 percent of the females had masturbated at some point (Hunt, 1974). Despite the widespread incidence of self-stimulation, most men and women still feel too ashamed of the practice to admit openly to friends, lovers, or spouses that they sometimes masturbate, even though they readily admit to other kinds of self-indulgence, like overeating or sleeping late. This lingering sense of guilt may be the unconscious result of their parents' disapproval when they touched their genitals as children, often too early in life to be consciously remembered.

Guilt feelings are being erased to some extent by the advice of medical doctors and psychologists that masturbation is a harmless form of sexual pleasure. According to current psychiatric theory, the tiredness and depression sometimes linked with masturbation is caused not by any debilitating physical effects but by mental conflicts over its use (Roth, 1975). Only a few people appear to use masturbation antisocially and neurotically, as a means of avoiding the problems of adult sexual relationships, as a weapon against a spouse, or as a tool to express hostility toward the opposite sex (Hunt, 1974). Sex therapists encourge masturbation as a simple, quick release for sexual tensions without any pressure to perform well. They also recommend self-stimulation to orgasm as a way to become more comfortable with one's own body in heterosexual lovemaking and a lifelong supplement to a normal sex life (Barbach, 1976; Kline-Graber and Graber, 1976). Masters and Johnson (1966) point out that masturbation at the onset of menstruation helps to free many women from menstrual cramps and backaches.

Despite more liberal attitudes toward self-stimulation, the practice does not necessarily meet people's emotional needs. While masturbation may provide release from sexual tensions, only half of the women who masturbate report that doing so is always satisfying; for 30 percent it is only sometimes satisfying, and for 20 percent it is not satisfying at all (Levin, 1975a).

PETTING AND ORAL SEX

Like masturbation, heterosexual petting—caresses, finger insertions, and perhaps oral-genital contact—is often an early substitute for copulation. It is a way for young people to experience intense sexual excitement without sacrificing technical **virginity** through actual penetration of the vagina by the penis. It may or may not culminate in orgasm, but for most it is part of the learning process upon which adult heterosexual intercourse ultimately rests. At the same time that they are discovering each other's most responsive parts and testing ways of exciting them, many petting couples develop feelings of tenderness and intimacy which go beyond sensual pleasure. Petting behaviors are later carried over into sexually mature relation-

Virginity. A state in which sexual intercourse had not been experienced.

ships as foreplay used to heighten sexual arousal in preparation for intercourse.

Like other advanced sexual behaviors, heavy **petting** techniques are more common among the better-educated. But the education gap in sexual permissiveness has narrowed considerably since Kinsey. While less than 60 percent of Kinsey's noncollege-educated married males frequently stimulated their wife's breasts with their lips and tongue, noncollege-educated men have now joined the college-educated in this behavior at a level of over 90 percent. The rise in cunnilingus, used by only a liberated few in Kinsey's time, is even more dramatic. While only 15 percent of Kinsey's married men whose education ended with high school had used cunnilingus at all in marriage, 56 percent of the high school-educated men interviewed in 1973 had done so, compared to 66 percent of college-educated husbands (Hunt, 1973c). Strongly taboo in Kinsey's time, oral-genital sex has become an acceptable part of sexual behavior in the United States. For many women, cunnilingus is the chief and sometimes the only way that they can reach orgasm (Levin, 1975a).

The old pattern of petting as a virginal substitute for copulation, with the boy trying to go as far as he can and the girl drawing the line on how far to go depending on the degree of affectionate involvement, appears to be a stage that is passed through more quickly now than formerly. Whereas Kinsey estimated that petting lasted an average of 6.6 years for females, a recent survey indicates that the median female now pets for only three or four years before progressing to either marriage or premarital intercourse (Hunt, 1974).

HOMOSEXUAL RELATIONS

While most Americans progress from early sex play and masturbation into petting and then heterosexual intercourse, some discover somewhere along the way an attraction toward partners of the same sex. Statistics on homosexuality are hard to gather, but contemporary sources estimate that 2–3 percent of all adult men and women are exclusively homosexual. Far more admit to some interest in people of the same sex, for about half of the people surveyed by the Research Guild agreed with the statement, "There is some homosexuality in all of us" (Hunt, 1974).

For most Americans explicit sexual contact with members of the same sex is a passing phase which usually occurs early in life. In the Research Guild sample, half of the males and more than half of the females who reported any homosexual experiences had stopped having them before they were 16 (Hunt, 1974). The young frequently choose friends of the same sex for their sexual experimentation, largely because at the time they are more available, open, and trusting than partners of the opposite sex. If discovered by disapproving adults, though, their behavior may be con-

Petting. Deliberate erotic stimulation of another's body by sensual caresses without actual copulation.

Tom Waddell and Charles Deaton, San Francisco professionals, consider themselves married—with all the traditional commitments—though without the sanction of any church or state. Both were once heterosexual, or bisexual. Deaton, formerly married, lost both his wife and child in a tragic automobile accident twenty years ago. A year after setting up their joint household, Waddell says, "...we are a very honest, very happy couple."

sidered "homosexuality" and burdened with meanings which are inappropriate at this stage (Gagnon and Simon).

When homosexual preferences persist over a long period of time, many people search for a cause rather than regarding this alternate form of sexual orientation as a matter of choice. Sometimes hormonal imbalances are blamed, and sometimes negative experiences—with a same-sex parent who is a poor gender-role model or with a threatening heterosexual partner, for instance—are thought to have interfered with socialization to heterosexual preferences.

The idea that homosexuality must be blamed on some unnatural cause stems from the Judeo-Christian religious tradition of encouraging forms of sexuality which lead to large, intact families and frowning on those which do not. But the current message from psychiatrists is that homosexuality should be viewed in the context of mental health, rather than sin. In 1973 the American Psychiatric Association announced that it would no longer label homosexuality a mental illness and would not try to "cure" homosexuals unless they were unhappy with their same-sex preferences (Lyons, 1973).

To social scientists, whether homosexuality is seen as normal or abnormal depends on social learning. According to a survey of research data on 76 cultures by Ford and Beach, 49 of these groups approve of some form of homosexual activity. Among the Siwans of Africa, for instance, all men and boys are expected to engage in anal intercourse; those who don't are considered peculiar. Women and girls of many cultures stimulate each other's clitorises, and some engage in simulated intercourse using local fruits as a substitute for the penis to simulate copulation (Ford and Beach, 1951). In our own society, those who engage in homosexual or bisexual behavior are considered abnormal; but models of normal sexual activity are themselves unnatural in the sense of being shaped by culturally imposed codes of behavior (Gagnon and Simon).

Bisexual. Participating in both heterosexual and homosexual relationships.

In arguing for public acceptance of their chosen gender identity, some gay liberationists voice their resentment of labels that emphasize the sexual aspects of their relationships with others. These relationships vary widely in physical and emotional intimacy; sexuality is not the central organizing principle in many homosexuals' lives, or might not be if public reactions were more tolerant. Open acknowledgment of their homosexual preferences makes it difficult for them to achieve major cultural goals and also has an important bearing on their mental health. For many, self-acceptance can only be won by withdrawing from the large community into gay bars and service organizations which cater to the social and emotional needs of large homosexual populations (Gagnon and Simon).

Despite widespread assumptions that most homosexuals use kinky techniques, manual stimulation to orgasm is the most common sexual technique for both sexes. Only 11 percent of the men interviewed by the Research Guild who have had any homosexual experiences have been fellated (orally stimulated) by another male and only 5 percent have themselves fellated another male. Only 20 percent of males with any homosexual experience have had anal intercourse as insertor and 18 percent as insertee. Women currently having adult homosexual relationships kiss each other's breasts and hug and about half use cunnilingus. Only about one-sixth had used a **dildo** (artificial penis to simulate copulation) within the year (Hunt, 1974).

INTERCOURSE AMONG SINGLES

To a far greater extent than homosexuality, heterosexual intercourse among single adults has become a common occurrence. While single men in the United States have always engaged in high levels of coitus (for instance, in one study 84 percent of men now over age 55 had intercourse before marriage), much of this activity was with prostitutes. Use of prostitutes by single males has probably dropped to about half of what it was in the forties, but intercourse with single women has increased enormously. While only 31 percent of married women now over 55 had coitus before marriage, 81 percent of those now under 25 have done so (Hunt, 1973a, 1973b).

Prostitute. A person who engages in sexual activity for money.

While six out of ten college-educated men and nine-tenths of all women in Kinsey's sample had moral objections to intercourse without marriage strong enough to prevent or restrict its incidence in their own lives, a large majority of those interviewed by the Research Guild feel that coitus among singles is acceptable for those who are engaged or in love. If the feeling between the partners is one of strong affection rather than love, a majority still see intercourse as permissible for single men and almost half find it acceptable for single women (Hunt, 1973b). Of those under age 25, about three-fourths of the males and half the females find intercourse acceptable for a single man even in the absence of strong affection; 29 percent of the women and 56 percent of the men think this is okay for a single woman (Hunt, 1974).

Some social scientists think that instead of examining motives for intercourse among singles, which was considered problem behavior in the past, we should be looking at motives for virginity, since they now consider this the more unexpected behavior. Gecas and Libby (1976) cite this as an extreme example of change in sexual attitudes.

Although the cultural reaction toward intercourse outside of marriage is increasingly tolerant, especially among the young, the experience may still be filled with tension and anxiety for the participants. Some have been pushed into coitus before they were ready by peer-group pressure, real or imagined; others find little enjoyment in coitus without strong affection. According to the Research Guild only four out of ten young unmarried males and two out of ten females found their first experience with coitus "very pleasurable." Over a third of the males and almost two-thirds of the females experienced feelings of regret and worry afterward. Some are bothered by ongoing moral and emotional conflicts, while others are concerned that they have not performed well enough. And for many there is the fear of pregnancy and venereal disease (Hunt, 1974).

On the other hand, for many couples, sexual intercourse before marriage eases sex of its great urgency and gives them time to get a clearer picture of the day-to-day workability of their relationship before making a lifelong commitment to each other.

There is, however, one factor that may have a negative effect on later marital happiness: the age of the woman at the time of first coitus. According to one survey, women who were 15 or younger when they first experienced intercourse were more likely than those who started later to share sex with many partners and use stimulating devices, masturbation, and marijuana in an effort to enhance sexual pleasure. But they were the least likely of all women to describe their marriages as good, the least likely to rate marital sex as being good, and the most dissatisfied with the frequency of intercourse in marriage. As a group, they are least likely to call themselves "mostly happy" and most likely to say that they are "mostly unhappy" (Levin, 1975b). There is no way of knowing whether these women are unhappy because they began intercourse when they were too young to handle its interpersonal aspects or began young because they already had unstable, unhappy personalities.

In the past, young people were warned that engaging in intercourse while single might jeopardize their later happiness and commitment in marriage. But research has shown this fear to be unjustified (Ard, 1974). Few young people believe it anymore anyway. The majority opinion seems to be that it is better to develop sexual and interpersonal skills and test compatibility before marriage than after. Many see lovemaking as a natural and satisfying activity that tends to deepen love and understanding in a relationship. Waiting until marriage is thought to be unnecessarily frustrating and perhaps even unhealthy (Finger, 1975).

SOCIAL ORIGINS OF SEXUAL BEHAVIOR

According to Freud and later Kinsey, sexuality is basically a biological drive. Since it presses so urgently for expression, it must be controlled by social laws, mores, or repressions internalized in childhood. Today, however, social scientists question this view. Instead, they see sexuality as something which is no more related to biological processes than other forms of human behavior.

The Freudian view that sexuality is instinctive, preordained by our biological nature, has blocked our full recognition of its social components. What we experience as sexual excitement is not purely automatic. It is learned. Socialization to sexuality—the learned scripts, meanings, values, fantasies, and gender identity people carry with them—begins with the warnings, teachings, examples, and reactions of parents during childhood. It is later influenced by the values of the adolescent peer group, specific partners, and the mass media, and continues developing throughout life. The sequence of physical responses that culminate in orgasm is usually possible only when stimulation is embedded in an appropriate social script (Gagnon and Simon).

SEXUAL SCRIPTS

Although sexual responses are sometimes spontaneous—and perhaps inappropriate, as when a man has an erection while pressed against a woman he doesn't know on a crowded bus—most of our sexual behavior follows **social scripts.** Learned ways of viewing sexuality define what constitutes an erotic situation, specify who the actors must be, and plot their behavior—as in a play actors learn their parts from the script provided by the author.

Social scripts. Learned patterns for how people should behave in particular social situations.

A sexual script has two basic components: the external or interpersonal, and the internal. The external part defines a sexual opportunity by means of certain interpersonal conventions. For adolescents, going to a drive-in movie might signal interest in petting. For adults, appearing at a singles bar might be a sign of readiness for sexual activity. The internal part of a sexual script specifies the psychic states and motivations necessary for arousal. A woman undergoing a medical examination does not usually respond erotically as the doctor feels her breasts and inserts instruments in her vagina. If her lover carried on the same activities, however, the different psychic state she reads into his touches—perhaps love and passion instead of clinical concern—and her own desire for lovemaking can trigger her sexual responsiveness (Gagnon and Simon).

The details of the sexual script are usually determined by some larger value system. Gecas and Libby have identified five distinct kinds of sexual scripts current in the United States at this time:

1. The traditional-religious script is rooted in the philosophy that sex outside of marriage is sinful. Unmarried women especially are expected to remain virgins. Marital partners are to be sexually faithful to each other. Sexuality is defined in terms of reproduction, though its relationship to affection is acknowledged.
2. The romantic script emphasized by our mass media makes love a prerequisite for sexual activity. In the absence of love, intercourse is thought to be meaningless or disgusting; in its presence, intercourse is

CASE STUDY—BRUCE AND SALLY

Bruce is a young man of 22, a university student, living with Sally, who is 20. Sally's two-year-old daughter lives with them also, and Bruce finds her an adorable child. Though still legally married to the child's father, Sally is in the process of getting a divorce.

Bruce and Sally had known each other for ten months before deciding they were in love with each other and wanted to live together. Since that time they have been very happy together, except for one problem. Though Sally says she is in love with Bruce, she insists on her right as a liberated woman to have sexual intercourse with other men when she feels like it. She considers this merely an expression of her independence and a totally separate activity from her relationship with Bruce. Bruce, however, is very much bothered by the idea of sharing Sally with other men. When he objects, she says, "That's too bad. Accept it. This is the way it's going to be."

For class discussion: (1) Is it possible to be in love with one person and enjoy sharing sexual intimacies with a number of others? (2) What advice would you give to Bruce in this situation? How should this conflict be managed?

justified even outside of marriage. In this script, the only eligible actors are those who are in love with each other, the required emotional state is one of uncontrollable loving passion, and the situation is supposed to be as spontaneous as possible. In our society, women are more likely to have been socialized to this script than men.

3. The recreational script defines sex primarily as fun. According to this concept, sexual activity need not be limited to marriage or loving relationships. It is justified as a way of getting pleasure for yourself and giving it to others. Although emphasis is placed on enjoyment, playfulness, and abandon, concern for perfecting techniques may involve hard work and performance fears, just like golf or tennis.

4. Friendly sex is an emerging variation which combines sex as recreation and sex as affection. It involves a single standard of sexual behavior for men and women, acceptance of sexual intimacies within casual but affectionate relationships, and tends to allow marriage to be sexually open rather than exclusive.

5. The utilitarian-predatory script defines sex as a means toward some other goal. Sex may not even be seen as pleasurable in itself, but it is used as a way to earn money, power, or prestige. A prostitute, for instance, uses sex for money, an ambitious woman may use sex to gain power over men, and an adolescent male may try to "score" to raise his status within the peer group.

Utilitarian. Aimed at usefulness rather than pleasure.

The scripts just described are abstractions or ideals; their acting out is often garbled and incomplete. Individuals may lack a clear awareness of the script they are following, switch between divergent scripts prescribed by family and peer group, or change scripts several times during their lifetime. They also may end up in confusion by trying to follow a script which differs from their partner's (Gecas and Libby).

Motive. Something, such as a need or desire, that causes people to act.

MOTIVES FOR SEX

Gerhard Neubeck (1972) does not dispute the idea of sexual scripts as a way of organizing our thoughts about the meaning of the sexual act and what we might hope to get out of it. However, he has made a different, perhaps more personal, kind of analysis of sexual behavior, which overlaps at points with the five sexual scripts suggested by Gecas and Libby.

Neubeck proposes a list of 14 motives which may be influential, together or separately, in any one person's sexual behavior. The specific motives for sex may vary from one partner to another or from one time to another, depending on the interpersonal relationship that exists between the partners. In fact, Neubeck closes his list with the idea that participation in sexual intercourse may be a highly individual and spontaneous action. Nevertheless, the idea of spontaneous sex is still consistent with the view of Gagnon and Simon that such behavior would not occur unless the individual had been previously socialized to regard this as acceptable or even expected behavior. The 14 motives listed by Neubeck are as follows:

1. Affection—seeking sexual intimacy out of feelings of love, romance, and desire for closeness.
2. Animosity—seeking to vent hostility toward the partner, for those who consider sex degrading, or as an expression of power.
3. Anxieties—seeking to use sex as temporary relief from feelings of fear and impotence in other spheres.
4. Boredom—seeking sexual excitement as an escape from a dull environment or boring routine.
5. Duty—agreeing to sex out of a sense of obligation to the partner.
6. Mending wounds—wanting to use sex as a way to make up after a fight or to forget sorrows.
7. Accomplishment—seeking to copulate to meet personal or cultural standards for frequency of intercourse, or perhaps to break the record.
8. Adventure—seeking sexual variety and excitement out of a sense of curiosity and creativity.
9. Recreation—wanting sex for the sport of it, producing pleasant sensations for each other.
10. Lust—a passionate hunger for sexual consummation.
11. Self-affirmation—wanting to engage in sex as an expression of one's sex role, to confirm one's masculinity or femininity.

12. Altruism—seeking sexual involvement with another in order to give pleasure or a feeling of being wanted and needed.
13. Idiosyncratic needs—wanting to act out unusual personal desires.
14. Situational influences—reacting to specific circumstances which trigger arousal, such as checking into a motel without the children.

THE FREQUENCY OF SEXUAL BEHAVIOR

Frequency is not considered the most important aspect of a healthy sexual relationship. Nevertheless, researchers have used frequency of sexual activity as an indicator of trends in attitudes and behavior. To some extent, these trends can be interpreted as clues to where U.S. society is headed. In this section, we will look first at some statistics on the frequency of certain sexual behaviors in adolescence, and then at how often adults engage in sexual intercourse.

ADOLESCENT BEHAVIORS

According to various surveys, adolescents are becoming increasingly sexually experienced. Vener and Stewart (1974) found that the percentage of high school students in one representative mid-western community who had engaged in coitus increased from 22 percent to almost 28 percent within a three-year period, 1970–1973. Other indices of sexual activity showed similar increases. In 1973, compared to 1970, more students were engaging in light petting, heavy petting, and coitus with two or more partners. Boys seem to be more precocious during early adolescence than girls. Twenty-eight percent of the males but only 10 percent of the females had experienced intercourse by age 13. By the time they were 17, however, the girls had caught up, erasing the effect of the double standard within this sample of high school students. In 1973, 35 percent of the 17-year-old girls and 34 percent of the 17-year-old boys, a little more than a third of each group, reported having "gone all the way."

Precocious. Exhibiting adult behavior at an exceptionally early age.

The effects of changing morality extend beyond sexuality, according to the research of Vener and Stewart. Those who are sexually active at the high school level are also likely to be involved in socially condemned nonsexual behaviors. Sexual activity is positively correlated with general delinquency (shoplifting, car theft, vandalism, assault, reckless driving), drug use, smoking, and drinking. It is also associated with lack of commitment to traditional institutions. Sexually active students tend to have negative attitudes toward police, church, school, and teachers. On the other hand, these researchers gained the impression that informal, egalitarian, mutually respectful interaction between the sexes is increasing.

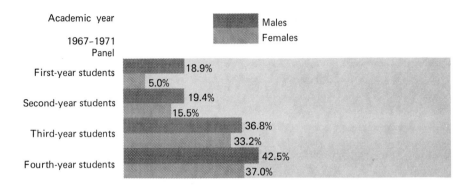

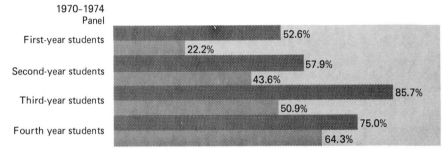

Fig. 11.1 Differences between males and females in self-reported involvement in premarital coitus by academic year. Data from a longitudinal study of two groups of college students shows increasing involvement in premarital coitus as students move through their college years. Differences between students who entered college in 1967 and in 1970 are also shown, and involvement in premarital coitus is seen to have increased substantially for both males and females. (Source: Ferrell, Tolone, and Walsh, 1977.)

ADULT INTERCOURSE

Growing cultural openness has affected adults as well as adolescents. According to a study by Cody Wilson (1975), although a majority of U.S. adults consider themselves sexually conservative, a large minority (40 percent) describe their sexual attitudes as liberal. Gender, education, and age are significant variables here. Males are more liberal than females, college-educated people more liberal than those with high school or elementary education, and young adults more liberal than older adults.

According to this survey, the median age for first intercourse is 18 years for males and 20 for females. The older people in the sample tended to have started intercourse later than the younger people. And even though they seemed to have more liberal attitudes on the whole, those with a college education tended to have started having intercourse later than those with less education. Three-fourths of these adults rate their sex lives as satisfactory, and over half of the women and men in the 21–29-year age bracket rate their sex life very satisfactory. Asked how often they engaged in intercourse, they reported a median frequency of once a week. This ranged from the 15 percent who had not engaged in intercourse at all during the previous six months to the 3 percent who reported having intercourse five or more times per week.

Coital rates decline with age, especially the man's age, suggesting that it is the man more than the woman who determines the frequency of intercourse. According to one study, each five years added to a man's age reduces frequency of intercourse by an average of ten times per year. Between the ages of 20 and 40, the average frequency of coitus for married men is cut in half, dropping from ten coitions every four weeks to five (James, 1974). As indicated in Chapter 5, however, many older couples continue to enjoy an active sex life, despite the decrease in the overall rate of sexual activity.

For married couples, having children seems to decrease the frequency of intercourse. Couples with no children have the highest coital rates. Perhaps this is because their lovemaking doesn't have to compete with night feedings, weariness after a day's worth of caring for children, images of each other as coparents rather than lovers, and the inhibitions to spontaneity of sexual activity posed by having children in the house (James).

PROBLEMS IN A SEXUAL RELATIONSHIP

Children are not the only barriers to richly satisfying lovemaking. In addition to the possibility that they may be reading from different scripts or resistant to the other's motives for sex, people may bring to sexual encounters a number of personal problems. In this section we describe some ways partners can prevent each other from enjoying sex, either intentionally or unconsciously, and then list some psychological difficulties that may underlie their problematic sexual behaviors.

SEXUAL SABOTAGE

People can make sexual relations unsatisfactory for each other through a variety of sabotaging maneuvers. Not all **saboteurs** intend to hurt their partners, some may be trying to throw up defenses for their own fears. Rather than encouraging each other's sexuality, they unconsciously find subtle ways of undermining it. Sex therapist Helen Singer Kaplan (1974a) describes four common antisex behaviors.

Sabotage. Destructive or obstructive action intended to hinder another person's efforts.

Tension Creation.   Rather than trying to create feelings of relaxation and self-esteem, some people habitually point out faults or raise anxiety-provoking issues like money problems as a prelude to lovemaking. They may do so innocently, but nonetheless effectively: "All right, but I hope your mother doesn't hear us through these thin walls." Specific sexual demands or criticisms are especially likely to inhibit sexual response.

Bad Timing.   While many lovers know intuitively when both are in the mood for lovemaking, some people repeatedly choose to make sexual demands when their partners are not interested or refuse advances when they are. Dr. Kaplan had one patient who, when he found his wife lying in bed, obviously freshly washed, perfumed, and ready, took off on a suddenly urgent hour-long errand to the hardware store. Some women habitually complain of being too tired for sex at night except when the male partner is exhausted or drunk, at which times the woman suddenly wants to make love.

Physical Repulsion.   Rather than going to great lengths to make themselves attractive to their lovers, antisex partners may unconsciously make themselves unappealing. They may gain weight, ignore personal hygiene, speak crudely or move clumsily, usually without recognizing that such behaviors may be defenses against sexual involvement. But as Kaplan remarks, it is no surprise if one partner is uninterested in sex when the other gets into bed dirty or smelly, without having made any effort to be physically attractive.

Frustrating Tactics.   A person who enjoys sex learns what the partner likes and tries to satisfy these needs; a sabotaging spouse does just the opposite. If the husband is excited by his wife's movements, she keeps still. If she likes to move, he lies on top of her. If she dislikes TV, he leaves it on during intercourse. If he likes to fondle her breasts, she says they hurt. So both end up frustrated.

PSYCHOLOGICAL BARRIERS

If such sexually destructive maneuvers are used out of sheer hostility between partners, there is little that can improve their sex life. But sex therapists speculate that often such defensive barriers to full sexual expression spring from personal problems, misunderstandings, or ignorance of normal and effective sexual behavior. Sexual adjustment involves both self-discovery and mutual accommodation. Both partners have to learn what their own needs are in the way of atmosphere, stimulation, timing of orgasm, duration of coitus, and frequency of lovemaking, express them openly and then resolve individual differences in some mutually agreeable pattern. This takes time, openness, awareness of body sensations, and a deep, unselfish commitment to each other.

Inability to Communicate.   Many adults retain childhood prohibitions against talking openly about sexual responses and desires. It is hard to unlearn the notion that people we care for will disapprove if we try to put such intimate thoughts into words. But this secrecy puts a great burden on sexual partners. They have to guess at what kinds of loveplay the partner likes, what turns the other off, and what new things the other would secretly like to try. To be able to speak to each other candidly and without accusation—"I think, I wish, I feel, I need, I'm afraid"—frees sexual adjusting from years of silent misunderstandings. According to a 1975 survey, 70 out of 100 women who never talk about sex rate the sexual aspect of marriage as fair to poor. On the other hand, 88 out of 100 women who regularly discuss their sexual feelings with their husbands say their sex lives are good to very good (Levin, 1975a).

Lack of a comfortable vocabulary for body parts and sexual behavior often inhibits communication between sensitive people. Four-letter street words seem too crude and clinical terms too cold. Some speak in **euphemisms** to sidestep the problem; a few creative lovers invent their own private words which are free from ugly associations. But sexual communication need not always be verbal. Partners often guide each other with their hands to indicate what pleases them. Lovemaking itself can be the ultimate in nonverbal communication of the strength of the bonds between two people, but if the couple have had nothing to say to each other aside from routine matters, if little emotional intimacy has been established before their lovemaking, they can hardly expect to communicate closeness and openness the minute their bodies touch.

Euphemism. Substitution of an agreeable or inoffensive word for one that may offend.

Fear of Rejection.   In order to function well sexually, people must relax their inhibitions and abandon themselves to erotic responsiveness. But learned behavior patterns and the dynamics of each interpersonal relationship frequently make people hold back from full sexual involvement. Fearing that they will be rejected and criticized rather than reassured, understood, and protected, they try never to allow themselves the total vulnerability of full sexual abandon.

Low Self-Esteem.   Letting go takes more than trust in a loving partner; it also takes self-love. Some people are unable to receive sexual pleasure freely because they feel unworthy of it, though they may enjoy giving pleasure. They are not free to explore their own needs without discomfort and even less free to ask a partner to help satisfy these needs. Only people with a good opinion of themselves are able to admit that even though they feel a bit awkward about it, they would like to try something new in lovemaking or ask for specific kinds of help. As psychiatrist R. Clay Burchell (1975)

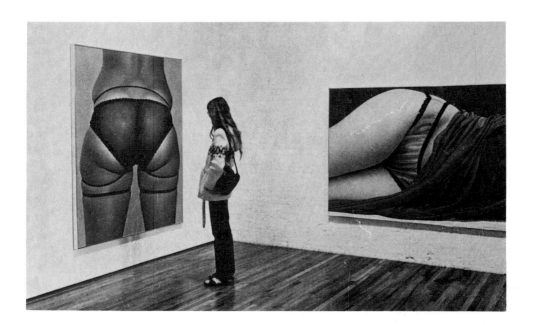

points out, "High-esteem provides a foundation for risk-taking and growth that is nurturing to any relationship" (p. 74).

Negative Body Image. People whose low self-esteem includes feeling physically unattractive often react tensely to sexual advances. Since they do not accept the way their own bodies look, they feel unlovable. Surprisingly, feelings about sex appeal do not center on the areas emphasized in erotic literature. According to a survey answered by over 62,000 readers of *Psychology Today*, people are more likely to be concerned with whether their mid-torsos bulge and how their faces look than with how big their breasts or penises are (Berscheid et al., 1973). Partners can help by assuring each other of their physical attractiveness.

Fear of Failure. Anyone who has ever tried to orgasm and failed is susceptible to worries about failure the next time. This kind of thinking is self-fulfilling. Fear of failure is the greatest immediate cause of impotence in men and is significant in women's inability to be orgasmic as well (Kaplan).

Men frequently lose their erections during extended lovemaking. Many accept this as natural, continue with foreplay, and eventually regain their erection. But if they lack self-confidence and start worrying about whether they will erect again, what would have been only a temporary loss of engorgement may become a total inability to carry intercourse to completion.

If such men have been using sexual activity to bolster their self-esteem, or if the partner is the demanding sort, performance failure may be especially disturbing.

Spectatoring. Orgasmic failure is frequently linked to what Masters and Johnson (1974) call **spectatoring.** People who fear their inadequacies often follow the progress of their own responses as onlookers from above rather than becoming deeply involved in a sense of union with the partner. Spectatoring is not unusual; even people who are secure in their sexuality do it sometimes, but it does interfere with full enjoyment of sexual relations.

Spectatoring. Mentally following the progress of one's own responses as if one were an onlooker instead of a participant.

Repression. Many adults have difficulty expressing their sexuality because they were forced to subdue it as children, treating it as something secret and evil. Even when marriage grants cultural approval to its expression, they may be unable to give themselves permission to enter into sexual behavior. This is particularly a problem for men who associate their wives with their mothers, with whom, of course, sexual intercourse is forbidden. The same is true for women who have repressed sexual feelings for their fathers and later identify their husbands with their fathers. As a defense against guilt and anxiety, they may deny feeling aroused by sensuous caresses, effectively killing their own sexual response.

Unrealistic Expectations. Some marriage counselors feel that most sex problems involve unrealistic expectations, including the myth that sexual responsiveness is natural rather than learned. Although all healthy humans are capable of sexual responses, good sexual functioning with a partner does not happen automatically. Individuals differ in the strength and character of their sexual responses, and anyone may experience a decrease in sex drive from time to time. It is unrealistic to expect that passionate sexual response can always be delivered on demand or that one partner can be completely responsible for the other's pleasure.

If people expect less from their lovemaking—in terms of earthshaking mutual orgasms—they get more out of it, in terms of full appreciation of all the sensuous giving and getting feelings which precede climax. There is no reason to assume that all loveplay should end with intercourse and/or orgasm. To insist on this goal every time makes sex more predictable, and therefore monotonous, and creates pressure to perform rather than relaxed mutual enjoyment in just being together.

Resistance to Change. To be workable, a sexual relationship must grow and change as the partners do. Biologically, the man's responses will inevitably slow down, while the woman's may become stronger as she reaches her late thirties and early forties. In an open, nurturing relationship, this shift can be accommodated without anxiety. The older he gets, the longer a man can delay his ejaculation since it gradually loses its urgency. This means a greater opportunity for foreplay and prolonged coitus, making it more possible for the woman to be orgasmic and to caress her husband at length. If he is secure in his self-esteem, he will find her increased responsiveness rewarding. But if he is haunted by comparisons with the peak of responsiveness he reached as a young man, he may find it hard to accept his diminished capacity for erection and may see her growing sexuality as a threat to his flagging powers. She, on the other hand, may be increasingly interested in her own orgasms and may subtly blame him for any failures to achieve them (Kaplan).

Sex-Role Conflicts. Many interpersonal difficulties can be traced to conflicting ideas about the proper roles of men and women. This is as true in the sexual sphere as in any other.

Victorian. Relating to the age of Victoria, Queen of England from 1837 to 1901.

In Victorian America, lovemaking was something a man did to a woman as a release for his sexual needs. She was thought not to have any sexual needs and was expected to submit to his advances out of a sense of duty. Neither found this very rewarding, so a new sexual ethic evolved. It required that the man make sex pleasurable for his partner as well as himself. At first he was expected to be tender and considerate; then he was told that she was capable of orgasm and that it was his responsibility to get her there; now he is expected to delay his own ejaculation while providing multiple orgasms for her. These demands place an enormous burden on the man and may make him feel sexually incompetent and insecure rather than assertive, confident, and sexually skilled, as the traditional masculine role dictates (Masters and Johnson, 1974).

At the same time, women have become more aware of their sexual potential and more open about wanting to enjoy it. Expecting equal rights in the bedroom as well as on the job market, many wives are abandoning their traditionally submissive sexual role. According to a recent survey, only 1 out of 135 women is passive in bed; the others all play a more or less active part in lovemaking (Levin, 1975a).

Marriage counselors are divided in their opinions of what effect this growing female assertiveness is having on sexual adjustment in marriage. Some professionals are expressing alarm that male impotence is on the increase, blaming this increase on the inability of men to function when assertive women place performance demands on them. Virginia Abernethy (1974) cites cross-cultural evidence from studies of the Hopi Indians and Trobriand Islanders that "female control of the conjugal relationship coincides with high rates of marital stress and instability." Ralph Greenson suggests that in our society as women are becoming more assertive, men are becoming sexually less active. "Before World War II," he writes, "the term 'frigidity' was used exclusively in regard to women. Today I find far more men who display sexual coldness or disinterest" (Greenson, 1970, pp. 261, 269). Some current courses and best-selling books encourage women to return to wifely submission in the interest of happier marriages. *Fascinating Womanhood*'s Helen Andelin and *The Total Woman*'s Marabel Morgan preach that wives should accept, admire, adapt to, and appreciate their husbands. They say responsibility for change and accommodation should be borne completely by the wife. If she stops nagging her husband, he will adore her, especially when she displays a new interest in sex. It is up to her to sustain or reintroduce romance and passionate lovemaking through playful, dependent, childlike behavior and such aids to sexual excitement as suggestive costumes. Many wives who have followed this advice claim that it has saved their marriages, delighting their husbands and enhancing their own sense of femininity (Emerson, 1975).

Critics of this point of view maintain that marriage and sex are best when men and women are equally and mutually involved in making them work. Masters and Johnson (1974) hold that liberation of the woman from her traditionally dependent role can also liberate the man from expectations that he always play the part of sexual expert and aggressor. Her willingness to take some of the responsibility for lovemaking frees him to relax and enjoy it more. The man will find her expressions of pleasure exciting and stimulating, heightening his own responsiveness and involvement.

SEX OUTSIDE OF MARRIAGE

For perhaps one-third of all married women (Levin, 1974b) and close to one-half of the married men in America (Hunt, 1974) marital lovemaking is not enough. These people have risked social disapproval, personal guilt, and possible marital disaster to make love to someone other than the legal sex partner. Extramarital sex as a marital problem is discussed in Chapter 14; in earlier chapters we considered the extent of cultural tolerance of adultery. Here we will briefly consider whether it is sexual frustration alone which makes so many people burst the bonds of monogamy.

Extramarital. Shared with someone other than one's spouse.

According to a 1975 survey, wives who have had extramarital sexual contact are more dissatisfied with their marriages or their sex lives than women who remain faithful to their husbands. And a large majority of those with poor marriages who have never engaged in extramarital sex nonetheless admit to a fairly strong desire for it. But about half of the wives who have had extramarital sexual experience claim to be happily married and find marital sex good to very good (Levin, 1975b).

The Research Guild's survey uncovered more surprising statistics about the sexual pleasure people derive from their extramarital lovemaking. Contrary to the common expectation that people involved in affairs would make love with passionate abandon, they actually seem to be more inhibited in

"We can't go on meeting this way, Daphne."
Copyright Glenn R. Bernhardt.

their range of sexual expression than marital partners. Ten percent of such couples limit their sexual contact to petting. Those who have intercourse are less likely than married partners to use positions other than the traditional missionary position. Whereas only 7 percent of all women never have orgasm in conjugal lovemaking, 35 percent never reach climax in extramarital coitus. Compared with the 67 percent of men and 55 percent of women who find marital sex very pleasurable, only 47 percent of the men and 37 percent of the women with extramarital experience rate its sexual aspect very pleasurable (Hunt, 1974).

There are a number of ways of interpreting these data, but they still raise this question: if romantic excursions outside of marriage provide less sexual satisfaction than marriage itself, why do so many people become involved in them, and why do they do so with a succession of partners? Only 40 percent of women who participate in extramarital sex have had only one extramarital partner; 44 percent have had two to five partners, and 16 percent have had from six up to as many as thirty (Hunt, 1974).

MOTIVES FOR EXTRAMARITAL SEX
It is difficult to generalize about behaviors which range from casual one-night stands to grand passions, the rare affairs of total involvement. But

researchers who have questioned people about their reasons for seeking extramarital sex have come up with a variety of motives.

Emotional boredom with marriage seems to overshadow all other reasons for **infidelity**. It is most common when people are in their thirties and forties, a time when monotony in marriage is underscored by the common feeling that the best years of one's life are rapidly slipping away and nothing exciting is happening. It is not instant love for a fascinating stranger that irresistibly transports people out of this emotional stalemate. Few people credit love as being the main factor in their first affairs, and a majority are drawn into extramarital involvement with someone they already know. Many are, however, seeking assurance that they are still lovable and capable of loving. Emotional responsiveness from someone who does not take them for granted is a boost to self-esteem (Hunt, 1969).

Some affairs are an expression of rebellion—against stability and maturity in general or against a mate they resent. Others are motivated to seek other partners because they have chosen poorly in the first place; extramarital satisfaction makes their unfortunate marriages more bearable, holding them together for the sake of children or social standing. Some people who seek extramarital sex do so because of long absence of their spouse. The beautiful people of the jet set may maintain lovers as **status symbols** (Hunt, 1969). And for people who are positively inclined toward the possibility of extramarital involvement, a good opportunity for it may be motivation enough (Johnson, 1970).

For an unknown number of Americans, extramarital affairs with people of the same sex are a way of expressing homosexual tendencies despite their heterosexual marriages, from which they draw different kinds of satisfactions. An estimated 20 percent of homosexual males and 35 percent of homosexual females have been part of a heterosexual marriage at some point (Bell, 1975).

OPEN MARRIAGES

For some people, extramarital sex is a way of expanding the range of their experience, of living life to the fullest. They do not expect their mates to meet all of their needs and feel no guilt about affairs which complement their marriages (O'Neill and O'Neill, 1972). This attitude may be shared by both partners. In an open marriage, husband and wife allow each other freedom to have sex with other people. Nonpossessiveness may involve sharing sex with a third person, mate-swapping or "swinging," or communal sex in which anyone in a group may have intercourse openly with anyone else. Such arrangements are supposed to be free from the deception and secrecy of conventional infidelity. But involving both partners in sexual experimentation with other people may still pose problems of jealousy and fear of abandonment, traditional reactions of the deceived partner when extramarital affairs are uncovered (Masters and Johnson, 1974).

Infidelity. Unfaithfulness to an obligation; especially marital unfaithfulness in the form of sexual intercourse with someone other than the spouse.

Status symbols. Possessions or attributes indicating a particular rank in the social hierarchy.

Table 11.1 Differences between intimate friendships and swinging as forms of extramarital involvement   As indicated in the text, married persons may decide to enter into a variety of interpersonal relationships outside the marriage, and these relationships vary in the emphasis placed on sexual activity compared with other activities. Ramey compares the characteristics of intimate friendships as he has observed them with characteristics of swinging relationships in a way that clarifies the nature of each of these types of co-marital involvement.

INTIMATE FRIENDSHIP	SWINGING
Individual activity	Couple-front activity
Emotional and personal involvement	Emotional and personal involvement taboo
Personal commitments	No personal commitments
Long-term relationships	Usually one-night stand or very short-term
Interpersonal interaction emphasis	Sexual activity emphasis
Much discussion/intellectual sharing	Talk limited, generally shallow
Intimate friendship philosophy permeates lifestyle	Usually male-dominant traditional marriage
Considerable family interaction	Family interaction avoided
Many kinship-type roles	No concerns except sexual activity
Considerable business involvement	No business involvement
Career ties and help	Avoid revealing professional information
May invest money in joint projects	Discussing money matters taboo
Tend to be politically liberal	Tend to be more conservative
Lean toward peer marriage and gender role equality	Swinging "compartmentalized"
Below average sexual frequency	Above average sexual frequency
Includes singles, divorceés, etc.	Almost exclusively a married couple activity but may include singles to make a couple
Includes male and female homosexuals	Avoids homosexuals
One out of three males bisexual	Extremely few male bisexuals
Wide age range	Usually compressed to approximate age peers
No youth cult	Heavy emphasis on youth and physical attractiveness

Source: James W. Ramey, "Intimate Groups and Networks: Frequent Consequence of Sexually Open Marriage," *The Family Coordinator* Vol. 24, No. 4 (Oct. 1975). Copyright National Council on Family Relations. Reprinted by permission.

Gagnon and Simon state that most women enter these relationships to meet their husband's rather than their own sexual needs. The wife becomes a token which can be used by the husband in sexual trading with other men. Sex with another man also enhances the erotic image of the wife, in opposition to her maternal role, and increases her desirability. However, sexual adventurousness solely for the sake of physical enjoyment has never drawn more than an estimated 1 percent of married people in the United States into swapping on a couples or group basis as a regular or frequent pattern. Only about 2 percent of all couples have tried mate-swapping; an estimated 18 percent of married men and 6 percent of married women have been involved in group sex at some time, often prior to marriage (Hunt, 1974). One swinger admitted in a discussion with Masters and Johnson (1974) that it is hard to find enough emotional energy to cope with the numerous relationships involved in swinging. Many men find that swinging creates performance fears as well as jealousy toward other men whom their wives might find more virile and sexually satisfying. In traditional two-people affairs, those which offer nothing but sexual gratification do not last very long. After the initial thrill of consummation of secret desires and the excitement of variety wear off, sex alone is not a powerful enough stimulus to keep these alliances going, and they may soon wither away (Hunt, 1969).

Although sex as the vehicle for being intimate with people other than one's legal mate is the only aspect of friendships outside of marriage considered taboo in U.S. society, it is not sexual satisfaction alone that most people seem to seek in extramarital involvement. Many may be looking—usually unsuccessfully—for what they had hoped to find in marriage, one deeply rewarding relationship. Compared to earlier generations, Americans now expect far more emotional satisfaction from marriage—warm companionship, romantic love, constant emotional support, and ever-exciting sex. People who work at building good sexual relationships, getting counseling and medical advice to help them if need be, may not always succeed. But if they do, they are likely to find that growth in sexual functioning is an expression of growth in themselves and in their relationship, leading to greater mutual trust, confidence in themselves, and pleasure in their marriage.

Summary

1. The purposes of this chapter are to consider the social origins of sexual behavior, how sexual behavior develops, and the problems that various kinds of sexual behavior can cause in a relationship.

2. In the relatively restrictive U.S. society, children frequently lack an education in sex and sexual behavior, getting most of their information (or misinformation) through hearsay. As they mature, adolescents engage in forms

of sexual behavior such as masturbation and petting which are stages in the learning process on which adult heterosexual intercourse rests. At some point in their development, there may be homosexual contact. This is usually a passing phase, but homosexual preferences may persist into adult life.

3. Sexual behavior is socially learned, even though biological in basis. We are socialized to sexuality by warnings, examples, and reactions of parents, peer groups, and the media. Sexual scripts are part of this process and define for us what constitutes an erotic situation, who the actors must be, and what their behavior must be. There are two parts to the script: the external (defines the opportunity in terms of interpersonal conventions) and the internal (specifies the psychic states necessary for arousal). Five basic scripts predominate in the United States: traditional-religious, romantic, recreational, friendly, and utilitarian-predatory. Motivations for sex, such as affection, boredom, and adventure also affect the form that sexual behavior takes.

4. Surveys indicate an increase in sexual experience of adolescents which is associated with trends toward changing morality and lack of commitment to traditional institutions. At the same time, informal and mutually respectful interaction between the sexes at the adolescent level is increasing. Adults are also affected by growing cultural openness as indicated by the large number of people who describe their sexual attitudes as liberal. Intercourse among single adults as well as co-marital and extramarital intercourse are now common and have become more culturally acceptable.

5. People may bring personal problems to sexual encounters which prevent them and their partners from enjoying sex. Some common problems are tension creation, bad timing, physical repulsion, and frustrating tactics. Sometimes these tactics are used on purpose, but frequently they are the result of personal problems, misunderstandings, or ignorance of effective sexual behavior such as inability to communicate, fear of rejection or failure, or gender-role conflicts. To resolve these problems both partners have to learn what their own needs are, express them openly, and then resolve individual differences in a mutually agreeable pattern. Often help from professional therapists may be needed.

Key Concepts

Sexual scripts	Sexual sabotage
Petting	Rape
Homosexual	Sodomy
Heterosexual	Adultery
Erotic	Extramarital
Euphemism	Co-marital
Virginity	Open marriage
Impotence	Swinging
Spectatoring	Status symbol
Oral-genital sex	Median

1. What are some of your state's laws concerning sexual behavior, both hetero-sexual and homosexual? Are they being enforced? Should they be?

2. What type of sex education course do you think should be taught in high schools—strictly biological, interpersonal? In elementary schools? Should contraceptive information be included.

3. How does our popular culture (ads, TV, movies, books) affect the attitudes of children toward sexual behavior? Of adults?

4. What are some possible results from current less restrictive attitudes toward sexual behavior? For example, what benefits might there be during adolescence? How might a marriage with sexual problems be helped by the increasing openness about sex?

5. Would you be willing to be part of an open marriage? Why or why not?

GAGNON, J. H., AND W. SIMON (1974).   *Sexual Conduct: The Social Sources of Human Sexuality.* London: Hutchison & Co., Ltd.

Discusses the sources and development of human sexuality. Includes coverage of social origins, pedagogy of sex, male and female homosexuality, pornography, and social change and sexual conduct.

KOGAN, B. A. (1973).   *Human Sexual Expression.* New York: Harcourt, Brace Jovanovich.

Based on the concept that human sexuality is an expression of the total personality, this book considers the importance of the self-image to sexual expression, reproductive structures and functions, marriage, and other topics related to human sexuality.

SMITH, J. R., AND L. G. SMITH, eds. (1974).   *Beyond Monogamy, Recent Studies of Sexual Alternatives in Marriage.* Baltimore: Johns Hopkins University Press.

A collection of sixteen essays on various experimental forms of sexual activity, such as swinging, group marriage, and co-marital sex.

TRAVIS, C. (1977).   Masculinity. *Psychology Today* 10:8, pp. 35–42.

Reports on the views of 28,000 Psychology Today readers who responded to a survey addressed to both sexes on what makes a "real man" and what his traits are. Results show that the tough, aggressive ideal is on the way out and that men have more trouble defining the new ideal than women have.

LAWS, J. L., AND P. SCHWARTZ (1977).   *Sexual Scripts: Social Construction of Female Sexuality.* New York: Holt, Rinehart and Winston.

A collection of original essays covering female sexuality and its relation to the social environment, and exploring such topics as the formation of gender roles, the effects of body processes, dating, and marriage.

Money Management: Cooperative Planning | *12*

THE FAMILY AS CONSUMERS

Over the past generations, the American family has changed from a unit of production to a unit of consumption. No longer do we grow it, make it, or do without. No longer is the whole family involved in serving the needs of a single enterprise. In today's family-business or farm most children do not automatically leave school at the first opportunity to ensure continuation of the operation. Now it is the exception rather than the rule to carry on a parent's life work. In fact, the majority of urban/suburban children have little idea of the production processes that provide for them, let alone have a hand in their success or failure.

To be a successful unit of production, yesterday's family had to work together. The hay had to be into the barn by winter or the animals would starve. It was in everyones' best interest to see to it that the animals did not starve. The community provided manpower and mutual protection against disaster. Today's family is part of a different social structure. We owe not neighbors, but various banks and corporations, the obligation for goods and services. In spite of hard times or illness, that obligation must be met week after week.

Small wonder many people are intrigued by the idea of returning to the land—of returning to a family unit that produces what it consumes. The complications seem fewer, as, indeed, they would be were it possible to take society back 200 years. But, as Mark Kramer (1976) points out, our mass production economy is no longer organized to supply the needs **subsistence farmers** are likely to experience. Nor does the social organization of the town include "the sort of mutual dependence that once provided a pool of manpower and special skills for the occasions when one's own resources weren't enough." Kramer doesn't define himself as a subsistence farmer, though he lives and farms in Vermont and is a faithful reader of the *Mother Earth News*, because he has a **cash crop**—writing.

That, for most people, the family is no longer a producing unit but a consuming unit is an inescapable fact of life. What is equally inescapable is that just as the producing family had to work together to be successful, so must today's consuming family. Just as the successful producing unit has control of the means of production, so must the consuming unit have control over the means of consumption—money.

Money Is the Number-One Cause of Friction in the Family Today. The section of this chapter on arguing about money takes a look at some of the background factors that aggravate the family's money problems—cultural, social, and family conditioning and personality; power struggles; failure in communication; and lack of knowledge. Successful money management can ease a family through the various stages of the family life cycle. Failure to

Subsistence farmer. A farmer whose system of farming provides for all or almost all household needs with no significant surplus for sale.

Cash crop. An agricultural yield which can be sold on the market as a source of income.

plan use of money can condemn a family to an ever-increasing spiral of debt and, thanks to inflation, a decreasing ability to repay.

Families Often Have an Easier Time Earning Money than Spending It Wisely.   Ignorance or lack of concern about personal finance creates many contradictions in American life. Individuals who are most careful about searching for the best bargains—saving pennies here and there—express complete ignorance when making major purchases, such as large appliances, automobiles, or even a house. People who snarl and protest seeing the price of a favorite product rise a nickel or dime may never fully understand the impact of paying 18 percent interest on **installment purchases** or **revolving credit accounts.** At the same time, these people insist on purchasing national-brand food items without realizing that national companies often sell the same product to food-store chains under the chain label, which sells for less. The section on Intelligent Consumerism touches upon the complex decisions facing both the individual and the family unit. These issues include shelter, household purchases, and transportation. Other sections discuss insurance, borrowing and credit, and savings and investment. These sections are by no means an exhaustive study of any single topic. There are an increasing number of books, magazines, and pamphlets available to help the indiivdual and the family become intelligent consumers. Rather, the material provided here should alert students to the complexity of the issues and the necessity of becoming further informed.

Installment purchases. Goods or services paid for through partial payments at fixed intervals.

American Families Often Lack Control over Their Finances.   Studies show that an average middle-class family will have over a half million dollars pass through its hands during the lifetime of the breadwinner—and yet this same family is likely to be struggling with financial difficulties throughout this time. The final section of the chapter on Financial Planning outlines the means by which a family unit or individual can gain and keep control of its resources and maximize the value of its income. Financial planning is the key to money management, no matter how much or how little money one may have. Cooperative financial planning is the key to a successful consuming unit—today's family.

But first, why do we fight, what do we fight over, and how can we stop all that fighting?

ARGUING ABOUT MONEY

Recent studies indicate that couples quarrel over money more than anything else and that economic stress is a major cause in marriage breakup. Evidence of this is found at all economic levels. Stress is by no means limited to those who lack sufficient funds for necessities. It is also present in so-called affluent families that cannot agree on how to use their discretionary income.

CULTURAL, SOCIAL, AND FAMILY CONDITIONING

American culture places a tremendous emphasis on the accumulation of material things. Newspaper, radio, and TV advertising assaults our senses daily urging us to spend. Overspending is hard to avoid, given the easy flow of credit. The young family that responds to the "buy now, pay later, enjoy it while you make easy payments" illusion can find itself quickly trapped in financial bondage.

But attitudes to money do vary within the overall social structure. Saving is more valued in some groups, conspicuous consumption in others. Ethnic, religious, and geographical influences have a strong effect on our consumer habits. Further, within a given subculture, an individual is conditioned by economic factors. The person raised in a family of limited economic means will likely have different perceptions of what's a necessity and what's a luxury than the person raised in a wealthy family (Donnelly, 1976).

Even within the same socioeconomic group, families will spend their money differently, will value different things. For example, one family will buy the best on the theory that it will last longer. Another will buy the least expensive because it has a low replacement cost. Both believe they are getting the most for their money.

PERSONALITY

When personality differences are added to the cultural-socioeconomic stew, little wonder that the mixture often boils over. Within a given family the children's personalities vary widely. One is a spender; one is a saver. Or, for example, look at the differences in attitudes toward **discretionary income** (money available after necessities have been paid for which may be used to improve the quality of life). For person *A* spending this money on an experience (a trip, a cultural event, a gourmet dinner) is the most pleasurable and satisfying way of improving the quality of life. For person *B* buying something that lasts and can be enjoyed every day (an antique, a new couch, a piece of jewelry) is the best use of discretionary income. The conflict starts when *A* marries *B*.

In our highly mobile society, it is likely that a person will marry someone with a different background, with a different set of values. Given these background factors, it's not surprising that, according to a 1974 survey, 54 percent of American families argue a lot about money (Donnelly).

CASE STUDY—HANK AND SHIRLEY

Shirley loves stylish clothes, fancy cars, and luxurious trips. During the time she and Hank were courting, Hank—who worked for his father in a successful family business—always had plenty of money when they went out on dates. Shirley was frank that this was part of his appeal for her. Religion was a barrier to their marriage, since Hank was a strict Catholic and Shirley was a Protestant. However, she decided to convert to Catholicism, and eventually they were married in an elaborate ceremony followed by a lavish reception.

Hank's two younger brothers often made remarks, both before and after the marriage, about Shirley's concerns for what other people thought of her or how much money something might have cost, but Hank ignored them.

When Shirley became pregnant with their sixth child, she wanted to have an abortion, but Hank wouldn't consent. One of the brothers said, "Buy her the biggest diamond you can afford and tell her it's to celebrate the new baby." Two days later, Shirley was happily showing off the biggest diamond their town had ever seen, and the relationship between Hank and Shirley seemed to improve.

As the children got older, Shirley pressed for more and more money to spend on them and on herself. Under this pressure, Hank, through a technical maneuver, was able to ease his brothers out of the very lucrative family business. Eventually he signed over half of all he owned to his wife, and she became an equal partner with him in the business.

Now the children are grown. Shirley has become active in politics and is trying to obtain a divorce in order to marry a state senator on whose campaign she has worked. She predicts he will be the next governor of their state. However, she refuses to give up her half of the family business. Hank still loves her and would gladly take her back if she would come. He feels very guilty about the business deal he pulled on his brothers, but they are not bitter, sympathize with him, and place all the blame on Shirley.

For class discussion: (1) Do you think there are many people who allow themselves to be manipulated by their spouses as Hank apparently has done? (2) This case is reported from Hank's point of view. Do you think Shirley might tell a different story of how she helped make her husband successful in the family business and is entitled to her share of the rewards?

POWER STRUGGLES

Money fights between husband and wife often come down to a fight for supremacy—who's in charge. Until recently, in most families the husband earned the money and controlled its expenditure. He had the power. Today, as a result of the feminist movement and the increased number of working wives, many women are demanding an equal voice in all aspects of the marriage relationship. Numerous studies have been conducted to determine the changing purchasing patterns of husbands and wives in the United States. Although specific assignment of decision-making authority may vary with income, age, and situational characteristics, across all categories the power of the husband in family purchasing decisions has declined (Green and Cunningham, 1975).

In some cases where both partners earn money, the pendulum has swung to the other side. Many wives tend to regard their husbands' earnings as "our" money and their own income as "my" money (Donnelly). Like yesterday's male breadwinner, today's female breadwinner sees the earning of money as involving the right to decide how it should be used.

Holmstrom notes that some couples use a double standard in evaluating their incomes. If the husband's career is seen as primary and the wife's career as secondary, a double standard of cost accounting creeps into their economic decisions. All expenses associated with her work are costs. For example, one professional woman described as follows how the costs associated with her working were so great that, despite her relatively high income bracket, her net income was very low:

Net income. Earnings remaining after the deduction of all charges, outlay, or losses.

[My husband] sat down and figured out one day . . . that when you consider household help, second car, professional clothes, a higher income bracket, the whole bit—and I was earning in the $10,000 a year category at that time—that I was making about 10 cents an hour. So that you can't say that it's a matter of bringing home a good second salary. (Holmstrom, 1972, p. 100)

This is "faulty accounting" for at least two reasons. First of all, the items in the quote—help, car, clothes—have an independent desirability. They may be necessary for the wife to work; but they are also pleasant in themselves. Yet despite their independent desirability, these items are subtracted from her income. They become part of an argument alleging that it really is not financially profitable for her to work. In contrast, things like a car which the husband's job requires—which also have independent desirability —are not viewed in the same way. They are not incorporated into an argument alleging that it is not financially profitable for him to work. In this case, the husband has retained the upper hand in the power struggle because, after all, his wife is only earning 10 cents an hour (Holmstrom).

Some power struggles can only lead to divorce or psychoanalysis. Sometimes, however, the reasons for arguing about money may be rooted not in a struggle for supremacy but in an inability to communicate.

FAILURE IN COMMUNICATION

A 1974 survey of American families by Yankelovich, Skelly, and White showed that of families that fight a lot, half are unable to communicate freely with each other about money matters. Obviously, it is very hard to resolve a problem without talking about it (Donnelly).

How to begin? Counselors offer two principles that may reduce the static in conversations about highly charged topics such as money. First, use the first-person for discussions, "I" not "you." This requires accepting the responsibility for thoughts, words, and actions. Thus, "I am angry," not "You make me mad."

Second, repeat what the other person said in your own words. Don't assume you understand his or her point of view. This allows both to correct any misapprehensions. If there is fighting rather than talking, counselors suggest starting the discussion by talking about why you have trouble talking.

Some people find it easier to communicate on paper. Writing ideas down may help to clarify a position or prevent being sidetracked by emotional flare-ups. Arrange your separate **priorities** in descending order and compare the lists. Negotiate a contract. Give a little, take a little. Hold a meeting. When the family includes children it is considered desirable to involve them in money matters. Many families do not do this. Yet familiarity with money problems will prepare children to handle their spending in a responsible way as adults. Family counselors urge parents to include the children's desires in money questions that affect them. The children should not be the decision-makers, but should know that their voices are heard (Donnelly).

> **Priorities.** The ranking of goals, preferences, or obligations in terms of their relative importance.

Even when partners sincerely try to communicate freely on financial matters, they often find the discussion growing emotional and nonproductive. The reason for this failure in communication may be rooted in different spending patterns as well as personal anxieties. People attach **subjective** meanings to spending. They are buying security or status, love or authority. These intangibles are even harder to discuss than money because they are part of each partner's unique personality. Couples who can remember that attitudes to money are the result of previous cultural and social experiences will have an easier time discussing and resolving money problems. It takes this understanding to be patient, to be flexible, and to be truly cooperative. However, cooperative planning can still flounder on the rocks of financial ignorance.

> **Subjective.** Peculiar to a particular individual; personal.

LACK OF KNOWLEDGE

Virtually overnight, fresh out of the romantic excitement of the wedding, the newly married couple is thrown into the position of making important financial decisions that will affect the long-term pattern of their lives. These early years of the family life cycle, when both partners are working and childless, are financially the most carefree, although they rarely seem so at the time. Most feel financially straitened because there are so many things they want and need. Too often these important decisions about buying or renting shelter, choosing a car, and buying furniture and clothes are made for subjective reasons. And too often couples enter the next stage, the addition of children, already in debt. With the coming of children the wife either stops working or provides for child care out of that "extra" income. Larger living quarters, more furniture and appliances, medical care, food, clothing, and baby-sitters all contribute to a continually growing list of expenses.

According to the Bureau of Labor Statistics, it costs approximately $70,000 to raise the average baby to adulthood in this country. In round figures, parents will spend $2500 on a child's recreation; $4000 for medical bills; $6500 for housing; $7000 for clothing; $13,000 for food; $14,000 on miscellaneous expenses, and $24,000 on a college education (Swift, 1976b).

A major financial crisis arises when children reach the age for college or vocational education. Total costs for tuition, room, board, and other basic expenses run around $5000 a year at private colleges, considerably more at prestige colleges. Even at state colleges and universities, the costs range from $2500 to $3500 a year (Margolius, 1976). According to economists, college and university costs throughout the United States will rise faster than costs of other goods and services, and unfortunately, faster than family income (Swift, 1976a).

Another change in the family financial cycle occurs when the children have left home. By this time the couple's home, furniture, and appliances are largely paid for and they are reaching their peak earning years. This should be a second period of relative affluence and comfort. However, substantial sums will be needed for retirement which is only fifteen or so years away. One in four retired people have no resources beyond their **Social Security payments,** but Social Security has never been sufficient for even bare subsistence. It should be viewed as a cushion to help stretch other funds which people must accumulate for themselves.

Consumerism. Promotion of the consumer's interests through comparison shopping and knowledge of testing programs and quality standards.

Intelligent **consumerism** and successful money management can ease a couple through these stages in the family life cycle. Even if one has made a conscious decision to live on a very simple, modest scale, rejecting the materialistic values of much of society, there is still the problem of balancing income against expenditures. Basic needs for food, shelter, clothing,

---

INFORMATION AVAILABLE TO CONSUMERS
Pamphlets providing practical consumer advice are available from the federal government, either free or at low cost, by writing to the Consumer Information Center, Pueblo, CO 81009. More than 250 pamphlets and leaflets on subject areas such as health and nutrition, budgeting and finance, home energy conservation, and purchasing a house, car, or household appliance are listed and described in the Consumer Information Index which may be obtained, without charge, by writing to the Center.

medical care, transportation, even recreation, continue as long as life continues. Failure to acquire the knowledge and skills necessary to act as a successful consuming unit is as risky as playing Russian Roulette.

INTELLIGENT CONSUMERISM

Consumers purchase a wide and diverse range of goods and services. Their purchases may be items for immediate consumption, several years' usage, or lifetime **investment.** A pair of shoes, an automobile, a month's rent, life insurance, college tuition, and income taxes indicate the range of consumerism. Taxes—whether sales, income, gasoline, or tobacco—represent payment for government services like fire and police protection, road maintenance, schools, and health services. Credit represents a double consumption: a product or service is purchased with someone else's money, for the use of which a fee is paid. One consumes a product or service and also consumes the use of money. How can individuals, couples, and families get the most for their dollars and cents?

Investment. An outlay, usually of money, in the expectation of gaining income or profit.

SHELTER

Since housing is the single largest expense for most families, people need to know all they can about the costs associated with various types of shelter. It is crucial to understand the economics of owning versus renting. However, the final decision probably will be one of personality, lifestyle, place in the family life cycle, and aspirations, as well as of income and savings.

Advantages of Renting.   Despite today's high rents, the average middle-income family pays less for housing when they rent than when they own a home. The cost of rental housing covers, in many cases, not only the rooms but also the major utilities, upkeep and repairs to buildings and grounds, the property taxes, and some depreciation of the value of the property. Renters know almost to the penny what their housing costs will be. On the average, renters paid about 23 percent of their annual income for gross rent in 1975 (U.S. Dept. of Commerce, CB77-64).

The renter has no **equity** invested in shelter. Any family savings are making money either in a bank or **stocks** or **bonds. Capital** is kept fluid. There is no obligation for upkeep, maintenance, or property improvement. In addition, the person who rents an apartment instead of a house has more time to spend on leisure activities since mowing, weeding, raking, shoveling snow, and painting are the landlord's obligation. The person who rents an apartment may also be closer to stores and other conveniences and thus less dependent upon owning a car.

Equity. The money value of a property or of an interest in a property.

Advantages of Owning.   The average home owner has housing and living conditions which are far superior to those of the average apartment dweller. The home owner may have more living space, more storage space, a garden and a backyard for recreation, a private garage, independence from landlords, and may other pleasant advantages.

Second, a community of private residences is generally a pleasanter place to live than the areas zoned for large apartment buildings. There are fewer people, less congestion, traffic, noise, and dirt. People who own property have an economic incentive to maintain the neighborhood in the best possible condition.

Third, some owners feel more secure financially. In a period of inflation, mortgage payments remain the same. While taxes rise, increasing land values tend to offset these costs. A home is a type of forced savings program and in 20 years the home owner will have solid equity. (However, the renter who saved and invested an amount equal to the buyer's monthly repayment of **principal** might show a larger dollar profit.) Home owners also have certain **income-tax** advantages over people who rent, since they may take a deduction of real-estate taxes and interest on the **mortgage** loan. Owning a **condominium** is somewhat of a compromise between the convenience of apartment living and the economic advantages of owning a home, but many people have been turned off from condominiums because they don't really have control of their property and expenses in the same way those who own houses do.

How Much Can You Afford?   The amount a buyer can afford to put into a house is the amount he or she can borrow, plus the cash available for a down payment, minus all settlement costs. The U.S. Department of Housing and Urban Development says that the value of owner-occupied homes in 1975 was about twice the income of their owners, though the ratio varies considerably according to income level (U.S. Dept. of Commerce CB77-64). When a mortgage is obtained, the buyer is taking out a loan using a house as **collateral** or security. A mortgage is a contract between the borrower and the lender in which a certain sum of money, plus interest, is promised to be repaid over a given number of years (usually 20, 25, or 30) in regular payments.

Mortgage companies use the Twenty-Percent Rule to determine what they will lend. This rule states that a debt-free person who has money for a 20–25 percent down payment on a home can spend 20 percent of his or her monthly income for carrying charges on the property which include **interest** and **amortization,** realty taxes, and fire insurance. On an income of $12,000 a year, a buyer could safely allocate $200 a month for these items. Roughly $50 of this might go for taxes and insurance and $150 for interest charges and payments on the principal of the loan. It is this pay-back rate

Principal. The actual amount of money borrowed or credit received, not including interest and service charges.

Collateral. Something of value put up as surety for a loan.

Table 12.1

$1000 BORROWED FOR	MONEY THAT MUST BE REPAID AT			
	8%	8½%	9%	9½%
20 years	$2008.80	$2083.20	$2160.00	$2239.20
25 years	2316.00	2418.00	2520.00	2622.00
30 years	2642.40	2768.40	2898.00	3027.60

which determines how much money the mortgage company or bank will loan. By shopping around individuals can save money. Even a difference of half of one percent in the interest rate can mount up over a twenty-year period. Table 12.1 shows costs of borrowing $1000 at various rates of interest for various periods of time.

In addition to the down payment, a buyer must have enough cash to cover settlement charges and lawyer's fees. These costs vary by locality and can be high. Federal law requires that the buyer be informed of the amount of closing costs at least 11 days before the actual sale, so that there is time to get the money together. A real-estate agent can provide a list of the items to be paid. Knowing these figures, as well as the amount of mortgage money he or she is eligible to borrow, the prospective buyer can go house hunting. It should be remembered, however, the costs of utilities, taxes, insurance, maintenance, care of the grounds, and, if need be, **commuting** must also be figured as monthly expense items. If the estimated cost of the mortgage payments plus the monthly running expenses multiplied by 12 months is more than one-fourth of annual net income (take-home pay), the family would be unwise to commit themselves to the purchase of that house.

The U.S. Bureau of Labor Statistics Bulletin 1823 called *Rent or Buy?* is a good source of additional information about evaluating alternatives in the shelter market.

Commuting. Traveling back and forth regularly, as between home and place of work.

HOUSEHOLD PURCHASES

Getting a dollar's worth out of a dollar is more difficult than one might think. The shopper must know value, comparative prices, and how to distinguish quality merchandise from shoddy. A great number of families find that the money that is not drained off in high credit charges is lost through poor shopping habits.

The prices for the same or equivalent items often vary widely, depending on the store, the neighborhood, the season, or even the type of sale. A wise consumer will recognize misrepresented merchandise, inflated prices, phony markdowns, and fictitious discounts. **Guaranties** and **warranties** are always limited in some way, so the consumer should read the fine print. *Consumer Reports* magazine is a valuable source of consumer information. Staff researchers and professional shoppers compare and evaluate packaged food, clothing, cameras, automobiles, appliances and many other consumer goods for durability, safety, effectiveness, and price value. *Consumer Reports* is published monthly by Consumers Union, a nonprofit organization, and may be obtained by subscription, on newsstands, or in public libraries. Consumers Union also publishes an annual *Buying Guide,* which covers the most popular consumer items. The Consumer Information Center at Pueblo, Colorado, a U.S. Government agency, is also a reliable source of advice and information for consumers. The Center makes available, either free or for a small fee, a large number of booklets and leaflets written in a simple, easy-to-read style.

The Supermarket. The yearly bill for food and household supplies varies from about 20 percent of income for an affluent family of four to over 25 percent for a family with a low income. Since such a large proportion of the family income is at stake, intelligent shopping and food preparation is very important for the family budget as well as for good nutrition.

Consumer experts agree that grocery shopping should be done with a list based on preplanned menus, and planning includes reading the news-

papers for advertised specials. Two rules, shop alone and shop on a full stomach, help cut down on impulse buying, reducing the chance of purchasing unneeded items that the store is promoting. However, when an often-used item is marked down, money can be saved by buying then, even if there is not an immediate need for this item.

In comparing prices, shoppers should look at **unit price** as well as **net price.** It sometimes seems that merchandizers deliberately package their products in odd quantities to make price comparisons difficult for the shopper. If all powdered detergents were packaged by the pound, it would be easy to know which one costs less. But if one package contains 10 ounces, and other 14 ounces, and another 17 ounces, the buyer needs to know the price per ounce in order to know which is cheapest. This is what is meant by the unit price. Shelf labels showing the price of the item are now required to show the unit price as well, but many shoppers fail to use this information. For liquid items, the unit price may be expresesd in pints or quarts instead of ounces but the principle is the same. Another use for unit pricing is in trying to determine whether it is actually cheaper to buy the giant size, the large size, the family size, or the trial size of an item. Buying the bigger sizes, whether it be toothpaste, soda, or dishwashing liquid, may be cheaper, but the buyer does not know without comparing the unit price for each size.

> **Unit price.** The price of an item per standard unit, such as ounce, pound, quart, or square foot.

Unit pricing applies under the **metric system,** now becoming standard in the United States also. However, switching to the metric system makes price comparisons even more difficult until consumers become used to the various metric weights and measures.

> **Metric system.** A decimal system of weights and measures based on the meter and the kilogram.

Shopping for food, like choosing a place to live, involves personal choices about lifestyle and individual needs. Using convenience foods and items from the bakery or the delicatessen adds a lot to the food budget, but the extra cost may be worth it to a person who hates to cook. The important thing is to know what the options are, rather than bumbling along spending money and wondering later where it went.

Clothing.   Clothing expenses can be cut substantially by planning ahead and taking advantage of seasonal sales. However, the shopper must beware of phony markdowns and close-outs, the substitution of lower quality sale merchandise for the store's regular line. The wise consumer buys only what he or she would buy anyway, even if it were not on sale. Buying something at a sale price that won't be used is certainly no bargain.

Some excellent values are featured in surplus shops and manufacturers' outlets. It is important to know something about textiles and construction, and to check labels for material content and laundering instructions. Even when the initial expense of a washable dress or suit is more, the upkeep may be so much less that it pays in the end.

"If you can give me some idea of how long you expect to be together, I can suggest a price range."

Drawing by Whitney Darrow, Jr., © 1975 The New Yorker Magazine, Inc.

Furniture and Appliances. For once-in-a-lifetime purchases like good home furnishings, the consumer needs to learn as much as possible about construction and style. Furniture is one item where buying top quality is the most economical as well as the most pleasing to the eye. Poor quality quickly breaks down and wears out. Good quality, with care, can last a lifetime and may even grow in value. Because there is generally no urgency in selecting furniture, householders should take time to plan in advance.

However, furniture of some kind is a necessity. For "make-do" pieces, to use until a couple can afford what they really want, it is wise to investigate sources of supply other than furniture stores. Large import stores offer "pier-to-pier" prices. Warehouse sales may offer bargains, especially damaged items. Often the shopper can refinish a piece or have it done professionally and still have a "good deal." The classified section in the papers is another place to look. People sell all sorts of things for all kinds of reasons. However, furniture should be sturdy, comfortable, and pleasant to look at whether it is a "permanent" or a "make-do" piece.

One merchandising swindle that every consumer should be aware of is the type of store known as a **borax store.** These stores specialize in selling furniture by the room. An ad reads something like "three rooms of furniture for $498." The person who responds is shown the advertised furniture stacked in a dark, dusty corner. The salesperson then leads the prospect to a different area with better lighting and display—and higher prices. This is called the **bait and switch** technique. Store operators count on the fact that many customers are unable to resist showing the salesperson that they can afford and have the taste to appreciate the "better" merchandise (often outrageously overpriced). The electronics, jewelry, appliance, and carpeting dealers also have their share of **swindles.** Carpeting seems to lend itself particularly well to the borax-store racket. In general, area rugs are more economical than carpeting. If carpeting is decided on, the consumer should be wary of misrepresentation or rackets, for carpeting is a major purchase and should be expected to give satisfaction for a long time.

On appliances, as with cars, last-year's models may be good buys. Building-supply companies often sell to the general public also and their prices are frequently lower than conventional dealers. Customers should check and compare guaranties, find out where the service centers are and whether they have a reputation for giving good service. In choosing appliances, the test results published in such journals as *Consumer Reports* can be extremely helpful.

TRANSPORTATION

With the exception of purchasing a place to live, an automobile is usually the highest cost item any individual or family buys. Today it is estimated that it costs 25 cents a mile to operate a car, which includes the purchase price, financing costs, gas, oil and maintenance, repairs, license, registration, taxes, and insurance. In essence, the automobile purchase is just the beginning of a series of automotive products and services consumed. Some of these allied purchases vary markedly in cost in different areas. A car owner living in a major **metropolitan area** may pay more than $1000 for insurance coverage while a person of the same age and sex pays a few hundred dollars, in some rural areas, for the same coverage. Insurance costs vary also with the value of the car being insured.

Many people, of course, never own a car and depend entirely on public transportation. For city dwellers, traffic jams and parking problems may make car ownership a burden. It often seems more desirable and, in fact, more economical, to rent a car for weekend trips or other special occasions than to own one. But for people living in suburban and rural areas, owning a car may be a necessity rather than a matter of choice.

Speaking strictly in terms of dollars and cents, a brand-new car is probably the worst investment possible. The value of a new car drops 25–30 percent the first year. It then depreciates another 18 percent of the original price the second year, and 14 percent the third year. At the end of three years, it is worth, at most, 40 percent of what it cost new. In short, it is economical to buy a used car if the buyer knows what he or she is doing. The **depreciation** of a used car is less, but the maintenance costs may be more. With any older car, the question must be asked, at what point is the saving in a car's depreciation balanced by the increasing costs of maintaining the aging car? Statistically, annual maintenance costs become greater than the annual depreciation half way through the fourth year. Buying a two-year-old car, to drive for two years and trade in on another two-year-old car, avoids the enormous initial depreciation of the first two years as well as the rise in repair costs.

Buying a Car.   Before looking at cars, new or used, the shopper should determine the most he or she wants to pay or can afford to pay for an automobile. The way to do this is to deduct from expected income for the next 12 months one's obligations for taxes, debt payments, and the necessities of living. The remainder is the amount of cash available for monthly payments on a car. The total can be found by multiplying the monthly amount by the number of months one is prepared to be paying on the car, and adding this to the total trade-in expected on the present car—if there is one. If this total is not sufficient to buy the kind of car selected, the shopper may then determine to use other resources such as savings to help pay for the car (DeCamp, 1972).

Trade-in. The value of used merchandise, such as an automobile, taken as part payment for a purchase.

The general rule is that cash in hand plus the **trade-in** should equal at least one-third the cost of the car, with the other two-thirds to be paid off in monthly installments. Conservative people finance no more than half of the total cost of a car and plan to pay off the debt within two years, but with the high costs of new cars, more and more people are assuming mini-mortgages on cars. According to the Federal Reserve Board one out of five automobile loans is now for more than three years (*Christian Science Monitor*, March 18, 1976).

There are many ways to save money in owning a car, such as shopping for insurance and relying as little as possible on high-interest financing for the purchase. Using 10 percent as an average interest rate to pay for financing an automobile, Table 12.2 shows how much it will cost to borrow various amounts for several standard automotive financing periods.

Saving Money through Good Driving Habits.   Money can be saved through good driving habits and careful maintenance. Moderate speeds substantially reduce gasoline consumption. Idling the car for more than a minute wastes more gas than it requires to restart the engine. Regular maintenance prevents costly repairs. The life of tires can be extended by maintaining the correct inflation pressures and proper front-end alignment and wheel balance. Two other well-established rules for increasing miles per gallon are to avoid rapid starts and stops and hard cornering and to drive at a constant speed (Shortney, 1971).

Ownership of a car may be a status-symbol and a source of pleasure. For many people it is also a necessity—for business reasons, for commut-

Table 12.2 Money that must be repaid when borrowing money at 10 percent for various periods of time

	MONTHS			
BORROWED	30	36	42	48
$1000	$1134.60	$1161.72	$1189.44	$1217.76
$2000	2269.20	2323.44	2378.88	2435.52
$3000	3403.80	3485.16	3568.32	3653.28
$4000	4538.40	4646.88	4757.76	4871.04
$5000	5673.00	5808.60	5947.20	6088.80

ing to and from work—and life in the suburbs often requires not just one but two or three cars per family. So care in purchasing and using cars is a major item in money management for the majority of Americans.

LIFE INSURANCE

The major reason for **life insurance** is to provide income protection for the beneficiary named in the **policy** in the event of the policy-holder's death. It is considered an essential form of protection in families with children, to compensate for the loss of income and services provided by either parent if one or both should die before the children are self-supporting. Even when there are no children, insurance on the husband is an important resource for nonworking wives when the husband's income is the principal support for the couple. Each life-insurance policy is a written contract between an insurance company and an individual which specifies the amount of money that will be paid should the individual die during the term of the contract. The contract also states the **premium** or price this coverage will cost (George, 1973).

Many working people are able to get insurance through group policies at their place of employment or through a union. Whether paid for by the employer or the employee, or jointly, **group life insurance** tends to be available at more favorable rates than individual policies. There are three basic kinds of life insurance: term, whole-life, and endowments.

Policy. A document by which a contract of insurance is made.

Premium. The price paid for a contract of insurance, usually broken down into weekly, monthly, or annual installments.

TERM INSURANCE

Term insurance provides the most coverage at the lowest cost. It is pure insurance with no frills. Premiums are paid for a fixed number of years, and the company pays the contracted amount of money to the **beneficiary** if the policy-holder dies during the term. If the individual does not die while the policy is in force, the company has no obligation. It pays nothing.

Term insurance is often labeled one-year term or five-year term because these are the common time-periods between premium increases. Premiums commonly go up every one to five years to reflect the rising probability of death as age increases. Therefore, it costs the 25-year-old relatively little to buy term insurance. It costs the 60-year-old a great deal. However, children of most 60-year-olds are no longer dependents and the premium burden can be reduced by reducing the amount of coverage.

A term policy is labeled **renewable** if the coverage can be continued at the end of each period simply by paying the increased premium. Term policies are commonly renewable through age 65 to 70 at which time all coverage stops. The renewability feature adds to the cost but is important to preserve the individual's insurability despite changes in his or her health. Without this feature the individual must have a new medical exam at the start of a new term. Another feature offered is **convertible** term insurance. Term insurance can be converted to whole-life without a new medical exam. One reason to convert might be to retain insurance coverage after age 65 or 70 (George).

WHOLE LIFE
Whole-life (or "cash value," or "permanent") is a combination savings and insurance program. Whole-life premiums normally stay level throughout the life of the policy. Therefore, the individual pays more than is necessary to cover the insurance company's risk in the early years and less than is necessary to cover the risk in the later years. The exact level of the premium is determined by the individual's age when he or she buys the policy. Unlike term, whole-life policies only expire at age 100 when the company pays the cash amount to the policy-holder rather than the beneficiary.

People faced with financial emergencies can fall back on their **whole-life insurance** by borrowing against it or cashing it in. But dropping a whole-life policy in its early years involves a big loss both in cash and protection. In Senate hearings, consumer advocate Ralph Nader pointed out that 25 percent of the policies issued by a major insurance company, the third largest in America, **lapsed** within one year. Another 10 percent lapsed in the second year. Some companies have lapse records even higher. This means, basically, that these individuals were sold insurance policies beyond their means to pay for and then had to give them up because they were unable to pay the premiums.

Lapsed. Was allowed to go out of existence through omission or neglect.

Cash value is the hallmark of a whole-life policy. But when pricing whole-life policies, an individual would be unwise simply to compare premiums. The wise consumer compares policies on the basis of "interest-adjusted cost," not "net cost," and this takes sophisticated accounting skills. *Consumer Reports* pointed out it took a team of skilled **actuaries** and a computer six months to gather and analyze cost data for the magazine's whole-life policy-comparison tables. Obviously, the individual cannot do such a comparison, yet is it very important to have this information. Consumer's Union (1974) estimates that a 35-year-old man buying $100,000 of whole-life insurance would be $12,000 better off in 20 years if he bought the best-rated policy rather than the worst-rated policy they tested.

Sellers of insurance like to say that whole-life is a bargain because the person gets back much or all of the money paid in premiums. However, money not being spent on high premiums could instead be invested where it would gather interest. Therefore, there are probably only two kinds of people who should consider whole-life: those who cannot save money on their own and those who are or expect to be in a very high income-tax bracket. Well-to-do people find whole-life a safe, tax-sheltered form of investment for their excess capital.

ENDOWMENTS

Endowments are the most expensive form of life insurance. They, too, are a combination insurance and savings program. An endowment matures after a specified number of years (usually 20 years or when the policyholder reaches age 65), at which point the holder receives the value of the policy in cash. It thus becomes a source of retirement income. Sometimes a 20-year endowment policy is written on a child at birth as part of a plan for meeting the cost of going to college. The net profit on this form of insurance is subject to federal tax (Blodgett, 1971).

WHAT KIND/HOW MUCH?

Unfortunately, there are no simple formulas to help a person decide how much or what kind of life insurance is the best choice. An effective insurance program requires careful research and realistic planning. The goal is a program that will cover most basic needs and be flexible enough to be adjusted as those needs change.

Some insurance companies sell direct to the public. Others are represented by insurance agents or brokers who are trained in sales. It is generally a good idea to use the same agent for all one's insurance needs: automobile insurance, property insurance, as well as life insurance. If this is done, the agent has a clearer picture of what the client's needs may be.

A good agent or broker can provide valuable help. But unless the client knows something about insurance, it is easy to be misled. Since insurance agents work on **commission,** the more coverage they sell, the more money they earn. This is, no doubt, one major reason why people are so often oversold on insurance. All potential buyers should evaluate their needs carefully and balance them against their ability to pay before committing themselves to any insurance policy (Blodgett).

BORROWING AND CREDIT

From colonial times until the end of the First World War, Americans generally believed that being in debt was sinful or, at least, something to be ashamed of. Except to buy a house or a farm, and often even then, they first saved, then spent. Today, people at all income levels are finding themselves deeply in debt without quite understanding how it happened. Despite the costs and misuses of **credit,** borrowing is now a way of life. Each person must develop a philosophy about the use of credit that realistically reflects his or her prospects and goals. Used wisely, credit can help a family buy a car, furnish a home, pay for medical care, or capitalize on a business opportunity.

THE COSTS OF CREDIT
Credit is the use of someone else's money for which there is a charge. This charge is called interest. It can be combined with overhead costs and called a service charge, a fee, a carrying charge, or a **finance charge.** There are, today, few places where credit may not be obtained. Some credit is, in a sense, free. Often, plumbers, carpenters, doctors, dentists, and others provide a service, do not bill until the end of the month, and allow the individual several further weeks in which to pay the bill. Stores sometimes offer free charge accounts so long as the bill is paid in full within 30 days after it is sent out. The costs of deferred payments are included in the prices charged for the service or item, so this credit is being paid for whether or not it is used. Interest-free charge accounts are a great convenience and provide a permanent record of expenses. In effect, the consumer is obtaining a free 30-day loan (DeCamp, 1972).

The great danger of running charge accounts is that they make buying too easy. The buy-now-pay-later syndrome has trapped many inexperienced or undisciplined consumers into purchasing luxury items, paying for dinners in fancy restaurants with a charge card, or taking expensive vacation trips that their income is simply not sufficient to cover. When the bills all come in at once, the individual is unable to cover them within the allotted 30 days and the credit charges begin to pile up. In the end, the person may have to declare bankruptcy, with all credit cut off as a result.

Credit costs vary a great deal from place to place. Inexperienced consumers often get confused. Under the Federal Truth in Lending Law, every credit agreement must clearly state both the annual percentage rate of interest plus any other costs of borrowing and the total dollar finance charge. An interest rate of $1\frac{1}{2}$ percent per month sounds easy to pay, but when the account runs on for a year, the annual rate is 12 times $1\frac{1}{2}$, or 18 percent and that's a big chunk. In other words, it requires the buyer to pay $18 for the use of $100 worth of credit for a year. Shopping for low credit rates

Credit. The use of someone else's money, for which there is a charge called interest.

can save individuals and families substantial money over a year's time. Only by comparing the annual percentage rates can the consumer decide whether credit is being extended at the going rate or a **usurious** rate. It is important to do this both for revolving credit accounts and for borrowing cash. The type of loan sought has a direct bearing on the cost. A mortgage may cost between 8 and 9 percent annual interest. A **debt-consolidation loan** from a finance company operating under State Small Loan Laws may cost from 24 to 48 percent. In other words, to borrow $400 for a year, the borrower may agree to pay back $500 or more (DeCamp).

Another factor in obtaining credit is the lender's assessment of the individual's ability to repay. If the lender thinks the person is a good credit risk, the interest rate is more likely to be favorable. Job, family situation, and **credit rating** are all checked. Ironically, a totally clean financial record (no previous loans) is actually a negative factor. Lenders would prefer to see that a person has repaid a previous debt on schedule. So there is reason to take out a bank loan early in a career, repay it on schedule, and thus establish a good credit rating for future borrowing. It has even been suggested that a person might wish to borrow money that is not actually needed and keep the borrowed money in a savings account during the time the loan is being repaid. Interest on the savings largely offsets the interest charged on the loan and the difference between interest received and interest paid out can be viewed as the cost of establishing a good credit reputation (Garrison, 1976).

> **Credit rating.** The evaluation of a person's qualifications to receive credit, based on his or her past credit performance.

Factors which affect one's credit rating include how long one has been employed at one's current job, how long one has lived at a particular address or in a particular community, one's marital status, and, despite laws to the contrary, one's gender. Women often have a more difficult time obtaining credit than men, particularly newly divorced or widowed women whose previous financial transactions have all been in the husband's name. If credit or a loan is refused, individuals now have a right, under federal law, to know the contents of their credit-information file. By supplying additional information or correcting misinformation, they may be able to get the unfavorable decision reversed.

TYPES OF CONSUMER LOANS

Installment Buying. Installment buying is one of the most widespread types of consumer credit. Repayment is made in regular monthly installments usually over a period of one to three years. Once the buyer's signature is on paper, that person is obligated to pay periodic installments on the purchase price plus high financing costs. An article bought on time payment remains the property of the **creditor** until the final payment is made. If a payment is late, the creditor may ask for immediate payment of all outstanding principal and interest. If the buyer does not pay, the creditor may repossess the article and keep all money already paid on the account. The revolving charge account is similar to installment buying in that regularly scheduled repayments must be made. It may be used like a monthly charge account as free credit, but when the bill comes due it changes to a long-term credit account at a fairly high interest rate (Blodgett).

Bank Account Loans.   Many banks offer "overdraft" checking accounts. When a check is written greater than the account's balance, the difference is charged against the account as a loan. Passbook loans are available from savings and loan associations and savings banks. Only customers can borrow and only up to the amount on deposit.

Personal Loans.   Money for a vacation, education, medical expenses, or bill consolidation may be obtained in several places. A person who belongs to a **credit union** would be wise to start there. Credit unions are in business to offer low rates to their members. Other lenders to investigate are commercial banks. They can be quite flexible about structuring the size and payments to the customer's needs. They are the biggest lenders of all, 40 percent of all installment credit in America. A final, last-resort, source of money is a **finance company.** They are willing to take more risks and are thus more lenient in their requirements for granting loans, but the interest rates they charge are correspondingly high (Blodgett).

Credit union. A cooperative association, sometimes of company employees or trade union members, which makes loans to members at low interest rates.

Credit costs vary tremendously and failure to compare and shop for a reasonably priced loan can result in needlessly expensive finance charges. If borrowers should become overextended and unable to meet their financial obligations, the best recourse is to talk it over with their creditors. They would far prefer being repaid according to a new schedule than risk losing their money completely.

SAVINGS AND INVESTMENT

There is no simple or single answer to the question of how much money to save. However, having some cash reserve should be a high priority goal for every individual and certainly every family. How much to save or what to save for are goals that are likely to change as the family life cycle progresses. Partners should decide jointly on these goals and work together to achieve them (DeCamp).

Most financial counselors recommend that a specified amount for savings be deposited on a regular basis. One relatively painless way to save is through a **payroll-deduction plan** at work. Or arrangements can be made for a bank to transfer a set amount from a checking account to a savings account automatically each month (Blodgett).

As a minimum, a family should have enough cash available to cover living expenses for three months should an emergency, such as unemployment or illness of the wage earner, arise. Savings accounts are both a safe and a convenient place to accumulate this cash reserve. Money up to $20,000 is insured by the Federal Deposit Insurance Corporation, a government agency. The money is instantly available and yet it is earning interest while on deposit in the bank.

SAVINGS INSTITUTIONS

The kind of institution—commercial bank, savings bank, **savings and loan association,** or credit union—chosen for saving is not nearly so critical as the interest rate offered. The distinctions among banks have blurred because of competitive pressure and changes in the banking laws. In choosing the place to put savings, depositors should consider their overall financial situation and what services might be needed in the future. An established relationship with a bank or a credit union can result in more favorable loan terms, for example. The customer might also want to look at what other services the bank makes available. Some banks offer checking accounts completely free of service charges; some impose a monthly charge unless a minimum balance is maintained (Blodgett).

People who are able to save in regular and systematic ways are providing a sound financial base to their lives. Setting a financial goal is often overlooked by those who think about money only in terms of paychecks, without ever considering the total amount of money that passes through a working person's hands over the years. A person who earns $500 a month ($6000 a year), working from the age of 20 to the age of 60, will have earned close to a quarter of a million dollars. At $24,000 a year a person will earn close to a million dollars.

One type of savings goal is to decide on a certain amount of money to be saved by time of retirement. Table 12.3 shows the monthly deposits needed to reach various savings goals. The advantage of starting early to save for retirement years is in the greater amount of interest that will be accumulated.

Table 12.3   Monthly savings needed at six percent interest (compounded annually) to attain predetermined amount of capital

AGE NOW	YEARS TO RETIREMENT	MONTHS TO RETIREMENT	DESIRED AMOUNT		
			$100,000	$200,000	$500,000
25	40	480	$ 51	$ 102	$ 255
35	30	360	99	198	495
45	20	240	213	426	1,065
55	10	120	596	1,192	2,980

Source: Adapted from Venita Van Caspel, *Money Dynamics: How to Build Financial Independence* (Reston, Va.: Reston Publishing Co., 1975).

INVESTMENT PROGRAM

Commodities. Economic goods, as a product of agriculture or mining, often purchased as an investment for later resale.

Once sufficient cash has been accumulated to meet an emergency and some form of life insurance arranged for, the family is able to look into other forms of investment. While savings accounts do pay interest, at the present time the amount the dollar earns in interest is less than the amount lost through inflation. The major emphasis with investing, such as the purchase of stocks, bonds, real estate or **commodities,** is on the distant future and upon long-term growth of capital. Two other factors to consider are safety and yield.

Bonds. A bond is evidence of the issuer's debt. Bonds are issued in return for money by all levels of government and a variety of corporations. Each bond has a date at which it is scheduled to be repaid, called **date of maturity.** Each issue has an interest rate, fixed when the bond is sold, with interest payable twice a year. Bonds vary in risk from the extremely safe to the highly speculative. The riskier ones usually carry higher interest rates because this is the only way investors can be persuaded to buy them. Investors can make money in two ways: through the interest paid and through selling the bond at a later date for more than they paid for it.

Dividends. Profits from a business which are distributed to stockholders on the basis of the number of shares each holds.

Stocks. A stock certificate is evidence of ownership of a share in the business enterprise issuing the stock. If a company has 1000 shares of stock and an investor holds 10, that person owns 1 percent of the company. If the company doubles in value, the share's value doubles. If the company's value declines, the share's value declines. Two other factors enter into the value of the stock as an investment. (1) Many stocks pay **dividends.** These are paid at management's discretion and can be raised or lowered depending on company profits. (2) There is also the possibility of a gain or loss on an investment in stocks through a change in the price of shares in that company. The company does not control the price. Instead, the price is determined by what people are willing to pay at a given moment in a public trading market such as the New York Stock Exchange. However, this price is generally a function of the value of the company in terms of what the company is earning and is anticipated to earn. Newspapers carry a daily account of stock-market transactions, and most investors follow changes in the market closely.

PROFESSIONAL INVESTORS

Anyone buying and selling **securities** must deal through a brokerage house. **Brokers** are paid a commission for their services. A potential investor in the stock market or in the market for bonds, real estate, or commodities, should have the inclination and the time to study that market in depth. Moreover, he or she would be wise to seek the advice of a competent broker as well. But even the experts cannot be sure which stocks, bonds, or commodities will be tomorrow's winners. Business conditions, new regulations, confidence or lack of confidence in the government, fads—these and many other factors influence prices almost on a daily basis. Investments inevitably involve a risk. But they also carry the possibility of substantial financial gain (Blodgett).

FINANCIAL PLANNING

Some reasons why families are often unsuccessful in working together in money management were discussed early in the chapter. Partners argue about money because they were taught different ideas about money as they were growing up. They argue because their personalities are different, or because they are trying to achieve supremacy in a struggle for power. They fight because they cannot communicate. As much as any or all of these causes, people argue over money because of basic ignorance of how to be intelligent consumers. To this point, this chapter has attempted to indicate some of the decisions involved in money management. Now it is time to consider overall financial planning as the means by which an individual or a family can gain and keep control of resources and maximize the value of income.

INVENTORY OF ASSETS AND LIABILITIES

The first step in financial planning is to draw up a balance sheet of the dollar value of **assets** and **liabilities,** what one has and what one owes. A listing of all the items that might be considered in making the **financial inventory** is shown in Table 12.4

In estimating the value of assets, it should be remembered they are worth not what was paid for them but what the owner can reasonably expect to get if they are offered for sale. If assets exceed liabilities, the financial planner is on solid footing. If the balance sheet shows as many or more debts than assets, then this is the time to curtail spending and reorganize spending habits. Assets and liabilities should be reviewed each year to see how the picture has changed. A once-a-year check will show whether a person or a family is accumulating equities or slipping further into debt. Everybody's financial position varies from day to day. Small variations are not important. The focus of concern is the overall, long-term increase of assets over liabilities.

A current statement of personal assets and liabilities is useful not only in planning one's own finances. It might be useful in filing insurance claims in case of fire or theft. It can help in establishing whether or not you would be eligible for a loan. And it can help in writing a **will,** an important element of financial planning even for very young persons, since sudden, unexpected deaths do occur.

Financial inventory. An itemized list of current assets, such as cash or property, and liabilities or debts.

Table 12.4   The financial inventory   Many people, especially young couples just starting out in life, will not need such a complete form as this one, but an examination of the list of items might lead to a clearer knowledge of just what the couple's long-term and short-term financial goals are.

ASSETS	Date: _____	Date: _____
FIXED DOLLAR ASSETS		
Cash on hand	_____	_____
Balance in checking accounts	_____	_____
Balance in savings accounts	_____	_____
Savings bonds and accrued interest bonds	_____	_____
Cash surrender value in life policies	_____	_____
Cash value in pension and other plans	_____	_____
Money lent to others	_____	_____
Other fixed dollar assets	_____	_____
EQUITIES (ASSETS WITH FLUCTUATING VALUES)		
Home (current worth)	_____	_____
Other real estate	_____	_____
Common and preferred stocks	_____	_____
Investments in mutual funds	_____	_____
Business investments	_____	_____
Other equities	_____	_____
PERSONAL PROPERTY (DEPRECIATING ASSETS)		
Household furnishings	_____	_____
Car(s) (current resale value)	_____	_____
Boat	_____	_____
Furs and jewelry	_____	_____
Other personal property	_____	_____
TOTAL ASSETS	_____	_____
LIABILITIES		
Balance due on mortgage	_____	_____
Loans payable: personal	_____	_____
Loans payable: bank	_____	_____
Installment payments payable on car	_____	_____
Installment payments on appliances	_____	_____
Other installment payments	_____	_____
Balances in revolving charge accounts	_____	_____
Other liabilities	_____	_____
TOTAL LIABILITIES	_____	_____
NET WORTH (ASSETS MINUS LIABILITIES)	_____	_____

Source: Catherine Crook DeCamp, *The Money Tree.* Copyright © 1972 by Catherine Crook DeCamp. Reprinted by arrangement with The New American Library, Inc. New York, N.Y.

The goal of the annual inventory should be to show an increase in net worth. Payments on a mortgage or any other debt provide a steady increase in **net worth,** as do savings. Managing personal finances differs, however, from managing a business. The business executive's success or failure is measured by the profit or loss that the business records show. But success in family management is not measurable only in dollars and cents. The success of a family's spending program is also measured by healthy, happy, well-educated, responsible individuals who live comfortable lives. This cannot be put down on paper, but it should not be overlooked (DeCamp).

THE SPENDING PLAN

Financial planning means directing the flow of cash in and out. Each person must direct his or her income where he or she most wants it to go. This involves setting priorities. There will never be enough money to buy everything wanted and needed. So-called affluent families can end up more deeply in debt than lower-income families. Everything a person does involves choosing between alternatives, and choosing one eliminates the possibility of the other. In money management, the technique for defining the choices and setting priorities is called a **budget.** A budget does not tell an individual or a family what to do with money; it merely sets forth the alternatives. If the decision is made to buy a car, what will that mean in terms of saving for a vacation or buying a dishwasher? A budget also is indispensable in providing a record of where the money is going. When actual expenditures are compared to planned expenditures, the budget becomes both a record and a plan (DeCamp, 1972).

Steps in Budgeting. Budgeting involves four basic steps. Sample forms (Tables 12.5–12.8) are provided to aid the student in understanding this process.

Table 12.5 Estimated income for _____ Some families may find it best to estimate income on an annual basis and then divide it by 12 to arrive at a monthly income figure on which to base a family budget.

ITEM	AMOUNT
Wage or salary of—	
Husband	$_____
Wife	_____
Net profit from business, farm, or profession	_____
Interest, dividends	_____
Other	_____
Total	$_____

1. List annual or monthly income from all sources.
2. List all fixed expenses, the expenses a family or individual must meet. These include taxes, rent or mortgage payments, premiums on insurance, and debt payments.
3. List semi-fixed or variable expenses. These expenses are absolutely necessary but their cost can vary. They include food, clothing, transportation, and medical expense.
4. List optional expenses over which the individual or family should have complete control. These items include recreation, entertainment, and luxury goods and services.

The fixed and variable expenses represent the family's major living expenses. If the estimated basic cost of living, plus debts, taxes, and other fixed expenses equal or exceed projected income, there is nothing for plea-

Table 12.6 Plan for family spending Sample budget forms may be changed by adding or deleting categories to suit your family's needs.

INCOME, SET-ASIDES, AND EXPENSES	AMOUNT PER MONTH	
Total income		$_____
Set-asides:		
Emergencies and future goals		$_____
Seasonal expenses		_____
Debt payments		_____
Regular monthly expenses:		
Rent or mortgage payment	$_____	
Utilities	_____	
Installment payments	_____	
Other	_____	
Total		_____
Day-to-day expenses:		
Food and beverages	$_____	
Household operation and maintenance	_____	
Furnishings and equipment	_____	
Clothing	_____	
Personal	_____	
Transportation	_____	
Medical care	_____	
Recreation and education	_____	
Gifts and contributions	_____	
Total		_____
Total set-asides and expenses		$_____

Table 12.7   Detailed plan for seasonal expenses this year

EXPENSE	DATE NEEDED	AMOUNT PER YEAR	AMOUNT PER MONTH
Taxes		$_____	$_____
Insurance			
School expenses			
Fuel			
Vacation			
Other			
Total		$_____	$_____

sure and nothing to put aside for reserves and investments. There may even be too little to cover various unexpected expenses not itemized in the plan. At this point, it is necessary to reexamine the tentative spending plan. Are there heavy debts because too many things are being bought on installments? Perhaps the problem is much less serious. Overly large sums for food or clothing may be included because the consumer has no real idea what these things cost. Anyone not sure how much to allow for variable expenses may want to begin the budgeting process by keeping a detailed record of current spending for two or three months. A sample form for

Table 12.8   Detailed plan for set-asides for emergencies and future goals

TYPE OF FUND	PROBABLE TOTAL COST	DATE DESIRED	AMOUNT TO SET ASIDE PER YEAR	AMOUNT TO SET ASIDE PER MONTH
Emergency	$_____		$_____	$_____
Education				
Home or business[1]				
Home improvement				
Major equipment				
Retirement				
Other goals				
Total	$_____		$_____	$_____

1. This fund might include money you set aside to make a downpayment, or money (in addition to fixed mortgage payments) you set aside to reduce remaining interest and principal cost.

keeping account of spending is shown in Table 12.9. Monthly totals for the various categories can be compared and used as a basis for determining where to cut, if necessary (Mork, 1972).

Allocating available funds to optional expenses in a family budget should take into account all members of the family. If the family discusses money and financial planning with a spirit of openness, children will develop an awareness of and competence in the world of consumerism.

A spending plan is basically a yearly plan. Many of the largest expenses, like taxes or insurance payments, are due only once or twice a year. Others, like doctors' bills, occur at random. Still others, like food, are substantially the same month in and month out. There are also peak spending periods like Christmastime or vacations. In well-managed financial plans, there are periods when income can be accumulated for the next round of heavy spending. Therefore, in building a sound spending plan, it may be necessary first to consider total expenses on an annual basis. Later this plan may be refigured to fit a monthly or weekly paycheck (DeCamp).

Since living costs have been going higher every year, and income also varies, no budget can remain an exact guide. Further, family needs change as the family moves through the life cycle. Therefore, a budget must be revised yearly to fit the particular family pattern. Using the old budget and

Table 12.9   Record of Your Expenses

DATE	ITEM OR SERVICE BOUGHT	FOOD AND BEVERAGES	HOUSEHOLD OPERATION AND MAIN- TENANCE	FURNISH- INGS AND EQUIPMENT	CLOTHING
		$	$	$	$
Total		$_____	$_____	$_____	$_____

the records of family spending for that time period to compare amounts planned with amounts actually spent will indicate ways the next year's plan can be drawn to better serve the needs and wishes of the individual budgeter or the family unit.

RECORD KEEPING

A major part of financial management is keeping accurate, complete records of money coming in and going out. They are invaluable for timing new purchases, for living successfully on credit, for preparing income-tax returns, and for collecting health insurance, as well as for planning the next year's budget. Record-keeping forms and pamphlets can often be obtained free of charge from life-insurance companies and banks who offer them as a customer service, or they may be purchased in variety and stationery stores. Keeping financial records should, of course, be a joint activity of the couple, so each will be prepared to carry on in case of death or sudden illness of the other. If proper records are not kept, families may find themselves making important decisions without sufficient information. Good records, an annual inventory of net worth, thoughtful budgeting, and careful spending are the basic tools for getting the most for your money and an aid to keeping peace in the family.

PERSONAL	TRANS-PORTATION	MEDICAL CARE	RECREA-TION AND EDUCATION	GIFTS AND CONTRIBU-TIONS
$	$	$	$	$
$_____	$_____	$_____	$_____	$_____

Summary

1. The main purposes of this chapter are to discuss the reasons why families argue about money, to show how money decisions can be based on intelligent consumerism, and to outline the steps in financial planning.

2. Couples quarrel more over money than anything else. Ideas about money and how to use it are a combination of cultural, social, and economic influences. Our culture influences us by its emphasis on accumulation of material things. Ethnic, religious, and geographical backgrounds and differences in personality influence our feelings about money. In addition, conflicts over money may be the result of power struggles, inability to communicate effectively, or lack of knowledge needed to make sound spending and saving decisions.

3. When making either long-term or short-term purchases, consumers can make intelligent decisions if they take time and effort to follow three basic steps. (a) Study the pros and cons of various aspects of the situation or product such as owning a home compared with renting, or whole-life compared with term insurance. (b) Become familiar with the product—its value or usefulness as well as comparative prices and the relation of price to quality. (c) Plan ahead in order to take advantage of sales or special opportunities. These steps can apply to purchases in all areas of family consumption: shelter, food, clothing, recreation, furniture, appliances, transportation, and insurance.

4. If ready cash isn't available at the time a family wants to make a purchase, they can borrow money by taking out a loan or they can use other forms of credit. However, credit also costs money, and easy credit can be a trap. Consumers should limit credit purchases so they won't get buried under bills they can't pay.

5. Individuals and families can gain and keep control of their resources and maximize the value of their income by financial planning. The first step in financial planning is to take an inventory of assets (what you own) and liabilities (what you owe). The difference between the two is net worth. The next step is to direct and control the flow of cash by making a budget which sets priorities and defines the choices the family wishes to make. This involves listing expenses (fixed, variable, and optional) and income from all sources. The third step in the financial management program is to keep accurate and complete records of money coming in and money going out. This information is an aid to making a realistic budget or spending plan for the following months or years.

Key Concepts

Consumerism	Interest	Financial inventory
Unit price	Securities	Assets
Net price	Dividends	Liabilities
Installment purchases	Mortgage	Net worth
Credit	Insurance	Budget
Finance charge	Premium	Will
Credit rating	Social Security payments	

1. Were you or are you actively involved in your family's financial planning? Do you think this is a beneficial experience for children and young adults? Why?

2. Consider your attitudes toward spending and saving money and those of a friend. Why do you think your friend's attitudes are similar to or different from yours?

2. List some recent purchases you have made, for example, clothing, a typewriter, an airplane ticket, make-up, or record albums. What factors influenced your decision to buy what you did in each case? Would you make the same decision today?

4. Make up a sample weekly or monthly budget for yourself. Would you like to change the way you handle your money?

5. At what point should a couple thinking of marriage begin to make up a specific budget of income and expenses for the first year of their marriage?

CHAMBERS, R. L. (1976). *The Buyer's Handbook: A Guide to Defensive Shopping.* Englewood Cliffs, N.J.: Prentice-Hall.

A brief book, easy to read and understand, which gives tips on how to shop wisely for any number of products. Also includes a list of agencies to contact for consumer aid and a bibliography of sources for help with special consumer problems.

DONNELLY, C. (1976). How to stop arguing about money. *Money* 5:1, pp. 24–27.

Explores the problems of arguing about money in a relationship. Includes opinions of marriage counselors and techniques for handling money conflicts.

GARRISON, M. L. (1976). Credit-ability for women. *The Family Coordinator* 25:3, pp. 241–248.

Explores the area of credit for women and problems of discrimination that women encounter when applying for credit. Also offers some procedures for women to follow to establish credit.

PORTER, S. (1975). *Sylvia Porter's Money Book.* Garden City, N.Y.: Doubleday.

The subtitle of this book tells what it covers and its purposes: "How to Earn It, Spend It, Save It, Invest It, Borrow It and Use It to Better Your Life." Gives the rules of survival in the marketplace, points out traps to avoid, and even covers easy appliance-repair problems. A basic book on personal and family finance with an index and a list of where to get help with consumer-protection problems.

RAIHALL, D. T. (1975). *Money Management for the Consumer: Readings and Cases from MONEY Magazine.* Boston, Mass.: Little, Brown.

Reprints of articles from Money *magazine cover a variety of areas such as lifestyles, budgeting, credit, cars, vacation, and retirement. Includes case studies for most topics.*

Dynamics of Parenthood

BECOMING A PARENT

Becoming a parent represents one of the major transition points in an individual's life. Parenthood confronts people with new problems to be solved, some inherent in parenthood itself, others related to the particular sociocultural environment in which they live. Often prospective parents do not realize the effect a child will have upon their lives and are not prepared to make the adjustments their new roles require. More and more Americans, however, are considering, in advance of the event, the substantial commitment involved in becoming a parent. In our society, it is no longer automatic for married couples to have children. Remaining childless is an option many couples can and do take, and a majority of the population is choosing to limit the number of children they will have.

Fertility rate. The number of births per year per 1000 women 15–44 years of age.

The birth rate in the United States—the number of births per 1000 people in the population—has been declining for more than a decade. The **fertility rate**—the number of births per 1000 women 15–44 years of age—has also shown a fairly consistent decline during that time. In 1975, the birth rate was 1 percent lower than it had been in 1974; the fertility rate was 2 percent lower. Live births in 1975 were estimated to be 3,149,000, a decline from 1974 of three-tenths of a percent. Nevertheless, the total population of the country has continued to rise because of the decline in the death rate; and an increase in the number of women of childbearing age (15-44) is expected to ensure a rising population over the next ten years. (USDHEW, 1976, 76–1120, 24:12).

EFFECT OF THE ARRIVAL OF THE BABY ON THE FAMILY

The changes that take place in the transition to parenthood have been defined by some researchers as a crisis. The married couple as a family is an integrated social system of roles and statuses, and adding or removing members forces a major reorganization of the system. Especially with the shift from a dyad (a two-person relationship) to a **triad** (a three-person relationship), as occurs with the arrival of a baby, there is a disruption of patterns of affection and intimacy (Russell, 1974). However, others who have done extensive research on this process of adjustment conclude that it is more accurate to think of beginning parenthood as a transition accompanied by some difficulty rather than a crisis of severe proportions (Hobbs and Cole, 1976).

Triad. Social unit of three persons interacting together.

Problems Experienced Differently by Husbands and Wives.   It is generally agreed that mothers experience more bothersome changes in their lives related to the arrival of the first child than fathers do. Russell's research with 271 married couples aged 16–47 shows that the five changes most frequently expressed as bothersome by wives cluster around the emotional and physical self:

1. Worry about personal appearance
2. Physical tiredness and fatigue
3. Interruptions of sleep and rest caused by the baby
4. Worry about "loss of figure"
5. Feeling edgy or emotionally upset

Russell found that a healthy mother experiences less bother, and that the longer the mother had been married the less likely she is to experience parenthood as a crisis. The husbands' concerns reflected a broader range, including problems external to the physical or emotional self. The five problems experienced most frequently by the 271 fathers in Russell's sample were:

1. Interruptions of sleep or rest
2. Suggestions from in-laws about the baby
3. Increased money problems
4. Necessity to change some plans because of the baby
5. Additional amount of work required

Older men in Russell's sample seemed to experience less of a crisis upon becoming fathers, and this is confirmed by data from Nydegger (1974) that men who became fathers later in life made a better adjustment to the role than did early fathers. Nydegger feels that older fathers may have a better sense of their place in the world and what they have to offer a child.

Factors that Provide for a Smoother Transition. Couples with high levels of marital adjustment in Russell's study were less likely to experience a high degree of crisis and also reported more positive feelings of gratification in the role of parent. The timing of the birth seems important. Ryder (1973) determined that wives who have a child in the first year or two of marriage are more likely to feel that their husbands do not pay enough attention to them. Ideally, according to Russell, there would be sufficient time for the couple to develop good communication, but not so much delay that the woman loses stamina and patience for the tasks of parenting. The family-development approach to the study of the family, described in the theory section in Chapter 4, suggests that there is a sequence of developmental tasks a family goes through. The more adequately the family completes prior tasks, the better it will be able to handle a current transition, such as the arrival of the first child (Russell).

The Costs of Having a Child. Measured in dollars and cents, the cost of having and raising a child has gone up substantially in recent years and is continuing to increase. According to the Health Insurance Institute, hospital care and the initial equipment for a baby now cost more than $1600. It is estimated that the average middle-class family spends $30,000 (not including college) to raise a child (Porter, 1975; Rollin, 1972).

These costs vary, of course, with the status of the parents, where they live, their expectations of providing for their child, and their resourcefulness in economizing. Maternity clinics, health plans, or a short hospital stay can reduce the cost of the birth. Elimination of fancy and often unnecessary equipment can reduce the initial outlay. A family that emphasizes simplicity of lifestyle will spend less raising its children than a family that indulges in commercial entertainments, private schools, fancy wardrobes, or luxury vacations. Yet no matter how simply they live, a couple with a newborn child face a substantial increase in the cost of living that will extend throughout the child's lifetime under the family roof and frequently beyond. Additional housing space may be needed, involving perhaps a move and the payment of higher rent. The cost of providing food and clothing continue to rise with the child's age: the costs of supporting an eighteen-year old are 30–45 percent higher than for a one-year old (Porter).

In addition to the direct costs of raising a child, certain indirect costs must also be considered. A mother who stays home to care for a child instead of working at paid employment is losing income. The higher her educational level, the more income she would have earned and the greater the financial loss (Porter). If both parents work, a large percentage of their income will be spent on substitute care for the child.

The economic impact of a child upon a family has many consequences, both long-term and short-term. Where income is low, parents may experience such anxiety in providing for the child's basic needs that they cannot focus on providing love or enjoy the child's presence. Even in families that have enough money for necessities, care of the child may use up the money formerly available for extras, such as entertainment or an annual vacation. Parents who took these luxuries for granted may find that without them, life seems all work and no play—a feeling that will be encouraged by the sheer physical labor involved in caring for a child. Economic factors thus influence the physical and psychological well-being of a family. The more a couple has anticipated the costs and personal sacrifices that will be required by a child, the better able they will be to adjust to them when they arise.

Isolation of the New Mother.   As we have seen, in our society, the arrival of a baby in the family has more of an impact on the mother's life than on the father's. While the employed father will continue to spend much of his time as he did before the child was born, the woman who takes on the traditional job of mothering will find her life entirely altered.

One of the major problems she faces is social isolation. Given the mobility of our population, she often does not have close family in her

immediate neighborhood or close friendships that require years to develop. Her husband may work at a distance from their home and be very much involved in his career. Thus the new mother is likely to find herself with little emotional support to smooth her adjustment to her new and demanding role as well as little practical support. Anxieties are readily bred in such a situation. Should an emergency arise, where is the mother to turn? Should she have a simple question, whom is she to ask? Doctors are rushed, difficult to reach, and frequently annoyed at requests for trivial information. The support that used to be provided by the extended family is now difficult to obtain.

Equally difficult for the new mother is the problem of loneliness. A child may fill many needs and provide many satisfactions, but there are limitations on what company a young child can offer an adult. The access to social contacts the mother had before the child was born is severely curtailed by the presence of the child. The inadequacy of child-care facilities and the problems of finding and transporting babysitters—apart from the cost of each—make it difficult for the new mother to carry on an adult life separate from her child.

MOTIVATIONS TO HAVE CHILDREN

Why, if there are so many difficulties, do so many people continue to want children? Some look forward to parenthood as a sign of adult status and welcome the responsibility. Others respond to pressure from relatives to bear grandchildren, to carry on the family name. In our society, pressure is often exerted by friends who have had children upon those who have not to do their part in providing a new generation to carry on the society. There is also in America a certain mystique about motherhood, related to the mystery of birth and the notion that this is woman's most fulfilling and most natural role. There are other romantic notions prevalent in our society. Many young people view children as adorable or fun and look forward to having their own (LeMasters, 1974). Still others may value warm and rewarding personal relationships and desire to establish such relationships with their own children. They may view themselves as creating a talented individual who will make an outstanding contribution to society and make the parents proud.

All of these reasons require close examination in making the decision to have a child. The opinions of parents, friends, and personalities in the media should not carry too much weight since they will not have the responsibility of providing for the child.

Myth. An ill-founded belief held uncritically.

The mystique of motherhood is a myth. Birth, of course, is a miracle every time it happens, but it is only a small part in the total experience of parenthood. Parenting for the mother, as for the father, is learned, not natural or instinctive. Not all women are suited to this particular kind of work and many women question whether it is the most fulfilling way to spend their time. Certainly, whatever romantic ideas were held about childbearing dissolve in the face of the constant physical effort required. Children are sometimes adorable and fun to be with. But to observe only this, one must have watched only a family picnic (on an exceptionally good day), not a meal-time scene or an angry battle between siblings. Parents, when

---

MOTHERHOOD

The greatest number of children produced by a mother in an independently attested case is 69 by the first wife of Fyodor Vassilet (1816–1872) a peasant of the Moscow Jurisdiction, Russia, who in 27 confinements, gave birth to 16 pairs of twins, 7 sets of triplets and 4 sets of quadruplets. Most of the children attained their majority. Mme. Vassilet became so renowned that she was presented at the court of Czar Alexander II.

Currently the highest reliably reported figure is a 38th child born to Raimundo Carnauba, 58, and Josimar Carnauba, 54, of Belem, Brazil. She was married at 15 and so far has had 14 sons and 24 daughters at yearly intervals. In May 1972, the mother said, "They have given us a lot of work and worry but they are worth it," and the father, "I don't know why people make such a fuss."

Source: *Guinness Book of World Records.* © 1974 by Sterling Publishing Co., Inc., New York.

asked, may call their work exciting or interesting, but rarely would they call it easy (LeMasters).

The relationship between parent and child may be warm and personally rewarding and one may produce an individual who will make a contribution to society: the question is, how much control over this do parents have? Having children is something of a gamble. The control of the parent over the child's intelligence, talent, or interests is debatable. The wisdom of having a child in order to create a certain kind of person, or a companion for oneself, is thus highly questionable. The reasons for having children should be weighed realistically against the responsibility and the potential difficulties that are involved.

ASSUMING THE PARENTAL ROLE

The responsibility for another human life is a task facing all parents, and this responsibility is more permanent and binding than any other. For most individuals, the birth of the first child requires psychological readjustment and complete reassessment of the self-concept.

Many problems relating to parenting are culturally determined. In contemporary American society, there is much confusion surrounding the parental role. This confusion exists at both the societal and the family levels. While parents have retained final responsibility for their children, formal institutions now fulfill many formerly parental functions. This division of labor has both diminished parental authority and blurred the nature of many tasks (LeMasters). For example, schools are responsible for a child's education, but parents are held responsible for the child's morality. Can education and morality be divided? What if the teacher's rules of conduct conflict with those of the parents—who prevails?

At the family level, shifts have occurred in the roles of male and female parents over the past decades. Early theories of psychology, particularly those of Freud, depicted the mother as the all-important influence in determining the child's personality. New theories have challenged this concept. Mothers, broadening the scope and focus of their lives, and fathers, rejecting the limited parental role traditionally assigned to them, have also challenged this concept. It is no longer clear what the father, the mother, or the parents as a couple are supposed to do in fulfilling their parental roles. Thus new parents in our society are faced with determining their roles for themselves.

> **Parental role.** The provision of care, training, and support for one's offspring.

Male Parents.   The role of father in the U.S. has traditionally been of secondary importance in a male's life. A man has been expected to identify with his occupational role more than with his family role. When asked what he does in life, it is not likely a man would reply, "I'm a husband and father," as a woman might answer, "I'm a wife and mother."

CASE STUDY—PAULA AND KEITH

Keith and Paula had been going together for nearly a year and both were aware that their deepening involvement with each other might lead to marriage. Trained professionals, both were happy in career-type jobs, but found ample time to be together outside of work.

One Sunday afternoon, Keith formally and seriously proposed marriage, and Paula accepted, happy and enthusiastic. "What a wonderful life we're going to have," she said, "and what beautiful children." Keith was dismayed, because he had long since made up his mind he did not want to have children. Not wishing to make an issue of the matter, he said lightly, "What children?" Neither of them saw this problem as serious. Both assumed they would come to an agreement on it later.

After the wedding, the question of children kept coming up and Paula would become very emotional in their discussion. Having children was to her a normal and expected part of every marriage, and Keith's salary was sufficient to live on if she stopped work to became a mother.

In one of these quarrels, Paula said, "You're never going to change your mind, are you? You won't even consider it." Keith replied that he had considered it, but that every time he came back to the realization that he didn't want to bring children into the world and that he didn't like the idea of sharing Paula's time and attention with a child. He admitted this was selfish but stated flatly that this was the way he felt. At last, the issue was in the open.

As the discussion continued, Paula recognized two things. First, she realized that it was more important to her to be married to Keith than it was to have children. Second, she realized that she didn't have very good reasons for wanting children. She was simply taking it for granted that children were a part of marriage. That very night, she formally committed herself to a childless marriage. "I still get sad about it sometimes and wonder what it would be like," she says, "but I know we made the best decision for us as a couple."

For class discussion: (1) Keith and Paula have been married for only two years. Do you think they will be able to live with this decision for the rest of their lives? (2) What are some of the trade-offs in having children? Though Keith might have less of Paula's time and attention if they have children, what might be gained in return?

A man's occupational role may be directly related to his family role, however. Economically, the pressure to provide is intensified both psychologically and actually by the presence of a child, especially as a wife may give up her paid job at this time. Even if the wife has not been employed, the husband's responsibility is increased. Supporting a wife does not carry the same psychological burden of necessity as does supporting a helpless newborn child. Moreover, the father often aspires to provide his children with a better standard of living than he himself had as a child. If he cannot provide this, he may feel himself a failure as a father.

Perhaps the greatest impact of the child on the father's life is on his marital relationship. Many women find themselves fully absorbed by the infant's demands and enthralled by the novelty of this new focus of their lives. Husbands may feel they are not only less important to their wives than formerly, but also that they are excluded from the mother-child relationship. This sense of loss may foster feelings of jealousy and resentment unless the father creates a place for himself within the family.

Parke and Sawin, along with other researchers, have found that fathers are much more skillful and nurturant in caring for newborn infants than was previously thought. Observations in the mother's hospital room, between 6 and 48 hours after delivery of the couple's first child, showed that fathers were just as involved as mothers in holding and rocking the baby, touching, looking at, vocalizing to, and kissing their newborn offspring. The babies consumed a similar amount of milk when they were bottle-fed by fathers and mothers, and fathers were equally responsive to signs of distress from the infant such as a cough, a spit-up, or a sneeze (Parke and Sawin, 1976).

> **Nurturant.** Furthering development; providing care and attention.

These researchers have suggested that fathers, like mothers, need social support in adapting to their new role. They recommend that the interest and involvement of fathers be supported by modifying hospital visiting arrangements, providing paternity leaves, and making available more training classes so that fathers will have the opportunity to learn and practice caretaking skills (Parke and Sawin). Confronted with an unclear role in the family and the conflicting demands of other roles, the father will usually have to work harder than the mother to establish a satisfactory relationship with his child.

Female Parents.   The role of the mother in America has changed dramatically in the past few decades. Smaller families, the development of household appliances, the need or wish to work outside the home, and changing ideologies have so altered the nature of her tasks that the traditional mother, devoting all her time to her children, rarely exists anymore.

One of the problems faced by the contemporary mother may be overcommitment. In his analysis of the mother's role in our society, LeMasters suggests that in recent years each of her commitments has expanded. As a wife, she is expected to be a total and equal partner to her husband, as friend, companion, and lover. The standards of mothering have risen, and she is expected to be informed about what is best for her children, in terms of health, schooling, and emotional well-being. The mother has retained the responsibility of managing the home, with the added chore of overseeing the budget, and she has expanded her community role. Finally, the majority of mothers in the country work outside the home, in addition to performing their family duties (LeMasters).

> **Overcommitment.** Allocation of resources beyond the ability for fulfillment.

The variety of options and the lack of guidelines to determine which options she should take can result in a sense of confusion for the mother of a first child. A young child's demands are enormous, and if the mother expects herself to meet these and other demands simultaneously, she may become distracted, overworked, and exhausted. The more clearly a woman has defined her overall life goals before she has children, the easier it will be for her to decide what emphasis she wishes to give her children, husband, career, and community activities after the children have arrived.

Research by McIntire, Nass, and Battistone suggests that women may be making their child-care roles more difficult for themselves than need be. A study among college students at the University of Connecticut indicates that young men are much more interested in early child raising than the women students thought them to be. Such misperceptions are possibly leading women to exclude fathers from child-care duties they are interested in sharing with the mothers.

Sixty-two percent of the men disagreed with the statement, "Most males don't think about their eventual role as father until their first child is born." Eighty-six percent agreed that, "Besides being a provider, husbands should help their wives with the housework and child care." On the statement, "A wife has a right to expect her husband to help feed and diaper-change the baby," 78 percent of the men agreed, but only 36 percent of the women thought the men would agree (McIntire et al., 1974).

The father's role in the development of older children has been widely acknowledged, but it has been thought to be inappropriate in our culture for fathers to be nurturant toward their infants. The importance of the mother has been stressed because of her biological capacity for nursing. However, the invention of bottle feeding made it possible for fathers to overcome this limitation on their role in caring for infants. The fact that historical, social, and economic arrangements have put them in other roles should not be interpreted to mean that men are incapable of assuming a caretaking function or unwilling to do so (Parke and Sawin).

Innovations in Male-Female Parenting.   Traditional concepts of masculine and feminine parental roles appear to be major factors contributing to the difficulties of contemporary parents. The father has been assigned the **instrumental** role in the family: he is responsible for the rational behavior of the family in its relationship to the outside world. The mother has been assigned the **expressive** role: she is considered the emotional or affective center of the family (Rossi, 1968). The limitations of these role designations were mentioned in Chapter 4 as a defect of structural functional theory. In her analysis of parenthood, Rossi has suggested that this traditional division is inappropriate for present-day family and social systems. The demands made upon a woman in her role as mother are in fact largely instrumental. Such tasks as household management and community organization are not carried out by the emotions; rather, they require the rationality and efficiency characteristic of the instrumental role. By contrast, success in the contemporary work world often requires that men make use of affective skills in interpersonal relationships. For example, in selling or in supervisory positions, they must be psychologically attuned to others (Rossi).

Rossi suggests that it is the extremely passive and dependent woman who would experience difficulty in her role as a mother today and the man who failed to integrate affective skills with his instrumental skills who would have difficulty as a father. In her opinion, it is more useful and accurate to view both types of skills as necessary to both the mother and father roles.

Many parents today, aware that the traditional roles are not suitable for their own lifestyle, are attempting to restructure these roles. It is no longer unusual to find mothers of young children employed outside the home, nor are men looked down on for changing diapers, feeding their children, or sharing household work. Some couples have gone still further in their efforts to redefine their parental roles, dividing child-care responsibilities equally between them, and there is indication that such an arrangement can be highly successful (Steinberg, 1972). More flexible parental-role definitions offer parents the opportunity to tailor these role to their personal abilities and needs. They can then experience their children in ways that are satisfying both for themselves and their offspring.

Instrumental. Concerned with rational and efficient behavior directed toward achievement of specific goals.

Expressive. Giving more importance to the emotional content of interpersonal relationships than to their effectiveness in accomplishing specific tasks.

RELATIONSHIPS OF PARENTS AND CHILDREN

Economic factors inevitably play a large role in parents' relationships with their children. Among groups below the poverty level, the physical and psychological strain of poor housing, inadequate food, and poor health may affect the quality of the time these parents spend with their children. Children's respect for parents and parents' expectations of children may be low in such circumstances. Yet if poverty directly causes certain difficulties for parents, higher income seems to alter rather than eliminate parental problems. Social scientists consider that parental stress is greatest among the middle class where ambitions to rise above one's social and economic level are often imposed on the children, creating tension between the two generations (LeMasters).

Parents' expectations for themselves, which tend to be high among the middle classes, may restrict the parents' freedom as much as poverty. A father who feels he must work at two jobs to achieve the economic and social status he desires for his family, and a mother who feels she is supposed to devote the bulk of her time to her children though she does not wish to, are restricting their own life choices. Researchers have found that middle-class parents experience fewer gratifications from the arrival of the first baby than do lower-class parents and that the initial experiences of parenthood tend to be more of a crisis for middle-class parents (Russell).

Future parents should consider what they have to offer their children in the way of material provisions. But they must also consider what their expectations are, both for themselves and for their children, and what sacrifices these expectations will require, if they are to predict future sources of tension in their lives and be prepared to deal with them.

DISCIPLINE AND SUPPORT

Social-class differences. Variations in lifestyle as determined by differences in educational attainment, occupation, and income.

Social-class differences in child rearing can be seen to depend on two factors. One is differences in lifestyle based on economic resources. The other is cultural differences in what is expected of children and parents. This factor seems to be influenced by the amount of education parents have. Scheck and Emerick (1976) asked a group of adolescent males about their perceptions of their parents, and found that the lower the socioeconomic status, the less likely are male adolescents to perceive their parents as being supportive, controlling, and consistent in their discipline. However, in all social classes, mothers were perceived as more supportive but less controlling and less consistent than fathers.

In general, these researchers feel that level of formal education is highly related to development of such personal characteristics as intellectual flexibility, breadth of perspective, and tolerance of nonconformity, and that parents possessing these characteristics would then be more supportive of

their children, helping them to develop a strong self-image. The more educated parents would also tend to be more democratic in their control and
show greater consistency in discipline, so that the children would experience
less confusion in knowing how they were expected to behave (Scheck and
Emerick).

THE WORKING MOTHER

The proportion of mothers who are employed outside the home has shown
a marked increase in recent years, and many people are concerned about
the effect the mother's absence from the home is having on the children.
Among single mothers—those separated, divorced, or widowed—55 percent of those with children under age 6 and 67 percent of those with children aged 6–17 were in the labor force in 1975. Among married women
living with their husbands, 37 percent of those with children under age 6
and 52 percent of those with children aged 6–17 were in the labor force in
1975. Thus, a majority of women who have children of school age are in
the labor force, as well as a substantial proportion of those who have children under age 6, whether the mothers are married or single. Figure 13.1,
comparing data for 1960 and 1975, shows the trend to employment of
women with children (U.S. Bureau of the Census, 1976, P-23:58).

Effects on Children.   After a review of recent research on the subject,
Claire Etaugh (1974) has concluded that maternal employment of itself has
very little influence on the behavior of children. She has grouped the various
research findings into the categories of personal adjustment, school achievement and intelligence, leisure activities, and perceptions and attitudes, and
summarized the results.

According to this analysis, young children are not adversely affected
by maternal employment in terms of their attachment to the working parent

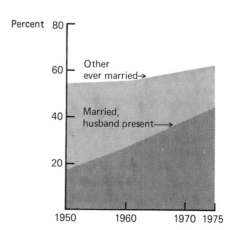

Fig. 13.1 Increase in labor force participation, ever
married women with children under 18 years of age.
(Source: U.S. Bureau of the Census, 1976, P–23:58.)

Cognitive. Pertaining to mental processes, such as those involved in problem solving.

or their **cognitive** development, provided there is frequent parent-child interaction during nonworking hours and stable, stimulating substitute care. The adjustment of elementary-school children to maternal employment seems to be directly related to the mother's attitudes toward working and homemaking. The mother who remains at home, although discontent in the homemaking role, may create more problems for her children than the one who provides good substitute care and works outside the home. It has been found consistently that "satisfied mothers—working or not—have the best adjusted children" (Etaugh).

In regard to schoolwork, research suggests that maternal employment may adversely affect boys' performance and have either a positive influence or none at all on girls' performance. The relation between cause and effect is not clear, however. In schoolwork, as in psychological adjustment, children of satisfied mothers functioned better than children of dissatisfied mothers, whether working or at home.

Maternal employment seems to have little effect on the leisure activities of children, but some influence on perceptions, attitudes, and life goals. In general, children of working mothers, especially girls, have higher educational goals and career expectations than those of nonworking mothers. They have a broader concept of the female role and perceive less difference between men's and women's roles. The attitudes of the children, however, depend largely on the success of the mother in combining her family and career roles (Etaugh, p. 77).

An undesirable consequence of maternal employment appears to be that sons of working mothers tend to show more disapproval of their fathers. Thus, while the self-image of daughters may be raised when the mother works outside the home, the self-image of sons may ultimately be lowered by their less favorable attitude toward the father. It may be that because maternal employment is usually based on need, the father is viewed by children as failing to provide an adequate income. As maternal employment becomes a more widely accepted cultural norm, this perception may change.

Fig. 13.2 Labor force participation rates, 1975—ever married women with children under 18. (Source: U.S. Bureau of the Census, 1976, P–23:58.)

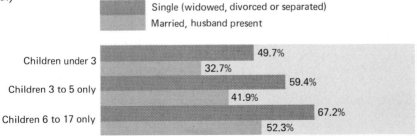

As suggested in Chapter 3, in the discussion of the problems of working mothers whether single or married, it appears that the mother's employment outside the home does not necessarily create problems for her children, provided she is able to integrate the two roles and provide adequate substitute care.

Child-Care Needs.   At the present time, the lack of adequate child-care facilities, such as day-care centers and centers for after-school supervision, is perhaps the working mother's biggest problem. In addition to her many responsibilities, she has the burden of establishing child-care arrangements on an individual basis. Such arrangements are likely to be more difficult to set up, more expensive to maintain, and also less able to provide the stability required by both parent and child than could be provided in community-based facilities.

McBride suggests in *The Growth and Development of Mothers* (1973) that too much time has been spent worrying about whether or not to encourage day-care rather than directing energy toward finding suitable day-care structures. Cooperative day-care in which parents put in time is one possibility. Family-style care could be combined with larger neighborhood activity groups. Research has amply revealed the importance of good substitute child care in the case of maternal employment. As more and more women join the labor force, it is becoming clear that new social structures will need to be developed to meet our changing social needs.

Day-care. A system for providing for the physical and emotional needs of children by persons other than their parents.

SPECIAL FORMS OF PARENTHOOD

Though most children in the United States spend their childhood in the company and custody of their two biological parents, a growing number are living in homes with a stepparent, adoptive parents, or under the temporary care of foster parents. Legal responsibilities are different in each of these cases. Adoptive parents have exactly the same legal relationship to a child as biological parents do. Foster parents are, in effect, employees of the state in caring for children placed in their care. In cases of remarriage, the new spouse of the mother or father has no legal relationship to the child at all. This is true whether the stepparent relationship is established after the death of the natural mother or father or after a divorce. However, relationships are likely to be more complex in the case of divorce, since the child has both a mother and a father and the role of the stepparent is more difficult to define. Sometimes stepparents go into court to adopt their stepchildren and thus establish the legal relationship to the children of biological parents.

MARRIAGE TO SOMEONE WITH CHILDREN

The rising divorce rate, together with a high rate of remarriage, has meant that it is no longer uncommon to marry an individual with children from a former marriage. Marriage to an individual with children presents a special set of problems. A study at the University of Toronto School of Social Work revealed that the three problems stepparents viewed as most difficult were disciplining the children, adjusting to the habits and personalities of the children, and gaining the children's acceptance (Schlesinger and Stasiuk, 1972).

Stepparent. A person related to a child through marriage to one of the child's biological parents.

The stepparent enters a situation in which roles are not clear. Should the stepparent act as a parent to the child, or should the role be something different since the child already has parents? However the role is defined, it must include the establishment of authority. The stepparent's values may differ from those of the former parent and if the child is old enough to have adopted the former parent's values, there is a potential source of conflict. The dimensions of the new parent's authority should probably be decided upon by the couple prior to the marriage so that there can be consistency in the way discipline is presented to the children.

It should be recognized, also, that time is needed to develop a parent-child relationship. A parent gradually adjusts to and influences the personalities and habits of the children as they mature. A stepparent, on the other hand, is presented with the child all at once. A period of adjustment is necessary for the new parent to find out who the child is, what the child's likes and dislikes are, and how the child responds in a variety of situations. The child may have annoying traits which the stepparent must learn to cope with. From the child's point of view, also, the new marriage brings adjustment problems. Such children are suddenly faced with sharing a parent they may have had to themselves for some time. They may well feel jealous and resentful of this new person who has entered their lives. Learning to know and trust a stepparent is a slow process for many children. Open and frank discussions between parents and children may help in this process (Schlesinger and Stasiuk).

The kinds of problems encountered in blending families are discussed further in Chapter 14, "Marital Problems, Marital Dissolution, and Remarriages." Despite potential problems in the remarriage situation, it does not appear that children inevitably suffer either psychologically or emotionally from having a stepparent. Two national surveys conducted in 1973 revealed that children in stepfather families did not differ from children in biological-father families in social or psychological characteristics (Wilson et al., 1975).

PARENTING AFTER DIVORCE OR WIDOWHOOD

Divorce or the death of a spouse leaves one parent with the major responsibility for the child and dramatically alters the parent-child relationship.

Both the widow and the divorced parent with custody face the kinds of problems of the single parent discussed in Chapter 3. In the case of divorce, however, where both parents are living but one is absent, parent-child relationships may be more complicated for all members of the family.

The Parent Who Has Custody.   The parent who retains custody has the advantage of a continuing relationship with the children. The sense of loss experienced by many individuals in divorce may be lessened somewhat by the ongoing parental role which has now been enlarged. It is this parent who is likely to exert the major influence on the children since the parent who has custody is in the desirable position of not having seemed, from the children's point of view, to have deserted them.

The problems faced by the parent who has custody, however, are more than equal to the rewards. The parent who must fulfill the roles of both mother and father on a daily basis is bound to be overworked, and the economic problems characteristic of many single-parent households make it more difficult to carry out the parent role effectively.

Single parent. A widowed, divorced, or never-married parent.

The Parent Who Does Not Have Custody.   The parent who does not get custody of the children has fewer overt problems than the parent with custody and probably more time and freedom than he or she has had for years. Yet because this independence is the result of the disruption of close relationships, it may be experienced more as a loss than as a gain. Anxiety about what the effects of the divorce might be on the lives of the children is a major problem in divorces where children are involved, and the parent who loses custody may feel keenly the loss of opportunity to direct and influence the upbringing of the children.

No matter how the parent tries to maintain closeness with the children, loss of daily contact creates a certain distance which it is hard to counteract. This may be intensified by the children's resentment that this parent has "left." The absent parent may be called upon to help make major decisions, but then left out of the minor decisions that form the bulk of the parent's role. The role of the absent parent varies with visiting agreements, geographical distance, the relationship between the former spouses, remarriage, and, more important, the parent's own attitude. Determination to maintain a relationship with one's children can overcome at least some of the difficulties. Some specific suggestions for reducing the harmful effects of divorce for children are given in Chapter 14 in the section called "Children and Divorce."

ADOPTION: REWARDS AND SPECIAL PROBLEMS

Adoption occurs in a variety of situations. A relative may adopt a child of deceased parents; a new spouse may adopt the children of the partner's former marriage; a couple, with or without children of their own, may adopt an unrelated child. The particular type of adoption obviously influences how the parent-child relationship will develop and what problems parents and child will face.

It has been estimated that there were 149,000 adoptions in the United States in 1974, including both relative and nonrelative adoptions. Adoptions by relatives are 64 percent of the total, and most of these are adoptions by a stepparent of children of the spouse by a former marriage (Bonham, 1977). There is supposedly a shortage of babies available for adoption compared to the number of couples applying for them. The shortage, however, refers specifically to healthy, Caucasian babies. There is in fact a surplus of "hard-to-place" children—those from minority or mixed racial background, those with physical or emotional handicaps, or those over the age of three (Johnson, 1975).

That these children are hard to place is not solely the result of a shortage of couples willing to assume the responsibility of more difficult children. State laws, social attitudes, and particularly the practices of adoption agencies have also contributed to the failure to find homes for them. It has been suggested that the policies of adoption agencies, based on middle-class prejudices, have emphasized income, social status, education, and home ownership in evaluating prospective parents, thus screening out many couples, especially members of the black community, who might well provide secure and loving homes (Aldridge, 1974).

One of the main difficulties experienced by adopted children is the psychological burden of feeling they were rejected by their natural parents. The question of why they were rejected may lie behind the need many adopted children feel to find out about their origins. Betty Jean Lifton, herself an adoptee, describes the search for the truth about one's origins as a prerequisite for establishing a sense of identity. Adoptive parents must be sensitive to this need in their children and not interpret it as a rejection of themselves but rather as a reflection of a human need to know who we are (Lifton, 1976).

Adoption. Taking voluntarily a child of other parents as one's own child.

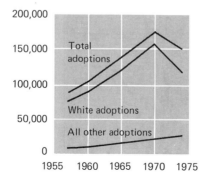

Fig. 13.3 Number of adoptions by color: United States, 1957–1974. In the United States, adoption is widely supported as a means of increasing family size, and about four percent of U.S. women have adopted a child other than a stepchild by the time they are 45 years old. People who adopt are found in all racial, religious, and socioeconomic groups. (Source: Gordon S. Bonham, Who adopts: the relationship of adoption and social-demographic characteristics of women, *Journal of Marriage and the Family* 39:2:297. Copyright 1977 by the National Council on Family Relations. Reprinted by permission.)

The advantages and rewards of adoption are many, for both parents and children. If adopted children bear the burden of feeling they were once rejected, they also have the pride of having been chosen as no natural child can be. There are no accidental adoptions. Parents are often in a position to choose the time for a child to enter their home. They can wait until they are financially secure while avoiding the pressure of health statistics to bear their children young. By this time they are more likely to be past the identity crises of youth and to have more stability to offer the child. Adoptive parents can experience the reward of knowing they have helped a child who needed help. They did not create that need, they fulfilled it.

FOSTER PARENTING

Like parents who adopt, foster parents fulfill an urgent social need. Nearly 300,000 children under the age of 18 have been removed from parental custody and placed in foster care, whether family homes, group homes, or child-welfare institutions (Mnookin, 1973). Yet because of the rules and regulations relating to foster parenting, as well as certain problems inherent in the arrangement itself, foster parents face an extremely difficult situation.

Foster parent. One who provides parental care though not related by blood or legal ties.

The foster home is viewed by all involved as temporary. Parents retain legal responsibility for the child and this responsibility is temporarily given not to the foster parents, but to the social agency involved. The agency's policies are usually related to the foster parents through a caseworker. Under these conditions, it is difficult for foster parents to define their role. Parents may be inhibited from developing a deep relationship with the child, since they feel the arrangement is temporary and they may soon be parted. Questions of policy relating to the child are decided by the social agency and the caseworker's decisions override the foster parents' should a conflict arise. Support for the child is provided by the state. Deprived of most of the functions of parenting, it is not surprising that many foster parents have trouble fulfilling their role or that foster children often experience difficulty in adjusting to the home.

In actual practice foster care is not usually a temporary arrangement. Most children, once they are placed in foster care, never return to their own homes (Mnookin). It has been suggested that agencies should recognize this reality and focus on finding long-term home situations for these children, preferably with the possibility of adoption. Adoption, however, might be limited since it could require people to give up the payments made for foster care and support the children on their own.

PROBLEM PARENTS

For a variety of reasons, some people do not successfully fulfill their parental roles. In some cases where parents have failed to carry out their responsibilities toward their children, the law will intervene and remove the child from the home. Broadly speaking, parents are legally required to provide their children with basic necessities, to maintain their health, ensure their education, and instill in them values of morality and respect. These obligations reflect community expectations but are, in themselves, highly abstract. In specific cases, whether or not parents have failed to fulfill their duties must be decided by the court (Katz, 1971).

Sanford Katz in *When Parents Fail* differentiates between two ways in which parents mistreat children: **child abuse** and **child neglect.** Child abuse refers to intentional behavior of a parent or a custodian which causes physical injury to the child. Child neglect refers to indifference to the child's needs, failure to carry out the expected duties of parenthood. We might call these active and passive forms of mistreatment. Abused children are harmed by certain acts against them. Neglected children are harmed by the omission of certain acts they need to develop their fullest potential.

Child abuse. Intentional behavior of a parent or custodian which causes injury to a child.

An extreme case of child neglect is the parent who willfully refuses to provide funds for food, clothing, shelter, education, and health care. This form of neglect is becoming increasingly common after divorce or when the breadwinner simply deserts the family.

CHILD ABUSE

The extent of the problem of child abuse is difficult to determine because so many cases are not reported and reporting practices vary so much from one state to another. It has been estimated that there are 60,000 reported incidents of child abuse each year in the U.S. However, David Gil, citing data from a 1965 survey, estimates that 2½–4 million children actually suffer abuse resulting in some injury each year. Vincent DeFrancis, Director of the Children's Division of the American Humane Association, places his estimate considerably lower than Gil does. He suggests that there are between 30,000 and 40,000 cases of battered children each year, plus at least 100,000 children who are sexually abused, and probably 200,000 to 300,000 who are psychologically abused (Cohen and Sussman, 1975).

The incidence of child abuse appears to vary with the sex and age of the child. Data from a nationwide survey indicate that under the age of 12, boys are more often abused than girls. Past puberty, however, girls far outnumber boys as the targets of physical abuse. Conflicts between parent and child concerning the heterosexual relationships of the adolescent girl may contribute to this, as may the increasing physical strength of boys. Certainly physical abuse is not limited to young children: nearly one-fifth of the cases in Gil's 1965 survey were teenagers (Gil, 1970).

Factors in Child Abuse. People who cause physical injury to their own children seem to be people who have themselves been raised without love and tolerance. Many abusing parents were abused themselves as children and are acting toward their own children according to the example that was set for them. They also seem to lack knowledge of what a child's ability may be at a certain age and how to go about getting the child to behave in the way they desire. They seem often not to realize that the child is not just being stubborn or willful but really does not understand or cannot perform in the way the parent wants (Spinetta and Rigler, 1972).

Abusing parents seem to suffer from deep feelings of inadequacy, especially a sense that they are failing to fulfill the roles expected of parents. This may be reflected in the child's misbehavior or failure to progress as expected. It may also be reflected in failure to meet the cultural definition of what a successful family is. A home in which the father is unemployed and the mother has taken over financial responsibility for the family is considered a breeding ground for abuse (Spinetta and Rigler).

Child abuse seems not to be related directly to economic deprivation but rather is found in families caught up in a tangle of individual and social problems (Erlanger, 1974). Whatever the cause, the problem is serious because indications are that children experiencing abuse are likely to become abusing parents themselves.

Broadening the Definition of Child Abuse.   Gil, interpreting the term abuse broadly to include all inflicted events that prevent the child's actualization of his or her potential, suggests that our society is characterized by child abuse at many levels. Schools and other child-care settings employ practices that are not conducive to optimal child development. Corporal punishment, threats, the inhibition of spontaneity and creativity, and insistence upon rigid conformity are all forms of abuse at the institutional level. At the societal level, Gil suggests that policies based on the prevailing social, economic, and political order deprive many children of basic requirements, such as adequate housing, food, and education, as well as occupational opportunities and ethical values (Gil, 1975).

One of the issues explored in Gil's survey was the inclination of people to inflict injury upon a child. He found that nearly six out of every ten respondents thought that "almost anybody could at some time injure a child in his care." Gil (1970) interprets this to mean that the infliction of physical injury upon children is viewed as an almost normal occurrence. Physical punishment is one more form of violence in U.S. society. In Gil's view, however, physical abuse of children is still less widespread and less serious a problem in undermining the developmental opportunities of children than such social abuse as poverty, racial discrimination, malnutrition, and inadequate provisions for medical care and education.

CHILD NEGLECT

In general, people are more aware of the incidence of child abuse than of child neglect. All American jurisdictions have legal procedures for handling

Child neglect. Failure to carry out the expected duties of parenthood.

abuse cases (Katz). Child neglect probably occurs six times as often as child abuse but it is not often brought to the attention of the courts and there are no standard procedures for dealing with neglect cases when they arise (Cohen and Sussman).

What are the reasons parents neglect their children? Because the majority of child-neglect cases are instituted against parents who are poor, it would seem that poverty is one of the major factors contributing to child neglect (Katz). Overwork, exhaustion, poor health, inadequate food, and substandard housing are conditions that drain parents of energy for caring for their children and make them indifferent to their needs. Moreover, the sense they may have that they will, in any case, fail their children because of their own inadequacies may lead them to give up trying.

Other social factors associated with poverty may further contribute to child neglect. Alcoholism and drug use, common escape routes from the reality of poverty, prevent the fulfillment of the parent role in an immediate sense: a parent who is drunk or high cannot function adequately as a parent. In a long-term sense, such escapes may lead to unemployment, transience, and other disruptions in family life that will further child neglect.

While it is likely that conditions of poverty do lead to child neglect, it may also be, as Katz remarks, that proceedings are instituted against the poor because wealth and societal standards protect middle- and upper-class parents. The poor, particularly if they are on welfare, are more subject to the scrutiny of officials. If they are indifferent to or neglectful of a child, it is visible. Wealthy parents who send their child to a private boarding school are not judged neglectful though they may in fact be entirely indifferent to the child. The wealthy have options for getting their children off their hands that the poor do not (Katz).

Whatever part poverty plays in child neglect, it is clear that other factors are also involved. Just as with child abuse, personality problems of the parents are considered a major factor in child neglect. Some individuals do not seem able to make the necessary adjustment to the parental role. They may have lacked good parental role models when they were growing up, or they may be too young to handle the responsibility with which they are suddenly faced. Children make great demands upon parents' emotional resources, and parents who lack emotional stability themselves will have difficulty meeting their children's needs. Economic factors may make the situation more difficult, but poverty alone is not a cause of child neglect. It may be that some individuals are just not suited to be parents (Katz).

NONSUPPORT

Nonsupport. Failure to meet the basic economic needs of a dependent.

Responsibility to provide for their children falls upon both parents equally, although the labor may be divided, with one parent serving as breadwinner and the other providing the domestic and child-care services that enable the breadwinner to fulfill that role. After a divorce, the couple is no longer a legal unit. Yet each spouse continues to bear financial responsibilities toward the offspring of the dissolved union. The specific financial arrangements made for child support vary with the circumstances of the couple, such as the number of children and the income of each parent. But according to the law, the burden of support falls equally upon each spouse, no matter which one has custody of the children.

From the point of view of society, it has been important to establish parental responsibility for support of the children, for otherwise the burden falls upon the state, putting a strain upon public funds. The law, as stated, makes parental responsibility clear (Eckhardt, 1968).

Yet however explicitly support is required by the law, nonsupport has been a common practice. A 1965 survey in Wisconsin revealed that 62 percent of divorced fathers studied were not providing child support though ordered by the court to do so (Cowley, 1975). The problem is nationwide and has led to the establishment of a federal law, administered by the Department of Health, Education, and Welfare, which provides for federal control over the search for fathers who are negligent in supporting their children. Though in some cases, fathers who can afford to pay have refused to do so, in other cases, an unemployed father may not be able to meet his child-support payments. Or if a father has remarried and there are offspring of the new union, he may find it impossible to support two families. With the rising frequency of divorce and remarriage, nonsupport has become a major problem. A solution will have to take into consideration the needs of each parent, setting reasonable expectations for both. The most important thing, however, may be for parents to set reasonable expectations for themselves, adjusting the number of children they have to the number they are likely to be able to support for a lifetime.

GOALS OF CHILD REARING

Becoming a parent is, for most people, a fairly easy accomplishment. It is rearing the child, once born, that many people find difficult. As we have seen, some people are unsuited to the task. There is, in fact, a booming business in parent-training courses attended by people who need help in coping with their children (Brown, 1976).

DESIRABLE BEHAVIOR IN CHILDREN

What are the traits people desire to encourage in their children? Baumrind and Black (1967) define eight personality characteristics as aspects of competence in preschool children. They consider self-reliance, self-control, and the ability to relate easily to other people to be highly desirable traits. Self-assertive and explorative behavior is valued over that of the withdrawn child who tends to retreat from new experiences. Finally, successful children are those who are realistic, contented, and buoyant, able to bounce back after a disappointment.

The purpose of the research by Baumrind and Black was to determine what parental practices could be found to lead to competence in preschool children. In general, they found that parents of competent children balanced highly nurturant behavior with high control of the children. They made firm demands of the children and were notably clear in communicating to the child what was required. However, firm, demanding behavior was not associated with punitiveness or lack of warmth. On the contrary, these parents were very loving, and when they gave a directive to the child, they accompanied it with a reason.

DEVELOPMENT OF SELF-ESTEEM

Other researchers have concerned themselves with the connection between child-rearing practices and the development of high self-esteem in young people. Coopersmith (1967) found that parents who have definite values, who have a clear idea of appropriate behavior, and who are able and willing to present and enforce their beliefs are more likely to rear children who value themselves highly. Self-confidence on the part of parents—knowing what to expect and what they want to do about it—seems to build self-esteem in the children.

In a study of fifth- and sixth-grade boys and their mothers, Cooper-smith found three specific conditions that lead to high self-esteem. The first of these is acceptance: total or nearly total acceptance of the children by their parents. These parents were concerned for the welfare of their children and were loyal sources of affection and support. The second condition is discipline: establishment of clearly defined and enforced limits on behavior, providing for the child a social map of do's and don't's. Establishment of limits gives children a basis for evaluating their performance. Areas of safety and hazard are also marked off and signposts set up that serve as a guide to the expectations, demands, and taboos of the community. The third condition is respect: allowing latitude for individual action, acceptance and tolerance of dissent within the established limits.

Self-esteem. One's sense of one's own worth or value.

Supporting the findings of Baumrind and Black and Coopersmith with younger children, Rollins and Thomas (1975) found that parental nurturance—accepting and loving behavior—is the key factor among adolescents in the development of self-esteem, conformance to appropriate authority, and acceptance of parental religious values and practices. In their view, parents' nurturance toward a child increases their ability to lead the child to do what they desire.

The child with high self-esteem is not always an easy child to be with, according to Coopersmith, and, in fact, can be a source of torment and anxiety. Baumrind and Black say that interaction between competent preschoolers and their parents is often vigorous and conflictful. But in the end, according to Rollins and Thomas, the basic interaction pattern between parents and children is the mutually rewarding exchange of parental nurturance for child compliance, and sheer assertion of power is not necessary to bring about conformity to parental wishes.

Why should development of high self-esteem be a major goal of child rearing? Coopersmith joins with others in asserting that the individual with low self-esteem feels helpless, vulnerable, and inadequate, while individuals with high self-esteem feel capable of coping with adversity and competent to achieve success. It is these latter characteristics most people are likely to desire for their children.

TWO PROGRAMS TO IMPROVE PARENT-CHILD COMMUNICATION

Among the families studied in the various research projects described in the preceding section, many parents were doing an excellent job of child rearing in terms of their goals for their children. Others were found to be having an unhappy time. Those chosen for study were average parents, just as likely to make mistakes in bringing up their children as any average group of people. The potential for conflict between parents and children is great. In some families, it may be intensified by conflict between the parents over how the children should be treated. Fortunately, more and more families are finding help with parenting problems through programs to improve communication between children and parents.

FAMILY-COMMUNICATION SYSTEMS

Concerned that the way parents interact with their children often leads the child to have low self-esteem, Benson, Berger, and Mease (1975) have developed a program for improvement of parent-child communication based on the concept of the family as a system of interlocking personalities. Parents in this program learn to make active interventions in their current relationship system aimed at developing mutual respect between family members and shared control of family life.

The program involves seven evening meetings at which parents become more aware of the effect on the child of their present communications and are provided with new alternatives through role playing in structured situations. Since the ability of a child to process information is limited—especially in very young children—misunderstandings by the child of what the parent wants are bound to occur. This problem is increased because the child is capable of a broad range of intense feelings, such as guilt and shame as well as pride and joy, even though intellectual understanding of the cause of the feelings is so limited (Benson et al., 1975).

© George Dole

"...and that's all I know about sex, so far."

Benson and his fellow researchers believe that most people want to be good parents—to help their children grow into mentally healthy adults—but often lack the communication skills to do this. The program, therefore, aims to improve skills in eight areas.

1. Listening: being sensitive to both the content and the feeling of what the child is saying.
2. Goal setting: applying the new awareness to specific situations where change is desired.
3. Identification of parenting styles: recognition of the effect on the child of one's present way of parenting.
4. Sending negative feelings: being able to express a negative reaction to the child's behavior without causing the child to feel rejected.
5. Sending positive feelings: reinforcement of behavior the parent wants continued.
6. Systems analysis skills: deciding what communication styles are having negative effects on the children so that these systems can be changed.
7. Creative problem solving: developing effective procedures for decision making in family matters.
8. Family rules: identifying hidden rules of family behavior that are having a negative effect and then changing them.

Changes measured in parents' attitudes before and after participation in the program support the belief that an educational training program in parent-child communication can produce significantly improved communication patterns. Parents who participated have been very positive in their comments about the program and its effect on their family life (Benson et al., 1957).

PARENT-ADOLESCENT RELATIONSHIP DEVELOPMENT

The program developed by Grando and Ginsberg to deal specifically with the problems of poor communication between adolescent boys and their fathers does not use role playing in the same way as the family-systems program of Benson, Berger, and Mease. In the PARD program, fathers remain in their roles as fathers and sons remain in their roles as sons. But each learns the special skills and requirements of being a Speaker and a Listener.

The Speaker role emphasizes openness, which Grando and Ginsberg define as including genuineness in communication; congruence, or consistency in the intellectual and the emotional content of the messages sent; and self-disclosure. In the learning situations they set up, fathers and sons took turns at being the Speaker, and when one was speaking, the other was the Listener. The Listener role requires **empathy,** understanding what the other is trying to say rather than concentrating on refuting it. The Listener must hold feelings and opinions in abeyance until a later time when he has a turn to be the Speaker. While the Listener, one must be accepting and non-critical, emphasizing warmth and genuineness. It is the Listener's task to be specific in stating what is being learned from the Speaker. The Speaker then gives feedback as to whether the Listener has understood correctly (Grando and Ginsberg, 1976).

As indicated above, Speaker and Listener roles are taken in turns by both fathers and sons. The group leader of the program and other participants comment upon how well each partner in the dyad is doing in fulfilling the obligation to speak openly and to listen perceptively. The pairs also practiced the Speaker-Listener roles at home and brought in tapes of their dialogue to be commented upon by the program leaders.

Grando and Ginsberg found that the needs and goals of these fathers and sons were in conflict both within each individual and within the relationship. Fathers were having difficulty in fulfilling the father role—as a guide and disciplinarian—and at the same time maintaining a close relationship with the son. Sons were torn between the growing desire for independence and the wish to gain the father's approval by fulfillment of his expectations. There was also interpersonal conflict between the father's desire to maintain a close relationship and the son's desire for increasing independence of action. The practice in communication skills as Speakers and Listeners in the PARD program enabled these fathers and sons to retain their separate developmental needs while working to be more in touch with one another, more able to reveal to each other their love and anger, affection and resentment, and their mutual desire to know more about each other.

While Grando and Ginsberg make no extension of their program beyond the father-son dyad, there may be an equal potential here for better communication between mothers and adolescent daughters, and, in fact, in any dyadic relationship which could be improved by greater openness on one the hand and willingness to listen on the other.

Summary

1. The purpose of this chapter is to focus on the adjustments required when children are a part of the family system.

2. Becoming parents requires a major reorganization of a couple's life patterns. Changes are experienced differently by the mother and the father. The transition from a dyad to a triad can be eased if the couple plans ahead for the costs, difficulties, and responsibilities of the task.

3. Problems related to parenting are often culturally determined. For example, sharing responsibility for child rearing with social institutions such as the school or the church may create conflicts for the parents, and shifts in definitions of male and female parental roles may require parents to restructure

roles to suit their particular situations. Other factors which influence the relationships between parents and children are economic circumstances, the parents' expectations for themselves, their ideas on child rearing, and whether or not the mother works.

4. Forms of parenthood other than biological involve different adjustments, problems, and legal responsibilities. (a) Stepparents: Three problems are especially difficult for stepparents: discipline, adjustment to habits and personalities of the children, and gaining acceptance of the children. (b) Adoptive parents: Special concerns of adopted children may be the feeling of having been rejected by their biological parents and the desire to know who their parents are as a part of establishing their own identity. (c) Foster parents: The foster-home situation is often temporary, and parental roles are not clear since parental responsibilities are shared with the state. (d) Single parents: As discussed in Chapter 3, single parents with children in their custody must try to fulfill the roles of both father and mother. The single parents without custody of a child may suffer anxiety about disruption of the parent-child relationships and loss of influence on the child's upbringing.

5. Some parents do not successfully fulfill parental roles in providing their children with basic necessities, maintaining their health, educating them, and providing for their emotional security. There are two ways in which parents may mistreat children. Child abuse is intentional injury of a child and can be related to the parent's own upbringing, lack of knowledge, or feelings of inadequacy. Child neglect is indifference to a child's needs and failure to carry out expected duties of parenthood. Neglect is associated with problems of poverty, alcoholism, and drug use, emotional problems of the parent, and parental upbringing.

6. Two basic goals in child rearing are to encourage desirable behavior in children through a balance between nurturance and control and to promote development of the child's self-esteem through parental acceptance of the child, establishment of limits to behavior, and respect for the child. To help parents achieve these goals, training programs have been developed to improve parent-child communication skills.

Key Concepts

Baby	Motherhood mystique	Foster parent
Child	Father	Child abuse
Adolescent	Mother	Child neglect
Adult	Nurturance	Nonsupport
Parenthood	Day-care center	Discipline
Triad	Stepparent	Family communication
Social isolation	Adoptive parent	system

Review and Discussion

1. Describe some realistic and unrealistic portrayals of parenting in the popular media (TV shows, books, movies). Why do you think they are realistic or unrealistic?

2. At what point in their relationship should a couple discuss their approach to child rearing, before or after marriage? Why?

3. Did your mother work while you were growing up? What benefits or disadvantages did the situation (working or nonworking) have for you and other members of your family?

4. Do you know anyone who has been brought up by parents other than the biological parents? Did this perhaps happen to you? Do you think such a person has problems, adjustments, and rewards different from children raised by their biological parents?

5. What are the laws about child abuse and child neglect in your state? Do you think laws are the way to solve these social problems?

Suggested Readings

BERMAN, C. (1974). *We Take This Child: A Candid Look at Modern Adoption.* Garden City, N.Y.: Doubleday.

Explores the experiences of parents adopting all varieties of children, including black, white, multiracial, and handicapped. The views of parents, social workers, lawyers, and others are combined to give a picture of the adoption process and what it is like to raise an adopted child. Includes a bibliography of books and articles on adoption and a list of organizations concerned with adoption.

JAMES, M. (1975). *Transactional Analysis for Moms and Dads.* Reading, Mass.: Addison-Wesley.

A book to help anyone who interacts with children—family therapists and teachers as well as parents. Diagrams and cartoons illustrate family relationships and communication between parents and children. Special chapters deal with divorced parents and stepparents.

MADDOX, B. (1975). *The Half-Parent: Living with Other People's Children.* New York: Evans.

Discusses the emotional problems and rewards of being a second parent. Considers myths, legal questions, etiquette, discipline, and communication between stepparents and stepchildren.

ROTHSCHILD, J., AND S. B. WOLF (1976). *The Children of the Counterculture.* Garden City, N.Y.: Doubleday.

Describes visits to several dozen communes and radical homes in the early seventies where the authors studied effects on children of living in alternative family structures. Reports some attitudes toward child rearing that the authors found helpful in relating to their own children.

WOODWARD, K. L., WITH P. MALAMUD (1975). The parent gap. *Newsweek,* Sept. 22, pp. 48–56.

Discusses the problems and pressures that parents face today when respect for them is declining and there is no longer agreement on what a good parent should be. Includes close-ups on how some parents are handling their problems.

Marital Problems, Marital Dissolution, and Remarriages | 14

Separation and divorce have become so common in the United States that it is no longer appropriate to assume that a marriage will last forever. Although people want companionship and intimacy, perhaps even more consciously than in the past, they may not be able to find them or sustain them in a first marriage, or even a second. If society can stop looking on divorce as personal failure and see it instead as a difficult time when people need social support in the movement toward greater self-actualization, perhaps it can be of more help in coping with the complex problems of divorce.

In this chapter we first explore some problems which are often behind the decision to undo a marriage—anger as an expression of incompatibility, violence, alcoholism, and extramarital sex. We examine divorce as a reasonable alternative to such problems on the one hand, but as an event charged with personal trauma for everyone involved on the other. At the end of the chapter we consider some ways of aiding troubled families in dealing with their problems.

ANGER AS A RESPONSE TO CONFLICT

A major factor causing marriages to fail is people's inability to deal with anger—their own and their partner's. **Companionate marriage,** according to Mace (1976a), is often attempted by couples who have never learned the interpersonal skills it requires—skills which were not needed so much in more traditional marriages held together by duty and patience rather than love.

Conflict is an inescapable component of intimacy. Seeking love, two people become more intimate, but as they get to know each other better, they discover differences of opinion and personality as well as similarities. Eventually, disagreements may escalate into angry conflicts which hurt and puzzle them. Those who do not have the skills to work through their anger may draw away from it into less intense relationships, sacrificing love and intimacy for the sake of peace (Mace).

WHAT IS ANGER?
Anger is a highly charged emotion, a strong feeling of displeasure and usually of antagonism. Biologically, anger is a survival response, a marshaling of the body's resources to deal with threat. Adrenalin output soars, heartbeat accelerates, and muscles tighten, along with other physiological changes. It is a normal, healthy response which drives us to action—to defend ourselves when physically attacked or unjustly accused, for instance.

Anger may be a reaction to **frustration,** as well as to insult or attack, for blocking of goal-directed behavior results in the same aroused state as insults and attacks (Rule and Nesdale, 1976). Most of us would become

Companionate marriage. A marriage which stresses love and intimacy and mutual enjoyment of the spouse's company.

angry, for instance, if someone snatched a sandwich away from us just as we were about to eat it, or blocked our way as we were intent on hurrying out the door to catch a bus. For two people accustomed to living independently, living together creates many frustrations: getting in each other's way in a shared bathroom, tripping over the other's dirty clothes, waiting for the other to finish dressing when you're already late for a party, and limiting expenditures to those which are jointly approved, for example.

Frustration. The state of the individual in a situation where movement toward a goal is perceived to be blocked.

The Relation of Anger and Aggression.   Anger is not the same thing as aggression, even though they may occur in the same context. **Anger** is an intense feeling; **aggression** is hostile or injurious behavior. It includes verbal attacks, gestures, bodily responses, and failure to respond, as well as actual physical attempts to harm another. Aggressive behavior is not always the result of anger and, as we will see later, anger need not lead to aggressive behavior.

Aggressive actions—such as purse snatching or discipline of a disobedient child—may stem not from anger but from cold-blooded, rational motives (to get enough money to buy food, for instance, or to help a child distinguish between acceptable and unacceptable behavior). Some kinds of aggressive behavior are even socially approved. Supervisors are allowed to criticize employees bluntly for inadequate performance; teachers are allowed to castigate unruly students; and parents are expected to scold and sometimes spank their children for misbehavior.

Aggression. Hostile or injurious behavior toward another.

Anger can be heightened, however, by factors other than frustration, insult, or attack. According to a number of experiments, if people are angry, environmental stimuli can increase emotional arousal and make them more likely to respond aggressively. Teachers are more likely to lose their tempers, for instance, when the room is too hot or outside noise intrudes into the classroom (Rule and Nesdale). This finding has implications for marriage, for people in close contact are quite likely to annoy each other without even meaning to, increasing the likelihood that they will overreact to actual conflicts.

POSSIBLE RESPONSES TO ANGER

As indicated above, anger does not necessarily result in aggressive behavior. After it is first felt, anger may be either dissolved or sustained. It dissolves when we determine that what set it off was a false alarm. If a man bumped into you on a city sidewalk, for instance, you might feel angry at him until you noticed that he was blind. Staying angry under such circumstances would be inappropriate, and the anger would subside. People who are slow to anger tend to interpret potential insults as false alarms. Their anger is dissipated by thoughts like "That person said that because of being tired"

... "drunk" ... "worried about something else." But when anger is not interpreted as inappropriate, it will be sustained until the situation is dealt with or until the person becomes too exhausted to sustain it any longer.

Even when anger is sustained it may, in some situations, be suppressed. Anger is dammed up in situations in which releasing it in a flood could be disastrous. It's inadvisable to punch a police officer or insult your boss, no matter how angry you are. Some people suppress their anger in less disastrous situations as well, either because they are ashamed to acknowledge it or because they think it is better to turn the other cheek than to fight back. The alternative to suppression of anger is **ventilation.** Continual suppression may cut people off from their feelings, but unrestrained venting of anger may be harmful in other ways (Mace).

Catharsis. Cleansing oneself of an emotion by bringing it to consciousness and affording it expression.

The Effects of Venting Anger.   There is a popular belief—encouraged by some marital therapists—that explosive expression of anger, getting it out of the system, relieves tension and allows anger to wear itself out.

In this view, fighting is good for a marriage. Relationships have an unhealthy undercurrent of hostility when partners try to suppress their angry feelings about each other under a mantle of politeness. This undercurrent, it is thought, might some day explode between them. It also poses a barrier to intimacy.

This theory is based on the notion of **catharsis,** the idea that all humans experience anger which, if bottled up too long, may someday erupt explosively in socially dangerous ways. To keep this from happening, people should let off steam frequently in minor eruptions to keep the potential major blast from building up. Couples in encounter groups focused on **therapeutic aggression** are therefore encouraged to release their anger in verbal arguments and even in attacks on each other with foam bats.

Therapeutic aggression. Release of anger in verbal arguments and mock attacks under supervision of a therapist.

According to sociologist Murray Straus (1974a), the idea of catharsis or cleansing oneself of anger is a myth. Experiments tend to show that, if anything, expressions of anger actually increase the tendency to aggression. Straus, for example, asked 385 students to fill out questionnaires about conflicts in their own families during the year when they were seniors in high school. They were asked to indicate how often their parents had used either verbal or physical aggression to resolve conflicts. If the catharsis theory were correct, the higher a couple's verbal aggression scores, the lower their physical aggression score should be. But the opposite was true. Couples with low verbal aggression had low physical aggression scores as well. As the level of verbal aggression increased, the level of physical aggression also rose dramatically. Straus concluded that verbal aggression cannot be seen as a substitute for physical aggression, for the two are closely linked. The more couples shout, stomp, and smash things, the more likely they are to hit, push, and throw things at each other as well.

Straus had also asked his students to rate their parents' use of intellectual rather than emotional modes of conflict resolution. He found that the more couples used rational approaches, such as attempts at calm discussion, use of specific examples, and even bringing in outsiders to arbitrate disputes, the less likely they were to engage in physical violence. He concluded from his own and other people's research that the advice to use "therapeutic aggression" to restore marital harmony is the opposite of what research indicates as the best approach for restoring harmony.

Venting anger is inappropriate in a love relationship anyway. People will only have an open relationship if they feel safe in sharing. They cannot feel safe if their disclosures are likely to be met with insults, ridicule, or even physical abuse.

Mace reviews three common beliefs about venting anger and rejects them all. Some theorists advise that door slamming and angry gestures are useful communications. The message they convey is, "Watch out! I'm really mad now!" But as Mace points out, as creatures who can speak, we don't need to use such primitive means of sounding the alarm. Instead, we can simply say, "Look, this situation is making me angry. What can we do about it?"

Another theory suggests occasional fights are good because they give partners a chance to break away from the restrictions of the marital relationship from time to time. Intimacy can be restored later. But again, Mace writes, there is a more acceptable way to handle this problem. Even though distance is sometimes desirable as relief from the intense closeness of marriage, there is no reason why partners can't just tell each other that they need to be alone for a while.

A final theory is that couples find their intimacy more rewarding after they have been alienated by fighting. Some couples, for instance, find that lovemaking is best after a fight. Mace observes, however, that such couples are probably a minority. For most, venting anger is painful and destructive to an intimate relationship.

Managing anger. Conducting oneself in a controlled and directed manner so as to avoid the divisive effects of anger.

Managing Anger.   Since both suppressing anger and venting it may have harmful consequences, Mace suggests a three-step procedure for managing angry feelings.

The first step is verbal acknowledgment that anger is building up. Instead of angry outbursts or insults, what couples have to do at this stage is simply to say, "I'm getting angry with you." Admitting anger can be just as constructive in marriage as communicating other states of emotion—"I'm tired," "I'm hurt," "I'm pleased."

The second step in managing anger is to renounce it as inappropriate. Although anger sometimes helps us to right wrongs and to assert ourselves when we must, these measures should not be necessary in a loving relationship. Lovers are not enemies. To keep from making an enemy of the partner by attack, thus inviting a return attack, each partner can instead express anger as a personal problem. He might say, "I'm feeling angry with you but I'd rather feel affectionate. I don't like to feel this way." She is unlikely to respond angrily to this neutralized statement.

The final important step is to ask the partner's help in getting to the root of the problem and perhaps in negotiating whatever differences are found. Such a request is not likely to be refused, for it is in both people's interest to figure out why they are angry with each other and to try to correct the problem. If they have accepted and admitted their differences, working them out as calmly as possible should not destroy their bond, and may even strengthen it. Thus carefully handled, Mace feels, marital conflicts "provide valuable clues that show us the growing edges of our relationship—the points at which we need to work together to make it richer and deeper" (p. 136).

VIOLENCE BETWEEN MARRIAGE PARTNERS

Unfortunately, anger is a constant presence in many marriages and often erupts into physical violence. Gelles, for instance, made an in-depth study of 40 families known to police and social agencies, and 40 neighboring families as well. As reported in his book, *The Violent Home* (1974), conflicts involved actual physical violence in 55 percent of the families, including 37 percent of the neighbors, whose behavior had never been brought to the attention of authorities. And these are not isolated incidents of pushing and shoving. In many cases, violence is patterned and frequent, and often causes broken bones and cuts deep enough to require stitches.

THE MEANINGS OF FAMILY VIOLENCE

Violence can be defined as behavior which threatens or causes physical harm to another person. Anger can be dissolved, suppressed, or handled calmly. But anger may lead to aggression. And when aggression is expressed physically with the intent to injure or abuse, it becomes violence. Violence is not subtle cruelty—it is vehement behavior, usually marked by extreme force or sudden, intense activity.

Violence. Behavior which threatens or does physical harm to another person.

There is some disagreement on where to draw the line between violent and nonviolent behavior. Although some physical discipline of children is socially approved, child abuse is not. Spanking a disobedient child is not usually considered violence, but spanking with a paddle until the child is black and blue would be considered by most people to be violence. Or, to look at marital disagreements, if a wife tries to leave the scene of an argument, and her husband pushes her back into a chair while continuing to shout at her, is this violence or isn't it? If he slaps her on the face, is that violence? The answer might depend on how much it hurts.

O'Brien has defined family violence as "behavior which openly threatens the physical well-being of some member of the family" (1971, p. 694). It involves either the intent to injure, or behavior which results in physical pain or injury, or both. Breaking a child's arm in the process of disciplining the child is violence even if the parent doesn't mean to do it. Throwing a plate at someone is violence, even if you miss. And pushing and shoving is violence even if it does not result in physical injury.

Attitudes toward Family Violence.   Many people, including social scientists, have long maintained the image of the family as nonviolent. When violence occurred it was blamed on sick individuals. Even the husbands and wives involved in use of physical force seem to invent accounts of the incidents which define them as something other than violence. In Gelles' interviews, for instance, wives explained that their husbands hit them because they "deserved" it, and husbands related that they sometimes had to slap their wives to "knock them to their senses." However, family violence has recently been perceived as a widespread social problem, and intensive studies are now being made of **battered wives,** abused children, and hostility between kin. One of the factors behind this upsurge of interest is the women's liberation movement. Its leaders have chosen wife battering as one of their targets, seeing implied or real physical coercion as one of the sources of masculine power.

Battered wives. Women who are subjected to physical brutality by their husbands.

Violent Family Events.   Men are more likely to beat their wives than women are to attack their husbands, perhaps because of the typically greater physical strength of men and traditional notions of male supremacy. Wives are more likely to resort to weapons like withholding of sexual interaction or threatening to leave. But many wives are also violent. In Gelles' sample, 32 percent had hit their husbands. Their methods differ from those of their husbands, with husbands more likely to use direct physical strength to dominate their wives (by pushing, punching, or choking them, for instance) and wives more likely to try to overcome the strength imbalance by hitting their husbands with hard objects.

Many violent husband-wife confrontations are set off by disagreements over how their children should be disciplined. Typically, when parents feel their spouses are being unreasonably harsh, they try to intervene. One wife recounted trying to prevent her husband from beating their infants with a belt when they cried, by standing in his way; another recalled hitting her husband to distract him from slamming their teenage daughter's head against a doorway for coming home too late. Such interventions frequently lead to secondary violent fights between the spouses themselves (Gelles).

Violent fights are often related to alcohol use. Liquor or large quantities of beer have such a strong effect on some people that they are often said to be different people when they are drinking—nonviolent and even pleasant when sober, but extremely violent when drunk. As one wife put it, "When he was sober he was very, very nice, but when he was drunk, he was terribly irrational. . . . I can't begin to tell you what fear is. . . . He was a big man . . . very irrational, very ugly like 'Mr. Hyde and Dr. Jekyll' " (Gelles, p. 78). In addition to disagreements over discipline of children and alchohol-related fights, violence is often triggered by sexual jealousy. According to Gelles, men have no monopoly on jealousy-related violence, for men and women are equally aggressive in this area.

GELLES' THEORY OF FAMILY VIOLENCE

Despite difficulties in analyzing family violence, Gelles has constructed a theory which sheds light on this social problem. Violence, he proposes, is a response to stress, frustration, or threats to identity. Stressful situations which are especially likely to prompt violence are unwanted pregnancy, unemployment, religious differences, and the wife's having higher educational or occupational status than the husband. This last possibility has been studied in detail by O'Brien. Examining divorce cases, he found that violence is most likely to occur in families in which the husband fails to live up to social expectations that he be the clear head of the household by virtue of superior competence, especially as wage-earner. Compared to marriages in which no violence was reported, husbands who were said to be violent were more likely to be dissatisfied with their jobs, to have dropped out of school to bring home wages which seemed inadequate, to be less educated than their wives, and to hold jobs with lower status than their wives.

Gelles' second proposition is that families with less education, occupational status, and income, even when husband-wife status is equal, are more likely to encounter stressful events and have stressful family relations. Family violence is most common in the lower classes, apparently because their lack of economic and social support leaves them with few resources for coping with problems and conflicts.

Gelles' third proposition is that exposure to violence in childhood provides a learning environment for the use of violence. Although violent TV programs and other such stimuli are often blamed for teaching aggressive behavior, the available data on child abuse, criminal violence, and husband-wife violence suggests that violence is most likely to have been learned in family interaction with the parents as models. People who commit violent acts are likely to have been raised in violent families and to have been the victims of violence themselves as children.

Family violence is thus explained by a combination of stressful family relationships and the learning of violence as an appropriate response to stress. Since stresses tend to be greatest in low-income, low-status families, members of these families are the people most likely to engage in violence. This pattern may be repeated in each generation, for socialization to violence breeds more violence. Although violence occurs in all social classes, some individuals are thus more susceptible to violence than others because of their position in the social structure.

Because family violence is a major social problem, it deserves intense research, new legislation, and efforts on the part of social agencies to help the families involved. Recognition of child abuse has already attracted funds and some preventive programs. And here and there, shelter homes are being provided for "battered wives," offering these women not only a safe physical refuge but also support and reassurance.

ALCOHOLISM AS A MARITAL PROBLEM

Another problem frequently found within troubled families is **alcoholism.** It affects not only the person who drinks but all family members. The spouse and children are stigmatized as well as disturbed. And how they react may in turn influence the alcoholic's behavior. While there are many women who are alcoholics, most studies on the effect of alcoholism on the family have dealt with male alcoholics. Their drinking may make it difficult for them to hold a job, posing a more basic threat to the stability of the family than the drunkenness of a wife who remains at home instead of going outside to work.

Alcoholism. Excessive and usually compulsive use of alcoholic drinks, to the extent that overt behavior is affected.

Some studies blame wives for their husbands' drinking, suggesting that they are disturbed women who have chosen mates with a tendency to alcoholism to satisfy neurotic needs of their own. Whether this is the case or not, once they have been subjected for some time to the ups and downs of life with an alcoholic, they often become disturbed (Jackson, 1958).

These wives receive little economic or emotional support from their husbands. Because of their drinking, the men often lose their jobs or spend what they earn on alcohol, lose their grip on domestic finances, break promises, and ignore the children or else behave cruelly toward them. Their sex life wanes, as do their social contacts. When the husbands are drinking, they are prone to unsettling mood shifts; when they are not, they experience—and their families must endure—increasing nervousness as the urge to drink grows stronger (Wiseman, 1975).

The children of an alcoholic may fare even worse than the spouse. Their personalities are molded in a highly unstable environment. The alcoholic parent may act one way toward them when sober, another when drunk, and another when suffering from a hangover. Damage to the children appears to be minimized if the nonalcoholic parent understands their special problems, offers them emotional support, is as consistent as possible, and explains the drinking problem as an illness for which they are not responsible (Jackson).

RELATIONSHIP OF ALCOHOLIC HUSBANDS AND THEIR WIVES
Alcoholism is often associated with a peculiarly rigid style of interaction in marriage. Stephen Gorad (1971) studied 20 couples in which the husband was an alcoholic and 20 couples in which the husband was not. Using an experimental game-playing situation, he found that there were significant differences between the two groups in the way that the husbands and wives interacted with each other.

Drunkenness, Gorad suggested, puts people in a position of unusual power. Since they are not behaving normally or even rationally, they cannot be reasoned with and are not held responsible for what they do or say. When they are "not themselves," any countermaneuvers by others are ineffective. Drinking, then, is a way of keeping control of a situation—remaining "one-up"—without having to exercise any responsibility. Gorad has demonstrated that alcoholics tend to display responsibility-avoiding behavior in communicating with their wives even when they are sober. The wives of alcoholics, on the other hand, tend to be more direct, open, and willing to accept responsibility than their husbands. Although they are typically portrayed as domineering, they are no more so than normal husbands and wives. But they do differ markedly from their own husbands in this respect.

Instead of being able to cooperate for mutual benefit as normal husbands and wives do, alcoholics and their wives seem to be locked in a

Domineering. Exercising arbitrary or overbearing control.

continuous battle for control of whatever situation is at hand. Judging from the way they play his game, Gorad suggests that alcoholics and their wives refuse to relinquish their competitive stance because neither believes that the other is capable of changing. Even though they get nowhere by their rigid adherence to the same old one-up style of interaction, neither seems willing to take risks, as normal couples do when they try different styles of interaction to see if they can find one which is more mutually satisfying.

INDEPENDENCE FOR WIVES OF ALCOHOLICS

Torn between the desire to escape from an unsatisfying and disturbing relationship and guilt over abandoning a man who needs help, some wives seek divorce; others live in despair and isolation. But as Wiseman's research with Finnish wives of alcoholics has shown, there is another alternative—building an independent life without actually moving out.

In Finland, divorce has rarely been a workable option. Laws make it difficult, child support is not assured, social stigma is attached to divorce, a serious housing shorting leaves wives no place to go if they move out, income for working women is low, living on welfare is considered disgraceful, and there are social pressures on the wife not to leave her husband or take her children away from their natural father. With divorce almost ruled out, many wives of Finnish alcoholics have instead built up satisfying lifestyles which exclude their husbands. They may do so knowingly, or an independent way of life may simply evolve as the distance between them and their husbands increases.

Social stigma. A mark of shame or discredit.

In the first stage, wives step back from the difficulties of trying to rescue or live with their husbands and try to see what they can do to improve the quality of their own lives. Resigned to the notion that they cannot change their husbands, they think about how they might change themselves. After this period of self-examination, many determine to develop a new skill or improve their old ones. Often taking a job or upgrading the one they have is a financial necessity since the husband has lost his. As they concentrate more of their energies on their work, they spend less time worrying about their domestic life. And being gone for perhaps eight hours a day allows them to escape to a different world. Their employment outside of the home cuts down on the amount of time wives spend with their husbands. Some carry this arrangement one step farther and set up living schedules which rarely coincide with their husbands'. Although they technically share the same house, spouses keeping different hours may rarely see each other.

A final form of readjustment may be the wife's establishment of an independent social life. Her husband's drinking may have cost her their mutual friends and in-laws. To break out of her isolation, she may form new friendships with people at work and perhaps with other wives of alcoholics. Once alcoholics' wives have reduced marriage to the barest minimum—sharing a house and a last name with a husband with whom they rarely interect—and built somewhat satisfying lives of their own, a husband who manages to sober up may find that his wife no longer cares to build her life around his. She, too, may have problems readjusting to his changed status and to his expectation that she give up her independence. One such wife told Wiseman, "In the beginning, this change was strange, but I'm getting used to it and guess it will be okay" (p. 178).

EXTRAMARITAL SEXUAL INVOLVEMENT

Alcoholism usually damages marriages in which it occurs: extramarital sexual involvement may or may not. Although many contemporary writers are advocating sexually open marriage and current statistics indicate that extramarital sexual behavior is frequent, our social norms against adultery remain strong. It is widely felt that marriage provides an approved sexual partner, so that married people are not altogether sexually deprived, and that outside involvement threatens the marital relationship. Common terms used for adultery—cheating, infidelity, unfaithfulness—all have negative connotations. And extramarital sex is one of the most frequently mentioned problems in broken marriages (Bell, Turner, and Rosen, 1975; Libby, 1973; Johnson, 1970).

EFFECTS ON MARRIAGE
Sometimes affairs destroy a marriage and severely hurt everyone involved; sometimes nothing happens and no one is hurt; and sometimes extramarital lovemaking contributes to personal growth. The outcome depends on the attitudes of the people involved and the meaning they give to the behavior.

Researchers now make a distinction between extramarital sex, in which the behavior is concealed from the spouse or causes the spouse distress if discovered, and what Della and Rustum Roy, authors of *Honest Sex* (1968), call **co-marital sex.** In co-marital sex, both marital partners approve and expect sexual relationships outside the marriage as a basic human right they grant each other. These relationships are not thought to compete with the marriage; they may have no effect on it or they may even improve it (Libby, 1973).

Even when extramarital sex is concealed from the spouse, many people consider it justified for certain reasons or under special circumstances. According to a study by Ralph Johnson (1970) of 60 family agency case histories involving extramarital sex, the nine most common explanations for the behavior were: the spouse's physical handicap made sex impossible, the spouse was having an affair, the spouse was frigid or unaffectionate, the spouse was too fat, the spouse was physically unclean, partners were separated by long business trips or imprisonment or armed service tours, the

Co-marital sex. Sexual relationships outside of marriage with the consent and approval of the spouse.

CASE STUDY—TONY AND LAURIE

Tony and Laurie had married very young and in a short time had two children, both boys. Needing additional income, Laurie went back to work for the telephone company. She made arrangements for a sitter to come when she went to work at 3 P.M. Then Tony was supposed to take over when he returned from his job, letting the sitter go.

However, Tony had gradually gotten into the habit of stopping over with friends after work for a few beers before going home, and was often late in relieving the sitter, who needed to go home and fix dinner for her own family. Other times he would arrive home, feed the kids, then take them over to his mother's house for the evening while he joined his friends at a bar.

Laurie could never be sure when she arrived home where the children would be or where Tony would be. This disturbed her and she also felt discouraged to think of the money Tony was spending on drinks and social activities while she was struggling to increase their limited income. One day, a friend mentioned that Tony was not "out with the boys" but hanging around with a mixed group of men and women who seemed to have nothing on their minds but having a good time. When Laurie questioned him about this, Tony acknowledged it readily and bragged about what a good time they were having. A little drunk, he told Laurie he was having a sexual relationship with one of the women. His attitude was that he should not be expected to stick around home with the kids just because Laurie wanted the extra money her job brought in to buy fancy things for the house.

At this point, Laurie decided to make an appointment next day with a marriage counselor a friend had told her about. When she asked Tony if he would go with her, he flatly refused, saying he was not going to discuss his private life with any stranger, and forbidding her to do so either.

For class discussion: (1) Tony thinks the main problem in their marriage is that Laurie is too serious about everything and never wants to go out drinking with him. If Laurie started socializing with him and his friends, would this be a step toward straightening out some of their marital problems? (2) What might be some advantages to discussing their marital problems with a professional counselor? Would a close personal friend be a better choice?

---

spouse could not provide sexual satisfaction, the spouse felt that the only reason for intercourse was reproduction, and the spouse disliked sex. In addition to these negative reasons, some people would probably add positive reasons as well, such as strong feelings of affection or attraction toward the extramarital partner.

No matter how broad-minded they are about sexual freedom, couples are found to experience difficulty if one of them feels more affectionate toward the extramarital partner than toward the spouse. In such cases, it is the emotional rather than the sexual involvement with a third party that poses problems within the marriage. And if income is limited, the uninvolved spouse may also resent the spending of money that is needed at home on the extramarital relationship (Libby).

FACTORS CONTRIBUTING TO EXTRAMARITAL INVOLVEMENT

Lovemaking outside of marriage is not a random occurrence. It doesn't "just happen" to some and not to others. Certain factors have been found to predispose people to this behavior.

Happiness in Marriage. The biggest determinant for both men and women is whether or not they are happily married. People who are unhappy in their marriages are generally more likely to become extramaritally involved than those whose marriages are happy. But some who are unhappy do not have affairs, and some who are very happy do. Researchers have found that certain sex differences and other factors must be considered along with marital happiness.

Johnson, for instance, found that there is a stronger relationship between dissatisfaction with marriage and extramarital involvement for males than for females. Men who find their marriages unsatisfactory are more likely to seek outside sexual involvement than unhappily married women.

Bell, Turner, and Rosen found from the questionnaire responses of over 2000 married women that while 55 percent who rated their marriages fair to very poor reported some extramarital involvement, 20 percent of those who rated their marriages good or very good reported extramarital involvement as well. For women, whether they have liberal or conservative sexual views seems to be an important factor to consider, along with how they feel about their marriage. Those who have unhappy marriages combined with liberal attitudes toward masturbation, cunnilingus, fellatio, and anal intercourse are more likely to have extramarital affairs than those who are unhappy but sexually conservative. Being happily married is not always a barrier to extramarital involvement for women if their sexual attitudes are liberal; having conservative sexual attitudes is a barrier to lovemaking outside of marriage even for unhappily married women.

Sexual Satisfaction in Marriage. If sexual satisfaction is considered separately from general marital satisfaction, it seems to have a significant bearing on extramarital behavior. The research of Edwards and Booth (1976) and Johnson, for example, indicates that for both men and women, those who are satisfied with the rate of marital coitus within marriage are less likely to seek sexual satisfaction outside of it. Sexual and marital satisfaction are interrelated, however. As Edwards and Booth's research suggests, marital conflicts may lower the frequency of coitus. And serious strains in the relationship—marked by threats to leave home and the like—lower the frequency of lovemaking even more and increase the likelihood that partners will seek sexual involvement outside the marriage.

Opportunity for Involvement. A number of studies reveal that more Americans approve of extramarital sex, especially if it is not hidden from the spouse, than have actually engaged in it. Apparently, the lack of opportunity—of willing partners and suitable times and places—is another important variable distinguishing between those who do and those who don't.

According to Johnson's study of 100 middle-aged, Midwestern couples, the husbands were far more likely than their wives to have found themselves in situations where they could have had intercourse with someone else. But the men were also more likely to justify extramarital sex and to think that other people desired extramarital sexual involvement (considered an indirect measure of their own desire) than their wives were. These findings suggest the possibility that those who approve of and desire extramarital sex create their own opportunities for involvement.

Edwards (1973) has suggested a theory of how opportunity leads to extramarital sexual involvement. Frequency of contact and maintenance of a high level of involvement with people of the opposite sex—perhaps at work—cause these people to be seen as alternatives to one's own mate. The more attractive these alternatives seem, the more likely one is to feel dissatisfied with the existing marriage. The combination of attractive alternatives, opportunity for involvement, and dissatisfaction with marriage increases the chances that the extramarital contacts will become sexual partners.

HOW IMPORTANT IS SEXUAL FIDELITY?

Extramarital sexuality has traditionally been considered deviant in the United States because it is thought to disrupt marriages and violate the exclusive sexual contract which ensures that those who conceive children will raise them to adulthood. But intercourse need not lead to conception, since effective contraceptive measures are now widely available. Sexuality can thus be viewed as entirely separate from reproduction and child rearing. And as more open marital styles emerge, seeing extramarital sex as deviant because it disrupts marriages is no longer necessarily valid.

Deviant. Failing to conform to established norms and social expectations.

Some social scientists assert that it is unrealistic to expect people to forsake all others when they marry. Attractions to others outside the marriage, they feel, should be accepted and examined realistically by marital partners to see what degree, if any, of outside involvement their union can tolerate and under what circumstances it might be allowed. Insisting that two people cannot possibly meet all of each other's needs, these writers urge a more open view of marriage. Its structure, they feel, must be shaped by the unique needs and personalities of each couple if it is to remain vibrant and growing and allow them to develop fully as individuals (Libby).

Nevertheless, traditional sexual norms still persist. The double standard continues to allow men more sexual freedom than women, although this social attitude is changing with the recognition that women also have sexual needs and rights (Bell, Turner, and Rosen). Many people still view extramarital sexual involvement of a spouse as the ultimate disloyalty, even though, as the research cited indicates, infidelity is more likely to be a sign of marital failure than a cause of it.

DIVORCE AS A REASONABLE ACTION

Accommodation. The social process of adjusting differences in ideas or goals so as to avoid conflict.

Some couples are unable to manage their interpersonal conflicts. Some lack the skills, others the desire, to do so; still others are basically incompatible, and should never have married in the first place. The continuing process of interpersonal adjustment described in Chapter 10 may lead not to compromise, understanding, or **accommodation** of differences, but to perpetual angry standoffs. Violence, alcoholism, or extramarital sex may seriously alienate partners, and efforts to balance each person's needs for independence and togetherness may not work. Divorce is gaining increasing acceptance as a way out of such unhappy marriages. Despite the problems termination of marriage brings, it may be seen as a reasonable alternative to trying to keep an unsatisfactory marriage together. The current high rate of employment of women in paid jobs is contributing to this view of divorce. Where the husband's income might not be sufficient to maintain two homes, this becomes more feasible when the woman has an income also. More job opportunities for women means that both men and women have greater freedom to escape from poor marriages (Norton and Glick, 1976).

There is evidence that staying in a miserable marriage is self-destructive. McIntire and Nass (1974) questioned couples whose marriages seemed stable and happy and others whose marriages had lasted but were unhappy. Tested with personality inventories when they had been married about seven years, and again ten years later, individuals in stable-happy marriages scored far higher in various self-actualization measures than unhappily married individuals. Self-actualization is the psychological state of functioning to the full extent of one's abilities, fully expressing one's inner self with minimal evidence of mental or physical ill health. This research suggested that couples in stable-unhappy marriages are concerned more with seeking social approval or avoiding disapproval than with directly meeting each partner's individual needs.

Since mate selection is so unplanned in this country, so subject to chance and compromise, it is no wonder that many couples find their part-

© George Dole

"Mom, meet Janet. She's going to be my first wife."

nerships unworkable. According to demographer Paul Glick, many divorces probably stem from the fact that compatible mates are few and that a person simply may not happen to run across someone who would be an ideal spouse at a time when marriage is a possibility for both of them. To increase the chances that people will choose partners with whom they will be able to establish satisfying and enduring relationships, Glick feels there is a need for more scientific methods of mate selection. Meanwhile, people proceed by trial and error, with divorce—and perhaps remarriage—sometimes the only practical solution to mis-marriages. (Glick, 1975).

DIVORCE AS A PERSONAL CRISIS

Even when divorce seems the only solution to an unworkable marriage, most people are unprepared for the experience. There is no socially prescribed way to mourn a divorce, although the loneliness of separation may bring grief equal to what people feel if a spouse has died. Self-esteem suffers as well, for it is painful to be rejected or to admit to having made a mistake. Although the community can be counted on for active support when there is a death, friends and relatives are of little help during a divorce. The separated person is likely to feel very much alone in struggling with its problems.

THE DIVORCING PROCESS—SIX OVERLAPPING EXPERIENCES

Paul Bohannon, author of *Divorce and After*, suggests that divorce is so difficult to cope with because six different processes are going on at once. We will describe them briefly here and then look at them separately in greater detail.

1. *The Emotional Divorce.* The failure of a marriage is often signaled by what is called "emotional divorce," when people begin to withhold emotion from their relationship in order to avoid revealing the hostility or ambiguity of their feelings for each other. Although they may still appear in public as a couple, they are no longer bound by love and trust. In healthy marriages, people may grow in different directions but still be emotionally interdependent; in failing marriages, people become so antagonistic that they repress or reject any lingering emotional ties to each other.

2. *The Legal Divorce.* When the emotional ties between a husband and wife have become this thin, they must go to court if they want to cut their legal bond. Once they do so, events seem to take over, giving them the feeling that they no longer have any control over what happens. But the legal process serves only to establish the right of each partner to marry someone else. The actual separation has already taken place.

3. *The Economic Divorce.* Along with the legal severing of their marital bond, couples seeking divorce must agree on how to divide their money and joint possessions. They may have to work with lawyers and judges on this property settlement because of tax complications and their bitterness over not having enough resources to support two independent lives. Both partners are likely to feel cheated by the eventual redistribution of money and property.

4. *The Coparental Divorce.* Parents seeking divorce must also deal with the problem of who gets custody of and chief responsibility for bringing up their children. **Visitation rights** for the parent who does not get custody must be worked out as well. And since some clear provision must be made for their continued financial support, the details of the coparental divorce must be ratified by the court. Although they are divorcing each other and not their children, the parents are likely to worry that the divorce will hurt their children and feel guilty about what they are doing to them.

5. *The Community Divorce.* Everyone going through a divorce from a spouse finds that relationships with friends are altered as well. No longer part of a couple, the former spouses are left out of certain social activities and may even encounter active social disapproval.

6. *The Psychic Divorce.*   The former partners' attempts to turn themselves into single social individuals again are, for many, the hardest part of the separation. Years of marriage accustom people to thinking of themselves as part of a pair, so being single and independent again may be a difficult adjustment. Those who married to avoid independence in the first place are especially likely to feel frightened and lonely (Bohannon, 1971).

GROWING APART—THE EMOTIONAL DIVORCE

Conflicts of some sort occur over the course of every marriage. For healthy couples, disagreements can lead to a clearer understanding of their differences, negotiated compromises, and extension of their awareness of each other into new areas. But in marriages which are not working, fighting over problems like money or use of leisure time increases the distance between partners. Their lives increasingly extend into areas that do not include each other—business, community, work, recreation, and friends—until their relationship only occupies a marginal and not very satisfying place in their lives. But the realization that there is not much feeling left in the marriage may bring acute grief. Just as we mourn the loss by death of people we love, we feel deeply saddened by the loss of a formerly meaningful relationship with a person who is still living (Bohannon).

In an effort to postpone the trauma of separation, people often seem to put off divorce as long as they can. According to various surveys, the decision to seek a divorce may be reached over a period of two or three or as long as ten to twelve years (Rose and Price-Bonham, 1973).

Persistence of the Marital Bond.   The pain of separation doesn't seem to have anything to do with how good the marriage was. A study of widows and widowers revealed that almost all of them suffered intense grief when their spouse died, no matter whether their marriages had been very good, adequate, or poor. And people facing separation have reported that even though their marriages are unhappy, the idea of ending them makes them feel anxious, even terrified. No matter how unhappy the relationship, marriage seems to provide a feeling of security which people are reluctant to give up.

Once a marriage has been disrupted, most partners continue to be drawn to each other even if they no longer feel love or respect. They find this emotional tug disturbing and hard to explain, but they feel it nonetheless. Their shared experiences, continuous intimate contact, and interwoven habits have forged an attachment that is not easily broken. It doesn't seem to make any difference whether a person has been rejected or has done the rejecting—both are likely to feel the same anxiety at no longer being accessible to each other. Instead of being relieved by their escape from a burdensome relationship, they may feel restless, lonely, panicky, guilty over having caused the separation, obsessed with thoughts of the ex-partner, and overcome with the desire to be reunited (Weiss, 1976).

Anger. At the same time that it brings the desire to be with the former spouse again, separation often causes anger as well. Each spouse may see the other as the cause of the divorce. The one who initiated the separation or refused to try reconciliation is an obvious target for blame. Even the spouse who has done the rejecting blames the other, thinking that it was the partner's weaknesses or refusal to change that caused the relationship to break down. Ex-partners may be angry with each other over real conflicts of interest as well. The legal divorce proceedings—placing blame, property settlements, support provisions, child custody, and visitation arrangements —may pit them against each other as adversaries (Weiss, 1976).

Ambivalence. Uncertainty as to which course of action to take.

Ambivalence. Since separated spouses are angry with and yet attached to each other at the same time, their relationship is highly ambiguous. They cannot fully express both feelings at once, so they try to hide their attachment, hide their anger, or express them alternately. Sometimes they express different feelings in different settings. They may be angry adversaries in court, but friends and even lovers outside. Their ambivalence toward each other confuses the course of the divorce—they want it because they are angry and disappointed with each other, but they don't want it because they are still drawn to each other. On the other hand, this ambivalence stands in the way of reconciliation, too. When they are in a loving mood, they may try living together again, but soon the angry conflicts reappear (Weiss, 1976).

LEGAL ASPECTS OF DIVORCE

As we saw in Chapter 3, the termination of a marriage in the United States still comes under legal scrutiny. And despite the good intentions behind the insistence on legal proceedings—the intention to make sure that children will be well cared for after their parents separate, for instance—legal divorce proceedings may intensify animosities and personal problems experienced by people seeking to end unworkable marriages.

Divorce as Punishment for Fault. Our society's use of legal divorce began in Massachusetts early in the 1700s, with the state justifying its authority to dissolve marriages on the basis that by stepping in, it could punish the partner who was at fault. This concept of divorce as punishment of the offending spouse is still with us, even though marital breakup is rarely caused by only one partner. In order to place blame on the partner, the one asking for a divorce must express the demand for freedom in terms dictated

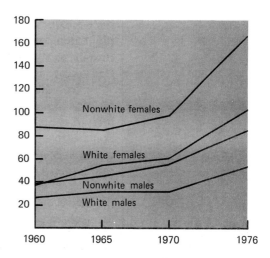

Fig. 14.1 Number of divorced persons per 1000 married persons with spouse present. The difference in number of divorced males reflects the greater tendency of males to remarry after divorce. Racial differences are thought to be related to the greater likelihood of economic problems as a factor in marital adjustment among nonwhites, though delay in remarriage may also be a factor. (Source: U.S. Bureau of the Census, 1977, P–20:306.)

by law. Instead of simply stating the unhappiness of the marriage, the petitioner still must, in many states, select one of the specific grounds for divorce recognized in that state, such as adultery, desertion, or cruelty.

The Right to Divorce. As is well known, it is far easier to get a divorce in some states than in others. The state variations in divorce laws thus discriminate against those who cannot afford to travel or pay expensive legal fees in order to dissolve a failed marriage. To give all Americans the same rights in forming and dissolving marriages, in 1970 a special national committee drew up a proposed Uniform Marriage and Divorce Act as a model for state legislatures to copy in reforming their laws. Among its other provisions, the Uniform Act recommends **no-fault** divorce, in which the only necessary grounds are irretrievable breakdown of the marriage.

No-fault. Settlement of a legal claim without regard for the question of which party is to blame.

The Uniform Act has not yet been uniformly adopted, although most states provide some version of no-fault divorce. Reluctant state legislatures may be prodded into further action by the Supreme Court, which has become involved in the question of the right to divorce. In 1971 it ruled in *Boddie vs. Connecticut* that inability to pay the legal fees involved could not prevent people from filing for divorce. The right to divorce, the Court ruled, is guaranteed by the due process clause in the Constitution. A state cannot restrict the right to due process unless it has an overriding interest in doing so (Kargman, 1973). In some states, people can now submit their petitions for divorce themselves, without the expense of hiring a lawyer.

Participation of Lawyers. Whether or not no-fault divorce, or dissolution of marriage, becomes widely available, there is still the problem that lawyers who handle divorce cases are not usually capable of counseling spouses in the personal problems they encounter. Although they are dealing with highly emotional situations, lawyers are generally trained only in law, not in family psychology and sociology. Many lawyers do not want to take on divorce cases anyway because they are time-consuming, but not lucrative or prestigious. Although the divorced are usually convinced that they have been overcharged, lawyers often feel that the fees they earn for handling such cases are much lower than what they could earn in other kinds of legal practice.

Divorce lawyers do what they can to offer guidance and comfort to their clients, but the fact that they must often work within a punitive legal system makes them contributors to the hostilities. For instance, marriage counselors have observed that once couples have been helped to define their differences in legal rather than emotional terms, they are much less inclined to seek reconciliation with each other. Once all the papers have been prepared, the actual divorce proceeding before a judge takes only a few minutes. Most cases are heard and decided within two or three minutes; few take longer than fifteen to twenty minutes. The brevity and superficiality of the judge's consideration of something so important and emotionally complicated comes as a shock to most people seeking divorce. Instead of being an emotionally charged event which allows participants to express and resolve feelings connected with the divorce, the court procedure is startingly impersonal and brief (Bohannon).

CHILDREN AND DIVORCE

Divorce of two people who are torn between their anger and attachment for each other is complicated enough; physical separation of one parent from the children as well, coupled with arrangements to somehow continue the couple's joint responsibilities to the children, may be traumatic. When a divorce is in the offing, parents may be too involved with their own hostilities, embarrassment, and distress to pay much attention to their children. But the children may be suffering emotional upheavals of their own—anxiety, grief, fear, guilt, and anger—and need the parents' emotional support. It is important to accept the fact that children will have mixed emotions about the divorce and to let them express these feelings honestly (Krantzler, 1973).

The emotional difficulties of children in divorce are intensified by the problem of divided loyalties. Parents with custody sometimes put strong pressure on children to reject the other parent. Torn between their attachments to both parents, young children may feel guilty about this, and try to hide from each parent the strength of their attachment to the other (Kelly and Wallerstein, 1976).

Are children from conflict-ridden homes better or worse off after their parents separate? There is no simple answer to this question. Kelly and

Wallerstein concluded that the divorce itself was not the central event in determining the child's response. Instead, a child was more likely to be influenced by a variety of factors related to the separation—the new family structure, continued disequilibrium or newfound stability, tension levels, the gratification or lack of it in relationships with parents—combined with the child's own **developmental needs** and personality.

Reviewing a number of other studies of children of divorce, Robert Weiss concluded that although divorce causes temporary distress, there is no evidence that children whose parents are divorced will suffer more emotional problems in later life than children from intact homes. In fact, few differences have been found between children of intact and single-parent households. Boys who are raised by divorced mothers, for instance, apparently learn the roles and responsibilities considered appropriate to their sex as well as those who have a father present as a model. Many parents report that after some initial anxiety, their children adjust to the new situation faster than the parents themselves. This is especially true when the parents, despite their own problems, make an effort to show that they are capable of managing their postmarital situation, of being good parents, and of keeping family life relatively free of stress (Weiss, 1975).

Custody and Support.   Perhaps the most disturbing thing about divorce for a child is the fact that one of the parents must leave the family circle. No matter how inept as a parent, that person is to the child someone whose absence will be keenly felt. Traditionally, custody was granted to the mother since she was assumed to be the more nurturant parent. But today, some men are taking custody of their children after divorce. Either way, the parent with custody normally has almost full-time charge of the children, with the other retaining visitation rights. In an effort to share both the burdens and the rewards of child rearing, some divorced couples have agreed to **joint custody** of their children. Some try taking them different parts of the week, some different years, or different seasons (with the father, for instance, having them all summer, or with parents changing places in the family home every three months). Some such arrangements are mechanically awkward and take the children away from their friends; some seem a bit more workable. But little is known of what effect these shifts have on the children (Weiss, 1975; Bohannon).

Which parent has custody and what arrangements are made for financial support are so important to the well-being of the child that some observers have recommended that children be represented by their own lawyers during divorce proceedings. Michael Wheeler, author of *No-Fault Divorce* (1974), notes that the child's best interests are beginning to take precedence over considerations of parental moral fitness in determining custody. (Mothers were sometimes denied custody, for instance, if they had

Developmental needs. Requirements for healthy, normal development of a human organism from conception to death.

Joint custody. The shared charge of children by a divorced couple.

Traumatic. Causing a disordered psychic or behavioral state through mental or emotional stress.

been guilty parties in the divorce action.) But he points out the danger that overinvolving children in the legal conflicts of divorce could be traumatic for them.

Sometimes parents themselves prolong their court battles long after their initial settlement is reached. The noncustodial parent may try to win custody by proving that the other has been a destructive influence on the children. The one with custody may have to get court approval before deciding, for whatever reason, to move the children out of state, since doing so will make it hard for the other one to see them. And people also bring their complaints about visitation privileges to court, with stories of the children's having been taken to bars or kept up late, ill-fed, and coming home sick or emotionally upset.

Support arrangements, too, can cause long-festering resentments. As discussed in Chapter 3, the economic problems of single-parent households are often severe. There never seems to be enough money to keep up with the needs of the growing children. Both parents are expected to help pay their expenses, but some are unwilling or unable to meet scheduled payments. Collecting support payments through the courts is expensive, slow, and sometimes ineffective. Continuing struggles over custody and support are apparently detrimental to children. A study of records from divorce courts and child-guidance clinics revealed that children from single-parent homes showed emotional stress if their parents' relationship continued to be stormy or if visits with the noncustodial parent were forbidden. In contrast, no children of divorced parents whose agreements on support and custody were mutually reached and mutually kept had needed help with emotional problems (Brandwein et al., 1974).

Children's Responses to Divorce.   To examine children's responses to divorce in greater detail, Kelly and Wallerstein began in 1970 to observe 131 psychologically normal California children whose parents were breaking up. Interviewed shortly after their parents first separated, the children were obviously disturbed by what was going on.

Most were very distressed at being separated from the parent who did not have custody—usually the father. Children of all ages seemed to feel a strong need for the father to continue playing a role in their lives. And despite the limitations of scheduled visits, many fathers had managed to do so, enriching and providing a sense of security to their children's lives. Most of the children studied wished their parents would get back together. Strong wishes for reconciliation may take the form of active attempts to bring their parents back together, or they may be expressed on a fantasy level with children secretly pretending that the absent parent is still with them. Preschool children are likely to feel that they were to blame for their parents' separation. They may explain that the father went away because they were too noisy or too naughty—and refuse to believe otherwise. Older children are less likely to feel personally responsible for the divorce, but for younger children, this anxiety is a common problem. Anxiety about their own future is another common reaction among young children. Frightened by the feeling of instability, they see the disruption of their family as a threat to their whole world. They fear that the family structure is no longer a safe refuge and that they, too, may be rejected (Kelly and Wallerstein; Weiss, 1975).

Despite these initial symptoms of psychological disorganization, children gradually adjust to the fact of the divorce. When Kelly and Wallerstein checked on their subjects a year after their parents had separated, they found that over half had returned to a normal developmental pattern. They were as lively and self-confident as they had been before the divorce, and their psychological problems had eased. A fourth of these children were already having trouble at school or home before their parents separated, and a year later their condition was about the same. However, the other fourth of the sample became progressively more troubled after their parents' separation. Their sadness lingered, their self-esteem dropped, and their relationships with other people were shallow and unrewarding (Weiss, 1975).

The Roles of Divorced Parents.   As discussed in Chapter 3, life with or without the children is not easy for divorced parents. In the case of the parent who has custody, role strain results from the effort of one person to do alone the various family tasks normally shared by two. On the other hand, single parenthood offers a life of greater independence. There is no one to countermand orders to the children, no other adult to have to cater to as they organize their life, no one to argue with about what to spend money on, no one to constrict their choice of friends. Free to make their own decisions, some adults clearly prefer the peace and lack of conflict of single parenthood, despite its loneliness and its burdens (Brown et al., 1976; Weiss, 1975).

> **Role strain.** Difficulty in carrying out the behavior patterns associated with a particular position in a social system.

As for the person who does not have custody—usually the father—separation means new freedom, but this may seem a hollow victory since it involves loss of contact with the children. And when he leaves the home, he loses his roles as final authority and symbolic protector of the family. Despite the frustrations, parents who do not have custody often manage to maintain a special relationship with their children and still support and influence their children's goals and interests. And they also give their children a sense of security by serving as what Weiss calls a "reserve parent," someone to fall back on in case anything ever happens to the mother (Weiss, 1975).

Ten Principles to Help Children of Divorce.   Weiss, in his book *Marital Separation*, has developed some suggestions for divorcing parents based on

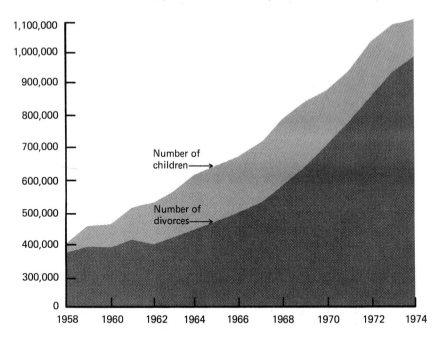

Fig. 14.2 Divorces and children involved: United States, 1958–1974. The couples that divorced in 1974 had an estimated 1,099,000 children under 18 years of age. The annual estimated number of children of divorcing couples has been above one million for every year since 1972. However, the average number of children per decree declined from 1.36 in 1964 to 1.12 in 1974, reflecting the overall decline in family size. (Source: USDHEW, 1976, Monthly Vital Statistics Report, HRA 76–1120 25:1 Supplement.)

a review of clinical research with children of broken families. While cautioning that his suggestions may not work well in all cases, he offers these ten principles to help separating parents help their children.

1. Children of all ages should be kept informed about the divorce. The evidence indicates that children whose parents had tried to explain what was going on showed less distress than those whose fathers suddenly disappeared without any explanations. Although there is no point in overwhelming children with information which is over their heads, lying to them about the situation prevents them from understanding it.

2. Since children are likely to be upset by the separation, they need soothing and reassurance. With adolescents, this may mean being sensitive to their feelings but letting them work out their hurt and anger on their own. For smaller children, it may be necessary to play with them more, be more available to them, or hire a stable caretaker who can give them emotional support along with attention to their physical needs.

3. A child who is still not back to normal a year after the separation may need special attention. Certain problems are normal to all children's development, but some may need help with troubles which seem definitely related to the divorce. A child might prefer living with the father

than the mother, for instance, or a different visitation schedule. If nothing else works, parents should seek help from a professional therapist.

4. The most important source of security for the child is the presence of a parent who is competent and self-confident as head of the household. The mother's ability to cope with her problems may help the children to deal with theirs. The noncustodial father can contribute to family stability by supporting her for the sake of the children, no matter what his personal feelings toward her are.

5. It is important for preadolescent children to have a parent's undivided attention some of the time. Although the custodial parent may be preoccupied with work, housekeeping, and building new friendships, it is essential to provide opportunities for communication with the children. Otherwise, they may feel that they have lost two parents instead of one.

6. Children usually benefit from continued contact with their noncustodial parent. If this person were to leave their lives entirely, they would suffer even greater deprivation than from the initial separation.

7. The children's world should be kept as stable as possible. They have already lost a parent; they should not lose other sources of safety as well. Taking them away from familiar friends, home, and school should be avoided, if possible.

8. Children need their parents' support in adjusting to the changes in their lives. The parents should try to help them feel comfortable with the new living arrangements and with their new relationship to the parent who no longer lives with them. If a move is unavoidable, they will need help in making new friends and coping with problems in a new school.

9. Children should be allowed to grow up at their own speed. There is a tendency in divorce either to initiate children prematurely into the adult world by making confidants of them, or to overprotect them from all risks and worries. Either way, children are diverted from the interests, activities, and problems which are normal for their age.

10. Instead of trying to live for their children, parents help them more by building satisfying lives for themselves. Parents who sacrifice too much for their children may burden them with guilt or feelings of being unworthy of so much sacrifice. And if they put all their energies into their lives with the children, they may find their morale slipping because life is insufficiently gratifying and, in the end, blame the children for their unhappiness.

RELATIONSHIPS WITH KIN AND FRIENDS—
THE COMMUNITY DIVORCE

Once the decision to separate or divorce has been reached, family and friends will be informed, but they may not offer much emotional support. Many people in our society still have mixed feelings about divorce. Should those going through it be encouraged to reconcile, criticized for acting irresponsibly, congratulated, sympathized with, or left alone? No matter how the community of family, friends, and coworkers reacts, their relationships with the ex-partners will undergo changes in response to the new situation.

Telling the Family.   If relatives do not live nearby, they may not know that the marriage is in trouble until they are told. People often avoid discussing their marital problems until after they have made the decision to seek a divorce. When they finally break the news, they may meet with various responses. Some families immediately offer help and moral support, some are critical and angry, some try not to get involved. Separation is still seen by some parents as a family disgrace. Siblings may worry that marital instability is contagious and that their marriages may be affected. Once the families know about the separation, the divorcing couple may find their status subtly lowered. They may no longer be treated as mature, responsible adults but as targets for unwanted advice on how to manage their lives (Weiss, 1975).

Returning to Live with Parents.   Despite their potential for making trouble, relatives may be helpful in ways that make a difference when a couple's emotional and financial resources are low. They may offer to help with the children, with meeting the bills, with meal preparation, or with household repairs. And they may even want the divorcing son or daughter to return home to live, bringing the grandchildren along. Parents' motives for offering their home as a refuge may include more than a simple desire to help. They may feel responsible for the unsuccessful marriage or for not having prepared the son or daughter properly for making marriage work. With the grown-up child back under their wing, they have a second chance to try to do things right. They may also want to make sure that their grandchildren have a good home. And having the grandchildren will give them a chance to play a nurturing role again.

For the separated mother with children, going back home has its attractions. It is a chance to have help with child care, to cut down on expenses, and to be with loving people. However, accepting the offer will usually mean a loss of independence and authority for her as well. Clashes over ideas about child rearing and other matters are likely to arise, so women who try this arrangement usually consider it a temporary one. Men who move back in with their parents after a separation don't seem to clash with them to the extent that women do. But for men, too, returning home means a loss of status, from head of a household to boarder in their parents' home. To most, living with parents is thus a matter of expedience, and a temporary one at that (Weiss, 1975).

Changes in Kinship Patterns.   According to a number of studies, divorce brings changes in the kin that people see and can call on for aid. Whereas interaction with one's own blood relatives remains at the same level after a divorce and may often increase, interaction with the ex-partner's family is likely to decrease. This pattern is especially pronounced among divorced men. Over 50 percent of the males in one study never saw their wife's parents again after the divorce, compared to the 14 percent of women who never saw their husband's parents. This difference in kinship contact reflects our general cultural pattern, in which contact with kin usually takes place through the women of the family. It also reflects the greater likelihood that the husband's parents will continue to offer financial aid to his ex-wife, helping in his traditional support role, than that her parents will offer to help him (Spicer and Hampe, 1975).

Unlike the divorced couple, the children have blood ties with both sets of relatives and might be expected to continue to provide a link between them. But interviews by Anspach (1976) with 128 married, divorced, and remarried women with children indicate that this is not necessarily the case. Some children seem to lose one set of grandparents—those on the noncustodial father's side—when there is a divorce. Whether they will continue to have close relationships with the father's relatives depends on whether they have contact with the father himself. In Anspach's study, 90 percent of the children who had no contact with their fathers saw more of their mother's family than of his; but over half of those who were in contact with their fathers saw as much of his family as of their mother's relatives.

Relations with Friends.   As with relatives, it is hard for the separating couple to know how to break the news to their friends. To say merely, "We've decided to get a divorce," is to leave them wondering what happened. To give too many personal details may expose more of the couple's private lives than they care to expose. This is especially true among work associates, but keeping the separation a secret becomes awkward also.

According to Robert Weiss, friendship patterns are almost sure to change once a couple decides on a divorce, especially among the network of married couples with whom the divorcing pair have been friendly. The initial reaction is likely to be one of rallying around to assist friends in trouble, and there is some choosing up of sides, depending on where the blame is being placed for the failure of the marriage.

After this first phase, a second phase occurs when married friends begin to recognize that the separated individual is moving to a new way of life, that of a single individual. No longer does a similar life situation provide them with conversational topics of mutual interest. Friendships maintained primarily through activities of the former partner, such as those formed through business associations, may be the first to go. Gradually a degree of social isolation sets in and the recently divorced person may be as cut off from community ties as if he or she had moved to another part of the country.

In the third phase, the divorced person begins to establish new friendships, and these are very likely to be with other divorced or separated persons whose problems and concerns are similar to his or her own. Ultimately, this new social life may become as satisfying as the old one, or for some even more so (Weiss, 1975).

BLENDING FAMILIES

Despite their problems the first time around, most divorced people eventually remarry. Men are somewhat more likely to do so than women, but the remarriage rates are high for both sexes: five-sixths of the divorced men and three-fourths of the divorced women in this country remarry sooner or later.

Remarriage. Marriage of a divorced or widowed person.

The fact that divorced women often have dependent children does not seem to account for the sex differences in remarriage rates. Although we might expect that women with children would have a hard time finding new mates who are willing to take them all on as a responsibility, remarriage rates for women with several children are about as high as those for women with few or no children. The main reason that more men than women remarry seems to be that men have more potential partners. They can choose from a pool which includes younger women as well as those more nearly their own age, while women are limited by custom to the available men their age or older. Men in our culture seldom marry women much older than themselves (Weiss, 1975; Westoff, 1975).

Falling in love again rejuvenates people who have been crushed by divorce. They look back on their first marriage as a mistake or a series of mistakes, a learning experience which prepared them to make a better marriage the second time around. However, second marriages end in divorce even more often than first ones. Second marriages involve stresses which were unknown in the first—interference by ex-partners, the complications of stepparenthood, reluctance of the community to accept the replacement partner, financial strain on the man of supporting two families—on top of the usual marital difficulties in getting along with each other. Despite their

unique pressures, there are many happy remarriages. But for those that aren't, the partners already know how to seek divorce and have demonstrated their willingness to use it as a solution to marital problems. This is also thought to be a factor in the high rate of divorce in remarriages (Weiss, 1975).

REDEFINING RELATIONSHIPS

Especially when there are children involved, remarriages suddenly swell the family tree, multiplying the number of people with whom one must establish relationships. If a divorced woman with children, for instance, marries a divorced man whose children from his former marriage visit him occasionally, the new relationships include those between the new husband and wife, the wife and the husband's children, the husband and the wife's children, the two sets of children who must at least sometimes live together, the husband and the wife's ex-husband, the wife and the husband's ex-wife, the new couple and the new in-laws on either side, the spouses' parents and their stepgrandchildren, and everybody with any new children conceived within the remarriage.

Stepparents and Stepchildren.   For the wife's children, gaining a stepfather means that they will no longer have their mother to themselves as they did when she was a single parent. But their acceptance of the step-

CASE STUDY—HELEN AND BILL

Bill was 38 when he met Helen, and until then he had never met anyone he had the faintest interest in marrying. They met through mutual friends at a rather large party, and it was only when he telephoned her the next evening that he learned she was a divorcée wtih four children.

Money was not an obstacle to their courtship. Bill was a partner in a flourishing law firm and had a good income. Helen received generous alimony and support payments from her former husband. The obstacle was the children. They had a close family relationship with each other and with their mother, and they saw their father regularly. They seemed to sense some threat in their mother's growing interest in Bill and resisted all his overtures of friendship.

After a courtship of about four months, Bill and Helen married, and Bill moved into the home Helen shared with her children. Their hope was that once Bill was a regular part of the household, the children would let down their guard and accept him as a member of the family. Before the marriage, Bill had tried being a pal, bringing the children gifts, but that hadn't worked. Afterwards he became a disciplinarian and tutor, thinking this was the kind of help and support his new wife needed. Finally, the eldest child refused a direct order and turned on him with, "You can't tell me what to do. You're not my real father." Helen was upset, of course. After the children were in bed that night, she and Bill had an open, honest, far-ranging discussion about what a stepfather might do to establish good relations with his stepchildren and just what his role should be in this particular household. They realized that perhaps they had pushed this new relationship too fast. They decided a family conference including all the children might help.

Next evening, the four children gathered in the living room with Bill and Helen, and Helen expressed in simple, direct terms her wish for them all to live together harmoniously. Bill, too, spoke simply and honestly of his desire to be friendly and helpful to them, and to assist their mother in their upbringing. Especially, he stressed that it was not his desire to take the place of their real father. The children, in turn, expressed objections to particular incidents when Bill seemed to them to have been too bossy or to have made unreasonable demands. This candid discussion cleared the air, and—over the succeeding months—formed the basis for the development of a more satisfactory relationship between Bill and his four new stepchildren.

For class discussion: (1) Do you think marriage to a divorced person with children would be easier if there were two children instead of four? What if there is only one child? (2) Do you think some distress and unhappiness might have been avoided if Helen, Bill, and the four children had had their family conference before the new marriage instead of after?

father is crucial to the happiness of their mother's remarriage (Weiss, 1975). In addition to redefining her relationship to her own children again, as she did when she was divorced, the mother must work out an acceptable way to relate to her new husband's children. She may want to be a friend, advisor, comforter, and supporter to them, but if she overplays these roles, their real mother may resent her interference. And as we saw in Chapter 13, both stepparents are likely to have problems disciplining and establishing authority over their stepchildren.

Reviewing the literature on step relationships, Lucile Duberman (1973) found several possible explanations for the difficulties stepparents have in establishing good relationships with their stepchildren. One is the Cinderella myth that stepparents are evil, a myth that children are likely to believe. But according to the surveys, stepparents are likely to be confused rather than malevolent, uncertain just what the stepparent role requires.

Another explanation is that American children are overdependent on their parents. They learn that their entire security depends on their parents and are never taught that other adults can be loved and trusted, too. As a result, they are unprepared to commit themselves to a stepparent.

A third explanation is that our society has no realistic specifications for the role of stepparent. What norms there are suggest that there are differences between stepparents and parents. But it is difficult for a stepfather, for instance, to be a replacement father to his stepchildren, for they still have a real father. Stepparents need a role of their own, as special additional parents, not as replacement ones.

Seen this way, many stepparents do manage to fill their roles as extra parents well, developing excellent special relationships with their stepchildren. Stepfathers are more often successful at this than stepmothers, and younger stepmothers are more likely to get along well with their stepchildren than older stepmothers (Duberman).

Stepsiblings.   Children of **blended families** must suddenly share with each other their parents, their rooms, and their toys, as well as their daily lives. They may experience the same jealousy and disruption of normal patterns children do when siblings are born, only more so. Friendship, or at least accommodation, between stepsiblings may develop only slowly.

> **Blended families.** Families formed by the remarriage of divorced persons so that stepparent and stepsibling relationships are established.

In Duberman's study of stepsibling relationships, less than a fourth were rated "excellent," with the rest evenly divided between "good" and "poor." She pointed out, however, that siblings don't always get along well, either. They often differ in age, sex, and personality and may see each other as rivals. Stepsibling relationships may be marred by the same factors.

Relationships between stepsiblings are more likely to be excellent if they live in the same house than if they don't. And they are more likely to get along well if the new set of parents have a child together. At any rate, the better the relationships between stepsiblings, the better the integration of the new family as a close-knit group (Duberman).

Cohabiting and Children.   While many divorced people establish joint living arrangements with friends of the opposite sex, often drifting into a relationship almost like marriage, those with children must give serious thought to the consequences of doing so. Lack of clarity in the roles each partner is to play can cause resentments about the fairness of the division of labor or the shared financial responsibility.

If a man moves in with a woman who has children, his relationship with them is something between what it was when he was only going with her and what it would be if he married her. He is not the children's step-father, but he has at least the authority of an adult guest. He can ask them not to make so much noise and he can stop them from being destructive. But he has no parental rights or responsibilities. Decisions about the children's upbringing and even about which TV programs they can watch are the mother's alone. Weiss suggests that adjustments will be better if the whole idea is presented to the children ahead of time and their acceptance obtained before the actual move takes place (Weiss, 1975).

GETTING HELP IN MANAGING FAMILY PROBLEMS

Families with problems usually struggle with them in private. Their attempts at resolving conflicts and remedying dissatisfactions are thus limited to their own resources and to the style of interaction which may have contributed to their difficulties in the first place. Though still emotionally attached to each other, some couples will separate because they see no other way out of their dilemma.

But it is possible that with some outside input, some restating and interpretation of their problems by perceptive and understanding friends or advisers, troubled couples might begin to work through their differences instead of ending the marriage in frustration. This would save everyone—including children—from the stresses of separation. And even if the couple decided to seek divorce anyway because their relationship was beyond salvaging, counseling might at least give them some perspective on what had gone wrong and help them to adapt to their new situations.

FAMILY THERAPY AS AN ALTERNATIVE TO DIVORCE

Conciliation. Reconciling of marital differences through counseling.

Troubled couples who go to lawyers to determine what their rights are may not be certain divorce is what they want, but once legal proceedings have been initiated, they may be swept along by events. Unless they have voluntarily sought help from marriage counselors, little is done to try to save the marriage. It has been suggested that applicants for divorce be required to seek **conciliation** through marriage counseling. Although this proposal would take money—for the states would have to set up good conciliation services—it would improve on the present system in at least three ways. (1) It would influence couples to try reconciliation, something the present system does not encourage. (2) It would allow objective examination of

---

AMERICAN ASSOCIATION OF MARRIAGE AND FAMILY COUNSELORS
Many troubled couples do not go to marriage counselors because they do not
know where to find the reliable ones. The American Association of Marriage and
Family Counselors, 225 Yale Avenue, Claremont, CA 91711, is a national organization concerned exclusively with marriage counseling. Members of this association include physicians, ministers, social service workers, sociologists,
educators, and psychologists. Standards for membership are rigorous, including
graduate training, advanced degrees, and supervised experience in the field of
marriage counseling. They will suggest qualified marriage counselors in the city
or town of the troubled couple.

---

their true problems in a more supportive and personal setting than the
courtroom. (3) It would demonstrate society's interest in supporting and
preserving family life (McHugh, 1975; Zuckman, 1975).

Demographer Paul Glick (1975) has another suggestion. He proposes
that married people be encouraged to visit a marriage counselor for periodic
marital "checkups," just as they routinely visit dentists and doctors for
routine examinations. If people could get used to this idea, going to the
counselor for help when major problems are threatening would seem natural
and appropriate, rather than awkward and embarrassing. Then, possibly
more people would make use of this resource.

FAMILIES HELPING FAMILIES

It is possible that many floundering marriages can be saved before they
get to the point of seeking divorce, before tempers are so high that reconciliation is impossible. Current efforts at divorce prevention include some
attempts to help families in a group, rather than a private counseling setting. We will briefly review three different ways in which families helping
families have helped people to achieve more satisfying relationships.

Network Intervention.   One method that has worked for some families
with problems they cannot solve on their own is to call in their close friends
and kin for group discussion of their difficulties. Uri Rueveni (1975) described the use of this process with a family torn apart by conflict between
the father and the 16-year-old son, David. The parents claimed that he was
not doing well at school and refused discipline, suggestions, and chores at
home. David, on the other hand, felt that he was growing up but still being
treated as a child. Distrust and physical confrontations, with dissent over
what to do marring the parents' relationship with each other, were so bad
that the father forced David out of the house. The mother then left to
stay with her sister. Both came back, but the problems did not disappear.
The father recognized that his family was in trouble and wanted desperately
for someone to help them resolve their difficulties.

Under the supervision of Rueveni and two family therapists, the family invited about 35 people—adult friends, relatives, neighbors, and David's peers—to their house for a series of meetings. Although the invited network seemed eager to help, the family's individual explanations of their points of view led initially to a generational split, with David's friends backing him and the adults backing the parents. But by the second meeting, David's friends had begun to press him to consider his father's point of view. David refused, and the meeting ended again in a standoff.

The hoped-for breakthrough happened in the third meeting. Rueveni suggested a mock death ceremony for the parents and David, to encourage network members to share their feelings about each of the three antagonists. The strategy worked, and the meeting ended with the three crying and holding hands. By the fourth meeting, the positive feelings their friends had evoked had led to active attempts by the family to work out a more comfortable relationship with each other. Their problems were not over, but the continuing active support and advice of a network of friends provided the impetus for ongoing efforts to help themselves.

Family clusters. Groups of families and unrelated individuals who share recreation and mutual support in the way extended families might.

Family Clusters.   In a less crisis-oriented experiment, people from a Dallas church tried forming artificial family "clusters" to supply each other with the emotional support that less transient families find in close kin or community networks. Each group consisted of about a dozen adults—some of them single or divorced—and their children. They agreed to get together regularly for fun, personal growth, and sharing of information, skills, joys, and sorrows in an atmosphere of mutual concern.

After several months of Ping-Pong, pot-luck suppers, campouts, kite-flying, group singing, sensitivity sessions, and the like, they evaluated their experiences. The cluster experiment, they agreed, had allowed them to get to know people in the group more intimately and honestly, made them aware of the goodwill in people different from themselves, provided contact with children for those who had none, given children the chance to be close to children and adults who were not in their family, and provided some insight into how other nuclear families operate. Although the intimacy established within the clusters proved to be no greater than that in good friendships, the cluster concept may be especially good for providing substitute network support when moves, divorces, or other changes prevent contact with a community of old friends or the extended family (Pringle, 1974).

A Prevention Program for "Well Families."   Another group experiment took place in New York City, where three family social workers (Papp, Silverstein, and Carter, 1973) set up a program designed to help families see the sources of stress in their relationships. It was offered for the "average family with everyday problems" that wanted to understand and revitalize its relationships.

The counselors thought their preventive methods were most likely to work if the problem interactions could be caught early enough. Accordingly, the experiment was not set up as "therapy" from a mental-health agency. Seeking professional help makes many families feel guilty and anxious and is generally used only as a last resort when all else has failed. By that time, problems have reached crisis proportions, and people have become so entrenched in their defensive positions that they may be unable to draw back from them to gain some perspective on what is going on. The "well" families who responded to the nonthreatening invitation often had serious problems, but these were felt as pressures and not yet as crises.

Since they came not to be cured or blamed but to learn about themselves, the participants were open to active involvement in changing their behavior. One of the basic ideas behind the experiment was that family difficulties can be reduced even if the behavior of only one person in the relationship changes. It is frustrating and unproductive for individuals to blame others, the social workers felt, rather than to change themselves. They tried to provide a safe, rather than threatening, atmosphere for self-understanding and change by concentrating not on problem individuals but on relationships, generational patterns, and family themes carried on from grandparents to parents to children.

The specific method used in these workshops was called **family sculpting.** To describe it briefly, it involved family members taking turns in arranging members of the family physically the way they saw them, and then rearranging them the way they would like things to be. A father, for instance, laid down and acted as though he were trying to swim upstream in mud, with his wife clinging to his feet, his daughter hanging onto his wife, and his son across his neck like a millstone. Asked to rearrange them to his liking, he tried standing up, but found that to do so he had to get his son off his neck, his wife off his heels, and his daughter off his wife's heels. After some intense symbolic interaction as each family member recognized what relationship was holding him or her back from standing independently, they finally ended up standing husband and wife, hand in hand, with the two children also standing, but at a slight distance.

In creating and redoing their living sculpture, the family members gained insight into the patterns that were causing their problems. But people's understanding their problems intellectually does not always result in their changing their behavior in ways that will resolve them. In this experiment in family therapy, as in the other two, the support, examples, and points of view of other families seem to have provided the impetus to change, sometimes alleviating family problems which might otherwise have led to divorce.

Therapy. Remedial treatment designed to cure bodily disorders or to bring about social adjustment.

Family sculpting. A method used in family-therapy programs to improve communication between family members.

Summary

1. The purposes of this chapter are to explore some marital problems which may lead to divorce, to examine divorce as a reasonable alternative to marital problems, and to consider ways of providing support for families with problems.

2. Marriages often fail because people don't know how to handle anger. Some marriage therapists believe that venting anger is good for a marriage. Others feel that there is a better way to manage angry feelings: acknowledge them, renounce them, ask the partner's help in getting to the root of the problem, and negotiate a solution.

3. Anger can erupt into violence which may cause physical harm to another person. Family violence is a widespread social problem often related to alcohol use, conflicting ideas about disciplining children, and sexual jealously, as well as to economic status, stress, and models provided in one's own upbringing.

4. Alcoholism of one family member affects all the others emotionally, economically, and sometimes physically. It is often related to other problems such as a struggle between husband and wife for control of the relationship. Spouses of alcoholics can choose to divorce, to live in despair, or to build an independent life for themselves without actually moving out of the home.

5. Extramarital sexual involvement is a frequently mentioned problem in divorce suits, but whether such activity leads to divorce depends on the attitudes of the people involved and the meaning they give to the behavior. It is viewed by many people as the ultimate disloyalty. For some couples, however, open discussion of extramarital relationships may contribute to personal growth and enrichment of the marriage.

6. In some situations, divorce may seem the best solution to family problems. In divorce, there may be six processes occurring simultaneously to which the individual must adjust. (a) Emotional divorce: repression or rejection of emotional ties. (b) Legal divorce: establishing the right of the partners to marry someone else. (c) Economic divorce: dividing money and joint possessions. (d) Coparental divorce: depending upon custody of the children, visitation rights, and financial support. (e) Community divorce: alteration of relationships with kin, friendships, and social activities. (f) Psychic divorce: turning oneself into a single, independent individual again.

7. When divorced persons remarry, they face some marital stresses and situations not found in first marriages, especially when children are involved. Relationships between stepparents, stepchildren, stepsiblings, new in-laws, stepgrandparents, and others may be difficult to work out.

8. Marriage or family counseling may help troubled families to cope with problems. Some types of counseling available for couples and for whole families emphasize support from family networks or family clusters and prevention programs for "well" families.

Companionate marriage
Anger
Frustration
Suppression
Ventilation
Catharsis
Aggression
Therapeutic aggression
Violence
Battered wives

Alcoholism
Deviance
Self-actualization
Ambivalence
Conciliation service
No-fault divorce
Developmental needs
Joint custody
Remarriage
Blended families

1. At what point in their relationship should a courting or engaged couple discuss their attitudes toward extramarital sexual involvement?

2. Should couples filing for a divorce be required to seek marriage counseling? Why or why not? Would such a requirement be an invasion of the right to privacy? If counseling services were available without charge, would more couples seek help?

3. What are the benefits and/or drawbacks to no-fault divorce? Do you think it is a good idea? Why or why not?

4. What are some of the ways in which divorcing parents can help their children adjust to their new situation?

5. Do you think family and friends should seek to become involved in helping a divorced or divorcing couple to work out a new relationship? Or should this be left to professional counselors?

BECK, D. F., AND M. A. JONES (1973). *Progress on Family Problems.* New York: Family Service Association of America.

A nationwide study of clients' and counselors' views on the services provided by family agencies. Reports were submitted on 3746 cases by 273 participating agencies. Contains many interesting charts along with the easy-to-read text.

EPSTEIN, J. (1974). *Divorced in America: Marriage in an Age of Possibility.* New York: E. P. Dutton.

Uses a combination of autobiography, novels, and social science literature to analyze why the divorce rate has increased. Reports on divorce from the male viewpoint and gives a picture of the author's life as a divorced man with custody of his children.

HETHERINGTON, E. M., M. COX, AND R. COX (1977). Divorced fathers. *Psychology Today* 10:13: 42–46.

Focuses on problems of newly divorced fathers and how they handled them. Three basic kinds of problems are those involved with the matters of day-to-day living; those associated with emotional stress and changes in self-concept; and those involving new definitions of relationships with ex-wives, children, and others.

KOCH, J., AND L. KOCH (1976). A consumers guide to therapy for couples. *Psychology Today* 9:10:33–40.

The authors point out some things to beware of and watch out for in the marriage-therapy market in general and sex therapy in particular. They also give some ideas of what to expect from therapy and how to find a marriage counselor.

SHERESKY, N., AND M. MANNES (1972). *Uncoupling.* New York: Viking Press.

Combines law, psychology, and sociology in an entertaining style to describe the process of getting divorced. Offers practical advice and information on what to expect during the divorce, legally and emotionally, so as to be prepared to cope with its problems.

Family Patterns in Middle Age and After 15

Forty-six million people in the United States are middle-aged (45–64) according to 1975 population estimates; another 22 million have passed age 65 and are living on in what is conventionally regarded as old age. Most of us will reach that age some day. But people in our youth-oriented society tend to avoid the idea of getting old. Some fear old age as something that changes people into sick, lonely, unhappy souls. This negative attitude toward aging sometimes extends to dislike of the aged themselves. Some older citizens are now fighting back, pushing for a better situation in a society which emphasizes youth and work and has little use for the elderly retired. Groups like the Gray Panthers and the American Association of Retired Persons are working to counteract the anti-aged prejudice and discrimination which pervade urban, industrial America.

The U.S. government has made some efforts to consider the needs of its senior citizens in its allocation of resources. Working people are required to contribute through taxation to Social Security, Medicare, and Medicaid benefits intended to help older people. Some sociologists note that the attempt by the government to take over the traditional family function of supporting the elderly may lead to a taxpayer's revolt of the young against the old. Because the old are living longer and births are declining, more old people must be supported by fewer young people and at inflating costs.

The concerns of the elderly are not only financial. They have emotional needs, too, just as younger people do. They are involved in interpersonal relationships, marital crises, parenthood, and sometimes even mate selection and communal living. This chapter will consider some of the special problems of the middle and later years, when the emptying of the parental nest, retirement, and eventually death of a spouse disengage people from their most important former roles.

THE DEMOGRAPHY OF AGING

Demography. The statistical study of human populations.

A common form of thinking about older people is to lump them all together. But the middle and later years span three or four decades, and there are dramatic differences between people aged 40, 60, and 80. In studying the older population, some sociologists like to classify older people according to their relationship to the traditional retirement age of 65. Doing this is useful for studying work and retirement patterns. Such a division of the middle and later years involves four decades by age:

1. Late maturity (45–54)
2. Preretirement (55–64)
3. Early retirement (65–74)
4. Late retirement (75 and over)

This division also fits conveniently into categories used by the Census Bureau in presenting its statistics on factors other than retirement. Using these age and retirement categories as markers for significant decades in later life, researchers can make some generalizations about what usually happens at each age level.

SOCIAL CHARACTERISTICS OF OLDER PEOPLE

During late maturity (45–54), 90 percent of Americans have been married at least once and the great majority of them live in their own homes with a spouse. More than half still have a child under 18 living at home, but this is the time of the "launching" process of watching offspring leave the parental nest. In terms of developmental tasks, parents must at this point disengage themselves from their children and reconsider their bonds with each other.

During the preretirement years (55–64), most people still live with their mates, in their own homes, but many, especially women, are widowed in this period. The relationship with their children has now changed from full responsibility to recognition that they are building independent lives of their own. During these years, health is still usually good enough that couples can enjoy leisure activities together; many begin to plan what they will do when they retire, and also to face the idea that one of them will be left alone when the other dies.

In the family of early retirement (65–74), the gap between the number of surviving men and women increases. Those who are still together, and have enough money, may enjoy new freedom to do whatever they please; for others, retirement is an unhappy struggle with boredom, loss of self-respect, and poverty.

By late retirement (over 75), less than 28 percent of women still have husbands living, dropping to less than 11 percent when they reach 85. This is a time of deteriorating health and increasing dependence on others, whether they like it or not, for residence, financial support, or at least the bulk of their emotional attachments as they gradually become disengaged from the rest of society (Thompson and Streib, 1961).

Although age categories are helpful in predicting the chances of survival of a spouse and other aspects of life for different segments of the older population, studies of their happiness, health, intelligence, and personality characteristics have shown that age is a relatively poor guide to the differences between people. The age of 65 was chosen as the time for retirement during the Great Depression of the thirties, when unemployment was high and it seemed to social planners better to pension off the older generation so more jobs would be available for young people. Thus the choice was based on economic and manpower considerations of the times rather than any indications that people themselves change dramatically

Categories. Divisions within a system of classification.

when they reach 65. Some retain their youthful outlook and vigor far longer; some begin to withdraw from life long before then (Neugarten, 1971).

THE FAMILY LIFE CYCLE

Some sociologists prefer to trace patterns of behavior which distinguish groups of older people according to where they are in the family life cycle. Vital events which constitute the ebb and flow of family life, rather than work and retirement, are used as marking-off points. For instance, one such division is:

1. Birth of the first child
2. Birth of the last child
3. Marriage or permanent departure from home of the last child
4. Death of one spouse
5. Death of second spouse

Some researchers add more stages, according to where the children are in their progress through school, for instance. In the division given here, the median age in the first three stages is controlled to some degree by the couple themselves and by the marital trends of their children; the timing of the last two stages is generally beyond their control.

As we have seen in Chapter 4, sociologists sometimes group people into these life-cycle stages by cohorts, all those who are born at the same period of time. Figure 4.1, showing trends in the median age of mothers at selected stages of the family life cycle, is an example of the use of this technique. The cohort concept is important because the people it refers to experience the same public and historical events at about the same period in their personal lives. For example, all women born in 1928 were about 18 years old when the soldiers came home at the end of the Second World War. Many of them married in the peak marriage year of 1946 and became mothers in a **baby boom** which lasted from 1946 to 1957. Their behavior is thus to some extent explained by the year in which they were born.

In order to draw a general picture of the timing of marriage, child-bearing, launching, and widowhood, studies of the family life cycle are based on certain assumptions about the typical family: (1) it consists of a man and a woman who remain married to each other until one of them (usually the husband) dies; (2) the wife has given birth to the average number of children born to all women in her cohort; (3) she marries and has children according to the median time schedule for all ever-married mothers in her cohort (Norton, 1974). Even though these assumptions do not always fit individual family patterns, they provide a standard or norm for statistical analysis of the life patterns within a cohort and reveal changes between cohorts. On the basis of these assumptions, if your mother was

Baby boom. An abnormally high number of births relative to the size of the population.

CASE STUDY—AL AND IRIS

Al and Iris married in 1943, in the midst of World War II, and after 35 years they both feel things have worked out pretty well for them. Though they were separated only a few months after marriage when Al was shipped overseas by the Army, Iris was already pregnant. When Al returned home, he was greeted by a sturdy two-year-old son. Later, there was a daughter and another son. All three children have married and now have children of their own. The only big quarrels Al and Iris have ever had were because Al has a tendency to drink a little too much. Once or twice he had been laid off from construction work for drinking on the job.

Now in his late fifties, Al is thinking about how he wants to spend his time after retirement. With maximum Social Security benefits, a substantial investment in the union pension fund, and some savings, he and Iris should be able to get by comfortably. Part of Al's plan is to sell the house they've lived in for 30 years, invest some of the proceeds in a nicely fitted out mobile home, and take off to see the U.S.A. He especially wants to check out what's happening in Alaska. Iris is interested in travel, too, but not in selling their home. Her five little grandchildren are the major focus of her life now, and she wants to be in touch with them through frequent visits and exchange of gifts.

Al says, "We have to do this while we still have our health." Or, "I've been tied down long enough by having to support you and the kids." Iris says, "The grandchildren will be grown up soon enough and off on their own. I want to be here in case they need me." But she is sure that, in the end, Al will have his way, because that's how it's always been in their marriage.

For class discussion: (1) Should the fact that Al has always been the one to provide financial support for the family give him more authority in making family decisions? (2) If Iris simply gives in to Al's wishes, instead of seeking some sort of compromise plan, what consequences might this have for their relationship?

in the ten-year cohort born from 1930–1939, she was likely to have married when she was 20, had her first child when she was 21.4, and her last child when she was about 31. She will marry off her last child when she is about 52, lose her husband when she is about 64, and die when she is about 68, according to current statistical projections (North, 1974).

These median ages are for ever-married mothers of all races; white women in the cohort born from 1930–1939 are likely to be 51 when their last child marries, while nonwhite mothers are likely to be 53 before this happens. At the same time, nonwhite mothers in this cohort started their childbearing earlier, sometimes even before they married. Their median age at first marriage was 19.7; they were statistically likely to have been 19.6 at the birth of the first child (Norton). Such statistics, of course, give only a broad picure of childbearing among U.S. women. The actual life histories of individual women are submerged in whatever figure is used to represent the "average" person.

FAMILY LIFE AFTER AGE FORTY-FIVE

It is difficult to generalize about the emotional quality of American life in later years. On the one hand, depression is so great among some of the aged that older people account for a higher rate of suicide than any other age group in the country. Twenty-five percent of all suicides are committed by people over 65, with the suicide rate reaching its peak in men over 85 (Smith, 1973). On the other hand, couples in their early postparental years with all children over 17 are reportedly one of the happiest groups of adults in America (Campbell, 1975).

Are most of America's older people lonely, useless, and unhappy, or are they happily involved with relatives and work or with other meaningful substitute relationships?

THE STATISTICAL PICTURE

In 1900, only 4.1 percent of the population had lived to age 65 or older, the phase of life conventionally regarded as "old age." But in 1975, over 10.5 percent of Americans fell into this age bracket, for there were 22.4 million people over 65 out of a total population of 213.1 million (U.S. Bureau of the Census, *Statistical Abstract of the U.S., 1976*).

When the population born during the baby boom reaches 65 around the turn of the century, the proportion of older people may rise to almost 13 percent (Rosenberg, 1970). And until our population stops growing, there will continue to be an increase in the total number of older people.

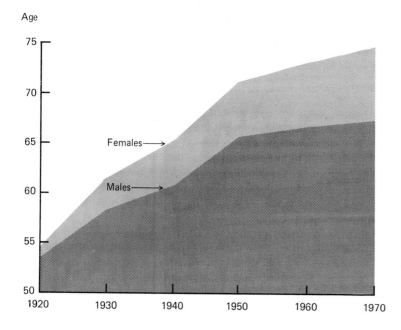

Fig. 15.1 Life expectancy in the United States, 1920 to 1970, by sex. Persons born in 1920 could expect to live, on the average, to the age of 54. Those born in 1970 are likely to live out the three score years and ten allotted in the Bible. However, life expectancy has increased at different rates for men and women. In 1920, women lived on the average one year longer than men. In 1970, the difference was almost eight years. (Source: U.S. Bureau of the Census, *Statistical Abstract of the United States, 1976*.)

Life Expectancy.   In 1920, the average **life expectancy** for Americans was 54.1 years; by 1974 it was 71.9. Over the last 50 years, there has been an increase of about 18 years in the average life span (U.S. Bureau of the Census, *Statistical Abstract of the U.S.*, 1976). Along with this dramatic increase in longevity, the **survival gap** between men and women has widened, as shown in Fig. 15.1. Women in 1974 had a life expectancy of 75.9 years, compared to 68.2 years for men. Scientists speculate that genetic differences between males and females, along with differences in the way males and females live their lives, are responsible for this survival gap. Both men and women are being kept alive longer through increased control over fatal childhood diseases, but male mortality exceeds female mortality by 100 percent or more for seven major causes of death: coronary heart disease, lung cancer, emphysema, motor vehicle and other accidents, cirrhosis of the liver, and suicide (Waldron and Johnston, 1976).

Life expectancy. A statistical expression of the average number of years lived by members of a given population.

Widowhood.   Since women tend to marry men an average of three years older than themselves, they now face the prospect of 10 or 11 years of widowhood at the end of their lives after their mates die. Over half of the women over age 65 in this country (52 percent of white women, 64 percent of black women) are widowed, compared with 14 percent of white men and 23 percent of black men (U.S. Bureau of the Census, 1974, *Current Population Reports*, P-23:57).

Survival gap. A term for the difference, on the average, between the life expectancy of women and that of men.

One reason widows are less likely to remarry than men who lose their wives is that there are fewer partners available to the women. Whereas in 1910, there were 101.2 men over 65 to every 100 women in that age group, the imbalanced sex ratio has swung so far in the opposite direction that by 1970 there were only 72.2 men over 65 per 100 females of that age (U.S. Census: 1970). Widows who would like to remarry are restricted not only by the scarcity of long-lived men but also—like the divorcées described in Chapter 14—by the cultural double standard regarding remarriage. It is considered quite acceptable for older widowers to marry younger women, but not for older widows to marry younger men. After the age of 55, men are five times as likely to remarry as women. The loss of a marital relationship thus is a more permanent event for women than for men.

Poverty.   Being left alone is not the only social problem of aging which affects women more heavily than men. An estimated 3.3 million people over 65 were living on incomes below the poverty level in 1975. Of over 2 million single or no longer married aged living below the poverty level, women outnumber men by more than four to one. This means that their income is below a figure established by the Social Security Administration as sufficient to provide a nutritionally adequate diet. The figure is adjusted yearly to allow for variations in prices. (U.S. Bureau of the Census, *Statistical Abstract of the United States: 1976*).

Being both old and poor brings other deprivations besides **malnutrition.** Compared to the aged rich, those who are poor are less healthy, less active, and more isolated from friends and family. Analysis of data on life satisfaction among older people reveals important links between life satisfaction and health, economic resources, and independence in later life (Watson and Kivett, 1976). A study of 6000 working-class people revealed that fully one-third of those who were over 65 and living on less than $3000 a year had not visited or spoken to a single friend or neighbor during the week before they were interviewed (Hochschild, 1973). However, the lives of the old should be improving, for in 1960 over 35 percent of those 65 and older fell below that year's low-income level, compared to 15 percent below poverty level in 1975 (U.S. Bureau of the Census, *Statistical Abstract of the U.S., 1976*). Social Security payments are largely responsible for the increased income level of the aged. In 1950, there were 1,771,000 Americans over 65 receiving retirement benefits. In 1975, many had qualified for retirement benefits by the age of 62, and 16,588,000 retired workers were receiving Social Security benefits (U.S. Bureau of the Census, *Statistical Abstract of the U.S., 1976*).

Living Arrangements. About 14 million households are headed by persons 65 years old or older. Although 18 percent of all families in the United States have at least one member who is 65 years old or older, the trend in the last two decades has been for older citizens to head their own households, whether as head of a family or as an individual living alone. Females living alone represent 34 percent of the households headed by persons over 65; males living alone represent 10 percent. Husband-wife households total 46 percent, and the other 10 percent represent households of two or more persons, such as brother-sister households or households including a nonrelative but with no spouse of the head of the household present.

Of more than a million persons over 65 living in public and private institutions, eight out of ten are in homes for the aged and another one out of ten are in mental hospitals and residential treatment centers. The remainder are hospitalized for physical reasons or are inmates of correctional or other institutions (U.S. Bureau of the Census, 1974, *Current Population Reports,* P-23:57).

KINSHIP STRUCTURE

Several decades ago, sociologists suggested that nuclear families in this country—young husbands and wives with their children—were cutting themselves off almost completely from their parents and grandparents. If this were true, the older parents would have only each other for family. Death of one would leave the other without any family at all. But according to sociological studies made during the 1950s and 1960s, this does not seem to be happening. After examining these surveys, Troll (1971) concluded that they point to the prevalence of a modified form of the extended family in which married offspring and their older parents keep in touch through close residence, visiting, and mutual aid. (This idea has been mentioned previously in the brief discussion of the trend to the conjugal family at the end of Chapter 1.) Troll suggests that the strength of kinship ties in the later years can be measured in terms of numbers of available kin, how close they live to each other, the extent of aid in the form of money or services, and indications of emotional closeness.

Number of Kin. Only 3 percent of people over age 65 who are not in institutions have no living relatives. Although mourning for family and friends who die off more rapidly as one approaches old age is a source of continuing pain for the elderly, few are left with no kin at all. Even though those of their own age may be gone, some older people nonetheless enjoy being at the top of a pyramid of descendants. Many older women keep a large supply of birthday and anniversary cards ready for the constant string of family events involving their children, grandchildren, and great-grandchildren.

The number or degree of relationships between kin may be less important than the nature of their interaction. For instance, a widow whose only child visits her once a week or whose cousin lives nearby may be richer in emotional support from kinship ties than one whose five children have married, moved far away, and rarely even telephone (Troll).

RESIDENTIAL CLOSENESS

The number of kin must thus be considered in relation to other factors. One of these is how close to each other relatives live. Degrees of geographical closeness may range from living in the same house or apartment building, living on the same block, or living close enough for an older person to walk between the two households, to residence within a half-hour's bus ride, within the same city, a few hours' drive away, or beyond convenient driving distance.

According to most surveys on housing for the aged, older Americans would rather live in their own homes than live with their children. Especially in urban areas, modern homes are likely to be too small for comfortable three-generation residence. Changing ideas about how children should be raised often cause conflicts between young parents and their parents if they live together. The grandparents are usually welcome to help with the care of the grandchildren, but in matters of their upbringing, the advice and interference of the older generation are often unwanted. The grandparents are probably no more eager than the parents for squabbles over child rearing, and, at any rate, they prefer to live as heads of their own households.

Although most older Americans prefer not to live with their children, some have to anyway, either because they cannot afford to live alone, are not healthy enough to care for themselves, or are just plain lonely. These joint households are not true three-generation families, however, because they usually consist of postparental couples and their aged parents. The grandchildren have usually grown up and moved away before the grandparents find it necessary to move in. Only 8 percent of the families in America are truly three-generational, with children, parents, and grandparents all living together in one house.

Even though they don't like to live with their children, older Americans do tend to live near them, especially in urban working-class families. According to a 1968 research report with Ethel Shanas as the senior author (cited by Troll), 84 percent of those over 65 in three industrial societies—the United States, England, and Denmark—live within an hour's traveling time of one of their children. There are indications, however, that during the middle years, when parents are middle-aged and their children are just starting families of their own, the generations are likely to keep greater geographic distance between themselves. This pattern seems to be strongest in middle-class families. But some years later, after the parents have retired, they tend to move back near one or more of their children (Troll).

Frequency of Interaction.   No matter how far from each other family members may live, they tend to contact each other often. Even middle-class families in which parents live too far from their children for weekly visits nonetheless keep in touch through letters, phone calls, and occasional extended visits. Eight-four percent of older Americans in the Shanas study had seen at least one of their children within the week, and 90 percent within the month. Older middle-class Bostonians in another survey contacted one-third of all their available relatives at least once a month. And despite the previously mentioned trend for middle-aged, middle-class parents to live some distance from their children, there is more visiting between middle-aged parents and their children than between any other age groups. Seventy percent of middle-aged parents in one study see their married children weekly, 40 percent see their own parents weekly, but only 10 percent of married young adults see their grandparents weekly. However, frequency of interaction is not in itself a reliable guide to family closeness. Children may feel obliged to take turns checking to see if an aging mother is all right without ever really communicating with her on an intimate level. Although one-third of the sons in one study who felt close to their parents visited them often, a third of those who felt distant did so too (Troll).

Generation. A group of individuals born and living in the same period of time.

Measures of Family Closeness.   Feelings of kinship strength are so subjective that no one has yet figured out how to measure them, except by indirect methods such as asking people to compare their closeness to relatives with attachments to friends. Such findings are still inconclusive, but suggest that people generally seem to feel closer to their children and their parents than to their friends. The long-term relationships between close kin are characterized by intimacy, concern, and feelings of obligation (Bahr and Nye, 1974). Friendships, on the other hand, may be held together by mutual values and interests. But unlike kinship ties, they may not survive over long periods of time and geographical separation. Friends, as equals, sometimes seem to take the place of siblings who have died, but they are less likely to act as emotional replacements for the dependent parent-child bond when a child dies. And despite the much-publicized generation gap, the traditional conflict in values between middle-aged parents and their college-aged children, family members are more likely to hold the same opinions than people of the same age who are not related (Troll).

Individual differences in the strength of the family bonds are often related to gender, stage of the family life cycle, social class, and geographic mobility. In adulthood, kinship ties seem to be strongest between women. Wives are expected to keep up correspondence with kin folk. They are the communicators in traditional family life (Bahr and Nye). Couples are more likely to live near the wife's parents and to get together with the wife's relatives: mutual aid and affection seem to be strongest between the women. Widows are more likely to move in with one of their children—usually a daughter—than are widowers. And even if women do not share the same values as their parents, they are more likely than men to feel close and visit often.

Social class does not seem to make as much difference in interaction frequency as the tie of female to female. Members of working-class families tend to live near and visit each other often; although middle-class families are more geographically scattered, they manage to maintain frequent contact in spite of their distance. When middle-class nuclear families move away from their relatives, they do not do so to get away from them but to further their careers. Working-class families usually do not need to move in order to find jobs and, therefore, tend to live closer to family.

Mutual Aid.   Many sociologists use the amount of economic interdependence as a measure of kinship strength. Mutual aid between generations may take the form of money and gifts or services, such as babysitting, housework, and shopping. Studies of whether more of this help flows from the young to the old or vice versa have produced conflicting results, from which Troll, in her comprehensive review of research on living patterns of

Generation gap. The difference in values and points of view often found between succeeding generations.

the older population, has extracted two general patterns: there is usually a flow of aid from the old to the young, but parents in the middle years give both to their children and to their aging parents. In general, parents seem to keep giving aid to their children as long as they can, until health or financial problems make this impossible. Families who live far from each other find it easier to exchange gifts than services. The middle-class old give money and gifts; the working-class gives services. Middle-class parents keep helping their children into old age; in blue-collar families, the middle-aged generation is more likely to help its older parents than the other way around. Such giving is greatest at the extreme income levels. The very rich have plenty to give, and they do so through gifts and divisions of property; the very poor need and ask for help from their kin. Social Security has made a difference in this pattern, for it has enabled the old to be more independent of economic support from their relatives. Except in cases of extreme need, the value of the aid may be more symbolic than real, as an indicator of affection (Troll).

FAMILY RELATIONSHIPS

There is a cultural expectation in the United States that when children marry, they will set up an independent household and rear their children by themselves according to the latest ideas on the subject. There supposedly should be no interference from the grandparents, who are frequently considered a bad influence, capable of disrupting the new family and interfering with the development of its children. However, most new couples actually live fairly close to both sets of parents, visit them often, and receive considerable help in the form of money and services like babysitting.

Statistically, grandparents are younger than they used to be, with earlier marriage, childbirth, and child launching making grandparents of people when they are middle-aged and still active rather than elderly and retired. It is the possibly still-living 70–80-year-old great-grandparents in the family who come closer to the rocking chair image, and who may receive as much of the grandparents' attention as do their grandchildren.

Grandparents vary considerably in terms of how they feel toward their grandchildren. Some seem to be glad to see them come and glad to see them go; some have strong ties of love and affection; and some see their grandchildren as allies against the parental generation in between. Grandparenting gives some a sense of purpose after they have retired from other life roles.

Unlike cultures in which reverence for the aged is automatic, in the United States we grant the status of valued grandparent only to those who have earned it by their personal qualities. Closeness to grandchildren and acceptability to parents is a matter both of cultural traits and of personality. Different people approach the role of grandparent in different ways. Some

Six-months-old Jemmy Tung and her grand-mother, Leong Toke Yon, are watching a balloon rise into the sky above a city playground in Boston.

are formal, some are fun-seeking, some try to be substitute parents (some-times against the will of the real parents), some assume the role of family sage, and some remain distant figures in the extended family structure.

The middle generation may feel a sense of rivalry with the grandparents for the affections of the children. Since some grandparents are less con-cerned than parents with what might be considered proper upbringing of children and more concerned with winning love for themselves, they may be more permissive and more liberal with gifts than the parents. Family contacts between older people and their children and grandchildren may not be as frequent and as close as the older people would like. But the gen-eral picture is that there is a mutual dependency between the generations, and that family relationships serve to give personal meaning to the lives of most Americans in an increasingly impersonal world (Bahr and Nye).

ROLE ADJUSTMENTS IN MIDDLE AND LATER YEARS

The major events of the middle and later years—the departure of children, retirement, often with reduced income, widowhood, and impaired health— result in loss of some social roles and major adjustments in others. While some sorts of interactions with close relatives often continue for the elderly, retirement and widowhood remove them from two social institutions which are more likely than any others to give meaning to contemporary adult life: the work system and marriage.

Retirement at the age of 65 has become the norm in the United States. Some feel that the average age of retirement may decline to 60 or even earlier (Blau, 1973). Unlike peasant cultures and planned societies like Israel which allow older people's work responsibilities to taper off gradually depending on their capabilities (Talmon, 1961), the pattern in the United States is for people to carry a full load of responsibilities until the day they are abruptly retired. This retirement from work has different meanings for different people. One could retire and be "released" to have more time for the family and other interesting social obligations. In this sense, one gains an opportunity. Or one could be retiring from a highly valued work role. In that case, the sense of loss at retirement is the predominant factor, and retirement is dreaded (Hochschild).

Death of one spouse—more often the husband—deprives the other of the intimate support of a long-term marital relationship. Widowhood means the end of the wife role for women who have outlived their husbands and do not remarry. As we will see in the next section, widowhood cuts deeply into the entire fabric of these women's lives, and they find that they have lost far more than a husband.

People do not usually recognize ahead of time how much their sense of identity, their social relationships, and their feeling that their daily lives have some meaning are bound to their jobs and their marriages. Newly retired men are often surprised, for instance, to find that they no longer have much in common with former work associates and may regret too late that they never had time to establish other friendships. Widowed women may likewise find themselves excluded from gatherings of couples with whom they and their husbands had formerly been joint friends (Blau).

THE CONCEPT OF ROLE EXIT

Role exit. Giving up a role because of a change in one's position in the social structure.

Role exits occur throughout life, for individual growth often depends on a person's willingness to give up roles that have already been mastered in order to take on new ones that are more challenging and ultimately more rewarding. But the role exits of earlier life are different from retirement and widowhood, for the earlier exits are followed by entrance into new roles, with new activities and new partners. Leaving a familiar and meaningful role—graduating from high school or college, for instance, or moving away to take a new job—may be accompanied by some emotional strain and sense of loss. But these feelings are cushioned by the promises of the new role, such as a career or independence from parents. The enticements of the new role are culturally emphasized during the socialization process; children learn to want to go to college, marry, raise a family, make money, and so on. But our society offers very little, except to the rich, to convince people of the joys of retirement, and certainly has no way of making widowhood seem attractive.

Some people—especially men—do remarry, and some take new jobs after their retirement, but they are in the minority. For many, it is retirement and widowhood, rather than aging itself, that cause the unhappiness associated with old age. It is important to recognize this distinction because, while aging cannot be prevented, older people may be helped to take up new, positively evaluated roles as substitutes for the ones they have lost. As it is, the new roles available are negatively defined and the number of roles decreased (Blau).

ANTICIPATORY SOCIALIZATION AND THE EMPTY NEST

During the 1960s, sociologists and psychotherapists warned of the prevalence of the **empty-nest syndrome.** When women lost their roles as mothers during the middle years as their last children grew up and moved away, they were thought to sink into depression, often turning to alcohol or adultery out of despair over the meaninglessness of their lives. But recent findings indicate that the majority of families face this change with something more like relief than gloom (Lowenthal and Chiriboga, 1972). The husband continues to work and the wife still has her wife role and often takes up new activities after the children have gone, or perhaps continues working at a job outside the home. The ways in which parents cope with exit from the parenting role may suggest some possibilities for preparing older people for the later adjustments of retirement and widowhood.

> **Empty-nest syndrome.** Depression experienced by some mothers at the time when the last child has left home for an independent life.

The term socialization, usually applied to the process through which small children learn the skills, customs, and attitudes of their society, can be applied to the lifelong continuation of social learning. Irwin Deutscher (1962) used the term **anticipatory socialization** to suggest that when people are moving toward a new status, they often have opportunities for learning about the new position ahead of time and then making the mental and emotional adjustments the new role will require. If workers have close friends and relatives who have retired ahead of them, they can observe their pleasures and problems and decide how they will behave at the time of their own retirement. They can learn to think of vacations or sick leaves as rehearsal for the time when they will be retired. The concept of anticipatory socialization applies also to the role adjustments required as children grow in independence and self-assertion and eventually leave the parental home to establish their own separate lives. Deutscher suggested a number of ways in which this particular form of anticipatory socialization occurs.

> **Anticipatory socialization.** A process by which people learn about a new status and role as they are moving toward it.

Acceptance of Change. The value placed on change for its own sake in America helps people of all ages to accept new situations. As Deutscher points out, "In a sense all Americans are socialized from early childhood to believe that change is both inevitable and good" (1962, p. 510). Since we are taught that nothing remains the same, such changes as children leaving home are easier to accept because they seem to be a natural part of life.

Earlier Breaks in the Family Circle.   For some parents, ties with their children are temporarily severed when they leave for college, jobs, or military service, easing the transition to the time when the children will be married and out of the parental household for good. As one middle-class mother put it, "The breaking point is when your children go away to college. After that you grow used to it. By the time they get married you're used to the idea of their being away and adjust to it" (Deutscher, pp. 511–512). Before these extended breaks, parents are often separated from their children for shorter periods by attendance at schools, summer camps, and out-of-town visits.

Extended Kinship Ties.   For families in which middle-aged parents are surrounded by a network of grown children, grandchildren, and other kin who live nearby and visit often, the departure of the last child from the family home may not cause any particular distress. The constant stream of relatives back and forth for outings, dinners, birthdays, and casual visits may keep the parents too busy for them to feel lonely (Deutscher).

The Pleasures of Disengagement.   Instead of regretting the loss of children as they leave home, many contemporary parents actually experience a welcome sense of freedom during their postparental years, freedom from the financial burdens and time demands of child rearing and freedom to give priority to their own needs for the first time in years. Women, traditionally expected to be hardest hit by the empty-nest syndrome, are now likely to have careers or other interests and to be less emotionally dependent on their children than earlier generations of women. Anticipating changes and planning ahead to adjust one's life to meet them enables both women and men to lead more fulfilling lives.

MARITAL SATISFACTION

Some researchers have considered that people's satisfaction in marriage is greatest as newlyweds and gradually declines to a low point in the later years. However, more recent studies indicate that marital satisfaction follows a U-shaped curve. It is high at the newlywed stage, declining through the infant, preschool, and school-age stages of the family life cycle, then begins to rise again when the children are teenaged. The rise in satisfaction continues through the launching and launched stages to a new high of marital happiness during the years of retirement (Harry, 1976).

A Study of Marital Satisfaction in Later Years.   In a study of 408 Oklahoma husbands and wives aged 60–89, Stinnett, Carter, and Montgomery found that 95 percent of their respondents rated their marriages happy or very happy. Over half (53 percent) felt that their marriages had grown better over time. Forty-one percent said they had stayed about the same. Only 4 percent felt their marriages were worse, and 2 percent were undecided.

This sample of older people rated companionship (18.4 percent) and being able to express their true feelings to each other (17.8 percent) the most rewarding aspects of their marriages. Rather than marital problems (only 5.4 percent), most said their major problems were housing (27.5 percent), poor health (21.2 percent), and money (20 percent).

This picture of conjugal bliss contradicts the stereotyped notion that elderly husbands and wives merely exist together. The high level of perceived satisfaction in older marriages probably is related to the increased amount of time older people have to spend enjoying each other's companionship. While many poor marriages may have broken up before this period, those that last may be based on years of growing understanding, acceptance, and communication, and increasing dependence on each other, rather than their children or their work roles, for the satisfaction of emotional needs (Stinnett, Carter, and Montgomery). Other studies have shown that older people who are still married are happier, better adjusted, and less lonely than people their age who are unmarried, divorced, or widowed (Stinnett, Collins, and Montgomery, 1970).

Sex in the Later Years.   Sexual satisfaction was rated the most important characteristic of a good marriage by only 7.8 percent of the old people in the Oklahoma study. While some older couples continue to make love during their later years, some cease sexual relations not so much out of disinterest as out of fear of failure or the embarrassed notion that sexual urges are abnormal at their age. But according to sex researchers, as we learned in Chapter 5, there is nothing unnatural about sexual desires in the elderly. Well-adjusted women continue to be sexually responsive during their later years, and though men's responses slow down with age, they are still capable of enjoyable sexual relations.

Duke University's Center for the Study of Aging has been following the course of older people's sexuality for over 20 years. The longitudinal research at Duke which has surveyed the same people every three years indicates that 15 percent of men and women actually experience a rising rate of sexual desire and activity as they age (Lobsenz, 1974). Sexual monotony, fatigue, obsession with work, liquor, overeating, and physical and mental illness can interfere with rewarding sexual relations. But when these factors can be controlled, sexual relations in later life can continue to make both partners feel wanted and needed. Even in old age, sex can serve as a gratifying expression of emotional intimacy.

Marital Adjustments to Role Changes. At the time of the empty-nest life-change, many women feel a need to take on new roles in order to fill the void left by the loss of their children. In general, Glenn's analysis of survey data indicates that middle-aged mothers adapt quite well (Glenn, 1975). Some go back to work if they are not already working, some take on volunteer work, some go back to school. Some husbands of women who work accept their wives' departure from the traditional female role and enjoy the lessening in their own share of the financial burden without hurt pride. For others, the changes are too much to take. Some bluntly refuse to allow their wives to work; in others, blocking attempts are more subtle. For instance, the policeman husband of a 40-year-old woman managed to have an accident requiring her attention every time she tried to go out to her weekly women's consciousness-raising-group meeting. Before the second meeting, he twisted his ankle on the front stoop; before the next, he sliced his thumb with a potato peeler; and before the next, he managed to pour boiling water all over his hand. At the time of Susan Jacoby's report, the wife was still attending her group meetings; the husband was still averaging two "accidents" a month (Jacoby, 1973).

Consciousness raising.
Teaching about social
realities in ways that
encourage the alteration
of social customs.

Later in the life cycle, it is the husband who gropes for new roles to sustain his self-respect when he retires. Readjustments within the marriage are difficult at this point, because if his mate is a full-time housewife, she continues to have a strong role through household routines established years before. To suddenly have her restless husband underfoot all day, perhaps trying to make himself useful by offering suggestions about how she could do her work more efficiently, makes many women resentful. When wives are thus obviously annoyed at having them around, newly retired men who have been told that working society no longer needs them may feel their loss of self-respect all the more keenly.

The same situation may arise when it is the husband who does the housework and then is pestered by his wife when she retires. In one marriage, the 75-year-old husband retired ten years before his younger wife. When she quit her waitress job at the age of 60, he confided, "You can't imagine how uneasy I feel having Sally around the house all day.... She doesn't mean to, of course, but she keeps touching everything and destroying the order I arranged. My castle's been invaded and I'm not a bit reconciled to it. I don't know how we're going to work it out" (Freilich, 1975, p. 21).

INDIVIDUAL MODES OF COPING
Older people's satisfaction in life and in their marriages depends not only on how well they manage to readjust to each other after various successive

changes in the life cycle but also on how well they cope with the changes as individuals. According to Bernice Neugarten's study of a large sample of people 70–79 years old in the Midwest, people's personality differences are more significant to their happiness than the specific ways they have of coping. For instance, some people are happy when they maintain active involvement with family and community during later life; but some people who are relatively inactive can also be happy.

Neugarten and her associates at the University of Chicago define happiness as taking pleasure in daily activities, seeing one's life as meaningful and accepting the past, feeling that one's life goals have been achieved, holding a positive self-image, and being optimistic. They found that both active and inactive people were capable of meeting these requirements. Seventy percent of those they studied had well-integrated, happy personalities of three distinct types. Those they called "reorganizers" were competently handling a wide variety of activities which they had substituted for their earlier roles. Those they called "focused" were more selective in their activities, doing only a few things which they truly enjoyed. A third group, those they called "disengaged," had adopted the rocking-chair approach to aging, withdrawing contentedly from role commitments to enjoy a calm, relaxed life.

There were two other kinds of people who managed to experience medium to high life satisfaction through defensive striving and tight control over their lives. Those with "holding-on" patterns coped by keeping too busy to feel any losses in their lives. "Constricted" people had limited their social activities, closed themselves to new involvements, and become preoccupied with defending themselves against the effects of aging.

Fig. 15.2 Problems receiving most agency services for persons over and under 65. Clients over the age of 65 served by family service agencies are eight times as likely as younger clients to be seeking assistance on health problems. They seek help five times as often on income or housing problems; four times as often on problems of social contacts; and three times as often on problems of money management. However, they are far less likely to seek assistance on problems of family relationships than are younger applicants to these agencies. (Source: Dorothy F. Beck and Mary Ann Jones, *Progress on Family Problems.* Copyright 1973 by Family Service Association of America, New York. Reprinted by permission.)

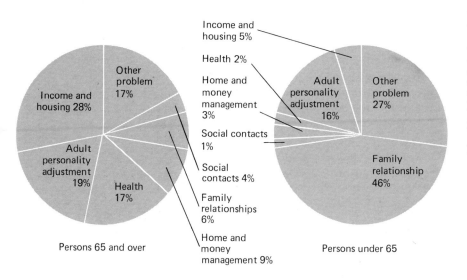

Income and housing 5%

Health 2%

Home and money management 3%

Social contacts 1%

Income and housing 28%

Other problem 17%

Adult personality adjustment 19%

Health 17%

Social contacts 4%

Family relationships 6%

Home and money management 9%

Adult personality adjustment 16%

Other problem 27%

Family relationship 46%

Persons 65 and over

Persons under 65

Even people whose response to age is passive dependency, leaning on one or more other people for support, were found to be capable of deriving at least medium satisfaction from life. The only two personality types that had not been able to cope with aging in ways that brought them happiness were the apathetic and those with severe psychological problems (Neugarten).

LOSS OF A SPOUSE

For many older people, loss of a spouse is more difficult to cope with than any former life change. The first year after the mate dies is especially difficult. This is a period of high death rates for the surviving spouse and of increased proneness to suicide. Once they have accepted their loss, men often remarry; as we have seen, older women are less likely to do so, and widowhood becomes the status they must accept for the rest of their lives.

MOURNING

Death of a family member is always experienced as a crisis because it is final. A unique human being has been lost and cannot be replaced. It is especially difficult because people usually have little prior experience in dealing with it. Death evokes a maze of emotions, sometimes including feelings of guilt, anger, relief, anxiety, helplessness, hostility, or fear, along with the feeling of loss, all of them normal reactions to bereavement. Healthy **grief work** requires allowing such emotions to surface so that they can be understood and worked through. In order to adjust to the finality of the loss, the surviving spouse must—after a period of mourning—relinquish the dead mate and accept the harsh reality of taking over or reassigning the dead person's roles.

If death is not sudden but expected, perhaps after a long illness, such mourning is prolonged but less intense than in the case of unexpected death. In some cases, adults who know they are going to die can help to ease the transition to life without them by helping to set up a life for their spouses in which factors like financial problems will not be such a burden (Stanley B. Goldberg, 1973).

ROLE-LOSS IN WIDOWHOOD

For a widow, financial problems and personal grief may be compounded by the stress of losing her central social role as a wife. In an intensive study of widows in Chicago, Lopata noted that American life puts unusual emphasis on the role of wife and makes many husbands and wives each other's only regular companions. Especially after the children are out of the home, the wife places the focus of her attention on her husband, who becomes the

Grief work. The effort required to adjust to the death of a person of significance in one's life.

only "client" for her activities. He, in turn, belongs to a group of co-workers with whom he spends most of his days, but job mobility and leisure activities which do not include co-workers keep this changing group from being as important to him as it would be if he had always known, worked, and played with them. His contact with his kin may be similarly unimportant. It is his wife who is likely to be his companion not only in the home but in almost everything he does outside of work.

Women in the United States are encouraged to invest much of their personality in their marriage, further burdening it with more sentiment and self-involvement than the institution carries in many other cultures. Husband and wife become a team which carries on not only residential tasks and pleasures together, but, increasingly, recreational and political activities, mutual friendships with other couples, involvement with community groups, and interactions with relatives. Togetherness in this kind of multi-level involvement with each other's lives sets the stage for a loss which cuts deeply into all aspects of life when one partner dies (Lopata, 1973).

Sentiment. An idea colored by emotion.

Different women react differently to the death of the husband, depending on how they interacted with him when he was alive. For some, the husband's death means the loss of a unique, deeply loved person with whom they shared a multi-dimensional companionship. They are likely to feel a crushing sense of personal loneliness when he dies and to find their lives seriously disorganized. For others, widowhood means a change in status, the loss of a social position and a couples-oriented lifestyle which they cannot recreate. These patterns are more likely to occur in middle- and upper-class widows. Wives of lower-class husbands may be more ambivalent toward them in death, as in life. The communication problems of working-class people described in Chapter 9 lead to greater emotional distance in these marriages. Many of these women never shift the focus of their roles to that of wife after their children leave home, and their husbands are less likely to be companions with whom they share the problems of everyday life. However, marital disruption through death almost invariably causes distress, regardless of the quality of the marriage (Weiss, 1976).

READJUSTMENT

In readjusting their roles after the spouse dies, most widows claim that they do not want to remarry. Some enjoy their new independence, free time, and lightened housework load; some claim they are too old to start again; and others feel that they should remain faithful to the dead spouse. Interestingly enough, remarriage is more often considered by women whose relationship with their lost husbands was most rewarding than by the survivors of poor marriages. But few expect to be able to find another good mate.

Of the Chicago widows interviewed by Lopata, half live alone and like it that way; half find loneliness the greatest problem in widowhood. All find that they are subtly stigmatized by their single status. They are usually excluded from gatherings of couples because they make an "odd" person. Widowed women often find that they have no one to escort them to social events, a lack felt most strongly by those widowed young, since most of their friends are still married (Lopata). Married women often regard them with some suspicion, as though they might try to steal their husbands, so interactions even with old friends may be marred by self-consciousness. Often the only people they can find for friends are other widows, and social clubs for people experiencing widowhood are helping to meet this need.

Our society ascribes no duties or regulations to the nonrole of widow. Women who identified strongly with the former role of wife are uncomfortable with the formlessness of their new status. But just as women who had strong marriages are most likely to remarry, they are also most capable of reorganizing their lives after their intense grief work is over. They have the self-assurance and know-how to enter new roles and relationships. Those who had been less involved with the role of wife seem to lack the personal resources to establish new links to society when their one minimal bridge with it is gone (Lopata).

Anticipatory socialization can be of value here. One major task might be discussion of the facts of death and widowhood between married couples. Each can encourage the other to think in positive terms of how one goes on living after the loss of a spouse. Another task would be open discussion of financial affairs, since change in financial status associated with loss of a spouse usually requires adjustment in the roles played by the survivor. A third task would be discussion of preferences as to funeral arrangements and purchase of a burial plot, if this is desired, rather than leave these decisions to the moment when the crisis of death arrives. The role of the widowed person, whether man or woman, is not a desired one, but it is one to which thousands of people, out of sheer necessity, adjust every year.

COMMUNITIES OF THE ELDERLY

In the face of retirement, separation from children, and widowhood, older people are increasingly turning to each other for companionship and mutual support. Many nonrelated older people are now living together in communities for senior citizens which range from public-housing projects and trailer parks to leisure communities for the rich.

LEISURE COMMUNITIES
Older couples have been migrating to warm climates like Florida and California for their retirement since the 1920s. But in 1960, when developers

began building Sun City, Arizona, a new town specifically for people over 50 with no live-in children, sociologists were skeptical. They thought the elderly would refuse to segregate themselves from the rest of the population. As journalist Thomas Meehan put it, they predicted that "people would resent being cordoned off into what amounted to a staging area in which to play shuffleboard and canasta while waiting for death" (Meehan, 1973, p. 18). But their predictions were wrong. Sun City has been so successful that its population is expected to reach 55,000 by 1980. Other developers quickly followed its lead, and there are now hundreds of retirement communities in the United States. Many are in cold parts of the country, for surveys indicate that some older people would rather retire to areas near their former homes than to sunnier climates. Although they like to maintain some sort of continuity with their former lives, they are glad to sell houses that are too big and too hard to maintain once their children are gone and to move into smaller dwellings in communities where maintenance and security are provided for them along with companionship, social activities, and hobbies.

What do people do in these retirement communities? At Heritage Village in the hills of rural Connecticut, people who have paid $30,000–$50,000 for their rustic-modern condominiums are kept busy with over 70 activities, from drama groups to courses like "Creative Survival." They can play at everything from woodworking to paddle-tennis, shop in the village's 50 stores, or attend a constant round of parties. Although some do volunteer community work, most indulge themselves solely in leisure activities. Many apparently feel that they have paid their dues and are only interested in relaxing and enjoying their last years. As one resident who struggled to make ends meet during the Depression and served in two world wars explained,

I earned it—I put in 33 years with the same company, commuting every day on the train to New York. Raised four children, too, all of whom are grown up now and married. . . . I gave a great deal of my time on weekends and in the evening to things like the P.T.A., the Boy Scouts, and the church, but my feeling is that I've done my bit. I'm finally going to relax and have some fun out of life. And if that means playing golf every day, I'm damned well going to play golf every day. (Meehan, p. 22)

SPONTANEOUS COMMUNITY AT MERRILL COURT

Life for those in lower-income elderly communities does not have this cruise-ship flavor. In some cases, the elderly live together almost communally as a sort of extended family. Although the trappings of life for today's oldest generation are very different from those of the young, the old are apparently no less capable of the spirit of cooperation and responsibility toward each other which makes communes work.

The 43 residents of Merrill Court, a San Francisco housing project, had no intentions of joining a commune. These conservative 60–80-year-olds from small towns in the Southwest and Midwest, 37 women and 6 men, would probably have been just as disengaged from social life as others their age if it had not been for the coffee machine that brought them together. When somebody's daughter placed a coffee machine in the unit's recreation room, people began to gather around it informally to share their morning coffee. After the recreation director joined in, a spontaneous fellowship sprang up so rapidly that half a year later Merrill Court was buzzing with joint activities, including a Bible study group, a service club, bowling, classes, birthday parties, a washtub band which visited old folks' homes, and a workshop for homemade articles to be donated to various charities. Along with these activities, the residents of Merrill Court took on responsibilities to each other and to society, adding shape and meaning to their lives (Hochschild).

The Social Structure.   According to Arlie Hochschild, who studied the community which developed at Merrill Court, social patterns there were centered on what went on "downstairs" in the recreation room, but they spread out to a network of informal friendships in the apartments upstairs. Downstairs, formal community organization took the form of the Merrill Court Service Club. Most of the residents and a few nonresidents belonged to it, and in its welter of committees and chairmanships, all but four club members had the chance to chair some activity during a three-year period.

Table 15.1   Social Security (OASDHI)—retirement benefits, by sex   The Social Security program of the federal government, though it does not provide complete support for retired persons, does allow vast numbers of people over the age of 62 a degree of financial independence they would not have otherwise. The consequences of this program for the structure of family life in the United States have been substantial.

	1950	*1960*	*1975*
Number over 62 Receiving Benefits			
Total	1,771,000	8,062,000	16,588,000
Male	1,469,000	5,217,000	9,164,000
Female	302,000	2,845,000	7,424,000
Average Monthly Benefit			
Male	$46	$82	$228
Female	35	60	182

Source: U.S. Bureau of the Census, *Statistical Abstract of the United States, 1975* and *1976.*

At any one time, perhaps a third of the members were in charge of something.

The apartments in which friends visited over coffee all tended to be furnished alike, with overstuffed chairs, floral sleep sofas for grandchildren spending the night, homemade artificial flowers, plants grown from slips shared among neighbors, and old photographs of grandchildren and occasionally the dead husband or the longer-dead parents. Refrigerators were filled with homemade butter, jam, and corn bread made by fellow residents who had once cooked for large families and still cooked food in such large quantities that they had plenty to share. Since all of the women distributed food in this way, Hochschild pointed out that it could be seen as an informal division of labor.

The Functions of Neighboring.   The informal system of visits and sharing, or neighboring, gratified residents' needs for friendship but it also served some other functions. Since upstairs gossip about each other's actions and conflicting opinions found its way downstairs, it served as a means of social control. In judging each other they set moral boundaries for themselves as well. Neighboring also served as a means for checking to see if the others were all right. If any residents had not opened their curtains by mid-morning, the others checked in on them to see if they were sick. Those who were healthy often adopted a few who were not, performing services like shopping, picking up mail, and writing letters for them. Those who received such care, like blind Little Floyd, were not usually able to offer services in return. Sometimes, however, people performed special services for others for a small fee. One woman, for instance, took in sewing but always told people what she would be spending their money for, such as bus fare to visit relatives in Montana, probably in an attempt to make the transaction seem less commercial (Hochschild).

The "Poor Dear" Hierarchy.   Although the residents of Merrill Court were all from the same social class, some held more honor than others, according to what Hochschild called a "poor dear" hierarchy, a multilevel structure of status rankings. They saw the differences between themselves as matters of "luck," and granted most honor to those with the most luck. Those with the luck to have good health won honor, as did those who had lost the fewest relatives and those whose children were still close to them. Others were referred to as "poor dears."

In this complex series of status levels, most people could find themselves superior to at least some "poor dear." Those who were active in politics and recreation referred to those who spent their time playing cards or reading the newspapers as "poor dears." Compared to themselves, all those in nursing homes were "poor dears." But to the young—the welfare workers, doctors, and Recreation Department employees with whom they interacted but avoided comparing themselves—the residents of Merrill Court were all "poor dears." Hochschild suggested that it was perhaps because younger people pitied them that Merrill Court's old needed to find someone of their own to pity.

"Sibling Bonds."   Despite the "poor dear" hierarchy, the residents of Merrill Court related to each other almost like brothers and sisters. They exchanged coffee, lunches, slips of potted plants, kitchen utensils, food, and curtain checks as equals. The things they wanted—such as Mother's Day cards—and the things they could give each other—such as home-canned peaches—were much the same from one person to the next. In their sharing of labor they showed little specialization, for they were likely to make and exchange the same things. Because of their similarity in skills and interests, they were understanding listeners for each other who could comfortably share old-age jokes and talk about illnesses or the past. This kind of bond does not always form in groups of older people. Thrown together in institutions with dependent relationships on nursing staff, they are unlikely to form mature "sibling bonds" because they do not live as independent adults. The residents at Merrill Court, on the other hand, took care of themselves for the most part, paying rent, shopping, cooking, making their beds, and helping each other (Hochschild).

Community as a Means of Adjustment.   As we have seen, social ties diminish with poverty and ties to the economy diminish with retirement, isolating the old. Against this background, the community which rose among people with modest means at Merrill Court was an adjustment to a bad situation. Feeling that they no longer had responsibilities to younger age groups, these men and women took on responsibilities toward each other. They learned to ignore the scorn of the young for those who do not "act their age," for with each other they could dance, joke, flirt, and sing, as well as talk candidly about approaching death. Together they worked out solutions to problems they had not had to face before.

Unlike many their age, the residents of Merrill Court came to recognize that they were part of a minority group with whose members they could feel a sense of solidarity. When strong family ties are absent, communities of the old may serve to raise "old-age consciousness" and thus give people a sense that they are part of an "us," not just a "me" (Hochschild).

TRENDS FOR THE FUTURE

Solving the problems of old age is not as simple as herding the elderly into housing developments and giving them coffee machines. Merrill Court's social life mirrored the very similar background of its occupants; it would not suit everyone. True intentional communes of the old are unlikely to form because older people are likely to want to hold on to whatever property they have, to prefer independent living units, and to lack the group identity and energy needed to form communal structures (Streib and Streib, 1975). Other kinds of solutions are being tried and suggested.

KEEPING BUSY

Assorted programs designed to give the old something meaningful to do with their time or ways to improve their living situation are of some help. To give a few examples, a Tax Aide program sponsored by the American Association of Retired Persons has placed thousands of capable retired volunteers specially trained by the Internal Revenue Service in communities around the country to provide free income-tax assistance to elderly people. In Santa Cruz, California, "Gray Bears" pay a dollar a year for the right to glean a weekly grocery bag of leftover fruits and vegetables from the land of local farmers who need their fields cleared after their harvests. Some of the "Gray Bears" apparently donate what they have picked to feebler friends. Self-help courses in "Senior Survival," covering such topics as adequate nutrition on a low income, and the ins and outs of applying for Social Security benefits, are now being offered to older people through some colleges (*Modern Maturity*, 1976). And the Foster Grandparents program has rejuvenated many lower-income older people, who are often very feeble themselves, by giving them a "poor dear" to take care of in the form of an institutionalized, emotionally deprived, and often retarded child. The foster grandparents are paid for their time, but more important, they and their

Still in the saddle, Gay Richmond has been traveling by motorcycle for 46 of her 72 years. Sitting on her bike, complete with sidecar, near her Michigan home, she declares she isn't about to give it up.

charges often develop a new interest in life. The old often seem to become younger again, and the young are drawn out of their isolation (Smith).

EMOTIONAL NEEDS

The problem with these and many other excellent work and housing programs for the elderly is that while they help to improve the lives of the old, they do not meet all their emotional needs. Ruth Shonle Cavan writes that in later life, people continue to feel a need for an intimate relationship with someone of the opposite sex, perhaps including intercourse; relationships with younger kin but not joint residence; inclusion in a peer group; and the feeling of belonging to a family, perhaps one of peers if relatives are not available (Cavan, 1974). While there is probably a limit to how far social planning can go toward making up for the multiple losses of later life, some sociologists are now speculating that alternative family forms might help to counter loneliness and meaninglessness in the lives of the old.

POLYGYNY AFTER 60—A VIABLE ALTERNATIVE?

Polygyny. The marriage of two or more women to the same man.

Victor Kassel, a specialist in the medical care of older people in Salt Lake City—where Mormons once practiced polygyny—suggests that if older men could marry two, three, four, or even five older women, many of their problems would be solved. Since there are so few older men to go around, this setup would offer more widows the chance to remarry and reestablish a meaningful family group. The women would have new clients and new incentives to use their household skills and perhaps everyone would eat better. Partners could take turns cooking to lessen the individual burden. Wives and husband could pool their economic resources so that all would live more comfortably. When anyone got sick, the others could take turns providing care in the familiar surroundings of their own home. Housework could be shared, lightening individual burdens.

The spouses would have the opportunity to engage in legitimized sexual relations once again. Kassel anticipates that competition among the wives for the husband's affection would reactivate their interest in keeping themselves attractive and therefore lift their morale. The man, in turn, would be inclined to keep himself in good shape because of his wives' flattering attention.

Despite disruptive jealousies which could be expected to arise among the wives, Kassel suggests that polygyny might provide a relationship which would be effective in relieving old people's loneliness and depression. The differing life experiences each would bring to the marriage could enrich the lives of the others, deepen their understanding of life, and help them to grow as people. Their intimate relationship would give them a feeling of belonging to a close family group and a reason for living. Those who found emotional gratification in such a relationship would then be more likely to take an interest in outside activities (Kassel, 1966).

Discussion of This Scheme.   Kassel made his suggestion back in 1966. There is no indication that old people are rushing to take his advice or that laws are being changed to allow polygyny for the old or anyone else. Clearly, the proposal is antagonistic to current values in the United States and would require radical resocialization.

Most obvious among the disadvantages is the probability that such an arrangement would be disrupted by jealousy over everything from housework to who sleeps with the husband. Since 90 percent of Americans get married at some point and are thus used to a monogamous marital structure which may have lasted for decades, a switch to polygyny late in life would require major personal readjustments. It is hard to imagine older people could be bent to the cooperative ways of thinking which multiple marriages would require. According to George Rosenberg, polygyny has declined around the world as ideas like freedom of mate choice, equality between husbands and wives, and emphasis on the emotional qualities of the conjugal relationship have taken hold.

Polygyny also sets up a situation in which one sex might be used by the other. The husband could act like a king, dominating the women and expecting them to wait on him hand and foot. On the other hand, he could become a pawn in a power struggle among the women. The way Kassel sees polygyny, traditional sex typing is strong, with the women doing all the housework and the man privileged to have sex with any of them he chooses. Polygyny does not exclude the possibility that such a marriage could function as a multiple-person peer group, with responsibilities shared on an equal basis, as if among friends. But it would probably be very difficult to achieve this balance without sacrificing the stimulating heterosexual incentives which Kassel sees as making polygyny more attractive than joint households of groups of widows, a type of family unit women rarely choose.

Death poses further problems. The increased chances for multiple bereavements would add to the continual losses an older person must face. The complex overlappings of combined kinship systems would make life more complicated for everybody. For instance, as members of the polygynous unit died, what kinship obligations would the others have to surviving stepchildren? Legally, polygyny could complicate matters of inheritance. Children might try to prevent their parents from joining such unions out of fear that they might be cut out of wills in favor of the new family members. This kind of interference from would-be beneficiaries is already influencing the liaisons of older people, thousands of whom are now cohabiting rather than remarrying in order to avoid dividing their estates, as well as to keep from losing their Social Security and pension payments (Lobsenz, 1974a).

Even considering the drift in U.S. society toward experimentation and change in family living, it does not seem likely that polygyny will take hold here, for the elderly or for any other age group. However, the imbalance in the sex ratio at older age levels, which prompted Kassel to make his proposal, is expected to persist.

A PICTURE OF THE FUTURE

According to sociologist Gordon Streib's predictions, all present trends in the older population will continue. While old age will not be appreciably extended any farther by modern medicine in the immediate future, women will continue to outlive their husbands, perpetuating the sex-ratio imbalance and the persistence of widowhood as a common fact of older life. Nine out of ten Americans will still probably marry at least once during their lifetime, with husbands usually about three years older than their wives. Families will be smaller and there will thus be fewer grandchildren.

Older couples will probably continue to prefer to live separately from their children, unless economic conditions get so bad that they have to double up on housing. Americans will gradually come to accept the fact that sexual activity is normal for the elderly and in line with a general relaxation of sexual restraints, to be tolerant of sexual relationships among the un-married aged (Somerville, 1972). Divorces after the children leave home will increasingly split up middle-aged marriages that had been held together only for the children's benefit. More divorced and widowed people will probably remarry, complicating parent-child relations in terms of visiting, inheritance, and family assistance.

Frequent contact between older people and their extended kin networks will continue and may even increase, in spite of the stereotyped notion that most of the elderly are isolated. The divorced and widowed will not be likely to live with their siblings, although the never-married may. Only 4 percent of today's old people are now receiving direct financial support from their children. Barring major economic collapse or social upheaval, this situation will probably continue. But mutual assistance will keep flowing between generations in the form of services and gifts.

The empty-nest syndrome will not be a major problem for most women. More will be working outside their homes, having small families, and finding new interests rather than investing most of their personalities in the mother role. During the postparental period, couples with sufficient financial resources will increasingly find satisfaction in travel and leisure activities, filling the void left by child-centered family activities.

Most older people will live in their own homes until they become physically unable to care for themselves, but there will be more age-segregated communities and housing developments. Because early-retirement benefits are increasing, more people will choose to retire before the age of 65. Although many people will move into smaller homes when they retire, most will not leave the general area of their long-term residence.

If there are no radical social changes, health, medical care, and Social Security benefits will increase, relieving the nuclear family of the expense

Drawing by Weber;
© 1976 The New Yorker Magazine, Inc.

"We haven't much time left, Jake. What do you say
we take a stab at la dolce vita?"

of care for the aged. But because of inflation, the old on fixed incomes will continue to be an economically underprivileged group.

Since it is the young who traditionally force social change and who are likely to overlook the special problems of the old, it is unlikely that society will do much to help the aged unless they themselves become militant to press their demands. But despite the limited successes of associations of senior citizens in making the younger population recognize their problems and grant them concessions, older people often have too little psychic and physical energy to assert their rights to their share of the American pie (Streib, 1970).

Significant losses of social contact are inevitable in later stages of the family life cycle. But whether the empty nest, retirement, and widowhood leave old people isolated and unhappy for the rest of their lives is largely determined by their personal resources. If the old have adaptable personalities, they can use their own strengths and the support they get from family and peers to create meaningful and satisfying lives for themselves.

Summary

1. The purpose of this chapter is to consider the special problems and opportunities of the middle and later years of life and some ways in which people can prepare for and adjust to changes in family situations.

2. Using statistics, researchers can make some generalizations about what happens to people as they age. Some researchers observe the social characteristics of people's lives at various age levels (late maturity, pre-, early, and late retirement) as a measure of change. Others discuss the changing patterns of

behavior in older people according to where they are in the family life cycle (as described in the discussion of family-development theory in Chapter 4).

3. It was formerly believed that people became isolated from kin as they aged, but recent studies have indicated that married offspring and their older parents keep in touch through residential closeness and patterns of mutual aid. The strength of kinship ties can be measured in terms of the number of kin, frequency of interaction, extent of aid (monetary or services), emotional closeness, and quality of the family relationship.

4. The major events of the middle and later years—departure of children from the home, reduced income, retirement, widowhood, and increasing health problems—result in loss or major adjustment of social roles. Anticipatory socialization can help people to learn about new roles ahead of time and anticipate the mental and emotional adjustments required.

5. When there are no pressing financial problems and the couple is still together, later years are often the happiest and most satisfying of a couple's life.

6. Loss of a spouse is a major change for people in middle age and later years. To adjust to the loss, the surviving spouse must allow a period of mourning, relinquish the dead mate, and accept the reality of taking over or reassigning the dead person's roles. For a widow, grief and financial pressures are accompanied by the stress of losing her central social role as a wife. This change in roles requires social and personal adjustments which may be made easier if couples plan together various aspects of life after the family circle is broken, in the process called anticipatory socialization.

7. Increasingly, older people turn to each other for companionship and mutual support in public-housing projects such as Merrill Court and leisure communities such as Heritage Village. If the elderly are adaptable, and if their economic and health problems are not too severe, they can continue to live meaningful and satisfying lives.

Key Concepts

Youth-oriented society	Widowhood	Empty-nest syndrome
Family life cycle	Life expectancy	Marital satisfaction
Launching process	Generation gap	Mourning
Postparental period	Mutual aid	Grief work
Late maturity	Role exit	Leisure communities
Retirement	Anticipatory	"Poor dear" hierarchy
Old age	socialization	"Sibling bonds"

Review and Discussion

1. Outline your family's kinship structure in relation to one of your parents and then to one of your grandparents. Take into account the number of kin, residential closeness, frequency of interaction, family closeness, and mutual aid. What differences do you find between family members at these two stages of life?

2. Marital satisfaction has been discussed in this chapter in terms of a U-shaped curve: a high degree of happiness as newlyweds, a low point when children are young, and a rise after the children leave home. How might this curve differ for married couples who have remained childless, such as those described in Chapter 3?

3. List three people you know in each of the following four stages of the life cycle: late maturity (45–54), preretirement (55–64), early retirement (65–74), and late retirement (75 and over). Decide which of the three in each group seems most satisfied with life and then try to think of why this might be so.

4. What is your view of the idea that people should have a number of children so that there will be someone to take care of them in their old age?

5. Do you think you would enjoy living in a community of elderly persons when you are elderly? Why or why not? Do you think that communities of this type are a good idea?

Suggested Readings

BART, P. (1977).   The loneliness of the long-distance mother. In P. J. Stein, J. Richman, and N. Hannon, *The Family.* Reading, Mass.: Addison-Wesley.

A brief study of the social status of middle-aged women in America and the stresses that affect their lives. Includes a case study of a woman placed in a . . . mental hospital as a result of being unprepared and unable to cope with the problems of middle age. Suggests ways in which our society could change to prevent this type of stress.

CAINE, L. (1974).   *Widow.* New York: Morrow.

This personal account of the author's experiences as a widow explores several aspects of widowhood: coping with grief, the sense of loss, and the roles of a single woman, single parent, and single provider.

KERCKHOFF, R. K. (1976).   Marriage and middle age. *The Family Coordinator.* 25:1:5–11.

Explores the problems of family life in middle age and how to deal with them in ways that lead to personal growth. Observations on middle age from literature and from people who took part in research studies are included.

LOPATA, H. Z. (1972).   Social relations of widows in urbanizing societies. *Sociological Quarterly* 13: 259–271.

Briefly describes the range of activities and lifestyles available to widows in communities from isolated rural areas to small towns to neighborhoods within large urban centers.

U.S. NEWS & WORLD REPORT EDITORS (1974).   *Teach Your Wife How to Be a Widow.* New York: Simon and Schuster.

A clear and practical guide to help husbands and wives face the realities of life and death. Covers many areas, such as Social Security, investments, taxes, and insurance.

Part IV

Will the Traditional Family Survive?

Alternatives to Traditional Marriage 16

Although formal, legal marriage continues to be the choice of the majority of Americans, many people are exploring alternative ways of achieving intimate, fulfilling relationships. The family was defined in Chapter 1 as a social group sharing a common residence and cooperating economically, usually based on the marriage of one or more sexually cohabiting couples. This definition includes the possibility of having children for whom the adults of the family would accept responsibility. The definition is broad enough to cover a wide range of family groupings, such as are found in many different parts of the world. Here in the United States, the standard form of the family has been considered to be one husband, one wife, and their children, cooperating to meet economic needs and to provide intimate and enduring personal relationships. However, as we have seen in preceding chapters, many U.S. families are single-parent units or childless units. Others are variants on monogamy, such as open marriages and swinging. In this chapter, we are looking at four other **alternative lifestyles:** communes, group marriages, and cohabitation, which are variant forms of the family; and singlehood, which is a temporary or permanent rejection of marriage.

Alternative lifestyles. Ways of living that differ from the customs of most members of a society.

COMMUNAL STRUCTURES AND RELATIONSHIPS

Communes and experimental forms of marriage are not new in American society. The Mormons, a religious community discussed in Chapter 1, practiced polygyny in the nineteenth century. The Oneida Community, described in this chapter, was an unusually successful experiment in communal living and group marriage that was begun in 1848 and lasted for over 30 years.

The last 10 years, however, have witnessed a flourishing of communal experiments in the United States—for a variety of reasons. Many communes have been organized to avoid, challenge, or replace the highly competitive, **materialistic** organization and atmosphere spawned in our urban-industrial society. Others have sought to find family systems and new marital forms that foster individual growth. Whatever the goals, communes tend to be formed by groups of people who believe they can create an ideal society in which their particular goals can be attained.

Materialistic. Stressing objects rather than intellectual or spiritual activities as sources of comfort and pleasure.

SEARCHING FOR A BETTER WAY
The search for **utopia,** a perfect society in which a perfect life can be lived, has a long history in the United States. As early as the seventeenth century, utopian communities were being formed by idealists who were critical of the established order and who believed they could create and perfect an alternative way of life. Utopian criticism has frequently been aimed at

marital and family patterns and these patterns have often been altered in utopian communities. But family life has by no means been the only focus of the utopian vision. Historically, in America, there have been three areas in which discontent has been sufficiently strong to motivate groups of people to form separate communities: the religious sphere, the political and economic sphere, and the psychosocial sphere (Kanter, 1973).

Religious Motivations.   The earliest communes formed in America were based on religious ideals. Many present-day communes have also been formed on religious principles, whether of Eastern mysticism or Christianity. The Hare Krishna is a well-established contemporary religious system of communes. Religious utopias have often organized around a **charismatic leader,** considered by followers to be invested with supernatural powers. For example, Mother Ann Lee of the Shaker community was believed to be the female counterpart of Christ (Caplow, 1964). Many of these communities have been extremely enduring. The Shaker community, though its membership is small now, has been in existence since 1787, and the Hutterian Brethren, another religious organization, was founded over 450 years ago in Europe and has been in existence in the United States since 1873 (Kanter, 1972).

> **Charismatic leader. An individual whose strong personal magnetism inspires an unquestioning loyalty in followers.**

Political and Economic Motivations.   Many utopian communities have been established on the basis of political or economic ideals, particularly since the **Industrial Revolution.** The problems that followed industrialization, such as overcrowding, dislocation, and an increased disparity between the wealthy and the poor, generated waves of criticism. Believing in the perfectibility of human society, utopians sought to create communities where work would be fairly divided and power and wealth would be shared. The North American Phalanx in New Jersey was one of these. It lasted from 1843 to 1856.

Psychosocial Motivations.   The majority of present-day communal groups have been formed on the basis of criticism of society's negative impact on the individual and on interpersonal relationships. Rejecting the isolation, alienation, and dehumanization of the individual in much of American society, these groups have tried to create settings which foster the individual's personal growth and promote intimate and healthy relationships with others. Synanon in California is a large and well-known example of such a commune.

All utopian communities past and present have shared certain basic features: (1) they reject the established order, (2) they envision a harmonious life, and (3) they believe that this harmony can be achieved here on earth—that human social life is perfectible. Many of these utopian communities, once established, have had similar lifestyles. The most successful ones have had communal arrangements for work activities, education and child care, and social life. Moreover, the utopian vision usually involves a total way of life. Thus, while religious or psychosocial factors may have been the prime reasons for the creation of a particular community, other factors will also have played a role. The Oneida Community, whose origins were mainly religious, was equally an economic, political, and social experiment; and it provided well for its members in all of these spheres (Kanter, 1972).

A SUCCESSFUL NINETEENTH-CENTURY COMMUNE

Many people interested in finding out why some communes survive over long periods of time while others last only a year or two have looked closely at the Oneida Community to see how it solved the problems of survival. Part of this interest has arisen because Oneida was an extremely radical community to be found in the United States in the mid-nineteenth century. It included group marriage, scientific breeding, and sexual equality (Kephart, 1963).

The Oneida Community was founded by John Humphrey Noyes, a deeply religious man and a dynamic leader. A graduate of Dartmouth College and the Yale Theological Seminary, Noyes believed in a doctrine that came to be known as **Perfectionism.** Rejecting the Calvinist view of all human beings as sinners, Noyes preached that Christ had already returned to earth, and thus people were capable of living a sinless life. Noyes' theories were considered heresy by his church, and his license to preach was revoked. Nevertheless, Perfectionism had attracted followers who formed a Bible class in 1839 in Putney, Vermont, under Noyes' leadership. By 1846, the Bible class had grown into the Putney Community where spiritual equality, the central religious theory of the group, was put into practice in economic and sexual activities as well. The economy of the group was collectivist; there was no private ownership. Monogamy, viewed by the Perfectionists as selfish, was replaced by sexual communism, where all adult females had marital privileges with all adult males in the community (Kephart).

Although the practices of the Putney Community were based on religious views, outsiders considered them sinful, and Noyes, charged with adultery, was arrested in 1847. He fled to New York State where he established a new community along Oneida Creek. Faced with the problem of supporting itself, the Oneida Community survived only with difficulty until one of its members, Sewell Newhouse, invented a steel trap. Production and sales of this trap, the best of its kind, became the economic mainstay of the Oneida Community. Later other industries were added. The community

Perfectionism. A doctrine that people are capable of living a sinless life on earth.

Table 16.1   Comparison of successful and unsuccessful nineteenth-century communities   Kanter's study of characteristics of successful and unsuccessful nineteenth-century communities is of interest because it may provide some clues as to ways modern communes can ensure their survival. The nine communities designated as successful by Kanter had all lasted more than one generation. The shortest duration of any of this group was 33 years. The 21 communities designated as unsuccessful had a much shorter existence. The longest any of these lasted was 16 years, never for more than one generation.

	SUCCESSFUL	UNSUCCESSFUL
Number	9	21
	PERCENTAGE THAT ADHERED TO THE PRACTICE	

GROUP RELATIONS

Communal family structure:

Free love or celibacy	100	29
Parent-child separation	48	15
Biological families not living together	33	5

Ritual:

Songs about the community	63	14
Group singing	100	73
Special community occasions celebrated	83	50

Mutual criticism:

Regular confession	44	0
Mutual-criticism sessions	44	26
Daily group meetings	56	6

PROPERTY AND WORK

Communistic sharing:

Property signed over to community at admission	100	45
Community-as-whole owned land	89	76
Community-owned buildings	89	71
Community-owned furniture, tools	100	79
Community-owned clothing, personal effects	67	28

Communal labor:

No compensation for labor	100	41
No charge for community services	100	47
Job rotation	50	44
Communal work efforts	100	50
Fixed daily routine	100	54

Source: Reprinted by permission of Psychology Today magazine. Copyright © 1970 Ziff-Davis Publishing Company.

was thus fortunate in solving the economic difficulties which have caused so many other communal experiments to fail (Robertson, 1970).

Rosabeth Moss Kanter, in her book *Commitment and Community* has identified some of the features of life at Oneida which seem to have made it a happy, well-integrated community of several hundred people. All members of the community lived in one house. Although each adult had a private room, large areas of the house, such as the dining hall and recreation rooms, were communal. In order to play down materialism and competition, the Oneidans eliminated the concept of private property. All property, even clothing, was jointly owned by all members of the community.

Job Rotation. Work was shared and each member was expected to take part. Specific jobs were rotated, so that everyone would have a turn at the more desirable jobs as well as the less desirable ones. At Oneida, as at other communal experiments, **job rotation** proved to be a significant way of promoting harmony and satisfaction among members. Although differences in natural ability were recognized, they were not rewarded or penalized; no one type of work was awarded higher status than any other. Equal respect was given to any member who did his or her work well.

Job rotation. Assigning work so that everyone takes turns at the dull jobs as well as the more satisfying ones.

Mutual Criticism. However strong the ties between members of a community, and however harmonious their principles and goals, interpersonal conflicts and some incidents of unacceptable behavior are likely to occur. The Oneidans dealt with such problems through a system called **mutual criticism.** If members were considered to be deviating in some way from group norms, they were required to meet with a committee that would evaluate them, analyzing both good points and bad points. The process, although painful, was felt by members to be cleansing. In fact, mutual criticism eventually came to be used as a method of self-improvement, with members who had committed no offense volunteering themselves for analysis.

Mutual criticism. Group evaluation of an individual's conduct, especially of behavior that deviates from group norms.

For the Oneida Community, mutual criticism was a highly effective means of integrating the group. Not only did it enforce the group's principles, it served to reinforce them—that is, to kindle the community's enthusiasm for its ideals. Other communes have made use of some group method of criticism in **encounter groups** or other meetings, and Kanter found that such communes have been more successful than communes that lack this feature.

Having and Caring for Children. In order to perfect society, Noyes believed that only those who were superior both mentally and physically should bear children. He thus instituted a system called **stirpiculture** whereby couples wishing to have children would be evaluated by a committee before receiving permission to do so. Couples not selected for stirpi-culture were expected to practice birth control.

During the ten years in which stirpiculture was practiced by the Oenida Community, 58 children were born. Infants remained with their mothers until the age of 15 months. Thereafter they were cared for communally. As all adults were supposed to love all adults, they were also supposed to love all children. A special relationship between parents and child was con-sidered out of keeping with the principles of universal love. All evidence indicates that the children born in the Oneida Community were well pro-vided for, both physically and emotionally. The children themselves, as adults, have reported that they had a very happy childhood (Robertson).

Reasons for Ending the Experiment.   In 1879, the Oneida Community dis-banded. Noyes had left for Canada in 1877, fearing legal prosecution, and no adequate leader was found to replace him. Weakened by increasing discontent and factionalism, the community was unable to withstand the external pressure which had by this time become extreme. The surrounding society was strongly opposed to the Oneida Community's radical practices of group marriage and stirpiculture. The Oneidans had created a society that eliminated legal marriages and the nuclear family, two institutions Americans had taken to be necessary, morally proper, and natural. Like the Mormons, the Oneida Community posed a threat to the country's beliefs and ideals. That the community had endured and prospered made their experiment seem even more threatening.

In attempting to evaluate the Oneida experiment as a model for other communes, Noyes' leadership must be taken into consideration. He was a charismatic leader with a profound devotion to his cause and an ability to transmit his enthusiasm to others. It is not surprising that leadership at Oneida failed when Noyes retired. It is possible that no one could really have replaced him, and that the Oneida Community could not have suc-ceeded at all without John Humphrey Noyes. But the Oneida experiment remains an example of an alternative system that did succeed for more than a generation in both an economic and a social sense. A business enterprise called Oneida, Ltd. was formed in 1880 to continue the business activities of the community, especially the manufacture of silverware, and stock in the new company was distributed among the members of the Oneida Com-munity. The company is still in existence today, and the Mansion House is still occupied by relatives and descendants of the original members (Kanter, 1972).

DECISION MAKING IN COMMUNES

The significance of a charismatic leader, such as Noyes was in the Oneida Community, lies in the effectiveness of such a leader in holding the group

Stirpiculture. A system by which only people considered to be men-tally and physically superior were allowed to have children.

together, making decisions and resolving problems as they arise in the day-to-day life of the commune. By definition, the sharing of communal living requires members of a commune to cooperate with each other and coordinate their activities in building a common life. However, some communes are more concerned with maintaining the voluntary nature of their association than they are with efficiency in meeting group needs. Such communes place a high value on freedom and spontaneity of individual behavior. Based on an extensive analysis of data on comtemporary communes compared with successful nineteenth-century communal groups, Kanter has identified four ways in which communes approach the problem of decision making. She calls these __anarchism, organized democracy, charisma, and variants of traditional systems. (Kanter, 1973).__

Anarchism. A philosophy that holds all forms of authority, rules, and regulations to be undesirable.

Anarchism. Anarchism tends to be associated with communes that are small in size and in the early stages of development, with a membership that shares rejection of the larger society more than they share any affirmative philosophy. The desire to be free—of rules and regulations, of commitment—does not provide a basis for order or productivity. Less stable than other types of organization, anarchistic communes are more transient. Where the commune survives, anarchy frequently has given way to some other form of decision making, such as organized democracy or charisma (Kanter, 1973).

Organized Democracy. In communes that operate on a system of __organized democracy,__ authority and responsibility are delegated to members in a well-defined and orderly manner. Organized democracy is characteristic of larger, more complex communes. Where the commune stresses equality, as, for example, in the Israeli kibbutz, leadership positions are rotated frequently. The system of the Hutterites, while still democratic, is more authoritarian and has been called **managed democracy.** Characterized by more control by officials or managers, as well as less participation in decision making by members, managed democracy shares some traits of communes centered around charismatic leaders (Kanter, 1973).

Democracy. Government by the people, especially rule by the majority.

Charisma. In communes directed by charismatic leaders, authority is invested in the leader who is considered to be in some way an extraordinary person, possibly **divine,** and whose teachings may form the basic beliefs of the group. Historically, communes led by charismatic persons have been fairly common: Oneida was founded on the teachings of Noyes; the Shaker community was founded by Ann Lee, considered to be divine; Synanon is led by Charles Dederich, highly revered by the commune's members. The notorious Charles Manson family was based on charismatic leadership. This form of organization is efficient, of course, for one person can make decisions more swiftly and easiy than many. It also carries with it the danger of **totalitarian** rule. The Farm, a rural commune in Tennessee, has been described as a dictatorship run by the leader Stephen Gaskin (Rothschild and Wolf, 1976). However, charismatic leaders need not be dictatorial and historically they usually have not been. Noyes, for example, was viewed as guiding the Oneida Community, not ruling it, and members participated in the decision-making process.

Variants of Traditional Systems.   Traditional systems allow persons to rule through ownership of the land or through their position in family or tribal councils. In one case, the oldest or wisest member of the commune may take the role of tribal leader. In another, a group of members who are most committed or who have been in the commune for the longest time may function as an aristocracy in controlling the behavior of newer members.

Caplow has said that in order to survive as social organizations, communes have to maintain stability, achievement, social integration, and voluntary participation. These goals are sought by contemporary communes in a variety of different ways, so that a commune may change its decision-making procedure from time to time, and communes resist being put into any neat and tidy system of classification. We will look at several different types of contemporary communes in trying to understand the complexity and diversity of this form of social organization as an alternative to traditional family life.

ANARCHISTIC COMMUNES

Anarchistic communes are generally hippie communes. Berger, Hackett, and Millar (1974), as part of their study of child-rearing practices in communal settings, have developed a rather complete statement of the values on which these communes are formed. The major stress is on full expression of feelings and unbounded freedom. No behavioral norm takes precedence over the search for self. A second major concern is for economic independence and **self-sufficiency.** Hippie communes seek to possess and consume as little as possible. In line with this, they value nudity, organic foods, and organic architecture over any synthetic material. A third strong emphasis is an affirmation of the present over any planning for the future. And finally, they emphasize brotherhood and equality. Unfortunately, conflicts arise between the values of freedom and communal solidarity. There are also problems in getting chores done, setting aside money for rent and taxes, or getting crops planted in time when the emphasis is on spontaneity and enjoyment of the present.

Morningstar Ranch.   The story of Morningstar Ranch, an early hippie commune in California, is an example of the problems that come with lack

Totalitarian. Characterized by centralized, absolute control over totally subjected individuals.

Self-sufficiency. Ability to provide for individual or group needs without outside help.

of restraint. Established in 1966 as an open-land commune by the owner, Lou Gottlieb, Morningstar was eventually destroyed by bad relations with the surrounding community and consequent legal prosecution.

When Gottlieb first declared his 30 acres open land, permitting anyone who wished to build there, he intended the area to be used as a sanctuary. He also felt that he was making a move against private ownership of land. Gottlieb and his cofounders refrained from making rules or setting up any structure. It was their hope that at Morningstar people could live in freedom and in harmony with the land.

Since Morningstar was established at the same time that Haight-Ashbury in San Francisco was on the decline, the commune was almost immediately deluged with hundreds of people drifting out of the urban hippie scene. The results were disastrous. The land was ravaged, buildings were wrecked, and with insufficient sanitary facilities, the area became polluted. The commune was closed as a health hazard by local authorities, the beginning of a series of legal hassles in which Gottlieb is still involved.

A description of Morningstar is essentially a description of its problems. It is impossible to speak of the commune's systems of marriage, child

rearing, or decision making, since the commune was based on a lack of system. As strictly defined, the term commune would not really apply to Morningstar. It might be described more as an experiment in lifestyle, communal insofar as there is sharing and mutual assistance as the need arises (Roberts, 1971).

Because of the severe problems at Morningstar, Gottlieb and Bill Wheeler of the Wheeler Ranch, another open-land commune, attempted to develop an ideology that might provide the commune with a sense of purpose (Roberts). Some Morningstar people moved to Wheeler's and some to other communes. The question raised by these anarchist experiments is, of course, whether communes can exist without organizational structure and, if so, for how long. Lack of rules within the commune concerning work, interpersonal relationships, and economic cooperation led to such internal disorder that the commune could not deal with external pressure. Oneida, by contrast, survived for 33 years under extreme external pressure.

Huw Williams, who started Freedom Farm, also in California, in 1963, stated to Sara Davidson in an interview that it's impossible to have "both a commune, where everyone lives and works collectively, and free land, where anyone can settle." Freedom Farm experimented with communal living but encountered so many problems that it converted to simply a cluster of nuclear families living near each other in an isolated rural setting and co-operating to about the same extent that villagers in a rural settlement might do (Davidson, 1970).

Anarchistic communes have been estimated to require from $40 to $60 per month per person to keep going. Sources of support are varied: collective enterprises such as leatherwork or pottery, welfare checks, food stamps, inheritances, birthday checks, and sometimes paid employment in the surrounding area (Berger et al.).

Although the anarchist communes seek to achieve warm and intimate relations among all members and a family feeling within the total commune, the emphasis on freedom to make individual choices and lack of commitment make this nearly impossible. In the absence of organization, work tends to be left undone. Group meetings may be valued, but they are seldom planned for or arranged on a regular basis. There is often a lack of any ideology stronger than general discontent with the larger society.

TRANSITION FROM ANARCHY TO DEMOCRACY

Twin Oaks was started in 1967 by eight individuals who had met at a *Walden Two* conference and wanted to test some psychological theories and principles that strongly appealed to them. *Walden Two*, a novel by psychologist B. F. Skinner, is a fictional account of a utopian community formed on the principles of **behaviorist psychology.** According to these principles, all human behavior is externally conditioned. Behavior that is reinforced or rewarded will continue, while behavior that is not reinforced is

Counterculture. A culture of people whose values and customs are opposed to those of the society as a whole.

eliminated. Thus reward, not punishment, is the most effective tool for teaching (Roberts).

Twin Oaks, although inspired by *Walden Two,* has developed its own structure and culture. Its philosophical base is a blend of behaviorist principles, **counterculture** values, democratic ideals, and managed organization. Making use of ideas from a wide variety of sources, Twin Oaks has been characterized by flexibility, and this has been one of its major strengths.

How the commune worked its way through the problems of the early years has been told in simple and direct terms by Kathleen Kinkade, one of the original eight founders of Twin Oaks, in *A Walden Two Experiment.* It is the story of their progression from anarchy to organized democracy, reluctantly adopting rules and requirements in order to ensure communal survival. Today it is a highly organized community. There is a board of planners, elected by the group, and a manager for each area of work. As the commune is still small—numbering about 50 members—every member is a manager of some area, and no prestige is accorded the role (Conover, 1975). Work is distributed on a labor-credit system and jobs are rotated. Interestingly, the reward system is based on personal preferences: a person who finds a particular job undesirable will receive more credit for doing that job than will someone who finds it desirable. All work is considered equally worthy and individual accomplishments are not played up (Kanter, 1972).

Equality in all things is one of the basic ideals of the community, and members feel that it has been achieved. Members have even replaced the personal pronouns "he" and "she" with the neutral pronoun "co" in speaking and writing (Kanter, 1973). The commune's policy on marriage is to allow members freedom of choice. Whether or not to marry, what kind of relationships to form, are decisions left to the individual. Child rearing is communal, and children are cared for by the "child-raising manager" according to the principles of behaviorist psychology. The commune hopes eventually to phase out the biological family, considered to be an outmoded social institution (Roberts).

Thus far, Twin Oaks has proved to be a workable experiment. While the commune is still not economically self-supporting, its hammock-making industry is doing well, its membership is increasing, and morale is high. Twin Oaks is antithetical in many ways to hippie communes. Organization and democracy prevail, modern technology is utilized where it is not enslaving, and drugs are prohibited. The prohibition on drugs has been strictly enforced as a means of encouraging good relations with neighboring communities.

HIGHLY STRUCTURED COMMUNES

Although basically democratic in organization, communes which have a strong leader such as Charles Dederich at Synanon in California or Stephen Gaskin at The Farm, a large hippie commune in Tennessee, tend to be more highly structured in terms of relationships and responsibilities of people in the communes. The same may be said of religious communes, since rules of behavior tend to be a part of the formal beliefs of the religion. An example of this "managed democracy" is The Bruderhof.

The Bruderhof.   A Protestant sect with Hutterite origins, The Bruderhof was first established in Germany in the 1920s and is now in its third generation. Settlements are found in Great Britain and North and South America. Three of these are in the United States, numbering about 800 members. Their religion, and the commitment to living by its teachings and actualizing their spiritual ideals, form the backbone of the Bruderhof community. Members view the community as a separate people. Linked by strong religious ties, they also view themselves as one family. Their oneness is emphasized in every feature of their organization.

Hutterite. Based on the teachings of Jakob Hutter, a sixteenth-century Moravian Protestant leader.

Unlike many successful communes, The Bruderhof has not eliminated the nuclear family. On the contrary, monogamous marriage and the nuclear family are strongly supported. Families are large—ten children are not uncommon—and they form the unit around which many community activities center. It is being single that is difficult in this particular communal setting, since both marriage and childbearing bring an improvement in status (Zablocki, 1971).

Despite its significant role, however, the nuclear family is not a self-contained unit in The Bruderhof. Child rearing is communal and children are considered to be the children of all adults in the community (Zablocki). The relationship of the married couple is supposed to be based on the spiritual brotherhood of the entire community and subordinate to the unity of the church. The marital relationship is thus much larger than a bond between two individuals. Founded in the eternal, it cannot be broken and divorce is not permitted. Married couples spend a good deal of time together, alone or with their families, as well as in the work areas, and, according to Zablocki, marriage relationships in The Bruderhof seem unusually happy.

Work and labor are shared in The Bruderhof. Although not all jobs are rotated, all are considered worthy. The emphasis in the community is on work as service, an attitude which denies the importance of individual achievement and plays up the benefits of cooperation. Property is shared, including personal property (members refer to "our cup," "our chair"), and money is not used (Zablocki).

The Bruderhof is economically self-supporting. The Bruderhof industry, Community Playthings, manufactures wooden toys of high quality. Begun in 1947, the business expanded until 1965 when, with over $1 million worth of business a year, The Bruderhof cut back on its sales for fear of becoming too affluent. The goal of their industry is not profits, but quality of the product and harmony among the workers.

The communistic system of work and property has been extremely successful in The Bruderhof. But, as Zablocki remarks, communism in The Bruderhof is more than just an economic arrangement. A way of life is shared by the whole community. Anyone may join The Bruderhof, but prospective members undergo a long trial period during which they must prove their willingness to devote themselves to the community life.

While ideologies at Synanon and The Farm differ from each other and from The Bruderhof, all three are strongly involved in schooling the children of the commune in the beliefs on which the communal life is based. Discipline at Synanon is maintained through encounter-group sessions, referred to as "the game," in which children participate from the age of four. At The Farm, adherence to Gaskin's ideas is promoted through the regular Sunday lecture by Gaskin, schooling for the children, and continual reference to Gaskin's teachings in daily conversations among children as well as adult members (Rothschild and Wolf).

SPECIAL FEATURES OF URBAN COMMUNES

Urban communes can be described in the same terms Kanter uses to describe rural communes—they are voluntary, value-based, communal social orders (Kanter, 1972). However, most investigators have noted that the physical and social boundaries of city communes are less clearly defined than when a group goes off to an isolated rural area to participate in a new lifestyle. Urban **communards** are thus more limited in the extent to which they can reject the surrounding culture. For instance, the nudity found in many rural communes would not likely be tolerated by city neighbors.

Berger, Hackett, and Millar also comment that their research indicates urban communes are easier to start since all it takes is a rented house and a group of willing people. As a result, membership tends to be more fluid and participation often represents a less serious commitment to the communal ideal.

Rothschild and Wolf noted the greater involvement of urban communards in the surrounding culture in their description of the Cosmic Circle. Three of the six adult members went daily to competitive professional jobs in the outside world, returning to communal living nights and weekends. Although several of the children had elected not to attend the local public school for that year, they were bored at home and looking forward to reentering school in the fall (Rothschild and Wolf).

Rural communes, therefore, seem to be a purer form of adherence to communal ideals than urban communes. Sometimes an urban group will talk about getting some land and moving their commune to the country as an expression of their desire for true communal living, but seldom do rural groups talk about moving as a commune back to the city (Berger et al.).

Communards. People who live in communes.

CHILD REARING IN COMMUNES

Communal child rearing is a convenient way of caring for children, since responsibility is shared by all in the group. Often, it is also the means by which the commune's ideals are taught to the children. The Oneidans' belief that people should all love one another equally required a form of child rearing where biological parents were not considered different from any other adults, nor brothers and sisters differentiated from other children in the group.

The Hare Krishna communes take indoctrination of children very seriously. At age five, Krishna children are separated from their parents and sent to a special boarding school in Dallas where they are taught Sanskrit and tutored to become the future priests of the movement. Money to run the school comes from an incense business which has made the Hare Krishna very wealthy. Communal child rearing at Synanon begins at birth and stresses nonviolence throughout, while in some religious communes children are beaten regularly as a means of discipline (Rothschild and Wolf).

On the other hand, Berger, Hackett, and Millar found that in hippie communes children tend to be viewed as autonomous, independent persons capable in large measure of caring for themselves. This corresponds to the hippie values of freedom, independence, and nonorganization. The children are given full rein and encouraged to lead independent lives. Adults in these communes are likely to think of themselves as big kids still finding their way through life and regard the communal children as just littler kids, less skilled, less experienced, and only perhaps less wise.

Zicklin noted that the perception of the hippie-commune child as autonomous is accompanied by an unwillingness on the part of the adults to exercise discipline. When children do something wrong, it is up to them to change their ways. As a result of the emphasis on autonomy, many of the distinctions between children and adults that exist in conventional society are eliminated (Zicklin, 1973). In contrast to the view of suburban middle-class mothers that children must be guided through successive developmental stages to reach adulthood in their twenties, children in hippie communes are allowed to raise themselves.

Children follow the example of the adults. They use hippie forms of speech and all the routine four-letter obscenities. There are no "bad words" in their language. Sexual intercourse is not hidden from them and they participate in the smoking of marijuana when joints are passed around. When things go wrong for the children, as for the adults, it's considered to be part of their fate due to some unfortunate crossing of astrological signs.

The liberation of the children from specific guidance and discipline by adults has its counterpart in the liberation of the parents from responsibil-

Indoctrination. Instruction in a partisan or sectarian point-of-view or principle.

ity for the behavior of the children. Both in historical times and at present, the predominant view in our society has been that the behavior of children reflects upon their parents who are in some sense responsible for it. In the straight world, people who get in trouble are thought to have been badly brought up. In the hippie communes, experiences had by children are in no way self-implicating for their parents (Berger et al.).

In all of the communes described by Rothschild and Wolf in their book, *The Children of the Counterculture,* the rule seems to be that when a child requires adult attention, the nearest person is the parent. The entire commune replaces the family in child rearing, just as it replaces the family as an economic unit for consumption and production. Thus, children tend to grow up as equals in sharing the resources of the commune. Despite the fact that resources are often very limited and there is a general scruffiness of the children, they seem to be leading healthy lives. They are not being groomed to compete and achieve. Nobody asks, "what are you going to be when you grow up?" Far more important to commune parents is that their children relate openly to other people in a simple and direct way. They want for them a kind of emotional goodness which they give them at the cost of the self-centered drive that leads to great personal achievement. Rothschild and Wolf ended their year-long visit to communes and counterculture parents with very positive feelings about the possibilities for competence and self-reliance of commune children when they are grown. Whether they will continue to live communal lives, it is too early yet to know.

Kanter (1973) has said that the greatest wave of activity in building a communal lifestyle occurred in the 1840s, and then subsided during the latter part of the century. Another such wave occurred in the late 1960s and early 1970s. None of these contemporary communes has yet had time to prove it can last for more than one generation. In fact, six months is a long time for a hippie commune to survive. If lessons can be learned from the past, it does seem likely that the communes which last will be the organized democracies rather than those which stress freedom over all other values.

GROUP MARRIAGE

Another alternative to traditional marriage that shares some of the features of the communes we have been discussing is group marriage. Group marriage involves a marriage-like arrangement among three or more adults in which each adult considers himself or herself married to at least two other partners (Constantine and Constantine, 1972a). The marital relationship, as we defined it in Chapter 1, must include not only sexual privileges but also

economic cooperation and public acknowledgment of the status and responsibilities of being married persons in that society.

Because of public hostility to the concept of group marriage in our society, such complex marital arrangements have not generally been made known by participants, nor would they be legally acknowledged by society. However, the acceptance of marital responsibilities, such as economic and emotional support, is openly made by partners within the group itself. Thus group marriage contrasts strongly with the transitory arrangements between swingers based solely on the sexual relationship and exclusive of emotional attachment or economic ties.

The similarities between communes and group marriages are mainly organizational, deriving from the typical problems and advantages of group living in general. In scope and focus, communes and group marriages are essentially different. Members of a commune are committed to changing their entire lifestyle which includes, but is not limited to, marital life. A commune may practice group marriage or it may retain the system of monogamy, depending on its overall goals. Group marriage, on the other hand, has one specific goal: to define and restructure the marital relationship. Apart from their unusual marital arrangements, partners in a group marriage seem to live otherwise conventional lives, whether urban, suburban, or rural.

As mentioned in Chapter 1, anthropologists have debated whether group marriage has ever really existed. While it is unlikely that this marital pattern was ever the most common marital form in any culture, it has probably existed within many cultures at different points in time (Ellis, 1970). The number of group marriages in our society is thought to have increased in the last decade, although exact statistics are difficult to obtain because of the secrecy with which such marital arrangements are kept.

REASONS FOR FORMING GROUP MARRIAGES

Among reasons given by participants for forming a group marriage, the most common is the desire to participate in a larger number of intimate relationships than monogamy permits. Group marriage has the potential to provide a sense of community or extended family not found in the nuclear unit. Moreover, by permitting an extension of the intimate and intense relationship usually limited to one husband and one wife, group marriage may provide more opportunity for personal growth. Other reasons given for the formation of group marriages include sexual freedom, economic efficiency, and approval of the idea of group marriage (Constantine and Constantine, 1972b). Sexual intimacy, as an important aspect of interpersonal relationships, is viewed by participants as a necessary and central feature of group marriage. The possibility of experiencing a variety of intimate relationships, both sexually and emotionally, of expanding one's capacity to give and receive love, and of being permitted and to some degree compelled to act out a variety of roles, all widen personal horizons. Women, in particular, are seen to have benefited in the group-marriage situation. According to the Constantines (1972a), an all but universal outcome of group marriage is that wives begin to discover their separate existence and grow in independence of their husbands.

There are also economic advantages to group marriage. The cost of living for a large family is lower per person than for a small one; equipment can be shared; if a member is temporarily unemployed the loss of income can be absorbed by the group. Domestic labor can be shared, undesirable jobs rotated, and rigid division of labor by sex avoided. Another advantage is the availability of joint child care which frees members for other types of work. The children themselves seem to do especially well in the expanded-family situation, thriving on the extra attention and additional playmates it provides. On the negative side, difficulty in finding suitable mates and convenient and adequate housing facilities prevents many couples from entering group marriages. A further initial problem is establishing an equitable financial basis on which a number of families, whose needs and incomes vary, can operate (Levy, 1973).

PROBLEMS IN GROUP MARRIAGES

Once a group marriage is established, there are certain problems which, if not inherent in the situation itself, are at least likely to arise and may lead to the group's dissolution. Cooperative living demands more compromise than most individuals in our society are used to making. A common source of friction is conflicting attitudes toward disciplining children. Jealousy can also be a problem, given the widespread cultural association between love and exclusive possession. In addition, there may be financial problems, personality conflicts, and the pressure of social disapproval (Levy).

Group marriages, like two-person marriages, do of course dissolve, and the effects are felt both by former partners and by children. A study of the dissolution of group marriages conducted by the Constantines provides an interesting analysis of the effects on the participants which seem to contrast with those which occur in the breakup of a two-person marriage.

The data were based on a study of 60 respondents, ranging in age from 23 to 60. The marriages included from three to six partners; some lasted as long as five years, but the median for dissolved groups was 16 months (Constantine and Constantine, 1972a).

The Constantines found that the main cause of group-marriage breakups was incompatibility of the partners in basic personality traits. Without exception, those group marriages which dissolved did so effectively without societal or legal intervention. Financial issues and property settlements, matters which are frequently disruptive in ordinary divorce, were handled efficiently and satisfactorily by the members themselves.

Typically, the original marital couples remained together after the group dissolved. But according to the Constantines, it may be difficult for them to return to their previous relationship. Group marriage, like an encounter group, tends to expose the games, or interpersonal strategies, on which particular relationships are based. This is one of the potentials for personal growth offered by group marriage. And such games, once exposed, are not easily resumed. The couple may be faced with the need to develop an entirely new relationship, based on new definitions of their roles.

The Constantines conclude that in general, despite the failure of the group, the participants were often better off for having made their experiment. "The vast majority evaluate the experience as beneficial even if difficult, and most state that they would try again, given the right people" (Constantine and Constantine, 1972a, pp. 93–94.)

The expectations one brings to an interpersonal situation play a major part in that situation, both in terms of what happens and in terms of how one feels about what happens. The high expectations many individuals bring to monogamous marriage serve to intensify the frustration they feel at a reality that almost always falls short of those ideals. As a new structure in our society, group marriage has as yet fewer norms associated with it; each group of individuals has had to work out their particular problems for themselves. This fluidity of form and the less idealistic expectations of marital partners have doubtless contributed to whatever degree of success, both in terms of endurance and benefits to partners, group marriage has thus far enjoyed. However, it does not seem likely that group marriage will become a very common alternative to traditional marriage. The difficulties in establishing such a marriage, the demands of maintaining it, and the well-established pattern of monogamy into which most Americans have been socialized make it unlikely that group marriage will become the preferred marital arrangement of U.S. society in the near future (Ellis).

COHABITATION

The term cohabitation has been given a variety of definitions, some broad and others more specific. As used here, cohabitation refers to two adults of different sex sharing a household while unmarried with or without children in the household. Cohabitation offers a variety of rewards, the most important, perhaps, being the sense of intimate involvement, both sexual and emotional, unrestricted by the taboos and legal rules of the marital arrangement.

In recent years, there has been an increase in the number of cohabiting couples in the United States and other countries, notably Sweden and Denmark. While commonly associated with young people (particularly college students), intellectuals, and entertainers, cohabitation is not restricted to these groups. Rather, it occurs among all age-groups and among different social classes. In our own country, many elderly people have discovered that living together permits them to pool pension and Social Security income that might be reduced if they were legally married. In Sweden, cohabitation is found as frequently among industrial and clerical workers as it is among students or intellectuals (Trost, 1975).

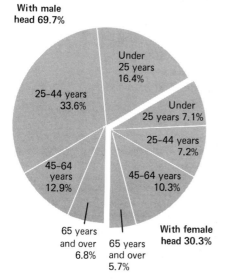

Fig. 16.1 Households shared by two unrelated individuals of different sex, 1976. In 1976, there were estimated to be 660,000 households shared by two unrelated individuals of different sex. Of this total, 460,000 had a male head and 200,000 a female head. A little less than half of these persons had never been married, 48 percent of the men and 43 percent of the women. It cannot be stated categorically that these people are cohabiting in the sense of sharing a sexual relationship since the data include households with a resident employee or a roomer of the opposite sex as well as households of partners. (Source: U.S. Bureau of the Census, 1977, P–20:306.)

Cohabitation, as we have seen in Chapter 8, does not serve the same function in all cases. It is viewed by some couples as a stage of courtship, by others as a trial marriage, and by still others as an alternative to marriage. Which viewpoint is held by the couple will be a factor in determining their marital future.

One of the problems indicated by the research on cohabitation of Lyness, Lipetz, and Davis is that couples living together appeared to have come to their arrangement with different expectations. While the women expressed a desire for marriage and thus view cohabitation as a stage in courtship or as a trial marriage, the men tended to view the arrangement as an alternative to marriage. These authors suggest that whether marriage would actually take place or not would depend on which partner's position prevailed (Lyness et al., 1972).

INTERPERSONAL RELATIONSHIPS IN COHABITATION

Certain problems are unique to couples who pursue alternative lifestyles, and cohabiting couples are no exception. In particular, cohabiting may create difficulties with landlords, employers, neighbors, and parents. Parental disapproval can be especially worrisome. Parents often feel that the female in the cohabitant relationship is being exploited sexually. For this reason, some cohabiting couples—even in their twenties and thirties—do not tell their parents they are living together. One extreme case involves a young woman in her later twenties who had her partner move out of the house whenever her parents were expected to visit. While this necessitated locking up certain rooms and putting away his possessions, the couple felt it was preferable to creating serious family disruption.

Decision Making. Cole (1977) interviewed 40 long-term cohabiting couples and found that within a year of living together primary decision making responsibility was undertaken by one partner rather than by the other or by both. Frequently the person most involved in a particular area had responsibility for making decisions in that area. For example, if one person had owned a car prior to cohabitation, he or she would continue to take responsibility for the car. All of the couples in Cole's interview indicated that some decisions were made jointly, but he observed that women were responsible for more areas than men were.

Gender Roles. A number of studies have found that there is a tendency for cohabiting couples to fall into traditional gender roles, especially with regard to housekeeping. Women tend to do the same housekeeping tasks as women in legal marriages, such as dishes and laundry. And, as in legal marriages, men take out the garbage. Interestingly the men perceive that they are sharing housekeeping tasks, while the women perceive themselves to be doing most of the work (Cole).

Sexual Relationships. While most long-term cohabiting couples say they believe in the idea of individual sexual freedom, the fact is that the majority practice monogamy. Otherwise, jealousy is likely to be a problem. Some non-monogamous individuals report that they find themselves feeling guilty about their sexual activities. It appears that it is difficult to shed one's cultural conditioning (Lobsenz, 1974).

1 at a time

Maintaining the Relationship. The factors that help to maintain an enduring cohabitant relationship seem to be very much the same factors that make for lasting marriages. Lyness, Lipetz, and Davis consider the following elements to be important: mutual trust, willingness to share personal feelings, the sense of needing one's partner, and sexual satisfaction. Cole cites research from Bower and others indicating that effective communication is vital to keeping a cohabitation relationship viable, just as it is in legal marriages.

Ending the Relationship. Dissolution of cohabitant relationships seems to follow much the same pattern as dissolution of a legal marriage. The divorce process may be seen as a series of stages in which the persons involved suffer loss, depression, and anger, then begin to reorient their lives and finally come to accept a new lifestyle. Cole believes that these stages apply equally to the dissolution of cohabitation.

POSSIBLE EFFECTS ON MARRIAGE

Some people view cohabitation as indicative of an erosion of marriage and the family and, by extension, an erosion of the fabric of society. By contrast, many social scientists view living together as functional and beneficial. Trost suggests that cohabitation, operating as a trial marriage, may in time become a social institution. Partners who discover they should not form a permanent relationship will be able to end the arrangement more easily than legal marriages and those marriages that do form will be more likely to last. There is the possibility that living together without the constraints of legal marriage serves to build happier, more durable relationships. As yet, it isn't clear to what degree cohabitation will serve as a prelude to marriage and to what degree it will be a true alternative to marriage. It does appear that many long-lasting cohabitant relationships lead to marriage.

CHOOSING TO REMAIN SINGLE

The proportion of single adults in our society has risen dramatically in the past ten years. As of March 1975, there were about 14 million women and 13 million men in the United States between the ages of 20 and 65 who either had never married or were widowed or divorced and not remarried (U.S. Bureau of the Census, *Statistical Abstract of the U.S., 1976*). Influencing the increase have been the spiraling divorce rate, later age at marriage, and a decline in the trend to early remarriage after divorce. More and more individuals are choosing to remain single, some permanently and others at least on a long-term basis.

Remaining single by choice is a surprising trend in a society where marriage has not only been associated with normality but has been considered nearly synonymous with "the good life" (Stein, 1975). As we saw in Chapter 8, being a single adult in the United States has traditionally been viewed as being in some way deviant. It was not considered that a healthy individual might choose to remain single. Rather, because of personal or social problems, the individual had failed to attain the ideal state of being married (Stein, 1975).

While some single people may in fact have problems that prevent them from marrying, sociologists have begun to recognize that singlehood may also be a choice of healthy, well-adjusted people. Peter Stein, who has done recent research on singles, views singlehood as a conscious and voluntary choice of growing numbers of people. A new wariness about marriage seems to figure importantly in the decision to remain single. Some singles who have not been married say they have seen their friends suffer through bad marriages. Others seem to be enjoying life too much to settle down, at least for now, and divorced people do not seem quite as eager as in the past to remarry.

Some caution is required in ascribing motivations to singles for their choice to remain unmarried. Despite a tendency of the general public, encouraged by the media, to view the unmarried in terms of the stereotype of the swinging single, the single population is in fact highly diverse. Those never married, those formerly married with children, and those formerly

DOONESBURY   by Garry Trudeau

© 1975, G. B. Trudeau/Distributed by Universal Press Syndicate.

married but childless show significant differences both in their motivations for remaining single and in the lifestyle their singleness will imply. As with any way of life, singlehood has as many subtle variations as there are individual personalities, and each variation is affected by social and economic realities.

On the whole, single life seems more satisfying for the upper-middle class than for any other group. To a large degree, the basis for this is economic. If singleness is attractive for the freedom it offers, it is affluence that makes this freedom possible to achieve. An unemployed parent with three children has little freedom, single or not. The substantial income of the upper-middle-class worker permits a choice in such basic aspects of life as housing; it also makes possible the entertainment, vacations, and trips which are a source of social contacts. Moreover, members of the upper-middle class are more likely to be involved in satisfying work, a focus of interest and involvement equal to interpersonal relationships, and, in itself, a further source of contacts (Jacoby, 1974).

GENDER DIFFERENCES

The state of being single is different for women and men. They confront different problems and must deal with a different set of stereotypes.

One of the major problems facing single women is economic: less education, fewer work options, and generally lower salaries are some of the factors which create severe money problems for single women, often compounded still further by the demands of caring for one or more children. Historically, women have not usually been trained to be financially independent. Rather, they have been used to having money both earned and managed for them, and they must make a psychological adjustment to their independent status. Even women with high-paying jobs have tended to make fewer investments in stocks, property, or pensions which might ensure their future economic security than have men with comparable salaries (Jacoby).

Although social norms are changing, they still reflect a double standard and further limit the single woman's life. For this reason, many unmarried women move from smaller to larger cities where anonymity affords them a higher degree of social freedom.

In some ways, men can lead single lives more easily than women. Raised to be independent, a man may not need to make as great a psychological adjustment to the single state as a woman will. Better trained and educated, he will probably have a better job and the economic and social benefits it provides. But single men too must face a negative stereotype that prevails in our society: that of the swinging single. In a survey of 50 major corporations, it was found that only 2 percent of the executives were single. Although a bias against singles was denied by the respondents,

60 percent said that they believed single executives tend to make snap judgments and 25 percent classified singles as less stable than married individuals. A faculty member at Michigan State University, 34 years old and unmarried, reported that no one in East Lansing would rent him a house. Owners feared that, as a single man, he would be likely to throw wild parties and wreck the place (Jacoby).

Whatever the problems of being single, uppermost in the attractions is the element of free choice, whether of job, house, friends, or sexual partner. When married or living with someone, one's identity is determined in part by another person's choices. Where one lives, for example, will probably be a matter of compromise. The choice of a job—which involves location, joint income and hours available for domestic life—is as much a family matter as an individual decision. Even personal friends are often determined by one's marriage: once married, the couple tends to become a social unit. Several of the singles in Stein's sample mentioned that while married, they had had to associate only with mutually satisfying friends. It was also mentioned that individual friendships, particularly with members of the opposite sex, were often seen as threatening by one's mate.

Singlehood, by contrast, offers the possibility of autonomy, the ability to live one's own life. Judith Thurman, in an article discussing her desire to remain single, emphasizes personal freedom as the main attraction. She describes how she has chosen with care every object that she owns, how she has determined in a sense her own world. She remarks that, "Choice . . . for people who live in twos and threes and fours, is a process. Agreement is a process—a necessary self-limitation. But alone, one is the author of every choice. One's choices are one's identity, even in petty things" (Thurman, 1975, p. 64).

The desire for self-direction extends to the interpersonal sphere as well. The desire to make contact with people, even passionate contact, yet at the same time to be able to remain oneself, or "intact," is a goal of singlehood. Such autonomy of course has its other, less attractive aspects. Living alone can sometimes be lonely. One must actively seek out the companionship that marriage automatically, if often unsatisfactorily, provides. Moreover, Thurman suggests that putting one's own freedom first, refusing to be bound, committed, or accountable to another person, may in effect limit the depth of the relationships one is able to form.

MEETING OTHER SINGLES

The desire to remain free of a binding relationship in no way implies, for most singles, an avoidance of relationships in general. On the contrary, the possibility of exploring a variety of relationships is often seen to be one of the major attractions of singlehood. Unfortunately, once a person is out of school, meeting new friends can be much harder (Starr and Carns, 1972).

In many communities social life revolves around married couples. The single person may feel uncomfortable in these groups and may also be viewed as a threat by married friends.

For upper-middle-class singles, work is a source of personal associations, and many indicate that this is one of the most satisfying aspects of their jobs. For blue-collar and low-level white-collar workers, however, jobs tend to be sex-segregated. Thus many lower-income workers, denied the social aspects of the work world as well as sufficient money to indulge in entertainment, recreation, or vacations, find it difficult to meet potential partners (Jacoby).

The singles bars provide a possible but, for many, unsatisfying source of personal associations (Starr and Carns). Studies indicate that singles frequent these bars in search of companionship, affection, excitement, and social acceptance. For many, the bars are disappointing and even depressing. The false glamour, hyped-up stimulation, and socially enforced role playing obstruct the development of meaningful relationships between men and women (Stein).

Other, equally unsatisfying, sources of personal contacts are the singles clubs and housing complexes. Focusing on the sexual aspect of singlehood, in regard to availability, need, and allure, these commercial enterprises tend to exploit and degrade the single population. In one housing complex, described by an observer as a "sexual Disneyland," the men, using sex almost as a drug, seem to be skittering along the surface of life, while the women were degraded as sexual objects. For anyone interested in a continuing relationship, a friendship, anything more than a one-night stand with a member of the opposite sex, the singles housing complex would seem to have little to offer (Proulx, 1973).

Finding a substitute for the traditional networks of human relationships has been cited as the greatest need single people feel (Kieffer, 1977). Stein believes that formal structures will develop to help meet the needs of single people for friendship and intimacy, and that in the large cities singlehood is emerging as a social movement. Reacting against the restrictions of marriage, singles are seeking self-development, freedom of choice, support structures, both social and personal, and the elimination of social and economic discrimination. The developing ideologies of other liberation movements—blacks, women, and gays—have been useful in helping singles define their own needs. Of further support have been such groups as Zero Population Growth and the National Organization for Non-Parents, which help to alter the stereotyped associations of normality with marriage and parenthood (Stein).

Network. An interconnected chain, group, or system.

THE SEARCH FOR INTIMACY AND VARIETY

Participation in all of the alternatives to marriage discussed in this chapter —communal lifestyles, group marriages, cohabitation, and remaining single —seems to be based primarily on a search for closer and deeper personal relationships and for relationships with more different people. Many Americans are no longer satisfied with a lifetime commitment to just one person, permitting only one deep and meaningful association with a person of the other sex. The cultural norm of restriction of sexual relationships to legally married couples is increasingly less significant in controlling behavior. Availability of reliable contraceptives and safe abortion procedures permits sexual relations to be viewed as a means to achieve intimacy without risk of unplanned parenthood. Whether these lifestyles, now described as alternatives to marriage, will eventually become the major forms of interpersonal relationships in American society, supplanting the traditional family, is discussed in the next chapter, The Future of the Family in the United States.

Summary

1. The purpose of this chapter is to explore alternative ways of seeking closer and deeper personal relationships (intimacy) and relationships with more different people (variety): communes, group marriages, cohabitation, and singlehood.

2. Communes are formed by groups of people who believe they can create an ideal society in which their particular economic, religious, or political goals can be attained. Communes are not new in American society. The Oneida Community is an example of one that flourished in the nineteenth century.

3. One of the main problems in holding a commune together is decision making. There are four common approaches. (a) Charisma: authority is invested in a leader with a magnetic personality (Oneida). (b) Anarchism: no rules or regulations; no structure (Morningstar Ranch). (c) Organized democracy: authority and responsibility are delegated to members in an orderly manner (Twin Oaks); may be highly structured (The Bruderhof). (d) Variants of traditional systems: authority invested in person who owns the land or has won a position of leadership in family or tribal councils (The Farm).

4. In addition to the more common rural communes, there are urban communes where membership is more fluid and there is less commitment to the communal ideal. In all communes, the responsibility for child rearing is shared by the group and is often the means by which the commune's ideals are taught.

5. Another alternative lifestyle in which a small number of people participate is group marriage. People may form group marriages to participate in a larger number of intimate relationships, to gain a sense of extended family, and to provide more opportunity for personal growth.

6. The most common alternative to traditional marriage is cohabitation. Cohabitation offers a variety of rewards, primarily the sense of intimate involvement unrestricted by taboos and rules of the marital arrangement, although there are problems cohabitating couples have to face that legally married couples don't (difficulties with landlords, employers, neighbors, and parents).

7. Remaining single is increasingly popular, although still chosen by a relatively small number of people. Singlehood brings different problems for women and men. Women face economic discrimination and double standards in sexual relationships; men are handicapped by the stereotype of the swinging bachelor and the biases against it. For both sexes, singlehood offers the opportunity to be self-directing, but it can also be lonely. Finding satisfactory substitutes for traditional networks of human relationships is the greatest need felt by singles, and some researchers believe that formal structures will eventually develop to meet their needs for friendship and intimacy.

Key Concepts

Traditional marriage
Alternative lifestyle
Commune
Group marriage
Utopia
Charismatic leader
Decision making
Job rotation
Mutual criticism
Stirpiculture

Anarchism
Organized democracy
Free land
Self-sufficiency
Ideology
Counterculture
Behaviorist psychology
Encounter group
Autonomy
Swinging single

Review and Discussion

1. What type of commune might you like to be a part of? Why? If you would not like to be a part of any commune, give your reasons.

2. Why hasn't the Twin Oaks commune been persecuted as the Oneida Community was? How does this difference reflect changes in attitudes and behavior in our society?

3. What are some of the advantages and disadvantages of parenting in a commune compared with parenting in a nuclear family?

4. What differences might there be in the interpersonal relationships in a group marriage of three people compared with one of four people?

5. Why is singlehood generally less satisfying for persons of lower economic status?

Suggested Readings

CONSTANTINE, L. R. AND J. M. CONSTANTINE (1973). *Group Marriage: A Study of Contemporary Multilateral Marriage.* New York: Macmillan.

An account of experimentation in new family forms by two sociologists who have been both participating members and observers of group marriage. Includes statistical data in appendixes.

HENDERSON, L. T. (1975). *The Holy Experiment.* New York: Exposition Press.

A novel about life in the Rappite (Harmonists) utopian community based on factual data. The story takes place in the late nineteenth century and revolves around the effects on the celibate religious commune of a lively, red-blooded woman who finds it impossible to observe the rule of celibacy.

KINKADE, K. (1973). *A Walden Two Experiment: The First Five Years of Twin Oaks Community.* New York: Morrow.

Describes the day-to-day problems of establishing a new commune, the choices which have to be made, the idealism, and the disillusionments. Interesting parallels can be seen between activities of a traditional farm family and the rural Virginia Twins Oaks commune.

STEIN, P. (1976). *Single.* Englewood Cliffs, N.J.: Prentice-Hall.

Through interviews and statistical data, the author analyzes lifestyles of single adults in America today and their experiences at work, in interpersonal relationships, and in society.

WEISBERG, D. K. (1977). The Cinderella children. *Psychology Today* 10:11:84–87.

Discusses the problems and benefits of children raised in urban communal households—problems such as too many rules, too many people ordering them to do things; and benefits such as learning responsibility, more bedtime stories, and more companionship.

The Future of the Family in the United States | 17

What will the average American family be like by the turn of the century? It's not likely to consist of a working husband, a housewife, and their dependent children. Already this description of the traditional nuclear family accounts for only 37 percent of the people in this country (Cole, 1977). The rest are divided among dual-career marriages, childless marriages, single-parent families, the once-married, the never-married, the group-married, the living-together, the homosexually paired, and other types of family units.

We might also ask whether, despite a changing format, the family unit of the future will be bound together by traditional family values—loyalty, duty, self-sacrifice, sharing, lasting love. Already some observers worry that growing cultural emphasis on self-actualization, individual autonomy, and mobility is weakening family bonds and may eventually override them. However, this projection may be unnecessarily gloomy. Many of the changes we are seeing in family life have potential for enhancing the warmth, understanding, and supportiveness among members. By the year 2000, emotional ties within families may actually be stronger than they are now.

In this chapter we will examine the picture of the future of the family from two angles. The first part of the chapter summarizes some of the present trends in family life and considers the question of which trends are likely to continue into the future. The second part of the chapter looks at some of the ways U.S. society can act to support family life, if there is national consensus that this is what we want to do.

The preceding sixteen chapters have presented a realistic unprejudiced conception of the state of marriage and family living in the United States in the seventies. Even the first two chapters, on cross-cultural variations in the family and historical antecedents of the U.S. family, were included to increase understanding of present-day family patterns. Much detail and depth of meaning were sacrificed in order to present a picture that college students could assimilate in one school term, but within these limitations, the overall image is as realistic as we have been able to make it.

In presenting this image, we have looked at the family as a social institution which meets the needs of the society for order and continuity. We have also looked at the family as a network of interacting personalities which meets the needs of individuals for intimate personal relationships. To do either of these things requires a lot of mental effort, for both are abstractions. To be able to "see" them, you have had to lift yourself out of your personal world and sit on an imaginary hilltop, looking down at U.S. society. From that vantage point, perhaps you can now see beyond current problems and upheavals to glimpse the rich possibilities family life holds for today and for the future.

Fig. 17.1 Percent favoring a single standard of sexual conduct for men and women.   More females than males reject the traditional double standard of sexual conduct. However, both males and females moved strongly toward endorsement of a single standard for both sexes over the three-year period between 1971 and 1974. (Source: Adapted from Ferrell, Tolone, and Walsh, 1977.)

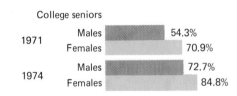

FLEXIBILITY IN SOCIAL ROLES

Today people in the United States are freer than they have ever been to seek satisfying interpersonal relationships, both in and out of marriage. There is increasing resistance by women and men to being locked into roles and lifestyles which restrict self-development. This trend toward growing freedom in sexuality, gender-role choice, and mate choice is expected to continue.

GREATER SEXUAL FREEDOM

Recent social movements—the youth movement of the sixties—the civil rights movement, women's liberation, gay liberation—reflect an increased emphasis in U.S. society on personal freedom. Though not always oriented toward changes in sexual behavior or gender-role norms, they all seem to have contributed to the increase in sexual freedom in the last ten years (Gagnon and Simon, 1974).

If current trends continue, sexual intercourse may become almost universal for single men and women of all classes. Yorburg (1973) states definitely that it will. Women are expected to be increasingly active in seeking and enjoying sexual encounters, no longer leaving it to men to take the initiative. Advances in contraceptive technology can already free them from fear of unwanted pregnancies, and growing social tolerance will increasingly free them from inhibitions to female sexuality inherent in the traditional double standard for males and females. The growing pool of divorced women is another factor in the expectation of greater sexual freedom. Divorce without remarriage may mean an increase in the number of women who are sexually experienced and available as partners outside of marriage. And as divorce loses its social stigma, divorcées may serve younger women as models of an alternative lifestyle which does not necessarily lead to marriage (Gagnon and Simon; Yorburg).

LESS DIFFERENTIATION IN GENDER ROLES

Traditional socialization to sharply differentiated identities as males and females has been decreasing at the following three important developmental stages:

1. During early childhood, parents are more likely than in the past to dress children of both sexes in similar clothes. They are also more likely to discourage aggressive behavior in boys and less likely to emphasize career preparation for males only, especially in middle-class families.

2. During adolescence, unisex clothes and haircuts are almost standard, and the attitudes of those reared along more traditional lines are influenced by the peer group in that direction.

3. Among adults, the effect of the women's liberation movement is to lessen the importance of gender differences in our society. At the same time, occupations are increasingly bureaucratic or service-oriented, requiring work skills which women can perform as well as or better than men, so that the lines between women's work and men's work are no longer so clearly drawn (Gagnon and Simon).

The reduction in gender differences will bring changes in interpersonal relationships. For instance, adolescent males may find it easier to develop friendships with females. Gagnon and Simon have predicted that boys will be less likely to belong to all-male peer groups, less likely to focus on sex in their relations with females, less likely to worry about sexual performance, less likely to be pushed toward sexual exploitation of females by the old male-achievement syndrome, and more likely to view sexual intercourse as an expression of affection. These trends have already begun in middle-class populations, but not among lower-class and minority groups, so tensions between males of different social classes may increase temporarily until adjustments are reached.

The expected decrease in pressure for male sexual aggressiveness may mean that females will no longer be defined largely by males as sexual objects. Instead of reflecting male attitudes, females may increasingly take the initiative in defining for themselves what a female should be (Gagnon and Simon).

GREATER FREEDOM IN MARITAL CHOICE

In the future, people will be even freer than now to fall in love and marry whomever they choose. Family pressures in mate selection are decreasing, and class, religion, and ethnic background are becoming less significant in marital choice as young people become more mobile, more highly educated, and less ethnocentric (Yorburg).

In some instances, the challenging of traditional sex roles may even alter the criteria by which females and males choose a possible mate. Safilios-Rothschild (1976) thinks we may before long see an increase in the number of matches in which a woman exchanges her occupational prestige for a man's sexual attractiveness and cooking skills, instead of the other way around. But for the present generations who have been socialized to stereotypes of male supremacy, it is unlikely that many men will fall in love with and marry women of higher status, or that many women will want to marry lower-status men.

ANDROGYNY FOR THOSE WHO CHOOSE IT

Stereotyped differences in the behavioral roles of women and men based on their sex alone are clearly less powerful now than even a generation ago. How far U.S. society will go in the direction of **androgyny**—behavior in which there is no gender-role differentiation—is uncertain. For some couples, however, this is already a reality of their daily lives. For these people, chores are done and career choices made without regard for sex, and they regard it as a trend which means greater opportunities for personal fulfillment for both females and males. Some men and women may prefer to be executives, some may choose to keep house and care for children. Some choose marriage; others prefer to remain single. If current trends prevail, choices requiring competitiveness and independence will not be closed to women; choices requiring passiveness and nurturant behavior will not be closed to men. And as their parents' gender roles become less rigidly defined, children will be aware of a broader range of acceptable options for developing their own talents and inclinations (Osofsky and Osofsky, 1972).

> **Androgyny.** Behavior in which traditional characteristics of men and women are merged and there is no gender-role differentiation.

OPPORTUNITY FOR ROLE MAKING

People learn their social roles through adoption of an accepted set of norms. However, in times of rapid change or in a new environment, it may seem that available role definitions are inappropriate. In such situations, interpersonal experimentation can lead to new role definitions, a process that Joan Aldous calls **role making.** The changes that have led 44 percent of the married women in the United States to take on paid jobs have rendered invalid many characteristics of the old male-female roles, for they were based on the man-working, wife-at-home setup. Twenty-five years earlier, in 1950, only 24 percent of married women were in the labor force, about 8 million women then, compared to 21 million in 1975 (U.S. Bureau of the Census, 1976, P-23:58). Many people are now experimenting and improvising to fit the realities of their situations.

> **Role making.** Improvising new role definitions to meet changing social conditions.

Today women have greater interest in role making than men, for they are often still saddled with traditional gender norm expectations that they cook, clean house, care for the children, and run errands in addition to their new occupational responsibilities. To lessen role overload, they are helping husbands to experiment with reorganization of family responsibilities and urging them to do the laundry, wash dishes, and change diapers, which, after all, are easily acquired skills. Although it may lead to conflicts, such role making can have positive effects. Couples who exercise the freedom to create a set of roles that work for them may develop more of their potential as individuals and as a social unit than if they moved only within prescribed traditional roles. And the flexibility they work into their relationship can help them adjust to change (Aldous, 1974).

FREEDOM TO REJECT FEMINIST GOALS

The existence of the women's liberation movement is a fact, and, according to Safilios-Rothschild, all people, whether they agree with it or not, are affected by it. One of the major changes is that women may now talk about unequal treatment without being ridiculed or punished by males for their "aggressive" behavior (Safilios-Rothschild, 1972). However, people who prefer to follow traditional behavior patterns will still have the freedom to do so. While many will feel that the best chances for rewarding relationships between men and women lie in relating to each other as equals and as individuals, others will probably continue to prefer the traditional differentiation between the sexes.

The women's liberation movement has already encountered considerable resistance from some of the very women it seeks to liberate. Some probably feel that it is more rewarding to cater to male friends or husbands who feel threatened by assertiveness in women. And many may be unwilling to give up the relative leisure and freedom from responsibilities of the traditional female role, recognizing that equal rights would also mean equal responsibilities. Yorburg suggests that to try to force the liberated female role on all women, regardless of their interests, values, and skills, would be just as destructive as trying to force them all into the dependent housewife mold, whatever their talents may be (Safilios-Rothschild, 1972; Bernard, 1972b; Yorburg).

FLEXIBILITY IN LIFESTYLES

Just as there is expected to be increasing flexibility in social roles in the years ahead, there is also expected to be increasing acceptance of varying forms of couple relationships and family life. Although patriarchal marriage may be on the way out in the United States, marriage itself will certainly continue as a social institution, in changed formats that better meet contemporary needs. There are, of course, many people who reject marriage altogether and choose alternatives like singlehood or cohabitation instead. But they are in the minority today and will probably remain so in the future.

MARRIAGE STILL POPULAR

Demographers cite statistical evidence that marriage is still the dominant family form in the United States:

1. In the 1970s, the percentage of women who never marry is the same as the average for this century: only about 7 percent.
2. In 1975, 84 percent of all families included a wife and a husband.
3. Less than 1 percent of all couples living together have been found to be cohabiting without marriage.
4. Although divorce may eventually dissolve one out of three first marriages if the divorce rate continues its current growth, two out of three marriages will last as long as both partners are alive.
5. Divorce does not mean a rejection of marriage since four out of five divorced people eventually remarry.
6. For those who divorce and remarry, one-half to two-thirds of these second marriages will probably last as long as both partners are alive (Glick, 1977; Norton and Glick, 1976).

There is also evidence from opinion surveys that marriage will still have a strong appeal in the future despite interest in alternative lifestyles. A recent survey by Leslie Strong (1977) of male and female undergraduates at the University of Connecticut revealed that the sexually monogamous, equalitarian marriage is the family form in which these students are most willing to participate. The traditional role-segregated marriage, though desired less frequently than the equalitarian marriage, is seen as a relatively appealing choice by males, and Strong thus concludes it will remain a part of the marital picture for the immediate future.

First marriages are likely to be delayed, however, if the present trend continues. Women under 25 are today getting married at an average age of 21, compared to 20 for their mothers who married during the late 1940s and early 1950s. This postponing of marriage is probably linked to an expansion of women into roles outside the home. More than three times as many women were enrolled in college in 1974 as in 1960 and the employment of women has sharply increased (Glick, 1975).

Cohabitation may be an additional factor in the later age at marriage. The average age at marriage for men also increased by almost a full year

Fig. 17.2 Marriage rate: United States, 1925–1975. The marriage rate in 1975 was 10 per 1000 of the population, almost the same as in 1925 when it was 10.3. However, there has been considerable fluctuation in between in response to varying social conditions. The lowest point in recent U.S. history was in 1932, at the depth of a severe economic depression. The highest point was in 1946 when large numbers of military men serving abroad returned home to enter into marriages postponed because of World War II. (Source: USDHEW, 1976, Monthly Vital Statistics Report, HRA 76–1120 25:2 Supplement.)

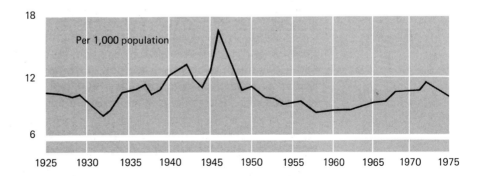

Demographers. People who study trends in the size, characteristics, and distribution of human populations.

between 1950 and 1975, from 22.8 years to 23.5 years. **Demographers** are watching these trends to see if they forecast an eventual decline in the popularity of marriage or simply a temporary delay in entering the married state (U.S. Bureau of the Census, 1977, CB77-24).

Many studies have shown that people find the greatest emotional gratification in stable, one-to-one relationships. Although marriage and parenting are often imperfect, they come closer than any other options to satisfying this emotional need. If anything, personal fulfillment will be stressed even more in the future than it has been in the past, as an antidote to increasing bureaucratization and mechanization outside the family. It is therefore predicted that marriage will remain popular, but for different reasons than in the past. Instead of marrying for motives like economic security for women, social pressure to be married, and making sex legal, future couples will tend to seek marriage as a vehicle for psychological satisfactions (Yorburg).

LIBERALIZING TREND IN SEXUAL ACTIVITY TO CONTINUE
More than 40 years ago, a scholarly treatise called *The Future of Marriage in Western Civilization* discussed the positive values associated with both premarital and extramarital sexual relationships, and suggested that acceptance of this behavior would become more widespread. Edward Westermarck, the author, predicted also that people would become more tolerant in their attitudes to homosexuality. While there have been changes in sexual attitudes since 1936 when he made his predictions, Westermarck might be dismayed to find how slow the process of change has been in this regard. In fact, it sometimes seems that sexual behavior has been changing faster than has public acknowledgment of it. Mace (1976b), on the other hand, suggests that by the year 2000, permissive attitudes will not have become so widespread as some present-day scholars are predicting. Nevertheless, he does believe that the liberating trends we see today have enough momentum to continue, at least for a short period.

Extramarital Sex.   The expected increase in sexual activity prior to marriage has been discussed earlier in the chapter. Extramarital coitus will probably become more common also, among both women and men. In part, this will occur because the penalty for adultery will decrease as divorce loses its social and economic stigma. At the same time, justification for extramarital sex will increase with the growing attitude that marriage can't supply all of a person's need for intimacy and that sexual expression is an important part of self-actualization. Participation in extramarital coitus is expected to remain a private adventure rather than a joint activity of the married couple, though swinging may still have its advocates (Gagnon and Simon).

Intimate Networks.   A pattern which may meet sexual and interpersonal needs for a small number of people is the formation of intimate networks, a series of interrelated close friendships which may or may not involve sexual intimacy. According to a study of already existing networks, a network may include married and single heterosexual and homosexual friends. The people who are married tend to be partners in sexually open marriages. They know about and accept each other's outside relationships; they accept and value emotional relationships with nonspouses, but they don't live with nonspouses for prolonged periods; and they usually carry on nonmarital sexual behaviors as individuals rather than as a swinging couple. Interpersonal conflicts are undoubtedly more complex in these networks than in isolated dyadic relationships, but participants claim to enjoy the challenge of working out problems on a deeply personal level. Since many of the married couples are childless and interact freely with single people, their activities may further liberate sexual expression from its traditional marriage-and-parenting context (Ramey, 1975).

Heterosexual. Relating to or including both males and females.

Homosexual. Pertaining to sexual desire for, or sexual activity with, members of one's own sex.

Cohabitation.   The liberalizing trend in sexual activity is also reflected in participation in other nontraditional ways of relating to people. Cohabitation is definitely expected to increase until it becomes almost universal among young people prior to marriage. Strong found in his sample of college students that there is a relatively high level of interest in long-term cohabitation, especially among males.

It is expected to spread from the upper-middle class to all levels of society and will also include older people whose marriages have been disrupted by death or divorce. Cohabitation will probably become a standard part of courtship and may serve as a screening device to filter out relationships that would make unworkable marriages. It is not likely to replace marriage, though increasing cohabitation may lower marriage rates somewhat and contribute to the trend toward delayed first marriages. Those who do choose living together as an alternative lifestyle, instead of a trial run before marriage, will add to the decline in the birth rate, for such couples usually intend to have no children (Yorburg; Cole).

Communal Living.   Constantine and Constantine reported in 1972 that there were probably only about a thousand group marriages in existence at that time in the United States, and most observers feel that interest in this lifestyle is not likely to grow much. Group marriage garnered little support in Strong's college sample. Urban collectives and rural communes will probably continue to be initiated, but our society's stress on individualism will probably limit participation in these alternatives to a small minority (Yorburg).

Singlehood. The state of being single by choice.

Singlehood.   One of the most noticeable aspects of the liberalizing trend in sexual activity is in the lifestyle of people who choose to remain single. Many of them place a high value on variety in sexual encounters and want to preserve their freedom to establish multiple sexual contacts rather than confine themselves to monogamous relationships in or out of marriage. However, total rejection of marriage in favor of singlehood is expected to appeal only to a small minority of adults in the United States, at least for the foreseeable future.

To summarize these trends, it seems likely that cohabitation and sexual activity prior to marriage will be almost universal. However, other alternatives to traditional patterns of marriage and family will each attract only a limited number of participants. Open marriages, swinging, homosexual pairing, group marriages, urban and rural communes, and the rejection of marriage in favor of remaining single are not expected to affect the lives of most people in the United States in this century.

In fact, Edward Shorter (1975) is one sociologist who thinks that instead of extending marital intimacy outward, conjugal couples will increasingly disengage themselves from all contacts—adolescent children, close friends, neighbors—and then be torn apart from within by conflict between the spouses in these overly intense relationships, thus destroying the last remnant of family life. Shorter is in the minority, however, in his dismal view of the future of marriage. Other sociologists consider that the availability of all these alternatives to the traditional family provides a safety valve to meet the needs of people who reject traditional forms of family life and is thus a protection to the nuclear family.

CHILDREN AND CHANGE

Changes in marital formats will probably continue to involve changes in parenthood and will be caused, to some extent, by changed attitudes to children. Firmly entrenched contraceptive use and still-controversial abortions will continue to limit the number of children born. Relationships between parents and children may become friendlier, including relations between adults and their elderly parents. Children whose parents have divorced and perhaps remarried may find their lives less stressful. And a new parenting style seems to be emerging.

EFFECTS OF THE FAMILY-PLANNING MOVEMENT
Influenced by persuasive arguments about overpopulation and effective methods of limiting the size of their families, couples are expected to continue two current trends: they will choose to have fewer children, on the average, and some will choose to have no children at all. Married women

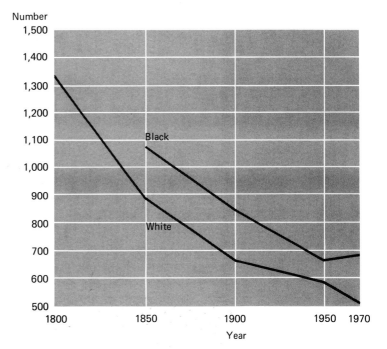

Fig. 17.3 Number of children under 5 years old per 1000 women 20–44 years old in the United States. The graph shows the substantial decline in the average number of children of pre-school age per woman of childbearing age from 1800 to 1970. It also reflects the long-term tendency for black women to bear more children than white women. (Source: Data from U.S. Bureau of the Census, 1975. *Historical Statistics of the United States. Colonial Times to 1970, Bicentennial Edition.*

under age 25 today report that they want to have only enough children for zero population growth. Although demographers note that the U.S. birth rate has risen and fallen substantially during this century in response to changing economic and political circumstances, they do not anticipate a repeat of the post-World War II baby boom (Glick, 1975).

Today's young mothers will probably have fewer children and have them in a shorter period of time than any other cohort of mothers who have married during this century. They are waiting later to start child-bearing than mothers of the 1950s and 1960s, and they are finishing sooner. They are expected to have their last child at an average age of 29.6 years, continuing a steady drop from the 32.9 years of the 1900s.

This projection of compressed childbearing years suggests a number of things about the family of the future. The spacing of the children's births will be planned to minimize ill effects on the mother's health; mothers won't have to spend many years giving full-time care to babies; parents may be better able to meet the emotional and financial needs of their children; and a longer period after their grown children leave the nest will give the parents more years alone together. In general, it seems clear that parents of the future, particularly mothers, will be making fewer sacrifices for the sake of their children and will have more time to devote to development of their own potential (Glick, 1977).

While remaining childless is a voluntary choice of substantial numbers of couples, other couples who strongly desire to become parents have been enabled to do so by recent advances in fertility control. Thus the techniques of family planning have given, and will continue to give, greater control over pregnancy, both when it is desirable and when it is to be avoided (Glick, 1977).

However, for some individuals, these family-planning choices—when and whether to have children—still do not exist. Their moral codes and religious beliefs require them to accept the number and timing of children as factors to be left mostly to chance.

CONFRONTATIONS OVER BIRTH CONTROL

In spite of expected decreases in family size, the problems of population growth and unwanted pregnancies will continue to be national issues. Since both personal lifestyles and environmental overloading are involved, conflicting moral issues are raised—the right of personal choice as opposed to the right of society to a livable future (Nettler, 1976).

On the one hand, many people feel that a continually growing population will soon overburden the earth's capacity to feed, clothe, and shelter humans. They see overcrowding as a threat to the quality of life as well, and unwanted birth as a favor to no one. But opponents of population control think that technology will somehow find ways to support infinite popula-

tion growth. They argue that no one has the right to deny birth to unborn souls or to deny parents the chance to reproduce (Nettler).

Abortion is one prominent issue which divides those desiring zero population growth and those preferring a **pronatalist** national policy. The dramatic struggle between these forces will continue, even though abortion is already a widespread practice. In a pluralist society like the United States, it is an infringement of individual rights to create laws that would make criminals of women choosing to end unwanted pregnancies through abortion. The Supreme Court ruling of 1973 avoided that dilemma, although it did place some constraints upon those desiring abortion. Despite efforts of militant antiabortion groups to undermine the now-legal right of women to determine the fate of their own bodies, the 1973 Supreme Court ruling will probably continue to be national policy.

LESS CONFLICT BETWEEN GENERATIONS

Yorburg believes that there will be less hostility between generations in the future than in the recent past. Part of the reason for this will be increasing government support for both children and old people, so that children will no longer be viewed as an investment to be repaid by support of parents in their old age. This will reduce feelings of resentment and guilt now experienced by many people faced with economic burdens too heavy for them to carry.

Conflict between adolescents, middle-aged parents, and their aged parents may ease with increasing education and the spread of similar values and lifestyles in all social classes. Increasing liberation of sexual expression for all ages may also limit the hostility of the old toward the young, for some social scientists think it is rooted in sexual frustration and envy. In addition, parents who have fewer children may be emotionally closer to them. And advances in transportation and communication should help families keep in touch despite the potentially divisive effects of rapid social change and mobility (Yorburg).

ACCEPTANCE OF BLENDED AND SINGLE-PARENT FAMILIES

Children today in single-parent families, or living with stepparents because of remarriage of a biological parent, are often found to experience more stress in their lives than children who are living with two biological parents. Some of these problems have been discussed in Chapters 13 and 14 and in the section on Single-Parent Families in Chapter 3. However, the special problems of these children are expected to diminish as divorce and remarriage become more standard behavior in U.S. society. In 1970, only 70 percent of children under 18 were living with two natural parents in their first marriage. The other 30 percent were children of separated, divorced, remarried, or never-married parents (Glick, 1975). The fact that so many children are growing up in nonstandard families can be expected to reduce the stigma to their lives and lead eventually to development of social resources to help meet their needs.

CHANGING STYLES IN PARENTHOOD

According to a recent national survey, a new breed of parent is emerging—one that is more self-centered, more permissive, and less authoritarian than the traditional parent. They may be raising a new breed of children (General Mills, 1977).

The traditionalists, who still make up 57 percent of parents of children under 13, strongly value having children and are willing to sacrifice for them. They emphasize old-fashioned child rearing—teaching respect for authority, discipline, different roles for boys and girls, and religious beliefs. They try to socialize their children to value money-saving, patriotism, marriage, and success.

By contrast, "new-breed" parents, the other 43 percent, feel that they have their own lives to live. They take a relaxed attitude toward parenting; they let children make their own decisions, raise both sexes the same way, are permissive with them, deny that their children have any future obligations to them, and view parenthood as an option, not a moral duty. On the average, new-breed parents are better educated and more affluent than traditional parents.

Table 17.1   Today's parents

THE NEW BREED—43%	THE TRADITIONALISTS—57%
Not Important Values:	**Very Important Values:**
Marriage as an institution	Marriage as an institution
Religion	Religion
Saving money	Saving money
Patriotism	Hard work
Success	Financial security
Characteristics and Beliefs:	**Characteristics and Beliefs:**
Parents are self-oriented—not ready to sacrifice for their children	Parents are child-oriented—ready to sacrifice for their children
Parents don't push their children	Parents want their children to be outstanding
Parents have a laissez faire attitude—children should be free to make their own decisions	Parents want to be in charge—believe parents should make decisions for their children
Parents question authority	Parents respect authority
Parents are permissive with their children	Parents are not permissive with their children
Parents believe boys and girls should be raised alike	Parents believe boys and girls should be raised differently
Parents believe their children have no future obligation to them	Parents believe old-fashioned upbringing is best
Parents see having children as an option, not a social responsibility	Parents see having children as a very important value

WHAT BOTH GROUPS TEACH THEIR CHILDREN

Duty before pleasure
My country right or wrong
Hard work pays off
People in authority know best
Sex is wrong without marriage

Source: The General Mills American Family Report, 1976–1977: *Raising Children in a Changing Society*. Minneapolis, Minn.: General Mills Consumer Center, 1977.

However, children of new-breed and traditional parents agree on a number of matters. New-breed parents are apparently still teaching some traditional values which they themselves no longer believe. Or perhaps the children learn these values at school and from TV. Both sets of children like their mother for her cooking and homemaking, their father for his role as chief breadwinner. They think that parents should stay together even if their marriage is unhappy, that parents should not take vacations without their children, that cooking and housekeeping are women's work, and that spanking is okay.

On the other hand, the fact that these children are being raised differently has made a difference in some of their attitudes. For instance, children of new-breed parents are somewhat more willing (58 percent) to see them separate if they are unhappy than children of traditional parents (47 percent). New-breed children tend to be more relaxed and to recognize that their parents place less emphasis on achievement in sports, school, social life, and personal behavior than some of their friends' parents. And they are more tolerant of differences, more willing to play with children from different ethnic backgrounds.

TERMINATION OF MARRIAGES

The divorce rate in the United States is extremely high and apparently is still climbing. There were slightly more than 2 million marriages in 1975 and just over 1 million divorces. The median duration of marriages which end in divorce or annulment is six and a half years, though, of course, many divorces occur in the first year of marriage and many others in marriages that have lasted twenty or twenty-five years (U.S. Bureau of the Census, *Statistical Abstract of the U.S., 1976*). The divorce rate has been increasing sharply since the mid-1950s and will probably remain high. But demographers predict that it will eventually level off.

DIVORCE RATES TO REMAIN HIGH

The rise in divorces does not necessarily mean that marriages are less happy than in the past. It seems instead that people with marital problems are less willing to maintain an unhappy marriage. Increasing public acceptance of divorce has made it more acceptable as a means of resolving marital conflict. And liberalization of divorce laws has made it easier and quicker to dissolve a marriage than in the past.

Marital dissolution is becoming an option people expect when they marry. The increasing numbers of divorced people in the community mean more models for divorce and singlehood as acceptable and sometimes desirable alternatives to marriages that aren't working. The fact that couples now have fewer children, or none at all, means that there will be less stringent financial, emotional, and social obligations holding them together when they are having problems. The decline in the number of children also makes it easier for the wife to enter paid employment, and if she can be independent of her husband, divorce becomes more practicable (Norton and Glick; Gagnon and Simon).

Although the divorce rate has not yet shown any signs of leveling off, it is expected to do so eventually. Yorburg points out that our society as a whole is becoming more affluent, and the intense marital problems associated with poverty may eventually affect fewer people. The difference in the divorce rates between upper-class and lower-class families may eventually become equalized as economic resources are distributed more equally. People's conception of marriage will also become more realistic. Today's high divorce rates have been partially blamed on rising expectations, rather than worsening realities. We are now in a transition period from old marital values and rules to new ones. Once new values and rules have become established, they may conform more closely to what can actually be expected of real life situations. Yorburg anticipates that there will be more tolerance of individual, subcultural, and cultural differences in family conceptions and behavior.

A third reason why divorce rates may level off is that people have access to more knowledge about how to deal with family conflicts. Interpersonal skills which were inappropriate to the old patriarchal system, in which father's word was law, are increasingly being brought to public attention in magazine articles, television discussions, and books. This knowledge is gradually becoming part of people's interaction in interpersonal relationships and can eventually lead to happier marriages (Yorburg; Norton and Glick).

INNOVATIVE CUSTODY AND SUPPORT ARRANGEMENTS

Increasing public awareness of the problems involved in providing for children of a dissolved marriage is leading to innovative arrangements for their support and custody. Some of these were suggested in the section on children and divorce in Chapter 14. For instance, instead of automatically assigning custody to the mother, the courts are beginning to listen to requests from fathers for shared custody. Men's rights groups are increasingly active in pushing for legal reforms in custody and support arrangements (Molinoff, 1977). Such activity can be expected to bring about more positive approaches to the particular problems of children affected by divorce.

NEED FOR FAMILY SUPPORT SYSTEMS

We have seen in this book that no family exists in a vacuum. The surrounding society impinges on families, and families on the society, at many points. As the basic unit that holds society together, the family deserves public attention and support to resolve ongoing problems. Reforms in public policies are needed in four major areas: (1) to modify marriage and divorce laws to provide more adequately for human needs, (2) to provide more extensive family-counseling programs, (3) to adjust occupational demands so that husbands and wives can more adequately meet their own and their children's needs, and (4) to provide an office of family advocacy in the federal government so that governmental policies can be directed to protecting and sustaining families.

CONTINUING REFORM NEEDED IN FAMILY LAW

The discussion of legal requirements for marriage at the beginning of Chapter 3 has indicated many of the areas in which reform in family law may be needed. One of these is the need to make marriage harder to enter and easier to dissolve. Sociologists have been urging for 50 years that people take marrying more seriously and divorcing less so, since continuing a destructive marital relationship is so harmful for the participants. No-fault divorces are a step in this direction, but more progress is needed (Glick, 1975).

De-legalizing Divorce. Some people feel that much of the trauma of divorce could be eliminated by taking divorce out of the hands of lawyers and turning it over to professional marriage counselors. Under the present system, lawyers are usually hired to handle the legal intricacies of divorce and to promote the interests of the partners as individuals. As a result, partners are adversaries before the courts and few or no official attempts are made at reconciliation.

Reformers suggest that society would be better served by a setup that encourages cooperation between partners instead of fierce protection of individual rights. They suggest that divorce requests be handled by family-preservation bureaus linked to the courts. Staffed by family therapists and marriage counselors, they could be funded by increased fees for marriage licenses so that no one would be denied their service for lack of money (Bach and Wyden, 1968; Auerbach, 1976).

Marriage Contracts. Since the requirements of traditional marriage law often do not fit the needs and desires of two people considering marriage to each other, some of them have sought to clarify their rights and obligations by drawing up a personal marriage contract. The advantages and weaknesses of such contracts were discussed briefly in Chapter 8. They are expected to be a subject of continuing interest. For example, a recent appeal for sample copies of actual contracts attracted 800 such documents —plus 8000 requests for information on how to draw one up (Sussman, 1975). A national effort should be made to resolve problems of conflict between personal marriage contracts and established family law.

*"Also in all times and in all places to condemn war, pollution,
and non-biodegradable containers, to support the Third World, and
to fight for a better life for the migrant farm worker."*

Adapting Policies to Alternative Lifestyles.   Traditional policies and laws
have been found to discriminate against nontraditional family forms. This
bias has been based on the persistent belief that the best family is an intact
one, that women belong in the home, and that community support to
families should be limited so that families will be encouraged to develop
their own resources rather than fall back on the government for help. Welfare policies in regard to aid to dependent children are often affected. Since
an increasing number of Americans are living in nontraditional family
structures, these assumptions and the laws based on them are now being
challenged (Cogswell and Sussman, 1972).

Although people who have chosen alternative lifestyles—such as cohabitation, communal life, or homosexual pairings—do not conform to
traditional ideas of what constitutes a family, they may behave very much
like one. Many hold traditional jobs, provide economic support, have children, and own possessions and property in common. Like a traditional
family, an alternative family unit can give children a protective environment, provide for their education, offer outlets for sexual expression, and
satisfy the psychological needs of family members. But because they have
no biological or legal family ties, they do not have the rights granted to
traditionally married people. They may be refused housing, insurance, citi-
zenship, food stamps, alimony, and survivor's Social Security, and face
potential arrest for adultery, sodomy, cohabitation, or fornication.

Extension of legal protection to alternative families may be slow to come. Although the attitudes and behaviors of many people are changing, court decisions lag behind, partly because they are based on outmoded laws. In the meantime, alternative families are in some cases trying to safeguard their rights by drawing up their own contracts. Such documents may define whether property is held jointly or individually and what should become of it in case of death or separation (Weisberg, 1975).

FAMILY ENRICHMENT AND COUNSELING PROGRAMS

Although laws will be slow to adapt to variant family structures, the years to come should see increasing professional efforts to support the family in all its forms. The **human potential movement** and concern over the forces that threaten to disrupt family relationships will help promote a nationwide push for applying the knowledge and skills of family counselors to everyday family living. Many of these programs will be preventive, dealing with "well" families before problems develop into crises. In the future, young people may even receive formal training for their possible roles as husbands and wives, mothers and fathers (Schaefer, 1972).

Self-help efforts are already underway, with families taking the initiative to apply to their own relationships the interpersonal skills described in the media (Yorburg). But government has been slow to underwrite the costs of providing professional counseling services to families. Although sociologists have for some time recommended federally supported marriage-counseling clinics where families could get annual "checkups" and suggestions for working out problems in their interpersonal relationships, such services are still very limited (Otto, 1972; Glick, 1975). But with increasing recognition that the family is our major resource for developing healthy, well-adjusted people, government support should grow.

In addition to the need for innovative new support programs for well families, existing programs for troubled families need to be reorganized and expanded. According to some critics, they should be decentralized, so that bureaucratic distance does not keep workers from dealing intimately with the families they serve. These programs should also be "de-specialized." Families in trouble are now offered fragmented attention from an array of specialists: family-planning counselors, nutritionists, health professionals, education aides, social workers, and public-health nurses. Instead of sending all these specialists into homes, it might be better to send one family advisor who could provide assistance and support in broad areas, based on the overall needs of the family.

Another problem with current programs is their bias in favor of the traditional nuclear family. When variant family forms are served, programs seem chiefly designed to restore the nuclear form. Instead, human-service systems should be flexible enough to accommodate the varying competen-

---

Human potential movement. Focusing of behavioral scientists and professional therapists on ways to ensure the maximum development of individuals in terms of their own needs and desires.

cies, values, and images of the good life held by single-parent, communal, and traditional families (Cogswell and Sussman; Schaefer).

CHANGES IN THE OCCUPATIONAL SYSTEM

Another way U.S. society could help support and strengthen families is by accommodating jobs to family realities, instead of forcing families to accommodate themselves to the requirements of business and industry.

Husbands and wives are increasingly trying to share responsibility for providing family income. However, full-time outside jobs often require overtime work as a sign of commitment and a prerequisite for raises or promotions. Putting in long hours at their separate jobs leaves couples little time or energy for domestic chores, leisure activities, and creative parenting. As a result, life is likely to be hectic in dual-career families, and responsibilities either at home or at work may be partially neglected. If people give higher priority to taking time off from work to be with their families, grow food, travel, or have fun, than to their occupational goals, they are considered irresponsible. But work discontinuity may be a source of personal and family revitalization which leads to high productivity and enthusiasm for work. Work schedules can and should be made more flexible to allow families the adequate leisure that is increasingly seen as contributing to the quality of life.

In Sweden, efforts have been made in this direction. During the child-bearing years, both fathers and mothers may work part-time without any financial or occupational penalty. They can also take a six-month paid leave when a baby is born and up to 21 days a year of paid leave for taking care of sick children. This time off for parenting can be divided between both working spouses (Safilios-Rothschild, 1976).

In the United States, dual-career marriages are increasingly common. For many, the two jobs are a financial necessity. According to the U.S. Bureau of Labor Statistics, a middle-class income is usually possible only when both spouses work. And studies have shown that marriages tend to be happier if the wife works and the husband lowers his career ambitions. But occupational policies are for the most part still based on the old male-breadwinner/female-homemaker family ideal, which no longer applies to over half the people in the country (Bernard, 1972a; Howe, 1972).

Flex-Time. Although it is unlikely that we will approach the flexibility Sweden grants its working families, reforms are possible within the U.S. economic system, and some are already underway. Some fathers have established the right to take child-care leaves (Peratis, 1976). Instead of the traditional nine-to-five work day, many industries are adopting more flexible schedules, such as shifts of people working three twelve-hour days, followed by four days off. Although industries that have experimented

Flex-time. Provision for variations in work schedules to permit individuals more freedom in scheduling their non-work activities.

with flexible schedules have been motivated by nonfamily goals, such as increased employee satisfaction and productivity, the new schedules can benefit the family. They may make it easier for spouses to take turns working and caring for house and children, or for both to work part-time with more time for leisure activities (Kanter, 1976).

Child Care.   Another major step businesses and government can take to support families which include a working mother is to expand and improve day-care facilities for children. In the 1960s, policymakers were reluctant to give up the traditional idea that men should work and women should stay home, and support for day-care centers was limited. It is increasing, however, as old gender-role attitudes are being discarded.

Some far-out alternatives to parental childcare have been suggested—paying trained couples to parent large families for a living, rearing children in age groups supervised by professionals, or encouraging every American adult to be responsible for rearing one child. Such schemes are unlikely to be tried on a wide scale. However, increasing recognition that childrearing is a social responsibility, not just a parental one, may eventually prompt the government to provide financial allowances for children's needs and extend the scope of day-care centers. Instead of just being places where young children can be parked during the day, they may increasingly offer educational and recreational programs, nursing care during sickness, psy-

chological services, and overnight and weekend care. Such services would not take the place of parental love, but they would allow couples to build more equal partnerships without necessarily giving up the joys of parenthood or depriving children of the emotional security they need (Lorber, 1975).

NEED FOR A NATIONAL FAMILY AGENCY

To bring about the various programs suggested here—legal reforms, expanded family counseling programs, and occupational changes—many sociologists feel that families need an advocate at the highest level of government. Family support measures in which U.S. society can and is involving itself range from flexible and part-time work schedules, child-care services, and paternity and maternity leaves to realistic no-fault divorce laws and recreational facilities placed close to homes so that parents need not act as chauffeurs (Cogswell and Sussman). Coordination of such efforts, revamping of old programs, development of new ones, and assessment of the effect of national legislation on family life requires an official at cabinet level, one with power to influence national policy (Sussman, 1971).

It is important to recognize that how we as a society solve family problems will determine the flow of the future. If we continue to neglect family concerns and treat problems only when they bother the neighbors, we will miss great opportunities. There are some hopeful signs that more attention will be given to both governmental and private programs that will enhance the intimate experiences of the family. Much planning and work on such programs are still to be done and will be an exciting mission for the future. But despite the potential for increased government concern and involvement, the success of family life will still largely depend on the behavior of individuals. If our families are to be the focus of warm, loving, supportive relationships, it is up to us to make them that way.

Summary

1. The purposes of this chapter are to consider trends related to future development of the family in the United States and to explore some of the ways our society can support family life, if this is what it wishes to do.

2. The trend toward growing freedom in sexual behavior, gender-role choice, and mate choice is expected to continue. These changes will offer opportunities for personal development that would not have been available if norms had remained unchanged.

3. Cohabitation and sexual intercourse between singles will be almost universal, while other alternatives to traditional marriage and family (group marriage, communes, and singlehood) will attract only a limited number of participants. Marriage will continue to be chosen by a majority of Americans.

4. The trend to smaller families and child-free families will continue as contraceptive techniques continue to improve. Increased government assistance to children and the elderly, increased education, and increased liberalization of sexual expression will tend to reduce conflict between generations. The stress of being part of blended or single-parent families will diminish as divorce and remarriage become more common.

5. Divorce rates will remain high and divorce will become a more acceptable means of resolving marital conflict. Increased public awareness of the problems involved in providing for children of a dissolved marriage will bring about more innovative arrangements for custody and support of children.

6. Support for the family under changing social conditions will require change in public policies in four major areas. (a) Marriage and divorce laws should be modified to provide more adequately for human needs. (b) Family-counseling programs should be expanded and provided as a public service for those in need. (e) Work schedules and occupational demands should be adjusted so that couples can more adequately meet their own and their children's needs. (d) An office of family advocacy should be established in the federal government to ensure that government policies will be directed to protecting and assisting families.

7. The ultimate responsibility for success of a marriage rests upon the two individuals involved.

Key Concepts

Androgyny	**New-breed parents**
Role making	**Family preservation bureau**
Women's liberation	**Human potential movement**
Men's liberation	**Maternity leave**
Equalitarian marriage	**Paternity leave**
Intimate networks	**Flex-time**
Pronatalism	**Family advocate**

Review and Discussion

1. Looking at your own family, can you see evidence of any of the trends discussed in this chapter? Which changes do you think are for the better? Which for the worse?

2. Compare traditional and new-breed approaches to parenting. What do you see as the benefits and/or disadvantages of each in terms of the effects on children?

3. What reasons might be given for leaving the process of divorce in the hands of lawyers? Would a team effort by lawyers and social scientists be more practical than "de-legalizing" divorce?

4. Do you think it is practical for businesses and industries to provide flexible working hours and irregular work schedules to permit parents to share homemaking and child-care responsibilities? Why or why not?

5. It has been suggested that too much emphasis on governmental support services to aid families in trouble may endanger the American citizen's right to privacy. What are your feelings about this problem?

BANE, M. J. (1976). *American Families in the Twentieth Century.* New York: Basic Books.

Challenges the belief that the American family is a dying institution. Focuses on the stability of the family and holds that there is now more concern for relatives, especially children and the elderly, than in the past.

BERNARD, J. (1972). *The Future of Marriage.* New York: World Publishing Co.

Discusses the evolution of marriage to its present state in America and what the marriage of the future may involve. Investigates the inequalities and inadequacies of the institution and concludes that people will continue to marry for the intimacy, stability, and unity it provides.

GENERAL MILLS (1977). *Raising Children in a Changing Society.* Minneapolis, Minn.: General Mills Consumer Center.

A statistical report on how parents are coping with the problems of raising children amid the rapidly changing values of our society. Provides information on aspects of child rearing such as health needs, television, schools, and working mothers. The numerous charts and tables and the explanatory text are easy to read and understand.

HOWE, L. K., ED. (1972). *The Future of the Family.* New York: Simon and Schuster.

A collection of essays, stories, studies, and personal accounts which sketch the behavior of mothers, fathers, and children and discuss ways that our society can meet the needs of families in the United States now and in the future.

NOVAK, M. (1976). The family out of favor. *Harper's* 252:1511:37–46.

Discusses why strengthening the family is necessary for the emotional and political health of the nation and explores the idea that choosing family life is "an act of intelligence and courage" in today's urban-industrial society.

Suggested
Readings

Glossary

Abnormality. A state or quality deviating from the normal or average; a psychological or behavioral disorder.

Aborigines. The first inhabitants of a region especially as contrasted with an invading or colonizing people.

Abortion. Termination of a pregnancy by separating the embryo or fetus from the woman before it is capable of existing on its own. An abortion may be surgically or chemically induced or it may occur naturally (a miscarriage).

Abstinence. Voluntary avoidance of bodily pleasures such as eating, drinking, or sexual activity.

Accommodation. The social process of adjusting differences in ideas or goals so as to avoid conflict.

Actuaries. People who calculate insurance premiums through use of statistical data, especially life expectancy tables.

A.D. Abbreviation for the Latin words *anno Domini,* meaning "in the year of the Lord." Used in the Western world to refer to the period of time since the birth of Jesus Christ.

Adolescent. A person undergoing the physical and psychological changes following puberty; someone approximately 13 to 20 years of age.

Adrenalin. A hormone that raises blood pressure and effects changes necessary for the quick release of energy in emergency situations.

Adultery. Sexual intercourse between a married man and someone other than his wife, or between a married woman and someone other than her husband.

Adversary proceeding. A legal action involving opposing parties, in which one person files suit against the other.

Aerosol foam. A chemical contraceptive containing substances which immobilize and kill sperm; used prior to sexual intercourse, the foam spreads throughout the vagina and acts as a physical barrier to sperm trying to pass through the cervix.

Affinal relatives. Persons related by marriage; in-laws.

Agape. A Greek word meaning altruistic, nondemanding, spiritual love. As such, it is one of three different kinds of love distinguished by the Greeks. See also **philos** and **eros**.

Aggression. Hostile or injurious behavior toward another, including verbal attacks, gestures, bodily responses, and failure to respond, as well as actual physical attempts to harm another.

AID. Abbreviation for artificial insemination with donor sperm. See **artificial insemination**.

Alcoholism. Excessive and usually compulsive use of alcoholic drinks, to the extent that overt behavior is affected. The alcoholic is usually psychologically and physiologically dependent on liquor, wine, or beer.

Alienation. Withdrawal or separation of an individual from the values of the society. A sense of powerlessness; a feeling of inability to control one's destiny.

Alimony. Money paid on a regular basis to a former spouse for support pending and after a legal separation or divorce.

Alternative lifestyles. Ways of living that differ from the customs of most members of a society, especially including behavior which differs from traditional forms of marriage and family life.

Amnesics. Drugs used medically which erase the memory of pain.

Amniotic fluid. A salty fluid which surrounds the embryo and later the fetus, filling the amniotic sac. It bathes and cushions the developing organism during pregnancy.

Amniotic sac. The protective membrane which surrounds the developing embryo and later the fetus, during pregnancy; contains the amniotic fluid.

Amortization. A payment plan which enables a borrower to reduce a debt gradually through regular payments of principal and interest.

Anal intercourse. Sexual activity involving insertion of the penis of one person into the anus of another.

Analgesics. Drugs used medically to decrease the sensation of pain.

Anarchism. A philosophy holding all forms of authority, rules, and regulations to be undesirable and advocating a society based on voluntary cooperation and free association of individuals.

Androgyny. Behavior in which traditional characteristics of men and women are merged and there is no gender-role differentiation.

Anemia. A condition in which the blood has a marked deficiency of red blood cells, of hemoglobin, or both. A person suffering from this condition lacks vitality.

Anesthetics. Drugs used medically which block all sensation, either by producing unconsciousness or by blocking the transmission of pain sensations to the brain.

Anger. A strong feeling of displeasure and usually of antagonism. An emotional reaction to frustration, insult, or attack.

Annulment. A pronouncement that a marriage is void and does not exist.

Anthropologist. One who studies the science of human behavior, especially in relation to physical characteristics, environmental and social relations, and culture.

Anticipatory socialization. A process by which people learn about a new status and role as they are moving toward it, and so make the mental and emotional adjustments required ahead of time.

Antisexual. Opposed to the enjoyment of sexual activity for moral or religious reasons.

Anus. The opening at the rear of the body through which wastes are excreted from the large intestine.

Aphrodisiac. A food or chemical which is thought to increase sexual desire and enjoyment of sexual activity.

Arranged marriage. A system of mate selection in which partners are matched by elder members of the family for social and economic reasons rather than through the free choice of the individuals concerned.

Artifact. A product of civilization, something created through human activity as opposed to something occurring naturally.

Artificial insemination. A procedure by which sperm obtained under medical supervision by masturbation are introduced into the vagina with a syringe so that fertilization might take place. Impregnation of a woman through artificial rather than natural procedures.

Assets. Things of value owned by a business or an individual, such as cash or real property.

Attitudes. Learned mental positions toward objects, events, or issues; also feelings or emotions toward a fact or condition.

Automation. Operation of machinery or equipment by mechanical or electronic devices instead of people.

Autonomous. Existing or capable of existing independently; having the right or power of self-government.

Baby boom. An abnormally high number of births relative to the population, as in the period from 1946 to 1957 during which U.S. birth rates were at very high levels.

Bag of waters. A lay term for the amniotic sac which contains the fetus and the amniotic fluid during pregnancy.

Bait and switch. A technique of merchandising in which customers respond to an advertisement for low-priced items and are then manipulated by the salesperson into buying more expensive merchandise, often beyond what they can afford.

Banns. A public announcement, especially in church, of a proposed marriage, to give persons who may object to the marriage an opportunity to make their objections known.

Barrenness. Failure to produce offspring; sterility.

Bartholin's glands. Two small mucus-producing glands located on each side of the vaginal opening; they contribute a small amount of lubricating fluid late in sexual arousal.

Battered wives. Women who are subjected to physical brutality by their husbands.

B.C. Abbreviation for the words "Before Christ," used in the Western world for providing dates for historical events, and calculated backwords through time from the birth of Jesus Christ. A person born in 200 B.C. lived at a later time than a person born in 300 B.C.

Behaviorist psychology. An approach to psychology, associated with B. F. Skinner and John B. Watson, which sees all human behavior as externally conditioned. In this view, all behavior that is reinforced and rewarded will continue and all behavior that is not reinforced will be eliminated.

Beneficiary. One that benefits from something. The person named to receive the proceeds or benefits of a life-insurance policy or the income from a trust fund.

Betrothal. A mutual promise or contract between a man and a woman for a future marriage; an engagement.

Bigamy. The act of entering into a ceremonial marriage with one person while still legally married to another.

Bilineal descent. Descent traced through both male and female lines instead of just one of them.

Biological factors. Determinants of behavior and experience which are based in the anatomy and physiology of an organism, as opposed to those acquired through social learning.

Birth canal. The fully dilated cervix (neck of the uterus) and the vagina through which a baby must pass in the process of being born.

Birth control techniques. Procedures which limit the number of children born by preventing or reducing the frequency of impregnation resulting from sexual intercourse.

Birthmark. An unusual mark or blemish on the skin of an infant at birth.

Birth rate. The number of births per year per thousand of a population. Used in making comparisons of the rates at which populations are reproducing at different points in time or in different societies.

Blackmail. The act of obtaining money or goods from an individual by threatening to expose some damaging knowledge about the person; also, the act of getting an individual to behave in compliance with one's wishes through such threats.

Bladder. The membranous, saclike structure that acts as a receptacle for urine.

Blended family. Family group resulting from the remarriage of divorced persons, so that stepparent relationships are established and children from two families may be blended into one.

Body image. One's perception of one's physical appearance as attractive or unattractive, ordinary or unusual looking.

Bonds. Certificates representing a loan of money by the purchaser to the issuer (as when a citizen purchases a government bond). The issuer repays the principal amount within a given period of time and pays interest on it periodically.

Borax store. A term used in describing stores where the merchandise or the terms of the sale may be misrepresented by the salesperson to the disadvantage of the customer.

Bourgeoisie. People of the middle class in Europe, often associated with commercial and industrial interests; people lower in social status than the nobility and higher than the peasants.

Breech birth. A delivery in which the baby is born bottom down or feet first, rather than the normal-head first position.

Bride price. A gift of money, goods, or property from a man or his family to the family of his wife at the time of the marriage.

Bride service. The performance of labor by a man for his prospective father-in-law; in some societies, a requirement to be met before a marriage could take place.

Brokers. People who act as intermediaries. Agents who negotiate contracts of purchase and sale, as of real estate, commodities, or securities.

Budget. A written plan for coordination of resources and expenditures, showing amounts of money available for, required for, or assigned to a particular purpose.

Bundling. A courting custom in colonial America, by which an engaged couple would spend the evening or the whole night lying together in bed, but physically separated from each other by a board or a feather bolster and fully dressed.

Caesarean section. An incision made into the womb or uterus of a pregnant woman for delivery of an infant; performed only when some abnormality prevents delivery through the birth canal. The name comes from the fact that the Roman emperor Julius Caesar was supposed to have been born this way.

Capital. A stock of accumulated goods and property, or the value of same; tangible or intangible long-term assets.

Capitalist. Pertaining to capitalism, an economic system based on private ownership and open competition, relatively free from government controls, in which individuals are theoretically free to acquire as much capital and economic power as their talent and energy permit.

Cash crop. An agricultural yield which can be sold on the market as a source of income.

Cash value. The amount of money that will be paid by an insurance company if a life-insurance policy is discontinued during the lifetime of the insured person, based on the amount of the premiums paid in. Applicable only to "whole-life" policies.

Caste. A social class in which membership is determined entirely and permanently by heredity. In India, caste membership restricts the occupation of members and their association with members of other castes.

Castration. Removal of the testicles of a male or ovaries of a female, resulting in inability to reproduce.

Catharsis. A purification of the emotions—such as anger, pity, or fear—by bringing them to consciousness and giving them expression; incorporates the idea that if such cleansing occurs, tension is reduced.

Caustic. Capable of destroying or eating away by chemical action.

Celibacy. The state of not being married. Abstention by vow from sexual intercourse or from marriage.

Ceremony. A formal act, dictated by protocol or convention and following a prescribed ritual.

Cervical cap. A rubber contraceptive device, smaller and deeper than the diaphragm, which fits over the cervix and may be left in the vagina from one menstrual period to the next.

Cervix. The narrow, slightly protruding lower end (neck) of the uterus with a narrow opening which connects uterus and vagina.

Chancre. The primary lesion of syphilis, appearing as a reddish ulcer at the site of the entrance of the infection.

Charismatic leader. A leader who conveys personal magnetism and appeal and inspires a special loyalty in his or her followers; sometimes considered by the followers to be invested with supernatural powers.

Chastity. Abstention from all sexual intercourse.

Child abuse. Intentional behavior of a parent or a custodian which causes physical injury to a child; an active form of mistreatment of children.

Childbirth. The action or process of giving birth to offspring.

Childfree. Childless by choice, based on a rejection of parenthood rather than an inability to conceive.

Child neglect. Indifference on the part of a parent or a custodian to a child's needs, or failure to carry out the expected duties of parenthood.

Child support. The allowance paid for the support of a child by a parent, pending and after a legal separation or divorce.

Chivalry. The system, spirit, or customs of medieval knighthood, marked by gracious courtesy and high-minded consideration, especially to women.

Chorionic gonadotropin. A hormone made by the body during early pregnancy which will appear in a urine sample from a pregnant woman. Testing for this hormone is therefore a test of whether or not the woman is pregnant.

Chromosome. A self-duplicating body found in the nucleus of higher plant and animal cells. Each human cell contains 46 chromosomes which are composed of long, coiled double-strands of DNA, molecules which contain genetic information.

Circumcision. The surgical removal of the foreskin of the penis, generally for hygienic reasons, often performed in our society shortly after birth.

Civil ceremonies. Ceremonies, as a marriage, conducted by an official of the state, rather than of the church.

Civil rights. Rights of personal liberty guaranteed to U.S. citizens by the Constitution. Civil rights imply that government will protect individuals from abuse by other individuals, private organizations, and government itself.

Clan. A group composed of a number of households whose heads claim descent from a common ancestor and who reside in one geographic area.

Clap. Gonorrhea, a venereal disease.

Clergy. Those who perform sacred rites and spiritual services within the church, such as bishsops and priests.

Climax. Orgasm, the release of peak sexual tensions.

Clinical psychologist. A person with special training who provides therapy for psychologically disturbed persons.

Clitoral hood. The partial covering over the clitoris.

Clitoris. A small, very sensitive, erectile organ in the female, consisting of a glans and shaft, which lies under the upper portion of the labia minora. Of similar embryonic origin to the male penis, it is the prime organ for sexual arousal in the female.

Codified. Reduced to a code; systematized, as in a set of laws; classified.

Cognitive. Pertaining to mental processes, such as those involved in problem solving; relating to thinking, as distinct from feeling.

Cognitive restructuring. A personality mechanism by which one rationalizes one's behavior to conform to one's self-concept; used to maintain a consistent and stable self-concept.

Cohabitation. Two adults of different sex sharing a household while unmarried, with or without children in the household.

Cohort. A group of individuals having a statistical factor such as age or class membership in common in a demographic study.

Coitus. Sexual intercourse; the insertion of a male's penis into a female's vagina.

Coitus-related. Directly related to sexual intercourse such that action must be taken shortly before or after intercourse occurs.

Collateral. Anything of value against which money may be borrowed. If the borrower fails to pay the debt, the lender is entitled to the collateral.

Comarital sex. Sexual relationships outside of marriage which are approved and expected by both marital partners.

Commission. A fee paid to an agent or employee for transacting a piece of business; the amount is usually a percentage of the total amount of the business transaction.

Commodities. Economic goods, as a product of agriculture or mining, often purchased as an investment for later resale.

Common-law union. A situation in which a man and woman live together as husband and wife without going through a legal ceremony. This union is recognized as a binding marriage in several states of the United States.

Communards. People who live in communes.

Commune. A group of people who live together, share rights and obligations, and collectively own and use property. The purpose behind their formation is usually to create an ideal society in which the particular goals of the group can be attained. Also, broadly, the area in which such a group lives.

Commuting. Traveling back and forth regularly, as between a suburb and a city.

Companionate marriage. A marriage in which the goal is harmonious companionship and intimacy, rather than mutual protection and economic cooperation.

Composite family. A family structure combining two or more nuclear families, usually based on the marriage of one man to several women (polygyny). May also refer to extended families of three or more generations sharing a household and cooperating economically.

Compound family. See **extended family.** Also **composite family.**

Computerized. Entered into a computer in such a way that records or calculations of data can be rapidly retrieved for evaluation or distribution to others.

Concept. Something conceived in the mind; an abstract or generic idea generalized from particular instances.

Conception. The fertilization of a ripe egg (ovum) by a sperm cell, which may result—after a period of pregnancy—in the birth of offspring.

Conciliation. Making compatible or agreeable; reconciling of marital differences through marriage counseling.

Concubinage. A custom by which the head of a household takes an extra female sexual partner who then lives with the family. However, the concubine does not have the full status of a wife.

Concubine. A woman living in a socially recognized state of concubinage.

Condom. A simple, disposable sheath of rubber, latex, or animal membrane which is placed over the erect penis before intercourse. In addition to being an effective contraceptive device, it provides protection against venereal disease. Also called rubber, safe, prophylactic, or skin.

Condominium. An individually owned unit of a multi-unit structure, as an apartment building; usually includes an individual interest in the common areas and facilities which serve the multi-unit complex.

Conflict management. The process of negotiation in a dyadic relationship in which conflict between the interests of the two people is not fully resolved, but is controlled through bargaining, compromise, and accommodation.

Conflict resolution. Settlement of disputes arising from conflict in a dyadic relationship, sometimes in ways that are not fully satisfactory to the parties concerned.

Conflict theory. A theoretical framework in which emphasis is placed on conflicting forces within social units (such as a society or a family) in explaining the behavior of individuals and groups.

Congenital. Existing at or dating from birth; acquired during development in the uterus and not through heredity.

Conjugal. Pertaining to the married state, especially the bond of intimacy between married persons.

Consanguineal. Of the same blood or origin.

Consciousness raising. Teaching about social realities in ways that encourage the alteration of social customs and behavior, as in the women's liberation movement.

Consensual union. A union based on the mutual consent of the two parties involved, and not on a legal marriage ceremony.

Consensus. General agreement; the judgment or opinion of most of those concerned.

Consort-mistress union. A Toda custom by which a man and a woman from two exclusive groups that do not permit marriage of their members with one another are permitted to become sexual partners; they are not married but a public ceremony is held and gifts exchanged.

Consumerism. Promotion of the consumer's interests through comparison shopping, testing programs, setting of government standards for quality, and legislation such as the truth-in-lending law.

Consummate. Complete; especially, make a marital union complete by sexual intercourse.

Contraception. Prevention of conception; voluntary and intentional prevention of pregnancy.

Contraceptives. Devices or chemical agents used to prevent conception.

Contraction. Shortening and thickening of a functioning muscle or muscle fiber, as when the fetus is being expelled from the uterus in the process of childbirth.

Convertible. Capable of being exchanged for a specified equivalent; a feature of some life-insurance policies and other investments.

Convulsions. A series of violent and involuntary contractions of the muscles; violent shaking with irregular spasms, often with loss of consciousness.

Copper 7. A plastic intrauterine device in the shape of a 7 wrapped with thin copper wire; placed in the uterus as a means of contraception.

Copulation. Joining together in sexual intercourse.

Corona. A crownlike ridge of the tissue which encircles the penis where shaft and glans join. Laced with nerve endings, it is particularly sensitive to erotic arousal.

Corporate wives. Wives of business executives who play a part in the success of their husbands through their appearance, personality, and skill in entertaining.

Counterculture. A culture of people, especially young people, whose values and customs are opposed to those of the society as a whole.

Courtly love. A code of conduct developed during the medieval period in which women were elevated to a pedestal of spiritual sublimity and beauty beyond the attainment of men. In this system of conduct, love exists only on a spiritual plane and no sexual gratification is expected.

Courtoisie. A behavior pattern developed by the nobility particularly in parts of France and Germany during the twelfth and thirteenth centuries, in which a ritualized adoration of women (who are usually married) is acted out by men (who are usually knights).

Co-wives. Women married to the same man, as in polygynous marriages or group marriages.

Cowper's glands. In the male, two glands embedded in the muscle of the urethra at the base of the penis; it is believed that these glands excrete a few drops of fluid into the urethra before ejaculation to neutralize the urethra and make the environment more hospitable to sperm.

Credibility. Trustworthiness; ability to be believed or accepted as reasonable.

Credit. Time given for payment for goods or services sold on trust; the use of someone else's money for which there is a charge called interest.

Creditor. One who has extended credit; therefore, one to whom a debt is owed.

Credit rating. The evaluation of a person's qualifications to receive credit, based on his or her past credit performance.

Credit union. A cooperative association that makes small loans to its members at low interest rates, usually composed of employees of a particular business or members of a particular trade union.

Cross-cultural. Describing and comparing the customs and beliefs of two or more different cultures or cultural areas.

Cross-sectional data. Information obtained through research with subjects who represent all the constituent parts of a social group or category and their relationships to each other at some particular point in time.

Cultural diversity. Variability in customs, beliefs, and standards of behavior; a blend of cultural elements from many different sources.

Cultural factors. Determinants of behavior and experience which are acquired through socialization such as norms, values, and laws, as well as tools and skills. See **biological factors.**

Cultural pluralism. A state of society in which members of diverse ethnic, racial, religious or social groups maintain their traditional culture or special interests while at the same time participating in the dominant society.

Cunnilingus. Oral stimulation of the female genitals.

Custody. Immediate charge and control exercised by a person in authority, as of a child by a parent or guardian. When a child's parents are divorced, the court decides who shall have custody of the child.

Cyclical. Characterized by a recurring succession of events which usually leads back to the starting point.

Dalkon shield. A crab-shaped, plastic intrauterine device; formerly used as a means of contraception but now off the market because of hazards connected with its use.

Dating. The process of experiencing a series of social engagements—usually with a person of the opposite sex—for recreational purposes.

Debt-consolidation loan. A type of loan where a person with many loans at differing rates of interest to be repaid on different schedules may borrow enough money to pay off all the other loans and then have only one regular loan payment to make. Helps to give an individual a clearer picture of what the total indebtedness is and how long it will take to pay it off.

Demographers. People who specialize in the statistical study of human populations, especially noting trends in size, distribution, and vital statistics. Information developed by demographers is useful in setting public policy.

Demographic. Relating to the dynamic balance of a population and its capacity for expansion or decline as determined from analysis of statistical data.

Depreciation. Reduction in the value of machinery, equipment, or other real property due to use and wear over a period of time.

DES (diethylstilbestrol). A drug containing synthetic estrogen, administered in cases of hormone deficiency in older women or as a "morning-after" contraceptive. Certain risks are involved in its use.

Deserted mother. A woman abandoned by the father of her children; she receives no financial aid from him and is not legally free to remarry. Desertion is sometimes called the poor man's divorce.

Developmental needs. Requirements for healthy, normal development of a human organism from conception to death. These requirements change as the organism proceeds through successive stages of development.

Developmental stage. A particular level of growth in an ongoing process. Attainment of each stage is thought of as a prerequisite to movement to the next stage. This concept forms the basis of the study of child development. The idea of developmental stages is now applied to the life cycle of a family as well as the life cycle of a human being.

Developmental tasks. Steps to be accomplished at various stages of the life cycle in accord with physical state, age, and social expectations so that the organism can move on to the next stage of development.

Used also in relation to the life cycle of a family from conception to death.

Deviant. Failing to conform to established norms and social expectations.

Diaphragm. A contraceptive device consisting of a fitted rubber dome with a wire rim. Used in conjunction with spermicidal jelly or cream, it is inserted into the vagina before intercourse so that it blocks the entry of sperm to the cervix.

Diffusion. The process by which nutrients and oxygen in a pregnant woman's bloodstream are transmitted through the placenta to the bloodstream of the fetus.

Dilation and curretage (D & C). A medical procedure in which a woman's cervix is dilated and the uterine contents removed by scraping with a spoon-like instrument. Sometimes used as an abortion procedure.

Dildo. An artificial penis or object of similar shape used by females to simulate copulation.

Discretionary income. Money available after necessities have been paid for which may be used to improve the quality of life.

Discrimination. Unfair or unequal treatment of individuals according to their placement in certain social categories; prejudiced outlook, action, or treatment.

Dividends. Funds of a business or industry which are divided up and distributed to stockholders on the basis of the number of shares each holds.

Divine. Proceeding directly from God; heavenly; godlike.

Division of labor. The assignment of tasks according to the skills and abilities of the workers. Breaking up a major production job into small elements and assigning different parts of the work to different people. Such assignments are frequently made on the basis of age and sex of the workers.

Divorce. The legal termination of a marriage.

Divorcée. A divorced woman.

Double standard. A principle or code that applies differently and usually more strictly to one group than to another. A common example of a double standard is a code of morals that applies more restrictive standards of sexual behavior to women than to men.

Douching. A contraceptive method in which a liquid is injected into the vagina immediately after intercourse to flush out the semen. Also used as a hygienic measure to prevent venereal disease.

Downward mobility. The movement of an individual downward in the social-class system, usually on the basis of changes in occupation and income.

Dowry. A gift of money, livestock, or goods transferred by the family of the woman to the new husband or his family at the time of a marriage.

Dual-career families. Families in which both husband and wife work at paid jobs.

Dualism. A view of humanity which holds that the demands of the spirit and of the flesh are in conflict with each other; a doctrine that the universe is under the dominion of two opposing principles, one of which is good and the other evil. Christian doctrine has traditionally associated spirit with good and flesh with evil.

Dyad. A term used in the study of interpersonal communication to refer to two people interacting with each other.

Dysfunction. Abnormal or impaired functioning; failure to fulfill needs. In sexual terms, the inability to orgasm or to participate satisfactorily in sexual intercourse.

Dysfunctional. Failing to fulfill the social requirements of the society, or having undesirable effects for some individuals, groups, or the society as a whole.

Dyspareunia. A sexual dysfunction in women in which intercourse causes intense pain in the clitoris, vaginal barrel, or soft tissues of the pelvis.

Ego. The self, especially as contrasted with another self or the world; also, the sense of self-worth. In psychoanalytic theory, the part of the psyche that organizes a person's relationship to the real world.

Ejaculation. The forcible, rhythmic discharge of seminal fluid from the penis during the male orgasm.

Elderly. Old people; senior citizens. Sometimes limited to the very old, as those past the age of 75 or 80.

Eligibility. The state of being qualified for acceptance; suitability.

Embryo. The developing human organism from the time of implantation to the end of the eighth week after conception; during this period, organs, systems, and tissues become differentiated.

Empathy. The capacity for sharing another's feelings or ideas; the skill through which partner's enter into each other's internal frame of reference.

Empirical. Originating in or based on experience or observation.

Empty-nest syndrome. The depression experienced by some mothers in middle age when children are working, married, or for other reasons not living at home. Such women become acutely depressed by loss of the mother role which has been central to their lives for so many years while others enjoy their new freedom.

Encounter groups. Groups, usually with a trained leader, that seek to apply psychological principles to promote the personal growth and psychological well-being of the participants.

Endogamy. Marriage within a specific group, especially as required by custom or law.

Endowment. A kind of life insurance which is a combination insurance and savings program; the policy matures after a specified number of years (usually twenty years or when the policyholder reaches age 65), at which point the holder receives the value of the policy in cash.

Engorgement. The filling with blood of the erectile tissue in the female's clitoris and in the vaginal area in general, or in the erectile tissue of the male's penis; results from sexual stimulation.

Enzyme. A complex protein produced by living cells necessary to certain biochemical reactions of the body.

Epididymis. A small organ lying within each of the male's testicles. It is composed of a long, tightly coiled mass of tubes and serves as a storage chamber for maturing sperm. It also adds an essential secretion to the seminal fluid.

Episiotomy. A small incision in the perineum made during childbirth, just before the baby's head appears; by enlarging the opening through which the baby will pass, a possible ragged-edged tear in the perineum is avoided.

Equalitarian.   Marked by equal rights and opportunities among the participants.

Equity.   A buyer's initial and increasing ownership rights in a house as a mortgage is paid off. When the mortgage is fully paid off, the buyer has 100 percent equity in the house.

Erectile tissue.   Soft tissue containing large venous spaces connected directly with the arteries. When stimulated, this tissue becomes firm and swollen with blood. See **engorgement.**

Erection.   The enlarged, stiffened state of the penis or clitoris when engorged with blood.

Erogenous zones.   Certain particularly sensitive areas of the body which respond to touch with sexual arousal; such areas include especially the genitalia, mouth, breasts, and neck.

Eros.   A Greek word meaning sexual attraction. As such, it is one of three different kinds of love distinguished by the Greeks. See also **philos** and **agape.**

Erotic.   Related to sexual arousal; tending to arouse sexual love or desire.

Eroticism.   Sexual impulse or desire, especially when abnormally insistent.

Estrogen.   A hormone produced by the ovaries which influences the development of female secondary characteristics (breasts, skin texture, etc.), stimulates the changes of the menstrual cycle, and contributes to enjoyment of sexual behavior.

Ethnic group.   A group socially identified by race, religion, language, or national origin and having a sense of common identity.

Ethnocentric.   Pertaining to the tendency to feel that one's own culture is superior, right, and natural, and that all other cultures are inferior and oftentimes wrong and unnatural.

Euphemism.   An agreeable or inoffensive word that is substituted for one that may offend or suggest something unpleasant.

Eustachian tube.   The tube in the ear connecting the middle ear cavity with the nasal passages.

Exchange theory.   A sociological theory based on the idea that social interaction involves a give and take similar to the economic marketplace; that is, people offer their own desirable traits and behaviors to bargain for social status and to bring about desired behaviors in another person.

Exogamy.   Marriage outside one's own group, especially as required by custom or law.

Exploitation.   Unjust or improper use of another person for one's own profit or advantage; behavior that benefits one person at the expense of another.

Expose.   Deprive of shelter, protection, or care; abandon (an infant), especially by leaving in the open.

Expressive.   Revealing thoughts and feelings; emphasizing personal qualities in interaction with others; giving more importance to the emotional content of interpersonal relationships than to their effectiveness in accomplishing specific tasks.

Extended family.   A family structure more complex than the nuclear family (a married couple and their children). May be based on the sharing of a household by three or more generations, including a number of married couples, or on plural marriages where one man has several wives or one woman several husbands.

Extramarital.   Relating to sexual intercourse of married persons with someone other than the spouse. See **comarital.**

Failure rates.   Measurements of the effectiveness of various birth control methods; the ratio of women who become pregnant while using a particular birth control method to those who do not. The ratio is expressed as the likelihood of pregnancy occurring during one year in 100 sexually active women using a particular method of contraception.

Fallopian tubes.   The two tubes in the female which link the ovaries to the uterus. Eggs released periodically from the ovaries are carried down these tubes toward the uterus.

Family.   Two or more persons related to each other by blood, marriage, or adoption, sharing a common residence, and cooperating economically.

Family of orientation. The family into which one is born and in which one is reared; the social group which gives one a place in society.

Family of procreation. The family established when one marries; includes the expectation that a married couple will procreate, or produce offspring.

Family planning. A system of controlling family size and spacing of children by appropriate use of contraceptive methods and/or methods for increasing fertility.

Family sculpting. A method used in family-therapy programs to improve communication between family members. Each person in turn arranges members of the family physically the way he or she sees them, and then rearranges them in the way he or she would like them to be.

Family-development approach. A way of organizing data from sociological studies of the family. Conceives of a family as having a life cycle which requires members to accomplish certain developmental tasks at each stage of its history. Accomplishment of these tasks enables a family to function effectively in meeting needs of family members.

Fecal matter. Feces; excrement; bodily waste discharged through the anus.

Feedback. In communication, giving an individual evaluative or corrective information about that person's behavior, both verbal and nonverbal. People in a communication set are continually providing feedback to each other.

Fellatio. Oral stimulation of the male genitals.

Feminism. The theory of the political, economic, and social equality of the sexes; organized activity in behalf of women's rights and interests.

Fertility rate. The number of births per year in relation to the number of women 15–44 years of age; a more highly refined indicator of trends in childbearing than the birth rate.

Fertilization. The union of male and female sex cells (egg and sperm) resulting in the formation of a zygote.

Fetus. A developing human from eight weeks after conception to birth.

Finance charge. Interest and carrying charges to be paid by a consumer for the use of credit in making major purchases.

Finance company. A company that grants personal loans; usually lenient in its requirements for references and willing to take risks, but charges high rates of interest.

Financial inventory. An itemized list of current assets and liabilities.

Forceps. A tonglike tool with large blades curved to fit the shape of a baby's head, sometimes used by doctors at childbirth to gently pull the baby from the woman's vagina.

Foreplay. Development of sexual responsiveness as a preparation for sexual intercourse through kissing, caressing, licking, and nibbling of sensitive body areas.

Foreskin. A loose, retractable fold of skin which covers the glans of the penis; this skin is commonly surgically removed in infancy by circumcision.

Fornication. Sexual intercourse outside of marriage, between unmarried persons, between a spouse and an unmarried person, or between spouses not married to each other.

Fraternal polyandry. Marriage of a group of brothers to one woman.

Frenum. A thin ridge of erotically sensitive tissue which joins glans to shaft on the underside of the penis.

Frustration. Dissatisfaction arising from unresolved problems. The state of the individual in a situation in which strong motives are perceived to be blocked.

Function. An action for which a person or thing is especially fitted or used or for which a thing exists. In sociology, includes purposes or uses of customs and beliefs as well as of objects and individuals. A function may be intentional (manifest), or it may be unintended, often unrecognized (latent).

Functionalists. Sociologists who make extensive use of structural-functional analysis in studying social organization and the behavior of individuals in society.

Gay liberation movement. The organized effort to promote equal opportunity for homosexuals; to eliminate discrimination against homosexuals from all major social institutions; and to improve the self-concept of homosexuals and the image of homosexuals held by society.

Gender roles.   Behavior patterns expected of men and women in a given society stemming from biological differences between males and females.

Gene.   A portion of the DNA molecule capable of determining the development of a specific hereditary trait.

Genetic defects.   Inherited variations in human anatomy or physiology which impair the structure or functioning of the body.

Genitalia.   The external sexual organs.

Geographic mobility.   Movement of people from one place of residence to another. Statistical data on trends in geographic mobility influences policy decisions of business and government.

Gestation.   Conception and development; carrying of young in the uterus.

Ghetto.   A densely populated inner-city area generally composed of minority-group members who are restricted by social or financial barriers from living in other areas.

Glans.   The smooth, conical structure at the tip of the penis or clitoris. It is a chief source of erotic response. In the male, it is covered at birth with a retractable foreskin sometimes removed by circumcision.

Gonoccocus.   A pus-producing bacterium that causes gonorrhea.

Gonorrhea.   A highly contagious venereal disease, caused by a micro-organism, the gonococcus. It is characterized by a discharge and painful inflamation of the mucous membranes of the genitals.

Grief work.   A term referring to the process of adjustment required after the death of a family member, especially the effort to understand and deal with one's own emotions.

Group life insurance.   Insurance coverage secured through group policies at one's place of employment or through a union, often at a more favorable price than individual policies.

Group marriage.   Marriage of two or more people of each sex, including sharing of sexual privileges and economic responsibilities.

Guaranty.   An assurance of the quality or the length of use to be expected from a product offered for sale, often including a promise of reimbursement if the buyer is not satisfied.

Gynecologist.   A medical doctor specializing in female disorders and the hygiene of women in pregnancy and childbirth.

Hedonism.   The doctrine that pleasure or happiness is the chief good in life.

Hereditary.   Transmitted genetically from parent to offspring.

Herpes.   A dangerous modern venereal disease caused by a virus known as Herpes simplex, type 2. Characterized by painful, blisterlike sores in the genital area and sometimes elsewhere on the body.

Hetaerae.   An elite group of mistresses or concubines in ancient Greece who provided the companionship and pleasure that Greek men did not expect from their wives. From Greek word meaning "female companions."

Heterosexual.   Relating to or including both males and females.

Hierarchy.   A graded or ranked series; an organization of orders or ranks.

Homosexual.   Pertaining to sexual desire for, or sexual activity with, members of one's own sex. Or a person who participates in such activities.

Homosexuality.   Erotic activity with a member of one's own sex.

Hormones.   Body substances secreted by endocrine glands, and carried by body fluids, which evoke specific responses in parts of the body far from the site of the glands where they originate.

Household.   All persons occupying a housing unit; this includes related family members as well as all unrelated persons like foster children, lodgers, or employees living in the house. One person keeping house alone also constitutes a household.

Human-potential movement.   Focusing of behavioral scientists and professional therapists on ways to ensure the maximum development of individuals in terms of their own needs and desires.

Humanist.   Pertaining to an attitude that asserts the dignity and worth of human beings, emphasizes reason, and often rejects elements of the supernatural.

Hyperventilate. To breathe at an excessive rate so as to cause an abnormal loss of carbon dioxide from the blood. Physical symptoms such as temporary loss of hearing, tingling in hands or feet, and loss of consciousness may result.

Hybrid model of equality. A more equalized definition of gender roles than the traditional assignment of tasks based on sex.

Hymen. A membrane, varying in thickness and shape, which stretches across the vaginal opening. The breaking of this membrane at a woman's first experience of sexual intercourse sometimes causes mild bleeding.

Hypocrisy. Pretense; deliberate creation of a false impression; appearing to have more virtue or religious devotion than one actually possesses.

Hypothesis. A tentative assumption that a researcher seeks to test through empirical research.

Hysterectomy. A medical procedure in which the uterus and sometimes the ovaries are removed. Usually a treatment for severe medical problems, the operation is sometimes performed as a permanent means of contraception.

Hysterotomy. An abortion technique in which the fetus is removed from the uterus through surgical incision in the abdomen.

Ideals. Standards of perfection; goals; the focus of endeavor.

Identity. The sense of one's own uniqueness, consistency, and continuity over time.

Identity bargaining. A process in social interaction by which people negotiate for acceptance of their own identities through acceptance of the identity another person is projecting; reaching a joint agreement to accept the identity of the other as defined in the interaction process.

Ideological. Concerned with ideas and ideals; relating to or based on an ideology.

Ideology. A systematic set of ideas, particularly about human life or culture; the integrated beliefs, assertions, and aims that constitute a sociopolitical program.

Illegitimate. Not recognized as lawful; born of parents not married to each other.

Implantation. The process by which the fertilized egg attaches itself to the uterine wall and draws nourishment from it until the placenta can be formed.

Impotence. Inability of the male to achieve an erection of the penis as a means to copulation; may be the result of either physical or psychological causes, generally the latter.

Inbreeding. The producing of offspring by two closely related individuals; sometimes used in agriculture to preserve and fix desirable characteristics and to eliminate undesirable characteristics from a stock.

Incest taboo. A rule forbidding sexual contact between certain closely related kin. Most commonly, it is the banning of sexual intercourse and marriage between parent and child and between brother and sister.

Income maintenance. The provision of income by governments or private organizations to enable indigent people to obtain the necessities of life.

Income tax. A tax based on the amount of income an individual has, often with elaborate exemptions and deductions intended to equalize the burden of paying the tax.

Incubator. An apparatus for maintenance of controlled conditions; especially an apparatus for controlling the oxygen intake and temperature of premature babies.

Index. A ratio or other number derived from a series of observations and used as a measure of a condition or characteristic.

Individualism. The doctrine that every individual should be free to pursue his or her own destiny, with emphasis on individual initiative, action, and interest.

Industrial Revolution. The period from 1760 to 1860 (the First Industrial Revolution) and from 1860 to 1914 (the Second Industrial Revolution) during which industry and agriculture became mechanized, power was applied to industry, the factory system was developed, and important developments in transportation and communication occurred.

Infanticide. Socially accepted killing of infants, usually by exposure or abandonment, often for economic reasons.

Infertile. Unable to reproduce; sterile.

Infidelity. Unfaithfulness to a moral obligation, especially a marital obligation; sexual intercourse of a married person with someone other than the spouse.

Installment purchases. Goods or services paid for through partial payments at fixed intervals. A form of buying on credit for which interest must be paid in addition to the actual purchase price.

Instinctive. Arising spontaneously and being independent of judgment or will.

Institution. A system of social relations organized to meet a basic societal need; the formal and stable cluster of norms, values, positions, and activities that centers around a basic social or individual need.

Instrumental. Task oriented; concerned with rational and efficient behavior directed toward achievement of specific goals.

Intercourse. Connection or dealings between persons or groups. Physical sexual contact between individuals that involves the genitalia of at least one person, most commonly the insertion of the penis of the male into the vagina of the female.

Interest. The cost, or charge paid, for borrowing money, usually figured as a percentage of the amount borowed and calculated daily, monthly, or yearly.

Intermarriage. Marriage between members of different groups, especially those of different racial or religious affiliations.

Interracial. Involving persons of different racial origin.

Intimacy. Very close association, contact, or familiarity; a relationhip of a very personal or private nature.

Intrauterine device (IUD). One of various small devices, usually made of plastic or metal, inserted by a doctor into the uterus and worn continuously as a contraceptive.

Intravenously. By means of the veins; through creating a passage into a vein.

Inventory. A list of traits, attitudes, interests, or abilities used to evaluate personal characteristics or skills.

Investment. An outlay, usually of money, in the expectation of gaining income or profit.

Involuntary. Against the will or without choice; not subject to control of the will.

Job fragmentation. The division of a work process into small steps or parts in the interest of greater efficiency. Leads to monotonous repetition of the same small operation, as on an automobile assembly line.

Job rotation. The practice of assigning jobs on a rotating basis so that all persons must take turns at the dull, onerous work as well as at the more creative and productive tasks; a practice in many successful communes.

Joint custody. The shared charge of children by a divorced couple, in which each parent takes responsibility for the children part of the time.

Joint family. A family unit, common in India, consisting of a number of brothers and their respective wives and children living in the same household and sharing mutual resources and obligations.

Jurisdiction. The power, right, or authority to interpret and apply the law; the territory within which authority may be exercised.

Juvenile delinquency. Antisocial behavior of a juvenile, usually a person under the age of 18, such that the individual is considered to be beyond parental control and therefore subject to legal action.

Karanavan. Among the Nayar of Southwest India, the head of the household or taravad, usually the oldest surviving male member.

Kibbutz. A collective farm in Israel, operated by a large group of people, often under very difficult environmental conditions.

Kibbutzim. Plural of kibbutz.

Kinship system. The way in which a society defines the relationships of persons connected to each other by blood, marriage, or adoption; a key element in the social structure, especially with respect to social rights and obligations.

Labia majora. An erotically sensitive outer fold of skin running downward and backward on each side of the vaginal opening.

Labia minora. The erotically sensitive inner folds of skin located on either side between the labia majora and the vaginal opening.

Language. A system for communicating ideas or feelings by the use of conventionalized sounds, gestures, or marks having agreed-upon meanings.

Laparoscopy. A medical procedure for the sterilization of females in which the fallopian tubes are seared or clipped and then tied off to prevent contact of ovum and sperm.

Lapsed. Was allowed to go out of existence; was terminated through omission or negligence.

Legal construct. A legal definition of the rights and obligations of persons toward each other in some specific context.

Legal entity. A social structure recognized by law and given formal status by law.

Legitimization. Making legal; giving legal status to; especially, putting a child into a state of legitimacy before the law by legal means.

Lesion. An abnormal change in the structure of an organ or part because of injury or disease.

Level of aspiration. The social status to which we think we are entitled, or which we think it is possible for us to achieve; the highest level in the social structure at which we think we will be able to gain acceptance.

Levirate. The marriage, sometimes compulsory, of a widow to the brother of her deceased husband.

Liabilities. Obligations; individual or corporate debts.

Liaison. A close bond or connection, especially an illicit sexual relationship.

Libido. Sexual desire; energy derived from primitive biological urges.

License. A permission granted by the proper authorities to engage in an activity that is otherwise unlawful; a document, plate, or tag as evidence of a license granted.

Life expectancy. A statistical expression of the number of years lived, on the average, by members of a given population. Varies with sex, year of birth, and environmental conditions.

Life insurance. A contract providing for payment of a sum of money to a designated beneficiary upon the death of an insured person provided premiums have been paid to keep the contract in force.

Lifetime family. The family seen in terms of progressive stages as members age and pass from one set of social roles to another; the family in terms of its career.

Ligament. A connecting band of body tissue which joins the extremities of bones to each other or supports an organ in place.

Lineage family. The family as a continuing structure, including the activities of successive generations of the same line.

Lippes loop. An intrauterine device made of plastic in a double-S shape, used as a means of contraception.

Longitudinal. Dealing with the growth and change of an individual or group over a period of years.

Lubrication. Something that lessens or prevents friction or wear; moisture collected on the wall of the vagina during sexual arousal which facilitates entry of the penis.

Lust. Intense sexual desire.

Lymph gland. A small, organized mass of tissue which produces cells that function in repair of tissue and in the formation of antibodies.

Maiden. Earliest, first; not married; never yet mated.

Malnutrition. Faulty or inadequate diet.

Managed democracy. A term used to define the social structure found in some types of communes which provides for substantial control of the decision-making process by leaders or managers.

Manually. Worked or done by hand.

Marriage. The set of laws and customs that specifies the ways in which the family relationship should be established, conducted, or terminated.

Marriage contract. A binding agreement to fulfill the legal and moral obligations of the married state as defined in a given society.

Marriage counselor. A trained professional who helps people experiencing marital difficulties to explore their problems and to develop a viable course of action in remedying them.

Marital adjustment. The process by which marriage partners adapt to each other's and their own conflicting needs; a process of accommodation between marriage partners.

Mass production. A system of industrial organization employing large numbers of people in the output of large quantities of goods, usually by machinery.

Masturbation. The practice of sexual arousal through erotic stimulation of genital organs commonly resulting in orgasm and achieved by manual or other bodily contact exclusive of sexual intercourse.

Matching hypothesis. The assumption, subject to further testing, that people are likely to choose dates and marriage partners who are like themselves in terms of social desirability.

Mate selection. The process of choosing a particular sexual partner, usually involving courtship rituals.

Materialistic. Pertaining to a stress upon material goods rather than intellectual or spiritual things.

Maternal instinct. The so-called natural or inherent aptitude, impulse, or capacity of a woman to fulfill the role of mother, no longer considered by behavioral scientists to be a valid concept.

Matriarchy. A system of social organization in which the power to rule rests in the female members of the family.

Matrilineage. A kinship system in which descent is traced through the females of the family.

Matrilineal. Traced through the female family lines only.

Matrilocal. Pertaining to the custom by which the place of residence of a married couple is with the family of the woman.

Maturity. The quality of being capable of making adult judgments; having completed growth and development.

Media. Channels of communication, such as newspapers, television, radio, and film, especially publications or broadcasts that carry advertising.

Median. A value in an ordered set of values, or scores, below and above which there is an equal number of values, or scores; a statistical measure of central tendency having somewhat the same function as the mean (average) or the mode.

Mediation. Assistance from an outside person or persons in arriving at a compromise or reconciling conflicting goals.

Membrane. A thin, soft, pliable sheet or layer of tissue.

Menopause. The time in a woman's life, usually between 45 and 50, when the menstrual cycle ceases, due to the cessation of ovulation and various hormonal changes.

Menstrual induction. An abortion technique in which the lining of the uterus is sucked out by means of a slender tube inserted through the cervix.

Menstruation. The final stage of the menstrual cycle when the menstrual fluid, consisting of blood, dead tissue, and glandular secretions, is discharged from the uterus.

Mental competence. Ability to function responsibly in social situations; sufficient intellectual development to be a responsible member of society.

Metric system. A decimal system of weights and measures based on the meter and on the kilogram.

Metropolitan area. A city and the area surrounding it, usually a densely populated area with considerable movement of people in and out.

Middle Ages. The period of European history from approximately 500 A.D. to approximately 1500.

Minnesingers. The German lyric poets and poet musicians of the eleventh to thirteenth centuries; the major theme of their poems and songs was courtly love. See **troubadours.**

Miscarriage. Expulsion of the human fetus before it is able to live, especially between the 12th and 28th weeks of gestation.

Miscegenation. Racial mixing; especially marriage or cohabitation between a white person and a member of another race.

Mistress. A woman who has power, authority, or ownership; a woman with whom a man habitually has sexual relations outside of marriage.

Moieties. Two basic complementary subdivisions of a tribe.

Mongolism. A congenital condition in humans associated with chromosomal abnormalities and characterized by both mental retardation and physical deformities. Also known as Down's syndrome.

Monogamy.   The state of being married to one person at a time.

Mons veneris.   The erotically sensitive mound of flesh which covers the female pubic bone.

Morality.   Conformity to ideals of right human conduct.

Mores.   The fixed, morally binding ideas of a particular group in regard to correct and incorrect behavior.

Mortgage.   A conveyance of property, as for security on a loan, on condition that the conveyance becomes void on payment or performance of the terms of the loan.

Mucus.   A slippery fluid secreted by mucous glands that moistens and protects the mucous membranes.

Mutual criticism.   A procedure found in some communes by which members, or a committee of members, evaluate an individual's conduct, especially in regard to behavior that is considered deviant from the group's norms.

Myth.   An ill-founded belief held uncritically, especially by an interested group.

Natural childbirth.   The process of giving birth without use of painkillers or anesthetics, in which special breathing is employed to prevent muscular tension and the woman takes an active part in labor.

Natural selection.   The "survival of the fittest" principle developed by Charles Darwin in 1859, which states that because all species tend to overproduce, there is a struggle for survival. In this struggle, those who have developed favorable variations survive and pass on their adaptive traits to succeeding generations.

Neolocal.   Pertaining to the custom by which a married couple sets up a new household separate from that of either spouse's family.

Net price.   The final or total price for which a product is sold.

Net worth.   The total financial value of a company or an individual, arrived at by preparation of a financial statement balancing assets and liabilities.

No-fault.   Pertaining to a system which settles legal claims without regard for the question of which party is to blame; a term applied especially in cases involving divorce and damages from automobile accidents.

Nonverbal behaviors.   Gestures, postures, facial expressions, tone of voice, touching, listening, and the physical placement of speaker and listener which convey messages in interpersonal communication.

Norms.   Cultural standards that define correct and incorrect behavior; principles of right action binding upon members of a group and serving to guide, control, or regulate proper and acceptable behavior.

Nuclear family.   A family composed of a married couple and their children, born or adopted, living by themselves. Also known as the conjugal family because of its emphasis on the conjugal bond, the strong tie between husband and wife.

Nurturant.   Furthering development; giving affectionate care and attention.

Obstetrician.   A medical doctor specializing in the care of women in pregnancy and childbirth.

Occupational mobility.   Movement of individuals from one type of job to another or one employer to another, often leading to a change in social-class position based on the change in work status.

Occupational status.   The social position of an individual based on the kind of work he or she does.

Offspring.   The young of an animal or plant; children.

Oral.   By means of the mouth.

Oral-genital contact.   Stimulation of the genitals of a sex partner by the mouth and tongue.

Organism.   A complex structure of interrelated parts; an individual constituted to carry on the activities of life by means of separate but mutually dependent organs.

Organized democracy.   A term used to define the social structure and decision-making process in certain types of communes; participation of members in management of the commune.

Orgasm.   The release of peak sexual tensions. It is characterized by involuntary, rhythmic, muscular contractions, a loss of self-awareness, and varying degrees of intense sensory pleasure.

Orgasmic platform. The engorged state of the vagina and nearby sexual organs in the female, during the plateau phase of sexual intercourse, which provides pleasurable friction for both partners and leads to the orgasmic phase.

Os. The opening of the cervix, which connects the upper end of the vagina to the uterus. Normally no wider than a thin straw, it is capable of stretching wide enough to allow a baby to pass through during childbirth.

Ovaries. Two almond-sized organs in the female which store and release the egg cells (ova) and the female sex hormones, estrogen and progesterone.

Ovulation. The process in the fertile female whereby the ovary releases an ovum, a mature egg, at regular intervals, usually once every 28 days.

Pater familias. Latin term meaning the father of the family or the male head of the household.

Paternity. The state of being a father.

Patriarchal. Characterized by the supremacy of the father of the family, or other male head, and the legal dependency of wives and children.

Patrilineal. Traced through the male family lines only.

Patrilocal. Pertaining to the custom by which the place of residence of a married couple is with the family of the man.

Payroll-deduction plan. A method of saving money whereby an employee authorizes the employer to deduct a specified amount of money from each paycheck and deposit it in the employee's savings account.

Peer group. People of equal standing; friends and associates of similar age and social status.

Pelvic. Pertaining to the pelvis, the basin-shaped structure formed by the pelvic girdle and adjoining bones of the spine; in humans, the lower part of the body just above the crotch.

Penicillin. A relatively nontoxic antibiotic.

Penis. The male organ of copulation, consisting of a root, shaft, and glans. Erect when sexually stimu-

lated, it is the most erotically sensitive area of the male body. Also contains the passage for the elimination of urine from the body.

Perception. The process of becoming aware of aspects of the external environment or internal states by way of the sense organs.

Perfectionism. A doctrine—preached by John Humphrey Noyes—that people are capable of living a sinless life on earth. This was the philosophy behind the nineteenth-century communes called the Putney Community and the Oneida Community.

Perineum. The erotically sensitive area between the anus and the genitalia.

Perjury. Deliberate lying under oath; swearing to what is untrue.

Permissiveness. The giving of consent or approval by someone in authority; often used in the sense of excessive tolerance.

Personality. The organization of an individual's attitudes, beliefs, habits, behavior, and other characteristics developed through interaction with others.

Petting. Deliberate erotic stimulation of another's body by sensual caresses without actual copulation.

Pheromones. Chemical substances produced by an organism which induce a physiological response in another of the same species; genital odors which may excite or repel a potential sex partner.

Philos. A Greek word meaning profound and enduring friendship. As such, it is one of three different kinds of love distinguished by the Greeks. See also **eros** and **agape.**

Physiological. Based on the function or malfunction of various systems of the body.

Physiology. The organic processes of a living organism or any of its parts; the functioning of various systems of the body.

Placenta. A mass of soft tissue attached to the inner surface of the uterus during pregnancy. It serves as a medium of exchange between maternal and fetal blood, nourishing the fetus and discharging its wastes.

Pleasuring. A term used by Masters and Johnson to describe a technique used in sex therapy in which each sexual partner gently explores the other's body with caresses without aiming for orgasm.

Policy. A document by which a contract of insurance is made.

Polyandry. A type of plural marriage in which a woman has two or more husbands.

Polygyny. A type of plural marriage in which a man has two or more wives; the most widespread form of plural marriage.

Pornographic. Pertaining to material, such as photographs or books, that depicts erotic behavior and is intended to cause sexual excitement.

Postpartum depression. A time of emotional upheaval in the weeks or months following childbirth in which mood swings of varying degrees are common.

Poverty level. The minimum income required for an individual or a family to provide a nutritionally adequate diet and other necessities of life, based on the "poverty index" of the Social Security Administration and adjusted annually according to changes in the Consumer Price Index.

Pregnancy. The period when unborn young are contained within the body.

Prehistoric. Relating to times before written history began.

Prejudice. An adverse opinion or leaning, without just grounds or without sufficient knowledge; an inflexible prejudgment of people belonging to certain social groups.

Premarital. Existing or occurring before marriage.

Prematurely. Before the proper or usual time, especially in reference to births occurring before completion of the full period of gestation.

Premenstrual tension. Feelings of irritability and depression which may precede menstrual periods due to hormonal and other body changes, especially retention of fluids.

Premium. The price paid for a contract of insurance, usually broken down into weekly, monthly, or annual installments.

Prerequisite. A requirement that must be fulfilled before an end or function can be carried out.

Primates. The order of mammals that includes man, together with apes, monkeys, and related forms. They are characterized by mobility of appendages (fingers and toes), replacement of claws by flat nails, development of simultaneous vision with two eyes, and a large brain.

Primitive. Belonging to an early stage of development; simple.

Principal. The actual amount of money borrowed (as on a mortgage) or credit received (as on a charge account) minus the interest to be paid and any service charges.

Priorities. Items requiring prior attention; the ranking of items—such as goals, preferences, or obligations—in terms of their relative importance.

Procreation. Propagation; the bringing forth of offspring.

Progesterone. A hormone produced by the ovaries and, during pregnancy, by the placenta. With estrogen, it prepares the lining of the uterus for the implantation and maintenance of the ovum, and it stimulates the mammary glands during pregnancy.

Progesterone T. A T-shaped intrauterine device, used in contraception, which continually releases tiny dosages of the hormone progesterone, making the uterus even more hostile to implantation than with other intrauterine devices.

Pronatalist. Morally opposed to the termination of pregnancy through abortion.

Prophylactic. Something which protects from disease; something used for preventing venereal infection such as a condom; also, a contraceptive device.

Prostaglandin. A hormonelike substance present in seminal, menstrual, and amniotic fluids and various mammalian tissues. Since prostaglandins stimulate contractions of the uterus, they may be used to induce labor, bring on delayed menstruation, or terminate unwanted pregnancies.

Prostate gland. A gland which passes alkaline secretions through its ducts into the urethra; these secretions mix with the seminal fluid and activate the sperm.

Prostitute. A person who engages in sexual behavior for money.

Protestant Reformation. The sixteenth-century religious movement in which groups of people broke away from the Roman Catholic church and established various Protestant denominations.

Psychohistorian. A historical researcher or student of history who is concerned with the influence of psychological factors in determining the course of historical events or patterns of behavior.

Psychosomatic. Pertaining to the influence of the mind or emotions upon the functioning of the body.

Puberty. The period when sexual maturity begins; at this time, functional sperm begin to be produced in the male and the female's menstrual cycle begins.

Pubic area. The pelvis; the lower part of the body just above the crotch.

Pubic hair. Body hair in humans, especially in the area of the pelvis and crotch, which usually appears just prior to or at the time of puberty.

Public assistance. Financial aid from a governmental agency—such as the Department of Health, Education and Welfare—to those who, for a variety of reasons, are unable to support themselves.

Puritans. A group of early Protestants whose aim was to cleanse their religion of all clerical power and rituals associated with the Roman Catholic church and return to the Biblical form of Christianity as they conceived it.

Racial minority. A group of people who, because of inherited physical characteristics, represent a distinct human type different from the human type, or race, represented by the majority of the people in a given society or geographical area.

Racism. Prejudice or discrimination against members of a particular race; the mistaken belief that race is the primary determinant of human traits and capacities and that racial differences produce superior and inferior races.

Radical. Extreme; marked by a significant departure from the usual or the traditional.

Rape. Sexual intercourse of a man with a woman without her consent and chiefly by force or deception.

Rapport. A relationship marked by harmony, conformity, and shared interests.

Reciprocate. To give and take mutually; to return, usually in kind or degree.

Reconciliation. The restoration of harmony after a period of conflict.

Rectum. The terminal part of the large intestine leading to the anus.

Refractory period. The period following the response of a muscle or nerve before it recovers the capacity to make a second response; especially, the rest period following a man's orgasm, during which he cannot produce another erection.

Remarriage. Marriage of a widowed or divorced person.

Renaissance. The period in Europe from the fourteenth to the seventeenth centuries, characterized by a flowering of the arts, literature, and science and a renewal of interest in the classical cultures of Greece and Rome. The transition period between medieval and modern times.

Renewable. Capable of being renewed or continued in force for another period of time, as with the loan of a library book; a feature of some insurance policies and other investments.

Retrospective. Based on memory; pertaining to what people recall about earlier periods of their lives.

Residential differentiation. The tendency for people to select housing on the basis of their age, income, race or ethnic affiliation, and stage in the family life cycle.

Revolving credit account. A loan by which a person can borrow for purchases and pay for them on an installment basis. Interest is based on the loan outstanding. However, if the full amount owed is paid within thirty days after the date of the billing statement, there is no finance charge.

Rhythm method. A contraceptive method in which the couple abstains from intercourse during the female's monthly fertile period (three to four days before ovulation and one day after).

Ritual. An established form for a ceremony; any formal and customarily repeated act or series of acts.

Role. Expected behavior pattern associated with a particular poition in a social system; a pattern of behavior that is appropriate to a particular social setting and exists outside the personality of the individual fulfilling the role.

Role exits. Giving up of roles because of a change in status, a process which occurs frequently in the course of the life cycle.

Role-identity. A term used to represent the combination of a role as defined by the society and an individual's personal conception of how a role should be fulfilled.

Role making. The process of defining new roles through interpersonal experimentation in times of rapid change or in a new environment.

Role models. Persons active in the socialization process who help to establish the social definition of particular roles through their own behavior patterns in carrying out these roles.

Role overload. Stress occurring when people are trying to fulfill more different roles than they have time or energy for.

Role playing. Carrying out the behaviors expected of an individual of a particular status in any given social interaction; involves modifying and adapting one's role behavior to the role behavior of other individuals.

Rules of residence. Customs determining where a newly married couple will establish their joint home.

Saboteurs. People engaging in action tending to hamper or hurt another; especially people who make sexual relations unsatisfactory for their partners by undermining the other's sexuality in subtle and indirect ways.

Sacrament. A formal religious act symbolic of a spiritual reality, especially one begun or recognized by Jesus Christ.

Saf-t-coil. An all-plastic model of the intrauterine device, in the shape of a ram's horn, used as a means of contraception.

Salient. Noticeable; standing out conspicuously.

Savings and loan association. A specialized kind of bank which uses the funds of its depositors primarily for mortgage-secured home loans.

Scale. A graduated series or scheme for ranking statistical data, as used in sociological research.

Scrotum. A pouch of loose skin which contains the testicles.

Securities. Evidence of debt or of ownership, as stock certificates or bonds.

Segregation. The isolation of a race, class, or ethnic group by discrimination in employment, housing, educational facilities, or other means.

Selective comparison. A personality mechanism by which we compare ourselves to others in ways that sustain our self-concept rather than in ways that might be disruptive to it.

Selective evaluation. A personality mechanism by which one changes an assessment of oneself and others in order to maintain a consistent self-concept.

Selective interaction. A personality mechanism by which one chooses to associate only with those people who support one's self-concept.

Self-concept. The mental image one has of oneself as an individual, including physical features, body image, personality, and ability; it is acquired through social interaction.

Self-disclosure. The act of revealing personal information to others.

Self-esteem. One's sense of one's own worth or value.

Self-marriage. The formation of a union by a couple who recite their vows to each other without the presence of any civil or religious official.

Self-presentation. A step in identity bargaining, in which one tries to convey a particular perception of oneself in a given role.

Self-preservation. A personality mechanism by which we present ourselves in ways that will gain a certain desired response from family or friends and that will support our self-concept.

Self-sufficiency. The ability to provide for individual or group needs without outside help.

Semen. The thick, whitish fluid produced by the male reproductive organs and ejaculated during orgasm; it consists of the sperm, their nutrient plasma, and various glandular secretions.

Seminal vesicle. A small pouch between the vas deferens and the urethra where sperm collect and are mixed with a secretion to form the semen or ejaculate.

Sense receptors. Bodily structures that receive stimuli from the internal or external environment and transmit the message to the brain which, in turn, interprets the sensation.

Separation. The ending of cohabitation of a married couple without the legal right to marry again.

Serial monogamy. A succession of marriages such that one may have several spouses in the course of a lifetime but only one at a time.

Sex objects. People viewed solely in terms of their usefulness in gratifying sexual desire.

Sex ratio. The number of males in a population per 100 females; varies with age level and environmental conditions.

Sex therapist. A counselor with special training who provides treatment for sexual dysfunctions.

Sexist. Exhibiting prejudice or discrimination against women or the belief that women are innately inferior to men.

Sexuality. The total of an individual's sexual characteristics, behavior, tendencies, attractiveness, and drives.

Sib. A group of people descended from one real or supposed ancestor along either the maternal or paternal line; a tribal division similar to a clan.

Sibling. One of two or more individuals having one common parent; a brother or sister.

Significant others. A term developed by George H. Mead to indicate those people whose judgment and opinion have the most influence in the formation of an individual's self-concept.

Smegma. A thick, cheesy, glandular secretion which sometimes collects under the foreskin of the penis.

Social indicators. Traits such as age, income, race or ethnic identification, political orientation, education, and religious affiliation, which correlate with behavior and can, therefore, be used as predictors of what a population is likely to do at a given time or place.

Social mobility. The movement of an individual upward or downward in the social-class structure on the basis of changes in age, income, or educational attainment.

Social organization. The way in which various groups, categories, or aggregates of people interact to form the structure of the total society.

Social psychology. An academic discipline which links the study of psychology and the study of sociology, focusing especially on the relationships between the individual and various groups in the society.

Social scripts. Learned ways of how one should behave in particular social situations and of how other people can be expected to behave; a pattern for social interaction.

Social Security payments. Retirement benefits for the aged, benefits for children of a deceased worker, or payments to disabled workers, from the government; these have been financed by regular contributions from workers and their employers. Payments vary, depending upon years of employment and wages earned.

Social status. A position in a social system which forms the basis for defining the role of a person having that status.

Social structure. The organized or patterned ways in which people interact with one another.

Social system. The interaction patterns of a set of interrelated and interdependent individuals and groups.

Social worker. One who is specially trained in procedures for investigation, treatment, and material aid of the economically underprivileged and socially maladjusted.

Socialists. Supporters of various economic and political theories advocating collective or governmental ownership and administration of the means of production and distribution of goods.

Socialization. The process by which an individual acquires the skills, norms, and values of a group or society; the process by which culture is transmitted to the individual.

Society. A relatively independent and self-perpetuating human group which occupies a particular territory and which learns and shares a particular culture.

Sociocultural. Relating to or involving a combination of social and cultural factors

Sociological. Pertaining to social behavior.

Sociologist. One who studies social organization and the behavior of humans in social settings.

Sodomy. Sexual behavior which includes anal and oral intercourse and copulation with animals.

Sororal polygyny. The form of plural marriage in which two or more sisters are married to one man.

Spectatoring. A term used by Masters and Johnson to describe a situation during lovemaking in which people mentally follow the progress of their own responses as if they were onlookers from above; may be linked to fear of sexual inadequacy.

Sperm. A mature male sex cell capable of fertilizing an ovum from the female, thus leading to development of a new individual of the same species.

Sperm bank. Facilities for storage of frozen human semen for use later in artificial insemination.

Spermicides. Chemical substances, used as contraceptives, which immobilize or destroy sperm.

Spouse. A married person, either husband or wife.

Standard of living. The necessities, comforts, and luxuries enjoyed or aspired to by an individual or group.

Statistics. A collection of data, expressed in numerical terms, which provides methods for describing, summarizing, and organizing events, and for making predictions and estimations.

Status symbols. Possessions or attributes indicating a particular rank in the social hierarchy.

Statutes. Laws enacted by the legislative branch of a government.

Stem family. A family system, common in agricultural societies, in which one child, usually the eldest son, inherits all the family property.

Stereotype. A conception of a group or category of people that represents an oversimplified, rigid opinion or attitude.

Stereotyped. Perceived in terms of an oversimplified, rigid opinion or attitude which does not correspond to reality.

Sterility. Inability to produce offspring; barrenness.

Sterilization. Rendering a person sterile through medical procedures such as vasectomy in males or tubal ligation and hysterectomy in females.

Stimuli. Events or things that arouse a person to activity; agents which act as excitants or irritants.

Stirpiculture. A system instituted by John Humphrey Noyes in the Oneida Community by which couples wishing to have children were evaluated by a committee; some received permission to do so and some were expected to practice birth control. Behind this is the belief that only mentally and physically superior people should bear children.

Stocks. (1) A device for public punishment, consisting of a wooden frame with holes in which the feet and hands of the offender could be locked. (2) Certificates representing the acquisition of ownership of a portion or share of a business enterprise.

Structural-functional analysis. A theoretical framework for the study of human behavior which holds that people behave in certain ways to fulfill social needs or functions and that the patterns of interaction best suited to fulfilling these needs form the structure of the society; implies a close interrelationship between structure—the patterns of social interaction—and function—the purposes accomplished by the interaction.

Structure. Pattern of organization; arrangement or interrelationship of parts as dominated by the general character of the whole.

Subfertile. Producing lower than normal quantities of sperm, in the male, or releasing ova irregularly, in the female, so that conception is unlikely to take place despite regular sexual intercourse.

Subhuman species. Varieties of living organisms which are less complex in organization than humans and lack the morality and intelligence normally associated with humans.

Subjective. Peculiar to a particular individual; personal.

Subsistence farmer. A farmer whose system of farming provides all, or almost all, the goods required by the household. Usually, there is no significant surplus for sale.

Substandard. Of low quality; falling short of the norm.

Suppositories. Solid but meltable cones or cylinders of substances that immobilize and kill sperm when inserted into the vagina before intercourse.

Surrogate. Appointed to act in place of another; as a babysitter is a surrogate parent.

Survival gap. A term for the difference, on the average, between the life expectancy of women and that of men.

Survival of the fittest. The doctrine of Charles Darwin that the healthiest and strongest organisms of a given species will survive and procreate and their superior adaptive traits will continue to improve the species.

Swaddling. The custom of wrapping the entire body of an infant with narrow strips of cloth to restrict his or her movements.

Swindles. Actions which enable one to obtain money or property by fraud or deceit.

Symbolic communication. The exchange of information through words, gestures, and facial expressions, and the interpretation of these symbols by the people involved.

Symbolic-interaction approach. A theoretical framework for the study of human behavior in which the emphasis is on individuals reacting and interacting with one another in a network of social roles.

Symbols. Acts, sounds, or objects having cultural significance and the capacity to excite or objectify a response.

Synthetic. Produced artificially rather than occurring in the natural world.

Syphilis. A venereal disease caused by a spirochaete bacterium and passed from person to person by direct physical contact. It is primarily a disease of blood vessels and thus may affect any part of the body if untreated.

Syringe. A device used to inject fluids or withdraw them from something, as a device used to suck mucus from a baby's mouth and nose immediately upon delivery.

Taravad. A term among the Nayar of Southwest India indicating both the mound on which a house was built and the kinship unit living there.

Technologically. Pertaining to the means employed to provide a society with objects necessary for sustenance and comfort.

Technology. Practical application of scientific knowledge; the totality of the means employed to provide objects necessary for human sustenance and comfort.

Term insurance. A type of life-insurance policy which covers the insured for a specific period of time rather than for an entire lifetime. Some term insurance is renewable, however.

Testicles. Oval-shaped organs, suspended in the scrotum by the spermatic cords, which produce sperm cells and the male hormone, testosterone.

Testosterone. A hormone which induces and maintains male secondary characteristics (facial hair, musculature, etc.) and masculine behavior patterns. Produced in the testicles of males and in the adrenal glands of both men and women, it is essential to sexual desire.

Tetracycline. An antibiotic used in the treatment of various venereal diseases.

Theoretical framework. A set of concepts used in the analysis of scientific data which helps to give order and meaning to observations and research findings.

Theorist. One who analyzes facts in their relation to one another in order to develop general statements or principles which account for research findings.

Theory. A set of general statements or principles which attempts to explain or account for one's observations, experiences, or research findings.

Therapeutic aggression. The releasing of anger in verbal arguments and in mock attacks (as with foam bats) in encounter groups or in other forms of therapy for couples.

Thromboembolism. A disease involving the possibly fatal blockage of a major blood vessel by a blood clot.

Total fertility rate. The number of children born per thousand women during their entire lifetime; computed only for those beyond childbearing age.

Totalitarian. Characterized by centralized, absolute control over totally subjected individuals.

Trade-in. An item of merchandise (such as an automobile) taken as payment or part payment for a purchase.

Transsexual. A person who adopts the gender role of the opposite sex from that in which originally reared, and has perhaps undergone surgery and hormonal treatment to bring about changes in sexual characteristics.

Trauma. An injury or wound; a disordered psychic or behavioral state resulting from mental or emotional stress.

Triad. A term used in the study of interpersonal communication to refer to three people interacting with each other. More complex than a dyad.

Trimester. A three-month period; one of three equal periods into which the nine months of pregnancy are divided.

Tripartite. Composed of three parts; made between or involving three parties, as a treaty or contract.

Troubadours. The lyric poets and poet-musicians who flourished in the eleventh to thirteenth centuries, chiefly in the south of France and north of Italy. The major theme of their poems and songs was courtly love. See **minnesingers.**

Tubal ligation. A method of sterilization of women in which a portion of the fallopian tubes is cut, tied, or removed so that eggs are blocked from moving down the fallopian tube and sperm are blocked from moving up, and conception cannot occur.

Ultrasonic. Pertaining to sound waves of frequencies above the hearing limit of the human ear.

Umbilical cord. The flexible cord, arising from the navel, which connects the fetus with the placenta and carries nutrients from the system of the pregnant woman to that of the fetus.

Unconstitutional. Not according to the written Constitution of the United States, which outlines the powers and duties of the government and the rights of the people under the government.

Unit price. The price of an item per standard unit, such as ounce, pound, quart, or square foot, in contrast to the price for the item as packaged; used in comparing the price of items which come in packages of assorted sizes.

Universal. Present or occurring everywhere.

Unmarried mother. A woman who has had a child outside of marriage.

Urban-industrial society. A society in which people tend to be concentrated in densely populated metropolitan areas and production is carried on in large, mechanized manufacturing and processing facilities.

Urethra. The duct in male and female mammals through which urine passes from the bladder to the outside. In the male it also functions as a passage for sperm.

Urinary. Pertaining to those organs concerned with the formation and discharge of urine.

Usurious. Characterized by an excessive rate or amount of interest.

Uterus. The hollow, muscular, pear-shaped organ in the female which nurtures the fetus. Its cavity opens into the fallopian tubes on either side above and into the vagina below.

Utilities. Services such as light, power, or water provided by a municipality or by a corporation organized for that purpose.

Utopia. A place of ideal perfection, especially in laws, government, and social conditions; an imaginary society in which a perfect life can be lived.

Vacuum curettage. An abortion technique used up to the twelfth week of pregnancy in which the cervix is dilated and the contents of the uterus sucked out by means of a tube and vacuum pump.

Vagina. The elastic sex organ of the female which extends like a canal between the external genitalia and the cervix or opening to the uterus.

Vaginismus. Involuntary muscular spasms of the vagina, caused by a woman's anxiety, which may tighten the vagina to the point of preventing intercourse.

Values. Principles or qualities which are highly esteemed; cultural standards for appraising people, behavior, experiences, and objects.

Variables. Measurable elements which influence and account for behavior; attributes or characteristics that change from individual to individual, group to group, place to place, or over time.

Varicose veins. Blood vessels which are abnormally swollen or dilated.

Vas deferens. A continuation of the duct of the epididymis which carries sperm on toward the seminal vesicles for storage.

Vasectomy. A male sterilization method in which a small piece of each vas deferens is removed and the ends tied off to prevent movement of sperm into the seminal vesicles; thus the ejaculate of the male during orgasm will not contain any sperm.

Venereal diseases. Dangerous infections which attack the genital area and may cause complications in other areas of the body. Very contagious, they are spread mainly by sexual contact.

Ventilation. Free and open discussion; especially, the free expression of feelings of anger and frustration.

Verbal. Involving or consisting of words, spoken rather than written.

Vibrator. Vibrating electrical devices used in massage, sometimes for purposes of sexual arousal.

Violence. Behavior which threatens or causes physical harm to another person.

Virginity. A state in which sexual intercourse has not been experienced.

Virility. Masculinity; manly vigor.

Visitation rights. The rights of a divorced parent who does not have custody of the children of the marriage to visit them at specified times.

Warranty. A written guaranty of the integrity of a product and of the maker's responsibility for the repair or replacement of defective parts.

Wedlock. The state of being married.

White blood cells. Almost colorless cells in the blood that form part of the defense mechanisms of the body against viruses, bacteria, and foreign particles. They move through the blood-transport system to damaged or infected tissues.

Whole-life insurance. A kind of life insurance which is a combination savings and insurance program; premiums usually stay level throughout the life of the policy and the regular payment of premiums builds up the cash value of the policy.

Widower. A man whose wife has died and who has not remarried.

Wife transfer. A custom among the Toda by which a man is permitted to choose a mate from among women already married. The husband or husbands are reimbursed with cattle for the loss of the wife.

Will. A written declaration, legally executed, of a person's desires as to the manner in which his or her estate should be disposed of after that person's death.

Witchcraft. The use of magic; sorcery; communication with the devil.

Withdrawal. A contraceptive method in which the penis is withdrawn from the vagina just before ejaculation. Also called **coitus interruptus.**

Women's liberation movement. Organized activity in behalf of women's rights and interests, especially activity directed to ensuring social equality of the sexes.

Work-role orientation. The feelings or attitudes about work that play a powerful role in shaping a person's overall outlook toward life. Variable attitudes to work as a job, a task, an occupation, or a career.

Zero population growth. A condition in which the number of births equals the number of deaths, thus creating a stable population size.

Zygote. A fertilized egg, or ovum.

Bibliography

ABERNETHY, VIRGINIA (1974). Dominance and sexual behavior: an hypothesis. *American Journal of Psychiatry* 131:7:813–817.

ALDOUS, JOAN (1974). The making of family roles and family change. *The Family Coordinator* 23:3:231–235.

——— (1972). Children's perceptions of adult role assignment: father-absence, class, race and sex influences. *Journal of Marriage and the Family* 34:1:55–74.

ALDRIDGE, DELORES P. (1974). Problems and approaches to black adoptions. *The Family Coordinator* 23:4:407–410.

ALEKSANDROWICZ, MALCO K., AND DOV R. ALEKSANDROWICZ (1974). Obstetrical pain-relieving drugs as predictors of infant behavior variability. *Child Development* 45:935–945.

AMENT, MARC (1974). The right to be well born. *The Journal of Legal Medicine*. 2:6:19–24.

AMERICAN COUNCIL OF LIFE INSURANCE (1976). *Youth 1976.* New York: American Council of Life Insurance.

ANSHEN, RUTH NANDA (1959). The family in transition. In Ruth Nanda Anshen (ed.), *The Family: Its Function and Destiny.* New York: Harper.

ANSPACH, DONALD F. (1976). Kinship and divorce. *Journal of Marriage and the Family* 38:2:323–230.

ARD, BEN (1974). Premarital sexual experience: a longitudinal study. *Journal of Sex Research* 10:1:32–39.

ARGYLE, MICHAEL (1969). *Social Interaction.* Chicago: Aldine.

ASKHAM, JANET (1976). Identity and stability within the marriage relationship. *Journal of Marriage and the Family* 38:3:535–547.

ASKINS, JOHN (1976). Natural birth control growing. *Boston Evening Globe,* March 10, 1976, p. 37.

AUERBACH, JEROLD S. (1976). A plague of lawyers. *Harper's* 253:1517:37–44.

BACH, GEORGE, AND PETER WYDEN (1968). *The Intimate Enemy.* New York: Avon Books.

BAHR, HOWARD M., AND F. IVAN NYE (1974). The kinship role in a contemporary community: perceptions of obligations and sanctions. *Journal of Comparative Family Studies* V:1:17–25.

BALSWICK, JACK O., AND JAMES A. ANDERSON (1969). Role definition in the unarranged date. *Journal of Marriage and the Family* 31:4:776–778.

BALSWICK, JACK O., AND CHARLES W. PEEK (1971). The inexpressive male: a tragedy of American society. *The Family Coordinator* 20:4:363–368.

BARBACH, LONNIE GARFIELD (1976). *For Yourself: The Fulfillment of Female Sexuality.* New York: Anchor Press.

BARDIS, PANOS D. (1964). Family forms and variations historically considered. In Harold T. Christiansen (ed.), *Handbook of Marriage and the Family.* Chicago: Rand McNally, pp. 403–461.

BAUMRIND, DIANA, AND ALLEN E. BLACK (1967). Socialization practices associated with dimensions of competence in preschool boys and girls. *Child Development* 38:2:291–327.

BAYER, ALAN (1975). Sexist students in American colleges: a descriptive note. *Journal of Marriage and the Family* 37:2:391–397.

BEALES, ROSS W., JR. (1975). In search of the historical child: miniature adulthood and youth in colonial New England. *American Quarterly* XXVII:4.

BECK, DOROTHY FAHS, AND MARY ANN JONES (1973). *Progress on Family Problems, A Nationwide Study of Clients' and Counselors' Views on Family Agency Services.* New York: Family Service Association of America.

BEIGEL, HUGO G. (1951). Romantic love. *American Sociological Review* 16:326–334.

BELL, ALAN P. (1975). Percentage of homosexuals who are married. *Medical Aspects of Human Sexuality,* Sept. 1975, p. 106.

BELL, ROBERT R., WITH NORMAN M. LOBSENZ (1974). Married sex: how uninhibited can a woman dare to be? *Redbook,* Sept. 1974, pp. 75, 176, 179, 181.

BELL, ROBERT R., STANLEY TURNER, AND LAWRENCE ROSEN (1975). A multi-variate analysis of female extramarital coitus. *Journal of Marriage and the Family* 37:2: 375–384.

BENSON, LOREN, MICHAEL BERGER, AND WILLIAM MEASE (1975). Family communication systems. *Small Group Behavior* 6:1:91–105.

BERGER, BENNETT M. (1966). Suburbs, subcultures, and the urban future. In Sam Bass Warner (ed.), *Planning for a Nation of Cities.* Cambridge, Mass.: The M.I.T. Press, pp. 143–162.

BERGER, BENNETT M., BRUCE M. HACKETT, AND R. MERVYN MILLAR (1974). Child-rearing practices in the communal family. In Arlene Skolnick and Jerome H. Skolnick, *Intimacy, Family, and Society.* Boston, Mass.: Little, Brown, pp. 441–463.

BERNARD, JESSIE (1972a). Changing family life styles: one role, two roles, shared roles. In Louise Kapp Howe (ed.), *The Future of the Family.* New York: Simon and Schuster, pp. 235–246.

———— (1972b).   Women, marriage, and the future. In Constantina Safilios-Rothschild, *Toward a Sociology of Women.* Lexington, Mass.: Xerox College Publishing, pp. 367–371.

BERNDT, RONALD M. (1965).   Marriage and the family in north-eastern Arnhem Land. In M. F. Nimkoff, *Comparative Family Systems.* Boston: Houghton Mifflin, pp. 77–104.

BERNSTEIN, GERALD S. (1975).   Use of vaginal spermicidal agents. *Medical Aspects of Human Sexuality,* July 1975, pp. 135–136.

BERSCHEID, ELLEN, AND ELAINE WALSTER (1974).   Physical attractiveness. In Leonard Berkowitz (ed.), *Advances in Experimental Social Psychology,* Vol. 7. New York: Academic Press, pp. 158–216.

BERSCHEID, ELLEN, ELAINE WALSTER, AND GEORGE BOHRNSTEDT (1973).   Body image—the happy American body: a survey report. *Psychology Today* 7:6:119–131.

BIBRING, GRETE L., et al. (1961).   A study of the psychological processes in pregnancy and of the earliest mother-child relationship. *The Psychoanalytic Study of the Child* 16:9–72.

BIENVENU, MILLARD J., SR. (1975).   A measurement of premarital communication. *The Family Coordinator* 24:1:65–68.

———— (1970).   Measurement of marital communication. *The Family Coordinator* 19:1:26–31.

BIRDWHISTELL, RAY L. (1974).   The idealized model of the American family. In Marvin B. Sussman, *Sourcebook in Marriage and the Family,* 4th ed. Boston: Houghton Miffllin, pp. 12–15.

BLAKE, JUDITH (1961).   *Family Structure in Jamaica.* New York: Free Press.

BLAU, ZENA SMITH (1973).   *Old Age in a Changing Society.* New York: Franklin Watts (New Viewpoints).

BLODGETT, RICHARD E. (1971).   *The New York Times Book of Money.* New York: New York Times Book Co.

BLUFORD, ROBERT W., JR., AND ROBERT E. PETERS (1973).   *Unwanted Pregnancy.* New York: Harper & Row.

BLUMBERG, PAUL M., AND P. W. PAUL (1975).   Continuities and discontinuities in upper-class marriages. *Journal of Marriage and the Family* 37:1:63–77.

BLUMSTEIN, PHILIP W. (1975).   Identity bargaining and self-conception. *Social Forces* 53:3:47–485.

BOCKUS, FRANK (1975).   A systems approach to marital process. *Journal of Marriage and Family Counseling* 1:3:251–258.

BOHANNAN, PAUL (1971).   *Divorce and After.* New York: Anchor Books.

BOLTE, GORDON L. (1970).   A communications approach to marital counseling. *The Family Coordinator* 19:1:34–40.

BONHAM, GORDON SCOTT (1977).   Who adopts: the relationship of adoption and social-demographic characteristics of women. *Journal of Marriage and the Family* 39:2:295–306.

BOOTH, ALAN, AND ELAINE HESS (1974). Cross-sex friendship. *Journal of Marriage and the Family* 36:1:38–47.

BOSTON WOMEN'S HEALTH BOOK COLLECTIVE (1976). *Our Bodies, Ourselves,* 2nd ed. New York: Simon and Schuster.

BRADLEY, ROBERT A. (1965). *Husband-Coached Childbirth.* New York: Harper & Row.

BRANDWEIN, RUTH A., CAROL A. BROWN, AND ELIZABETH MAURY FOX (1974). Women and children last: the social situation of divorced mothers and their families. *Journal of Marriage and the Family* 36:3:498–514.

BRECHER, RUTH, AND EDWARD BRECHER, EDS. (1966). *An Analysis of Human Sexual Response.* New York: Signet Books.

BRODERICK, CARLFRED B. (1971). Beyond the five conceptual frameworks: a decade of development in family theory. *Journal of Marriage and the Family* 33:1:139–159.

BROWN, CAROL A., ROSLYN FELDBERG, ELIZABETH M. FOX, AND JANET KOHEN (1976). Divorce: chance of a new lifetime. *Journal of Social Issues* 32:1:119–133.

BROWN, CATHERINE CALDWELL (1976). It changed my life. *Psychology Today* 10:6: 47ff.

BRUCE, JOHN ALLEN (1974). The role of mothers in the social placement of daughters: marriage or work? *Journal of Marriage and the Family* 36:3:392–397.

BRUNDAGE, JAMES A. (1975). Concubinage and marriage in medieval canon law. *Journal of Medieval History* 1:1:1–17.

BURKE, RONALD J., AND TAMARA WEIR (1976). Relationship of wives' employment status to husband, wife and pair satisfaction and performance. *Journal of Marriage and the Family* 38:2:297–287.

BURCHELL, R. CLAY, GABRIEL V. LAURY, AND BERNARD SOCHET (1975). Self-esteem and sexuality. *Medical Aspects of Human Sexuality,* Jan. 1975, pp. 74–90.

CAMPBELL, ANGUS (1975). The American way of mating: marriage sí, children only maybe. *Psychology Today* 8:12:37–43.

CAPLOW, THEODORE (1964). *Principles of Organization.* New York: Harcourt, Brace.

CAVAN, RUTH SHONLE, ED. (1974). *Marriage and Family in the Modern World.* New York: Thomas Y. Crowell.

CENTERS, RICHARD (1975). Attitude similarity-dissimilarity as a correlate of heterosexual attraction and love. *Journal of Marriage and the Family* 37:2:305–312.

CHAIKIN, ALAN L., AND VALERIAN J. DERLEGA (1974). *Self-Disclosure.* Morristown, N.J.: General Learning Press.

CHAMBLISS, WILLIAM J., ED. (1973). *Sociological Readings in the Conflict Perspective.* Reading, Mass.: Addison-Wesley.

Christian Science Monitor: 4-year car loans increasing in U.S. Boston, Mass.: *Christian Science Monitor,* March 18, 1976.

COGSWELL, BETTY E., AND MARVIN B. SUSSMAN (1972).   Changing family and marriage forms: complications for human service systems. *The Family Coordinator* 21:4:505–516.

COHEN, STEPHEN, AND ALAN SUSSMAN (1975).   The incidence of child abuse in the United States. *Child Welfare* 54:6:432–443.

COLE, CHARLES LEE (1977).   Cohabitation in social context. In Roger W. Libby and Robert N. Whitehurst (eds.), *Marriage and Alternatives: Exploring Intimate Relationships*. Glenview, Ill.: Scott, Foresman, pp. 62–79.

COLLINS, JOHN K., JUDITH R. KENNEDY, AND RONALD D. FRANCIS (1976).   Insights into a dating partner's expectations of how behavior should ensue during the courtship process. *Journal of Marriage and the Family* 38:2:373–378.

CONNELL, ELIZABETH B. (1975).   The pill revisited. *Family Planning Perspectives* 7:2:62–71.

CONOVER, PATRICK W. (1975).   An analysis of communes and intentional communities with particular attention to sexual and general relations. *The Family Coordinator* 24:4:453–464.

CONSTANTINE, LARRY L., AND JOAN M. CONSTANTINE (1973).   *Group Marriage*. New York: Macmillan.

———— (1972a).   Dissolution of marriage in a non-conventional context. In M. B. Sussman (ed.), *Non-Traditional Family Forms in the 1970's*. Minneapolis: National Council on Family Relations, pp. 89–94.

———— (1972b).   The group marriage. In M. Gordon (ed.), *Nuclear Family in Crisis: The Search for an Alternative*, pp. 204–222. New York: Harper & Row.

CONSUMERS UNION (1974).   A guide to life insurance: part III. *Consumer Reports* 39:3:219–223.

COOPERSMITH, STANLEY (1967).   *The Antecedents of Self-Esteem*. San Francisco: W. H. Freeman.

COUNCIL OF STATE GOVERNMENTS (1976).   *The Book of the States*, Vol. XXI. Lexington, Ky.: The Council of State Governments.

COWLEY, SUSAN CHEEVER (1975).   Paying their dues. *Newsweek*, Feb. 24, 1975, pp. 55–56.

COZBY, PAUL C. (1973).   Self-disclosure: a literature review. *Psychological Bulletin* 79:2:73–91.

CROMWELL, RONALD E., AND DAVID H. OLSON, EDS. (1975).   *Power in Families*. New York: Halsted Press.

DAVIDSON, SARA (1970).   Open land: getting back to the communal garden. *Harper's Magazine* 240:1441:91–102.

DAVIS, ADELLE (1972).   *Let's Have Healthy Children*. New York: Signet Books.

DAVIS, JOSEPH E. (1972).   The reversibility of male sterilization. In Lawrence Lader (ed.), *Foolproof Birth Control*. Boston: Beacon Press, pp. 191–197.

DAY, RICHARD L. (1967).   Factors influencing offspring. *American Journal of Diseases of Children* 113:2:179–185.

DECAMP, CATHERINE CROOK (1972).   *The Money Tree.* New York: Signet Books.

DELISSOVOY, VLADMIR (1973).   High school marriages: a longitudinal study. *Journal of Marriage and the Family* 35:2:245–255.

DELORA, JOANN S., AND CAROL A. B. WARREN (1977).   *Understanding Sexual Interaction.* Boston: Houghton Mifflin.

DEMAUSE, LLOYD, ED. (1974).   *The History of Childhood.* New York: The Psychohistory Press.

DEMOS, JOHN (1974).   The American family in past time. *The American Scholar* 43:3:422–446.

——— (1973).   Infancy and childhood in the Plymouth Colony. In Michael Gordon (ed.), *The American Family in Social-Historical Perspective.* New York: St. Martin's Press, pp. 180–191.

DEUTSCHER, IRWIN (1962).   Socialization for postparental life. In Arnold M. Rose, (ed.), *Human Behavior and Social Processes.* Boston: Houghton Mifflin.

DIETRICH, KATHERYN THOMAS (1975).   A Reexamination of the myth of black matriarchy. *Journal of Marriage and the Family* 37:2:367–375.

DONNELLY, CAROLINE (1976).   How to stop arguing about money. *Money* 5:1: 24–27.

DOSSENBACH, HANS D. (1971).   *The Family Life of Birds.* Maidenhead, England: McGraw-Hill.

DRINAN, ROBERT F. (1969).   American laws regulating the formation of the marriage contract. *The Annals of the American Academy of Political and Social Science, Progress in Family Law* 383:4:49–57.

DUVALL, EVELYN MILLIS (1965).   Marriage makes in-laws. In Ruth Shonle Cavan, (ed.), *Marriage and Family in the Modern World.* New York: Thomas Y. Crowell, pp. 383–387.

DUBERMAN, LUCILE (1973).   Step-kin relationships. *Journal of Marriage and the Family* 35:2:283–292.

DYTRYCH, ZDENEK, ZDENEK MATEJČEK, VRATISLAV SCHÜLLER, HENRY P. DAVID, AND HERBERT L. FRIEDMAN (1975).   Children born to women denied abortion. *Family Planning Perspectives* 7:4:165–171.

ECKHARDT, KENNETH W. (1968).   Deviance, visibility, and legal action: the duty to support. *Social Problems* 15:470–477.

EDWARDS, JOHN N. (1973).   Extramarital involvement: fact and theory. *The Journal of Sex Research* 9:3:210–224.

EDWARDS, JOHN N., AND ALAN BOOTH (1976).   Sexual behavior in and out of marriage. *Journal of Marriage and the Family* 38:1:73–81.

EDWARDS, MARGOT E. (1973).   Unattended home birth. *American Journal of Nursing* 73:1332–1335.

EIBL-EIBESFELDT, IRENAUS (1970).   *Ethology—The Biology of Behavior.* New York: Holt, Rinehart, and Winston.

ELDER, GLEN H., JR. (1975).   Age differentiation and the life course. *Annual Review of Sociology* 1:165–190.

ELKIN, MEYER (1973).   The conciliation courts: the reintegration of disintegrating families. *The Family Coordinator* 22:1:63–71.

ELLINWOOD, EVERETT H., JR., W. J. KENNETH ROCKWELL, RICHARD D. CHESSICK, GABRIEL G. NAHAS, AND PAUL CUSHMAN (1975).   Effect of drug use on sexual behavior. *Medical Aspects of Human Sexuality*, March 1975, pp. 10–32.

ELLIS, ALBERT (1970).   Group marriage: a possible alternative? In H. A. Otto (ed.), *The Family in Search of a Future, Alternate Models for Moderns.* New York: Appleton-Century-Crofts, pp. 85–97.

EMERSON, WILLIAM A., JR. (1975).   Traditional wife: adoring husband. *Woman's Day*, Nov. 1975, pp. 75, 170–172.

ERLANGER, HOWARD S. (1974).   Social class differences in parent's use of physical punishment. In Suzanne K. Steinmetz and Murray A. Straus (eds.), *Violence in the Family.* New York: Dodd, Mead, pp. 150–159.

ETAUGH, CLAIRE (1974).   Effects of maternal employment on children: a review of recent research. *Merrill-Palmer Quarterly* 20:2:71–98.

FELDMAN, HAROLD, AND MARGARET FELDMAN (1975).   The family life cycle: some suggestions for recycling. *Journal of Marriage and the Family* 37:2:277–284.

FERGUSON, BRUCE (1971).   Birth at home: the precise considerations. In Stewart Brand (ed.), *The Last Whole Earth Catalog.* Millerton, N.Y.: Book Organization (Portola), p. 218.

FERIN, MICHEL, FRANZ HALBERT, RALPH M. RICHART, AND RAYMOND L. VANDE WIELE (1974).   *Biorhythms and Human Reproduction.* New York: Wiley.

FERRELL, MARY Z., WILLIAM L. TOLONE, AND ROBERT H. WALSH (1977).   Maturational and societal changes in the sexual double-standard: a panel analysis. *Journal of Marriage and the Family* 39:2:255–271.

FINGER, FRANK W. (1975).   Changes in sex practices and beliefs of male college students: over 30 years. *Journal of Sex Research* 11:4:304–317.

FINK, PAUL J. (1975).   Couples who are troubled about oral-genital sex. *Medical Aspects of Human Sexuality*, March 1975, pp. 85–86.

FISHER, SEYMOUR (1973).   *The Female Orgasm.* New York: Basic Books.

FLEMING, WILLIAM L. (1975).   Syphilis rates partly controlled, gonorrhea at all-time high. *Medical Aspects of Human Sexuality*, Feb. 1975, p. 125.

FORD, CLELLAN S., AND FRANK A. BEACH (1951).   *Patterns of Sexual Behavior.* New York: Harper.

FOX, ROBIN (1967).   *Kinship and Marriage.* Baltimore: Penguin Books.

FREILICH, LEON (1975).   December song. *New York Sunday News*, Nov. 16, 1975, pp. 12–14, 21.

FREUND, MATTHEW (1972).   The use of frozen semen banks to preserve the fertility of vasectomized men. In Lawrence Lader (ed.), *Foolproof Birth Control.* Boston: Beacon Press, pp. 197–201.

FRIEDENTHAL, RICHARD (1967).   *Luther, His Life and Times.* New York: Harcourt Brace Jovanovich.

FRIED, MARC A. (1966).   The role of work in a mobile society. In Sam Bass Warner (ed.), *Planning for a Network of Cities.* Cambridge, Mass.: The M.I.T. Press, pp. 81–104.

FURSTENBERG, FRANK F., JR. (1974).   Industrialization and the American family: a look backward. In Marvin B. Sussman (ed.), *Sourcebook in Marriage and the Family,* 4th ed. Boston: Houghton Mifflin, pp. 30–40.

FURSTENBERG, FRANK F., JR., THEODORE HERSHBERG, AND JOHN MODELL (1975).   The origins of the female-headed black family: the impact of the urban experience. *Journal of Interdisciplinary History* 6:2:211–233.

GAGNON, JOHN H., AND WILLIAM SIMON (1974).   *Sexual Conduct.* London: Hutchinson.

GARRISON, MARTA L. (1976).   Credit-ability for women. *The Family Coordinator* 25:3:241–248.

GECAS, VICTOR, AND ROGER LIBBY (1976).   Sexual behavior as symbolic interaction. *Journal of Sex Research* 12:1:33–49.

GELLES, RICHARD J. (1974).   *The Violent Home.* Beverly Hills, Calif.: Sage Publications.

GENERAL MILLS (1977).   *Raising Children In a Changing Society.* Minneapolis, Minn.: General Mills Consumer Center.

GEORGE, CHARLOTTE (1973).   Insurance for your health, car, life. *Handbook for the Home.* Pueblo, Colo.: Consumer Information Public Documents Distribution Center.

GERSON, MENACHEM (1971).   Women in the kibbutz. *American Journal of Orthopsychiatry* 41:4:566–573.

GIL, DAVID G. (1975).   Unraveling child abuse. *American Journal of Orthopsychiatry* 45:3:346–356.

———— (1970).   *Violence Against Children.* Cambridge, Mass.: Harvard University Press.

GILBERT, SHIRLEY J. (1976).   Self-disclosure, intimacy and communication in families. *The Family Coordinator* 25:3:221–231.

GLENN, NORVAL D. (1975).   Psychological well-being in the postparental stage: some evidence from national surveys. *Journal of Marriage and the Family* 37:1:105–110.

GLICK, PAUL C. (1977).   Updating the life cycle of the family. *Journal of Marriage and the Family* 39:1:5–13.

———— (1976).   Living arrangements of children and young adults. *Journal of Comparative Family Studies* VII:2:321–33.

———— (1975).   A demographer looks at American families. *Journal of Marriage and the Family* 37:1:15–26.

GOLDBERG, HERB (1973). The psychological pressures on the American male. *Human Behavior* 2:4:73–75.

GOLDBERG, STANLEY B. (1973). Family tasks and reactions in the crisis of death. *Social Casework* 54:7:398–405.

GOLDSMITH, SADJA (1974). Early abortion in a family planning clinic. *Family Planning Perspectives* 6:2:119–122.

GOODE, WILLIAM J. (1972). Social change and family renewal. In *Families of the Future*. Ames: Iowa State University Press, pp. 116–133.

——— (1964). *The Family*. Englewood Cliffs, N.J.: Prentice-Hall.

——— (1963). *World Revolution and Family Patterns*. New York: Free Press.

GORAD, STEPHEN L. (1971). Communicational styles and interaction of alcoholics and their wives. *Family Process* 10:4:475–489.

GORDON, HARVEY L. (1974). Daily production of sperm. *Medical Aspects of Human Sexuality*, Aug. 1974, pp. 119–120.

GOUGH, E. KATHLEEN (1968). Is the family universal?—the Nayar case. In Norman W. Bell and Ezra F. Vogel (eds.), *A Modern Introduction to the Family*, Rev. ed. New York: Free Press.

GRANDO, ROY, AND BARRY G. GINSBERG (1976). Communication in the father-son relationship: the parent-adolescent relationship development program. *The Family Coordinator* 25:4:465–473.

GREEN, ROBERT T., AND ISABELLA C. M. CUNNINGHAM (1975). Feminine role perception and family purchasing decisions. *Journal of Marketing Research* XII:325–332.

GREENBERG, M., I. ROSENBERG, AND J. LIND (1973). First mothers rooming-in with their newborns: its impact upon the mother. *American Journal of Orthopsychiatry* 43:783–788.

GREENSON, RALPH R. (1970). On sexual apathy in the male. In Jhan Robbins and June Robbins, *An Analysis of Human Sexual Inadequacy*. New York: New American Library, pp. 261–270.

GRIFFITH, JANET (1973). Social pressure on family size intentions. *Family Planning Perspectives* 5:4:237–242.

GROUP FOR THE ADVANCEMENT OF PSYCHIATRY (GAP) (1973). *Human Reproduction*. New York: Scribner.

——— (1970). *The Right to Abortion*. New York: Scribner.

GROVER, JOHN W. (1971). *VD: The ABC's*. Englewood Cliffs, N.J.: Prentice-Hall.

GUTTMACHER, ALAN F. (1973). *Pregnancy, Birth, and Family Planning*. New York: Viking Press.

——— (1970). *Understanding Sex: A Young Person's Guide*. New York: Signet Books.

GUTTMACHER, ALAN F., WINFIELD BEST, AND FREDERICK S. JAFFE (1969). *Birth Control and Love*, 2nd ed. New York: Macmillan.

GUTMAN, HERBERT G. (1976). *The Black Family in Slavery and Freedom, 1750–1925*, p. xvii–xxviii. New York: Pantheon Books.

HARRY, JOSEPH (1976). Evolving sources of happiness for men over the life cycle: a structural analysis. *Journal of Marriage and the Family* 38:2:289–296.

HAVEMANN, ERNEST (1967). *Birth Control*. New York: Time-Life Books.

HAWKES, GLENN R., LEE BURCHINAL, AND BRUCE GARDNER (1958). Size of family and adjustment of children. *Marriage and Family Living* 20:65–68.

HAZELL, LESTER D. (1969). *Commonsense Childbirth*. New York: Tower Publications.

HEER, DAVID M. (1974). The prevalence of black-white marriage in the United States, 1960 and 1970. *Journal of Marriage and the Family* 36:2:246–259.

HEIMAN, JULIA R. (1975). The physiology of erotica: women's sexual arousal. *Psychology Today* 8:11:90–94.

HEISS, JEROLD (1976). *Family Roles and Interaction*, 2nd ed. Chicago: Rand McNally.

——— (1975). *The Case of the Black Family*. New York: Columbia University Press.

HEROLD, EDWARD S. (1973). A dating adjustment scale for college students. *Adolescence* VIII:29:51–61.

HICKMAN, ADDISON C. AND MANFRED H. KUHN (1956). *Individuals, Groups, and Economic Behavior*. New York: Dryden Press.

HILL, CHARLES G., ZICK RUBIN, AND LETETIA ANNE PEPLAU (1976). Breakups before marriage: the end of 103 affairs. *Journal of Social Issues* 32:1:147–168.

HILL, REUBEN (1974). Modern systems theory and the family: a confrontation. In Marvin B. Sussman (ed.), *Sourcebook in Marriage and the Family*, 4th ed. Boston: Houghton Mifflin.

HITE, SHERE (1976). *The Hite Report, A Nationwide Study of Female Sexuality*. New York: Dell.

HOBBS, DANIEL F., JR., AND SUE PECK COLE (1976). Transition to parenthood: a decade replication. *Journal of Marriage and the Family* 38:4:723–731.

HOCHSCHILD, ARLIE RUSSELL (1975). Disengagement theory: a critique and proposal. *American Sociological Review* 40:553–569.

——— (1973). Communal life styles for the old. *Society* 10:5:50–57.

HOLDEN, CONSTANCE (1974). Sex therapy: making it as a science and an industry. *Science* 186:330–334.

HOLMSTROM, LYNDA LYTLE (1972). *The Two-Career Family*. Cambridge, Mass.: Schenkman.

HOWE, LOUISE KAPP, ED. (1972). *The Future of the Family*. New York: Simon and Schuster.

HUMPHREYS, ALEXANDER J. (1965). The family in Ireland. In M. F. Nimkoff, *Comparative Family Systems*. Boston: Houghton Mifflin, pp. 232–258.

HUNT, MORTON (1974). *Sexual Behavior in the 1970's.* New York: Dell.

—— (1973). Sexual behavior in the 1970's. *Playboy,* Oct. 1973a, pp. 84–88, 194–207; Nov. 1973b, pp. 74–75; Dec. 1973c, pp. 90–91.

—— (1969). *The Affair.* New York: World.

HUNTER, ALBERT (1975). The loss of community: an empirical test through replication. *American Sociological Review* 40:5:537–552.

INSTITUTE OF LIFE INSURANCE (1976). *Current Social Issues: The Public's View.* New York: Institute of Life Insurance.

JACKSON, JOAN K. (1958). Alcoholism and the family. *The Annals of the American Academy* 315:90–97.

JACOBY, SUSAN (1973). What do I do for the next twenty years? *New York Times Magazine,* June 17, 1973.

—— (1974). 49 million singles can't all be right. *The New York Times Magazine,* Feb. 17, 1974, pp. 12 ff.

JAMES, WILLIAM H. (1974). Marital coital rates, spouses' ages, family size and social class. *Journal of Sex Research* 10:3:205–218.

JOHNSON, ELMER H. (1973). *Social Problems of Urban Man.* Homewood, Ill.: Dorsey Press.

JOHNSON, RALPH E. (1970). Some correlates of extramarital coitus. *Journal of Marriage and the Family* 32:3:449–456.

JOHNSON, SHEILA K. (1975). The business in babies. *New York Times Magazine,* Aug. 17, 1975, pp. 11 ff.

JONES, STELLA B. (1973). Geographic mobility as seen by the wife and mother. *Journal of Marriage and the Family* 35:2:210–218.

KAATS, GILBERT R., AND KEITH E. DAVIS (1970). The dynamics of sexual behavior of college students. *Journal of Marriage and the Family* 32:3:390–399.

KAGAN, JULIA (1975). The new doubts about abortion. *McCall's* 102:9:121–123.

KANTER, ROSABETH MOSS (1976). Combating occupational segregation, the policy issues. Presentation VI. *Signs* 1:3:Part 2:282–291.

—— (1973). *Communes: Creating and Managing the Collective Life.* New York: Harper & Row.

—— (1972). *Commitment and Community.* Cambridge, Mass.: Harvard University Press.

—— (1970). Communes. *Psychology Today* 4:2:53–57; 78.

KAPLAN, HELEN SINGER (1974a). *The New Sex Therapy.* New York: Brunner/Mazel.

—— (1974b). No-nonsense therapy for six sexual malfunctions. *Psychology Today,* pp. 76–86.

KARGMAN, MARIE W. (1973). The revolution in divorce law. *The Family Coordinator* 22:2:245–248.

KASSEL, VICTOR (1966). Polygyny after 60. *Geriatrics* 21:1:214–218.

KATCHADOURIAN, HERANT A., AND DONALD T. LUNDE (1972). *Fundamentals of Human Sexuality.* New York: Holt, Rinehart, and Winston.

KATZ, JUDITH MILSTEIN (1976). How do you love me? Let me count the ways (the phenomenology of being loved). *Sociological Inquiry* 46:1:17–22.

KATZ, SANFORD N. (1971). *When Parents Fail.* Boston: Beacon Press.

KAUFMAN, MICHAEL (1973). Spare ribs: the conception of woman in the Middle Ages and the Renaissance. *Soundings* LVI:2:139–163.

KAUFMAN, SHERWIN A. (1970). *New Hope for the Childless Couple.* New York: Simon and Schuster.

KELLY, JANIS (1972). Sister love: an exploration of the need for homosexual experience. *The Family Coordinator* 21:4:473–475.

KELLY, JOAN B., AND JUDITH S. WALLERSTEIN (1976). The effects of parental divorce. *American Journal of Orthopsychiatry* 46:1:20–32.

KENKEL, WILLIAM F. (1973). *Family in Perspective,* 3rd ed. New York: Appleton-Century-Crofts.

KEPHART, WILLIAM M. (1972). *The Family, Society, and the Individual,* 3rd ed. Boston: Houghton Mifflin.

——— (1963). Experimental family organization. *Marriage and Family Living* 25:3:261–271.

KEPHART, WILLIAM M., NATALIE SHAINESS, WILLIAM KILPATRICK, DAVID B. MARCOTTE, FREDERICK LEMERE, SANDER J. BREINER, AND MARCIA F. CURRY (1974). Viewpoints: is sex overrated? *Medical Aspects of Human Sexuality,* Sept. 1974, pp. 8–23.

KHATRI, A. A. (1975). The adaptive extended family in India today. *Journal of Marriage and the Family* 37:3:633–642.

KIEFFER, CAROLYNNE (1977). New depths in intimacy. In Roger W. Libby and Robert N. Whitehurst (eds.), *Marriage and Alternatives: Exploring Intimate Relationships.* Glenview, Ill.: Scott, Foresman, pp. 267–293.

KINKADE, KATHLEEN (1973). *A Walden Two Experiment: The First Five Years at Twin Oaks Community.* New York: Morrow.

KINSEY, ALFRED C., W. B. POMEROY, C. E. MARTIN, AND P. H. GEBHARD (1953). *Sexual Behavior in the Human Female.* Philadelphia: W. B. Saunders.

KINSEY, ALFRED C., W. B. POMEROY, C. E. MARTIN (1948). *Sexual Behavior in the Human Male.* Philadelphia: W. B. Saunders.

KIRKPATRICK, CLIFFORD (1963). *The Family as Process and Institution.* New York: Ronald Press.

KLINE-GRABER, GEORGIA, AND BENJAMIN GRABER (1976). *A Guide to Sexual Satisfaction: Woman's Orgasm.* New York: Popular Library.

KOGAN, BENJAMIN A. (1973). *Human Sexual Expression.* New York: Harcourt Brace Jovanovich.

KOMAROVSKY, MIRRA (1964). *Blue-Collar Marriage.* New York: Random House.

KUTNER, NANCY G., AND DONNA BROGAN (1974).   An investigation of sex-related slang vocabulary and sex-role orientation among male and female university students. *Journal of Marriage and the Family* 36:3:474–484.

KRAIN, MARK (1975).   Communication among premarital couples at three stages of dating. *Journal of Marriage and the Family* 37:3:609–618.

KRAMER, MARK (1976).   Subsistence farming: a pipe dream? *Country Journal* III:1:37–39.

KRANTZLER, MEL (1974).   *Creative Divorce.* New York: Evans.

LADNER, JOYCE A. (1972).   *Tomorrow's Tomorrow, The Black Woman.* Garden City, N.Y.: Anchor Books.

LANTZ, HERMAN R., JANE KEYES, AND MARTIN SCHULTZ (1975).   The American family in the pre-industrial period: from base lines in history to change. *American Sociological Review* 40:1:21–36.

LASLETT, BARBARA (1973).   The family as a public and private institution. *Journal of Marriage and the Family* 35:3:480–492.

LEACOCK, ELEANOR BURKE, ED. (1971).   *The Culture of Poverty: A Critique.* New York: Simon and Schuster.

LEBOYER, FREDERICK (1975).   *Birth Without Violence.* New York: Alfred A. Knopf.

LEMASTERS, E. E. (1974).   *Parents in Modern America.* Homewood, Ill.: Dorsey Press.

LENTZ, WILLIAM D. (1975).   Constitutional law: marriage rights, homosexuals and transsexuals. *Akron Law Review* 8:2:369–374.

LESLIE, GERALD R. (1973).   *The Family in Social Context,* 2nd ed. New York: Oxford Press.

LEVIN, ROBERT J., AND AMY LEVIN (1975a).   Sexual pleasure: the surprising preferences of 100,000 women. *Redbook,* pp. 51–58.

————— (1975b).   The *Redbook* report on premarital and extramarital sex—the end of the double standard? *Redbook,* pp. 38–44, 190–192.

LEVY, HYIM J. (1973).   What about group marriage? In R. H. Rimmer (ed.), *Adventures in Loving.* New York: Signet Books, pp. 2–22.

LEWIS, DIANE K. (1975).   The black family: socialization and sex roles. *Phylon: The Atlanta University Review of Race and Culture* XXXVI:3:221–237.

LEWIS, ROBERT A. (1973a).   A longitudinal test of a development framework for premarital dyadic formation. *Journal of Marriage and the Family* 35:1:16–25.

————— (1973b).   Social reaction and the formation of dyads: an interactionist approach to mate selection. *Sociometry* 36:3:409–418.

LIBBY, ROGER W. (1977).   Creative singlehood as a sexual life-style: beyond marriage as a rite of passage. In Roger W. Libby and Robert N. Whitehurst (eds.), *Marriage and Alternatives: Exploring Intimate Relationships.* Glenview, Ill.: Scott, Foresman, pp. 37–61.

LIBBY, ROGER W. AND ROBERT N. WHITEHURST (1973).   *Renovating Marriage.* Danville, Calif.: Consensus Publishers.

LIEBERMAN, E. JAMES, AND ELLEN PECK (1973). *Sex and Birth Control.* New York: Thomas Y. Crowell.

LIFTON, BETTY JEAN (1976). The search. *New York Times Magazine,* Jan. 25, 1976, pp. 15 ff.

LILEY, H. M. I. (1969). *Modern Motherhood.* New York: Random House.

LIPPES, J., T. MALIK, AND H. J. TATUM (1975). The post-coital copper T. Paper presented at annual meeting of Association of Planned Parenthood Physicians. *Family Planning Perspectives* 7:4:151–152.

LOBOTSKY, JULIA (1974). Prostaglandins and reproduction. *Family Planning Perspectives* 6:1:62–63.

LOBSENZ, NORMAN M. (1974a). Sex and the senior citizen. *New York Times Magazine,* Jan. 20, 1974, p. 8.

———— (1974b). Living together: a newfangled tango—or an oldfashioned waltz? *Redbook* 143:2:86–87; 184; 186.

LONG, HUEY B. (1975). Women's education in colonial America. *Adult Education* XXV:2:90–106.

LOPATA, HELENA ZNANIECKI (1973). *Widowhood in an American City.* Cambridge, Mass.: Schenkman.

LORBER, JUDITH (1975). Beyond equality of the sexes: the question of the children. *The Family Coordinator* 24:4:465–472 .

LOWENTHAL, MARJORIE FISKE, AND DAVID CHIRIBODA (1972). Transition to the empty nest. *Archives of General Psychiatry* 26:8–14.

LYNESS, J. L., M. E. LIPETZ, AND K. E. DAVIS (1972). Living together: an alternative to marriage. *Journal of Marriage and the Family* 34:2:305–311.

LYONS, RICHARD D. (1973). Psychiatrists, in a shift, declare homosexuality no mental illness. *New York Times,* Dec. 16, 1973, pp. 1, 25.

MACE, DAVID R. (1976a). Marital intimacy and the deadly love-anger cycle. *Journal of Marriage and Family Counseling* 2:2:131–138.

———— (1976b). Sex in the year 2000. In Sol Gordon and Roger W. Libby (eds.), *Sexuality Today and Tomorrow.* North Scituate, Mass.: Duxbury Press, pp. 396–403.

MACKLIN, ELEANOR D. (1974). Going very steady: cohabitation in college. *Psychology Today* 8:6:53, 55–59.

MANDELBAUM, DAVID G. (1938). Polyandry in Kota society. *American Anthropologist* 40:574–583.

MARGOLIUS, SYDNEY (1976). The sources of funds for college. *Boston Evening Globe,* March 30, 1976, p. 7.

MARSHALL, DONALD S., AND ROBERT C. SUGGS, EDS. (1971). *Human Sexual Behavior, Variations Across the Ethnographic Spectrum.* New York: Basic Books.

MARTINDALE, DON (1960). *The Nature and Types of Sociological Theory.* Boston: Houghton Mifflin.

MASTERS, WILLIAM H. (1974). Phony sex clinics—medicine's newest nightmare. *Today's Health* 52:11:22–26.

MASTERS, WILLIAM H., AND VIRGINIA E. JOHNSON (1974). *The Pleasure Bond.* Boston: Little, Brown.

——— (1970). *Human Sexual Inadequacy.* Boston: Little, Brown.

——— (1966). *Human Sexual Response.* Boston: Little, Brown.

MCBRIDE, ANGELA BARRON (1973). *The Growth and Development of Mothers.* New York: Harper & Row.

MCCALL, GEORGE J., AND J. L. SIMMONS (1966). *Identities and Interactions.* New York: Free Press.

MCCARY, JAMES LESLIE (1975). *Freedom and Growth in Marriage.* Santa Barbara, Calif.: Hamilton Publishing Co. (Wiley).

——— (1973a). *Human Sexuality.* New York: D. Van Nostrand.

——— (1973b). *Human Sexuality: A Brief Edition.* New York: D. Van Nostrand.

——— (1971). *Sexual Myths and Fallacies.* New York: Schocken Books.

MCCLEARY, ELLIOTT H. (1974). *New Miracles of Childbirth.* New York: David McKay.

MCDAVID, JOHN W., AND HERBERT HARARI (1974). *Psychology and Social Behavior.* New York: Harper & Row.

MCEADDY, BEVERLY JOHNSON (1976). Women who head families: a socioeconomic analysis. *Monthly Labor Review* 99:6:3–9.

MCHUGH, JAMES T. (1975). No fault divorce. *The Jurist,* Winter 1975, pp. 17–31.

MCINTIRE, WALTER G., GILBERT D. NASS, AND DONNA L. BATTISTONE (1974). Female misperception of male parenting attitudes and expectancies. *Youth and Society* 6:1:104–112.

MCINTYRE, JENNIE (1966). The structure-functional approach to family study. In Ivan F. Nye and Felix M. Berardo (eds.), *Emerging Conceptual Frameworks in Family Analysis.* New York: Macmillan, pp. 52–73.

MCINTIRE, WALTER G., AND GILBERT D. NAS: (1974). Self-actualizing qualities of low and high happiness stable marriages. *Research in the Life Sciences,* University of Maine at Orono 21:5.

MCWHIRTER, NORRIS, AND ROSS MCWHIRTER (1974). *Guiness Book of World Records.* New York: Sterling.

MEADOWS, DONELLA H., DENNIS L. MEADOWS, JORGEN RANDERS, AND WILLIAM H. BEHRENS, III (1972). *The Limits to Growth.* New York: Universe Books.

MEEHAN, THOMAS (1973). Letting the rest of the world go by at Heritage Village. *Horizon* 15:16–25.

MIDDLETON, RUSSELL (1962). Brother-sister and father-daughter marriage in Ancient Egypt. *American Sociological Review* 27:5:603–611.

MILLER, BRENT C. (1975).   Child density, marital satisfaction, and conventionalization. *Journal of Marriage and the Family* 37:345–347.

MILLER, SHEROD, ELAM W. NUNNALLY, AND DANIEL B. WACKMAN (1976).   A communication training program for couples. *Social Casework* 57:1:9–18.

MILLER, SHEROD, RAMON CORRALES, AND DANIEL B. WACKMAN (1975).   Recent progress in understanding and facilitating marital communication. *The Family Coordinator* 24:2:143–152.

MISHELL, DANIEL R., JR. (1975).   Assessing the intrauterine device. *Family Planning Perspectives* 7:3:103–111.

MITCHELL, JOHN J. (1976).   Adolescent intimacy. *Adolescence* XI:42:275–280.

MNOOKIN, ROBERT H. (1973).   Foster care: in whose best interest. *Harvard Educational Review* 43:4:599–638.

Modern Maturity (February–March 1976) pp. 5–7, 17–19.

MOLINOFF, DANIEL D. (1977).   Men's rights groups fight to change divorce laws. *Parade*, April 3, 1977, pp. 27–28.

MOLLER, HERBERT (1959).   The social causation of the courtly love complex. *Comparative Studies in Society and History* 1:137–163.

MONAHAN, THOMAS P. (1976).   An overview of statistics on interracial marriage in the United States, with data on its extent from 1963–1970. *Journal of Marriage and the Family* 38:2:223–231.

MONTREAL HEALTH PRESS (1974).   *Birth Control Handbook*. Montreal: Montreal Health Press, Inc.

MORGAN, EDMUND S. (1973).   The Puritans and sex. In Michael Gordon (ed.), *The American Family in Social-Historical Perspective*. New York: St. Martin's Press, pp. 282–295.

MORK, LUCILE F. (1972).   *A Guide to Budgeting for the Family*, Home and Garden Bulletin No. 108. Washington: U.S. Dept. of Agriculture.

MORRIS, EARL W., SUE R. CRULL, AND MARY WINTER (1976).   Housing norms, housing satisfaction and the propensity to move. *Journal of Marriage and the Family* 38:2:309–320.

MORRIS, EARL W., AND MARY WINTER (1975).   A theory of family housing adjustment. *Journal of Marriage and the Family* 37:1:79–88.

MOVIUS, MARGARET (1976).   Voluntary childlessness—the ultimate liberation. *The Family Coordinator* 25:1:57–63 .

MURDOCK, GEORGE P. (1957).   World ethnographic sample. *American Anthropologist* 59:664–687.

——— (1949).   *Social Structure*. New York: Free Press.

MURSTEIN, BERNARD I. (1974).   *Love, Sex, and Marriage through the Ages*. New York: Springer.

NETTLER, GWYNN (1976).   *Social Concerns*. New York: McGraw-Hill.

NEUBECK, GERHARD (1972).   The myriad motives for sex. *Sexual Behavior* 2:7:50–56.

NEUGARTEN, BERNICE L. (1971).   Grow old along with me! The best is yet to be. *Psychology Today* 5:7:45.

NGUYEN, TUAN, RICHARD HESLIN, AND MICHELE L. NGUYEN (1975).   The meanings of touch: sex differences. *Journal of Communication* 25:92–103.

NORTON, ARTHUR J. (1974).   The Family-life cycle updated. In Robert F. Winch and Graham B. Spanier (eds.), *Selected Studies in Marriage and the Family.* New York: Holt, Rinehart, and Winston.

NORTON, ARTHUR J., AND PAUL C. GLICK (1976).   Marital instability: past, present, and future. *Journal of Social Issues* 32:1:5–20.

NYDEGGER, CORINNE (1974).   The older father: late is great. *Psychology Today* 7:11:26–27.

NYE, F. IVAN (1952).   Adolescent-parent adjustment: age, sex, sibling number, broken homes, and employed mothers as variables. *Marriage and Family Living* 14:328.

NYE, F. IVAN, AND FELIX M. BERARDO (1973).   *The Family: Its Structure and Interaction.* New York: Macmillan.

O'BRIEN, JOHN E. (1971).   Violence in divorce prone families. *Journal of Marriage and the Family* 33:4:692–698.

O'CONNOR, JOHN F., EDWARD M. SHELLEY, AND LENORE O. STERN (1974).   Behavioral rhythms related to the menstrual cycle. In Michel Ferin et al., *Biorhythms and Human Reproduction.* New York: Wiley, pp. 309–324.

OLSON, DAVID H. (1972).   Marriage of the future: revolutionary or evolutionary change? *The Family Coordinator* 21:4:383–393.

O'NEILL, NENA, AND GEORGE O'NEILL (1972).   *Open Marriage.* New York: Avon Books.

ORENSTEIN, HENRY (1961).   The recent history of the extended family in India. *Social Problems* 8:341–350.

ORTHNER, DENNIS K. (1975).   Leisure activity patterns and marital satisfaction over the marital career. *Journal of Marriage and the Family* 37:1:91–102.

OSMOND, MARIE WITHERS, AND PATRICIA YANCEY MARTIN (1975).   Sex and sexism: a comparison of male and female sex-role attitudes. *Journal of Marriage and the Family* 37:4:744–758.

OSOFSKY, JOY D, AND HOWARD J. OSOFSKY (1972).   Androgyny as a life style. *The Family Coordinator* 21:4:411–418.

OTTO, HERBERT A. (1972).   New light on human potential. In *Families of the Future.* Ames: Iowa State University Press, pp. 14–25.

OTTO, LUTHER B. (1975).   Class and status in family research. *Journal of Marriage and the Family* 37:2:315–332.

OTTO, LUTHER B., AND DAVID L. FEATHERMAN (1975).   Social structural and psychological antecedents of self-estrangement and powerlessness. *American Sociological Review* 40:6:701–719.

PALME, OLAF (1972). The emancipation of man. *The Journal of Social Issues* 28:2:237–246.

PAPP, PEGGY, OLGA SILVERSTEIN, AND ELIZABETH CARTER (1973). Family sculpting in preventive work with "well families." *Family Process* 12:2:197–212.

PARELIUS, ANN P. (1975). Emerging sex-role attitudes, expectations, and strains among college women. *Journal of Marriage and the Family* 32:1:146–153.

PARKE, ROSS D., AND DOUGLAS B. SAWIN (1976). The father's role in infancy: a re-evaluation. *The Family Coordinator* 25:4:365–371.

PENGELLEY, ERIC T. (1974). *Sex and Human Life.* Reading, Mass.: Addison-Wesley.

PERATIS, KATHLEEN W. (1976). Director, Women's Rights Project, American Civil Liberties Union. Personal Communication, April 16, 1976.

PETERMAN, DAN J., CARL A. RIDLEY, AND SCOTT M. ANDERSON (1974). A comparison of cohabiting and noncohabiting college students. *Journal of Marriage and the Family* 36:2:344–354.

PETERS, MARIE FERGUSON (1974). The black family—perpetuating the myths: an analysis of family sociology textbook treatment of black families. *The Family Coordinator* 23:4:349–357.

PILPEL, HARRIET F. (1975). Abortion: USA style. *The Journal of Sex Research* 11:2:113–118.

PLANNED PARENTHOOD OF NEW YORK CITY, INC. (1973). *Abortion: A Woman's Guide.* New York: Abelard-Schuman, Ltd.

POPENOE, DAVID (1973). Urban residential differentiation: an overview of patterns, trends, and problems. *Sociological Inquiry* 43:3–4.

PORTER, CEDRIC W., JR., AND JAROSLAV F. HULKA (1974). Femal sterilization in current clinical practice. *Family Planning Perspectives* 6:1:30–37.

PORTER, SYLVIA (1975). *Sylvia Porter's Money Book,* Vol. 2. Garden City, N.Y.: Doubleday.

PRINGLE, BRUCE M. (1974). Family clusters as a means of reducing isolation among urbanites. *The Family Coordinator* 23:2:175–179.

PROULX, CYNTHIA (1973). Sex as athletics in the single complex. *Saturday Review of the Society* 1:4:61–66.

PUMPHREY, RALPH E. (1966). The reinstitutionalization of social welfare. In Sam Bass Warner (ed.), *Planning for a Nation of Cities.* Cambridge, Mass.: The M.I.T. Press, pp. 285–297.

QUEEN, STUART A., AND ROBERT W. HABENSTEIN (1974). *The Family in Various Cultures,* 4th ed. Philadelphia: J. B. Lippincott.

RAMEY, JAMES W. (1975a). Intimate groups and networks: frequent consequence of sexually open marriage. *The Family Coordinator* 24:4:515–530.

———— (1975b). Intimate networks. *The Futurist* IX:4:175–181.

———— (1972). Communes, group marriage, and the upper-middle class. *Journal of Marriage and the Family* 34:4:647–655.

RAO, S.L.N. (1974). A comparative study of childlessness and never-pregnant status. *Journal of Marriage and the Family* 36:1:149–157.

RAPOPORT, RHONA, AND ROBERT N. RAPOPORT (1969). The dual-career family: a variant pattern and social change. *Human Relations* 22:1:3–29.

RAPOPORT, RHONA (1973). The transition from engagement to marriage. In Marcia E. Lasswell and Thomas E. Lasswell (eds.), *Love-Marriage-Family, A Developmental Approach*. Glenview, Ill.: Scott, Foresman.

READ, GRANTLY DICK (1953). *Childbirth Without Fear*. New York: Harper.

REISS, IRA L. (1960). *Premarital Sexual Standards in America*. London: The Free Press of Glencoe (Collier-Macmillan Limited).

RICHARD, J. A., AND ALBERT HYMA (1956). *Ancient, Medieval and Modern History*. New York: Barnes and Noble.

RIDLEY, CARL A. (1973). Exploring the impact of work satisfaction and involvement on marital interaction when both partners are employed. *Journal of Marriage and the Family* 35:2:229–237.

ROBBINS, NORMAN N. (1974). End of divorce—beginning of legal problems. *The Family Coordinator* 23:2:185–188.

———— (1973). Have we found fault in no fault divorce? *The Family Coordinator* 22:3:359–362.

ROBERTS, R. E. (1971). *The New Communes: Coming Together in America*. Englewood Cliffs, N.J.: Prentice-Hall.

ROBERTSON, CONSTANCE NOYES, ED. (1970). *Oneida Community, An Autobiography, 1851–1876*. Syracuse, N.Y.: Syracuse University Press.

RODGERS, ROY H. (1973). *Family Interaction and Transaction: The Developmental Approach*. Englewood Cliffs, N.J.: Prentice-Hall.

ROLLIN, BETTY (1972). Motherhood: who needs it? In Louise Howe Kapp (ed.), *The Future of the Family*. New York: Simon and Schuster, pp. 368–378.

ROLLINS, BOYD C. AND DARWIN L. THOMAS (1975). A theory of parental power and child compliance. In Ronald E. Cromwell and David H. Olson (eds.), *Power in Families*. New York: Halsted Press, pp. 38–60.

ROSE, VICKI L., AND SHARON PRICE-BONHAM (1973). Divorce adjustment: a woman's problem? *The Family Coordinator* 22:3:292–297.

ROSENBERG, GEORGE S. (1970). Implications of new models of the family for the aging population. In Herbert A. Otto (ed.), *The Family in Search of a Future*. New York: Appleton-Century-Crofts, pp. 171–181.

ROSSI, ALICE S. (1968). Transition to parenthood. *Journal of Marriage and the Family* 30:1:26–39.

ROTH, NATHAN (1975). Neurotic fears that sex is debilitating. *Medical Aspects of Human Sexuality*, Sept. 1975, pp. 91–92.

ROTHSCHILD, JOHN, AND SUSAN BERNS WOLF (1976). *The Children of the Counterculture*. Garden City, N.Y.: Doubleday.

ROWE, GEORGE P. (1966).   The developmental conceptual framework to the study of the family. In F. Ivan Nye and Felix M. Berardo (eds.), *Emerging Conceptual Frameworks in Family Analysis*. New York: Macmillan, pp. 198–217.

ROY, DELLA, AND RUSTUM ROY (1968).   *Honest Sex*. New York: American Library.

RUBIN, ISADORE (1966).   Sex after forty—and after seventy. In Ruth Brecher and Edward Brecher, *An Analysis of Human Sexual Response*. New York: Signet Books, pp. 251–266.

RUEVENI, URI (1975).   Network intervention with a family in crisis. *Family Process* 14:2:193–203.

RUGH, ROBERTS, AND LANDRUM B. SHETTLES (1971).   *From Conception to Birth*. New York: Harper & Row.

RULE, BRENDAN GAIL, AND ANDREW R. NESDALE (1976).   Emotional arousal and aggressive behavior. *Psychological Bulletin* 83:5:851–863.

RUSSELL, CANDYCE SMITH (1974).   Transition to parenthood: problems and gratifications. *Journal of Marriage and the Family* 36:2:294–302.

RYDER, NORMAN B. (1973).   Contraceptive failure in the United States. *Family Planning Perspectives* 5:3:133–142.

RYDER, ROBERT G. (1973).   Longitudinal data relating marriage satisfaction and having a child. *Journal of Marriage and the Family* 35:4:604–606.

SAFILIOS-ROTHCHILD, CONSTANTINA (1976).   Dual linkages between the occupational and family systems: a macrosociological analysis. *Signs* 1:3:2:51–60.

——— (1974).   *Women and Social Policy*. Englewood Cliffs, N.J.: Prentice-Hall.

——— (1972).   *Toward a Sociology of Women*. Lexington, Mass.: Xerox College Publishing.

SALK, LEE (1970).   The critical nature of the post-partum period in the human for the establishment of the mother-infant bond: a controlled study. *Diseases of the Nervous System* 31:11sup.:110–116.

SATIR, VIRGINIA (1972).   *Peoplemaking*. Palo Alto, Calif.: Science and Behavior Books.

SAUNDERS, LAVELL E. (1975).   Collective ignorance: public knowledge of family law. *The Family Coordinator* 24:1:69–74.

SCANZONI, JOHN (1975).   Sex roles, economic factors, and marital solidarity in black and white marriages. *Journal of Marriage and the Family* 37:1:130—144.

——— (1971).   *The black family in modern society*. Boston: Allyn and Bacon.

SCHAEFER, EARL S. (1972).   The family and the education process. *Families of the Future*. Ames: Iowa State University Press, pp. 26—43.

SCHAIE, K. WARNER, AND KATHY GRIBBIN (1975).   Adult development and aging. *Annual Review of Psychology* 26:65–96.

SCHECK, DENNIS C., AND ROBERT EMERICK (1976).   The young male adolescent's perception of early child-rearing behavior: the differential effects of socioeconomic status and family size. *Sociometry* 39:1:39–52.

SCHLESINGER, BENJAMIN, AND EUGENE STASIUK (1972).   Children of divorced parents in second marriages. In Irving R. Stuart and Lawrence Edwin Abt (eds.), *Children of Separation and Divorce.* New York: Grossman Publishers, pp. 20—35.

SCHMIDT, A. M. (1975).   Intrauterine contraceptive devices: professional and patient labeling. *Federal Register* 40:22796.

SCHNAIBERG, ALLAN, AND SHELDON GOLDENBERG (1975).   Closing the circle: the impact of children on parental status. *Journal of Marriage and the Family* 37:4:937–953.

SCHNUCKER, ROBERT V. (1975).   Elizabethan birth control and Puritan attitudes. *Journal of Interdisciplinary History* 4:655–667.

SCHULMAN, MARION L. (1974).   Idealization in engaged couples. *Journal of Marriage and the Family* 36:1:139–147.

SCHVANEVELDT, JAY D. (1966).   The interactional framework in the study of the family. In F. Ivan Nye and Felix M. Berardo (eds.), *Emerging Conceptual Frameworks in Family Analysis.* New York: Macmillan, pp. 97–123.

SECORD, PAUL F., AND CARL W. BACKMAN (1974).   *Social Psychology,* 2nd ed. New York: McGraw-Hill.

SELIGMAN, JEAN (1975).   Life without father. *Newsweek,* Sept. 22, 1975, p. 87.

SELIGSON, MARCIA (1973).   *The Eternal Bliss Machine: America's Way of Wedding.* New York: Morrow.

SEWARD, RUDY RAY (1973).   The colonial family in America: toward a socio-historical restoration of its structure. *Journal of Marriage and the Family* 35:58–70.

SGROI, SUZANNE M. (1974).   *VD: A Doctor's Answers.* New York: Harcourt Brace.

SHAH, FARIDA, MELVIN ZELNIK, AND JOHN F. KANTER (1975).   Unprotected intercourse among unwed teenagers. *Family Planning Perspectives* 7:1:39–44.

SHANAS, ETHEL, PETER TOWNSEND, DOROTHY WEDDERBURN, HENNING FRIIS, PAUL MILHHOJ, AND J. STEHOUWER (1968).   *Older People in Three Industrial Societies.* New York: Atherton Press.

SHAPIRO, ARNOLD, AND CLIFFORD SWENSON (1969).   Patterns of self-disclosure among married couples. *Journal of Counseling Psychology* 16:2:179–180.

SHORTER, EDWARD (1975).   *The making of the modern family.* New York: Basic Books.

SHORTNEY, JEAN RANSON (1971).   *How to Live on Nothing.* New York: Pocket Books.

SIDEL, RUTH (1973).   *Women and Child Care in China.* Baltimore: Penguin.

SKIPPER, JAMES K., JR., AND GILBERT NASS (1966).   Dating behavior: a framework for analysis and an illustration. *Journal of Marriage and the Family* 38:4:412–420.

SKLAR, J., AND B. BERKOV (1974).   Abortion, illegitimacy, and the American birth rate. *Science* 185:909.

SLATER, PHILIP E. (1970).   *The Pursuit of Loneliness: American Culture at the Breaking Point.* Boston: Beacon Press.

SLOTKIN, J. S. (1947).   On a possible lack of incest regulations in old Iran. *American Anthropologist* 69:4:612–617.

SMITH, BERT KRUGER (1973).   *Aging in America.* Boston: Beacon Press.

SMITH, DANIEL SCOTT, AND MICHAEL S. HINDUS (1975).   Premarital pregnancy in America, 1640–1971: an overview and interpretation. *The Journal of Interdisciplinary History* V:4:537–570.

SOMERVILLE, JAMES K. (1974).   The Salem (Mass.) woman in the home, 1660–1770. *Eighteenth-Century Life* 1:1:11–14.

SOMERVILLE, ROSE M. (1972).   The future of family relationships in the middle and older years: clues in fiction. *The Family Coordinator* 24:4:487–498.

SORG, DAVID A., AND MARGARET B. SORG (1975).   Sexual satisfaction in maturing women. *Medical Aspects of Human Sexuality,* Feb. 1975, pp. 62–79.

SPANIER, GRAHAM B. (1976).   Measuring dyadic adjustment: new scales for assessing the quality of marriage and similar dyads. *Journal of Marriage and the Family* 38:1:15–28.

SPICER, JERRY W., AND GARY D. HAMPE (1975).   Kinship interaction after divorce. *Journal of Marriage and the Family* 38:1:113–119.

SPINETTA, JOHN J., AND DAVID RIGLER (1972).   The child-abusing parent: a psychological review. *Psychological Bulletin* 77:4:296–304.

SPIRO, MELFORD E. (1968).   Is the family universal—the Israeli case. In Norman W. Bell and Ezra F. Vogel (eds.), *A Modern Introduction to the Family*, Rev. ed. New York: Free Press.

SPREY, JETSE (1972).   Family power structure: a critical comment. *Journal of Marriage and the Family* 34:2:235–238.

——— (1971).   On the management of conflict in families. *Journal of Marriage and the Family* 33:4:722–731.

——— (1969).   The family as a system in conflict. *Journal of Marriage and the Family* 31:4:699–706.

STAPLES, ROBERT (1971).   Towards a sociology of the black family: a theoretical and methodological assessment. *Journal of Marriage and the Family* 33:1:119–137.

STARR, JOYCE R., AND DONALD E. CARNS (1972).   Singles in the city. *Society* 9:4:43–48.

STAUFFER, JOHN, AND RICHARD FROST (1976).   Male and female interest in sexually-oriented magazines. *Journal of Communication* 26:1:25–30.

STEIN, PETER J. (1975).   Singlehood: an alternative to marriage. *The Family Coordinator* 24:4:489–503.

STEINBERG, DAVID (1972).   Redefining fatherhood: notes after six months. In Louise Kapp Howe (ed.), *The Future of the Family.* New York: Simon and Schuster, pp. 368–378.

STEMBER, CHARLES H. (1975).   Interest in breasts vs. buttocks. *Medical Aspects of Human Sexuality,* Feb. 1975, pp. 88–89.

STEPHENS, WILLIAM N. (1963). *The Family in Cross-Cultural Perspective.* New York: Holt, Rinehart, and Winston.

STINNETT, NICK, LINDA MITTELSTET CARTER, AND JAMES MONTGOMERY (1972). Older persons' perceptions of their marriages. *Journal of Marriage and the Family* 34:4:665–670.

STINNETT, NICK, JANET COLLINS, AND JAMES E. MONTGOMERY (1970). Marital need satisfaction of older husbands and wives. *Journal of Marriage and the Family* 32:3:428–434.

STONE, LAWRENCE (1975). The rise of the nuclear family in early modern England. In Charles E. Rosenberg (ed.), *The Family in History.* Philadelphia: University of Pennsylvania Press.

STRAUS, MURRAY A. (1974a). Leveling, civility, and violence in the family. *Journal of Marriage and the Family* 36:1:13–29.

———— (1974b). Letters to the editor. *Journal of Marriage and the Family* 36:3: 442–443.

STREIB, GORDON F., AND RUTH B. STREIB (1975). Communes and the aging: utopian dream and gerontological reality. *American Behavioral Scientist* 19:2:166–189.

STREIB, GORDON F. (1970). Old age and the family: facts and forecasts. *American Behavioral Scientist* 14:125—139.

STRONG, LESLIE D. (1977). The relative attractiveness of alternative marriage and family forms to persons of a marriageable age. Unpublished manuscript, University of Connecticut.

STRYKER, SHELDON (1968). Identity salience and role performance: the relevance of symbolic interaction theory for family research. *Journal of Marriage and the Family* 30:4:558–564.

SUBAK-SHARPE, GENELL (1975). The venereal disease of the new morality. *Today's Health,* March 1975, pp. 42–45, 55.

SUSSMAN, MARVIN B. (1975). The four F's of variant family forms and marriage styles. *The Family Coordinator* 24:4:563–576.

———— (1974). The isolated nuclear famliy: fact or fiction? In Marvin B. Sussman (ed.), *Sourcebook in Marriage and the Family,* 4th ed. Boston: Houghton Mifflin, pp. 25–30.

SUSSMAN, MARVIN B. et al. (1971). Changing families in a changing society. Report to the President; White House Conference on Children. Washington: Government Printing Office.

SWEET, JAMES A. (1974). Differentials in the rate of fertility decline: 1960–1970. *Family Planning Perspectives* 6:2:103–107.

SWIFT, PAMELA (1976). Keeping up with youth. *Parade,* Feb. 1, 1976a; Feb. 15, 1976b.

TALMON, YONINA (1961). Aging in Israel, a planned society. *American Journal of Sociology* LXVII:3:284–295.

TANNER, JAMES M., AND GORDON RATTRAY TAYLOR (1968). *Growth.* New York: Time-Life Books.

TAYLOR, PATRICIA ANN, AND NORVAL D. GLENN (1976).   The utility of education and attractiveness for females' status attainment through marriage. *American Sociological Review* 41:484:–498.

THOMPSON, BARBARA, AND DUGALD BAIRD (1972).   Follow-up of 186 sterilized women. In Lawrence Lader (ed.), *Foolproof Birth Control.* Boston: Beacon Press, pp. 142–159.

THOMPSON, WAYNE E., AND GORDON F. STREIB (1961).   Meaningful activity in a family context. In Robert W. Kleemeier (ed.), *Aging and Leisure.* New York: Oxford University Press, pp. 177–211.

THURMAN, JUDITH (1975).   Living alone—by choice. *Ms.* IV:1:64–67; 115.

TOOLAN, JAMES M. (1975).   Adolescent concerns about being "normal" sexually. *Medical Aspects of Human Sexuality,* Oct. 1975, pp. 79–80.

TORTORA, GERALD A., AND NICHOLAS P. ANAGNOSTAKOS (1975).   *Principles of Anatomy and Physiology.* San Francisco: Canfield Press.

TROLL, LILLIAN E. (1971).   The family of later life: a decade review. *Journal of Marriage and the Family* 33:2:263–290.

TROST, JAN (1975).   Married and unmarried cohabitation: the case of Sweden, with some comparisons. *Journal of Marriage and the Family* 37:3:677–682.

U.S. BUREAU OF THE CENSUS (1977).   Current Population Reports P–20:306. *Marital Status and Living Arrangements: March 1976.* Washington: U.S. Government Printing Office.

———— (1976).   Current Population Reports P–23:58. *A Statistical Portrait of Women in the United States.* Washington: U.S. Government Printing Office.

———— (1976).   *Statistical Abstract of the United States: 1976.* Washington: U.S. Government Printing Office.

———— (1975).   Fertility expectations of American women: June 1974. Current Population Reports P–20:277. Washington: U.S. Government Printing Office.

———— (1975).   School enrollment social and economic characteristics of students: October 1974. Current Population Reports P–20:286. Washington: U.S. Government Printing Office.

———— (1975).   Households and families by type: March 1975. Current Population Reports P–20:282. Washington: U.S. Government Printing Office.

———— (1975).   Social and economic characteristics of the metropolitan and nonmetropolitan population: 1974 and 1970. Current Population Reports P–23:55. Washington: U.S. Government Printing Office.

———— (1974).   Fertility expectations of American women: June 1973. P–20:265. Washington: U.S. Government Printing Office.

———— (1974).   Marital status and living arrangements: March 1974. Current Population Reports P–20:271. Washington: U.S. Government Printing Office.

———— (1974).   Social and economic characteristics of the older population, 1974. Current Population Reports P–23:57. Washington: U.S. Government Printing Office.

——— (1974).   The social and economic status of the black population in the United States, 1974. Current Population Reports P–23:54. Washington: U.S. Government Printing Office.

U.S. BUREAU OF LABOR STATISTICS (1975).   U.S. working women: a chartbook. Bulletin 1880. Washington: U.S. Government Printing Office.

U.S. DEPARTMENT OF COMMERCE (1977).   News Release CB77–64, Increase in housing costs outstripping income gains, census-HUD report shows. Washington: U.S. Department of Commerce.

——— (1977).   News Release CB77–24, Youth waiting longer to wed, Census Bureau reports. Washington: U.S. Department of Commerce.

——— (1976).   News Release CB76–256, Census-HUD survey shows high income households critical of public transit, low income households find shopping inadequate. Washington: U.S. Department of Commerce.

——— (1976).   News Release CB76–210, Renters about four times as likely as homeowners to move, census-HUD survey shows. Washington: U.S. Department of Commerce.

——— (1976).   News Release CB76–119, Nearly one-half of U.S. households moved during 1970–1974 census reports; new data on household financial characteristics shown. Washington: U.S. Department of Commerce.

U.S. DEPARTMENT OF HEALTH, EDUCATION, AND WELFARE (1977).   Monthly Vital Statistics Report (HRA) 77–1120 26:1. Births, marriages, divorces and deaths for January 1977. Washington: U.S. Government Printing Office.

——— (1976).   Monthly Vital Statistics Report (HRA) 76–1120 25:7 Supplement. Contraceptive utilization among currently married women 15–44 years of age: United States, 1973. Washington: U.S. Government Printing Office.

——— (1976).   Monthly Vital Statistics Report (HRA) 76–1120 25:2 Supplement. Advance report, final marriage statistics, 1974. Washington: U.S. Government Printing Office.

——— (1976).   Monthly Vital Statistics Report (HRA) 76–1120 25:1 Supplement. Advance report, final divorce statistics, 1974. Washington: U.S. Government Printing Office.

——— (1976).   Monthly Vital Statistics Report (HRA) 76–1120 24:12. Births, marriages, and deaths for 1975. Washington: U.S. Government Printing Office.

——— (1975).   Monthly Vital Statistics Report (HRA) 76–1120 24:5. Summary report, final marriage statistics, 1973. Washington: U.S. Government Printing Office.

——— (1975).   Monthly Vital Statistics Report (HRA) 76–1120 24:4. Summary report, final divorce statistics, 1973. Washington: U.S. Government Printing Office.

——— (1975).   Monthly Vital Statistics Report 23:13. Annual summary for the United States, 1974, births, deaths, marriages, and divorces. Washington: U.S. Government Printing Office.

———— (1975). Monthly Vital Statistics Report (HRA) 75–1120 23:11. Summary report, final natality statistics, 1973. Washington: U.S. Government Printing Office.

———— (1975). Vital statistics of the United States, 1971. Vol. 1—Natality. (HRA) 75–1113. Washington: U.S. Government Printing Office.

———— (1973). Remarriages, United States. DHEW Publication No. (HRA) 74–1903, Series 21:25. Washington: U.S. Government Printing Office.

VAN CASPEL, VENITA (1975). *Money Dynamics.* Reston, Va.: Reston Publishing Co.

VEEVERS, J. E. (1973). Voluntarily childless wives: an exploratory study. *Sociology and Social Research* 57:3:356–366.

VENER, ARTHUR M., AND CYRUS S. STEWART (1974). Adolescent sexual behavior in middle America revisited: 1970–1973. *Journal of Marriage and the Family* 36:4: 728–735.

WALDRON, INGRID, AND SUSAN JOHNSTON (1976). Why do women live longer than men? *Journal of Human Stress* 2:2:19–30.

WARNER, SAM BASS, ED. (1966). *Planning for a Nation of Cities.* Cambridge, Mass.: The M.I.T. Press.

WATKINS, BEVERLY T. (1976). This year's freshmen reflect new views of women's role. *The Chronicle of Higher Education,* Jan. 12, 1976.

WATSON, J. ALLEN, AND VIRA R. KIVETT (1976). Influences on the life satisfaction of older fathers. *The Family Coordinator* 25:4:482–488.

WATZLAWICK, PAUL, JANET H. BEAVIN, AND DON D. JACKSON (1967). *Pragmatics of Human Communication.* New York: Norton.

WECHT, CYRIL H. (1975). A comparison of two abortion-related legal inquiries. *The Journal of Legal Medicine* 3:8:26–34.

WEINBERG, MARTIN S., AND COLIN J. WILLIAMS (1974). *Male Homosexuals.* New York: Oxford University Press.

WEINSTOCK, EDWARD, CHRISTOPHER TIETZE, FREDERICK S. JAFFE, AND JOY G. DRYFOOS (1975). Legal abortions in the U. S. since the 1973 Supreme Court decisions. *Family Planning Perspectives* 7:7:23–31.

WEISBERG, D. KELLY (1975). Alternative family structures and the law. *The Family Coordinator* 24:4:549–559.

WEISS, BRIAN (1974). Earlier menstruation, longer adolescence. *Psychology Today* 8:6:59.

WEISS, ROBERT S. (1976). The emotional impact of marital separation. *Journal of Social Issues* 32:1:135–145.

———— (1975). *Marital Separation.* New York: Basic Books.

WEITZMAN, LENORE J. (1975). To love, honor, and obey? Traditional legal marriage and alternative family forms. *The Family Coordinator* 24:4:531–548.

WELLS, J. GIPSON (1976). A critical look at personal marriage contracts. *The Family Coordinator* 25:1:33–37.

WELLS, ROBERT V. (1974).   Household size and composition in the British colonies in America, 1675–1775. *The Journal of Interdisciplinary History* IV:4:543–570.

WESTOFF, LESLIE ALDRIDGE (1975).   Two-time winners. *The New York Times Magazine*, Aug. 10, 1975, pp. 10–15.

WILSON, CODY W. (1975).   The distribution of selected sexual attitudes and behaviors among the adult population of the United States. *Journal of Sex Research* 11:1:46–64.

WILSON, EDWARD O. (1975).   *Sociobiology: The New Synthesis*. Cambridge, Mass.: Harvard University Press.

WILSON, KENNETH, LOUIS A. ZURCHER, DIANA CLAIRE MCADAMS, AND RUSSELL CURTIS (1975).   Stepfathers and stepchildren: an exploratory analysis from two national surveys. *Journal of Marriage and the Family* 37:3:526–536.

WINCH, ROBERT F. (1970).   Permanence and change in the history of the American family and some speculations as to its future. *Journal of Marriage and the Family* 32:1:6–15.

WISEMAN, JACQUELINE P. (1975).   An alternative role for the wife of an alcoholic in Finland. *Journal of Marriage and the Family* 37:1:172–179.

WHEELER, MICHAEL (1974).   *No-Fault Divorce*. Boston: Beacon Press.

WOOD, CLIVE (1969).   *Human Fertility: Threat and Promise*. New York: Funk & Wagnalls.

YORBURG, BETTY (1973).   *The Changing Family*. New York: Columbia University Press.

YOUNG, T. R. (1976).   Some theoretical foundations for conflict methodology. *Sociological Inquiry* 46(I):23–29.

ZABLOCKI, BENJAMIN DAVID (1971).   *The Joyful Community*. Baltimore: Penguin Books.

ZAJONC, ROBERT B. (1975).   Birth order and intelligence: dumber by the dozen. *Psychology Today* 8:8:37–43.

ZEMLICK, MAURICE J., AND ROBERT I. WATSON (1953).   Maternal attitudes of acceptance and rejection during and after pregnancy. *American Journal of Orthopsychiatry* 23:570–584.

ZICKLIN, GILBERT (1973).   Communal child-rearing: a report on three cases. In Hans Peter Dreitzel (ed.), *Childhood and Socialization*. New York: Macmillan, pp. 176–208.

ZUCKMAN, HARVEY L. (1975).   Recent development in American divorce legislation. *The Jurist*, Winter 1975, pp. 6–16.

Photograph Acknowledgments

5, Marjorie Shostak/Anthro Photo; 11, William Gladstone/Anthro Photo; 26, Black Star/Alain Keler; 31, Photograph by Ken Heyman; 35, Library of the University of Heidelberg; 59, Culver Pictures; 65, Owen Franken/Stock Boston; 72, Suzanne Arms/Jeroboam; 79, Jean Boughton, Boston; 88, Dave Bellak/Jeroboam; 93, Jean Boughton, Boston; 97, Rick Smolan; 101, Mike Mazzaschi/Stock Boston; 108, K. Rosenthal/Stock Boston; 117, Donald Dietz/Stock Boston; 123, Rick Smolan; 130, Fredrick D. Bodin/Stock Boston; 133, Peter Simon/Stock Boston; 167, Eve Arnold/Magnum Photos; 191, Jean Boughton, Boston; 216, Milton Rogovin, Buffalo, New York; 219, Rick Smolan; 221, Frank Siteman/Stock Boston; 224, Ellis Herwig/Stock Boston; 225, Jeff Albertson/Stock Boston; 250, Elizabeth Hamlin/Stock Boston; 255, Mike Mazzaschi/Stock Boston; 258, John Launois/Black Star; 264, Ken Graves/Jeroboam; 278, Frank Siteman/Stock Boston; 283, Karen Preuss/Jeroboam; 287, Rick Smolan; 301, Wide World; 309, Susan Ylvlsaker/Jeroboam; 315, Frank Siteman/Stock Boston; 322, Michael Alexander, *People Weekly*, © Time Inc.; 325, Frank Siteman/Stock Boston; 334, Harry Wilks/Stock Boston; 345, Fredrick D. Bodin/Stock Boston; 356, Jean Boughton, Boston; 359, Peter Southwick/Stock Boston; 379, Black Star/Robert B. Goodman; 383, Anthony Wolff; 388, Anna Kaufman Moon/Stock Boston; 401, Cary Wolinsky/Stock Boston; 402, Ulrike Welsch/Boston Globe; 409, Marshall Henrichs; 413, Jean Boughton, Boston; 430, Jim Ritscher/Stock Boston; 439, Phil Preston/Boston Globe Library; 449, Jean Boughton, Boston; 456, Ellis Herwig/Stock Boston; 461, Stan Grossfeld/Boston Globe Library; 475, Wide World Photos; 482, Rick Smolan; 485, David Powers/Jeroboam; 494, Henri Cartier-Bresson/Magnum Photos; 501, Susan Ylvlsaker/Jeroboam; 506, Rick Smolan; 510, David Krathwohl/Stock Boston; 515, M. C. Escher, "Bond of Union," Escher Foundation—Haags Gemeentemuseum—The Hague; 526, Patricia Hollander Gross/Stock Boston; 527, Elizabeth Hamlin/Stock Boston; 536, Julie O'Neil/Stock Boston.

Index